1945
VICTORY
IN THE
WEST

PETER CADDICK-ADAMS

PENGUIN BOOKS

PENGUIN BOOKS

UK | USA | Canada | Ireland | Australia
India | New Zealand | South Africa

Penguin Books is part of the Penguin Random House group of companies
whose addresses can be found at global.penguinrandomhouse.com

Penguin
Random House
UK

First published by Hutchinson Heinemann in 2022
Published in Penguin Books 2023

001

Maps by Darren Bennett

Typeset in 11.2/15 pt Minion Pro by Jouve (UK), Milton Keynes
Printed and bound in Great Britain by Clays Ltd, Elcograf S.p.A.

The authorised representative in the EEA is Penguin Random House Ireland,
Morrison Chambers, 32 Nassau Street, Dublin DO2 YH68

A CIP catalogue record for this book is available from the British Library

ISBN: 978–1–529–15773–4

www.greenpenguin.co.uk

To A.L. LeQuesne
who taught me history
at Shrewsbury School (1974–1978)
&
Paul Beaver and Cate Pye
who have kindly accommodated, wined and dined
the wandering historian
during his many travels

Contents

Military Tool Kit And Glossary

Military folk worldwide, like many other communities, tend to adopt their own abbreviations, which they forget puzzle those outside. Military algebra, by which I mean the designation of divisions, brigades, regiments, battalions and so on, is particularly vexing to the uninitiated, hence this briefest of tool kits for your enlightenment.

Units of all the nations covered here followed much the same approach, in that their basic formation was the division. By 1945 German divisions had often shrunk to perhaps 10,000 and sometimes much less. Allied ones tended to vary between 12,000 and 15,000 men, depending on purpose (airborne, armoured or infantry). Divisions (usually commanded by a Major General, Generalmajor or Generalleutnant) were self-supporting, with their own reconnaissance, artillery, anti-aircraft and anti-tank, engineers, signals, machine-gun, supply, transport, ordnance (for repair), workshop (for vehicles), medical and military police elements.

All divisions were numbered, and often had a secondary title, which indicated where they recruited, for example 15th Scottish, 43rd Wessex and 53rd Welsh under Montgomery; or the 36th Texas and 42nd Rainbow (the latter drawing recruits from across the United States). Two divisions or more – often many more – made an army corps. Allied corps possessed their own heavy artillery (an AGRA, Army Group Royal Artillery in the Anglo-Canadian forces), anti-aircraft, armoured and reconnaissance units, a Mechanized Cavalry Group (in US corps), plus other assets.

Allied infantry divisions were broken down into three infantry brigades (regiments in US terminology), each of around 3,000 personnel, commanded by a Colonel or Brigadier (Brigadier General, or Général de Brigade). The Cottonbalers was the unofficial title of a US Army regiment, more formally titled the 7th Infantry. A brigade, in turn, comprised three battalions, led by lieutenant colonels, which remain the basic building blocks of military formations. Tank battalions (sometimes called armoured regiments) fielded around sixty tanks, infantry battalions contained 600–1,000 riflemen, whilst artillery battalions (or regiments) comprised anything from nine to forty-eight guns, depending on type and calibre. Each generally included three infantry companies, armoured squadrons or artillery batteries, plus headquarters elements.

American and British airborne forces, with minimal transport, who deployed into battle by glider and parachute, fielded fewer numbers, as did British Commandos. The latter, all numbered, were split between the Navy (Royal Marine Commandos) and Army, each unit being the equivalent of a highly-trained, well-armed, but small battalion. Their US equivalents are Ranger battalions.

American battalions and regiments were numbered, while the Anglo-Canadians retained a variety of exotic and confusing titles for their battalions, evoking nineteenth-century antecedents. These included the 13th/18th Hussars, 22nd Dragoons and Staffordshire Yeomanry (all British tank battalions); 3rd Scots Guards (also a tank battalion); 13th Royal Horse Artillery (an artillery battalion); the Algonquin Regiment and the Cameron Highlanders of Ottawa (both Canadian infantry battalions, the latter fielding machine-guns); and 4th/5th Royal Scots Fusiliers, 5th Duke of Cornwall's Light Infantry and (bizarrely) the 12th King's Royal Rifle Corps (all British battalions).

Now, for some TLAs (Three Letter Abbreviations) and others, which have crept past the censors and into this volume.

30 Assault Unit	British commando unit, raised by Ian Fleming, tasked to capture German codes, technical documents, equipment and personnel
AEF	American Expeditionary Force, which fought in World War One
AFS	American Field Service; an all-volunteer US force of ambulance drivers
AGRA	Army Group Royal Artillery; corps-level medium and heavy artillery units
AGRE	Army Group Royal Engineers; fielded troops for corps and army activities
AVRE	Armoured Vehicle Royal Engineers, based on the 40-ton Churchill tank
Army Group 'B'	FM Model's central German force; 5th Panzer, 7th and 15th Armies
Army Group 'G'	SS Gen. Hausser's force defending southern Germany; 1st and 19th Armies
Army Group 'H'	Defended Holland with 1st Parachute and 25th Armies under Blaskowitz
BAR	Browning Automatic Rifle; US Army squad light machine-gun, 20-round magazine, 0.30-06-inch calibre
Bagration	Soviet operation, 23 June 1944, to compliment D-Day in Normandy
BLA	British Liberation Army
Blackcock	British XII Corps operation to clear Roermond Triangle, 13–27 January 1945
Blockbuster	Canadian operation to clear Rhineland, 26 February to 3 March 1945
Blue and White Devils	Nickname for 3rd US Infantry Division (Maj. Gen. John W. O'Daniel)

Bren Carrier	British-Canadian 3-ton armed and armoured, tracked carrier for moving combat supplies and towing equipment
Bren gun	British-Czech .303-inch calibre, 30-round, magazine-fed, light machine-gun
Bronze Star	US decoration for achievement or bravery in a combat zone
C-rations	(US) canned combat rations, also gum, matches, cigarettes, toilet paper
CEF	(French) Corps Expéditionnaire Français, under Général Alphonse Juin
CIC	US Counter Intelligence Corps; provided tactical intelligence from captured documents, interrogations, or civilian sources
CIGS	British Chief of the Imperial General Staff, FM Sir Alan Brooke
Combat Command	US all-arms combat grouping in armoured divisions, designated 'A', 'B' and 'R'
Cottonbalers	(US) nickname for 7th US Infantry Regiment (Col. John A. Heintges)
Crocodile	Churchill flame-throwing tank, towed armoured trailer of fuel; range 100yds
Curtiss C-46	(US) twin-engined transport, forty troops, aka 'Commando'
DD tank	Duplex Drive Sherman tank, able to float using canvas side screens
DESt	Deutsche Erd und Steinwerke, SS-run German Earth & Stone Works
Deutsche Reichsbahn	German railways
Division-Leclerc	(French) 2nd Armoured Division, led by Général Philippe Leclerc
Douglas C-47	(US) twin-engined transport, twenty-eight troops, aka 'Dakota' or 'Skytrain'
Douglas C-54	(US) four-engined, long-range transport, fifty troops, aka 'Skymaster'
Dragoon	Anglo-US amphibious assault of southern France, 15 August 1944
ETO	(US) European Theater of Operations
Fallschirmjäger	(German) parachute troops, forces
Festung	(German) fortress; if so designated, area obliged to fight to the last bullet
Flakhelfer	German teenaged anti-aircraft assistant personnel; females designated as Flakhelferinnen
Flashpoint	Ninth US Army operation to cross the Rhine, 24 March 1945
FOO	Forward Observation Officer (for artillery)
Franconia	Old Germanic region centred on northern Bavaria and eastern Württemberg

G-1	(SHAEF/US, later NATO) designation for administration and personnel issues
G-2	(SHAEF/US) personnel and departments responsible for intelligence matters
G-3	(SHAEF/US) personnel responsible for operations, plans and training
G-4	(SHAEF/US) personnel and departments devoted to supply issues
G-5	(SHAEF/US) personnel and departments responsible for civil-military matters
Gauleiter	Powerful regional political leader, senior to Kreisleiter and Ortsgruppenleiter
Gebirgsjäger	German mountain troops or formations
Goldflake/Penknife	Anglo-Canadian operation to bring troops from Italy to North West Europe
Grenade	US Ninth Army operation to clear Rhineland, 23 February to 10 March 1945
Hauptbahnhof	Main railway station
Herbstnebel	German 'Autumn Mist' Ardennes attack, beginning on 16 December 1944
Hitlerjugend	Hitler Youth movement for males aged 14–18; heavily militarised
Jagdpanther	German turretless, tracked vehicle, mounting 88mm gun on Panther chassis
Jagdpanzer IV	German turretless, tracked vehicle with 75mm gun on Panzer IV chassis
Kaiserreich	German Empire of 1871–1918 (Second Reich); preceded by the Holy Roman Empire of 800–1806, first established by Charlemagne (First Reich)
Kampfgruppe	German temporary all-arms combat grouping
Kangaroo	Armoured personnel carrier, based on M7 Priest or Canadian Ram tank
King Tiger	German 70-ton heavy tank, mounting 88mm gun, armour up to 7.5 inches
K-rations	US emergency rations, included chocolate, crackers, powdered drinks
LCM	Landing Craft Mechanised, capable of carrying a tank, 50-foot long
LCVP	(US) Landing Craft, Vehicle, Personnel; the 36-foot- long Higgins Boat
Lumberjack	US First Army operation to clear west of Rhine, 1 to 25 March 1945
LVT	Armoured tracked amphibious carrier, nicknamed 'Buffalo' or 'Alligator'
M4	Sherman: US-designed 32- to 42-ton medium tank in general Allied service
M5	Stuart: US light tank, with 37mm gun in revolving turret

M7	Priest: US tracked, armoured motor gun carriage with 105mm howitzer
M8	US 6-wheeled armoured car with 37mm gun in revolving turret
M10	US tank destroyer on Sherman chassis, 3-inch gun in revolving turret
M26	Pershing: 46-ton heavy US tank with 90mm gun, introduced early 1945
M29	Weasel: US rubber-tracked, amphibious load carrier, with a crew of four
M36	US tank destroyer; development of M10, with 90mm gun
Manhattan Project	US operation to develop atomic weapons
Market Garden	Anglo-American airborne and ground operation, Holland, 17 to 25 September 1944
Marne Division	US 3rd Infantry Division, named 'Rock of the Marne' from service in 1918
Monty's Moonlight	Reflecting searchlights on low clouds, creating night-time illumination
Nashorn	German self-propelled 88mm anti-tank gun on Panzer IV chassis
Nebelwerfer	German multi-barrelled mortar tubes, wheeled or towed into position
Nordwind	'North Wind' German attack against US Seventh Army, 1 to 25 January 1945
Oberbürgermeister	(German) lord mayor, senior to Bürgermeister (mayor)
Oberrhein	Himmler's Upper Rhine army group, November 1944–January 1945
Oflag	Abbr. of 'Offizierslager', (German) prison camp for officers
OKW	Oberkommando der Wehrmacht, the German Armed Forces High Command headquarters near Berlin
Overlord	Anglo-American-Canadian invasion of France, from D-Day, 6 June 1944
P-47	US single-seat ground attack fighter, aka 'Thunderbolt'
P-51	US long-range, single-seat fighter, aka 'Mustang'
Panzerfaust	German shoulder-launched, single-shot anti-tank weapon
Panzergrenadier	German armoured infantry personnel or units
Panzerjäger	German anti-tank units, weapons or personnel
Panzerschreck	German stove-pipe-like two-man anti-tank weapon, modelled on bazooka
Paperclip	US operation to remove to America German scientists, engineers and technicians from post-war Soviet influence, 1945
PFC	(US) Private First Class, rank above private, for military service of one year
Phantom	British liaison unit of teams with special communications; equivalent of US Signal Information and Monitoring (SIAM) Companies

PIAT	Projector, Infantry, Anti-Tank (Anglo-Canadian bazooka)
Plunder	British-Canadian Rhine crossing operation, 23 to 24 March 1945
PTSD	Post Traumatic Stress Disorder, modern term for shell shock (WW1), or battle exhaustion (WW2)
PX	(US) Post Exchange, front-line store, where troops could buy non-issue items
RAD	Reichsarbeitsdienst (Reich Labour Service), 6-months' compulsory service for those aged 18–25, before joining the Wehrmacht or SS
Ram	Canadian training tank; turretless, converted into Kangaroo armoured personnel carrier for 10-man infantry section or squad
Rathaus	(German) city or town hall
Repple Depple	(US slang) Replacement Depot, where troops are processed before combat
SAS	(British) Special Air Service; air-dropped or Jeep-equipped special forces operating forward of Allied troops
SCAEF	Supreme Commander Allied Expeditionary Force, General Dwight David Eisenhower
Schmeisser	German MP-40 machine-pistol, 9mm calibre, 32-round magazine
SHAEF	Supreme Headquarters Allied Expeditionary Force, forward base in Reims
Silver Star	US award for bravery in battle from 1942, above Bronze Star
Sten	British-Canadian submachine-gun, 9mm calibre, 32-round magazine
Sturmgeschütze	German tracked, turretless vehicle with 75mm gun, abbreviated to StuG
T-4	German programme to murder individuals designated 'of no use to the Reich', disguised as euthanasia
TAC	Tactical Command Post/HQ
Task Force	US all-arms grouping, usually two per armoured combat command
T-Force	Anglo-US military mission in 1945 to secure German scientific and industrial technology before it could be destroyed or fall into Russian hands
Torchlight	British XII Corps attack on Xanten, 24 March 1945
Turnscrew	Anglo-Canadian XXX Corps assault on Rees, 23 March 1945
Typhoon	RAF ground attack fighter, 4x 20mm cannon, 8x rockets plus 2x bombs
Ultra	Strategic intelligence gleaned from cryptoanalysis of German radio signals
V-1	*Vergeltungswaffe* (vengeance weapon) flying bomb
V-2	German rocket, assembled by slave labour in underground facilities

Varsity	Anglo-American airborne operation beyond Rhine, 24 March 1945
Veritable	Anglo-Canadian operation to clear Rhineland, 8 February to 11 March 1945
Volksgrenadier	German infantry soldier or formation, designated from autumn 1944
Volkssturm	German armed civilian militia, established in battalions from 25 September 1944
wald	German for 'wood' or 'forest', hence Hochwald, Pfälzerwald, Reichswald, Schwarzwald
Westwall	German western frontier defences, aka the Siegfried Line
Widgeon	British Commando attack on Wesel, 23 March 1945

Order of Battle, Allied Forces Western Europe, at the Time of the *Plunder/ Varsity* Rhine Crossings, 24 March 1945

Note: this is a snapshot of Eisenhower's ninety-one full-strength divisions and other forces on a significant day. No more divisions arrived after this date. Allied divisions changed between corps frequently, and several senior commanders changed. John Millikin had just been replaced at III US Corps on 17 March by James A. Van Fleet. On 23 March, Dan Spry had been replaced by Ralph Keefler as commander of the 3rd Canadian Infantry Division. On 24 March, Tom Rennie (51st Highland Division, Second British Army) was killed in action and replaced by Gordon MacMillan. Maurice Rose (3rd US Armored Division) was killed on 30 March and replaced by his deputy, Doyle Hickey; on 4 April, Simpson's Ninth US Army would revert from Montgomery's control to Bradley's Twelfth US Army Group. On 22 April, Van Fleet's III US Corps would be switched from First to Third US Army in exchange for VIII US Corps joining First Army. On 17 April, John Wogan (13th US Armored Division) was wounded and replaced by John Millikin, recently sacked from III Corps. On 20 April, Manton Eddy at XII US Corps was replaced for medical reasons by Leroy Irwin. Matthew Ridgway's XVIII Airborne Corps was moved frequently between armies in the last month. US V Corps joined Patton's Third Army from Hodge's First at the beginning of May 1945.

SUPREME HEADQUARTERS ALLIED EXPEDITIONARY FORCE
Gen. Dwight D. Eisenhower

FIRST ALLIED AIRBORNE ARMY (Lt Gen. Lewis H. Brereton)

XVIII US Airborne Corps (Maj. Gen. Matthew B. Ridgway)
13th US Airborne Division (Maj. Gen. Elbridge G. Chapman Jr)

515th and 517th Parachute Infantry and 326th Glider Infantry Regiments
17th US Airborne Division (Maj. Gen. William M. Miley)
507th and 513rd Parachute Infantry and 193rd Glider Infantry Regiments
82nd 'All American' Airborne Division (Maj. Gen. James M. Gavin)
504th and 505th Parachute Infantry, 325th Glider Infantry Regiments
101st 'Screaming Eagles' US Airborne Division (Maj. Gen. Maxwell D. Taylor)
502nd and 506th Parachute Infantry, 327th Glider Infantry

I British Airborne Corps (Lt Gen. Sir Richard Gale)
1st British Airborne Division (Maj. Gen. Robert E. 'Roy' Urquhart)
1st Parachute Brigade, 1st Airlanding Brigade
6th British Airborne Division (Maj. Gen. Eric Bols)
3rd and 5th Parachute Brigades, 6th Airlanding Brigade
1st and 2nd (UK), 3rd and 4th (French) and 5th (Belgian)
Special Air Service (SAS) units
1st Polish Independent Parachute Brigade (Lt. Col. Stanislaw Jachnik)
(3 parachute battalions; brigade later joined
1st Polish Armoured Division)

TWENTY FIRST ARMY GROUP
Field Marshal Sir L. Bernard Montgomery

2nd Tactical Air Force, RAF (Air Marshal Sir Arthur 'Maori' Coningham)
No. 2 Group (medium bombers), No. 83 Group (supported British),
No.84 Group (supported Canadians),
No. 85 Group (night fighters/light bombers)

FIRST CANADIAN ARMY (Gen. H.D.G. 'Harry' Crerar)

2nd Canadian Independent Armoured Brigade (Brig. G.W. Robinson)
(1st Canadian Hussars, Fort Garry Horse, Sherbrook Fusiliers)

4th Commando Brigade (Brig. Bernard W. 'Jumbo' Leicester)
(41, 46, 47 and 48 RM Commandos)
1st and 2nd Canadian Army Groups Royal Artillery

I British Corps (Sir John T. Crocker)
(lines of communication and military government duties)
49th West Riding Infantry Division (Maj. Gen. Stuart B. Rawlins,
later to I Canadian Corps), 56th, 146th and 147th Infantry Brigades
1st Polish Armoured Division (Maj. Gen. Stanisław Maczek,
later to II Canadian Corps): 10th Polish Armoured Brigade,
3rd Infantry Brigades

I Canadian Corps (Lt Gen. Charles Foulkes)
Arriving from Italy, 1st Canadian Infantry Division
(Maj. Gen. Harry W. Foster) 1st, 2nd and 3rd Canadian Infantry Brigades
Arriving from Italy, 5th Canadian Armoured Division
(Maj. Gen. Bert H. Hoffmeister)
5th Canadian Armoured Brigade, 11th Canadian Infantry Brigade
Arriving from Italy, 1st Canadian independent Armoured Brigade
(Brig. William C. Murphy: Ontario, Three Rivers and Calgary Regiments)

SECOND BRITISH ARMY (Gen. Sir Miles C. 'Bimbo' Dempsey)

30th Armoured Brigade (Brig. Nigel W. Duncan: Flail Tanks)
31st Armoured Brigade (Brig. Gordon S. Knight:
Crocodiles, LVTs and Kangaroos)
33rd Armoured Brigade (Brig. Henry B. Scott: DD tanks and LVTs)
1st Assault Brigade, Royal Engineers (Brig. Philip St. B Sydenham:
AVREs and LVTs)

II Canadian Corps (Lt Gen. Guy G. Simonds, under command)
4th Canadian Armoured Division (Maj. Gen. Chris Vokes)
4th Canadian Armoured Brigade, 10th Canadian Infantry Brigade
2nd Canadian Infantry Division (Maj. Gen. A. Bruce Matthews)
4th, 5th and 6th Canadian Infantry Brigades

VIII British Corps (Lt Gen. Evelyn H. 'Bubbles' Barker)
11th Armoured Division (Maj. Gen. G.P.B. 'Pip' Roberts)
29th Armoured Brigade, 159th Infantry Brigade
6th Guards Independent Tank Brigade (Brig. Walter D.C. Greenacre)
(4th Coldstream Guards, 4th Grenadier Guards, 3rd Scots Guards)
Arriving from Italy, 5th British Infantry Division (Maj. Gen. Richard A. Hull)
13th, 15th and 17th Infantry Brigades

XII British Corps (Lt Gen. Sir Neil Ritchie)
7th Armoured Division (Maj. Gen. Lewis O. Lyne)
22nd Armoured Brigade, 131st Infantry Brigade
15th Scottish Infantry Division (Maj. Gen. Colin M. 'Tiny' Barber)
44th and 46th Lowland Brigades, 227th Highland Brigade
52nd Lowland Infantry Division (Maj. Gen. E Hakewill-Smith)
156th, 157th, 158th Infantry Brigades
53rd Welsh Infantry Division (Maj. Gen. Robert K. 'Bobbie' Ross)
71st, 158th and 160th Infantry Brigades

1st Commando Brigade (Brig. Derek Mills-Roberts)
(3 and 6 Army Commandos, 46 and 45 RM Commandos)
4th Independent Armoured Brigade (Brig. R. Michael P. Carver)
(Sharpshooters Yeomanry, Royal Scots Greys, 44th Royal Tank Regiment plus
2nd Kings Royal Rifle Corps, infantry battalion)
34th Independent Tank Brigade (Brig. William S. Clarke)
(107th and 147th Royal Armoured Corps, 7th and 9th Royal Tank Regiment)
3rd, 8th and 9th Army Groups Royal Artillery

XXX British Corps (Lt Gen. Sir Brian G. 'Jorrocks' Horrocks)
Guard Armoured Division (Maj. Gen. Alan H.S. Adair)
5th Guards Armoured Brigade, 32nd Guards Brigade
3rd Infantry Division (Maj. Gen. Lashmer G. 'Bolo' Whistler)
8th, 9th, 185th Infantry Brigades
3rd Canadian Infantry Division (Maj. Gen. Ralph H. Keefler,
later to II Canadian Corps)
7th, 8th and 9th Canadian Infantry Brigades
43rd Wessex Division (Maj. Gen. G. Ivor Thomas)
129th, 130th, 214th Infantry Brigades
51st Highland Division (Maj. Gen. T.G. Rennie,
killed in action 24 March, then Maj. Gen. G.H.A. MacMillan)
152nd, 153rd and 154th Infantry Brigades
4th and 5th Army Groups Royal Artillery

8th Independent Armoured Brigade (Brig. Gen. Erroll Prior Palmer)
(Sherwood Rangers Yeomanry, 4th/7th Royal Dragoon Guards,
13th/18th Hussars
12th King's Royal Rifle Corps, infantry battalion)

NINTH US ARMY (Lt Gen. William H. Simpson)
XXIX Tactical Air Command (Brig. Gen. Richard E. Nugent)

XIII US Corps (Maj. Gen. Alvan C. Gillem)
11th Mechanized Cavalry Group
5th 'Victory' Armored Division (Maj. Gen. Lunsford E. Oliver)
10th, 34th and 81st Tank, and 15th, 46th and 47th Armored Infantry Battalions
84th 'Lincoln' Infantry Division (Maj. Gen. Alexander R. Bolling)
333rd, 334th and 335th Infantry Regiments, 771st Tank Battalion
95th 'Victory' Infantry Division (Maj. Gen. Harry L. Twaddle)
377th, 378th and 379th Infantry Regiments, 709th Tank Battalion
102nd 'Ozark' Infantry Division (Maj. Gen. Frank A. Keating)

405th, 406th and 407th Infantry Regiments, 709th Tank Battalion

XVI US Corps (Maj. Gen. John B. Anderson)
15th Mechanized Cavalry Group
8th 'Thundering Herd' Armored Division (Brig. Gen. John M. Devine)
18th, 36th and 80th Tank, and 7th, 49th and 58th Armored Infantry Battalions
30th Infantry 'Old Hickory' Division (Maj. Gen. Leland S. Hobbs)
117th, 119th and 120th Infantry Regiments, 743rd Tank Battalion
35th Infantry 'Santa Fe' Division (Maj. Gen. Paul W. Baade)
134th, 137th and 320th Infantry Regiments, 784th Tank Battalion
75th Infantry Division (Maj. Gen. Ray E. Porter)
289th, 290th and 291st Infantry Regiments, 701st Tank Battalion
79th 'Cross of Lorraine' Infantry Division (Maj. Gen. Ira T. Wyche)
313th, 314th and 315th Infantry Regiments, 717th Tank Battalion

XIX US Corps (Raymond S. McLain)
113th Mechanized Cavalry Group
2nd 'Hell on Wheels' Armored Division (Brig. Gen. Isaac D. White)
66th and 67th Armored Regiments, 41st Armored Infantry Regiment
29th 'Blue and Gray' Infantry Division (Maj. Gen. Charles H. Gerhardt)
115th, 116th and 175th Infantry Regiments, 747th Tank Battalion
83rd 'Thunderbolt' Infantry Division (Maj. Gen. Robert C. Macon)
329th, 330th and 331st Infantry Regiments, 736th Tank Battalion

TWELFTH US ARMY GROUP
Gen. Omar N. Bradley

FIRST US ARMY (Lt Gen. Courtney H. Hodges)
IX Tactical Air Command (Maj. Gen. Elwood R. 'Pete' Quesada)

III US Corps (Maj. Gen. James A. Van Fleet)
14th Mechanized Cavalry Group
7th 'Lucky Seventh' Armored Division (Maj. Gen. Robert W Hasbrouck)
17th, 31st and 40th Tank and 23rd, 38th and 48th
Armored Infantry Battalions
9th 'Old Reliables' Infantry Division (Maj. Gen. Louis A. Craig)
39th, 47th and 60th Infantry Regiments, 746th Tank Battalion
99th 'Checkerboard' Infantry (Maj. Gen. Walter E. Lauer)
393rd, 394th and 395th Infantry Regiments, 786th Tank Battalion

V US Corps (Maj. Gen. Clarence R. Huebner)
102nd Mechanized Cavalry Group

9th Armored Division (Maj. Gen. John W. Leonard)
2nd, 14th and 19th Tank Battalions; 27th, 52nd and 60th
Armored Infantry Battalions
2nd 'Indianhead' Infantry Division (Walter M. Robertson)
9th, 23rd and 38th Infantry Regiments, 741st Tank Battalion
28th 'Keystone' Infantry Division (Maj. Gen. Norman D. Cota)
109th, 110th and 112th Infantry Regiments, 777th Tank Battalion
69th Infantry Division (Maj. Gen. Emil F. Reinhardt)
271st, 272nd and 273rd Infantry Regiments, 777th Tank Battalion

VII US Corps (Maj. Gen. J. Lawton Collins)
4th Mechanized Cavalry Group
3rd Armored 'Spearhead' Division (Maj. Gen. Maurice Rose)
32nd and 33rd Armored Regiments, 36th Armored Infantry Regiment
1st 'Red One' Infantry Division (Maj. Gen. Clift Andrus)
16th, 18th and 26th Infantry Regiments, 745th Tank Battalion
8th 'Arrow/Pathfinder' Infantry Division (Brig. Gen. Bryant E. Moore)
13th, 28th and 121st Infantry Regiments
78th 'Lightning' Infantry (Edwin P. Parker Jr)
309th, 310th and 311th Infantry Regiments, 774th Tank Battalion
86th 'Blackhawk' Infantry Division (Maj. Gen. Harris M. Melasky)
341st, 342nd and 343rd Infantry Regiments
104th 'Timberwolf' Infantry Division (Terry de la Mesa Allen)
413th, 414th and 415th Infantry Regiments, 750th Tank Battalion

THIRD US ARMY (Lt Gen. George S. Patton Jr)
XIX Tactical Air Command (Maj. Gen. O.P. Weyland)
6th Mechanized Cavalry Group (Army reporting and liaison)

VIII US Corps (Maj. Gen. Troy H. Middleton)
11th Mechanized Cavalry Group
87th 'Golden Acorn' Infantry Division (Maj. Gen. Frank L. Cullin, Jr)
345th, 346th and 347th Infantry Regiments, 735th Tank Battalion
89th 'Rolling W' Infantry Division (Maj. Gen. Thomas D. Finley)
353rd, 354th and 355th Infantry Regiments, 748th Tank Battalion

XII US Corps (Maj. Gen. Manton S. Eddy)
2nd 'Dragoons' Mechanized Cavalry Group
4th Armored Division (Brig. Gen. William M. Hoge)
8th, 35th and 37th Tank, 10th, 51st and 53rd Armored Infantry Battalions
6th 'Super Sixth' Armored (Maj. Gen. Robert Grow)

15th, 68th and 69th Tank, and 9th, 44th and 50th Armored Infantry Battalions
5th 'Red Diamond' Infantry Division (Maj. Gen. S. Leroy Irwin)
2nd, 10th and 11th Infantry Regiments
26th 'Yankee' Infantry Division (Maj. Gen. Willard S. Paul)
101st, 104th and 328th Infantry Regiments, 778th Tank Battalion
76th 'Onaway' Infantry Division (Maj. Gen. William R. Schmidt)
304th, 385th and 417th Infantry Regiments
90th 'Tough Ombres' Infantry Division (Brig. Gen. Herbert L. Earnest)
357th, 358th and 359th Infantry Regiments

XX US Corps (Maj. Gen. Walton H. Walker)
16th Mechanized Cavalry Group
3rd Mechanized Cavalry Group (later SHAEF reserve)
11th 'Thunderbolt' Armored Division (Brig. Gen. Holmes E. Dager)
22nd, 41st and 42nd Tank, and 21st, 55th and 63rd Armored Infantry Battalions
65th Infantry Division (Maj. Gen. Stanley E. Reinhart)
259th, 260th and 261st Infantry Regiments, 748th Tank Battalion
80th 'Blue Ridge' Infantry Division (Maj. Gen. Horace L. McBride)
317th, 318th and 319th Infantry Regiments, 702nd Tank Battalion
94th Infantry Division (Maj. Gen. Harry J. Malony)
301st, 302nd and 376th Infantry Regiments, 778th Tank Battalion

SIXTH US ARMY GROUP
Gen. Jacob L. Devers

SEVENTH US ARMY (Lt Gen. Alexander 'Sandy' M. Patch)
XII Tactical Air Command (Brig. Gen. Glenn O. Barcus)

Reserve: 13th US Armored Division (Maj. Gen. John B. Wogan)
24th, 45th and 46th Tank, and 16th, 59th and 67th
Armored Infantry Battalions

VI US Corps (Maj. Gen. Edward H. Brooks)
117th Cavalry Reconnaissance Squadron
14th Armored Division (Maj. Gen. Albert C. Smith)
25th, 47th and 48th Tank, and 19th, 62nd and 68th
Armored Infantry Battalions
4th 'Ivy' Infantry Division (Maj. Gen. Harold W. Blakeley)
8th, 12th and 22nd Infantry Regiments, 70th Tank Battalion
42nd 'Rainbow' Infantry Division (Maj. Gen. Harry J. Collins)
222nd, 232nd and 242nd Infantry Regiments, 48th Tank Battalion
36th Texas Infantry Division (Maj. Gen. John E. Dahlquist)

141st, 142nd and 143rd Infantry Regiments, 753rd Tank Battalion
103rd 'Cactus' Division (Maj. Gen. Anthony C. McAuliffe)
409th, 410th and 411th Infantry Regiments, 761st Tank Battalion

XV US Corps (Maj. Gen. Wade H. Haislip)
106th Mechanized Cavalry Group
2nd French Armoured Division (Général de Division Philippe Leclerc)
12th Chasseurs d'Afrique, 12th Cuirassiers, 501st Régiment de Chars
(tank battalions)
Régiment de Marche du Tchad (3 battalions mechanised infantry)
3rd 'Marne' Infantry Division (Maj. Gen. John W. O'Daniel)
7th ('Cottonbalers'), 15th and 30th Infantry Regiments
44th Infantry Division (Maj. Gen. William F. Dean)
71st, 114th and 324th Infantry Regiments
45th 'Thunderbird' Division (Maj. Gen. Robert T. Frederick)
157th, 179th and 180th Infantry Regiments, 191st Tank Battalion
63rd 'Blood and Fire' Division (Maj. Gen. Louis E. Hibbs)
253rd, 254th and 255th Infantry Regiments, 740th Tank Battalion

XXI US Corps (Maj. Gen. Frank W. Milburn)
101st Mechanized Cavalry Group
10th 'Tigers' Armored Division (Maj. Gen. William H. H. Morris, Jr)
3rd, 11th and 21st Tank, 20th, 54th and 61st Armored Infantry Battalions
12th 'Hellcats' Armored Division (Maj. Gen. Roderick R. Allen)
3rd, 11th and 21st Tank, and 20th, 54th and 61st Armored Infantry Battalions
70th 'Trailblazers' Infantry Division (Maj. Gen. Allison J. Barnett)
274th, 275th and 276th Infantry Regiments, 772nd Tank Battalion
71st Infantry Division (Maj. Gen. Willard G. Wyman)
5th, 14th and 66th Infantry Regiments, 761st Tank Battalion
100th 'Century' Infantry Division (Maj. Gen. Withers A. Burress)
397th, 398th and 399th Infantry Regiments, 781st Tank Battalion

FIRST FRENCH ARMY (Général Jean De Lattre De Tassigny)

I French Corps (Général de corps d'armée Émile A. Béthouart)
1st French Armored Division (Général de Brigade Aime Sudre)
2nd Moroccan Division (Général de Division Maurice Carpentier)
4th Moroccan Mountain Division (Général de Division René de Hasdin)
9th Colonial Infantry Division (Général de Brigade Jean-Étienne Valluy)
10th French Infantry Division (Général de Brigade Pierre Billotte)

II French Corps (Général de corps d'armée Joseph de Goislard de Monsabert)
5th Armored Division (Général de Brigade Guy Schlesser)

French 1st Motorised Infantry Division (Général de Division Pierre Garbay)
French 1st Infantry Division (Général de Brigade Jean Callies)
French 3rd Algerian Infantry Division
(Général de Division Augustin Guillaume)
French 14th Infantry Division (Général de Brigade Raoul)

Detachment Army of the Alps (Général de corps d'armée Paul Doyen)
French 27th Infantry Division (Col. Jean Valette d'Osia)

SHAEF RESERVE

FIFTEENTH US ARMY (Lt Gen. Leonard T. Gerow)
(Inward processing, training of troops)

XXII US Corps (Maj. Gen. Ernest N. Harmon)
16th US Armored Division (Brig. Gen. John L. Pierce)
Arrived ETO 11 February 1945
5th, 16th and 26th Tank, and 18th, 64th and 69th Armored Infantry Battalions
20th US Armored Division (Maj. Gen. Orlando Ward)
Arrived ETO 21 February 1945
9th, 20th and 27th Tank, and 8th, 65th and 70th Armored Infantry Battalions
66th Infantry Division (Maj. Gen. Herman F. Kramer)
262nd, 263rd and 264th Infantry Regiments (training French Army)
97th Infantry Division (Brig. Gen. Milton B. Halsey)
Arrived ETO 3 March 1945
303rd, 386th and 387th Infantry Regiments
106th 'Golden Lions' Division (Maj. Gen. Donald A. Stroh)
422nd, 423rd and 424th Infantry Regiments

Prologue

'You are in enemy country! These people are not our allies or
our friends. You must remain an alert soldier. Protect yourself at
all times.'

US Army Pocket Guide to Germany, 1944[1]

'We were over Germany,' wrote Martha Gellhorn, 'and a blacker, less
inviting piece of land I never saw.'[2] In early 1945 General Dwight
D. Eisenhower had assembled seven Allied armies, totalling 4 million
men and women, to invade the Western Reich. This is the story of the
last hundred days of their war.

Let us begin on one of them, 14 March 1945. The weather still hovered
between the seasons. The raw edge of winter had gone, but the penetrating damp had not. 'Warm days and cold nights,' noted one GI. Captain
Earl E. Swanson's diary told him it was a Wednesday – not that days mattered in combat. He lifted his binoculars and surveyed the terrain ahead.
Standing in France, he looked over to the village in Germany. Across the
morass of rain-soaked soil, his eyes focused first on Utweiler. Then five
miles beyond, where he knew lay the true ramparts of the Reich. Called
the *Westwall* by the natives, it was marked 'Siegfried Line' on Swanson's
map. Built before the war, its five belts of anti-tank obstacles, barbed
wire, ditches, minefields, machine-gun nests and bunkers, thousands
of yards deep, hugged the contours and awaited his men.

In these lonely southern borderlands of France and Germany there
was no frontier fence or wall. Just marker stones in the corners of
fields, observed only by generations of farmers, for few travelled this

way. In 1769, Marshal Ney, Napoleon's finest warrior, was born in the nearby fortress town of Saarlouis and grew up speaking both German and French, which reflected the frequent changes of nationality in the region. In Hitler's day, Ney's hometown had been renamed Saarlautern. Even here, in this tiny place, the shadow of past conflicts loomed large. Always an area of Franco–German tension, it had lost eight of its menfolk in the Great War, including three pairs of brothers.[3] History mattered not to Swanson, but he had read the Seventh Army assessment that 'the people and their cows live together in thick-walled buildings and manure is piled neatly in the streets'.[4] He knew the French Army had occupied the area for a few weeks in September 1939, when the German population had been evacuated. Swanson expected the locals to have again been removed, including prisoners forced to work on the surrounding farms. His job was to clear these outposts.

Aerial photos picked out the low rolling ridgelines topped with trees that ringed the village. His map indicated Utweiler lay just three hundred yards inside the Reich. A 700-year-old hamlet, one of the smallest settlements in the region, he could see it comprised no more than a couple of farms, a few dozen houses and a tiny church grouped around a crossroads.[5] Instinct had told his superiors this collection of stone and wood structures, a symbolic gateway into Germany, would be symbolically defended. Swanson viewed the glossy black-and-white air imagery, taken days earlier. They highlighted machine-gun posts, mortars, minefields, and trenches.[6]

Swanson's men were known as the 'Cottonbalers'. In January 1815 at New Orleans, their predecessors had repelled English redcoats from behind walls of cotton bales, and the moniker had stuck. As the US 7th Infantry Regiment, they had campaigned throughout the Civil War, notably at Gettysburg, where they had taken over 50 per cent casualties in the Wheatfield. Alongside their Anglo compatriots 128 years later, they had waded onto the sands of Morocco in November 1942, splashed ashore in Sicily the following July, and in September 1943 passed through the newly won Salerno beachhead in Italy towards Monte Cassino. January 1944 saw the three battalions of the 7th Infantry – more than 3,000 GIs – assault the port of Anzio.

It was at Anzio that their German opponents first labelled everyone in the US 3rd Infantry Division, Cottonbalers included, the 'Blue and White Devils', after the distinct, diagonal stripes all wore on their helmets and uniform sleeves. This was their second nickname, for the 3rd Division were also known as the 'Rock of the Marne' after their combat service in France during 1918. The 3rd prided themselves on being 'Eisenhower's favourite division', not least because Ike had commanded one of their battalions before serving as their chief of staff in late 1940.

The Cottonbalers' next amphibious landing had seen them arrive on the French Riviera in August 1944 and fight their way to the German frontier. Following 188 days of continuous operations, latterly in the Colmar Pocket of France, on 18 February 1945 exhausted Cottonbalers, commanded by German-born Colonel John A. Heintges, were pulled out of the line to rest and absorb replacements. Now they were returning to the fray, attacking fifteen miles east of Saarbrücken, in the middle of German-held terrain known as the Saar-Palatinate Triangle. They spent a couple of weeks in March training for village and street fighting, including night operations, then teamed up with other divisions as the Seventh Army's spearhead to punch their way through the Siegfried Line.

Before Swanson and the rest started out, their divisional commander, Major General John 'Iron Mike' O'Daniel, gave them all a pep talk about the opposition ahead. Their mission, he told the Cottonbalers, was part of a larger divisional operation called *Earthquake*. Friendly troops would be to their right and left. However, he warned them, the Germans were waiting, determined to defend their homeland at all costs. O'Daniel ordered that 'gas masks with protective eye ointment must be carried'.[7] Staff Sergeant Eldon Berthiaume, a former military policeman assigned to Company 'G', recalled the anxiety that caused many to skip their meals that afternoon. At six in the evening the men of the 7th Infantry started out in the dark towards their objective. The ground was unforgiving caramel: 'every step was agony', remembered one, as GIs wrestled their boots out of the mud. 'We was sweating like pigs, and when we stopped, the sweat froze on us.'

In many ways Utweiler resembled the French village of Pournoy-la-Chétive, a southern suburb of Metz, which the Cottonbalers had just left, where the 7th Infantry had trained with demolitions, grenades, rocket launchers and flame-throwers, and worked with tanks and tracked tank destroyers.[8] As a result, the Americans considered themselves expert at night-fighting. At one in the morning on the 15th, Captain Swanson's Fox Company led the way, followed by Easy and George, advancing downhill in the half-light. Searchlights bounced their beams off clouds to create 'artificial moonlight', a tactic borrowed from the British.

All was quiet, with the Germans either absent or asleep.[9] Ben Loup, carrying a BAR (Browning Automatic Rifle) with First Platoon, recalled their orders were to follow the white tape placed by another unit through a minefield. A mile short of Utweiler, Loup observed, 'the officer who was supposed to lead us through the mines pointed out the engineer's tape to Captain Swanson and took off for the rear. Swanson led, followed by his radio operator, my squad's scout, then myself and my assistant BAR-man.' After twenty yards or so, the tape ended. The captain looked around for more, found none and assumed no more tape equalled no more mines.[10]

Ten yards later, Loup recalled, 'Swanson's radio operator set off a bouncing mine that killed him and destroyed the radio on his back. Almost simultaneously, there were two other explosions farther back in my squad. Swanson immediately gave us the order to stop in our tracks, to not move our feet, and gently feel around where we were standing. If we felt nothing, lie prone.' As his men groped blindly in the freezing mud and clotted leaves, the captain sent a runner back to battalion HQ alerting them to his predicament, but now had no wireless communications. Flares soared into the sky and tracer stabbed the dark: the noise had alerted their opponents, who deluged the GIs with anti-aircraft fire in flat trajectory, machine-guns, and mortars.

At this juncture Loup was wounded in the cheek by a shell fragment and told to make his way back to the battalion aid station for treatment. Rifleman George Corpis, in action for the first time, saw what happened next. A shell landed next to his captain. Earl Swanson – the veteran of every campaign since 1942 and already wounded in the arm – was killed instantly by the blast. Corpis then witnessed his own platoon commander, Lieutenant Robert W. Rankin, step on a mine blowing him into the air. He came down on another mine, which eviscerated him.

Fox Company was soon badly disorganised, with dead and wounded lying everywhere. The commander of Easy, Captain James Powell, stepped forward to lead the rest around the minefield while Fox sorted itself out. Under fire, the companies extracted themselves with difficulty, skirted right and found a new route into what they now knew was a heavily defended position. Corpis remembered Fox Company retracing their steps away from the mines and following Easy into Utweiler, 'where we charged the German defenders, firing from the hip, just like in the movies'. The rest stormed downhill into the village, finding it ringed by zigzag trenches and felled trees, and took sixty prisoners.

It was 06:00 by the time they had mopped up, but the Cottonbalers' first visit to Germany had been unexpectedly costly. As he moved his command post into the village, the CO, Lieutenant Colonel Jack M. Duncan, mused that his Second Battalion had grown careless. The minefield delayed the laying of telephone lines from Duncan to other units, but he was more concerned that almost half his battalion, which in the preceding month had been brought up to strength by 'reppledepples' – replacements from training depots and rear areas, many of them without combat experience – had failed to arrive at all. Presumably the 'greenhorns' had been disorientated by the minefield, the shelling, the darkness, and their own fear.

Pondering how to better grip his battalion, Duncan waited for communications to be restored and the arrival of his supporting armour, which had no night-fighting capability and tended to operate only in daylight. However, all was not well back at the line of departure, where four tanks lay disabled by mines and shellfire. Other armoured vehicles refused to move forward until engineers had 'deloused' the road ahead of munitions, objecting that the ground was too soft to go cross-country. While the Cottonbalers' CO, Colonel Heintges, persuaded some vehicles to move, the GIs in Utweiler were unaware that their friendly armour would be delayed.

However, none of this was an issue to Duncan, whose men consolidated their positions and grabbed a hasty breakfast. George Corpis recollected that Company 'F', now officerless, was told to occupy the small Catholic church and adjacent graveyard and wait for their armour to catch up before resuming the advance. Once in the church they relaxed, reflecting on their nightmare in the minefield, just glad to be alive.

Another GI, Joseph Corrigan, recalled that his squad leader, Sergeant Jacob Cohen, was soon 'off with a German woman'.

At 08:00, Corpis had put down his rifle and unbuckled his trousers to answer a call of nature in the churchyard when he happened to glance uphill. On the slope above lurked a German tank, surrounded by small specks – infantrymen.[11] It was one of several that suddenly surrounded the village and began firing at the surprised GIs who had been off their guard and inattentive. Corpis dashed back towards the church to raise the alarm but was wounded in the shoulder by shrapnel that hit the church wall. PFC Hubert 'Kly' Kleiboeker was killed instantly when a tank shell burst near him. A devout Lutheran, Kleiboeker had just written home, 'I hope if you ever hear I am wounded, don't get all excited and worried, because nine out of ten that go to hospital make it OK.'[12]

Although each rifle company carried bazookas, their inexperienced handlers had yet to learn to let enemy armour crawl to within sniffing distance, to be sure of a kill. They soon used all their ammunition firing at extreme range. Once the bazookas fell silent, German tracked assault guns nosed their way into Utweiler, demolishing each house, while their supporting infantry overran Duncan's men. Eldon Berthiaume, the former military policeman of Company 'G', and five of his buddies took shelter in the cellar of a nearby barn, where they were captured by a young German soldier. 'He was a kid no older than fifteen or sixteen,' remembered Berthiaume, who was marched away with his hands up. He regretted not having eaten the previous day and had no idea when he would next be fed. They happened to pass a wounded German officer and put a tourniquet on his leg to stop the bleeding, which resulted in better treatment during their captivity.[13]

Machine-gunner Ross West was a 'repple-depple' newcomer, in Europe for only two months when he was taken prisoner. Utweiler was his first and last day of combat. He recalled German cameramen snapping pictures, muttering 'infanterie, gut, gut', sharing a big vat of beer, before trucking their captives away from the front.[14] Sergeant Robert Cook and ten others from Company 'F' were in the church with the injured Corpis and Sergeant Cohen, who had rushed back from his fraternisation. A tank shell crashed through the door and skidded along the floor. They all watched and held their breaths. It did not explode: a dud. At about 11:00 Cook recollected he was at a window firing when 'Sergeant Cohen yelled at me to stop shooting because we were going to have to surrender. One of our German prisoners, taken in the first firefight, signed that he would go and negotiate the capitulation. As he stepped outside, he was felled by a German machine-gun.'

Cook observed, 'an SS officer came in with several infantrymen; he was waving a potato-masher grenade over his head and yelling, "Amerika ist kaput". He began arguing with one of our German prisoners in a loud and threatening voice. Later, one of our guys who could understand German said that the SS officer wanted to kill all of us but was talked out of it by one of our prisoners who told him we had taken good care of their wounded. We were then marched out of town, picking up other groups from Fox Company along the way.'[15] The 7th Infantry's official history noted the Germans 'closed in on the town with a combination of four flak wagons and nine tanks and tank destroyers, which included two Tigers. It was a tough situation to be in without support of any kind. Attached armor had not gotten through to the battalion and without communication, artillery could not be called into play.'[16]

In a short morning, the Second Battalion of the 7th Infantry Regiment had ceased to exist. Colonel Duncan and three others survived by immersing themselves to their necks in a water-filled bomb crater for almost eight hours. Dale Schumacher of Company 'F', his pelvis and femur damaged by shrapnel, played dead for almost twenty-four hours before rescue by friendly medics. For the rest, with small arms useless against armour, without radio or telephone communication to friendly aircraft or artillery, and without supporting tanks, there was no alternative but for the Blue and White Devils to surrender.

When they saw the signature SS runes on the collars of their opponents – panzermen of the 'Götz von Berlichingen' Division, and infantry of the First Battalion, 37th SS Panzergrenadiers – the surviving Cottonbalers understood why they had been outfought. These units, who had an appalling reputation for brutality in Normandy, had orders to 'keep the enemy out of the Reich at any cost'. They were not merely fighting for their Homeland, but everything they believed in. Mostly in their late teens, these were fanatics who had no fear of death.

Back home and safe on the other side of the Atlantic, in their diners, apartments and farmhouses over morning coffee, Americans read the Associated Press communiqué in their newspapers. 'Lieutenant General Alexander M. Patch sent his Seventh Army into its first major action since the Colmar Pocket fight, at one o'clock yesterday morning, striking silently without the usual artillery preparation. Only light resistance met the first assault forces, and the enemy began at once to fall back into the Siegfried Line, behind thick minefields. Then massed American guns opened up with a thunderous barrage and only scattered fire met the attackers.'

More intent on eggs or toast, they might have missed the last paragraph, where Colonel Duncan's Second Battalion of the 7th Infantry were rewarded forty-five words: 'Fifteen miles east of Saarbrucken, other forces broke into the Saar on a two-mile front, penetrated the basin as far as a mile and were locked in a swirling battle near the border town of Utweiler where the Germans threw in their first tanks.'

That 'swirling battle', a footnote on the Seventh US Army's front, cost the Second Battalion 456 missing personnel. More than at Gettysburg. Ten GIs per word of the press notice. By the war's end, military accountants would assess the bill as twenty-one killed, seventy-two wounded; 222 had been captured, while seventeen men remain missing to this day.[17] Lieutenant Colonel Duncan's 640 men had been reduced to a cadre of 'scattered and ineffective personnel' in a mere forty-five words.

Although the 'Marne' Division and its 7th Infantry were experienced outfits, the darkness, confusion, shelling, mines and panzers terrified the many newcomers that made up all US Army formations in 1945. In this case there were clearly tensions between the engineers, infantry and armour. All were cautious; many were tired; no one wanted to be the last to die. Even before 1945, the Marne Division's turnover had exceeded 100 per cent, which included the killed, wounded, captured and the missing, but also those claimed by illness, injury and battle fatigue. The Blue and White Devils would sustain the most casualties of any division in the European Theatre.[18] These losses fell disproportionately on its nine infantry battalions and their junior leadership. Captain Earl Swanson, Fox Company's commander, was one of these: an experienced GI who had worked his way up through the ranks; in Sicily he had been a staff sergeant.[19]

By March 1945, many US platoons and companies were being led by outstanding GIs who had bubbled to the surface as natural leaders. The same was true in the British, Canadian, French and Polish forces. Elsewhere in the US 3rd Division, First Lieutenant Audie Murphy (who would emerge as the US Army's most decorated soldier of the war) and Second Lieutenant Michael Daly (a month away from earning himself a Medal of Honor in the ruins of Nuremberg), both recipients of battle-field commissions, were serving in the neighbouring 15th Infantry Regiment. Yet, success or failure in combat can be random. When Murphy and Daly attacked Epping and Ormersviller on the 7th Infantry's right at the same time, they compelled a German withdrawal. It was Swanson's misfortune to alert his opponents by triggering landmines in the middle of the night.

To be fair, their 17th SS opponents were in much the same condition. Comprising conscripts and volunteers, they made up with fanaticism what they lacked in experience. They had recently disengaged from heavy combat in Operation *Nordwind*, a smaller version of the Ardennes assault but further south, and in January, much of the divisional staff had been sacked and replaced with veteran army officers. A week later the divisional General was captured and was replaced temporarily by a Wehrmacht colonel. This was the *tenth* change of command in a year, surely an indication that by March 1945, the 17th SS lacked professionalism, never mind personnel and equipment.[20]

However, it was 283 days since the Allies had first set foot in northern France. Both sides had fought without respite since those first landings on German-occupied soil and were very tired. Across the armies, morale during the shockingly awful weather of the Bulge had been tested. Now it would be equally tested in victory. The 15 March setback at Utweiler indicated that any invasion of the Reich, even in 1945 with the Germans seemingly on the run, was going to be a slow and costly affair.

No one would have believed there were just fifty-four days of conflict left before the permanent demise of Nazi Germany. World War Two in Europe would officially finish on Tuesday 8 May – or some 336 days after the Normandy invasion. The Western Allies would call it VE (Victory in Europe) Day. For Germany, it was *Stunde Null* (Zero Hour), marking the beginning of a new era.[21]

Introduction

'You are not in Germany to carry a chip on your shoulder or brutalize the inhabitants. We are not like the Nazis. But you are not there on a goodwill errand either. Don't take chances. You are in unfriendly territory.'

US Army Pocket Guide to Germany, 1944

This volume concentrates on the last hundred days of war in the west against Nazi Germany in 1945. It does so without diminishing the achievement of those squeezing the Reich from the opposite direction. While there are no Russian voices here, there are also few Germans', and fewer still from the Allied air forces that enabled victory. These omissions resulted from a conscious decision to relate this account from the point of view of the Western Allied ground forces. The reader will encounter each of the seven Allied armies involved, including the First French and Seventh US of the lesser known Sixth Army Group who fought in the south. The First, Third and Ninth American Armies of the Twelfth Army Group, which campaigned in the centre. Finally, the British Second and Canadian First of the Twenty-First Army Group, who invaded Germany's northern flank.

The tale of these last days is one rarely told. Standard accounts of the war in Western Europe tend to dwell on the 1944 D-Day landings (analysed in the first volume of this trilogy, *Sand and Steel*) and summer battles in Normandy; the autumn stalemate of Operation *Market Garden* in Holland; and the winter campaign in the Ardennes forests (focus of the second volume, *Snow and Steel*). The subsequent months of 1945 then rush through to victory in May, like a movie suddenly speeded up. Even the participants are at fault here, as though hurrying to the end of a bad dream with indecent haste. Once across the Rhine, the advance into Germany of March–May often passes in a few paragraphs, with the end seemingly predetermined, as if it only remained to occupy territory and mop up a few diehards.

As the Prologue has demonstrated, the opposite was true. Much hard campaigning remained to be done. We will see there was bitter fighting all along the front until the last moments. On 4 January 1945 in the midst of the Ardennes fighting, Third Army commander General George Patton had confided to his private diary 'We can still lose this war.' He immediately qualified the observation with, 'However, the Germans are colder and hungrier than we are, but they fight better.'[1] This remained as a malevolent shadow sitting on the shoulders of many Allied commanders well into 1945. The British Prime Minister did not help matters when on 24 March, Winston Churchill expressed his view to Eisenhower: 'My dear General, the German is whipped. We've got him. He is all through.'[2] The next month, former journalist Major Bill Deedes of the 12th King's Royal Rifle Corps, a British infantry battalion, railed against 'the damned papers, which are full of propaganda and pretend the war is as good as won. By golly, it's not,' he wrote home to his wife. 'Lots of sixteen-year-olds are keen to die for Hitler.'[3] From crossing the Rhine to 4 May, when he took the German surrender in the north, Montgomery in his *Memoirs* allowed himself only ten pages, Bradley, and Eisenhower scarcely double that. The early post-war narratives by journalists such as Alan Moorehead, Chester Wilmot and Milton Shulman, as well as most modern ones, all fall into the same trap of offering their readers only the sketchiest coverage of the last days of the Reich.[4]

For the Allied commanders, led by Eisenhower, ever since Normandy there remained the obstacle of the River Rhine, the greatest water barrier in Europe. It is impossible to overstress the extent to which its 820 miles, an international waterborne highway that rises in Switzerland and passes through six countries before emptying into the North Sea, had dominated their thinking.[5] The September 1944 thrust at Arnhem had been an attempt to force a passage over it. The waterway loomed as large an obstruction in their minds as had the English Channel before

June 1944. The Rhine had last been crossed with hostile intent by Napoleon; long before that, for much of its length, the river marked the eastern boundary of the Roman Empire. Beyond, as in 1945, maps might as well have carried the legend 'Here be Dragons'.

The first code name for the 1944 Ardennes assault had been *Wacht am Rhein* ('Watch on the Rhine'), itself the title of Germany's foremost patriotic anthem. With its Rhinemaidens and Rheingold, it dominated the Wagnerian folklore so beloved of the Reich's hierarchy. Thus, as far as the Allies were concerned, breaching what amounted to Germany's natural western frontier would tap deep into the nervous system of the Nazi state. Flying over it, war reporter Martha Gellhorn opined 'the land itself looked actively hostile'. It was impossible not to believe that traversing the waterway would be a major undertaking, and one the Germans were bound to oppose with all their resources, cunning and passionate determination.

The river loomed large in Allied minds for another reason. There was among the western generals a sense of unfinished business. After the Versailles Peace Treaty of 1919, Germany's Rhineland had been demilitarised and came under Allied control for up to a decade. The Americans, British and French had maintained large occupation forces there, in which Charles de Gaulle, army group chiefs Bernard L. Montgomery and Jacob L. Devers, and army commanders Courtney H. Hodges of the First, Miles C. Dempsey of the Second, Alexander M. Patch of the Seventh, and William H. Simpson of the Ninth had served. Many of their subordinates had also learned their trade in the area. Third Army's George S. Patton Jr, with his strong sense of military history which redefined the professionalism of the US Army, had extensively studied the bloodlands on both banks of the Rhine.

A Major Eisenhower, of whom no one had heard, was posted to the region in the 1920s to write a guidebook, *The American Armies and Battlefields in Europe*, for the American Battle Monuments Commission.[6] Remembering that 19 per cent of Americans in the 1940 national census regarded themselves as of Germanic descent, maybe there was also a sense of puzzlement, disbelief and shame – stretching from Eisenhower (whose ancestors left Karlsbrunn, a stone's throw from Utweiler, in 1741) to Private Henry A. Kissinger (who migrated with his family from Bavaria in 1938) – that their kinsmen had departed so far from the norms of decency and democracy.

Other aspects of the western war in Europe evolved with common themes. For the landings in Normandy, it was fear of drowning in the hostile English Channel and landing on an equally hostile shore. The sky soldiers in Market Garden recollected the billow of silk and matchstick-fragility of their gliders. All the warriors in the snow-covered Ardennes discovered the misery of plunging outdoor temperatures and frozen feet. What then is the shared experience you will encounter in this volume? The answer may come as a surprise and will emerge throughout the narrative. It was not combat.

Invading Germany in the spring of 1945 was rather like conducting a series of archaeological digs on a fresh piece of terrain. As maps, aerial photographs and human intelligence provided only hints of insight into what lay beneath, there was great uncertainty as to what the Third Reich had created, both in a material and spiritual sense. None of the Allies really knew what was under the topsoil. Discovery would come only by systematic probing and examination of the ground. Making sense of the whole – as we can today – would only come after long and patient analysis.

Put simply, most of Eisenhower's people stumbled over the Holocaust in some form or other. Not just the awfulness of the concentration camps, but the far more numerous slave labour camps, and their pitiful inmates making their way home after liberation.[7] These were often referred to as 'Displaced Persons' (DPs) in memoirs and accounts, which obscures the depth of their suffering. In early November 1941 Hitler had stated, 'The area that works for us now includes more than 250 million people, but the area indirectly at our disposal has more than 350 million human beings.'[8] The Third Reich was able to release huge numbers of men into its armed forces and give its citizens a reasonable standard of living only by enslaving millions from neighbouring states. According to documentation cited at the Nuremberg trials, over 12 million people were used as serfs, enduring differing degrees of hardship. This was the Nazi policy of *Ausländereinsatz* (use of foreigners), most usually without recompense. By 1944 these unfortunates comprised 26 per cent of the entire workforce within Greater Germany.[9]

The advancing troops knew nothing of this. Nor did their commanders. Even today we are still coming to terms with how the Third Reich operated. There were about 45,000 camps of all kinds run by Hitler's Germany. Such a figure strikes the reader like a sledgehammer, proving there is always something new to learn.[10] This included all the prisons and other types of detainment facilities established at some stage between 1933 and 1945. These comprised well over 30,000 *Arbeiterziehungslager* (slave labour camps), which could range from huge factories to farms employing a dozen; Jewish ghettos (all 1,150 of them); and the 980 sites designated as concentration camps, only a very few equipped with gas chambers, but most sporting perimeter fences of barbed wire and sentry towers.[11] Factories were the 'slow-death camps for the still useful', noted one GI, as opposed to 'quick-death camps for the unwanted. Nearby townspeople closed their minds and their hearts to ignore the screams of men being whipped, the gutters, the miles of hasty graves, the smell of death and dirt and rotting food and fear.'[12]

Between 1941 and 1945, 6 million Russian soldiers ended up in restricted sections of POW camps assisting the German war effort or wasting away through sheer neglect. They were starved and brutalised more than their Western counterparts, their suffering witnessed by American, British and Commonwealth prisoners held in separate compounds. Post-war, it was assessed that 3 million Russian POWs had died in captivity. All these nationalities were conveyed to their camps or factories by Deutsche Reichsbahn (German Railways), in closed wagons, like cattle. After the war, Albert Speer, Hitler's architect and former minister of armaments and war production, conducted a successful obscuration of the full impact of the slave labour programme and his role in it. Instead, the prosecutors at Nuremberg turned their attention towards the plight of the Jews. The true nature of German war crimes uncovered by Allied troops in 1945 was the intertwining of three separate factors, each designed to kill. The Nazi use of slave labour. The camp system where many died. And the 47,076 miles of railway track, every single mile marking the spot where someone died of malnutrition, exposure – or a guard's bullet. Yet, until March 1945, no Western soldier had encountered any large-scale civilian atrocity, much less seen a camp.

One reason for the desperate fighting of April–May 1945 was to buy time. Time for the Nazi regime to burn archives, dismantle buildings, move or exterminate its victims, and hide the evidence of its crimes. Yet the skeletal appearance of those that were left, with their feverish eyes, shaven skulls, malnourished and shuffling gait, whether of camp inmates or the surviving slave labourers, betrayed the reality of life imposed by the SS and Speer's minions. Nearly all of these facilities were within the borders of Germany, whom the policy was designed to enrich. As the greatest proportion of the Fatherland was occupied by Eisenhower's troops until the country was divided into East and West in July 1945, it was the Western armies who encountered more camps of all types and their survivors than Soviet forces.

Thus, it turns out that stumbling over the dead, far more of them outside the camps than within, as well as releasing the living, was a surprisingly common experience for Eisenhower's personnel advancing into Germany in 1945. For these men and women, the images of fire and steel and death continued up to the last seconds of the European war. They found the shock so traumatic that, decades later, they were still reliving the moment in nightmares and panic attacks, with an inability to share what they had seen with anyone outside their comrades of those far-off days. They were only released of such visions with their departure from this world to join the Great Muster Beyond.

PART ONE

To The Rhine

Throughout the advance from Normandy and the French Riviera, the sheer weight and speed of the Allied war machine crushed their opponents. (*Above*): German prisoners had to endure the repressed emotion of the French, Belgian and Dutch populations, but left many booby traps behind. (*Below*): A Jeep and trailer have driven over a mine. Beyond, its two-man crew are receiving aid from red-cross helmeted medics, but the threat of mines reduced road movement to a crawl.

From Normandy to the Reich

On 28 January 1945, Master Sergeant Forrest Pogue, US Army historian attached to V Corps, carefully noted in his diary: 'Cold. Snow. Must be about zero. Today is D + 236.' This was the number of days since the Allied forces first landed in Normandy. Their leaders had long since expected to be in Berlin. Supreme Allied Commander Dwight Eisenhower had even bet Bernard Montgomery, leading one of his army groups, that the European war would end before Christmas – and had lost five pounds. Colonel Ernest 'Tex' Lee, Eisenhower's senior aide, recorded the 'Agreement entered into, 11 Oct 1944, between Generals Eisenhower and Montgomery. Amount £5 – General E. bets war with Germany will end before Xmas 1944. Local Time.' Eisenhower had promptly paid up.

The Allies had broken out of Normandy in August, driven headlong through France, and were nestling along the German border when Hitler's panzer onslaught, code-named *Herbstnebel* ('Autumn Mist'), erupted out of the Ardennes forests on 16 December. It caught Troy Middleton's VIII US Corps, guarding that sector, completely by surprise. General Omar Bradley's Twelfth Army Group had been on the receiving end and its First and Third Armies played a vital part in defeating this last major German assault. By 28 January the German Bulge into Allied lines had been pinched out.[1]

On this day – officially, the last day of the Bulge – the war in Europe had exactly one hundred more days to run. The same January Sunday saw one of Bradley's men – Sergeant Henry Giles of the 291st Engineers – reading his copy of the US Army's newspaper, *Stars and Stripes*. 'The headlines are – Bulge is gone. The Krauts are running hard to get back

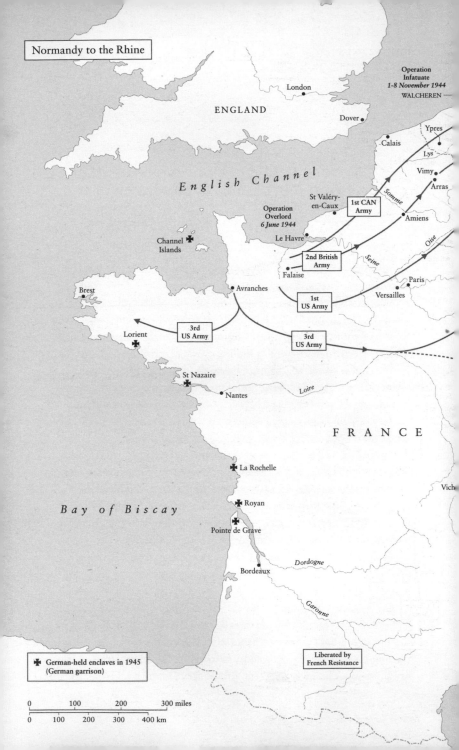

Normandy to the Rhine

ENGLAND

London

Dover

*Operation
Infatuate
1-8 November 1944*
WALCHEREN

Ypres

Calais

Lys

Vimy

English Channel

Arras

St Valéry-
en-Caux

1st CAN
Army

Somme

Amiens

Operation
Overlord
6 June 1944

Le Havre

2nd British
Army

Oise

Channel
Islands ✠

Seine

Falaise

Paris

Versailles

Avranches

1st
US Army

Brest

3rd
US Army

3rd
US Army

Lorient ✠

St Nazaire ✠

Nantes

Loire

FRANCE

La Rochelle ✠

Vich

Bay of Biscay

Royan ✠

Pointe de Grave

Dordogne

Bordeaux

Garonne

✠ German-held enclaves in 1945
(German garrison)

Liberated by
French Resistance

0		100		200		300 miles
0	100	200	300	400 km		

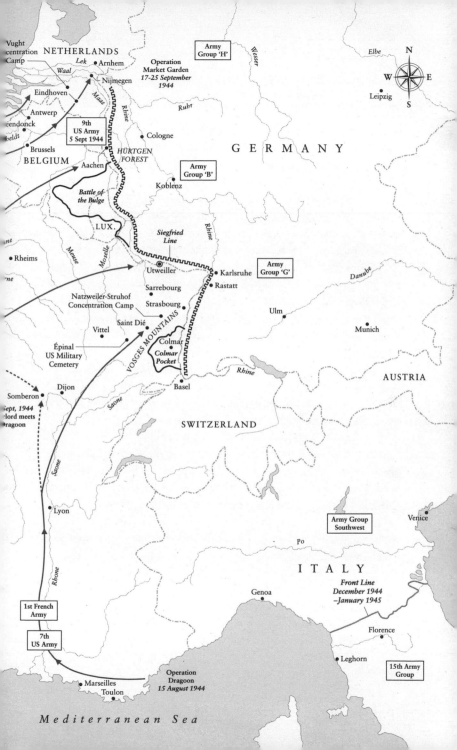

into Germany. The British and Ninth Armies up north are back to the Roer River. Six weeks and a lot of good men lost, and we're back where we were on 16 December.'[2]

The Battle of the Bulge had played out with estimated German losses of over 90,000 men, 500 tanks and 800 aircraft – all irreplaceable. These almost exactly matched the casualties inflicted on the US defenders, but the Americans could replace their lost tanks, planes – and, at a pinch, their manpower.[3] Hitler's last throw of the dice would delay the Western Allies by two months, but not much more. Meanwhile Bradley, headquartered at the 1930s Hotel Alfa opposite the main railway terminus in Luxembourg City, was still hankering after the return of General William Simpson's Ninth US Army, loaned to Montgomery on 20 December to help eliminate the north half of the Ardennes Bulge. Simpson had jokingly telephoned Bradley from his own HQ in Maastricht. 'Hey, Brad, what can you do to save us? If this goes on much longer, they'll begin thinking that we were given to them along with a shipment of Lend-Lease.'

Hiding the slight Bradley felt at this deprivation of a valuable resource by his old friend Eisenhower, his jocular response was, 'There's nothing we can do. You'd better polish up your British accent. You may be needing it for some while yet.'[4] At times during these short, grey, January days, the coalition glue lost its strength. The sun rose at eight and set at four thirty, but some days it never really got light before the afternoon gloom set in. Bradley's army group would fight much of the 1945 campaign without Simpson's Ninth, detached to Montgomery's command. It would not return to Bradley's fold until 4 April.

After exhaustive preparation, the North West European campaign had begun back on 6 June 1944 in Normandy when 156,000 Allied soldiers stormed five separate beaches and dropped from the air in three landing zones. Omar Bradley, then commanding First US Army, watched his Americans assault the terrain opposite their training areas in southern England. The first week saw elements of V Corps landing on Omaha beach and VII Corps further west at Utah beach, building up at a rate of over a division a day. In the east, under General Miles Dempsey's Second British Army, three more corps had also landed on D-Day.

The Canadians were initially under the British, though eventually they formed their own corps, and finally an Army, which started operations on 23 July.

The Anglo-Canadians, as planned, were soon sucked into the bitter attritional battles around Caen, which as they had foreseen, would be bloodily contested by the Germans. The ancient city was the main route centre in and out of Normandy, and the choke point through which panzer and infantry divisions would have to pass to attack the beaches and US forces in the west. It took five weeks to subdue Caen, which had been a naively optimistic D-Day objective, by which time the burial place of William the Conqueror was a total ruin.

Collectively, the Anglo-Canadian forces served their purpose in drawing most German armour to the Caen area where it was destroyed, rather than be permitted to approach the beaches or engage in large numbers with the Americans further west. Transatlantic tempers frayed at the time taken to crush the Caen garrison, but once achieved, in early August an irresistible Anglo-Canadian-Polish steamroller of men and tanks advanced south to Falaise, birthplace of the Conqueror and the region where the army group commander's ancestor, Roger de Montgomerie, had been born.

Further west, despite support from two American airborne divisions, it had taken time to expel the defenders from behind the landing beaches. The terrain of small fields bordered by dense hedgerows, the Normandy *bocage*, played to the defensive tactics of the Germans, already perfected in Russia. It was not until seven weeks into the campaign that the combination of American logistical might and erosion of German forces tipped the balance. On 25 July, the First US Army launched Operation *Cobra*, which saw the German front across the Cherbourg Peninsula suddenly rent asunder by J. Lawton Collins, commanding VII Corps, preceded by a massive preliminary aerial bombardment.

Although the carpet bombing of the Germans on a very narrow front of eight miles caused significant friendly fire casualties, Collins pushed for two days before breaking through. Troy Middleton's VIII Corps then joined the effort and later Charles Corlett's XIX Corps, all plunging down a narrow funnel through the German lines, kept open by tactical air power. Rather like punching a small hole in a huge dam, the German Seventh Army was unable to resist the momentum of the American pressure and rapidly crumbled away. The break-in rapidly evolved into a breakthrough and then a breakout.

The timing for General George Patton's entry into the fight could not have been more fortuitous. His Third Army was officially activated at noon on Tuesday 1 August, with three corps on the extreme right of the Allied line. Within four days, seven of his divisions had swept through Avranches and into Brittany. Other Third Army elements captured Le Mans, formerly the German Seventh Army's headquarters, on the 8th. *Cobra* had taken Bradley's Twelfth Army Group, the fusion of First and Third US Armies, beyond the stalemate of hedgerow warfare and into open country beyond, transiting from static operations to a fluid, rapid pursuit. This was exactly the kind of warfare that best suited Patton, sweeping manoeuvres and envelopments from a flank.

By this stage in the east, General Harry Crerar's First Canadian Army was operational, which included John Crocker's I British Corps, Stanisław Maczek's 1st Polish Armoured Division, as well as Guy Simonds' II Canadian Corps. With two armies comprising four British and one Canadian corps advancing from the north and north-east,[5] and Bradley's Twelfth Army Group swinging in from the west and south, the remnants of the German Fifth Panzer and Seventh Armies found themselves bottled up in a pocket east of Falaise. By 21 August, the area had been sealed and the 50,000 within killed or captured, which added to the 400,000 who had already suffered similarly. The Allied casualties of 210,000 in the campaign, beyond the worst-case planners' scenarios, hinted at a manpower crisis all the Western Allied armies would face by the year's end.

The American breakout, *Cobra*, which led to the unplanned Falaise pocket, emphasised the US Army's ability to move great distances at high speed. On the evening of 19 August Patton's foremost elements had crossed the Seine, and by 10 September were advancing on the Moselle département of eastern France, named after the river which flows through the area and into the Rhine, and five hundred miles distant from Normandy. Thereafter, Third Army, exhausted from their four-week trek across France, ground to a halt in the face of stiffening German opposition, poorer weather and difficult terrain. This was not the high point of Patton's career, for he relished swift advances and despised set-piece battles. For the next three months, until the Bulge began, he advanced sixty miles at the cost of 50,000 troops. However, Third Army wore down their opponents, who lost 180,000, but Third Army's 'romp through France' had concluded.

Despite its own breakout and achievement in creating and sealing the Falaise pocket, Montgomery's Twenty-First Army Group had come to be seen as a slow, plodding juggernaut in the way it had moved little, but bled heavily, during its two months in the wider Caen area. Yet this was always the plan, with the Anglo-Canadians crumbling away the panzers and German infantry at huge cost to themselves, enabling an American breakout south and east. Each nation played to its strengths: Twenty-First Army Group cautious, slow but well resourced, and the Twelfth US Army Group, more adventurous and richer in vehicles, dashing around Normandy. However, this interpretation became a springboard for innumerable criticisms of Montgomery by American, British and Canadian veterans, journalists, and historians, and misses a couple of points.

Only *by comparison* with the Americans did the British seem slow. Both wings of the Normandy assault made progress, but their intentions and methodologies were different. US forces were engaged in hedgerow warfare, where progress through the *bocage* was measurable. The Anglo-Canadians were often involved in static urban warfare around Caen, a slower kind of battle. Moreover, Twenty-First Army Group's task was to absorb the blows coming from German tanks and their panzergrenadiers. The American task was to seize ground, Montgomery's to destroy the opposition's forces by attrition.

As soon as the battles around Falaise were over, all the Allies thrust beyond the Seine in mid-August. There was little opposition, for most German combat power in France had already been spent. While the 51st Highland Division of I British Corps stayed behind to capture St Valéry-en-Caux, where they had been surrounded by Rommel in 1940, the rest of that corps took the port of Le Havre on 12 September. The remainder of Twenty-First Army Group moved forward in a three-week period known as the 'Great Swan', for its swift passage, devoid of German resistance. This was a time of Montgomery's fully mechanised army group, on Bradley's left, covering astonishing distances by road, following the German advance of 1940 in reverse, and far more efficiently.

Meanwhile, a Franco-American army group, the Sixth, led by General Jake Devers, had also entered the fray along the French Riviera coast in August 1944. Originally timed to coincide with *Overlord* in Normandy, logistics and political differences delayed this second D-Day for nearly two months. Unlike the northern landings, which initially failed to capture a usable port, the Franco-US invasion of 15 August quickly yielded two major deep-water harbours, Marseilles and Toulon, which brought logistical heft. Led initially by Alexander Patch of the Seventh US Army, who commanded all Franco-American forces until Devers took over, this second invasion exceeded all expectations in the way it seized the entire southern French coast within days and moved rapidly inland, exploiting the movement corridor of the Rhône Valley. On 11 September, *Dragoon* met *Overlord*, when French troops linked up with Patton's Third Army, ensuring a continuous Allied front. By the winter, Devers' Franco-American force had fought their way through the Vosges mountains and reached the west bank of the Rhine.

With their flanks protected by the Resistance, Patch's Seventh and the First French Army of Général Jean de Lattre de Tassigny (usually referred to as de Lattre) soon had their own lines of communication stretching back to the ten basins and thirteen miles of quay in the major port of Marseilles. By mid-October, French and American engineers had repaired German sabotage attempts in both harbours which were then open to merchant shipping. Thereafter, over 500,000 tons of military cargo was landed at Marseilles and Toulon each month, meeting between a third and a half of the entire Allied needs, excluding vehicles and fuel.[6]

The refurbished main highway, National Route 7, and double-track rail links daily facilitated the movement of up to 10,000 tons of supplies northwards, up the Rhône Valley as far as Lyon, which were then collected from railheads and distributed to both of Devers' armies in a vast fleet of trucks. Villagers along the route of the N7 remember the long columns of speeding American vehicles which posed more of a danger to their children than the Germans had ever done. Thus, the advancing GIs and French troops avoided some of the logistical constraints affecting Eisenhower's northern armies, where stability of supply was only achieved with the opening of Antwerp on 28 November 1944.[7] That September, General Wade Haislip's XV Corps was transferred from Patton's Third to Patch's Seventh Army, doubling the latter's combat power. The Seventh would gain a third corps and more divisions, particularly in early 1945, controlling eighteen at various stages, and finishing the war with fourteen, but it never grew to the size of the First or Third.[8]

Until 4 September 1944, soldiers in Montgomery's Anglo-Canadian Twenty-First Army Group had been fighting a military campaign. Few Western troops or their leaders possessed any understanding of the immorality towards civilians of their German opponents. On this day, as they sped down the main road from Brussels to Antwerp, the 11th Armoured Division in General Neil Ritchie's XII Corps discovered the old Belgian army fort of Breendonk. The 23rd Hussars described it as a 'large sinister grey fortress', where the Reich's 'enemies' had been herded for onward transit to camps further east, and members of the Belgian resistance tortured for information. 'The Gestapo made special runnels in the cement floors for the blood,' noted one witness. Some inmates left their details etched in the plaster walls and several hundred died through torture, executions and neglect.'[9]

Though captured empty, WRAF Officer Eileen M. Younghusband recalled that all RAF personnel in the area were ordered to visit the prison. 'In the courtyard, daily shootings took place; the victims were tied to wooden stakes already brown with the blood of those who had died before. In a nearby area, the guards buried Jewish prisoners up to their necks and left them to suffocate and perish. The policy of the Kommandant was to eliminate the weak by any conceivable method, and he pursued this policy with sadistic vigour.'[10]

The Canadian Army's II Corps followed the Channel coast and liberated Dieppe on 1 September, scene of the humbling of their own 2nd Division in August 1942. On the 6th of the month, Maczek's Polish troops in II Canadian Corps freed Ypres, another echo from an earlier war. On their right, XII Corps of General Miles Dempsey's Second British Army passed Arras on 1 September, north of the Somme bloodlands, and Vimy Ridge, scene of Canada's great triumph of 1917. By 4 September the 11th Armoured Division in the same corps had captured Antwerp, three hundred miles from Caen. Further right, on Second Army's southern flank, the Guards Armoured Division of XXX British Corps entered the capital of Belgium on 3 September, a similar distance from Normandy. Appropriately, Brussels was liberated on the fifth anniversary of Britain's declaration of war on Germany.

A sense that the German Army in the West was finished, as demonstrated by the easy advance experienced by all the Allied armies, was what undoubtedly led to the *Market Garden* operation of 17–25 September. In an attempt to circumvent the twin barriers of the German *Westwall* and the River Rhine, despite American airborne troops seizing Eindhoven and Nijmegen, the British 1st Airborne Division at Arnhem was tactically defeated. It prompted Montgomery to a rare admission that he had 'underestimated the difficulties of opening up the approaches to Antwerp'.[11]

If there was an operational benefit bequeathed by *Market Garden* in September 1944, it was the sixty-mile salient carved into German lines, which constantly threatened an Allied breakout. It was one which their opponents never possessed enough combat power to close by land or air. It would prove advantageous subsequently when Twenty-First Army Group launched its operations in 1945. Of *Market Garden*, Montgomery would soon claim the operation had been 'ninety-percent successful', to which Prince Bernhard of the Netherlands responded, 'My country can never again afford the luxury of another Montgomery success.'

The Twenty-First Army Group staff system had broken down in persuading its chief of the necessity of immediately capturing both German-held banks of the Scheldt Estuary, which ran from Antwerp, the largest seaport in Northern Europe, to the North Sea. Without control of the estuary, Antwerp – vital to Allied logistics at the operational level – was useless. The inability to use the port and having to haul supplies all the way from the Normandy beaches, created crushing shortages of everything from fuel and spare tyres to vehicles and artillery shells. Thus, the 'Great Swan' came to an abrupt halt equally for Montgomery and Bradley in mid-September. The fault was Montgomery's in opting to undertake *Market Garden* before first clearing the Scheldt, and Eisenhower's for backing him.

By 26 October, the Allies had fought their way into Holland but the campaign turned sour when Crerar's Canadians uncovered a concentration camp in Vught, a southern suburb of the city of 's-Hertogenbosch. Among others, Jewish diamond dealers from Amsterdam had been sent there as labour for the nearby Phillips Electric Company. The 4th Canadian Armoured Division had already overrun several POW camps, but this was beyond their ken. Lieutenant Colonel John Proctor, the divisional quartermaster, took a Jeep to investigate, returning 'badly shaken'. Addressing his commander, Major General Harry Foster, he reported, 'You'd better see this for yourself, Sir.' Vught was laid out like an army camp with barracks and a rail spur that ran into workshops. The main gates had been left open. They were shown around by an ashen-faced officer of the South Albertas. What he, the 7th Black Watch and the 96th Battery, 5th Anti-tank Regiment, had found were five hundred corpses left in piles, executed that morning by a rearguard of SS. Eight rope nooses dangled from an overhead beam. Nearly six hundred inmates were still alive, due to be executed that afternoon.

From them they learned the full extent of Vught. It was modelled on Dachau (encountered later), with wooden barracks, twelve-foot-high fencing, watchtowers built a hundred yards apart, and a crematorium. From January 1943 the main site and its associated fifteen sub-camps, where detainees operated lumber and woollen mills, had (in the German terminology of the era) 'processed' 31,000 Dutch Jews, political prisoners, resistance fighters, Roma, Jehovah's Witnesses, homosexuals, homeless people, black-market traders and criminals. These unfortunates had been transferred to other camps in Germany as the Allies approached, eighty at a time shoehorned into freight cars for the four-day journey to another hell. At Vught, the records show 750 perished, of whom 329 were shot just outside the wire.[12] The discovery resonated through the Canadian division, and British troops were aware of it, but it did not feature in the international press.

That autumn, Eisenhower and General Jake Devers, commanding the Franco-American Sixth Army Group in the south, had clashed twice. In mid-November when the Sixth had first arrived on the Rhine, Devers saw an opportunity to cross the river and advance into Germany. This was consistent with Eisenhower's immediate objective of 'destroying the German Army west of the Rhine in order to enable river crossings', contained in a written order of 23 October, and a Supreme Headquarters Allied Expeditionary Force (SHAEF) directive of five days later to 'take any opportunity to gain a bridgehead over the river'.[13] To Devers and his staff, such a bold manoeuvre in their area would seal off the German Nineteenth Army in Alsace and cut behind the Wehrmacht's First Army, then opposing Patton in Lorraine. In a flash, opposition to the US Third and Seventh Armies could be neutralised, and a southern axis opened into the Reich.

Logistically, Devers had strong lines of supply back to Marseilles. His Seventh Army was bullish they could overcome the twin barriers of the Rhine and Siegfried Line. His intelligence staff had already determined that most of the *Westwall* bunkers opposite were empty. Devers' chief engineer, Brigadier General Henry C. Wole, had assembled over three hundred assault boats, and stockpiled bridge components and pontoons. He had studied the 750-foot-wide waterway, which flowed at six miles per hour, and assessed that Seventh Army's XV Corps was ready and capable of mounting a two-division assault. Patch envisaged using the 45th and 79th, crossing south-west of Karlsruhe, in the first week of December, with 150 DUKW amphibious trucks in support.[14]

First used in support of *Husky*, the July 1943 landing on Sicily, the amphibious DUKWs were a game-changer for the Allies in Western Europe. Essentially a floating, six-wheeled cargo truck, the letters stood for a complicated factory code: D (Year of Design, 1942), U (Amphibian), K (all-wheel drive) and W (dual rear axles). More than 2,000 had been used in Normandy and subsequently six companies – fifty vehicles each – had arrived with the August *Dragoon* landings and unloaded ships in southern France until sabotage and demolition in the major ports had been repaired and railway lines leading to the front overhauled or re-laid.[15] Eventually DUKWs would carry supplies to the German frontier, participate in the Rhine crossings, and become troop carriers in the spring of 1945. Twenty-seven other companies (1,350 vehicles), using non-amphibious trucks, had also operated in the Riviera ports, which after November 1944 would also switch to supporting Devers' army.[16]

Devers kept both the US Army Chief of Staff, George C. Marshall, and Major General Harold 'Pinky' Bull, chief operations officer at SHAEF, apprised of his plans, but somehow this development escaped Eisenhower. The latter's attention was focused on Bradley's army group further north and Devers' slower-than-planned progress through the High Vosges, an extensive sandstone massif, with peaks stretching to between 3,000 and 4,000 feet. This rugged, pine-forested mountain range that runs from the Saverne Gap east of Strasbourg to the Belfort Gap sixty miles due south, lies parallel to the Rhine, and had witnessed some of the costliest fighting of World War One. Rommel had learned his military trade here in 1915–16. The Germans had avoided it in 1940 and later used slave labour to exploit its geographical features as a deadly defensive maze they hoped would hold the Allies until the spring of 1945.

Devers' men spent the autumn and winter grinding their way through its various passes but at an agonisingly slow pace. One of his sergeants noted the scenery 'full of Christmas trees and lousy with snipers; the winding streams through the valleys only made our feet wetter. We cursed, thinking of the long climb, and the mud, and more mud on the other side.'[17] To their north Patton's Third Army was equally behind schedule, spending the same months slithering through the slush of Lorraine to its capital, Metz. On 24 November, Eisenhower journeyed to Devers to warn Sixth Army Group that he was planning to switch some of their troops to aid Patton. However, he was also concerned that the Germans had not fallen back across the Rhine as expected but formed a pocket below Strasbourg which would pose a threat to Devers' southern flank for any future activity.

When Eisenhower, with Bradley in tow, visited Seventh Army's XV Corps headquarters at Sarrebourg, he found its commander, Wade Haislip, busy making plans for a Rhine crossing the Supreme Commander knew nothing about. The same picture greeted him hours later, on visiting Major General Edward Brooks' VI Corps in Saint-Dié. That evening, the spa town of Vittel played host to a dinner and subsequent discussion between Eisenhower, Bradley and Devers at Sixth Army Group headquarters in the Hôtel de l'Hermitage.[18] After dining with the staff, the three generals adjourned to Devers' office and the door was shut.

Devers, who had previously been unaware of Eisenhower's lack of knowledge of his plans, had maps, charts and briefing notes already laid out, and explained his scheme of manoeuvre to cross the Rhine. From the other side of the door, staff heard 'a lot of yelling'. No stenographer was present, but as Devers recalled, he found the Supreme Commander not only uninterested in changing his strategy and backing a new axis in the south but ordering him to send two divisions to Bradley's Twelfth Army Group, which would go to Patton.[19]

At Sixth Army Group headquarters, the consensus was that none of Bradley's formations were able to cross the Rhine in 1944, but their own Seventh Army had enough combat power to leap the river, though not exploit much beyond it. This would not deviate from the SHAEF strategy of a main axis in the north – where Montgomery and Bradley were to envelop the Ruhr – and a secondary axis further south, where Patton would attack the Saar. Arguing that he was still adhering to Eisenhower's original plan, Devers observed that Seventh Army could greatly assist both these axes with a surprise crossing in his sector, where the opposition was known to be weak. Then his men could head north to attack other Wehrmacht units lining the Rhine, taking them from behind. Unhinging the German front in this way would allow both First and Third Armies to cross unhindered.

Thus, Devers pleaded, it was he, not Patton, who should be reinforced. He even had it in mind to lobby for Patton's Third Army to be detached from Twelfth Army Group (which already contained Hodges' First and Simpson's Ninth Armies) and given to him. Such a strong force, well balanced logistically, would certainly succeed, he argued. At 02:00 on the 25th, Devers later recollected, Eisenhower compromised. 'You won't cross the Rhine – and you won't send two divisions to Bradley.'[20] The meeting finished leaving both men angry. According to one contemporary source, the Supreme Commander was 'mad as hell' with Devers, while the latter was left 'wondering if he was a member of the same team'.[21] Professionalism overrode pique the next day when the trio descended on de Lattre's headquarters at Besançon, then toured the French Army, betraying not a hint of their disagreement.

To their consternation and surprise, Devers' staff immediately received orders to cancel all river-crossing plans and turn around the bridging.

There were long faces at the Hermitage, feeling they were being 'denied the opportunity' to exploit the moment. As the Sixth Army Group's war diary tactfully observed, 'Gen. Devers was anxious to make a crossing of the Rhine by Seventh Army Group, but Gen. Bradley preferred the maximum of close-in support west of the Rhine.'[22] The relevant chapter of the US Army narrative, *Riviera to the Rhine*, is labelled 'Lost Opportunities', with the paragraphs relating to Vittel headed 'The Dubious Decision', its two official historians observing, 'Eisenhower and his major subordinates remained preoccupied with their existing plans.'[23] Other historians, including David P. Colley, whose *Decision at Strasbourg* deals extensively with this episode, have not been kind about Eisenhower's judgement at Vittel, calling it 'questionable', 'surprising' and 'inflexible', and assessing Devers' proposed operation as sound, logical and workable.[24]

Significantly, Patton – who would have benefitted from the manoeuvre – thought it practicable, writing on receipt of the news, 'I personally believe they should have crossed the Rhine.'[25] On the face of it, Eisenhower's opposition comes across as petty and illogical. However, for two months the Supreme Commander had received a series of tough setbacks. First with Montgomery's failure of *Market Garden*, then Patton's loss of momentum before Metz. Latterly, there had been Hodge's inability to subdue the Hürtgen Forest, an ongoing attritional battle south of Aachen that would eventually cost 30,000 American casualties over three months. Now another subordinate was proposing a new variation of the SHAEF strategy, which still carried risk: Eisenhower's patience was at an end. For Devers, it was probably a case of right solution, wrong time.

Apart from the remaining German garrison west of the Rhine, which Eisenhower regarded as a huge threat to Devers' rear, we now know the reason why the front opposite Sixth Army Group was only lightly held. Most of the available German forces were massed east of the Ardennes to launch what would become the Battle of the Bulge, three weeks hence. It is now assessed that the 16 December assault would have been postponed if not cancelled altogether, had Devers been allowed to continue. Wehrmacht formations would have to have been dispatched to counter Seventh Army's dangerous incursion, reinforcements which could only have come from the troops about to strike in the Ardennes.

The Germans opposite Seventh Army had lost 17,500 men in the November fighting alone, 13,000 of them taken prisoner. At the precise moment Devers was planning his river crossing, only 14,000 poorly equipped and demoralised Volksgrenadiers (the Nazi moniker for German infantrymen since October 1944) faced Patch's divisions. His Rhine crossing would almost certainly have succeeded and the defenders opposite Patton also crushed. The risk to Eisenhower was, in fact, minimal – but he did not know that.[26]

Pondering the Vittel decision years later, Brigadier General Garrison H. Davidson, Patch's Chief Engineer, observed, 'I have often wondered what might have happened had he [Eisenhower] had the audacity to take a calculated risk as General Patton would have, instead of playing it safe. Perhaps success would have eliminated any possibility of the Battle of the Bulge; the casualties there could have been avoided, and the war shortened by several months, saving more thousands of lives.'[27]

On 25 November, it was Seventh Army men who tripped over something which hinted, only vaguely, of the darkness they would uncover in 1945. GIs of Company 'K', 7th Infantry, the Cottonbalers we have met already, were scouting the area around Schirmeck, thirty miles southwest of Strasbourg. They followed a well-built road which climbed the 2,400-foot-high north slope of Mont Louise past a granite quarry and discovered Natzweiler-Struthof concentration camp. Deep in the Vosges mountains and hidden by pine forests, it was a series of purpose-built wooden huts, neatly laid out, surrounded by a double electric fence, and equipped with watchtowers, a gas chamber and crematorium. At its peak, it also administered fifty sub-camps in Alsace-Lorraine and the adjacent German provinces of Baden and Württemberg, typically holding around 7,000 in the main site, but over 20,000 in its satellites.[28]

Twelve days after its capture, the *New York Times*'s Milton Bracker was taken to the site. 'It might have been a Civilian Conservation Corps camp, from the winding road to the bald hilltop, the sturdy green barracks looked exactly like those that housed forestry trainees in the United States during the early New Deal.'[29] He was shown a room full of empty burial urns (for which relatives could pay fifty Reichsmarks to have a few spoonfuls of a prisoner's ashes sent to them), storerooms full of prisoners' shoes and civilian clothing, meat hooks from which prisoners were hung, dissection tables and the nearby granite quarry where inmates died of overwork and undernourishment. But no bodies. The camp was 'clean'.[30] Bracker's comment about a Civilian Conservation Corps camp betrays the innocence with which the Western Allies approached the whole concept of concentration camps. It would take until April 1945 to enlighten them.[31]

In Montgomery's northern sector, during the first week of November, both sides of the Scheldt Estuary, which flowed into the North Sea, were captured in appalling weather. Operation *Infatuate* combined attacks by II Canadian Corps with an amphibious assault against Walcheren, a former island at the estuary's mouth. This was the first major blooding of 52nd Lowland Division, the last infantry formation to arrive in 1944, which remained with II Canadian Corps for two months. It is worth noting that the First Canadian Army in 1944 was the smallest of all the four major national contingents to serve under Eisenhower's command. Until reinforced the following year, the Canadian element of Crerar's force never totalled more than 185,000 of the 4 million under SHAEF in North West Europe.

Yet, overall Canadian casualties were 20 per cent higher than in comparable British formations, as a direct result of more days spent in close combat. The burden fell on General Guy Simonds' II Canadian Corps, which in its securing of the Channel ports and opening the approaches to Antwerp, placed it among the most consistently utilised of all Allied formations. In terms of infantry losses, by the close of 1944, 3rd Canadian Division had suffered the highest casualties in Twenty-First Army Group, with the 2nd close behind them. Similarly for tank formation casualties, 4th Canadian Armoured Division was at the top, as was the nation's 2nd Armoured Brigade. Several scholars have sought to argue that this represented a failure in command. However, this more reasonably hints at the toughness of the Canadians' opponents, the weather in which they fought, and their length of time in battle.[32]

We must remember that the Western Allied campaign in Europe was only one half of the battle to destroy the Third Reich. At the highest level, the Big Three of Churchill, Roosevelt and Stalin were loosely able to coordinate their grand strategy. To complement the invasion of

Normandy, from 23 June 1944 Operation *Bagration* enabled the Red Army to recapture Belarus, Lithuania and Poland during the ensuing month. While the Western Allies were stumbling through the orchards and lanes of Normandy, the Soviet Union was destroying twenty-eight of Army Group Centre's thirty-four divisions, killing, wounding or capturing around 400,000 Axis personnel.

Bagration was a blow from which the German Army in the East would never recover and caused a not dissimilar casualty rate to that imposed by the Western Allies on Army Groups 'B' and 'G' in France.[33] However, Stalin's way of war was victory at any cost, with a complete disregard for his own casualties. Russia's losses in *Bagration* were possibly 800,000, double that of their opponents. In Normandy, the Western democracies, mindful of having to account for military deaths to their future electorates, would suffer a mere quarter of the Russian sacrifices, though still a high at 225,000, over a much longer period – the twelve weeks of 6 June to 30 August 1944.[34] Yet the unprecedented length and speed of the Red Army's advance, 450 miles in five weeks, but more importantly the erosion of its human capital, explains why Marshal Georgi Zhukov, Stalin's premier general, was unable to exploit the Wehrmacht's rout and move any further in the autumn of 1944. His halt on the River Vistula would last nearly six months.

Once consolidated and reinforced, on 12 January 1945 the Russians would follow *Bagration* with a further offensive that took them another three hundred miles westwards from the Vistula, as far as the River Oder. Outnumbered by 2.2 million to 400,000 along the six hundred miles of their front, from the Carpathians to the Baltic, Germany's Army Group 'A' was forced back as far as the Reich's last water barrier in the East. At those points along the Vistula chosen for their assaults, the imbalance was even more marked: the Wehrmacht's General Staff calculated the numbers were eleven to one in infantry, seven to one in tanks, and twenty to one in artillery, in the Russians' favour.[35]

Zhukov and Marshal Ivan Konev, the former's rival and commander of the First Ukrainian Front (equivalent to an army group), would consolidate on the Oder in another operational pause before resuming their advance on Berlin, just thirty-seven miles away, on 16 April 1945. Through the haze of ruins still smouldering from RAF and US air raids, the thunder of the Russian guns would be heard on 20 April, Hitler's fifty-sixth birthday. The journey of those *Ivans* (as they were collectively known by the Germans) from the gates of Moscow and ruins of Leningrad and Stalingrad, was longer and more arduous that that of their Western comrades, and no less heroic. Yet the manoeuvrings of Stalin's men (and a sizeable number of women) had only a minimal impact on Eisenhower's forces as all fought their way into Germany during the last hundred days of this narrative.

While there was broad Allied strategic alignment, the operational campaigns in the East and West were conducted completely separately, coordinated only as the two forces met. Lieutenant Belton Cooper with the 3rd US Armored Division would discover this when he visited a G-2 (Intelligence) officer to look at his situation map in the spring of 1945. Cooper noted blue grease pencil marking American units and red identifying German outfits. 'I was curious to see if there were any markings for the Russians. I saw none, so I asked one of the G-2 lieutenants. He said he didn't know. "We can pick up their voices on the radio and know they must be within a range of fifty miles. We've assumed they're on the other side of the River." '

Throughout the campaign, Western Allied casualties would turn out to be dreadful. From D-Day to VE-Day they were recorded as 766,294, of which American losses were 586,628, including 135,576 dead. The British, Canadians, French and other Western allies lost approximately 60,000 dead.[36] Many senior officers, including Eisenhower himself, Patch and de Lattre, had sons serving, which added to their personal burdens. One of Patch's subordinates, the Marne Division's commander, Major General John O'Daniel, whose men assaulted Utweiler, had news of his eldest son's death on 20 September. His namesake was fighting as a private with Company 'A', 505th Parachute Infantry Regiment, at Nijmegen. Hit in the chest his last words to his platoon sergeant were, 'Sarge, tell Dad I tried damned hard, won't you?' O'Daniel, whose brother had been killed serving during World War One, struggled with his loss, writing to a fellow general, 'It has been tough losing the young fellow. I am grateful though, that if he had to go, he went as he did – attacking the enemy.'

The following month, Patch in his headquarters at Lunéville was told of the death on 22 October 1944, of the CO of Company 'C' in the

315th Infantry Regiment. Captain Alexander McCarrell 'Mac' Patch III, his only son, was serving with the 79th Infantry Division when he was killed in action. De Lattre (whose own son, Bernard, was serving with him) was not alone in noting Patch's grief, recalling the 'sensitive man, who spoke tenderly of his wife, and dearly loved the son who fell in the Vosges'.[37] Patch, distraught like O'Daniel, buried his son, who had graduated from West Point only in May 1942, in the American military cemetery adjacent to his army's main field hospital at Épinal. Perturbed at being unable to comfort Julia, his wife, over their loss, he was also aware of his wider responsibilities.

As he pointed out in a letter to her, they were 'far from unique' in their situation.[38] Seventh Army staff observed their commander 'was never the same man after the loss of Mac'. Yet Patch soldiered on, providing a worthy example of devotion to duty in a higher cause. In February 1945 he would pen Julia a further heartfelt letter. 'In my quiet moments alone, I too get a great sense of depression . . . Am getting so very, very many letters from parents of boys who have been killed, wounded, or missing from this Army. Nothing is more devastating than that – There is so little I can say.'[39]

(*Above, left to right*): Two US Army Group commanders, Devers of the 6th and Bradley of the 12th, flank two cavalry officers: Patton of the Third Army and Patch of the Seventh. (*Below*): Dempsey of the Second British, Hodges of the First US, Simpson of the Ninth US and Crerar of the First Canadian Armies surround Montgomery, leader of the 21st Army Group

2

Allied Leadership

Dwight David Eisenhower had just turned fifty-three when he was named as Supreme Commander of the Allied Expeditionary Force (SCAEF) that would invade France.[1] He had earlier overseen all operations in the Mediterranean theatre and was well versed in the challenges of senior alliance leadership. Based in London then France, the Kansan would hold this elevated position until the end of hostilities, afterwards becoming Military Governor of the American occupation zone and subsequently succeeding George C. Marshall as US Army Chief of Staff.

Marshall's British opposite number as Chief of the Imperial General Staff (CIGS), Sir Alan Brooke, watched Eisenhower at a conference in May 1944. There was perhaps a hint of sour grapes – through not having the Supreme Command, which Churchill had implied earlier might be his – in his observation of the SHAEF commander. 'The main impression I gathered was that Eisenhower was no real director of thought, plans, energy or direction! Just a coordinator – a good mixer, a champion of inter-Allied cooperation, and in those respects, few can hold a candle to him. But is that enough?'[2] In retrospect, Brooke's bias seems shocking and indefensible. However, what were the prerequisites for Eisenhower's post? There was no job description. Eisenhower's core belief was the sanctity of the Anglo–US relationship, which for him assumed the status of a religion when he took up his new post of SCAEF in England on 14 January 1944.

One of his junior officers, Group Captain Desmond Scott, a New Zealander in charge of the Typhoon-equipped No.123 Wing, based at RAF Thorney Island, West Sussex, remembered a visit from Eisenhower before D-Day. 'The impression he made on me was a revelation. Some people you take to immediately – Eisenhower was one of them. Most of the British generals I met during my time in England were as stiff and unbending as the silly little sticks they carried. Eisenhower's authority, humility and broad friendly smile made you feel when meeting him that you had made his day.'[3] The American was a 'natural' with soldiers, as Major George Chambers of the 8th Durham Light Infantry, a battalion in 50th Northumbrian Division, recalled when the Supreme Commander addressed his battalion. 'At this stage the troops were bored stiff, bolshie, and had had all this so many times before. But, you know, at the end of his speech, the troops burst into spontaneous applause, which was tremendous praise of the man. His personality carried across to the troops.'[4]

Eisenhower was a man of humble origins who had emerged as the premier general of West Point's finest year, the vintage in question being the Class of 1915. His undisputed qualities lay in being an excellent organiser and planner, the pick of this generation – and in his ability to lead a multinational coalition of forces, each with their own national jealousies, characteristics and sensitivities. He was more of a politician than a soldier, thought Montgomery, who noted in a letter to Brooke of 4 April 1943: 'Eisenhower came and stayed a night with me on 31 March. He is a very nice chap; I should say probably quite good on the political side. But I can also say, quite definitely, that he knows nothing whatever about how to make war or to fight battles; he should be kept away from all that business if we want to win this war. The American Army will never be any good until we can teach the generals their stuff.'[5] These may have been fair criticisms in April 1943 when the US Army was fresh to combat and command, but what their British colleagues failed to appreciate was that the Yanks were *very* quick learners.

Most were won over by Eisenhower's natural charm and humility. Sergeant Norman Kirby, in charge of Montgomery's personal security detail, recalled that while de Gaulle refused to show his identity card, expecting to be recognised, Eisenhower had no such pretensions when challenged. He wrote later of 'Eisenhower putting his hand on my shoulder, handing me his wallet and saying, "Help yourself, son".'[6] Montgomery, too, was occasionally won over. The two dined quietly together on 2 June 1944 in Monty's headquarters on the eve of the invasion, after which the Briton uncharacteristically wrote of his boss, 'Eisenhower is just the man for the job; he is a really "big man" and is, in every way, an Allied commander – holding the balance between the Allied contingents. I like him immensely; he is a generous and lovable character, and I would trust him to the last gasp.'[7]

Yet the pair were fundamentally different. After the death of his wife in 1937, Montgomery shunned female company and neither smoked nor drank alcohol. Eisenhower's busy life was fuelled by caffeine, chain-smoking Camel cigarettes and, of an evening, the odd glass of Johnnie Walker Black Label Scotch, while he was never far from his British driver and companion, Captain Kay Summersby. Like Churchill, Eisenhower used painting as a release, producing over 260 canvases, including a very fine portrait of Montgomery which now hangs in the British Embassy in Washington DC. It is inscribed 'To my friend Monty from Ike', a magnanimous gesture despite Eisenhower's private, post-war view that 'I cannot forget his readiness to belittle associates in those critical moments when the cooperation of all of us was needed'.[8] Many commanders acquired pets as another form of stress-release; Montgomery was famous for his various dogs, including a spaniel named *Rommel* and a wire-haired fox terrier that answered to *Hitler* – presented to him by BBC reporters attached to his HQ – while Eisenhower relaxed with his headquarters cat, called *Shaef*.[9]

Needing to stay close to each of the army group commanders, Montgomery, Bradley and Devers, Eisenhower's headquarters of SHAEF Forward had initially opened on 19 September in the grounds and clubhouse of the Athletic Club of Reims. SHAEF Main was meanwhile located in Versailles and the Rear HQ at Bushy Park in West London. On 17 February 1945, once threats from German counter-attacks had receded, Eisenhower himself moved from Versailles to the centre of Reims, placing his G-3 (Operations) war room in the city's technical college. By that time, to run the European campaign, SHAEF Forward included 318 officers and 4,713 other ranks of central staff, with another 70 officers and 2,500 other supporting personnel.[10]

Battling their way into Germany in 1945, Eisenhower commanded three Allied army groups. Two were led by Americans, one by a Briton, but each was very different in structure and national make-up. Further-more, the Supreme Commander was at odds with two of their leaders, Montgomery and Devers. Contrary to popular belief, the wheels of high command turned, but only falteringly.

In the south, stretching from the Swiss border to south of Luxem-bourg, was Lieutenant General Jacob L. Devers' Sixth Army Group, as we have seen containing Patch's Seventh US and de Lattre's First French Armies. A good manager of the increasingly divergent interests of these two nations, Devers remains a relatively obscure figure in World War Two history, overshadowed by the big personalities of Eisenhower, Bradley and Montgomery, which inadequately reflects his contribu-tion to the war. Moreover, because Anglo-American historiography of the last offensive into Germany tends to be overly critical of the French effort, Devers is tainted in some accounts by his close associ-ation with de Lattre, the French commander, and thus marginalised. There is perhaps no better indication of his flexibility and willingness to learn and adapt than to observe that Jacob Devers began his mili-tary career as a horse-drawn artilleryman in 1909 and retired forty years later, ushering in ground-based tactical missiles and helicop-ter aviation.[11]

Although three years older than his Supreme Commander, Devers and Eisenhower were cut from the same cloth as interwar protégés of George C. Marshall, who would be appointed US Army Chief of Staff on 1 September 1939. Despite the sponsorship of Marshall, a coolness developed between Devers and Eisenhower, which was played down at the time and in histories and memoirs. A degree of antipathy arose between the studious, talented Devers, who preferred tea to strong drink and eschewed profanities, and the likeable and forthright Eisenhower, who may have felt threatened by his contemporary. For all Eisenhower's legendary tact and charm, when it came to his fellow countryman Jake Devers, Ike had a blind spot. Brigadier General Reuben E. Jenkins, Sixth Army Group's chief operations officer (G-3), noted that Devers 'felt that Eisenhower should have given him much greater latitude. There was not the warmth between those two men that you normally expect.'[12]

Devers was fully involved in planning for the 15 August French Riviera invasion (originally code-named *Anvil*, but at the last moment rechristened Operation *Dragoon*).[13] The French initially wanted to control the landings, but eventually conceded the Americans had more experience of amphibious war, and it was Patch, commanding the US Seventh Army, who oversaw the invasion phase and initial advance inland. Once his left flank had met Patton's right, Sixth Army Group was activated, for which Marshall had long earmarked Devers.

The latter saw his function as assigning objectives to his two subordinates, Patch and de Lattre, and observing his corps commanders fight their battles. At 311 officers and 1,221 enlisted men, Devers' headquarters staff was small for the power it wielded. Administratively, they intruded little on their subordinates and mostly coordinated between the armies, SHAEF, and logistical and personnel staff of the rear area, the so-called Communications Zone, usually abbreviated to 'Com-Z'.[14] However, it was immediately apparent that Eisenhower regarded Sixth Army Group's role as secondary – securing the southern flank – while Montgomery's and Bradley's army groups undertook the main task of thrusting into the industrial region of the Ruhr to seize the industries that fed the Wehrmacht.[15]

Yet without the *Dragoon* landings and Devers' two armies, SHAEF would still have had to allocate other forces to protect the southern flank of *Overlord*. This was a factor that Churchill and Brooke – through their entrenched hostility to *Dragoon*, which in their eyes drew men and resources away from the Italian campaign – failed to appreciate and never accepted. As the historians Jeffrey J. Clarke and Robert R. Smith wrote in the US Army official history, *Riviera to the Rhine*, in 1993, 'SHAEF had no real role to assign the newly created Sixth Army Group. From a theatre point of view, a major effort in the south seemed pointless. Devers' forces faced a daunting array of obstacles, starting with the Vosges Mountains, followed by the Rhine River and the *Westwall*.' Finally, they observed, the Black Forest represented another thirty miles of almost impenetrable terrain, all highly favourable for defence. They concluded the 1944 thinking was that 'even if Devers' Franco-American forces were somehow able to push through these barriers, which was extremely unlikely, the seizure of Nuremberg or Munich – just about the only prizes on the other side – did not seem especially worthwhile objectives.[16]

Furthermore, Devers not only had to compete for resources with the two northern army groups, but with Sir Harold Alexander's Fifteenth Army Group in Italy, for logistically he remained under control of the Allied Forces Mediterranean HQ in Italy, for administration and supply until 20 November.[17] Biographers have tended to overstress the Ike–Devers rift, asserting the pair were not old friends, like Patton and Bradley, and the little that is written about Sixth Army Group is often seen through the lens of their personality clash, which according to eyewitnesses varied between a crack and a chasm.[18]

Far more important to the last days of World War Two was not the frostiness between SHAEF headquarters and Devers, but the relationship between Devers and his French colleagues. Throughout his career, Devers was assessed by Marshall as bright, and one 'who showed great restraint from interfering in the work of subordinates, which became his secret method for accomplishing more in a short period of time'. In his dealings with the French, Devers held the reins loosely, by instinct avoiding petty conflicts which threatened to escalate. He 'quickly mastered the essential points of most problems and used all his skills to demolish bureaucratic roadblocks'.[19] De Lattre noted that Devers possessed 'an even temper which never deserted him' and was adept at not only deputising but in appointing able subordinates.

One was Lieutenant Colonel Henry Cabot Lodge Jr, chief liaison officer to de Lattre. Educated in Paris, Lodge was a Republican senator for Massachusetts and Army Reserve officer who had served with distinction with the 1st US Armored Division in North Africa.[20] In 1944 Lodge had resigned his seat to return to duty, the first senator to do so since the Civil War, and was assigned to the First French Army, where his fluency in language and knowledge of French history and culture immediately won him many admirers. Devers did not speak French well, despite having spent three months at the French artillery school in Trier in the summer of 1919. He found in Lodge a subordinate who did, and was a canny political animal in understanding their coalition partner. Lodge later praised Devers from the Senate floor, observing that his command philosophy was 'I want the French to be successful'.[21]

There was no precedent for Devers to consult, as Pershing's American Expeditionary Force (AEF) in World War One had been subordinated to the French. Thus, the success of Sixth Army Group in 1944–45 provides a good example of how to manage coalition operations with a challenging ally, for de Lattre had two masters. Militarily, he answered via Sixth Army Group to Eisenhower. However, as chief of a national contingent, the Frenchman's loyalty lay with the mercurial Charles de Gaulle, self-styled as leader of Free France. He saw de Lattre's army not just as a part of the Sixth Army Group, but as an instrument of France's post-war political agenda.

In 1918, France had provided the Supreme Commander, Ferdinand Foch, for the Allied coalition, which included Pershing's AEF. However, de Gaulle would never accept the role reversal of 1944. While he was as committed to defeating the Germans as Eisenhower, de Gaulle felt humiliation at his military reliance on the United States to achieve his post-war vision of the return of France as a world power. His delicate relationship with his Allies stemmed also from Roosevelt's recognition of the Vichy government in July 1940, which only ended when Germany occupied southern France in November 1942. Roosevelt's ambassador at the court of Maréchal Philippe Pétain, who headed the pro-German collaborationist government, was Admiral William Leahy, recalled on 1 May 1942 to become the first Chairman of the Joint Chiefs of Staff.

De Gaulle's response to Vichy was complicated by the fact that his mentor and patron during the interwar years had been none other than Pétain, for whom he had ghost-written papers and speeches, while the latter had advanced his career and secured postings for his protégé. De Gaulle had even named his son Philippe in the Maréchal's honour. In his eyes, Pétain had not only betrayed France, but in a very personal sense, had betrayed de Gaulle. However, making matters worse, Roosevelt had subsequently backed Général Henri Giraud over de Gaulle as leader of the Free French, unaware that Giraud and de Gaulle had clashed ever since the former had been the latter's instructor in military strategy at the *École de Guerre* in 1922–4. Later, when de Gaulle warned Roosevelt's special advisor Harry Hopkins that 'the French have the impression that you no longer consider the greatness of France necessary to the world and to yourselves', he was advertising a difference of opinion between France and America that would last down to the present day.[22]

The American half of Devers' Sixth Army Group comprised Lieutenant General Alexander McCarrell Patch's Seventh Army. Under George Patton, this had been the first field army to see combat in World War Two, being born at sea en route to Sicily, when the First US Armored Corps was redesignated Seventh Army on 10 July 1943. It would be the first to reach the Rhine. The son of a West Point-educated cavalry officer, 'Sandy' Patch, so named after his close-cropped reddish hair, was an experienced battalion commander who served with the 1st Infantry Division ('The Big Red One') in 1918. He loved horses and was instantly recognisable by his cavalry-issue breeches, highly polished riding boots and an elegant pistol strapped to his side.

Patch took over the Seventh in March 1944, preparing it for the Riviera landings near St Tropez and St Raphael on 15 August 1944, alongside their French comrades-in-arms. His opposite number, Général Jean de Lattre, later described him as 'of high and clear intellect, exceptional steadfastness, quiet, somewhat taciturn . . . deeply religious, of mystic turn of mind and charming manner. To drive away the blues he played the accordion like a virtuoso. General Patch impressed one with his affecting, bright blue eyes.'[23] The Frenchman recollected a moment when his American colleague, 'full of shyness brought out his pocket book and from it took a flower with two stems. "Look," he said, breaking it in two and handing me one stem. "A young girl gave it me on the slopes of Vesuvius on the day before we embarked. She said it will bring me luck. Let us each keep half and it will take our two armies side by side, on the road to victory." '[24]

Patch's style was less of an active tactical director, letting his corps commanders do the heavy lifting, yet offering avuncular advice and assistance. Weather permitting, he was forever being flown around 'his' battlefields by Technical Sergeant Robert F. Stretton Jr, who on one occasion was caught with his boss on board by a Messerschmitt-109 intent on their destruction. Stretton – named 'Sea Level', on account of his diminutive stature – later reckoned he used up all his flying luck to escape.

In complete contrast to their northern neighbour, Third Army, whose antics Patch found 'greatly amusing', Seventh Army took pride in their logistically balanced, intelligence-led, methodical approach to battle. They had none of the speed or élan of Patton, who would eventually, perhaps unfairly, symbolise the American effort in Europe.[25] Accomplished and modest, with a deadpan wit and love of the outdoors, Patch avoided public attention, preferring to remain focused on military operations. When his image appeared on the front cover of *Time* magazine on 28 August 1944, the Seventh Army's Chief Public Information Officer rushed in with a copy, only to have his boss express no interest and ignore the journal.[26]

The multinational force that Patch directed not only liberated the Riviera coast but had gone on to advance four hundred miles up the Rhône Valley (the so-called 'Champagne Campaign') and link up with their comrades who had broken out from Normandy and headed south. On the night of 10–11 September, Seventh Army contacted the 2nd French Armoured Division, operating with Patton's Third Army at Sombernon, west of Dijon. On 15 September, Patch's Seventh with de Lattre's First officially left the Mediterranean Theatre and came under Eisenhower's direct control. Both immediately became subordinate to Devers, whose army group was activated at the same time.

The French half of Sixth Army Group – named French Army 'B' until 25 September 1944 – was led by Jean de Lattre, a former cavalry officer born in 1889 – the same year as his opposite number, Patch, and his chief opponent, Adolf Hitler. Like de Gaulle, who was a year younger, de Lattre was wounded at Verdun (in his case, five times), recovered and had risen through the ranks during the interwar period to become an army chief of staff in 1939 and divisional commander in 1940. His career continued under Vichy until Pétain's Armistice Army was disbanded in November 1942.

De Lattre had been taught by de Gaulle's father at school but did not follow the self-styled leader of the Free French after his call to arms of 18 June 1940, feeling loyalty instead to Weygand, Pétain's first Minister of Defence.[27] It was Weygand who secretly directed the Armistice Army to send its best men and equipment to Tunisia, away from German eyes, and train them there as a future, non-Vichy force. Although Madame de Lattre admired de Gaulle's stance in London, her husband shared Weygand's belief that the regeneration of national self-respect and its armed forces should spring from within France itself.[28]

In the Armistice Army, de Lattre developed an excellent reputation as a trainer of men, and his imprisonment when the Germans marched into Vichy and subsequent escape to London aided by the British Special Operations Executive (SOE), cemented his credentials as an able leader, loyal to the Allied cause. From London he was immediately flown to join de Gaulle in Algiers and promoted to command the French Army 'B', a merger of the former Vichy Army of Africa (anchored on Tunisia, Algeria and Morocco) and Free French Forces, mostly raised in the Francophone African colonies.

However, de Lattre nearly didn't get his army, for the Allies had championed his compatriot, the colourful Alphonse Juin, instead. The latter had led the *Corps Expéditionnaire Français* (CEF), the four-division French North African force that had campaigned in Italy, and fought with great distinction in the first and fourth battles of Monte Cassino.[29] Juin and his men redeemed France's military reputation, proving to his coalition partners the whatever the malaise afflicting his country in 1940, the French were back in business.

It was essentially Juin's old CEF, but renamed Army 'B', that landed in southern France alongside Patch's American troops. They were an eclectic bunch of French *pied noir* (white settler) officers and indigenous troops, who were great fighters but clung to old-fashioned ways. In August 1944, the inhabitants of Rougiers, a village on the Côte d'Azur, witnessed Moroccan *Goums* (Berber tribesmen) liberating their settlement. What the civilians particularly recollected was the sound of a night-time caravan of military camels, mess tins clanking on the sides of the beasts. On closer inspection, they noted the North African soldiers were wearing trophies of war strung around their necks – male genitalia.

De Gaulle needed these fighters but was equally determined there could be no hint that France had been rescued by her colonies. Hence the overtly racist *blanchiment* (or whitening, as it was then known) of de Lattre's force throughout the autumn and winter of 1944–5. This saw many of the battle-hardened Berbers, Senegalese and Cameroonians hand over their weapons, helmets and even greatcoats, to former fighters of the French Resistance. The young teenagers knew no discipline and had little training, but they were white.

De Gaulle needed a compliant general to do his bidding and was aware that friction existed between Juin and de Lattre. In the spirit of keeping one's friends close and one's rivals closer, the leader of the Free French appointed the less recognised de Lattre to Army 'B' and made Juin his chief of defence staff, the first in French military history. The choice proved inspired, for Juin was soon expert at smoothing the feathers that de Gaulle – known among his staff as *deux metres*, or *la grande asperge* (the great asparagus), on account of his six-foot-five beanpole stature – all too often ruffled.

The best-known of Eisenhower's three army groups, the Twelfth, was led by General Omar Nelson Bradley. He was a contemporary of Ike's from West Point, and had risen to command a corps in Sicily before being appointed to lead First US Army prior to D-Day. From August 1944, he led the newly formed Twelfth Army Group. Before the landings, his group's job was to devise the methodology of planning and operating at higher levels, for which there was no precedent. Pershing had worked directly through his own headquarters to the forces below him. Marshall decreed that Eisenhower's SHAEF would devolve land power and tactical air power decisions to the army groups, who then directed their field armies.

Only twice in American history had generals previously commanded more than one field army. At the end of the US Civil War, Sherman had led three, although these totalled less than 100,000 men. In 1918, Pershing's two American armies, totalling 500,000, fought in combat for only a few weeks, leaving little in the nature of doctrine or a template. Thus, Bradley and Devers were on their own, but under the watchful eyes of Eisenhower, and his ultimate boss, Marshall. For Bradley, the responsibility was huge. On 1 August 1944, the day of its inception, his Twelfth Army Group possessed two field armies, six corps and twenty-one divisions, including airborne, armoured, and infantry formations.

As Bradley later recorded, 'I was free in a tactical sense to command however I wished. I chose to pattern my administration somewhat on the model set by Sir Harold Alexander, who had led army groups in Tunisia, Sicily and Italy.' In contrast to Devers' far more laid-back approach at Sixth Army Group, he observed, 'I would issue broad missions but at the same time would watch the situation very closely and suggest orders or modification as I thought required, even to the movement of specific divisions. In sum, I would exercise the very closest control over Hodges and Patton,' his First and Third Army commanders.

As US Army Staff College doctrine, taught at Fort Leavenworth to all future commanders, advised, Bradley divided his Twelfth Army Group headquarters, code-named 'Eagle', into two. From 14 August he began operating from a smaller command post called Forward or TAC (tactical). The bulk of his staff worked in a larger Main HQ, which undertook most of the bureaucracy of sending reports and returns to Eisenhower at SHAEF, allowing Bradley to command in relative seclusion, closer to the front. Eagle TAC, being small and compact, would move more frequently than Main.[30]

Writing in 1950, Bradley noted the contrasts between army and army group. 'At First Army the pace was harder, faster, and more rattling than that at Army Group . . . where the pace was leisurely, the staff seemed mild, unhurried, and unworried except during an occasional tussle with Monty. However, if the staff at Group was less tempestuous than that at First Army, its performance was no less efficient.'[31]

The different mood at First US Army reflected the personality of its new commander, Courtney Hicks Hodges, who would command from 1 August 1944 until the war's end. Under him, the rhythm of the army headquarters became less easy-going. To scholars of World War Two, Hodges was a vastly different personality from Bradley and something of an enigma. Arriving at West Point in June 1904 with George Patton, Hodges dropped out after a year on academic grounds, being unable to master geometry, but showed determination in joining the US Army as a private, and by 1918 was a battalion commander in the 6th Infantry, winning a Distinguished Service Cross in the Meuse-Argonne campaign.

Hodges had been in danger of missing the war until rescued by Bradley. From February 1943, he was commanding Third Army, a training formation based in San Antonio, Texas, preparing GIs to deploy to England. When Patton was given Third Army in January 1944, Hodges was brought over to supervise First Army's pre-invasion training as its deputy commander, while Bradley planned the assault. Thus, Hodges' chief value was initially less that of future battle captain and more an instructor and coach of men destined to enter combat, a role he executed flawlessly.

In his memoirs, Bradley's upbeat post-war assessment of Hodges (or rather that of his eloquent ghost-writer and aide, Chet Hansen) was, 'A soft-voiced Georgian without temper, drama or visible emotion, Hodges was left behind in the European headline sweepstakes. He was essentially a military technician whose faultless techniques and tactical knowledge made him one of the most skilled craftsmen in my entire command. He probably knew as much about infantry and training as any man in the army. But Hodges was unostentatious and retiring and occupied an almost anonymous role in the war.' Bradley continued, 'Hodges successfully blended dexterity and common sense in such equal portions as to produce a magnificently balanced command. I had implicit faith in his judgement, in his skill and restraint. Of all my Army commanders he required the least supervision.'[32]

There is much to be read between the lines of this analysis, with no reference to decisiveness in command, intuition, energy, leadership or tempo. Thus, Bradley's memoir can be read as a whitewash of his subordinate, and one interpretation of the bland platitudes in this passage might conclude that it damns Hodges with faint praise. The First Army chief required the *most supervision of Bradley's senior commanders*, for certainly Patton and Simpson required little guidance, and Bradley is on record as visiting Hodges most often of the three.

When surprised on 16 December 1944 by the German assault that became the Battle of the Bulge, Hodges was suffering from influenza, but may have had – if not a nervous breakdown – certainly, a crisis of confidence. He withdrew to his bed, issued no orders and the man who ran First Army at this crucial period was Bill Kean, his chief of staff. Kean's military secretary noted that 'For two days General Hodges stayed in his office alone, not taking calls, nor seeing visitors or staff'.[33] David W. Hogan's choice of title for his 2006 study of Hodges' First Army headquarters was *A Command Post at War*, which reflected the fact that it was not only battling the Germans but was at war with itself.

While all agree that Hodges lacked Eisenhower's charm, Bradley's decisiveness or Patton's flair, scholars remain divided as to whether Hodges was merely a safe pair of hands, or 'clearly in over his head'.

Perhaps indeed 'a battalion-level tactician by inclination and experience', an extreme view was that Hodges 'was a moron'. The latter observation, characteristically but unfairly, was penned by Patton.[34] The contrast with Third Army and its headquarters staff could not provide more of a contrast. Tongue in cheek, one staff officer observed, 'When you did a sitrep [situation report] for Third Army you showed the positions of the regiments. When you did one for First Army, you had to show platoons.'[35]

It was George Smith Patton Jr, who presided over the Third US Army in France and Germany, having previously led the First Armored Corps in Tunisia and Seventh Army in Sicily with great spirit and élan. However, he had lost credibility in the eyes of some Americans, due to the slapping of two GIs in separate field hospitals, who were suffering from shell shock. His critics in the United States included members of Congress and the former 1917–18 commander in France, Pershing. Secretary of War Henry L. Stimson and Marshall eventually agreed that Patton be retained due to 'his aggressive, winning leadership in the bitter battles which are to come'.[36]

While Patton was under this dark cloud, the more even-tempered Bradley, commander of II Corps in Sicily, and thus Patton's junior in both rank and experience, was selected in September to command the army that would assault France the following summer. Bradley emerged as an outstanding leader of men, not for nothing dubbed 'the Soldier's Soldier' by war correspondent Ernie Pyle in 1943. The newspaperman warmed to the 'ordinary' general precisely because he was not Patton. The latter was eight years older and had started the war as Bradley's superior in rank, both in North Africa and Sicily. Yet by August 1944 their roles had reversed, with Bradley as Patton's commanding officer.

They were as chalk and cheese. Bradley was born in a Missouri log cabin into rural poverty, working his way into West Point through sheer hard work. The United States Military Academy represented not only his college education, but a ticket out of the lifelong destitution that threatened to claim him. Commissioned from West Point into the infantry, World War One ended before he could reach France. Patton, by contrast, had an extensive military ancestry stretching back to the Revolutionary and Civil Wars and stemmed from Antebellum Virginian plantocracy.

He followed his father and grandfather into the Virginia Military Academy almost by right, studied fencing and designed the M1913 cavalry sabre, later named after him, and competed in modern pentathlon at the 1912 Summer Olympics in Stockholm and was selected for that of 1916. At one time the wealthiest officer in the US Army, material advantage also came from his maternal grandfather who was the second elected mayor of Los Angeles. Monied, aloof and regarding himself as martial aristocracy, he joined the cavalry, led a tank brigade in 1918, was wounded, but won both the Distinguished Service Cross and Medal, and promotion to colonel.

Although Patton's superior from 1944, throughout the war Bradley was continually eclipsed by his daring subordinate. The more so during the remaining thirty-six years of his own life after Patton's untimely death in 1945.[37] By instinct Bradley seems to have known how to handle the fiery, mercurial, shoot-from-the-hip George Smith Patton, and got the best from his Third Army commander in the way no one else could have done. Their fates seem intertwined; Patton brought military glory to Twelfth Army Group, completely outclassing other leaders, while Bradley gave him the opportunities to do this. Theirs was a symbiotic relationship, each reliant on the other.

Major (later Colonel) Robert S. Allen, a pre-war journalist, and Executive Officer of Third Army's G-2 (Intelligence) Section, and in charge of Patton's war room, noted of his general's first appearance, 'Very smartly attired – every stitch of him obviously tailored – from overseas cap to boots and combat jacket. West Point ring on left hand – two rings on right and riding crop. Every inch of him was highly polished.' Patton's battle jacket was adorned with four brass buttons, and four rows of medal ribbons. On his shoulders, his shirt collar and on his well-buffed helmet were a total of fifteen large brass stars, denoting his rank of lieutenant general. Later the stars would rise in number to twenty.

While at 2nd Armored Division in 1940–2 as its second commander, Patton had created 'Armored Diesel', a cocktail to further his unit's identity. With great ceremony, its officers were taught how to add the elements: bourbon (symbolising the United States), white wine (for France), ice ('coolness in battle'), and a shot of cherry juice to represent 'the blood of our opponents'. As I have discovered to my cost, it remains a spirit to be reckoned with.[38]

A firm believer in reincarnation, his after-dinner conversations illuminated Patton's beliefs that he had led other lives. Before the 1943 invasion of Sicily, British General Sir Harold Alexander had told him, 'You know, George, you would have made a great marshal for Napoleon if you had lived in the nineteenth century.' In all seriousness, Patton replied, 'But I did.' Other discussions ranged around his ancestors: one had been killed in the Battle of Princeton during the Revolutionary War. His paternal grandfather and great-uncle Tazewell were Confederate lieutenant colonels who died in the Civil War, Tazewell killed in Pickett's Charge at Gettysburg. In moments of personal concern, he 'chatted with the dead colonels', and other historical figures, at whose side he believed he had fought in historical campaigns.

Fluent in French, a family friend described him as 'the most literate man I have ever known and the most well-read', despite suffering from severe dyslexia and only learning to read aged eleven.[39] Characteristically, Patton lampooned his own inability to spell, once advising a nephew, 'any idiot can spell a word the same way time after time. But it calls for imagination and is much more distinguished to be able to spell it several different ways, as I do.'[40] It is worth observing that Patton graduated from West Point forty-sixth out of 103 and were it not for his dyslexia, would undoubtedly have been at or near the top of his class. Despite the affliction, Patton found time for Homer, Caesar, Napoleon and Shakespeare; memorised huge chunks of the Bible, knew the Book of Common Prayer backwards, and had read the Koran. His conversations were laced with quotes from these and many more. His men were often surprised to find that a deep, almost mystic, Christian faith was a cornerstone of his being.[41]

On 5 September 1944, an additional US Army arrived in France, the Ninth, which also came under Bradley. It had been activated just eight weeks before D-Day and was led from its inception by Lieutenant General William H. Simpson, a West Point contemporary of Patton's, class of 1909.[42] Simpson had risen to become Commanding General of the Eighth US Army, whose headquarters he accompanied to England. At his initial meeting with Eisenhower, the latter suggested Simpson's army be redesignated the Ninth, to avoid confusion with the British Eighth, which although it was fighting in Italy, was Montgomery's old command. Simpson readily assented. In France, his force took over the task of subduing Brest from Patton, and by November was at the Franco-German border, on Montgomery's southern flank.

The 300,000-strong Ninth Army, radio call sign 'Conquer', had been operating on the northern flank of Twelfth Army Group when the Ardennes erupted. It came under Montgomery's Twenty-First Army Group on 20 December 1944, when loaned by Eisenhower as a temporary measure to eliminate the north half of the Bulge. Of all senior Americans, Simpson, an ambitious but quiet Texan, was easily the most personable and respectful of his generation. Due to Montgomery's legendary abrasiveness, no one in the US Army relished the prospect of working under the Briton. Yet, as luck would have it, Simpson turned out to be the ideal candidate, although his attachment was not pre-planned.

The son of a Confederate veteran (whence a disproportionate number of US Army officers originated), Simpson was only six months younger than the British field marshal and went out of his way to ensure good Anglo–American relations. Standing six foot two, lean, fit, with a warm smile, and signature shaven head, 'Texan Bill' Simpson was unmistakable. He was always sharply attired in a close-fitting uniform, correctly knotted tie, polished boots and helmet: smart, but not aloof or brash like his Third Army counterpart. While Hodges often appeared nervous, even shifty in photographs, and Bradley resembled a GI dressed for combat, Simpson, like Patton, conveyed presence and radiated self-confidence. As a result of their working together during the Bulge campaign, Bill Simpson and the Canadian Guy Simonds rapidly became the only two non-British generals of whom Montgomery approved. Both, he realised, were calm in a crisis.

Before turning in each night, the Ninth Army chief would telephone each of his corps commanders, then discuss these calls informally with his Chief of Staff, and department heads. For larger undertakings, Simpson would chair conferences with his corps and divisional commanders, encouraging their advice and wargaming through options. In contrast to the gut instinct of Patton, Simpson was a great planner and insisted on hearing the opinion of his G-4 (Logistics chief) before signing off on any mission. By involving his subordinates in this way, Simpson sought collective responsibility, so that they would accept and carry out the plan as partly their own. He also encouraged his staff to visit their opposite numbers at corps and divisional level, a habit actively discouraged by Hodges.

Colonel Armistead D. Mead, the G-3 (Operations) at Ninth Army, opined that Simpson's 'genius lay in his charismatic manner, his command presence, his ability to listen, his unfailing use of his staff to check things out before making decisions, and his way of making all hands feel that they were important to him and to the Army. I have never known a commander to make better use of his staff than General Simpson.'[43]

Later that year another field army also joined Twelfth Army Group. This was the Fifteenth, which arrived in France and received orders on 25 November 1944 to work under Bradley's command. This brought to five the number of American armies deployed in Northern Europe by 1945. Only odd-numbered US armies served in Europe, while the even-numbered trained troops in America, or fought in the Pacific.[44] On 16 January 1945 Lieutenant General Leonard T. Gerow (former V Corps commander, whose men landed on Omaha beach on D-Day) was appointed to lead it. From mid-January until March 1945, the Fifteenth would be charged with rehabilitating, re-equipping and training various American units that had suffered heavily during the Ardennes campaign. Later, it would process new units arriving in northern France and Belgium, provide an emergency SHAEF reserve force, and eventually oversee the first occupation administration.[45] Thus, by the war's end, Bradley's Twelfth Army Group came to oversee four armies, totalling forty-five divisions, and 1.3 million men.

The Anglo-Canadian Twenty-First Army Group, which operated in the north of Eisenhower's front, was defined by one word – Montgomery. The very name was a litmus test among the Allies, Britons included. No one was neutral about 'Monty', as he was known to all, from the humblest private to his fellow generals. One either admired or loathed him. There was no middle ground. Outspoken and opinionated, Sir Bernard Montgomery, with his signature beret and informal dress that verged on scruffiness, was a 'brand' that was, and remains, a lightning rod to soldiers, military historians and Americans.

Appointed Eighth Army commander in the Western Desert in August 1942, Montgomery had been given a series of opportunities to deploy his own unique views on leadership and management on the battlefield and had delivered in style, beginning at Alamein in October–November 1942. He was rewarded on 6 January 1944 with the great prize of Twenty-First Army Group. Having led his Eighth Army in theatres far away from the critical gaze of the War Office in London, Monty had developed a command structure of his own and a relaxed attitude to dress, for which he would have been severely reprimanded had either been first attempted in England. However, the Montgomery formula had resulted in victory after victory, and the Prime Minister and Chief of the Imperial General Staff, who together had shoehorned him into Eighth Army, were content to leave him alone, if he continued to deliver.

The fact that he had survived the Great War endowed Montgomery with infectious self-confidence, high self-esteem, a strong personality and the ability to impose his will forcefully. From these characteristics stemmed a well-developed, positive ego. Armed with this self-knowledge, and aware he was holding all the cards, Montgomery insisted he bring his significant headquarters staff with him from Eighth Army in Italy to Twenty-First Army Group in London. This was an indication he intended to conduct operations as the commander of a large army, treating corps like divisions, rather than revising his ideas and attempting to think on a higher plane, as Bradley and Devers were doing.

There was a difference of scale: at its peak, the headquarters of Eighth Army totalled at most around 200 officers and 1,200 other ranks. By contrast, Twenty-First Army Group's HQ was huge, having to administer two armies and handling all its own administrative requirements, including piping fuel to forward dumps, running hospitals and being directly responsible for Civil Affairs in rear areas and, from early 1945, for Military Government as it advanced into Germany. Eventually the combined three headquarters – TAC, Main and Rear – of Twenty-First Army Group numbered over 1,000 officers and 3,500 other ranks.

What had worked for Montgomery in the desert and northern Mediterranean was maintaining a very small tactical command post (TAC), with a much larger Main HQ located at some geographical distance and, further away still, a Rear headquarters. Monty's TAC was tiny, around twenty officers and 250 other ranks. At TAC, the General, or Field Marshal as he became on 1 September 1944, was accommodated in three field caravans – one an office, another a bedroom, and the third and largest a map room – while other personnel were under canvas.[46]

In the fall of 1944, autumnal weather drove the set-up indoors, but they re-emerged, like hibernating animals, in the spring of 1945. A man of rigid habits, with a strong Christian faith and a daily reader of the Bible, Monty rose at 06:30 and went to bed at 21:30. There were no exceptions. Even when King George VI or Churchill visited, Monty left them with his ADCs and liaison officers. Rather like Patton, his style of leadership was to select good youngsters whom he could trust, inform them fully of his plans, then let them get on with their job. If they were good, and most of them were because Monty had an eye for talent, they survived.

These young men mattered hugely to the successful operation of TAC. They roamed far and wide, using Jeeps, scout cars and, on occasion, aircraft, to cover the great distances between Montgomery's armies, corps and divisions, reporting back on the successes and failures of every formation – and their commanders. Monty's TAC always had a couple of spotter planes available on a nearby airstrip, and his personal C-47 and a B-17 stationed at a handy airbase. When Monty's C-47 was destroyed by a huge Luftwaffe raid during New Year's Day 1945, Eisenhower with characteristic generosity sent Monty his own as a replacement.

Montgomery had another tool for measuring the performance of his commands, bringing accuracy to his battlefield picture. He created the GHQ Liaison Regiment, alternatively known as Phantom, which amounted to a second, private system of communication, the usual channels nearly always proving too slow. The network involved officer-led 'patrols', four or five strong, established at every divisional, corps and army HQ within Twenty-First Army Group and down as far as corps headquarters in the US Army. Their vehicles were marked with a white 'P' on a black background, giving them priority over all other traffic. Phantom had its own cipher system, good radio equipment and always an adequate supply of frequencies.

Monty's chief of staff, Major General Freddie de Guingand, ran everything at Main headquarters, coordinating the activities of the army group's staff, including Brigadier E.T. Williams, an Oxford history don turned Ultra-cleared chief of Intelligence.[47] The closely-guarded Ultra programme, secret until 1974, involved the supply of strategic intelligence to Allied military formations gleaned from messages sent between German Enigma enciphering machines. All Reich headquarters, ships, police and railroads used this supposedly secure technology, unaware it had been compromised by gifted linguists and mathematicians based at Bletchley Park in central England, aided by early computers of their own invention. 'Bill' Williams and his opposite numbers at Twelfth and Sixth Army Groups had access to these 'Ultra top secret' insights, as did intelligence cells in the seven Allied army headquarters, but no formations below, this material being so sensitive and its sources well concealed. Subsequent scholarly debate has assessed this intelligence as shortening the war by several months.

De Guingand acted both as enforcer, making sure army group tasks were actioned, and as gatekeeper to his commander, for one of the purposes of TAC was for Montgomery to isolate himself and concentrate on his battle. Yet de Guingand himself was not at TAC, but at Main, flying up each day with others to brief Monty at 15:00 sharp. An important weakness was the distance between TAC and Main. In the early days in the North African wastes, they were a few miles apart across the desert scrub. By 1945, TAC was frequently isolated not just by geography and sometimes by weather – but isolated mentally, too. Bradley noted, 'Whereas I preferred to live, work, and eat in the field with my staff, Monty sought the solitude of a lonely camp, removed and isolated from his Main command post.'[48] The purpose of Monty's TAC was really to play to his own strengths of being able to cut through the fog of war and set great plans in motion, which it achieved, but at a cost.

Montgomery was poor at keeping SHAEF and Twelfth Army Group informed of his activities, leaving that to de Guingand, which contributed to bad relations with Eisenhower and Bradley. Monty preferred that his Chief of Staff deal with all such matters, and rarely spoke with his American colleagues. He was genuinely uncomfortable with them, arrogantly believing himself to be a more experienced and therefore better soldier than Eisenhower, Devers or Bradley, or – in Patton's case – acutely aware of a competitor, as skilled as himself, but backed by better resources. Monty's approach to the Americans was that of a stern Victorian father, reluctant to show any approval. He reflected the British establishment view, built on a centuries-old reputation, that however hard their transatlantic cousins strove as a professional military force, they would generate only cold, hard disappointment. However, it has to be said that there were plenty of Britons working at SHAEF, directly under Eisenhower, who took a more enlightened view of coalition operations.

While the army group had its weaknesses, Churchill made the matter far worse on 1 September 1944, by promoting Montgomery to field marshal, a five-star rank the Americans did not possess, and thus technically outranking everyone else in Western Europe. The Royal Navy's Admiral Sir Bertram Ramsay, Supreme Allied Maritime Commander, understood the insult, writing in his diary, 'Monty made a Field Marshal. Astounding thing to do and I regret it more than I can say. I gather that the PM did it on his own. Damn stupid, and I warrant most offensive to Eisenhower and the Americans.'[49] Patton wrote to his wife the same day, 'The Field Marshal thing made us sick, that is Bradley and me.' Brooke was only told the day before. It took Congress until December 1944 to initiate five-star ranks and restore the balance for Monty's American superior.

The 1 September promotion was designed as a sweetener, for this was the same day that Montgomery relinquished control of ground forces to Eisenhower at SHAEF. In practice, ever since Bradley had become Monty's equal in running Twelfth Army Group from 1 August, the Briton's control was nominal rather than actual. Doctrinally, this was a weakness in the Allied chain of command, for in an ideal world, there should have been a dedicated land forces headquarters coordinating the three army groups of Monty, Bradley and Devers. SHAEF's task was as a tri-service headquarters, looking up to the Anglo-American Combined Chiefs of Staff Committee, and beyond them to London and Washington DC. Montgomery spotted the gap and periodically lobbied to undertake this role himself, though behind his back even his fellow countrymen, never mind every American commander, agreed he would have been unsuitable, lacking the required political sensitivity.

Montgomery oversaw two field armies, the Second British and First Canadian, hence the 2+1 Army Group. The former, known as the BLA (British Liberation Army), was commanded by General Miles Dempsey, universally known as 'Bimbo', the name of his horse at Staff College, and the latter by the Canadian Harry Crerar. Dempsey had commanded a battalion in France in 1940, and at Dunkirk took over 13 Brigade, covering the withdrawal of Montgomery's 3rd Division, for which he received a DSO. This is where the pair first met. Rapid promotion to brigadier on the staff of the Canadian Corps followed, then divisional commands, before receiving the call to join Montgomery in Eighth Army. He and Oliver Leese commanded Monty's two corps in the invasion of Sicily and southern Italy, and when summoned to Twenty-First Army Group, Montgomery left Leese to run Eighth Army in Italy, bringing back Dempsey to lead the Second.

Second Army's chief was shy and retiring and sought no limelight for himself, abhorring the idea of a personality cult, which is precisely why Montgomery selected him.[50] The XXX Corps commander, General Sir Brian Horrocks (of whom, more later), Dempsey's Staff College contemporary from 1931, described the pair as 'complementary – Montgomery the extrovert who loved the headlines; Dempsey the introvert who shunned publicity but got on with the job. Dempsey also went out of his way to iron out any friction so often caused by the other's tactlessness.'[51]

Dempsey was one of the ablest of his generation of senior commanders, yet subject to Montgomery's micro-management. Command philosophy taught at the Camberley Staff College was to issue orders in broad terms, allowing subordinates considerable lassitude in their implementation. This did not happen in Twenty-First Army Group for two distinct reasons. First, Montgomery maintained his habit of treating subordinates as staff college students, with himself as their instructor. Thus, against all doctrinal teaching, Dempsey was frequently bypassed when his chief intervened to order Second Army's corps and divisions about.

The second reason for Montgomery's obsessive grip was that Dempsey's Second Army was all that Britain could afford to commit to the European campaign. Labouring under the 'shadow of the Somme', Montgomery felt a duty to safeguard his troops' well-being, the pick of another generation. Besides, whatever went wrong for Second Army would impact on the army group commander's high-profile reputation, far more than Dempsey's low-key presence.

Canadian forces had originally been led by General Andrew McNaughton, a gunner whose expertise had contributed greatly to his nation's success at Vimy Ridge in 1917. During the training for D-Day, he had lost the confidence of his fellow gunner, Brooke (also at Vimy), who as CIGS of British and Empire forces was essentially the gatekeeper to senior command appointments for the approaching European campaign. Brooke engineered McNaughton's replacement by General Harry Crerar in December 1943, who had already led I Canadian Corps under Montgomery in Sicily.

Herein lay another problem. Monty did not care for Crerar, who was somewhat shy, a stickler for dress and favoured long written orders. Montgomery preferred oral orders, dressed casually and was a shameless showman. Only a year younger than his immediate chief, Crerar was a prickly Canadian nationalist who regarded his troops as equal in every way to their British counterparts. Alas for him, Montgomery was inclined to look down on non-British personnel as second-class citizens. As Brian Horrocks, the XXX Corps commander we have just met, observed, Crerar 'was much underrated, largely because he was the opposite of Montgomery. He hated publicity, was full of common sense and always prepared to listen to the views of his subordinates.'[52] Crerar was a heavy smoker, something else that Monty abhorred, and grew unwell into the winter of 1944–5, when his senior corps commander, Guy Simonds of II Canadian Corps, took over.

Simonds, though too young at forty-one, was the man Monty wanted to run First Canadian Army. Another gunner, like McNaughton and Crerar, he had attended the British staff college, an important pre-war credential, and rose fast through the Canadian ranks, taking over two successive divisions in Sicily and southern Italy under Montgomery's ever-watchful eye. However, his battlefield successes and meteoric rise from major to lieutenant general in three and a half years excited Crerar's jealousy, who tried to get the younger man sent home. Monty blocked the move, which reaffirmed Simonds' loyalty to Montgomery, and exacerbated the distance between the latter and Crerar. Strong-willed, quick of temper and personally ambitious, some found Simonds cold, but contemporaries felt 'we might have been served better with Guy in command . . . lots of the corps and divisional plans were Guy's. He then got Crerar's okay.'[53]

(*Above*): Général de Lattre, commanding the First French Army, confers with Frank Milburn of XXI US Corps during the Colmar campaign. (*Below*): German-speaking GIs from the Seventh US Army quiz female military prisoners, similar to those captured by the 3rd Division in Bischwihr. The *Fräulein* on the left is attired as an auxiliary plane spotter; the right hand pair wear men's uniforms, presumably those of their boyfriends.

3

The Colmar Pocket

Eisenhower's overall aim for the winter of 1944–5 was for each of his three army groups to assault the German *Westwall* and cross the Rhine. To his mind it was the Sixth Army Group down in the south that was most behind schedule in failing to take the Colmar Pocket, an 850-square-mile chunk of terrain due south of the regional capital, Strasbourg, and between the Vosges and the Rhine. Was Lieutenant General Jake Devers' career on the line? The latter could but wonder, but certainly understood he was under acute pressure to eliminate the remaining German presence in Alsace. His army group, and his own generalship, would be judged on its rapid destruction.

Up to this point Devers had left de Lattre's French Army to clear the region from the west and south. However, this was precisely the moment when the Frenchman's colonial troops had reached the end of their tether. They were not merely battle-weary, but exhausted and suffering from the cold, low morale and logistics shortages. Both de Lattre's corps d'armée made only slow progress. However, German resistance actually intensified as SS-Reichsführer Heinrich Himmler, overseeing all internal security forces within the Reich, from the SS, Gestapo and police to concentration camps, rounded up more manpower and threw it into the Colmar sector. This was on the basis that he was additionally commander of Heeresgruppe Oberrhein (Army Group Upper Rhine), a personal appointment made by Hitler. Sending more forces west of the Rhine was against all military logic but in accordance with the Führer's wishes. Himmler also engineered the departure of General Hermann Balck from Army Group 'G' and his replacement with Johannes

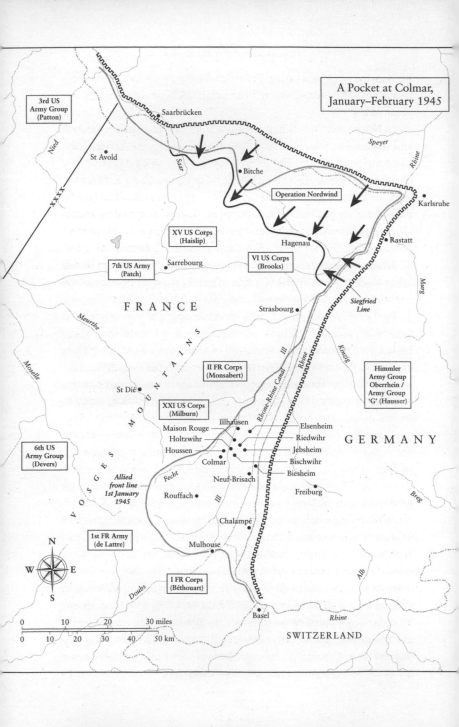

A Pocket at Colmar, January–February 1945

Blaskowitz, likewise sacking Friedrich Wiese and substituting Siegfried Rasp at Nineteenth Army. Both men, he felt, would be more compliant to his will.

In November, Devers had already let the Division Leclerc (French 2nd Armoured Division) make a run for Strasbourg, the Alsatian capital. It was not a military objective, but de Gaulle argued strongly for its liberation as the last French city in German hands. Using local knowledge, de Lattre's men had set out at night along country roads and tracks through the Vosges, bumper to bumper, headlights on, bypassing known German positions. Leclerc's men entered the city early on 23 November, Thanksgiving Day for their American comrades. Reflecting the eclectic nature of French forces, the advance was led by the Régiment Blindé des Fusiliers Marins (RBFM), a unit of naval personnel fighting a land war with American M10 tank destroyers.

For Leclerc it fulfilled an oath he had made to his fellow countrymen in the Libyan desert at Kufra. In March 1941, when the then Colonel Leclerc had achieved the first victory of Free French forces over their opponents, he had vowed, 'We will not stop until the French flag flies over Strasbourg.' The iconography of the moment was extreme. It was also a happy result for de Lattre, who had several times complained to Devers that his army was mostly assigned covering, rather than offensive, roles. In his mind, Patch's Americans were stealing all the military glory. Though there was good reason for this, it still offended French pride.[1]

However, the Colmar Pocket due south of Strasbourg refused to be subdued, due to the ferocity of the German defence driven by Himmler, French logistical challenges, combat fatigue, and the revolting wintry weather which precluded the use of close air support by the attackers. With Sixth Army Group fuming over Hitler's stubborn refusal to relinquish the Colmar area in the dregs of 1944, on 16 December the Führer unleashed *Herbstnebel* in the Ardennes.[2] Eisenhower ordered Patton to withdraw his own XII Corps (under Manton Eddy, with three infantry and two armoured divisions) from the line, swing them left through ninety degrees, spectacularly changing axis from facing east to glancing northwards, and with John Milliken's III Corps, relieve Bastogne and lance the underside of the German salient in the Ardennes. Eddy's place was taken by elements of Patch's Seventh Army, whom SHAEF instructed to extend their frontage by an extra fifty miles. They shuffled left, from Bitche to Saint-Avold, and there joined up with Walton H. Walker's XX Corps, under Patton's command.

Units were rushed up to bolster the thinly held front, including three infantry regiments of the 42nd National Guard Division. With them was Corporal Donald J. Carner, leading a machine-gun squad in Company 'C', 232nd Infantry. He had already experienced an adventurous war, joining an artillery unit of the California National Guard in 1938 and finding himself stationed at Pearl Harbor on 7 December 1941. After lengthy service in the Pacific, he was reassigned to the 42nd in the autumn of 1944.

'I left New York and docked at Marseilles, debarked the ship and when the Bulge started was bundled into a forty-and-eight [a rail boxcar that took forty men or eight horses] and arrived at Metz four days later.' These boxcars haunted many Great War-era memoirs and were still the most practical way of shifting large numbers of troops around Europe decades later. Deutsche Reichsbahn also used captured rolling stock to move other populations to camps, in grimmer fashion. Carner continued, 'We were trucked straight into line without artillery or other support as Task Force Linden, named for the Assistant Division Commander.'[3] They slotted into position north and south of Strasbourg, helping to defend Brooks' VI Corps sector of thirty-one miles along the Rhine. With Patch's men now stretched to holding an eighty-four-mile front with virtually no depth, this move repeated the same gamble that had led to Middleton's VIII Corps being thinly strung along the Ardennes prior to *Herbstnebel*.

On 19 December, Eisenhower ordered Devers to halt all offensive operations. Over the next few days all Allied military attention was fixed on the Ardennes, thus de Lattre's struggling French and US forces around Colmar were given a chance to draw breath and reorganise. By the new year, Eisenhower was confident the German assault would be contained then eradicated. However, on 31 December Hitler followed his dying Bulge campaign with Operation *Nordwind* ('North Wind'), a lesser German attack against precisely the extended sector now thinly held by Patch.

Nordwind was mounted by Himmler's Heeresgruppe Oberrhein which fielded four attacking corps and included powerful formations such as the 6th SS Gebirgs (Mountain), 17th SS Panzergrenadier, 21st Panzer and 25th Panzergrenadier Divisions. Two German pincers punched into stretches of Patch's front, now relatively denuded of troops, with VI Corps initially on the receiving end. The German aim, having correctly divined that some of Patton's forces would be drawn away to the Ardennes, was to seize Strasbourg then turn the lower flanks of Third Army.

Ultra, which had been found wanting before *Herbstnebel*, was afterwards in overdrive with every signal scrutinised, and SHAEF was able to alert Devers and Patch to the threat of *Nordwind* beforehand. The ability to break German Enigma ciphers at Bletchley Park in England remained a closely guarded secret, and a fiction was maintained to those in receipt of its insights that the material was gleaned from a highly placed spy, rather than cryptoanalysis and computer-driven code-breaking. Patch's chief intelligence officer, Colonel Bill Quinn, made the most of the hints he was given on 24 December ('Excellent agent sources report enemy units building up in Black Forest are for offensive. Imperative that all defensive precautions be immediately effective') to work out that *Nordwind* would initially fall at Bitche, on the boundary between US XV and VI Corps.[4]

The newly arrived Task Force Linden was caught in the southern pincer on 24–25 January, managing to hold on against tremendous odds, for which their 222nd Infantry Regiment received a Presidential Unit Citation. However, the main German effort erupted out of the Saar region, where the Reich's frontier left the Rhine and doglegged its way westwards to Saarbrücken. It was an area many of the same units would contest again in mid-March. Those on the receiving end were exclusively Seventh Army units, including the 70th 'Trailblazers' Division, who had only arrived in Marseilles in December. Corporal Frank Yarosh, born in Pennsylvania of Russian and Polish stock, remembered being assigned to a Maginot Line pillbox near Bitche with Company 'C' of the 274th Infantry on 20 January.

'The wind was cold and biting, minus fifteen or twenty Fahrenheit, the snow up to my rear end. Three buddies and I occupied a bunker with thick walls, a big heavy door, covered with snow three or four feet deep.' He recollected that he'd just lit a cigarette in the small hours when there was 'a blinding noise and a flash. I remember seeing stars just like in the movies. Then we heard a voice: "You are our prisoners. Come out."' A German had tossed a grenade through one of the loopholes. The squad had been captured by a Harvard-educated SS officer and his men dressed in snow-parka uniforms, who beat Yarosh and threatened to kill him unless he divulged military information. Yarosh revealed only his name, rank and serial number; 'I'm still proud of that,' he told me in 1992.[5]

The whole region of hills, forests and villages isolated by the terrain between Bitche and Hagenau was a lonely, frozen battlefield, where many from both sides were killed or captured, and some remain to this day. The wounded – unless given immediate medical attention – stood little chance of survival in such extreme conditions. It is difficult to identify what motivated the Germans to carry on. For some it was fear, for others it was military professionalism. Another grenadier observed, 'Call it loyalty if you have to call it something. Had we fought in Lapland, at the Volga, and in Africa, just to throw away our weapons the moment you Americans entered the Reich?'[6]

During *Nordwind*, both Brooks' VI and Haislip's XV Corps were forced to give ground; with two ongoing campaigns in the Ardennes and Colmar, there were no Allied reserves. Patch was able to absorb the blows, but a nervous Eisenhower, given what had just happened in the Ardennes, felt a temporary shortening of the Allied line was required. He ordered Devers to pull back two divisions from a large chunk of Alsace north of Colmar and form a defensive position on the eastern slopes of the Vosges. Strasbourg, only recently liberated, was to be abandoned. The French were understandably furious, for de Gaulle had just given a rousing speech there, announcing the city would never again be under German domination. He immediately went over Eisenhower's head to telegraph Roosevelt, who refused to intervene.

Duff Cooper, newly installed British Ambassador in Paris, warned Churchill of 'dire political consequences' following any evacuation, 'to the detriment of the Americans'.[7] Fearing massacres by a returning Gestapo, de Lattre was ordered by his national commander to defy

Eisenhower and 'make a Stalingrad out of Strasbourg' if the Americans withdrew. Patch sided with Général Schwartz, the French military governor, in arguing the city should be protected.[8] Devers was committed to implementing SHAEF's directive but listened to impassioned pleas from Colonel de Souzy (de Lattre's liaison officer), as well as Patch, and compromised by trying to delay implementation of his commander's instructions, sending his chief of staff to SHAEF to plead the French case.

Juin and de Gaulle both stressed the symbolism for the whole of France were the city to fall into German hands again, never mind the propaganda value for Hitler's Reich. Captured Volksgrenadiers revealed they were being exhorted 'to seize Strasbourg as a present for Der Führer'. Lieutenant Colonel Lodge, Devers' liaison officer to the French, observed that Strasbourg was where *La Marseillaise* (France's stirring national anthem) was written and first sung in 1792 when it was originally titled 'War Song for the Army of the Rhine'.

Official letters of increasing outrage flew back and forth. Possibly exaggerating, de Gaulle suggested he feared insurrection throughout France. Unmoved, Eisenhower and Bedell Smith warned that any disobedience would result in the withholding of fuel and ammunition. Juin retorted that de Gaulle would deny the Americans use of the French railway network, rolling stock and signals system. Bedell Smith became so angry with Juin he later wrote that had the Frenchman been in his own army, he'd have punched him in the face.[9]

Devers, caught in the middle, was blamed for the intransigence of the French, which further cast Sixth Army Group in poor light with Eisenhower's headquarters. However, even the Deputy Supreme Allied Commander, Air Chief Marshal Sir Arthur Tedder, privately warned Ike the abandonment of Strasbourg might be unwise. Sensing trouble, Churchill and Brooke flew from London to Paris on 3 January to lobby on France's behalf, though in his memoirs the Prime Minister wrote, 'I chanced to be at Eisenhower's headquarters.'[10]

Devers had made many friends in London before his posting to Algiers at the end of 1943; Churchill and Brooke shielded him as well as advancing de Gaulle's cause to retain Strasbourg. This was where political considerations overrode the military situation. Faced with such a line-up of heavy artillery, Eisenhower conceded and issued new instructions at noon on 3 January to defend Strasbourg, but the whole issue – which had the potential to fracture the Allied coalition – served also to widen the rift between him and Devers. This amounted to their second major confrontation, the first being Sixth Army Group's aspiration to cross the Rhine the previous November. However, a potential rift *within* Sixth Army Group, between the Americans and French, had been averted, largely due to the efforts of Colonels Lodge and de Souzy, which also reflected well on Devers' diplomacy and his ability to collaborate with his subordinates. De Lattre wrote later of 'our friendliness, cemented in the difficult days at Strasbourg'.[11]

De Lattre immediately dispatched the 3rd Algerian Division to Strasbourg, and the threat to the city diminished. *Nordwind* itself degenerated into half a dozen separate attacks directed against weak spots in Seventh Army's lines. At times ground was given, US units were forced back, prisoners taken, armour and vehicles captured, but by 25 January the offensive had spent itself. Seventh Army suffered losses of 13,000, but it had cost the Germans 23,000 killed, wounded and taken prisoner, plus the destruction of their last major armoured formations west of the Rhine.

However, in the larger picture, on 12 January the Russians had begun their campaign from the River Vistula to the Oder. Berlin could no longer countenance *Nordwind*'s piecemeal attacks in the West when this major new offensive, every bit as large as *Bagration* of the previous summer, threatened to undermine what remained of the Eastern Front. On 22 January Himmler relinquished the reins of Heeresgruppe Oberrhein after a far from stellar performance, his place taken by SS-Oberst-Gruppenführer Paul Hausser until the 29th, when the command itself was dissolved. Hausser went on to command Army Group 'G' from the same day, replacing the capable, but avowedly anti-SS, Johannes Blaskowitz. This was the Group's third change of commander in eight months, and more symbolic of Hitler's mood changes than professional competence.[12]

Those German units which had survived *Nordwind* reasonably intact were dispatched eastwards to halt the Red Army. Because of the enormous Franco-American effort in the West, it is easy to overlook that

Berlin's attention would remain focused on the Eastern Front. The pins on Hitler's strategic map boards tell the story. In January 1945, there were 146 German units assessed as being of divisional size stationed on the Eastern Front; in the West, there were seventy-nine; the following month, the Western Front had declined to sixty-eight, with 173 opposite the Russians as they neared Berlin. However, by this time not a single German unit was at full strength. Hitler's inclination was to raise new units, rather than reinforce old ones; thus most divisions could muster one or two thirds of their allocated manpower.[13]

To this day, the achievements of Devers and Patch in stemming *Nordwind* remain remarkably little known, possibly due to SHAEF's antipathy, partly because of the reluctance of both men to blow their own trumpet, but it was also deliberately under-reported. The war-weary American public had no stomach for reading of a second crisis immediately after the Ardennes. Recognition of defeating both German assaults is today vested in the US Army's 'Ardennes-Alsace' campaign streamer – acknowledging the destruction of *Herbstnebel* and *Nordwind*.

Devers spent the rest of the winter preparing his army group for its role in the final offensive against the Reich. However, the threat of the Colmar Pocket remained, where the German Nineteenth Army fed in eight divisions and other units totalling 30,000 men to hold the salient with the potential to again threaten Strasbourg. To Devers' embarrassment, both his armies had struggled to seal the area in December, until interrupted by *Herbstnebel*, then *Nordwind*. The new year saw Patch's Seventh more stretched than ever, holding a longer front with fewer men, while his supply of combat reinforcements had slowed to a trickle. The prospect of lancing the festering German boil around Colmar seemed as remote as ever.

That winter, for every nine American replacements arriving in Europe, Devers only received one to Bradley's eight, SHAEF directing most towards First and Third Armies in the Ardennes, despite his needs. Seventh Army meanwhile used the time to integrate new outfits such as the 42nd, 63rd and 70th Infantry Divisions, later joined by the 71st, 100th and 103rd, mostly arriving through Marseilles, demonstrating the value of that port.[14] From late January, Patch gained the recently constituted US XXI Corps, which had originally controlled SHAEF reserve divisions as they arrived. De Lattre was most impressed on first meeting its commander, Major General Frank W. Milburn, at his head-quarters on 25 January 1945. 'Lean and muscular and straight of eye, with the energetic features of a fighter,' the Frenchman noted, observing his 'leader-like authority'.[15]

The day before the French *chef* met XXI Corps' chief, Bradley's headquarters had received a phone call from SHAEF requesting the loan of two divisions to aid Devers in finishing off the Colmar Pocket. Bradley shared Eisenhower's dim view of his fellow army group com-mander. This persisted long after the war, when he asserted quite openly in his memoirs, 'Because of the ineptitude he had shown in the so-called Colmar Pocket operation, I had little faith in Devers and less in de Lattre. I foresaw a long bloody campaign going nowhere at great cost to us.'

Bradley wrote that the French had 'lazily and ill-advisedly failed to clear about 50,000 Germans west of the Rhine in a thirty-by-fifty-mile area'.[16] At the time, in answer to SHAEF's request for two of his divi-sions, Bradley slammed the phone down, warning Ike, his boss and friend, 'I trust you do not think I am angry. But I want you to impress upon you I am godamned well incensed.'[17] Having inspected the rele-vant papers at the US Army's Military History Institute this is not only word for word the text in the archives, but the strongest confrontation between US headquarters I have read anywhere. It neatly illustrated Allied tensions that winter and how little SHAEF, and Twelfth Army Group, sympathised with the difficulties facing Sixth Army Group.[18]

Devers warned the French that operations in Colmar must resume on 5 January 1945, but the Ardennes offensive took longer to defeat than he anticipated, never mind fighting off *Nordwind*. The weather, too, was hostile, with de Lattre assessing the winter as 'truly Siberian'. He con-tinued, 'though smiling on fine days, the Alsatian plain resembled an immense city of the dead, covered with a thick shroud of snow, from which emerged the skeletons of trees, haunted by croaking clouds of crows. And the sky, low and constantly grey, was lit only by the sinis-ter gleams of fires or the blood-red flashes of gunfire. It was 20 degrees below zero, the wind howled, and there was over three feet of snow.'[19]

PFC Bob Lynch, of the 15th Infantry's Company 'K' in 3rd Division, wrote home to his folks in Rye, New York, 'Our company was so high in the mountains that we had to be supplied by pack mules. To keep us warm at night we put three blankets over our bodies and two under; it didn't solve the problem.' The highlight of his Christmas mail had been a box containing socks. 'I don't know how I could have survived without them. I'll wear them until they cry for help. Unfortunately, my army-issued socks wear out in about two weeks. After that you are stuck with them unless you have another set – or lose a foot.'[20]

One of Lynch's platoon commanders recalled of this time, 'the night is filled with the clump, clump of pick and shovel gnawing at the rock-hard earth. The efforts are futile, but the exercise keeps us from freezing. When we finally give up trying to chew holes in the ground, we stamp up and down to stir up heat in our bodies. We take turns at staying on watch. I fall asleep. My hair freezes on the ground. A gun cracks. I jerk awake, leaving patches of my hair in the ice. Wind whistles through the barren tree limbs. Few words are spoken. Huddling in the snow, we open cans of greasy rations and attempt to eat.'[21]

Even out of the line the GIs suffered. Staff Sergeant Charles K. Blum leading a platoon with Company 'E' of the 7th Infantry, also 3rd Division, noted that when 'Company kitchens were brought up and the men fed three hot meals a day, nine out of every ten acquired a case of bellyache and the runs, and had to make hurried trips to the battalion aid station for a strong dose of Paregoric, a dose which proved to be an effective and immediate cure in most cases'.[22]

Dr M. Bedford Davis Jr was a surgeon attached to the neighbouring 109th Infantry, a regiment commanded by the D-Day hero James Earl Rudder, of the 28th Division. He observed of conditions in the Vosges, 'The snow was so soft that with every step we sank to our mid-thighs. A conditioned infantryman was only able to walk at one mile an hour. Even in a six-wheel drive truck, with snow tires, chains, and a snow-plow attached to the front, a platoon of soldiers with snow shovels was required to help us to move forward. Patrols robed in white field coats brought in POWs for interrogation. From them we learned the Germans were doing the same. Fighting was impossible.'[23]

In the event, because of Nordwind, the proposed French counter-offensive at Colmar, optimistically code-named Operation *Cheerful*, did not materialise until 20 January, in the half-light of a freezing, snowy morning. Turning the terrible weather to their advantage, and targeting the southern edge of the pocket, the colonial forces of Général Antoine Béthouart's I French Corps – four divisions of experienced veterans – achieved surprise by attacking during a snowstorm, then fought for eleven days before grinding to an exhausted halt. The Frenchmen tried to let their artillery do the hard work for them, employing 102 field batteries, and consequently were soon short of 105mm ammunition. Meanwhile, from the south-west Général Billotte's 10th Infantry Division, containing Moroccan Goums and a regiment of former Resistance fighters, held the high ground of the Vosges and vigorously raided their opponents.

Both armies were channelled by terrain, which the Germans turned to their advantage. Roads outside the towns were not paved and soon churned into seas of mud by the snow, wheels and tracks. Everywhere, it seemed, roads, forests, streams and small towns all led to killing zones carefully sited between German strongpoints. These positions were built in sturdy stone farmhouses, organised in depth, and surrounded by tiered minefields. The mines were frequently made of plastic or glass, undetectable by mechanical means, and further concealed by snow and ice. Schu-mines were designed to injure, not kill; the fiendish logic being that two soldiers would be needed to carry a third off the battlefield, thus diminishing the number of opponents. These devices contained half a pound of explosives in a small wooden box or glass jar, enough to sever feet or damage the groin. As the only metal was in the detonator, these mines were easily missed by the engineers' detectors. The alternative was to probe by hand, using a rod or stick: a laborious and frightening task. This was exactly the challenge the 7th Infantry, whom we met in the Prologue, would encounter at Utweiler.

From the southern edge of the pocket, the focus switched northwards with a II Corps Franco-American assault on 22 January. Massive bombardments also accompanied these attacks, with the African-American 969th Field Artillery Battalion, under French command and initially supporting the Marne Division, recording that its twelve guns fired 912 rounds of ammunition on the first day alone. With prior service in Normandy and the Bulge, the 969th was one of several experienced artillery battalions attached to de Lattre's force for the twenty-day campaign, equipped with the 155mm 'Long Tom', which could hurl a 127-pound projectile to a range of 13 miles. Général Joseph de Monsabert's own three divisions, including Leclerc's 2nd Armoured, began their drive with O'Daniel's 3rd Marne also under his command. The latter had managed to borrow a fourth infantry regiment, so deployed with twelve infantry battalions (belonging to the 7th, 15th, 30th and 254th Regiments). Some elements of the 5th French Armoured were in support, despite the earlier fighting having reduced their combat strength by 80 per cent, down to a mere sixty-one armoured vehicles.

From 25 January, Milburn's XXI Corps also came under de Lattre's control and piled in from the north-west with another three American divisions, including Norman D. Cota's understrength 28th (still licking its wounds after being shredded twice, once in the Hürtgen Forest, and a second time in the Bulge), Ray E. Porter's 75th and Roderick R. Allen's formidable 12th Armored. It was a mark of faith and respect for de Lattre that Devers, in the face of opposition from many of his own staff, placed first the Marne Division and later the whole of XXI Corps under the French.[24]

The immediate aim was to strike to the north of Colmar itself and neutralise the threat to Strasbourg. At the same time, the Franco-American force would reach to the German rear, cutting the defenders' communications and supply lines. Naming his offensive Operation *Grand Slam*, de Lattre noted it was the first anniversary of John O'Daniel leading his US 3rd Division ashore at Anzio.[25] 'It had travelled a long road since then', he observed, describing its commander whose features 'might have been carved out with an axe', and his 'uncommon dynamic personality, will and energy, which had turned his division into a tool of exceptional quality'.[26] A legend throughout the army, O'Daniel was nicknamed 'Iron Mike' for his doggedness in battle. He had won a Distinguished Service Cross in 1918 and had taken over an infantry company when his predecessor, Captain Mark W. Clark, was promoted to command the battalion. Sporting an impressive bayonet scar across one cheek, the envy of many a Prussian officer, and gained in hand-to-hand combat at Saint-Mihiel, O'Daniel's favourite expression when inspecting his Blue and White Devils was 'Sharpen your bayonet!'

The Colmar campaign, as elsewhere during that unusually bitter

January–March, was fought in the woods that surrounded the open fields, all blanketed with recent falls of thick snow which made the going heavy. GIs called their awkward walk through the Alpine white, slush or mud the 'paddle-foot shuffle'. They were weighed down with 'a full belt of ammunition, plus four extra bandoleers. Every man carried four hand grenades, three fragmentation, and one white phosphorus. One day's K-ration was issued, gas masks were carried, and white camouflage suits, known as spook suits, worn. To give greater freedom to the individual, both pack and cartridge belt were worn over the suit. Hoods were not worn, as they proved a disadvantage in hearing for the wearer.' Most were not purpose-made suits, but bedsheets, tablecloths and pillowcases, that flapped around, got muddy or wet, and froze, and were soon discarded.[27]

'Control was difficult in the snow-laden forests,' noted a platoon commander. 'Each man's snow shoes, crunching in the snow, made the only sound in his world, until he stopped and could hear the same subdued crunching from the man nearest him. The sense of being alone was strong upon all. Dark splodges showed where mines or shells had already exploded. Sounds of an intense small arms fight broke out to the east. The crackle of rifles came sharp and clear, with the swift, sudden rap of German automatic weapons answering, while in the lulls, could be heard the cries of American leaders shouting orders. A sudden, fierce crescendo came, then in an instant, complete silence from the same area, a silence that told neither of success, nor of failure.'[28] 'Sleep is not among our rations,' wrote another. 'The snow has turned to slush; we slog from objective to objective on leaden feet.'[29] Yet GIs soon found their opponents were just as demoralised and tired. One remembered the surrender of a gaggle of Volksgrenadiers: 'A sad, muddy lot, they throw their helmets down and stand with raised hands while we shake them down. Their eyes are dead and indifferent. They seem more exhausted than we.'[30]

On 23 January, one of O'Daniel's regiments, the 30th, captured a small bridge over the River Ill near a red-painted farmstead called La Maison Rouge (the Red House) and pushed forward to the next villages of Holtzwihr and Riedwihr, where they ran into groups of German infantry and armour. Rushing to bring up tank support for the beleaguered GIs, the 35-ton deadweight of the first Sherman across proved too much for the ancient wooden structure, and Lieutenant John F. Harmon's vehicle 'dropped like an elevator' into the river below amid the debris of the bridge. While engineers worked frantically on repairs, the 601st Tank Destroyer Battalion noted that night 'ice forming in the firing mechanisms [of their main three-inch guns], rendering them unable to fire'.[31]

By dusk, all three battalions of Colonel Lionel C. McGarr's 30th Infantry had withdrawn to the riverbanks, while frustrated tank destroyer crews watched the glow of 'German tank fire [which] sprayed our helpless doughs, so they retreated and jumped into the river. We covered their retreat by firing our .50-caliber machine-guns, and that gave our position away in the darkness.' Icicles formed on the soaked uniforms of the shivering men. The American vehicles came under fire themselves from what they assessed as several Mark IVs and 'a new Jagdpanther, a heavy German tank destroyer with an 88mm gun'.

Later, O'Daniel unleashed a second regiment, the 15th Infantry, to secure the area, which they did at first light on the 24th, crossing by engineer-constructed footbridges. They were immediately counter-attacked by a company of infantry from the 2nd Gebirgs (Mountain) Division – newly arrived from Norway – and thirteen Sturmgeschützen (23-ton, turretless, tracked assault guns, mounting a 75mm gun). These overran and destroyed Item and King Companies, holed up in and around La Maison Rouge. Some GIs were crushed under the tracks of the German armour, others machine-gunned where they lay or shot trying to surrender. PFC Robert Lynch was caught in this maelstrom as part of Company 'K': 'I and members of my squad, fully clothed, crossed the icy river and joined the isolated and outnumbered troops of the 30th Regiment. Some Jerry tanks overran our positions, and we were forced back into the river to save our lives. Everyone was soaking wet and frozen; there was no place to dry off. That same night the order was given to move out. Once again, we forded the icy river.'[32]

The battle for the little bridgehead over the River Ill, fast-flowing and some sixty feet wide at this point, swung to and fro before artillery and an assault by a fresh battalion drove the German armour and infantry back, with the 15th Infantry entering Riedwihr on the night of 25–26 January. The price of this action was ninety-four GIs, four tank destroyers and two Shermans, but the Germans had more casualties and lost four panzers. Sergeant Rudy Larsen of the 601st TD Battalion wrote home laconically describing how he had 'cost the army another $75,000. My tank got hit and burned up, so I also lost everything to my name, except for the clothes I was wearing. You'd be surprised how fast we can move in a case like that. We got out OK except for some scorched eyebrows and a big scare.'[33]

Simultaneously, ten miles upriver from La Maison Rouge, on the road between Illhäusern and Elsenheim, the 8th Régiment de Chasseurs d'Afrique (8th RCA), a cavalry outfit attached to the French 1st Infantry Division, was advancing on the Marne's left.[34] It made perfect sense for the Franco-US force to be closely integrated, given that they wore identical uniforms, and operated the same weapons and vehicles. The 8th RCA, for example, possessed thirty-six Detroit-manufactured M10 Tank Destroyers, a three-inch anti-tank gun mounted in a rotating turret, built onto the hull of a Sherman. Resembling a thirty-ton regular tank, they normally deployed in three squadrons of twelve.

In his memoirs, de Gaulle ungallantly described the goodwill of Roosevelt's United States as *maigre* (literally 'skinny', but meaning scanty), which was far from the truth.[35] During the war, the American arsenal supplied 1,400 tanks, scout and armoured cars, including 227 M10 tank destroyers, as well as 27,000 half-tracks and Jeeps produced by Ford and Willys-Overland at half a dozen sites across America, Dodge ambulances made by Chrysler in Michigan, and six-wheeled trucks supplied by GMC, assembled in Pontiac, Michigan and by Chevrolet at St. Louis, Missouri. Apart from consumables like rations, gasoline and medical supplies, 2,000 artillery pieces and mortars, 166,000 rifles and carbines, 30,000 machine-guns, over a million rounds of artillery and mortar ammunition, and 50 million rounds of small arms ammunition were sent to de Lattre's forces. Equally important was the formal training of eleven French divisions before the war's end.[36]

Opposite the French Chasseurs, clad in American-supplied olive-drab uniforms but sporting French headgear and badges of rank, lurked four battalions of the 708th Volksgrenadiers. De Lattre wrote later that the surrounding terrain was riddled with 'blockhouses and protected by an inextricable network of ditches', and subdued only by 'hand-to-hand fighting with grenades, submachine-guns, and daggers'. As a dismounted battalion of French Foreign légionnaires advanced, supported by a squadron of M10s from the 8th RCA, a party of Volksgrenadiers suddenly lunged out of the woods supported by Nashorn (Rhinoceros) tank destroyers, a Panzer IV mounting the deadly 88mm gun. Known as the long-range sniper, it was a Nashorn that duelled with the Chasseurs d'Afrique.[37]

Although the setback caused was temporary, in a couple of hours of daylight the French lost three M10s, two Shermans and 121 soldiers. One of the tracked casualties was *Porc-Epic II* (Porcupine-2), a tank destroyer in the 8th RCA's 3rd Squadron, immobilised near the Illhäusern Mill. Three of its crew – René Garnier, René Cardot and Claude Beaufils – died and were buried on the spot. They are commemorated with four officers and three other crewmen who also perished alongside the tank destroyer. The vehicle remains exactly where it was knocked out as a roadside memorial, a striking sight on this tiny route to the Rhine, the hole drilled by the 88 round clearly visible.[38]

Further south, back in the Marne Division's sector, PFC Jose F. Valdez with the 7th Infantry – the Cottonbalers – was the BAR-man in a squad on patrol at a small railway station near Houssen on the northern outskirts of Colmar, when confronted with a local German counter-attack. Valdez covered the rest of his patrol, sprayed automatic fire on a German tank so effectively that he forced it to withdraw, and killed several infantrymen. As the Germans surged forward with an estimated two companies, Valdez continued to give covering fire, while he and his comrades escaped. Valdez was hit and died three weeks later from his wounds, but his actions brought him a Medal of Honor, and his valour is now commemorated on the spot with a memorial.[39]

Another Medal of Honor was gained in the nearby village of Holtzwihr, where for two days the Germans launched company-strength assaults against the incursions made by the 15th Infantry. It was during one of these attempts on 26 January that two companies of Volksgrenadiers plus armour attempted to clear the woods north of Holtzwihr, held by the 15th Infantry's Company 'B'. As he ordered his company to withdraw, a young second lieutenant remained, and used a field telephone to call down artillery fire on his attackers. He then climbed onto a nearby M10 tank destroyer belonging to the 601st TD Battalion that had been hit and was slowly burning. First removing the vehicle's dead commander, and dragging the telephone into the turret, he used its machine-gun to slay more of his attackers who came as close as twenty yards, all the while relaying fire missions to the field guns behind.

As he later wrote in a memoir, when the artillery sergeant at the other end enquired 'How close are they?', the officer responded, 'Just hold the phone and I'll let you talk to one of the bastards.' The lieutenant was concealed by smoke from the burning vehicle, and the Germans were mystified as to where their opponent was located. In their minds, certainly not on the M10 which, packed with fuel and ammunition, was clearly about to explode. Although the vehicle was further struck by German tank fire, the officer remained in position until, wounded and burned, he saw the opposition finally stop and retreat. Only then did he crawl back to his own lines. An eyewitness, Sergeant Elmer C. Brawley of Company 'B', later recorded the scene. 'Silhouetted vividly against the nude trees, dark evergreens, and deep snow, without cover of any kind, he stood there, as the flames moved closer to the gasoline tank and ammunition in the tank destroyer. All around him, 88mm, and bullets from machine-guns, machine-pistols, and rifles, shook the forest and sent up flurries of snow and dirt.'[40]

The young man's name was Audie L. Murphy, recent recipient of a battlefield commission, and later renowned as the most decorated American serviceman of World War Two. Post-war he pursued a career as a movie star, appearing in the 1955 film *To Hell and Back* (also the title of his 1949 war memoirs), where he portrayed himself re-enacting the incident. De Lattre later recorded the pleasure of awarding Murphy (whom he called André) the Cross of the Chevalier of the Legion of Honour in the courtyard of Les Invalides in 1948.[41]

A while ago, I paid a visit to Holtzwihr and easily identified the route taken by Murphy's Company 'B'. The open meadow across which the Germans advanced beyond the outskirts of the village is plainly evident. At its far end is the treeline where the M10 was burning. At one stage the wrecked tank destroyer was bulldozed off the road, for in a ditch I found parts of its tank tracks and numerous .50-inch cartridges. In the surrounding woods, I came across the remains of German equipment and GI-issue Shoepac over-boots. The rubber-bottomed, leather-topped footwear was a belated attempt to deal with the problem of trench foot, though the ones I found had been abandoned in the flurry of combat. So too had a magazine for a Thompson submachine-gun, fully loaded with .45-inch ammunition, that had been dropped by a startled or injured GI. In January 2000, the people of Holtzwihr erected a memorial on the site of Murphy's bravery to both the Marne Infantry Division and Combat Command 4 (of the 5th French Armoured) who supported them.

However, the Colmar Pocket was not defeated by the 'Blue and White Devils' alone, though there are a disproportionate number of accounts featuring them. Other French and American divisions played equally important roles. On the Marne's left, the 254th Infantry (of the 63rd US Division) attacked Jebsheim, east of Colmar, on 25 January, alongside Colonel de Lavilléon's Combat Command 6, the French Parachute Battalion and légionnaires of the 3rd Foreign Legion. Initially the attack stalled as the men found their weapons had frozen solid in the extreme cold. Being on the German Hauptkampflinie (main line of resistance), the settlement was bitterly contested by detachments from the 2nd Gebirgs Division. De Lattre described how the town was utterly destroyed, changing hands three times, where 'every house was a redoubt, every air-vent concealed a bazooka. Hardly had we taken a small block than the back-surge of the wave took it away from us again.'[42]

At one stage, Colonel James E. Hatcher commanding the 255th Infantry remembered a conversation, 'held in clear over the radio-telephone with Captain Howdy Wilcox of our Company "E". I asked him what the steady popping sound was I kept hearing. He replied that it was his pistol shots. He found it necessary to keep shooting with his free hand while he talked, because the Germans had succeeded in surrounding a considerable number of his men in a barn and had set it on fire. Of course, the conversation was promptly discontinued.'[43] Bill Gold, a GI with the 254th, was caught by a brace of German stick grenades, one of which injured his right forearm and left ear, and flung shrapnel in his eyes. Semi-conscious he applied a tourniquet and was dragged by German medics into a bunker. He had the presence of mind 'to destroy my dog tags to prevent the Germans from learning I was Jewish. I worried they would kill me if they saw the 'H' [for Hebrew] on them.' After a couple of days, he was freed and immediately sent back to a field hospital.[44]

While civilians hid in their basements and cellars, the Germans were ejected from Jebsheim only after three days of hand-to-hand fighting and continued to send in panzer counter-attacks until 2 February. Much of the German armour belonged to Panzerjäger-Abteilung (Anti-Tank Battalion) 654, operating Jagdpanthers. On 26 January, vehicle No. 131 was commanded by Unteroffizier Karl-Heinz Danisch, but his mount was soon immobilised by an overheated engine. As Danisch was lifting the engine covers with his driver, Stabsgefreiter Rensen, they came under fire. In a flash, Rensen's head was removed by a French tank shell and Danisch scuttled back inside. After sixteen hits by anti-tank rounds, he and his remaining crew bailed out, escaping back to their lines. His *Abteilung* left behind at least four destroyed Jagdpanthers, which together with the smouldering wrecks of three French Shermans and another three M10 tank destroyers littered the area after the battle.[45]

'Five hundred German corpses transformed its streets into a regular charnel-house,' related de Lattre of Jebsheim. 'We ourselves had 300 men *hors de combat* and the Americans at least as many. But we had taken 750 prisoners there and the Americans more than 300. Jebsheim was truly a symbol of the Franco-American brotherhood which reigned in the hearts of the French First Army.'[46] A local resident recorded how 'People walk on bodies. They are everywhere, in the streets and in the orchards. All the houses are gutted, charred remains of vehicles lie here and there, and the dead, some of whom have been crushed by tanks, litter the streets and gardens.'[47]

The morale of the defenders had been shredded, and those who survived were often happy to enter captivity. Sergeant Bob Ross of Company 'G' was guarding about forty German prisoners, when 'an 88mm shell landed in the middle of them. Those that were not killed scuttled for cover.' Ross was momentarily stunned. 'My immediate thoughts were, My God, they're getting away from us. We'll have to do this all over again.' Yet his captives got back into line and ran to the rear, obediently and in formation. 'They wanted out!' he observed.[48] For their struggles, the Second Battalion, 254th Infantry, were awarded a Presidential Unit Citation. After the war, Jebsheim's citizens erected a concrete Croix du

Moulin (Mill Cross) on the edge of town. On it, a text in English, French and German reads: 'You are united in Death; we unite in Peace.'

On 27 January, Milburn's XXI Corps took over part of the French sector, with the 28th, 75th, 12th Armored, French 5th Armoured, as well as the Marne Divisions under command, which put at 125,000 the number of GIs serving in the sector under de Lattre. However, the 'Blue and White Devils' were spent, with some of their rifle companies down to thirty effectives. Murphy's Company 'B' numbered just eighteen at one stage. Like Verdun in World War One, Colmar became a mill that ground the life out of human bodies. Audie Murphy recalled the trail of burnt-out GIs 'sent to the rear with frozen feet and shattered nerves'. He recollected the moment when, under artillery fire, battle fatigue claimed one of his best men. 'His mouth sags; his speech becomes jerky; and his hands shake so that he can hardly insert an ammunition clip into his carbine. Whether he knows or wants it, he is through. Finished.'[49]

Robert Lynch, also with the 15th Infantry, observed, 'Of all the tough places I've been in combat, I'd say this was the worst. We had more men go completely out of their minds than any other campaign. It is simply terrible to see grown men laying in the dirt, crying. It burns me up to have so many men in the armed forces having plush jobs while we in the infantry are expected to do all the fighting. You have absolutely nothing in the world to look forward to except fighting your heart out until this war is over. The only rest you get is when you're wounded and end up in hospital.'[50]

On 29 January, the 3rd Division's artillery recorded firing a barrage of 16,438 rounds, while the 441st Anti-Aircraft Battalion, equipped with 40mm guns, loosed off 22,300 rounds at ground targets. French artillery was equally active, but already noticeably short of shells, consequently firing 1,491 rounds of the 1,500 available at its gun lines. The entire Franco-American force later calculated they had used 24,000 tons of ammunition, which in retrospect may have been as injurious to the firers as it was to those on the receiving end.[51] Surgeon Bedford Davis determined that his fellow medics 'were having nightmares at night. It was not possible to sleep soundly. We had become so conditioned to sudden noise that even a door slamming found most of us automatically flat on the ground.' He recorded that those wounded in the cold went into shock faster, observing that all suffered from sleep deprivation, which 'sucked out a man's energy'.[52]

Sergeant Troy D. Cox of the 15th Infantry remembered how 'you were completely exhausted most of the time, but you were forced to stay alert, in order to survive. You walked like you were in a trance and kept talking to God to help you.'[53] This was the kind of exhaustion that could kill. W. Bert Craft with the 7th Infantry was haunted by the moment one of his comrades 'who was so tired he couldn't function properly, didn't get out of the way of a tank and it backed over him. I will never forget the death scream he gave as he was crushed beneath the tank. It was nerve racking to know that a life had been taken so needlessly by one of our own.'[54]

Tiredness, too, played havoc with a soldier's emotions. During a German attack, Craft came across a GI who had his head down and was crying. 'What in the hell is wrong with you? Why aren't you shooting those damned Krauts?' The soldier in question was of German descent and sobbed, 'I can't shoot my flesh and blood.' Craft threw his empty rifle at the man and demanded, 'Load it, and give me yours.' Curiously, given the number of GIs with Germanic ancestry, already noted, reactions such as this were remarkably rare.

With French II Corps on their left, in Operation *Kraut Buster*, the Franco-American XXI Corps lunged towards the octagonally walled town of Neuf-Brisach, an old Vauban-designed frontier fortress which guarded the German escape route out of Colmar and over the Rhône–Rhine Canal. The town came with an intimidating history: in 1870, during the Franco–Prussian war, the French garrison had held out for an entire month. GIs feared the Wehrmacht would try to repeat the act. De Lattre joked that 'enclosed within its ramparts, in the century-old moats and raised drawbridges, the strange military city remained enigmatical. We made ready for medieval assault, with ladders and battering rams.'[55] In fact, despite the twenty-foot-thick battlements, locals showed 3rd Division GIs a secret tunnel under the moat, whereby the town fell without a shot being fired.

In nearby Bischwihr, Company 'L' of the 7th Infantry started searching a group of grenadiers found hiding in a cellar. On frisking one captive, a GI felt inside the German's breast pocket. The American stiffened and 'paused, not quite sure if what he felt was real, and then felt again. The reality set in. "For Christ's sake," he exclaimed, "it's a woman!" A large group of GIs began mingling with prisoners: out of thirty captured, fourteen were found to be women.' In trying to find volunteers to escort the POWs back, Captain Orville Dilly, the company commander, had no shortage of volunteers. These were unlikely to have been combatants, as female auxiliaries usually working in communications or anti-aircraft roles, and known as *Helferinen*, had their own uniforms, including a skirt. Instead, they were probably girlfriends of troops within the garrison, which in German-speaking Alsace would not have been unusual.[56]

Women served in uniform with the Allies, too. De Lattre had welcomed 5,000 into his AFAT (Armée Feminine de l'Armée de Terre) as secretaries, radio operators, nurses and ambulance drivers, whose numbers would grow to 14,000 by May 1945.[57] They were joined by hundreds of AFS (American Field Service) volunteers, a unit of male ambulance drivers originally founded in 1915 to rescue wounded soldiers on the Western Front. When reactivated in 1940, as in World War One, many were from prominent, wealthy families and graduates of Ivy League universities. They were later joined by conscientious objectors, and other Americans rejected by military recruiters who nevertheless wanted to serve.[58] One of many who answered a call addressed to Harvard students and alumni to join them was Philip Moulton Mayer. A gifted linguist, he soon found himself in the 3rd Field Service Unit, an ambulance company of 120 civilian volunteers and one hundred AFS vehicles supporting the 5th French Armoured Division.[59]

It was this division that clattered over the cobblestones and into Colmar's main square, La Place Rapp, on 2 February, with the US 28th Division securing the suburbs. However, the German rearguard was still active. Texan William M. Pena, an officer with the 109th Infantry, remembered the sound of a huge explosion as a French-driven tank was hit by an anti-tank gun. As the commander tried to get out, a sniper picked him off. 'A French ambulance came whizzing down the street as if to an auto accident. An aid man got out and climbed the tank. The sniper's bullet dropped him to the ground. Instead, a French nurse in overalls carried the aid man towards the ambulance where other hands took over.' Pena never forgot the gallantry of what he next witnessed. 'Then she climbed the tank, hauled the commander out of its turret, methodically pulled him down and dragged him to the ambulance. The sniper had gallantly spared her.'[60] The unfortunate aid man was probably one of Philip Moulton Mayer's colleagues from their all-volunteer AFS unit. Despite his role as a non-combatant, Mayer would later win a Croix de Guerre for similar acts during his progress through Vosges and Colmar.[61]

'The Colmariens,' wrote Richard Johnston of the *New York Times*, were 'oddly reserved' towards the Allies, and he puzzled that in taking down the Third Reich's Gothic-scripted signage, de Lattre's French troops 'enjoyed the liberation of the city more than its citizens'. Johnston quoted one GI as saying, 'They don't seem to give a damn. They don't seem to appreciate how lucky this burg is. Why, we didn't even throw in artillery!'[62] Yet the *New York Times* correspondent was overlooking the fear throughout the pocket – as demonstrated already in parts of the Ardennes – that liberation would be temporary, and their grey-clad neighbours would return. However, resistance was crumbling, and in the early hours of 5 February, armour from the 4th Régiment de Spahis Marocains of French I Corps advancing from the south met elements of the US 12th Armored Division coming from the north in Rouffach, splitting the pocket into an inner and an outer.[63]

Over the remaining three days of the campaign the Allies cleared out isolated German groups still resisting, then raced for the Rhine. As noted in the Prologue, on particularly dark nights the Americans started to deploy anti-aircraft searchlights, bouncing light off the clouds to create 'artificial moonlight', the first occasion being on 3 February, supporting an attack east of Colmar. This coincided with a thaw in the weather, turning the snow to unpleasant slush, which by day allowed Brigadier General Glenn O. Barcus's XII Tactical Air Command to mount ground attack sorties to hasten the Wehrmacht's departure. The clearer skies also tempted the Luftwaffe into the skies, where Bedford Davis one day spotted 'a small combat plane with a German cross on its fuselage. It was bat-winged and had no propeller.' This was the legendary Messerschmitt-262, the world's first jet fighter. It made a single strafing run, but with no control of the air, Davis noted, 'almost as rapidly as it had appeared, the German jet returned whence it came'.[64]

Concealed by a permanent smokescreen, the Germans kept their two main bridges across the Rhine open for as long as possible, but the night of 8 February proved to be the last that the Third Reich spent in Colmar. At 08:00 the following morning a violent explosion announced the disintegration of the railway bridge at Chalampé; French patrols arriving on the scene minutes later watched the twisted metal subside slowly into the Rhine. The Battle of the Colmar Pocket was finally over. Completely irrelevant to the course of the war, it had cost the Oberrhein command – or Army Group 'G' as it had reverted to at the end – an unnecessary 23,000 casualties, including 17,000 prisoners and 3,450 dead. Almost more important was the loss of all sixty-five panzers stationed in the salient and sixty-six artillery pieces.

I followed the route of the Marne Division and both French corps, basing myself in Rouffach. It escaped destruction during 1914–18, despite the nearness of the front lines in the mountains to the west, and suffered a bitter occupation in 1940–4, when the use of French was banned. Seventy-seven Rouffachois were killed, even before the town was caught in the sharp combat of February 1945. With its thirteenth-century stone buildings and fortifications, Rouffach today is a pretty Cinderella village of half-timbered houses with angular roofs, surrounded by vineyards. The first grapes were grown in the area on the estate of an early Roman villa, whose remains are under the present town hall. I couldn't help noticing, too, in the wider Colmar area, there are many streets named 'Devers' – a fitting compliment. As importantly, I discovered the reward for a day of hard battlefield walking: a chilled glass of Alsatian sparkling wine – there are four growers around Rouffach alone.

Walking the surrounding mountains is instructive, as they contain trenches, foxholes and barbed wire, but the many cartridges encountered in the loam could have been fired in anger in either world war, such is the violent history of this corner of eastern France. One can sit amid the pinecones on the lip of an old trench, now shallow with age, and ponder the adrenaline and fear of men in battle. Last time I did so, quite by chance among the pine needles, my fingers alighted on a German soldier's brass belt buckle bearing the Bavarian crown and a motto, *In Treue Fest* – 'In steadfast loyalty'. It dated from the 1914–18 war, but sums up that ethereal spirit, perhaps the only bond that kept young men going in both world wars.

From the beginning of the campaign in late November 1944 to February 1945, Sixth Army Group had suffered around 29,000 casualties, two-thirds of them French. In addition, over 7,000 had been hospitalised for illness, mostly trench foot, frostbite or respiratory problems including pneumonia. The Seventh Army assessed their French compatriots as 'incapable of offensive action until they undergo a thorough retraining and refitting program for a minimum of six weeks'.[65] This was not due to any lack of fighting spirit but a dearth of numbers and shortages of equipment. Franco-American losses among armoured crewmen stood at 5 per cent, whereas the campaign had eroded Devers' infantry by 20 per cent. This was on top of the corrosion sustained since they had landed in France which equated to another 20 per cent. However, these blows were unevenly spread. As Audie Murphy noted of his own division, 'In seven weeks we had suffered over forty-five hundred casualties'.[66] The end of the Colmar campaign on 9 February, though Sixth Army Group could not know, meant the European war had eighty-eight days to run.

(*Above*): An LVT (landing vehicle tracked) unloading from its transporter. Over 100 of these amphibious carriers, known variously as Alligators or Buffaloes, were available for the Reichswald operation. (*Below*): Scottish infantry advance on Bren carriers (*left*) and a column of Shermans (*right*) during Operation *Veritable*. The Jeep (*centre*) is for movement control, an almost impossible task on the few roads available.

4

Veritable Mud

Away from the festering Colmar Pocket, Allied offensive plans for 1945 were those of December 1944. They had been dusted off and improved from their predecessors, which the Ardennes campaign had interrupted. The immediate strategic aim remained the destruction of German forces west of the Rhine, which would be achieved by several operations. Initially, *Blackcock* followed by *Veritable* were attacks by Montgomery's army group to clear the Rhineland in the north, supported by *Grenade* mounted by Simpson's Ninth Army. Of these, the key manoeuvre was *Veritable*, beginning on 8 February. The next operation would see Bradley's army group launch attacks in the centre, eventually commencing on 23 February, with an operation called *Lumberjack*. Afterwards, Patton's Third along with Devers' army group would attack and eliminate the German garrison in the Saar, beginning on 15 March. This would bring all three groups level with the Rhine, which SHAEF's planning staff felt would be crossed in late March.

Back in November, Montgomery's TAC had moved indoors for the first time since before D-Day. His circus-like collection of trucks and caravans descended on the small town of Zonhoven, due east of Brussels, in Flemish-speaking Belgium. This would be their winter quarters while their vehicles were parked up. The staff took over the surrounding schools and houses, while Monty himself decamped to the red brick 'Villa Magda', which, according to his friend, the Member of Parliament A.P. Herbert, was 'of simple but appalling taste, with only one bath, a heating system that did not work, full of the rumble of tanks and guns and lorries driving down the single street, and Doodlebugs (V-1 flying

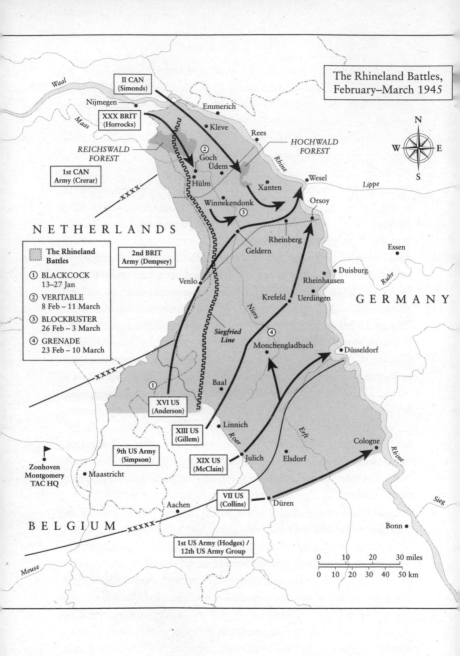

The Rhineland Battles,
February–March 1945

The Rhineland Battles

① BLACKCOCK
13–27 Jan

② VERITABLE
8 Feb – 11 March

③ BLOCKBUSTER
26 Feb – 3 March

④ GRENADE
23 Feb – 10 March

II CAN
(Simonds)

XXX BRIT
(Horrocks)

1st CAN
Army (Crerar)

2nd BRIT
Army (Dempsey)

XVI US
(Anderson)

XIII US
(Gillem)

9th US Army
(Simpson)

XIX US
(McClain)

VII US
(Collins)

1st US Army (Hodges) /
12th US Army Group

Zonhoven
Montgomery
TAC HQ

NETHERLANDS

GERMANY

BELGIUM

REICHSWALD
FOREST

HOCHWALD
FOREST

Siegfried
Line

Waal
Maas
Nijmegen
Emmerich
Kleve
Rees
Rhine
Lippe
Goch
Üdem
Hülm
Xanten
Wesel
Orsoy
Winnekendonk
Rheinberg
Geldern
Essen
Duisburg
Ruhr
Venlo
Rheinhausen
Krefeld
Uerdingen
Niers
Monchengladbach
Düsseldorf
Baal
Linnich
Erft
Roer
Cologne
Rhine
Julich
Elsdorf
Maastricht
Aachen
Düren
Bonn
Sieg
Meuse

N
W   E
S

0   10   20   30 miles

0   10   20   30   40   50 km

bombs) roaring overhead'. The choice of location was a mistake, but by the time all realised, it was too late into winter to change. Their stay, of just over three months until mid-February, would be longer than anyone intended, due to the German Ardennes assault.[1]

In midwinter, one of Monty's dogs was run over by a passing military truck. A brass plaque on the entrance gates records: 'In grateful remembrance. In this Villa, Field Marshal Montgomery of Alamein, Commander of the British Liberation Army in Europe, resided from 12 November 1944 to 7 February 1945. His beloved companion from Normandy to Holland, the cocker spaniel *Rommel*, died and was buried here on 18 December 1944.' This is when the army group commander came to rely on his aides and liaison officers, to lift him out of himself with their convivial after-dinner banter. Zonhoven has not forgotten. The 'Villa Monty' is still there on Houthalenseweg, and to this day, the brass plaque outside is still regularly polished.

Second Army spent the rest of 1944 exploiting the salient in the German line that it had created during Operation *Market Garden*, to advance on the Rhine and Meuse rivers (the latter known as the Maas in Belgium and the Netherlands). With Bradley's army group recovering from the severe mauling it had received in the Bulge, it remained for Montgomery's troops to retain the initiative and resume the advance in mid-January 1945. The first area selected to, in Monty's words, 'be cleansed of Huns' in *Blackcock* was a corner of German-held Holland, which protruded below Roermond, east of the Maas and west of Roer rivers. The task was undertaken by three divisions of Neil Ritchie's XII Corps.

Ritchie had experienced a 'good' World War One fighting the Turks in Mesopotamia, for which he had twice been decorated. A contemporary of Miles Dempsey's at Staff College in 1930, he had been an army commander in North Africa, until replaced in June 1942 in the merry-go-round of British generals that marked the high point of Rommel's desert advance. Brooke still had sufficient regard for Ritchie's operational capabilities to offer him a corps in December 1943, with the result that, admirably re-educating himself to handling a lesser formation, he led XII Corps from Normandy until the war's end. The jovial, pipe-smoking Ritchie later complained of feeling he was all the while under 'Monty's microscope', for both his desert army and XII Corps had once been led by his field marshal.

Also deploying the 43rd Wessex and 7th Armoured Divisions, Ritchie directed *Blackcock* in revolting weather, from 13 to 27 January, slowly ejecting the Germans from the Roermond area. The assault was launched in a 'thick, milky white fog, bayonets fixed, waiting for the high-pitched screech of a Spandau', according to the notes of Charles Whiting, later a prolific military historian, who had lied about his age to join the army in the summer of 1943, when aged sixteen. He found himself in the Reconnaissance Battalion of the 52nd Lowland Division, which had returned to the British fold after their Scheldt campaign, and recorded many of its campaigns, including *Blackcock*. His division alone suffered 752 killed and wounded, of whom 258 (34 per cent) were non-battle casualties, laid low by the bitter cold and wet of a nasty winter.

Whiting recalled a fellow soldier, 'Fusilier Dennis Donnini, son of an Italian ice-cream seller from Northern Ireland, who had already lost a brother in action', and was serving in the 4th/5th Royal Scots Fusiliers, an experienced infantry battalion. In the advance, the young fusilier was knocked unconscious by a blow to the head on the morning of 18 January. Yet on regaining consciousness and bleeding heavily, Donnini dragged a wounded comrade to safety, lobbed hand grenades at German positions and, seizing a Bren gun, embarked on a lone charge against their trenches. 'Weaving and swaying like a battered boxer, he staggered on until a German stick grenade was flung at him from ten yards away. This time he went down for good. The Bren dropped from the suddenly nerveless fingers and his legs collapsed from beneath him like those of a new-born foal.' Later analysis found a bullet had hit a grenade he was carrying, which exploded and killed him, but his bravery was recognised with the posthumous award of a Victoria Cross.[2]

Throughout *Blackcock*, the British and Canadians fought their opponents in sub-zero temperatures, where the weather was equally hostile to both sides, with rain, sleet and snow, as well as shellfire, grinding the terrain to a treacle-like goo. With rifle bolts sometimes frozen and useless, stress and exhaustion also took its toll. Losses were as high from exposure, frostbite and respiratory problems as from combat.

Meanwhile, at the operational level, Harry Crerar's Canadians were planning an operation to clear the rest of the German terrain west of the Rhine, which would bring them up to the great river in March. In the autumn of 1944 several projects were actively considered for Twenty-First Army Group to retain the tactical initiative and keep up pressure on the Germans. One such was to use the only useful legacy of *Market Garden*, the salient that reached to Nijmegen and Groesbeek, and cross the frontier into Germany, penetrate the vast former Imperial Forest that dominated the west bank of the lower Rhine, and overwhelm the Siegfried Line that ran through it. In early December 1944 it was decided to adopt this plan, then dubbed *Valediction*, with a proposed start date of 1 January 1945. Allocated to First Canadian Army to plan and implement, ten days later the Ardennes offensive threw all Crerar's plans into the air and effectively pushed back the assault, now renamed *Veritable*, by a month.

In its final conception, two corps, operating left and right, were to clear the terrain between the Rhine and the Maas on the German-Dutch border for a distance of fifty miles. On the left, Guy Simonds' II Canadian Corps would clear the flooded area between the Rhine and the former Imperial Forest and beyond, upriver to Xanten, another west-bank former Roman military outpost.[3] To Brian Horrocks' XXX Corps, loaned to Crerar for the operation, fell the task of dealing with the wood itself. The trees stretched as far as the ancient townships of Kleve and Goch, the former town best known to generations of British schoolchildren for its associations with Anna von Kleve (Anne of Cleves), fourth wife of King Henry VIII, to whom she was married for six months in January 1540.

Four hundred and five years later, the Anglo-Canadians, who knew the sixty square miles of wood by its German name of the Reichswald, would visit massive destruction on the area to ease their passage through the formidable network of defensive bunkers, trenches, minefields and artillery positions. They were so well built, that many are still evident today. Meanwhile, to their south, the US Ninth Army, still under Montgomery's operational control, would mount a complementary assault, *Grenade*, which would take them from the Roer to the Rhine. Both the *Veritable* and *Grenade* advances were designed to function as sharp-toothed pincers, to isolate and destroy any Germans caught west of the

Rhine when the claws snapped shut. Beyond Ninth Army's right flank, Courtney Hodges' First Army would launch a synchronised attack from the Roer to the Rhine at the same time.

Eisenhower thought Horrocks 'the outstanding British general under Montgomery', an accolade shared by XXX Corps and the rest of the Second Army.[4] This in no way belittled his friend and contemporary, Dempsey, but reflected Horrocks' larger-than-life personality, and photographic memory for faces and names, which resulted in war correspondents flocking to his briefings. His First World War was unusual, in that he had been wounded and captured by the Germans in 1914, spent the war behind bars, but was awarded an MC for his persistent escape attempts. Having learned Russian from fellow prisoners of war, from 1919 to 1920 he served in Britain's military mission to assist the White Army against the Bolsheviks during Russia's Revolution.

Horrocks was captured for a second time, by the Reds in January 1920, obliging him to spend the next nine months in detention, until released in a government-brokered deal. He rapidly caught up in the interwar years, shadowing his exact contemporary, Miles Dempsey, at Staff College and in postings to the War Office, and by 1940 was commanding the 2nd Middlesex, a battalion in Montgomery's 3rd Division. At the end of that short campaign Horrocks was a brigadier, and thereafter rose swiftly before receiving the summons to North Africa, where he led several different corps under Montgomery between June 1942 and June 1943.

However, it was the Luftwaffe which then intervened in Horrocks' active career when bullets from a roving German fighter struck him as he was preparing for the Salerno landings. Out of the war for the next fourteen months, Brooke offered him XXX Corps in August 1944, after sacking its previous commander, and Horrocks led them with dash and élan for the rest of the war. He emerges as a sort of mini-Montgomery, too junior to be a threat to the Great Man, but with the same self-confidence, drive and energy, leavened with a congenial personality which welcomed collaboration with all. 'Monty owed more to Horrocks than Horrocks owed to Monty', was the verdict of his biographer, Philip Warner.[5] Ranked among the top three of British corps commanders, Horrocks would no doubt have risen to lead an army were it not for his wounding, as the other two – Leese and Dempsey – both received promotion in 1944.

As one hundred days remained of the war in the West, rumours rippled through XXX Corps that a big 'push' was imminent. Serving with the Coldstream Guards, a regiment associated with his family since 1769, Lieutenant Bob Boscawen noted in his diary, 'Suspicions of an impending action are more than confirmed as a week of intensive maintenance on tanks has been ordered. In the morning I went to a lecture on Regimental History. Interesting. Colonel Roddy of the 5th Battalion gave us a poignant description of battle-weary officers in the last war bursting into tears of relief in November 1918 when they heard the Armistice had been signed. In retrospect it seemed incredible to me that those who are now battalion commanders could describe such events which some of them witnessed as young officers. Was it really so brief an interval of peacetime before this madness began all over again?'[6]

A sense of impending action was shared by Lieutenant Colonel Martin Lindsay, commanding the 1st Gordon Highlanders, a battalion of the Highland Division. He had just received a briefing from Horrocks. A 'most sumptuous, really quite pre-war, lunch' followed. 'This is a feature of all the General's final conferences before an important operation, and it is always known as the Last Supper.'[7] At the hundred-day mark, on 28 January, billeted in Holland, Sergeant Trevor Greenwood, a vehicle commander with the 9th Royal Tank Regiment, noted the extreme cold in his diary, continuing, 'Skating is now in full swing and many of the lads are joining in with borrowed skates'. He was in ignorance of the coming campaign, only a week later recording, 'We have to remain out of sight for secrecy. All unit signs, cap badges, etc. removed. Something very big is brewing – very big.'[8]

Preceding *Veritable* was a 'Monty touch', the battering of the area by 750 four-engined aircraft from RAF Bomber Command, which reduced Kleve and Goch to rubble. Horrocks later asserted that the decision to bomb Kleve had been 'the most terrible I had ever taken in my life'. He felt 'physically sick' when he saw the bombers overhead unloading 1,400 tons of explosives that reduced the eleventh-century town to dust.[9] The ground attack went in at 10:30 the next morning, 8 February 1945, following a 'Crerar touch', an artillery bombardment of

1,034 guns, as befitted a former gunner. Both precautions were necessary, for the area contained three separate belts of bunkers, ditches,
dragon's teeth anti-tank obstacles, and all the other structures associated with the German *Westwall*. Lance Corporal Rex Wingfield in the
1/5th Queens Royal Regiment, an infantry battalion of the 'Desert Rats'
(7th Armoured Division), recalled he was readied for *Veritable*, with
the words, 'This Reichswald forest will be a tough nut to crack. It's a
game preserve owned by Uncle Hermann Goering. So, watch out for
his bloody gamekeepers.'[10]

Waiting for the start, Lieutenant Colonel George Taylor commanding the 5th Duke of Cornwall's Light Infantry (DCLI) in the 43rd Wessex
Division noted, 'It was difficult to realise, packed in those silent woods
and houses that surrounded us, that here was the greatest concentration of men, artillery, and tanks, since our Normandy bridgehead days.'[11]
This was an era when infantry brigadiers were mostly in their mid-
thirties, while battalion commanders ten years younger. Taylor – about
to be promoted to brigadier – had already forged an outstanding reputation with two DSOs to his name in a division that would lose thirty-
six commanders of nine infantry battalions, a turnover rate of 400 per
cent, between June 1944 and May 1945.[12]

By this stage of the war, scale was everything. XXX Corps had been
massively reinforced to the size of nine divisions, a small army. With
200,000 troops and 3,500 vehicles, including 500 tanks, Horrocks' formation was more powerful than the entire British Expeditionary Force
which had fought in France in 1940. After eight months of front-line
battle experience, his men were at the zenith of their efficiency, and
incredibly well resourced, as were Simonds' Canadians. Due to combat
losses their ranks were supplemented by the 'six-week killers', a reference to the training that artillerymen culled from air defence regiments
received to serve as infantry. Even the Canadians, who were promised
'no conscription' in 1940 by their Prime Minister, Mackenzie King, had
to resort to that much abhorred necessity in the end, such was the pressure on Allied manpower.

Yet, terrain imposed a very narrow start line of just seven miles
for the opening phase of *Veritable*, before the troops could fan out,
II Canadian Corps on the left adjacent to the Rhine, XXX Corps on

the right. Horrocks noted in the post-war British Army of the Rhine study guide of the campaign that 'By the evening of 7th February our concentration was complete, and the woods and outskirts of Nijmegen were thick with troops, guns, vehicles, workshops, tanks – all the paraphernalia of modern war. It would have been almost impossible to drop a pea into the area without hitting something. This was probably the last of the old-type set piece attacks because, in face of the threat of tactical atomic missiles, no concentration like this can ever take place again.'[13]

Both the flooded water meadows adjacent to the Rhine, and the boggy, densely forested terrain further away, would dictate the tempo of operations, removing the Allied advantages of manpower and armour. However, *Veritable* was but the northern jaw of a pincer movement, which had to be sequenced with *Grenade*, the southern jaw. As soon as *Veritable* began, the Germans released winter floodwaters held back by upriver dams on the Roer, and the ensuing rising river level and its speed delayed Ninth Army's advance for two weeks, until 23 February. The rising Roer did not affect *Veritable*, whose troops were advancing from the north, but did allow the Germans to concentrate combat power against the Anglo-Canadians. However, the whole Reichswald area was soft from winter rain and snowmelt, muddy and freezing cold.

Despite the narrow start line, five infantry divisions began the assault, with Simonds' 3rd and 2nd Canadian Divisions advancing through the waterlogged ground on the left, and the 15th Scottish, 53rd Welsh and 51st Highland Divisions heading for the Reichswald. More formations were on call in reserve. These units rode into battle in 'Kangaroos', turretless tanks that could carry a ten-man section (equivalent to a US squad) of infantry. 'Since the substitution of the musket for the crossbow, there has been no development in infantry equipment which is comparable to the Kangaroo,' enthused a Twenty-First Army Group report.[14] In the later stages of the Normandy campaign, Simonds' Canadian Corps had developed the concept of removing the 25-pounder or 105mm cannon from within tracked M7 Priest self-propelled guns. However, he soon had Canadian-built Ram tanks used for crew training shipped over to France in large numbers for specific conversion to Ram Kangaroos, which became the world's first tracked armoured personnel carriers. For *Veritable*, Twenty-First Army Group possessed enough to move an entire infantry brigade, three battalions, at the same speed as tanks, cross-country.

Infantry battalions had spent much of January rehearsing forest warfare. One battalion commander recorded the 'four days near Eindhoven training in street fighting and the crossing of obstacles, with an operations room organised, stocked with maps and air photos'.[15] Newcomers to the 43rd Wessex Division were ordered to dig in and then, to their surprise, were mortared by their own colleagues, who landed bombs within sixty yards of the startled soldiers' positions. 'Death will come as a happy release to you lads after this,' warned the Divisional Battle School instructors who had fired the weapons.

By 1945 warfare looked very different, even from a year previously. Tank-busting, rocket-firing Typhoons and their American equivalent, P-47 Thunderbolts, were on call to Forward Air Controllers. Infantry were supported by Sherman 'Crabs' (minesweeping flail tanks) and heavier Churchills. Some of the latter were engineer tanks carrying much-needed bridging for the swampy conditions, while others were Churchill 'Crocodile' flame-throwers, and 'Wasps', another design which lanced fire, based on a Bren Carrier, both of which had a profound effect on their opponents. The Royal Electrical and Mechanical Engineers used bulldozers to remove felled trees, while other engineers were kept busy installing Bailey bridges or assembling corduroy roads of sawn logs and defusing booby traps left everywhere.

When they could get them, British and Canadian battalions also made much use of M29 'Weasels', small, Jeep-like amphibians with wide rubber tracks, built by Studebaker, which replaced Bren Carriers for transporting supplies and towing anti-tank guns over difficult terrain. To traverse the flooded areas, they also used American LVTs – landing vehicle tracked – an armoured amphibious craft, developed by the US Marines in the Pacific and capable of carrying thirty men and a Jeep, Weasel or Bren Carrier. In Western Europe, LVTs were dubbed 'Buffaloes' or 'Alligators'.[16] All this Horrocks had at his fingertips as he climbed into his command post in the early hours of 8 February.

'It was a cold, grey, miserable dawn with low clouds and rain, heralding several days of stormy weather,' the general recollected. He was on a small platform halfway up a tree, from where he had 'a wonderful view over most of the battlefield. The noise was appalling, and the sight awe-inspiring. All across the front shells were exploding. We had arranged for a barrage, a curtain of fire, to move forward at a rate of 100 yards every four minutes in front of the troops. To mark the end of the four-minute period, when the guns would increase their range by 300 yards, they all fired a round of yellow smoke.' His main concerns were mines and the mud. 'I am certain that this must be the chief memory of everyone who fought in the Reichswald. Mud and still more mud. It was so bad that after the first hour every tank going cross-country got bogged down, and the infantry had to struggle forward on their own.'[17]

Captain Ian Hammerton of the 22nd Dragoons, a war-raised tank battalion equipped with Sherman Crab mine-clearing tanks, remembered nosing out of Groesbeek, past the 'crashed and broken gliders, US airborne division left-overs from the airborne operation intended to capture Arnhem [*Market Garden* of the previous September]'. He had been awakened earlier with 'that most stomach-churning breakfast of bacon sandwiches washed down with strong, hot tea', then started flailing at one and a half miles per hour. 'Forward we creep, chains throwing up mud and grass. Progress was painfully slow as the fields were so waterlogged; in fact, every Crab in the squadron was soon bogged in the morass.' Behind them followed 32nd Guards Brigade, who fought attached to the Highland Division. Hammerton and his Crabs had to remain glued into the treacle, protected by the Guards, while 'a bulldozer demolished two farmhouses to provide hard core and dragged us out, ignominiously, one by one, onto the hard road. Another route was under water and our traffic on it had to rely on the trees lining its sides to see where the path lay. It was not a nice place for a holiday.'[18]

I walked the ground of Hammerton's attack with him on a British Army staff ride one December, during real *Veritable* weather. Of necessity, we started the day with mugs of hot chocolate rather than sweet tea, but the climate and terrain instantly transported him back to 1945. Yet the freezing mud and sleet we encountered reminded him not of February 1945, but of his father's tales of Passchendaele in 1917. The Reichswald was the penance his generation had to bear, he thought. This was the same, gloopy Flanders caramel his father was once obliged to navigate. To me, a student of both, I could see the precise similarities.

At the same time, Hammerton was delighted to be reminded that newsreel footage of the battle, shown in cinemas back home, actually featured his tank in the advance. From it we were able to pinpoint exactly where his troop had been swallowed up by the mire. According to the original maps in his possession, ahead lay a German anti-tank position. Hammerton was beyond amazed when we discovered in the shallow depression a single artillery-shell case, a relic from February 1945. Later, on my own, I explored the wood, where the shrapnel in every tree has hindered post-war forestry work, destroying saws. Decades later the dense undergrowth still contains the contours of trench lines and coils of barbed wire belonging to the former *Westwall*. In one place lay a battered aluminium mess tin of the kind issued to the British and Canadian troops. This one clearly bore its date of manufacture, 1944.

During *Veritable*, a single, narrow road ran parallel with the Allied central axis running from Nijmegen to Kleve. It remained just above the surrounding morass, with the result that four Allied divisions gravitated towards it. Despite the best efforts of 1,500 military policemen and 13th Army Group Royal Engineers (AGRE), the route proved unable to cope with several fully mechanised divisions crawling along its surface, laid down in earlier times for hooves and wooden wheels. Crerar, Simonds and Horrocks were furious with the four formations – two Canadian, and the 15th Scottish and 43rd Wessex – which reduced the advance to a crawl. In fact, Horrocks later admitted his 'grave error' in causing the traffic jam, by releasing his reserves too soon, which he assessed as 'one of the worst mistakes I made in the war'.[19]

Fortunately, the low grey clouds and inability of the Luftwaffe to contest the skies ensured the ten-mile, nose-to-tail logjam of valuable vehicles was never attacked. George Taylor of the 5th DCLI remembered the evening traffic of 10 February. 'The long night was bitterly cold, with flurries of icy rain and driving sleet. There were few handholds on the cold steel surface of the tanks on which the men travelled and no room to lie down. There were frequent stops but no official halts as the column wound its apprehensive way forward. No one knew if these stops would last five minutes or five hours, so it was only possible now and then to jump down and stamp life back into frozen feet.'[20]

For those operating within the great wood to their right, conditions were infinitely worse. The 5th/7th Gordon Highlanders of 51st Highland Division noted that 'all tracks through the forest were hopelessly blocked by trees, felled both by enemy demolitions and our own shellfire. They had not been able to get a single vehicle into the Reichswald.'[21] The official history of the 1st East Lancashires, a battalion with the 53rd (Welsh) Division, detailed the 'almost overpowering smell of spent explosive that hung like a cloud in the forest. Trees lay smashed and shattered, their broken branches strewn about, leaving stumps standing like grotesque scarecrows to discourage invaders'.[22] Lieutenant Colonel Martin Lindsay of the 1st Gordons was disappointed that searchlights bouncing illumination off clouds to generate 'Monty's moonlight' hardly penetrated through the trees at all. With Canadian units nearby, he was 'afraid that some enthusiast might shoot at us, so I passed word back to the two pipers to play the regimental march, and before long we heard the distant strain of *Cock o' the North*', but minutes later he and his men walked into a minefield. 'There was a loud bang and Danny fell down with a groan.'[23]

On the other side, twenty-one-year-old Kurt Herdina had just been promoted to NCO in the 6th Fallschirmjäger (Parachute) Division, in charge of a platoon of four heavy machine-guns. After the Normandy battles, together with an older veteran of the Crete campaign, he had retreated through Belgium in a requisitioned Fiat car, sustained by cigarettes and tins of tuna from a Kriegsmarine warehouse. His weapons were 7.92mm MG-42 machine-guns, about which much nonsense has been written.

An improved version of the original MG-34, with its increased 1,500 rounds-per-minute (rpm), the '42' gained many monikers due to the staccato signature of its rate of fire, including 'Hitler's bandsaw' and the *Todessense* (death scythe). A popular weapon with German troops, it was mostly deployed resting on a bipod and designated a 'light' machine-gun. Its high rate of fire caused vibration, meaning accuracy was poor, and the guns were mostly sited in pairs, catching opponents in crossfire. When mounted on its tripod, as in Herdina's platoon, the MG-42 was designated a 'medium' weapon, having reduced vibration, greater accuracy and longer range. In either configuration, it was not only wasteful of ammunition, but its barrels overheated very quickly if used for sustained fire.

Users were taught to change barrels every 150 rounds and to 'squirt' rounds in small bursts, bringing its actual rate of fire down to around 450rpm in the heavy role, and even less in its light role. This was closer to the 500rpm of the British Vickers .303-inch medium machine-gun, and the American M1917 Browning of .30-06-inch calibre. Although at least double the weight of the MG-42, both of the latter sat on tripods, giving them stability and therefore accuracy, and were water-cooled, thus more able to sustain high rates of fire.

Even the Czech-designed, British-built Bren, with its 500rpm, proved a handy opponent to the MG-42 due to several factors. It was magazine-fed, slowing its rate of fire, but preventing overheating of the air-cooled barrel. Its magazines prevented ammunition from getting dirty (a common cause of stoppages) and it was lighter than belt-fed automatic weapons. The Bren was still in use when I served in a British reserve unit, so I have some experience of its advantages and foibles. The same factors contributed to the success of the magazine-fed US Army's Browning Automatic Rifle (BAR), a rugged light machine-gun which had first seen service with the AEF in 1918. Thus, the Allies had more of an equivalence against 'Hitler's bandsaw' than most writers generally realise.

In the Reichswald, Herdina's weapons were entrenched in depth positions to take advantage of their extended range. With the tripod assembly came a telescopic sight, enabling them to take on targets over two miles away. Herdina's thirty-man platoon fell back gradually to a series of pre-prepared positions, taking care not to be caught by Allied artillery. While the smoking remains of Kleve fell into Allied hands on 11 February, Goch only succumbed eight days later. Fourteen days into *Veritable*, on 22 February 1945, Herdina was hit by artillery fire south of Goch, wounded in five places and evacuated. We will catch up with him later.[24]

On arriving in Kleve, the Wessex Division lamented the 'oafish stupidity of the attack by Bomber Command, which with its deep cratering, completely blocked the roads within the town'.[25] The 4th Dorsetshire Regiment, another Wessex battalion, echoed the fact that 'No house, building or even a single tree was left intact. The roads were cratered everywhere, and dead Germans and civilians were numerous.'[26] Similarly, in attacking Goch in the early hours of the 19th, John McGregor, a company commander with the 5th Black Watch in the Highland Division, noticed of Goch that 'most of the houses were in ruins from the heavy bombardment and many had cellars which were frequently found to be occupied by Germans'.

War photographers were roaming the area and several images confirm that even if the walls were still standing, every roof was missing its tiles from the concussion of aerial bomb blasts. McGregor observed, 'One method previously used was to open the cellar door and toss down a grenade, but that proved messy, if effective, and so a new technique was adopted. Instead of a grenade a large stone was tossed down the cellar steps which invariably had the desired effect of producing a scramble of Germans anxious to surrender.'[27]

Despite the employment of flame-throwers in the woods, the Black Watch charged into Goch with a sense of chivalry, noted McGregor. 'A rather shaken German lieutenant came up [from a cellar] with his hands aloft, shortly followed by a major bearing a white flag and closely behind him a colonel who was OC Troops in Goch, and some eighteen soldiers'. The senior German had been wounded, and as he was carried away by his own men on a stretcher, the attacking 'D' Company men 'saluted him, and this gesture persuaded more to come out of the surrounding buildings in surrender'.[28]

However, the ferocity of the defence of Kleve and Goch was partly down to Heinrich, Freiherr von Lüttwitz's 47th Panzer Korps and Herdina's tough 6th Fallschirmjäger Division, which had dug in around both towns. Lüttwitz, looking every inch the Prussian general with his signature monocle, had surrounded Bastogne the previous December and demanded its surrender. Now the boot was on the other foot, for his 116th Panzer and 15th Panzergrenadier Divisions barely amounted to 10,000 men and seventy panzers. Despite this, they had fought hard and their determination, as much as climate and terrain, combined to slow down the Allies.

Lance Corporal Rex Wingfield of the 1/5th Queen's found himself playing 'Hide and Seek in the Reichswald'.[29] Having breakfasted on 'Armoured Pig' and 'Armoured Dog', as his canned meat rations were called, but leaving the 'Yellow Peril' vitamin C pills, the Oxford-educated

Wingfield and his section made ready to advance beyond Goch to Üdem, with the Princess Patricia's Canadian Light Infantry on their left. In the town they witnessed a duel between a Churchill tank and a sniper who 'was blasted to his feet, danced a jig on the bullets, slowly tilted and fell headlong, sprawling in the rubble'.

Revenge was swift. A panzerfaust warhead looking 'like a flying gas lamp' smashed into the tank. Translating as 'tank fist', the weapon was essentially a disposable bazooka and weighed around ten pounds. It consisted of a three-foot-long hollow tube containing propellent and a rudimentary sight. At one end was a warhead capable of penetrating up to eight inches of armour at between 100 and 300 feet. 'Brown smoke gushed up from the turret and down the gun barrel, which drooped down, lifeless. From the smoke, the tank commander spilled out of the turret. He wasn't injured, just dazed. We climbed up to rescue the others but were stopped by a feeble cry from the commander. "The rest have had it." Soon it was a mass of flame, rocked by the ammunition exploding in the white-hot hull.'[30] At the tactical level, panzerfäuste were game-changers against Allied armour and initiated the era of disposable anti-tank weapons that led directly to the Rocket Propelled Grenades (RPGs) of modern times.

The Nebelwerfer, a wheeled, multi-barrelled mortar, was also an important tool in inflicting losses on their Allied opponents out of all proportion to the numbers fielded. They possessed a psychological dimension, too, as their projectiles were designed to whistle. The noise eventually undermined the morale of those frequently mortared, hence their nickname of 'Moaning Minnie'. Its real effectiveness lay in its mobility as a 'shoot-and-scoot' weapon, but when fuel supplies to tow them around the battlefield dried up, they were soon discovered and destroyed.

As originally conceived at Canadian Army headquarters, *Veritable* would take three weeks to reach Xanten. However, two weeks into the assault, II and XXX Corps had penetrated the Siegfried Line and had taken Kleve and Goch but were well short of Crerar's aspirations. This was primarily because the flooding of the Roer River had delayed the complementary American attack, *Grenade*, which would have split and overwhelmed the Wehrmacht reserves west of the Rhine. Instead, all available German combat power had been directed to the Reichswald itself, which had become a slaughterhouse for both sides. The Canadians counted 11,778 prisoners taken in the first two weeks of *Veritable*, and estimated another 12,000 killed or wounded, yet the attrition to the Allies was comparable. Over the same period, Anglo-Canadian casualties amounted to 490 officers and 8,023 other ranks, killed, wounded and missing.[31] The 53rd Welsh Division's 2,445 battle casualties in *Veritable* represented a quarter of the division's total for the whole 1944–5 campaign.[32]

There was also a striking uplift in psychological and battle exhaustion casualties, around 950 British and 350 Canadian soldiers at this time. 'Shell shock', defined as PTSD today, had become a widely accepted, if misunderstood, by-product of extended combat. In April 1944, the British Army had banned use of the First World War term, substituting 'battle exhaustion', in an attempt to imply a more temporary form of affliction, but the old colloquial diagnosis persisted, as did – in people's minds – the stigma. The Germans made no attempt to understand this, and generally shot the afflicted for cowardice.

Though some Allied commanders remained sceptical, it was the huge rise in cases, first in Normandy, then during the winter months, which persuaded senior officers that psychological wounds were real and every bit as debilitating as torn flesh. Some sufferers, as in the earlier world war, were good leaders who had been gradually worn down. Typical medical case notes included one experienced Canadian corporal, who 'had led a section for several months, had been blown up eight times, but had always carried on with his duties. Recently he had lost his confidence, was unable to make decisions, had become unduly cautious and felt that he was a bad influence on his section.'[33] Major John Wishart, psychiatrist attached to XXX Corps, concurred that 'very few could be returned to combat'.[34]

Of those who carried on, though wounded, Captain Stan Perry of the Sherwood Rangers Yeomanry, a Sherman tank regiment of 8th Armoured Brigade, observed that he bore three scars from the war. 'The first is your conscience, that you actually killed some young chap who was probably not very different from you. The second was, had you been a better soldier, could you have deployed differently and have saved the lives of some of your men? The other scars you have, of course, are the physical scars from wounding.'[35]

Meanwhile, having spent a sleepless night in the ruins of Üdem, smoking incessantly, 'lighting one cigarette from the remains of the previous one, until our tongues were sore, and our stomachs began to rumble', Rex Wingfield's section was about to advance three and a half miles to the Hochwald, a smaller forest between Üdem and Xanten. Fired in by artillery, and preceded by tanks, they hit dug-in German infantry. 'There was only one thing left to do. No one wanted to give the order. I gulped and turning to my section, shouted "Fix (pause) bayonets!" That seemed to bring us all to life. I heard the nasty snick of the bayonets locking home. I pulled the safety of my Sten [submachine-gun] and stood up.' Wingfield and his men lolloped off through the mud. 'We broke into a trot, a run, a mad charge, screaming, yelling, ready for the kill. Suddenly we saw the lip of the ditch opposite lined with bits of waving white paper. Carried away with the unreasoning atavistic bloodlust of combat we yelled "So you're trying to pack up now, you bastards! It's too bloody late" we roared and swept on. I sprayed a burst at the paper. It went down.'[36]

The papers were small leaflets dropped in their tens of millions over German lines encouraging the recipient to hide it on their person and then use it to surrender at the right moment. With Eisenhower's facsimile signature, it guaranteed they would not be harmed. Yet, as Wingfield observed, it was easy to wind men up to kill, but took time for that white fury to dissipate. Even in 1945 there existed a fine line between shooting at an opponent firing a machine-gun, and, the same soldier having surrendered, dispatching him in cold blood, though his weapon was not yet cold. It is a line drawn even finer in the twenty-first century, the era of helmet cams and close political and media scrutiny. Minutes later, Wingfield himself was wounded, and as a German stepped on his badly wounded abdomen, he was cut down in turn. 'A horrid sound, midway between a cough and a belch, and a body fell heavily across my legs, quivered, thrashed and lay still. His Schmeisser [machine-pistol] toppled over my shoulders and clouted me over the left ear.'[37]

Wingfield's charge was not unusual. 'The Hun will not face a determined man with the bayonet,' observed an immediate British report of the Reichswald fighting. 'On one occasion an SP [self-propelled] gun supported by a company of infantry was holding up the advance across a clearing in the Forest. They were some two hundred yards away, maybe a little more. After all ordinary methods to shift the Hun had failed, the commander led his whole company in a bayonet charge across the open ground. The enemy did not wait for it to arrive and a PIAT [hand-held infantry weapon, standing for: Projector, Infantry, Anti-Tank] finished off the SP [self-propelled] gun. There were five casualties only to our troops.'[38]

To try and speed up the end of *Veritable* and reduce the daily trickle of casualties, Crerar's headquarters quickly planned an extension, code-named *Blockbuster*, which commenced in the early hours of 26 February, deluged by icy rain. It started well, with Kangaroo-borne infantry following a forty-five-minute barrage, securing their objectives and beating off counter-attacks aided by overhead tracer and searchlights, horizontal and vertical. Essentially, *Blockbuster* started as a II Corps fight, following the Rhine, with XXX Corps protecting their right flank, but it soon sucked in much of the rest of Second Army. At various times, eleven armoured and infantry divisions were employed, for the length of river-bank to their left was the stretch already earmarked for Montgomery's great assault crossing later in March.[39]

Early March found Sergeant Trevor Greenwood, whom we last met skating in Holland, commanding a Churchill tank, attached to the 53rd Welsh Division, in Hülm, a couple of miles south of Goch. The dying settlement typified the destruction wrought throughout the area. 'Whole scene is rather fantastic and surreal,' he wrote. 'My troop harboured in a church. Several gaping holes in roof and walls. Slept on floor between two pews last night. Huge brazier made from dustbin for warmth located in centre of main aisle. Plenty of timber for fuel. Graveyard surrounding church now resembles a poultry farm. Several tank crews keeping live hens for eggs, wire netting enclosures around gravestones. In between graves infantry have dug slit trenches. Wooden cross now serving as hen-perch.'[40]

The armour crews were lucky; the infantry had to cope without abandoned churches, or keeping chickens, and had been reduced to thieving. Greenwood went on to note, perhaps to assuage his own conscience, 'Tank crews having a good time looting here. There are many empty houses, mostly well battered, and much stuff is being unearthed, particularly clothing, sheets, towels, pillowcases, etc., mostly new, and significantly Dutch labels. It would appear the looters are now being looted!'[41]

Another six miles beyond Hülm, 9th Infantry Brigade of 3rd Division and a squadron of tanks from the 3rd Scots Guards (6th Guards Tank Brigade) found the village of Winnekendonk strongly defended by veteran Fallschirmjägers on 2 March. An infantry battalion, the 2nd Lincolns, put in an attack over 1,200 yards of open ground, with the rest of the brigade on hand in fifty troop-carrying Kangaroos.[42] The Guards' War Diary summarised the British attack. 'All went well for the first four hundred yards, but immediately the leading troops came into the open they were met by a hail of fire from the front and flanks.' Machine-guns scythed through the infantry as five Churchill tanks were struck, one five times, and the FOO's (Forward Observation Officer of their attached artillery) tank blew up.

Sergeant Jim Alldred and Lieutenant Robert Runcie immediately drove their tanks, named 'Elgin' and 'Lochinvar' respectively, beyond the cover of some farm buildings. Alldred destroyed an 88mm cannon and Runcie bagged a Sturmgeschütze self-propelled gun. 'They also dealt with a number of machine-guns holding up the infantry from that flank, thus enabling the infantry to get into the town.'[43] This action cost the Lincolns twenty-two dead and ninety-five wounded, but without the armour, the infantry would have been massacred. 'This battle over a forgotten town with an unpronounceable name' brought Runcie a well-deserved Military Cross.

'So open was the approach, so strong the anti-tank screen, that it was impossible to believe, when examining the ground later, that one infantry battalion and a squadron of tanks could have captured it against the pick of Germany's infantry. It is suggested that this may rank as one of the finest small-scale tank-infantry co-operation battles ever executed and well worthy of more close study,' enthused the Guards' war diary.[44] Mounted aloft in 'Lochinvar', the young officer became known as 'Killer Runcie', but took Holy Orders after the war, partly as a result of having investigated the panzer he destroyed and seeing its four dead crewmen. To the surprise of his fellow officers, Runcie was installed as Archbishop of Canterbury in 1980, spiritual head of the Church of England and the worldwide Anglican Communion.[45]

Meanwhile, as Montgomery was conferring with Dempsey about riverine assaults, bridgeheads, breakouts and objectives deep into Germany, he uncharacteristically left Crerar to fight *Veritable* and *Blockbuster* on his own.[46] Despite the awesome firepower at the Canadians' disposal, *Blockbuster* soon proved to lack the punch needed to bring *Veritable* to a hasty conclusion. Due to the weather, close air support was not always available, and it soon degenerated into another series of infantry assaults over terrain the Allies could not reconnoitre in advance. It imposed further casualties of close to 4,000 men, 2,600 of them Canadian. As a result, *Blockbuster* has been roundly condemned by Canadian historians as unnecessary because the Roer floods were by then receding, which meant that Simpson's Americans would soon begin *Grenade*.[47]

In delaying the Allies for exactly thirty days, General Alfred Schlemm was obliged to commit the entire armoured reserve of Army Group 'H', 15th Panzergrenadier and 116th Panzer Divisions, and its infantry reserve, 7th Fallschirmjäger. As Schlemm noted later, 'Once the battle was joined, it was obvious I no longer had a free hand in the conduct of the defence. My orders were that under no circumstances was any land between the Maas and the Rhine to be given up without the permission of the Commander in Chief West [von Rundstedt], who in turn first had to ask Hitler. For every withdrawal, I had to send back a detailed explanation.'[48]

Yet Schlemm's men fought ferociously. In the outskirts of Xanten, the Algonquin Regiment (4th Canadian Armoured Division, and named after an indigenous tribe from Ontario) noted in their war diary on 7 March, 'During this action most of our casualties were caused by small arms fire from reinforced houses, which it was impossible to neutralise, even with tanks. On one occasion after a tank had fired three rounds of high explosive through a window, a German soldier stuck his head out and thumbed his nose at the oncoming infantry. Resistance was fanatical and very few prisoners were taken. Artillery concentrations, although magnificently placed, only served to put the Boche's head down momentarily, then he would come up to murder our men in the final assault.'[49]

Blockbuster and thus *Veritable* culminated with the capture of Xanten on 10 March. This was also the day Schlemm, and the remnants of his Parachute Army, withdrew across the Rhine to Wesel, taking care to blow the remaining bridge in his sector. He knew that somewhere in Berlin lurked a piece of paper bearing his signature agreeing to forfeit his life if any crossing points remained viable. A heavy weight to bear in addition to fighting a formidable foe. As he later told his interrogator, Canadian Major Milton Shulman, 'Since I had nine bridges in my sector, I could see my hopes for a long life rapidly dwindling.'[50] None knew there were now sixty-nine days of the war left.

(*Above*): This smoking Mark V Panther tank was destroyed outside Cologne cathedral on 6 March 1945 by 'Eagle 7', one of the first M26 Pershings in the European Theater of Operations. The neat hole made by one of the killer 90mm armour piercing warheads can be seen in the hull's side. (*Below*): Major General Maurice Rose, commanding the 3rd 'Spearhead' US Armored Division, whose men took the city.

5

The Road to Cologne

Opposite the Ninth US Army's sector lay General Gustav von Zangen's German Fifteenth Army, which was outnumbered ten to one.

Zangen could field 271 guns of all calibres against the Ninth's 2,000. His forces possessed eighty-five assault guns and thirty-two tanks (the sum total of the 9th and 11th Panzer Divisions), against four American armoured divisions. His five weak infantry divisions, assessed at 67 per cent strength and critically short of NCOs, compared poorly with General Bill Simpson's nine, all at full strength. Zangen's logistical situation was the inverse of the Americans'. Bombing had so disrupted transport that almost all rail lines were destroyed. Due to the Allied Oil Plan air offensive, refineries and fuel processing plants were so damaged that they were unable to meet even minimum Wehrmacht requirements. Thus, effectively immobile, none of Fifteenth Army's commanders felt prepared to fight any kind of battle. Perhaps more damning, all Zangen's units were rated Kampfwert (Fighting Quality) III, fit for defensive actions only.[1]

Simpson briefed the press on *Grenade* from his headquarters in Maastricht, Holland, on 8 February. The footage still exists; he gave a short introduction, stating he was 'feeling very confident' about his part, though emphasising 'the main effort would be that of the Twenty-First Army Group' to his north.[2] The atmosphere was relaxed, all the correspondents were smoking, an air of informality prevailed. Simpson was addressed as 'General'. It was unlike a Montgomery press conference in so many ways, where the attendees were instructed to call the Field Marshal 'Sir' and tobacco was *verboten*.

This was before the German-generated floods intervened. All through *Veritable*, Simpson's Ninth Army then had to cool their heels on the sidelines, unable to begin due to the deluge which increased the Roer's depth by three feet and its width to nearly a mile. Still under Montgomery's operational control, Simpson's men were anxious to get on with *Grenade*, which would take them over the Roer and to the Rhine, their biggest assault to date. To their right flank, Hodges' First US Army were equally impatient to launch their attacks and would take their cue from the Ninth.

By February 1945, Simpson had built his Ninth up to 303,243 men, 1,400 tanks and tank destroyers, and 2,000 field guns (130 battalions) in three corps totalling seven infantry and three armoured divisions, plus Collins' VII Corps of two infantry divisions and one armoured on loan from First Army.[3] These thirteen divisions in four corps then had to spend the next fifteen days on the west bank of the Roer River, itching to cross, while the waters subsided, and riverbanks dried out. However, Simpson's engineers had been active, calculating precisely when the floodwaters would subside. On their advice, he reset Ninth's start date for *Grenade* to 23 February, one day before the floods would cease.[4]

He hoped the Germans had made the same computations and he could therefore surprise them by launching a day early, when the waters would be a foot lower. Ninth Army had two river crossings to contemplate, beginning with the Roer, and followed by the lesser challenge of the Erft. The former, on average twelve feet deep, flowing at ten miles per hour, was the obstacle they had been attempting to cross in mid-December 1944 when the Ardennes offensive delayed all offensive manoeuvres by a couple of months. Now, in February, they were trying again.

Simpson's own corps commanders were extraordinarily able and experienced. John B. Anderson was an artillery officer who in early 1918 had served with the British Expeditionary Force in Ypres before reverting to his own army where he led an artillery battalion at Cantigny. Starting World War Two as commander of the 2nd Division's artillery, Anderson then commanded the 102nd Division in training before taking over XVI Corps on its activation in December 1943, taking it to France the following autumn at Simpson's request. Raymond S. McLain was another artilleryman, but unusually a National Guardsman, and the only one to command a corps during World War Two. He had led the 45th Division's artillery on Sicily and at Salerno, which won him two Distinguished Service Crosses and command of the 90th Division, before being elevated to XIX Corps in October 1944.

Destined for a military career, Alvan C. Gillem was the grandson of a Union general in the Civil War and son of a cavalry colonel. Although missing the usual Western Front experience, he served in the offbeat AEF Siberian campaign of 1918–19, before becoming an armoured warfare expert after graduating in 1923 from Leavenworth in the same class as Patton. The outbreak of war found him leading the 3rd Armored Division, which he named 'Spearhead', when Patton was heading the 2nd. The pair are considered fathers of the US Army's Armored Force, having written to Marshall in May 1940 recommending one be raised. The early armour guru was first given a corps in training before arriving in Europe with XIII Corps, in September 1944, personally requested by Simpson.

During 19–20 February, Simpson ordered his assault units to rehearse on the Maas behind them, in a similar flood, but away from German eyes. The attackers in the north included 84th and 102nd of Gillem's XIII Corps, who were to lunge east across the river, swing northwards to link up with the Canadians, then resume their eastwards axis towards the Rhine. To their right in the centre, the 29th and 30th from McLain's XIX Corps would storm the Roer, then move north-east, clearing out the Wehrmacht as they went. To the south, guarding the Ninth Army's right were two further divisions, the 8th and 104th from Collins' VII Corps, with 3rd Armored in reserve, loaned to the Ninth for the first phase of *Grenade*, which on reaching the Erft would revert to First Army.

Each corps had an additional armoured division in reserve, which once over the Roer, would be released like packs of hounds, and provide each formation with an iron fist. Bradley remembered selecting Collins, one of his most experienced commanders, as the sheepdog 'to shepherd XIII & XIX Corps as far as the Rhine'. Anderson's XVI Corps, as Ninth Army reserve, contained the 35th and 79th Infantry, plus the 8th Armored, and were to follow using the bridges made by their comrades. Overhead, XXIX Tactical Air Command was on call, weather permitting, with 375 aircraft, mostly P-47s, principally for interdiction of German reinforcements, expected from the north, south and east.

At 02:30 on 23 February, General von Zangen was woken by the distant rumble of 130 battalions of US field artillery, totalling more than 2,000 guns, firing a forty-five-minute barrage. Collins alone had 936 guns supporting him. American artillerymen look back on this as their heaviest artillery concentration of the war, with one gun barrel for each ten yards of front. They later calculated that McLain's XIX Corps in the centre received 8,138 tons of supporting fire in the opening six days. This illustrated just how the Allied logistics chain had matured since the famine of the previous autumn, with its need for the Red Ball Express supply lines. Combat supplies were now routed through Antwerp, which possessed the largest docks and freight-handling facilities in Western Europe – and had been captured intact.[5]

This logistical largesse allowed Simpson to stockpile 46,000 tons of ammunition (enough for twenty days), ten days' worth of fuel (3 million gallons), and everything from spare jerrycans and cans of self-heating soup, to blood plasma, medical syringes and grave markers. The Ninth Army chief knew that even before *Grenade* began, he possessed an overwhelming superiority in every category of supply and equipment: a rare situation for a commander to experience. Underlining his trust of his G-4 logisticians' advice, in case of bridge failure or hold-up, Simpson had some five hundred C-47 transports, fully loaded with a selection of combat supplies, at dozens of airbases, ready to undertake airdrops.

One officer marvelled at the intelligence knowledge of their opponents. 'The day before the offensive started, we received new 1:10,000 scale maps, marked "German positions as at 09:00, 21 February 1945". Days before, low-flying recon fighters had passed over and photographed the entire area. The images were rushed back to the Signal Corps map section which made red overlays of the enemy fortifications. They showed zigzagged trenches, anti-tank guns, artillery emplacements, foxholes, and machine-guns.' Amazed at the depth of detail, a photographic interpreter later explained that 'the rapid blast of an automatic weapon left a trace on the ground several feet long, enabling his colleagues to distinguish machine-gun positions from those of a rifleman. Freshly turned earth showed where mines had been laid.'[6]

The assault divisions were encouraged to supplement the fierce barrage with their own anti-aircraft guns, tanks, tank destroyers, chemical mortars and other infantry weapons. This would keep the Germans' heads down and muffle the sound of oars and motors. For the XIII Corps assault in the North, Alexander R. Bolling's 84th Division, with the 102nd on their right and the 5th Armored behind them in reserve, crossed twenty miles downriver from Düren and where the Roer was narrowest. It was an area they had planned to traverse the previous November. Already veterans of the Bulge and named the 'Railsplitters' after their divisional badge of an axe striking a tree – though some GIs liked to swear the weapon was buried in a German skull – the 84th comprised 14,253 men hailing mostly from Illinois, Kentucky and Indiana.

The First Battalion of Colonel Charles E. Hoy's 334th Infantry had slithered their way to the Roer in the dead of night, under cover of a smokescreen. Their progress looked like this. In silent, Indian file they felt their way along routes cleared and marked with tape by the 309th Engineers. These took them from their final assembly areas to a series of boat group areas, where scouts with hooded flashlights waited. From the latter, more guides led them along thirty-five cleared lanes to the water's edge, in all about a thousand yards. Here, engineers waited with fifteen-man assault boats. At 03:30, the first wave of thirty-five boats, carrying two companies – over four hundred GIs – entered the water.[7]

These were steered by one engineer, with two more to propel the craft back, but for the outward journey, which took about ten minutes, it was the dozen infantrymen who paddled their way across the swirling, coffee-coloured current. With heavy weapons, wirelesses and spare ammunition there was no room for clumsy life jackets. Reaching the equally marshy east bank, they then had to haul themselves and their equipment through more mire, while the boats returned for more passengers. The current swept some craft away to God knows where, others capsized or were swamped, but their opponents were caught by surprise. The following waves were peppered by mortars and machine-guns, but the Germans were firing blind, working from map coordinates, and casualties remained light.[8]

Soon the 334th Regiment's battalion had seized a 1,000-by-4,000-yard bridgehead; by mid-morning a second battalion was across, and by early afternoon the entire 334th was over, in a little over twelve hours. They were immediately followed by their buddies of the 335th, who started crossing by a newly assembled footbridge and were complete on the far bank by midnight. They in turn peeled right and were soon in contact with elements of the 407th Infantry of the 102nd Division who had crossed the Roer upstream at the same hour.[9] Along the entire fourteen-mile front, using motorised pontoons and supplemented by hastily erected footbridges, cable ferries and amphibious vehicles, Simpson's assault forces slid in one continuous, unstoppable wave across the still-flooded river, completely surprising their opponents. Once ropes were strung over the water, enabling craft to pull themselves back and forth over the flood, their task became considerably easier. Astonishingly, by the end of the day some twenty-eight battalions had crossed, nearly 25,000 American infantrymen.

The arrival of the 84th Infantry Division opposite a German inter-corps boundary meant the two weak defending battalions reported separately, up different chains of command to other divisions and corps, liaising little with each other. Their situational awareness was so poor that the Germans launched their first counter-attack just as a sixth American battalion had arrived and dug itself in. The Railsplitters had to fight off multiple German counter-attacks, while one GI hung a provocative sign in a nearby settlement. It read 'Annexed to Texas'.

Once the initial German defences had been penetrated, its two resident formations – the 12th Korps of the SS and 81st Korps of the Wehrmacht, who already had a strained relationship – were split and remained out of contact for two days, preventing the coordination of proper defensive measures.[10] This meant that Gillem's XIII Corps were able to outmatch the German decision-making cycle to replicate what the military theorist Basil Liddell Hart called 'the concept of the expanding torrent'. The latter observed that once a dam is holed, unless the breach is plugged immediately, there soon comes a point where the pressure of water and expanding gap make it impossible to repair the damage, and the whole structure gives way.[11]

Both sides traded shots throughout the 24th and though accompanied by three panzers, the Germans were so comprehensively ejected from the vicinity that the following day Simpson changed XIII Corps' mission. They had been originally tasked with finding and securing crossing sites further north over the Roer for Anderson's XVI Corps. Gillem's undeniable momentum and scent of victory induced Ninth Army to order Anderson to cross on his own. Henceforth the 84th, now reinforced with the 102nd, were released from their mission of finding crossing sites and got on with the task of pursuing their opponents. Not for nothing did Associated Press label the XIII Corps commander, Alvan Gillem, the 'small, hard-fisted general who was leading the breakout'.

Trusting subordinates to deviate from the plan to achieve the overall aim was an inspired example of mission command at every level, army, corps and division. Meanwhile, as the American bridgeheads mushroomed in size then merged, General von Zangen was hampered by the snail's pace at which his reinforcements arrived. This was as much due to lack of fuel as to Allied air interdiction. He observed, 'as units arrived, they were thrown into various crisis points in a piecemeal fashion; since these points developed more rapidly than our reserves arrived, the American breakthrough widened quickly in areas which we had not reinforced'.[12]

As the Roer's water level dropped, construction of nineteen bridges, seven of them vehicular, began. This allowed the 771st Tank Battalion to roll into the bridgehead, and though attacked by two Messerschmitt-262s, twin-engined jet fighters, the offenders were immediately brought down by quad 0.50-inch Brownings in Battery 'C', of the half-track mounted 557th Anti-Aircraft Artillery Battalion, the first downed by anyone in the corps. The doctrine of immediately deploying air defence to protect a major corps asset paid off handsomely.

With two divisions across the Roer, XIII Corps immediately started to push eastwards. Its logistical effort was such that when several bridges had to be shut for repairs on 25 February, their temporary closure had no serious effect on offensive operations, due to the stockpile of stores already dispersed on the eastern bank. Two days later, the 84th faltered in their advance west of Monchengladbach, tripping over a bunch of fanatics from the 8th Fallschirmjäger Division. Company 'G' of the 334th Infantry took the most punishment, losing forty out of 125 riflemen.

It proved the point that Ninth Army could not afford to be careless, and that for every Volksgrenadier keen to surrender, an indoctrinated Hitler Youth, paratrooper or SS man lurked around the corner. Their comrades fought literally to the death, with a senseless devotion that none in the US Army could understand. In this case the Railsplitters were obliged to remove their opponents at bayonet point with the result that only two of the garrison of fifty surrendered. Far more significantly, the Ninth had linked up with Hodges' First Army in the south to form a twenty-five-mile-long bridgehead over the Roer, as far South as Düren.

In the centre, McLain's XIX Corps (29th and 30th Infantry and 2nd Armored Divisions) was also returning to the scene of their planned attempts to force the Roer the previous November before the Ardennes offensive intervened. This time their passage over the Roer was by Alligator LVT, the amphibious vehicles whose capability the Canadians were exploiting at the same moment in the Reichswald. For *Grenade*, they provided an undramatic, but vital passage over water, mud and swamp. To assault in this fashion required the services of the 1115th Engineer Combat Group of four engineer battalions. That each divisional crossing site over the Roer required such a huge investment of specialist manpower is illustrative of how large the US Corps of Engineers had grown. Some seventeen LVTs were assigned, seven to the 29th, ten to the 30th, plus fifty DUKWs and M29 Weasels to each division, the latter being the rubber tracked Jeep-type vehicle used in *Veritable*.

Lieutenant Hatton of Company 'A' in the 234th Engineer Combat Battalion led the first Alligators across the Roer with the 30th Division. In complete contrast to the 84th's crossing, there was no opposition. He took his first troops over at 03:30 and started ferrying across supplies in daylight at midday, noting carefully that his four craft made fifty-three journeys with Jeeps and trailers, 105mm anti-tank guns, M29 Weasels, rations, water, ammunition, lumber, gasoline, and motor oil. On the return trips he brought back the wounded and prisoners of war.[13]

Hatton's colleague, Lieutenant Norman E. Cusick of Company 'C', supporting the 29th Division, had a more eventful time. 'As the lead Alligator started forward, it hit a mine, blowing the track and bogies off the right side. We backed a bulldozer up to pull the Alligator off the road and hit another mine disabling the dozer.' Cusick led the rest around and through a field, where another Alligator 'set off four *shu-mines*, none of which had any apparent effect of the tracks'. He crossed the Roer under machine-gun and sniper fire, observing, 'The far bank was very steep, about six feet high, with only about seven inches of it above water. The lead Alligator failed in its first attempt to climb out but made it on the second. Five Alligators entered the water about twenty-five yards apart and each reached the far shore, though one had to make five attempts before a successful exit.'[14]

McLain's subsequent progress towards the Rhine was swift, with a single regiment of the 29th Division taking Monchengladbach on 1 March without a fight. As the official history observed of this phase, 'It was all a typical pursuit operation, a return at last to the halcyon days of August and early September. The setting no longer looked like a battle-field. In one town electric lights were on, trolley buses running. Many a village bore no scar. Returning to the fight after two days of rain, tactical aircraft lent a kind of discordant note with their noisy attacks on fleeing German columns. Almost all firing seemed to have an air of unreality.'[15]

The following day, the 2nd Armored Division reached a Rhine bridge at Uerdingen, near Krefeld. Although a six-man engineer patrol slipped past the defenders, crossing all the way to the east bank before returning, snipping away at every wire they could find, they missed the critical circuits, or a backup, for at 07:00 the next morning, the Germans blew the structure in their faces. McLain's XIX Corps tried for other bridges at Rheinhausen, south-west of Duisburg, during 5 March, but on finding they were already down, XIX Corps had completed its role in *Grenade* by reaching the Rhine, though having failed to seize an intact bridge.

Meanwhile, on Ninth Army's right, on temporary loan as a flank guard, Collins' Roer assault was sequenced with that of the rest of First and Ninth Armies. He felt as though VII Corps were in the centre of a highly complex engine in motion. With so many simultaneous moving parts, one tiny mistake could disrupt the entire advance of the two armies. It was a heavy responsibility, which is why Bradley had temporarily switched him to help Simpson.

Two infantry divisions spearheaded Collins' advance, the 104th 'Timberwolves' led by Major General Terry de la Mesa Allen, and the 8th, known variously as the 'Pathfinders' or the 'Golden Arrow' Division, who had first landed in Normandy on 4 July, Independence Day. Illustrating that even Simpson's careful preparations could be challenged by the unexpected, two days into *Grenade*, the 8th's commander, William G. Weaver, in worrying about his own open right flank, suffered the fourth in a series of heart attacks on 25 February, and had to be immediately replaced by Brigadier General Bryant E. Moore. The latter was well known throughout the corps as the former Assistant Divisional Commander of Allen's 104th.[16]

Terry Allen was a legend in the US Army.[17] Of American and Spanish heritage, a thorough professional who valued weapons drill over clean clothes, he had led 1st Division in Sicily in his own informal but very efficient way. A favourite of Patton's (with whom he was on first-name terms) and Eisenhower's, he fell out with Bradley, his corps commander, and was relieved of command towards the end of the campaign. Allen was replaced at 1st Division by Clarence R. Huebner, who had by 1945 become V Corps commander in First Army, thus a job that might have been Allen's. Yet, within two months of losing 1st Infantry Division, the still highly regarded Allen was selected to take over the 104th in the States, lick them into shape and take them into European combat.

His corps commander, Collins, was at first suspicious of Allen's erratic track record, but quickly revised his judgement, as did Bradley and Eisenhower, who were soon congratulating the Timberwolves' leader on 'possessing one of the top three assault divisions in the ETO'. One of his men later observed of Allen, 'There wasn't a whole helluva lot of saluting. He didn't stand on that kind of protocol. He would be up front with them, he'd be in regimental headquarters in a battle, go down to battalion HQ, sometimes would even get up to an infantry company. Major generals aren't supposed to do that. They are supposed to be more valuable than us punk kids who were out there as cannon fodder'.[18]

Deploying the Timberwolves left and Pathfinders right, Collins' VII Corps stormed across the Roer in as dramatic fashion as the other corps, and with little opposition soon reached the Erft network of waterways. Collins managed to break open his sector by simple and unrelenting attacks all along the corps front for seventy-two hours. As one German commander observed, 'Contrary to their former customary manner of fighting, the Americans fought day and night. They could always bring

new infantry into the conflict, while our side it was always the same soldiers who had to continue fighting.'[19]

On the eve of the next crossing, Colonel Anthony Touart, the CO
of Allen's attacking regiment, the 414th Infantry, threw a roast chicken
dinner for his superiors, Brigadier General George A. Smith, the new
Assistant Division Commander (who had replaced Bryant Moore, now
leading 8th Division), and Allen. Shortly afterwards Allen left to watch
the Erft assault go in. Within minutes a shell had landed on Touart's
headquarters, killing him and Smith. Of the two attacking battalion
commanders, one was killed and the other wounded, along with a company commander and another staff officer. Altogether, five were killed
and eleven wounded in the explosion. Instantly, Allen was on the scene,
his sheer professionalism rising to the fore. Forgetting his own near-
death experience, for he had seen and heard the projectile, and putting
aside the deaths of his friends, he appointed new leaders, and reorganised the attack, which went in on time.

As Allen gave orders to his new command team, he counselled them,
'Now go in there cheerful. God help you if I catch you with a long face
today. Go in there smiling.' One of Allen's staff officers wrote later, 'I
was awestruck. I knew so well how the deaths of soldiers he didn't even
know tore the general to pieces inside, and here he was, after losing some
very dear personal friends, counselling cheer. But it worked. For in this
heavy hour, the 414th went smoothly ahead, hardly missing a beat in
the rhythm of the attack.'[20] Allen's behaviour offers a model for inspirational leadership - and is an indication of the loneliness of command.

One of Allen's GIs, Private John H. Light with Company 'G', 414th
Infantry, recollected the fateful shell, which killed officers he knew and
respected. Henceforth for him, all things German were suspect, nothing was sacred. 'While moving across the Cologne Plain,' he wrote, 'the
first sighting of the next town would be a church steeple. There would be
some target practice until the steeple had been destroyed, for we knew
the Germans would be watching for us from these vantage points.'[21]

On the same day, 27 February, Simpson let loose his armoured divisions, to nudge forward his three corps. The 5th Armored Division had
already started to trickle into Gillem's XIII Corps bridgehead. McLain's
XIX Corps called forward the 2nd Armored from behind the Roer, and

Anderson's XVI Corps, the reserve, crossing via their own sites, likewise alerted a combat command of the 8th Armored Division to take the fight to their northern flank. The drenching fire onto the far bank was such that one GI from the 2nd Armored observed 'a young German soldier sitting fully erect in his foxhole, holding his rifle. He had been struck by a single projectile, and I could see daylight through the two-inch hole in both sides of his helmet and his head. He hadn't fallen over; he just sat there passively staring out into eternity.'[22]

With Collins' corps having reverted to First Army, on 1 March, in a move he had anticipated, Simpson pushed his reserve formations forward to keep up the pressure on his opponents. In the north, he transferred the 75th Infantry Division to Anderson's XVI Corps (35th and 79th Infantry, 8th Armored), who were rapidly advancing northwards towards Geldern and Wesel in the Canadian Army's sector. In the centre, he attached the 79th Division to Gillem's XIII Corps (84th and 102nd Infantry, 5th Armored), striking east towards Moers and Düsseldorf, and placed the Ninth Army's reserve, the 95th Division, with McLain's XIX Corps (29th and 30th Infantry, 2nd Armored), thundering south-east.

The move was immediately justified for, invigorated with fresh troops, Gillem reached the Rhine opposite Düsseldorf the next day, though the spans had all been sabotaged. On 5 March, the 84th Division cleared Moers and Homberg but found the bridges at Duisburg, where the Ruhr flowed into the Rhine, already destroyed. 'They looked like a series of buckled, twisted Meccano construction sets,' reported a Canadian journalist, referring to the children's toy assembly kits.[23] Far more importantly, Anderson had linked up with the Canadians.

On 3 March, James Graff and his buddies of Company 'C', 134th Infantry with the 35th Division, had mounted tanks for an attack on Geldern. 'With us was an outfit of coloured tankers, the 784th Tank Battalion,' he recalled. 'As we moved out, their commander popped out of his turret hatch and asked if I could man the .50-inch machine-gun. "They done told us to button up and for you to watch for bazooka-men along the road."' Graff's column soon came under accurate fire, and as the lead tank began to cross a bridge over a canal, the span was blown in their faces. Then one of the dreaded 'bazooka-men', armed with a panzerfaust, hit that tank, knocked it out and blocked the route.[24]

'We were now road-bound because of mines along both shoulders,' remembered Graff. 'A Jeep pulling a trailer drove onto the grass, and there was one hell of an explosion. The Jeep's motor flew fifteen feet in the air and came down through the vehicle.' Those nearby were all wounded, and Captain Chappel, Graff's company commander, narrowly escaped injury when a piece of shrapnel sliced through his pistol holster. 'The coloured tankers were really laying down a barrage. Their muzzle blast firing over us was terrific. They hollered out of their tanks, "Hey, white boy, pick 'em out, and we'll shoot 'em." The combination of the mine explosion and those muzzle blasts still affects my hearing to this day,' recounted Graff.[25]

'We all scrambled along a ditch, over the remains of the destroyed bridge and into Geldern. I climbed into the loft of a barn and tore off some roof tiles to get a good field of fire. Soon we noticed a line of men coming toward us. As we were about to open fire, one of our runners cried out they were British. Just in time, or we would have inflicted some serious casualties upon our allies,' observed Graff.[26] They were men of the 1st East Lancashires, an infantry battalion in the 53rd Welsh Division, supported by 8th Armoured Brigade, under Canadian command. The East Lancs commander later described the fighting as 'terribly wearing business for the men. Psychologically and mentally. It was nearly all bayonet, Sten and grenade work. The Boche reserves fought very well, stubborn and had to be dug out with the bayonet.'[27]

At Geldern on 3 March, Crerar's First and Simpson's Ninth joined hands. *Grenade* had yielded for the latter around fifty miles of valuable river frontage, and 36,000 German prisoners. The casualty bill amounted to 7,300 Americans. As Operations *Veritable* and *Blockbuster*, *Grenade* and *Lumberjack* died down in the first days of March 1945, leaving the western banks of the Rhine in Allied hands, Eisenhower's troops looking across the twisted girders of numerous bridges, now washed by the river, wondering how and when they would cross the water.

At a level higher even than SHAEF, the Combined Chiefs of Staff had met in Malta, on their way to the Yalta conference with Stalin, and were pondering the same question. The Yalta gathering, code-named *Argonaut*, and held over 4–11 February, would loom over the later military operations of March–April and the post-war reorganisation of Germany and Europe. The manpower crisis affecting all the Allied armies continued to bite deep, exacerbated by the Ardennes.

The Reichswald operation had cost more and taken longer to subdue than planned. How many more casualties would 'bouncing the Rhine' cost? The Chiefs' eyes turned towards the Italian front. For political reasons of wanting to be in on the death throes of Nazi Germany itself, the Canadian premier, Mackenzie King, proposed bringing I Canadian Corps – essentially all his remaining combatant units in the Mediterranean – over to North West Europe. The 5th British Infantry Division could tag along, too, at a stroke easing, though not solving, each of those nations' shortage of infantrymen.

Thus was born Operation *Penknife*, for such a large movement of vehicles, personnel and equipment had to be concealed from German eyes. In Italy, Canadian tactical road signs were as usual erected and displayed where Fascist sympathisers could read them. Maple Leaf clubs, bars, hostels, leave centres and hospitals were kept open, though not necessarily patronised by Canuck soldiers. The Royal Canadian Corps of Signals maintained their normal level of wireless traffic by sending pointless messages. Equally pointlessly, the Germans tried to jam them. The Canadian forces newsletter, *The Maple Leaf*, continued to be published in Rome, though for a non-existent readership.

The wider migration, known as *Goldflake*, saw over 60,000 troops gradually thinned out from the front lines and sent to coastal areas for 'recuperation', which happened to be near the ports of Naples and Leghorn (Livorno). Beginning on 22 February, as their comrades were wading through the Rhineland mud, men were trickled unobtrusively onto ships which conveyed them to Marseilles at a rate of 3,700 personnel, 650 wheeled vehicles, fifty tracked carriers and forty tanks per day. US-operated French railways did the rest, whisking the troops in forty-and-eight boxcars, and their equipment under tarpaulins on flat wagons, intermingled with SHAEF's usual daily logistics, to the front. The Germans were completely fooled, as captured maps revealed. Only in mid-April were the Wehrmacht made aware of the absence of Canadian troops, by press reports of their arrival in Holland, where I Canadian Corps under Charles Foulkes joined their own army, and Richard Hull's 5th Division were absorbed into VIII British Corps. At thirty-seven, Hull was then the youngest divisional commander in the British Army. In twenty years, he would become Chief of Defence Staff but in 1945, in a fashion only the British could devise, his rank was substantive (permanent) captain, temporary major-general.

With *Grenade* winding down, leaving Simpson in possession of 'fifty miles of desirable waterfront overlooking the Rhine', as a real estate agent turned planner on his staff observed, the headquarters pondered what might be done with so valuable an asset. Ninth Army's headquarters felt sure it had the answer. With their opponents in disarray and good assault sites, since 1 March they had been planning a swift bridgehead across the waters between Düsseldorf and Uerdingen.

Despite intense G-2 analysis of the possible opposition, and G-3 assessments of the dangers – both were concluded to be negligible – when Simpson lobbied his chief at Twenty-First Army Group to make the 'risk-free operation', the response was a testy negative.[28] The British threw up a smokescreen of the dangers of 'wandering into the industrial wilderness of the Ruhr', but the truth was otherwise.[29] Under no circumstances was an impromptu American crossing going to endanger Field Marshal Montgomery's own plans for his grand, set-piece assault across the river.

While Simpson's Ninth Army was busy with Operation *Grenade*, the lower pincer to envelop the Rhineland, in tandem with the Anglo-Canadian *Veritable* forming its upper, Hodges proceeded with his own lunge at the Rhine, christened *Lumberjack*. It was a curious title, for the terrain assaulted by *Grenade* was comparatively dense with trees and in need of lumberjacks, whereas the object of Hodge's attack was the mostly open, flat, boggy Cologne plain.

By 1945, First Army was fielding three army corps, J. Lawton Collins' VII in the north, John Millikin's III in the centre, and Clarence R. Huebner's V in the south. Each corps generally had three or four infantry divisions, one of armour, plus a cavalry group for forward reconnaissance, assigned to it. All were seasoned, tested leaders, but Millikin was new to First Army and Huebner fresh to corps command. Collins was the youngest corps commander with the US Army and one of the very few with experience of the Pacific. He had led VII Corps ashore at Utah beach and fought at its helm all the way through the gruelling Normandy campaign and across France.

Known as 'Lightning Joe' for his momentum, the moniker was also a pun on his headquarters code name of 'Lightning'. His unflappability and decisiveness were highly respected by Eisenhower and Bradley, the latter observing that 'Had we created another ETO Army, despite his youth and lack of seniority, Collins certainly would have been named the commander'. As we have noted, during the early stages of *Lumberjack*, Collins was working under the control of Simpson's Ninth Army in the north. A well-connected cavalryman, John Millikin had served under Patton from October 1944, and his was one of two corps that had executed the deft change of axis through ninety degrees, to face north during the Bulge and relieve Bastogne. On 10 February, he and III Corps had come under First Army's command.

Affectionately labelled by Bradley as 'hardboiled', it was Huebner who had led the 1st Infantry Division ashore at Omaha beach on D-Day, remaining in command until stepping up to V Corps in January 1945 when his predecessor, Leonard T. Gerow, took over the newly arrived Fifteenth Army. Huebner's own story was one of the most dramatic in the US Army. A farm boy from Kansas of Germanic ancestry (both origins he shared with Eisenhower), he joined the army as a private, rising to sergeant in the 18th Infantry, and receiving a commission in 1916. He served in World War One with the 1st Division, and by 1918 was one of the youngest regimental commanders in the American Expeditionary Force, having amassed two Distinguished Service Crosses, a Distinguished Service Medal and a Silver Star.

After jumping the Roer and Erft rivers, First Army's main objective was Köln (Cologne). It was Germany's fourth largest city and a former Roman garrison on the west bank of the Rhine, its name deriving from *Colonia Agrippina*. Since 1940 it had endured 261 air raids which released 44,923 tons of munitions, destroying 61 per cent of the built-up area and killing 20,000. Since 1929, it had housed the German branch of Ford in a northern suburb, whose first production model was the Ford Köln of 1933. Surreally, troops were amazed to find that many parts of Fordwerke's Wehrmacht trucks and automobiles were identical to those manufactured for US Army vehicles.[30] 'Everywhere was the familiar Ford symbol,' noted one GI. 'In the beautifully panelled executive boardroom were large plate glass windows, intact, facing the river. The walls were festooned with swastika symbols and Ford badges, and gazing at them from one end was a life-sized portrait of Hitler.'[31] The plant was one of the few structures left standing, despite the best efforts of Operation *Millennium*, RAF Bomber Command's first thousand-bomber raid, directed against the conurbation on 30–31 March 1942.

Three years later, all but 50,000 of the city's pre-war population of 750,000 had fled these endless air assaults and were living in the surrounding settlements. One of the few major buildings still standing was its Gothic cathedral, one of Europe's finest. Begun in 1248, it was only completed dozens of generations of stonemasons later, in 1880. Widely regarded as a German national landmark, and not just a place of worship, its prized stained-glass windows, the earliest dating to between 1260 and 1330, and medieval carved pews had been removed for safe keeping leaving an empty shell.

'Inside,' remembered a visiting GI, 'was a tremendous amount of rubble. Benches and chairs plus gargoyles and statuettes had fallen to the floor. At least one 500-pound bomb had penetrated the transept on the south side. The explosion blew off a large section of the roof, but the main stone buttresses did not appear to be structurally damaged.'[32] Church services had ceased in 1943. Collins gave orders that it should, if at all possible, be spared. Its twin spires, skylined and visible from far away, beckoned like a gateway to the land across the Rhine.

Challenged by an early thaw after an uncommonly severe winter which saw the roads turned to a thick, syrupy goo, First Army's forestry engineers were busy laying corduroy roads of tree trunks, to bring troops, supplies and armour forward to the Roer – the origin of the *Lumberjack* title. They understood this never-ending task would need to be repeated beyond the Roer as far as the Erft, and possibly all the way to Cologne. After the war, George C. Marshall would admit, 'I dreaded the crossing of the Roer and the advance to the Rhine more than any other operation during the war. In fact, I dreaded the crossing of the Roer more than the cross-Channel attack.'[33]

As we have seen, the assault all along the line should have gone in much earlier, but the Germans' opening the sluice gates of a series of dams further upriver, sending winter snowmelt and rain thundering down the Roer, delayed crossings for over two weeks. The water deepened and widened alarmingly, preventing the entire Ninth and First Armies from making any progress eastwards. Poor weather, too, prevented air cover, parachute drops or glider assaults. The great offensive from the west was stymied yet again. Originally planned for early December, then postponed by two months because of the Bulge, and now delayed once more. Not until 23 February, when the floodwaters had passed on their way to the North Sea, did Ninth Army attack, triggering First Army's simultaneous assault.

On that morning, an impressive barrage along Hodges' front began at 03:30, which stunned or killed most Germans guarding the Roer, but the principal challenge for the attackers was the river current. Boats turned turtle or were swept downstream, drowning some, but enough made it across within the first hour. Bridging took much longer as German observers were able to direct fire onto the crossing sites, which meant no armoured support was available during the day. The real gains came on 24 February when the Roer was spanned, hostile artillery positions overrun, and tanks were rolling eastwards. They attracted the attention of the Luftwaffe, but the GIs were rich in air defence and more than able to fend off the puny air raids.[34]

By 26 February, with hundreds of armoured vehicles over the Roer and racing beyond, First Army's war diary noted, '3rd Armoured Division twice changed its command post to keep up with its rapidly pressing forces', which demonstrated that the bridgehead was entering its breakout phase. The same source also observed, 'All our other armies, with the exception of the Seventh and French, were likewise on the attack yesterday', which illustrated why the Germans were unable to hit back.[35] The Wehrmacht was under pressure all along their lines, in vindication of Eisenhower's broad front policy, which gave the Reich no ability to concentrate their reserves in a single locale. This was despite Allied air support being 'non-operational all day on our front due to the weather. According to Dickson [the colonel in charge of First Army's G-2], 'all reserve German divisions on the Western Front have now been committed', noted the war diary. 'The Germans are unable to quickly switch divisions because of the present state of their railways and lack of gas'.[36]

Between the Roer and Rhine stretched the twenty-five miles of the Cologne Plain. This was open countryside and dotted with towns and villages along the main routes radiating out from the city. To GIs, these settlements all resembled one another, 'each with its main streets barricaded, vehicles overturned and buildings smouldering in ruin. German dead lay by the roadside among the pagan effects of their falling empire. The swastika flags, official papers of Nazi government, and litter of Iron Cross-marked personal belongings,' as in one unit history.[37]

Opposite, the Germans fired on any of their compatriots' dwellings that displayed a white flag of surrender. The long winter was proving equally cruel. Soldiers on both sides had learned to be hard; all had lost friends. At the slightest suspicion, villages were drenched with Allied high explosive. Consequently, shell craters littered the landscape, filled with rainwater, snowmelt – and bodies, human and animal. At night GIs billeted themselves in German homes, first forcing the civilians to move. Tired and stressed, some looted at will, occasionally indulging in mindless orgies of destruction. At the very least, dining off clean plates then throwing the dirty crockery out of a window was an attraction of living indoors.

Once over the Roer, the second obstacle, halfway to Cologne, was the mostly canalised Erft (Bradley dismissed it as a 'muddy stream between the Roer and the Rhine'). Collins' men advanced the ten and a half miles to it in four days, which was enough to secure Ninth Army's southern flank. On 27 February, VII Corps was released from Simpson's clutches and reverted to First Army, whose sights were set not on the Rhine, but the huge west bank conurbation of Cologne. The city needed seizing before the Rhine itself could be contemplated. Meanwhile, Collins' engineers, under Luftwaffe air attack, erected six Class 40 Bailey bridges (able to take forty tons – in other words, a Sherman tank) over the Erft, enabling massed armour to move forward. Apart from three independent tank battalions (the 740th, 786th and 750th) accompanying the 8th, 99th and 104th Divisions respectively, VII Corps' concentrated armour was furnished by the 3rd 'Spearhead' Armored Division, whose radio call sign was 'Omaha'.

Spearhead was led by Major General Maurice Rose, an intensely private man who shunned publicity. Though listed as Protestant by his dog tags, Rose was the son and grandson of rabbis from Poland, but non-practising himself. Nevertheless, he technically ranked as the senior-serving Jew in the US Army. As a very young officer, born in 1899, Rose had served and been wounded in World War One, later graduating from Leavenworth in the class of 1937. Marked out for early promotion, he was Chief of Staff in Patton's 2nd Armored Division before the war, staying with it for combat in Tunisia.

Rose led its Combat Command 'A' in Sicily, after which he was given his own division, the 3rd Armored, in August 1944. Likeable and destined for corps command, Rose was soon known for his aggressive pursuit of the Germans, and was highly regarded by his own GIs and professional colleagues alike. Collins thought him 'the top-notch division commander in the [armour] business', while war correspondent Andy Rooney assessed that Rose 'may have been the best tank commander of the war. He was a leader down where they fight. Rose had a good reputation among the people who knew what was going on, but his name was not in the headlines so often as Patton's was. Rose led from the front.'

Once across the Roer, 3rd Armored had a unique combat grouping of Rose's own devising. In battle, all US armored divisions routinely formed Combat Commands, labelled 'A', 'B' (CCA, CCB) and if necessary 'R' (for Reserve, CCR). These combined armour, infantry, artillery, tank destroyer, engineer and other assets under a single, unified command. Rose created six smaller Task Forces, each based on a battalion of his own armoured infantry or riflemen borrowed from the 8th Division, with whom the 3rd Armored operated. Usually named after the battalion commander, to each were added companies of tanks, engineers and tank destroyers, and batteries of air defence and artillery, to form a self-sustaining, mobile miniature army.

After the Erft, CCA's two task forces deployed on Rose's right, while CCB's pair charged straight ahead. Of the remaining two, Rose kept one in reserve, while the sixth remained as a bridge between his two forward combat commands. It was a configuration optimised for speed.[38] Rose once explained to Rooney the relationship of a divisional commander with his superior. 'I take orders from the corps commander. He just tells me where he wants the Third Armored to go. He doesn't tell me how to get there.'[39]

It was Rose's CCB that had stumbled upon German armour of the 9th Panzer Division in Elsdorf on 27 February. With them that day was a brand-new M26 Pershing tank, one of twenty sent to the Spearhead Division for evaluation. Weighing in at nearly fifty tons, far more than a thirty-ton Sherman, the Pershing came equipped with a 90mm main gun. Of completely new design, it was the US Army's answer to the Panthers and Tigers of the Wehrmacht, but its arrival into Europe had been delayed by Army Ground Forces headquarters who were initially hostile to the new design. Three panzers lay in wait for the Americans in Elsdorf, and would have bested them, were it not for the lone Pershing. At a thousand yards, it hit and destroyed two Mark IV panzers, easily drilling holes through their thick side armour, and put out of action a near-invincible Tiger.[40] Elsdorf also demonstrated the value of CCB's combined arms grouping, for its engineers had soon demolished the settlement's roadblocks and field defences, while infantry entered the village, riding on the armour, with fire support from the artillery.

Within five days, most of Collins' VII Corps had arrived at the outskirts of Cologne. On the Corps' left were the 3rd Armored and 99th Divisions, to the right, the 104th and 8th, with the 4th Cavalry screening their southern flank. With the proximity of German forces, there was a real fear of friendly fire, so the US armour carried canvas air recognition panels stretched out over their rear engine panels. These came in different shades, a fluorescent red over a white base or garish yellow. Colour codes changed by arrangement with their supporting air cover, to prevent the Germans imitating them.

On the receiving end were the woefully understrength 363rd Volksgrenadier, 9th Panzer and 3rd Panzergrenadier Divisions. Supporting them were the anti-aircraft defences of the city, comprising a ring of 88mm flak (an abbreviation of Fliegerabwehrkanone, literally air defence cannon) artillery in direct-fire role. Meanwhile, the city's Hitlerjugend (Germany's teenaged Hitler Youth organisation), policemen, firemen and Volkssturm built roadblocks out of tram cars filled with rubble and dug trenches through the city's parks. The latter were the Home Guard of the Reich, first raised in October 1944, generally from those deemed too old or medically exempt from combat. Later, we shall encounter them in more detail. Bradley noted that 'the hastily-trained and astonished defending troops were by no means the equal of those we had met earlier in the campaign'.

A few tanks from Panzer Brigade 106 had trickled into town but were surprised by the lack of infantry to support them. The brigade's honorific title of *Feldherrnhalle* referred to the Field Marshal's Hall, a memorial building in Munich, where German military and Nazi heroes were commemorated. Hitherto, their combat reputation was such that the formation was also known as the Feuerwehr der Westfront (the Fire Brigade of the Western Front) for the way they were rushed to every military catastrophe. However, their panzer crewmen joked among themselves, 'One of our panzers is better than ten American ones. But they always have eleven!'

The usual tensions arose between Cologne's military defenders, who fell back or dug in as combat logic dictated, and the Nazi authorities, in this case Gauleiter Josef Grohé, who took to barging in on military conferences, waving his pistol around and demanding *unerbittliche Verteidigung* (unrelenting defence), and that the city be contested 'metre by metre'. Defending the Reich in 1945 were 43 Gauleiters, each the head of his Gau (regional government), and answerable only to Hitler. To the older professionals of the Wehrmacht, it was obvious they were on the losing side. The question was not whether they would be defeated, but how bad their annihilation would be. Occasionally, German civilians shared Grohé's fanaticism, as one 3rd Armored Division patrol recalled when they entered a farmyard barn to find 'an entire German family, father, mother, and a teenage daughter, hanging from the rafters. Even their dog, a loyal dachshund, lay strangled at their feet. There was no sign of a struggle. The family had taken their own lives just before the Americans arrived.'[41]

However, neither the local 81st Korps commander, General Friedrich Köchling, nor his subordinate, Generalmajor Harald Freiherr von Elverfeldt, leading the shattered remnants of 9th Panzer Division, paid Grohé, a virulent anti-Semite since the earliest days of Nazism, any heed. As in many larger German cities, city centre inhabitants lived in apartment blocks several storeys high. During air raids, they retreated to their basements, from which mouseholes had been burrowed into neighbouring blocks for rescue purposes. Now the city was threatened, these tunnels allowed the defenders to move around unmolested.

Just before the last assault, on 2 March, the Allied air forces paid Cologne their 262nd, and final, visit. In broad daylight, which emphasised the impotency of the Luftwaffe, two waves, comprising 531 Lancasters and 303 Halifaxes, led by twenty-four Mosquito pathfinders, scattered high explosives throughout the city. The raid may have achieved little, apart from shattering the Germans' already jittery morale, but it under-lined the power of RAF Bomber Command at that moment. However, it was Köchling's men who suffered the most, with many defensive pos-itions and communications wiped out. Allied propaganda leaflets urging surrender rained down at the same time adding to the broken glass, plaster dust, brick rubble and other litter in the streets. Overhead wires from Cologne's tram network dangled down; most of the city's trees had long since disappeared for firewood.

'Everything is going with clockwork precision,' noted Hodges' war diary on 3 March. 'VII Corps, taking almost 2,000 prisoners, were tonight looking at the spires of Cologne from a distance of not more than six miles.'[42] The final act began at 04:00 two days later, when Combat Command 'A' of Rose's Spearhead thundered into the city ruins along-side the 415th Infantry of Allen's 104th Timberwolves, their boundary being Cologne's main thoroughfare, the Venloer Strasse.

At the same moment, General Bryant Moore's 8th Division struck out for the Rhine, south of the city. Several combat cameramen accom-panied the GIs and recorded the mixed columns of Spearhead Sher-mans interspersed with half-tracks from their 36th Armored Infantry Regiment navigating their way through the debris-strewn streets, where scarcely a building remained intact. Using their tanks to guard every intersection, the 3rd Armored had also borrowed the 13th Infantry Regi-ment from the 8th Division and with this troop density felt able to take on urban combat. Earlier fighting in Stalingrad, Cassino and Aachen had indicated to both sides that cities were no place for armour, unless protected by foot soldiers. Each had learned to use tank-hunting teams with bazookas or panzerfäuste to creep up on their opponents. GIs rode on the slow-moving tanks whenever they could, dismounting when battle dictated.

The defence was spasmodic, but the city took time to subdue because of its sheer size. The pungent smell of unburied corpses, caught in the last bombing raids, hung heavy with the lingering scent of phosphorus from airdropped and land-fired munitions. By nightfall, the Spearhead Shermans and armoured infantry had penetrated a mile into built-up area and General von Elverfeldt had been killed. As American armour demolished roadblocks and engineers pulled away the rubble-filled trams, GIs were surprised when the locals emerged from their cellars – and the extensive network of air-raid shelters – to greet the Americans as liberators, not conquerors. German civilians now began to refer to their own troops as *der Kriegsverlängerern* (the war-extenders). This outraged Gauleiter Grohé, who placed General Köchling under arrest for defeatism and dereliction of duty, but then promptly fled across the Rhine in a small boat himself.

Around noon on 6 March, the second full day of urban combat, all heard a dull roar as the Germans sabotaged the great Hohenzollern bridge, the last of Cologne's crossings over the Rhine. Overnight, reinforcements led by Leutnant Wilhelm Bartelborth with three panzers, had trickled into the city, but now their route to safety was cut off. One of these, a Mark V Panther, parked up in front of the cathedral, determined to make a last-ditch stand. As several Shermans approached, it opened fire, destroying two of the American vehicles.

A late-war, fully loaded Sherman carried around eighty 76mm shells and 170 gallons of gasoline. Even a glancing blow from a German anti-tank gun would be enough to cause sparks, igniting the shells, fuel and 7,000 rounds of machine-gun ammunition on board. A crewman's life depended on his ability to exit his tank in seconds, but sometimes the forward hatches were blocked by the angle of the main gun. Three crew of one Sherman failed to escape but their commander, Second Lieutenant Karl Kellner, a Silver Star recipient, tumbled out of his turret, his right leg torn off at the knee. He was carried to a shell hole but bled to death in the arms of nearby war correspondent Andy Rooney.

Several cameramen had their lenses trained on the Panther, which they assumed had been knocked out earlier, when it sprang to life, so the incident was caught in several photographs and a newsreel. In a side street loitered one of the brand-new M26 Pershing tanks, called 'Eagle 7' by its Second Platoon crew – all the tanks in Company 'E' of the 32nd Armored Regiment began with the same letter. The US photographers had heard there was a new tank about but had never seen one, much less in action.

Earlier in the day Eagle 7's crew had already disabled a Mark IV panzer hidden behind a city block by the simple expedient of loading three-foot-long shells into their massive gun and firing at the building concealing their opponent. They let loose an avalanche of bricks which tumbled on top of the German tank, rendering it inoperable. Its commander, Rolf Millitzer, and radio operator, Gustav Schaeffer, managed to escape their iron coffin, and were soon scooped up by other Spearhead GIs.

Under the shadow of the cathedral, Staff Sergeant Robert Early ordered his Pershing forward, and Technician Fifth Grade Bill McVey, the driver, took them past the two damaged Shermans. Corporal Clarence Smoyer, the nineteen-year-old gunner, who had grown up with a hawk's eyes and steady hands, engaged the Panther as soon as he saw it, while their tank was still rolling. The distance was no more than seventy yards. A good loader could anticipate the kind of ammunition the gunner required, whether HE (high explosive), AP (armour piercing), or the grey-painted warheads that indicated white phosphorus. Normally used for marking targets, white phosphorus was deadly against infantry sheltering in static positions, like foxholes or basements. Today the need was for AP.

'I noticed through my periscope that the Panther's gun was turning to meet us. I fired, and – bingo – a hit with an armour-piercing 90mm under the Panther's gun shield,' recollected Smoyer. 'That was followed by two more shells, which I sighted and fired as fast as my assistant gunner – Private John DeRiggi – could load. All this happened so fast that I had no time to be nervous. It was just intense, fast work.'[43] With the bow gunner, Private Homer Davis, firing tracer at any movement, each of Smoyer's twenty-four-pound projectiles hit home with such muzzle velocity that they drilled through the armour plate on both sides, like a pencil through butter. The German turret crew of three managed to escape, but the remaining pair died in the inferno that followed. Cameras caught the great gouts of flame that emerged from the Panther's turret and forward hatches, as the fuel and ammunition caught fire, GIs remembering the roar of the furnace as the panzer died.

The duel soon became famous, not just because it was a very public baptism of fire for the new Pershing against a well-matched opponent, but because it was captured by so many photographers and a newsreel camera crew. In the following days and weeks, the hulk of the burnt-out Panther against the backdrop of Cologne's Gothic cathedral proved an irresistible composition for many photographers. Every newspaper carried the story with a photograph, as did the newsreels. For some it seemed to symbolise the survival of old Germany over the new. To others it underlined the superiority of American technology against that of the Reich. It was a dramatic duel, but only in 2019 was each surviving crew member of Eagle 7 recognised for their bravery with the award of a Bronze Star.[44]

This was the defenders' last major show of defiance and by 18:45 GIs had reached their objective of the adjacent Hauptbahnhof (main railway station) and the now-destroyed Hohenzollern bridge behind it. To the Spearhead's south, the Timberwolf Division had made equally significant progress, supported by the 750th Tank and 629th Tank Destroyer Battalions, while the 8th Division cleared the south-western outskirts. By 7 March, all resistance had been crushed, and Cologne had fallen. The war had sixty-two days to run.

Many GIs went into looting mode. For the infantry, limited as to what they could carry, this might amount to wristwatches, German badges or patches (those of the SS were highly prized) and maybe a pistol or two. Others, like artillerymen, armoured infantry riding in half-tracks, the cavalry in their armoured cars and tank crews, had room for more. One GI on the prowl noted the closets 'crammed with Nazi leaflets and Nazi books and Nazi uniforms and Nazi ceremonial daggers'.[45] Many were sent home to relatives and sweethearts, but others were kept for trading with rear echelon troops, for there was money to be made from Germany's humbling.

It was during a flag-raising ceremony at the city's Müngersdorf sports stadium on 11 March that 'Lightning Joe' addressed 2,500 representatives of his VII Corps. He told them this was the first time since 1923, when an earlier American Expeditionary Force withdrew, that the Stars and Stripes had flown over the Rhine. 'We pause to remember those men who gave their lives so that we might be here,' he intoned, as a flight of

P-47 Thunderbolts passed overhead in salute. Two months later, the former Oberbürgermeister (Lord Mayor) of Cologne, Konrad Adenauer, who had lost his job in 1933, and would one day become the first Chancellor of West Germany, was reinstated, a standard policy widespread across the occupation zones. Under the watchful eyes of an Allied military commandant, Weimar-era Bürgermeister of proven anti-Nazi credentials led civil servants, often former card-carrying National Socialists whose uniforms and insignia had become hot ashes days earlier, to get their settlements up and running.

Their priorities were food distribution, allocation of housing, and the restoration of electricity and water supplies. Issues of firewood for winter, rubble clearance and denazification of staff would follow later. Adenauer's job was both easy and difficult. Easy because Cologne contained only 40,000 residents left of the 770,000 it had recorded in 1939, but difficult in that many of its bureaucrats had also departed.[46] Elsewhere, the 22-year-old Henry A. Kissinger, a native of Bavaria but then serving in the US 84th Infantry Division, acted as Krefeld's first commandant, within eight days establishing that city's new administration following its occupation.[47]

In Cologne, as in all large settlements, the arriving troops found they were liberators to one group, even if they did not understand who they were – the slave labourers. In addition to those of many nationalities, the liberated included German civilians wedded to Jews, termed *Mischehe* (mixed married), and others deemed half-Jewish. None were recognised as acceptable citizens of the new Reich, and all had been obliged to act as forced labour in factories and private homes, daily trekking back and forth from camps to workplace. Years later, a Polish Jew, Helen Siegal, later a teacher in a Pennsylvanian college, would recall as a girl of nine her relief at being liberated by men 'wearing a wolf patch' – the Timberwolves. Some liberated slave labourers were the survivors of interrogations at the Gestapo headquarters on Appellhof Platz, freed by the 3rd Armored Division. This was one of the few undamaged buildings in the city centre, where American troops found ten basement cells, each with steel doors, and the graffiti of the inmates left on the walls. Up to thirty victims were crammed into each cell before being taken for interrogation.

Captured documents indicated the detainees were political dissidents, black marketeers and those suspected of sabotage; the numbers were not small – in August 1943 alone, the Cologne Gestapo arrested 2,090. After torture and execution in the courtyard, their bodies were hauled off to the Westfriedhof cemetery in municipal rubbish carts. GIs learned the last shootings took place on 2 March 1945 – four days before they reached the city – among them a fifteen-year-old Cologne youth, and a Polish forced labourer, Josef Biczszak, killed after working for the Gestapo as an errand boy and murdered because he knew too much. Of the 1,800 inscriptions preserved on the walls of the Gestapo building today, mostly names, written in Cyrillic, of those from Eastern lands about to die, there is only one in English: 'Earl Huge, Cleveland, Ohio. Third Armored Division.'[48]

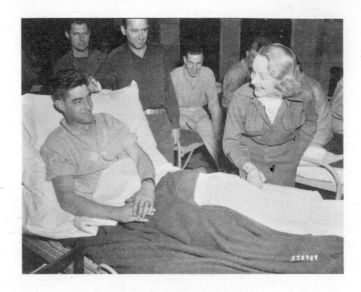

(*Above*): The USO entertainer Marlene Dietrich, a naturalised American who was born in Berlin, put heart and soul into maintaining the morale of 'her boys'. (*Below*): Colonel Edward Fickett's 6th Cavalry Group acted as Patton's personal eyes and ears for the Saar-Siegfried campaign. Each US army corps possessed a cavalry group with light tanks and armoured cars, which provided invaluable service liaising between units, protecting flanks and scouting ahead.

6

The Saar and the Siegfried

In the southern sector, having finally eliminated the Germans at Colmar, Sixth Army Group's doughboys and 'grognards' – grumblers, the old guard – belonging to Patch and de Lattre now paused to draw breath. For Jake Devers there was a moment to celebrate his promotion to four-star rank, full general, on 8 March. None of this mattered to his men, for whom hot showers, movies, recreation and, above all, sleep beckoned. Some communed with their Maker, and there was time, for those who appreciated smooth liquor and rough women, for leave passes to cities like Nancy.

The lure of hot food pulled GIs into restaurants, where they wolfed down steaks. Upon inspection the beef was invariably horse, 'but they was steaks. The meat was a little bit coarser than beef, but it was good. Anything would be good after C-rations,' reminisced Staff Sergeant Paul F. Jenkins of the 707th Tank Battalion.[1] Reims also offered 'R & R' facilities but was heavily patrolled by military policemen. It was an open secret that it housed SHAEF's forward headquarters.

For Eisenhower's millions in uniform, three-day furloughs to Paris or Brussels were offered to the battle-weary, where the delights of carousing in bars or indulging in 'Pig Alley', Place Pigalle, Paris's red-light district, suddenly made the rigours of combat endurable. In February 1945 Second Lieutenant Lee M. Otts with the 328th Infantry of 26th Division, recalled of his seventy-two-hour pass in Paris: 'We had no sooner entered a café in Pigalle than we were approached by women propositioning us. It was the same everywhere.' This was a revelation to many strait-laced GIs from small-town or rural America. Next day Otts dined

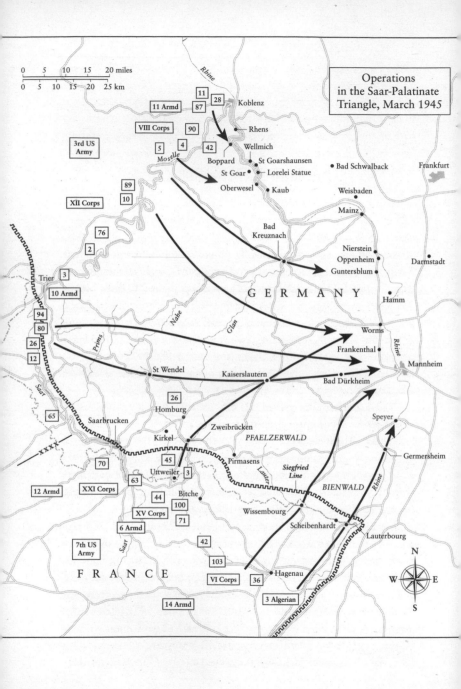

Operations
in the Saar-Palatinate
Triangle, March 1945

in an officers' club that was 'jammed and packed with officers of all ranks and all branches of the service, also with all types of women from army nurses to French prostitutes'. He soon moved on to take in a floor show in the Casino de Paris, where 'The scenery and costumes, when they had any on, were beautiful; for the most part the women in the show wore only a G-string or some feathers. It was just a musical stage show featuring pretty girls and much bare flesh.'[2]

The big cities were also places to make money. GIs witnessed a huge market for military souvenirs, particularly captured pistols (highly prized were P-38s and Lugers, at $100 each), uniform items such as headgear, and medals (an Iron Cross generally went for $10), sold to rear-echelon troops who would never see a German during their entire war. Rations, especially cigarettes, were traded for gifts, such as embroidered linen and perfume, to send home. Lieutenant Otts recalled his 'supply sergeant kept a stack of cigarette packs on hand just for men to trade when going on pass, so I loaded my musette bag with them and D-bars [chocolate].'[3] Every C or K ration meal came with chocolate and a four-pack of V-cigarettes, but GIs were also entitled to a twenty-pack daily and could buy more in the PX for fifty cents a pack.[4] Hence soldiers noting issue tobacco (Old Gold, Philip Morris, Lucky Strikes, Chesterfields and Camels were the favourites), Hershey chocolate D-bars and booze openly on display in the street markets.

The economic instability of liberated Europe meant that few items were valid means of barter for civilians. Even though cigarettes were widely available in military circles, with an instant, universal exchange value, they became the principal currency across war-torn Germany, Italy, Belgium, Holland and France. This led inevitably to the fact that, as Harald Jähner eloquently observed in *Aftermath*, 'The cigarette became the cowrie shell of the era. Its exchange rate may have fluctuated, but it remained one of the more dependable currencies of those years.'[5] GIs could quote the price of everything, from a seat at the Opéra to a moment of passion with a prostitute, in cigarettes. Thus, shortages arose, and in the hands of gangsters, the price of cigarette packs, whether issued or bought for fifty cents, climbed.[6] Yet that was just the tip of the iceberg: for everything and anything could be found on the black market. Hidden in garages, stolen Jeeps, trucks and vehicle parts were available for inspection, with jerrycans of gasoline offered at 5,000 francs.[7]

Jerrycans, the metal fuel containers holding five US gallons, became valuable commodities in themselves, capable of holding endless liquids, from gasoline to wine. Modelled on the twenty-litre German design, hence its name, they too were traded. At this stage in Europe, 21 million Allied-made jerrycans were in circulation, interchangeable with the *Wehrmachtskanister* originals. Combat soldiers often threw them away after use, to be retrieved after the war by thrifty farmers; 1.3 million new ones were shipped into theatre each month to replace those 'lost'.

The black market matter came to Eisenhower's attention when supplies of his favourite Johnnie Walker Black Label Scotch were diverted by thieves and in one thirty-day period only 11 million out of 77 million packs of cigarettes reached US troops in Europe. This was at a time when 55 *billion* cigarettes were supplied to the US War Department in the last six months of 1944 alone.[8] Ike, a three-packs-a-day man, ordered an immediate inquiry. What the US Army's Criminal Investigation Branch found shocked him.

Webs of highly organised American deserters, armed to the teeth, who used a vast array of stolen uniforms and weapons, forged passes and hijacked vehicles, operated in several major cities. Some had their own 'military policemen' and ambulances for transporting their booty, keeping their loot in freight cars on obscure railway sidings. Between June 1944 and April 1945, the CIB handled a total of 7,912 cases – 40 per cent involving the misappropriation of US supplies.[9] Returning to the front Lieutenant Otts reflected on the 'soldiers in soft jobs. Almost every man in Paris was wearing combat boots, while many of our troops had spent the whole winter in muddy, frozen leggings and GI shoes because we could not get enough combat boots'.[10]

For those who made it back to their units on time – and a substantial number were late or reappeared with venereal disease (which affected up to 5 per cent of GIs)[11] – there were endless training exercises. Replica sections of the German defences were built, dummy minefields laid, and trenches dug for the GIs to attack repeatedly. French villages, like Pournoy-la-Chétive, were taken over and literally shelled to pieces in an effort to perfect methods for penetrating the Siegfried Line and the urban warfare tactics needed to fight through German towns and cities beyond.

Meanwhile, their commanders fell in line with Eisenhower's overall plan for each of his seven armies to reach the western bank of the Rhine then mount a series of assault crossings. North of Strasbourg, where Seventh Army had been forced to give ground during *Nordwind*, there remained a large hostile garrison in the Saar Basin, a significant part of Germany west of the great river. Here, the Wehrmacht held a huge triangle of terrain, protected by the Siegfried Line, with its eastern edge stretching between Koblenz and Hagenau, and its two sides meeting at a point seventy-five miles west.

Subduing this area corresponded to Eisenhower's report to the Second Quebec Conference of September 1944, code-named *Octagon*, when the Combined Chiefs of Staff confirmed 'SCAEF's broad intention to press on with all speed to destroy the German armed forces and occupy the heart of Germany. The best opportunity of defeating the enemy in the West lies in striking at the Ruhr and Saar, where SCAEF is convinced that the enemy will concentrate the remainder of his forces in the defence of these areas. SCAEF's first operation will be to break the Siegfried Line and seize crossings over the Rhine, where his main effort will be on the left. He will then prepare for a deep thrust into Germany.' Of course, these plans, made in September, had been delayed on account of the German *Herbstnebel* and *Nordwind* offensives, and the wintry weather, but they remained unchanged in tactical and operational detail.[12]

In Patton's Third Army territory, the triangle's northern edge followed the Mosel River from Trier until it flowed into the Rhine. The southern flank was overseen by Patch's Seventh Army, following the line of the Saar River, and thence to Hagenau and the Rhine. An ordinary roadmap of the region does not suffice, for geology is the key. The Vosges mountain range, which had so bedevilled combat through the winter, snakes its way north into the centre of this triangle, where it is known as the Pfaelzerwald (Palatinate Forest). Its heights take the form of heavily afforested sandstone hills, of anything from 500 to 1,500 feet, where movement is restricted to a few roads and tracks. The Pfaelzerwald ends fifteen miles west of the Rhine, where numerous small rivers flow from the hills across flatlands into the main river. The wider region, with the Saar coalfield and several industrial towns, of strategic importance to the Reich, was labelled the Saar-Palatinate Triangle. After extensive rehearsals it was to be the target of a huge attack by both Third and Seventh Armies, dubbed Operation *Undertone*, beginning on 15 March.

For their first venture into the Fatherland, Sixth Army Group's part in the campaign – a lunge from the south – would be launched simultaneously with Third Army assaults from the west and north. For Patch's Seventh, several natural gaps in the terrain beckoned, of which the principal stretched from Saarbrucken north-east to Kaiserslautern, with an autobahn extending from there to Worms. A smaller movement corridor lay to the east beginning at Wissembourg, which had been much studied in staff colleges, due to its use twice by armies in the eighteenth century and by the Prussians in 1870. The region was as well known to the legionaries of the Caesars as to the grenadiers of Napoleon or Bismarck.

Initially, Seventh Army would have to win back the ground between Bitche and Hagenau lost during *Nordwind*. Then Eisenhower directed that Devers' task was not only to attack and penetrate the Siegfried Line defences, but then to swing east and establish bridgeheads over the Rhine between Mainz and Mannheim. The false dawn of crossing the great river four months earlier was forgotten.

Although under no illusions that their opponents would fight like tigers once the *Vaterland* was directly threatened, PFC Robert Lynch of the 15th Infantry Regiment summed up the buoyant mood: 'No passports were required. Nothing could stop us! We were on a roll; the die was cast.'[13] Seventh Army's own attack was to be made along a forty-seven-mile front between Saarbrücken and Hagenau. It involved, reading from the west, Milburn's XXI Corps, covering a twenty-mile front, fielding the 101st Cavalry Group, the 70th 'Trailblazers' and 63rd 'Blood and Fire' Divisions, and 12th Armored, known as the 'Hellcats'.[14] The Cavalry Group comprised 1,500 New York National Guardsmen arranged in three battalion-sized troops.

The cavalrymen operated M8 scout cars and jeeps, mostly acting as Milburn's eyes and ears, scouting ahead of the rest to locate the opposition, though some acted as security for corps headquarters. The 63rd had arrived in Marseilles in December, and its 264th Infantry Regiment had fought at Colmar attached to the Marne Division. Previously it had been the resident formation at Camp Van Dorn, Mississippi, responsible for the combat preparation of GIs fresh from boot camp. After the staggering casualties sustained in Normandy more men were needed in Europe and the army raided its Army Specialized Training Program (ASTP) for manpower. These were conscripts of above average IQ who were given college education and were destined for officer or aircrew training. The ASTP was dissolved, and many of its former students found themselves as infantry in the 63rd, which consequently became known as the 'Smart Division'.[15]

The main effort against Utweiler and Bitche would come from the centre, where Haislip's XV Corps consisted of six formations – the 44th, 45th, 3rd, 100th Infantry, followed by the 71st Infantry and 6th Armored Divisions. The first four were battle-scarred and experienced as was the 6th Armored, borrowed from Patton specifically for the assault. Having removed all their divisional badges from their uniforms and vehicles, the 6th embarked on a 150-mile journey south from the Ardennes, as the latter's history noted. 'We faded like mist from the ranks of the Third Army, and like a huge ghost reappeared as a part of the Seventh Army, ready to plunge across the Rhine.'[16] However, Willard G. Wyman's 71st had only arrived at Le Havre on 6 February and *Undertone* would be their initiation into the mysteries of combat. Among its rifle platoon leaders was Second Lieutenant John D. Eisenhower, commissioned from West Point on 6 June 1944. Understanding the impact the death of 'Mac' Patch had had on his father, Bradley was so worried about the effect on Ike, were the younger Eisenhower to be killed or captured, that he had him transferred to staff duties.

The 45th were a National Guard formation led by the tough and uncompromising Robert T. Frederick, who had earlier raised the US-Canadian 1st Special Service Force. It had fought near Cassino and Anzio in Italy; his subsequent command, the Anglo-US 1st Allied Airborne Task Force, had landed behind German lines in Operation *Dragoon*. On 3 December 1944, aged thirty-seven, he had taken over the 45th, becoming with Jim Gavin, who was born eight days earlier, the youngest US divisional commanders in the war. On their left shoulders, Frederick's men had once sported an ancient American Indian symbol of good luck, reflecting the heritage of the four states whence they came – Oklahoma, New Mexico, Colorado and Arizona. However, when the Third Reich also adopted the same symbol – the swastika – the division looked for an alternative. In 1939, their choice alighted on a Thunderbird, a Native American symbol signifying 'sacred bearer of unlimited happiness'. In May 1943, just before departing overseas, some of the division's 1,500 Indigenous Americans, from twenty-eight tribes, put on a campfire war dance. Thereafter, the 45th was always the 'Thunderbird' Division.[17]

That February, the division's popular cartoonist who worked on the *45th Division News* had just transferred to *Stars and Stripes*. This was Sergeant Bill Maudlin, an Arizona National Guard volunteer in 1940, who crafted some of the war's most enduring images. These included two unshaven, scruffy dogfaces, 'Willie' and 'Joe', who were forever complaining about rations, the weather and generals. At heart, Maudlin remained a Seventh Army GI, often ridiculing the spit and shine of their neighbours in Patton's Third through his characters. Publishing six cartoons a week, at the war's end he would be awarded a Pulitzer Prize for his collected wartime work which had done so much to keep spirits high.

Echoing their corps boundaries of January, when the sector had been hit by *Nordwind*, was Brooks' VI Corps with the 42nd, 103rd, 36th Infantry, 3rd Algerian and later the 14th Armored Divisions. All were old hands under Devers. The 42nd was known as the 'Rainbow' Division, a moniker that dated back to 1917 when its Chief of Staff, Colonel Douglas MacArthur, observed that the formation, which took men from across the United States, 'spanned the nation like a rainbow'. Consequently, they wore a red, gold and blue arc shaped like a rainbow, to emphasise the point.

The 103rd's commander since 11 January – his promotion for defending Bastogne so well during the Bulge – was the unflappable Anthony C. McAuliffe. His men wore a cactus badge on their shoulders, a nod to their home states of Arizona, Colorado and New Mexico. Although the Thunderbirds recruited in the same area, their soldiers were originally National Guard volunteers, whereas the Cactus men were draftees. Not untypical of their conscript officers was a twenty-year-old who had graduated from Officer Candidate School in May 1944 and was assigned to the 410th Infantry, in command of a platoon of Company 'F'. In the autumn of 1944, Second Lieutenant Paul Fussell Jr and his division had arrived in the foothills of the Vosges Mountains at a time when the average life expectancy for a junior officer there was just seventeen days.

In late November, Fussell's company lost four of its six officers, his platoon shrinking from forty to twenty-seven men. Of suffering his first combat casualties, he wrote later, 'My boyish illusions, largely intact to that moment of awakening, fell away all at once, and suddenly I knew that I was not and would never be in a world that was reasonable or just.' For their Saar offensive, they – like the other divisions – were rested and back at full strength. Fussell would provocatively conclude of his service, 'not merely did I learn to kill but I learned to enjoy the prospect of killing. You learn that you have much wider dimensions than you had imagined before you fight.'[18] In the vanguard of Augustine Guillaume's 3rd Algerian Division on the far right was the 3rd Régiment de Spahis Algériens de Reconnaissance, whose splendid unit insignia was full of both military and cultural significance – a crouching leopard astride a Muslim crescent moon.

The deployment of ten infantry divisions was an acknowledgement that the Siegfried Line would be a tough nut to crack. First, the troops had to advance between five and twenty miles just to reach it. A phase of battering their way through at chosen points would follow. Finally, once gaps had been made, the armoured formations and cavalry groups would be unleashed to race for the Rhine. At this stage, Patch alone was fielding around 250,000 men, more than double the 120,000 in the ranks of First and Seventh Armies in Hausser's Army Group 'G', which the Oberst-Gruppenführer had petitioned Hitler to withdraw to the east bank of the Rhine. As usual, his Führer had refused, abandoning the twenty-three divisions in the region to their fate.

In the Prologue we encountered the night onslaught of O'Daniel's Marne Division against Utweiler in the early hours of 15 March. They were dispatched with typical 'Iron Mike' aggression: 'The attack will be pressed with the ruthless vigor that has routed every formation opposing the 3rd Division. Bayonets will be sharpened!' The 'Blue and White Devils' started at 01:00, a few hours ahead of the other formations, and struck in the dead centre of the Seventh Army assault. Through no fault of their own, they were the only division to receive a significant counter-attack in the whole Saar Basin on the first day, the one which all but destroyed the Cottonbalers' Second Battalion.[19]

A few hundred yards away on their right the story was different, where other formations attacked in daylight, with air support. As PFC Robert Lynch with the 15th Infantry explained, 'Our planes continuously flew over German positions and saturated the area with surrender instructions. Many captured Germans carried these papers in their pockets or waved them at us so we would not shoot them.'[20] By now the weather had changed, and in addition to dropping leaflets, XII Tactical Air Command and other Allied sky raiders were able to provide close air support to ground troops.

The Cottonbalers' Third Battalion avenged their comrades the same afternoon but suffered from the attentions of the 'American Luftwaffe'. Besides driving the SS from Utweiler, killing or capturing nearly five hundred of them, James A. Little with Company 'I' witnessed, 'our P-47s bombed and strafed the retreating Germans, then almost got me. One dove with its guns roaring and dropped a bomb. I hit the ground near a brick wall and was covered with dirt when the bomb exploded. I made a dash for a building before the plane dove again. At that moment someone threw a yellow smoke-grenade into the street to let our planes know it was us they were bombing and not the enemy. They got our signal, thank God.'[21]

Also counter-attacking Utweiler in the afternoon of the 15th was First Lieutenant Arthur F. Richter, with a column of Shermans from Able Company of the 756th Tank Battalion, who would win himself a Silver Star for his leadership that day. This demonstrated just how vital infantry–armour–air cooperation was in defeating their opponents. The absence of the latter two had been lethal the night before for the Second Battalion of the Cottonbalers. Within hours the Marne Division had moved on, leaving Utweiler in ruins. Just as Pournoy-la-Chétive, where they had trained south of Metz, had been smashed beyond repair. Too often it was the civilians who bore the brunt of the fighting, losing everything, if not their lives, yet having no voice in the history of those times.

To the right of Utweiler, Major General Withers A. Burress' 100th 'Century' Division were given the task of subduing the much fought-over fortress town of Bitche, an important military centre since the 1300s. Its central citadel had been upgraded by Vauban and resisted capture during the Franco–Prussian War. In the 1930s it had been integrated into the Maginot Line defences and ringed with five forts. To the Century men this would be déjà vu, for the area had been taken by their division in early December 1944. They withstood counter-attacks from the 17th SS Panzergrenadier Division, but a month later, during the opening days of *Nordwind*, the same SS formation returned, and this time prevailed.[22] Knowing of their impending return to the town (by now the Century Division had taken to calling themselves Sons of Bitche), Colonel Paul S. Reinecke Jr, the division's G-2, initiated extensive observation: aerial photography, reconnaissance patrols and interviews with members of the French First Army, some of whom had designed or occupied the network of forts, tunnels and bunkers in the 1930s and campaign of 1940.

With the main XV Corps effort opposite Utweiler, the Century Division made no advance until 05:00 on 15 March. Meanwhile a four-hour artillery programme rained down on Bitche, commencing at the same hour the Cottonbalers first strode out on their ill-fated mission to the west. The Volksgrenadiers responded with mortars only when they saw GIs approaching the town, as PFC Andrews with Company 'F' of the 398th Infantry recorded: 'The Jerries did not see us until we left the woods and were going down a dirt road. Then it all began. It was the first time most of us had heard the mortar shells and rockets that came down constantly. No one hesitated to jump into a roadside ditch and lie down flat. I was so close to the ground that my nose was buried into the earth.' They were pinned down for two hours, 'each man's head was touching the next man's feet from end to end', while other companies and tanks worked their way around behind the German position.[23]

The end of the action came swiftly. 'The entire fortified area fell like a ripe fruit because we eliminated all of the fort's supporting weapons, capturing the dregs of a regiment of Nebelwerfers and many mortars. We took 293 prisoners, including a battalion commander of the 225th Volksgrenadier Regiment, four of his staff officers and more than seventy NCOs. All indicated ignorance of our intentions and amazement at the thoroughness of our knowledge of their situation.'[24] By this time, throughout the Reich, the Wehrmacht had devolved into scattered regiments and battalions, with the traditional structure of divisions broken beyond repair.

The following morning Captain Thomas H. Garahan led Company 'E' of the 398th into Bitche. The owner of the Auberge de Strasbourg, George Oblinger, welcomed them, and produced an American flag made in secret by his wife, Maria. A *Stars and Stripes* photographer was on hand to record the moment when Garahan unfurled it from an upstairs balcony. He later wrote home to his wife, 'I was shocked to learn that the photo had been published. Apparently, it was printed all over the United States. This flag had been hidden in a pillowcase for two years under the noses of the Germans. It is the first to have been displayed in the city.' Garahan never returned to Bitche, but in 2007 his son Frank visited the town. He was welcomed with open arms because the image of his father with the flag remains the symbol of the town's liberation, and a major event in the history of its inhabitants.[25]

The armoured fist of the Century Division was the 781st Independent Tank Battalion, the 'Red Raiders', so-named because all wore red scarves, a tradition initiated by their CO, Major Elery Zehner. A popular leader, widely known for his disdain of danger and risk, Zehner often dismounted to scout the terrain ahead himself, and when necessary, shouldered his radio man's heavy wireless set. Reflecting their easy infantry–armour relationship, it was Garahan's men of the 398th who cleared the mined roads, allowing Zehner's Shermans into the town.

All US infantry divisions had independent tank battalions assigned to them, which were usually parcelled up into tank platoons to support regiments. This was against US tank doctrine which insisted that armour should be deployed en masse, rather than broken up and dispersed, yet in eight months of combat since landing at Marseilles in October, the 781st was never once employed as a battalion. However, the 100th Infantry were the beneficiaries of this 'slippage' of doctrine, knowing they could always rely on immediate armour support; although Bitche cost the 781st five tanks lost to mines, with two crewmen killed.[26]

Back at Fort Knox, Kentucky, they had taken part in a round-the-clock tank marathon, testing forty different models of Sherman to find the best configuration of engine, gearbox, armour, main weapon and suspension. The results of the 'Million Dollar Tank Test' showed without doubt that the up-armoured Sherman M4E8, dubbed the 'Easy Eight', powered by a Ford V8 gasoline engine, and mounting a 76mm gun with an improved rate of fire and better accuracy, was the best type. These were the models with which the 781st Tank Battalion had shipped out to France.[27]

The 71st Division followed the Century men through the German defences, understandably anxious about the forthcoming baptism of fire. Sergeant Dean Joy, in charge of a mortar squad with Company 'G', 5th Infantry, was moving up at night through the woods towards Bitche, all his men labouring under the weight of their heavy weapons. 'Climbing an open slope strewn with fallen logs in the dark, we were utterly exhausted. Gasping, I made my way to a dark lump I took to be a log and sat down. I felt softness and smelled something putrid. Then I saw the shape of a coal-scuttle helmet nearby and was suddenly horrified to realize that I was sitting on a dead Kraut.'[28]

Texan John H. Atterbury, Jr, also 5th Infantry, recalled, 'One of our lieutenants in Company 'B', a southern boy from Mississippi, got into an argument over the Civil War with his men, who were mostly from the Northeast. He was reassigned and I took over his platoon. The first contact and action our division had with the Germans, was by my platoon. We were selected to seize an emplacement 600 yards in front of our lines at night. None of us had never been in combat before. To say we were a little nervous is an understatement. First thing we ran into was a dead GI from the 100th Division hung up on the wire. That didn't help our nerves.'

Brooks' VI Corps had the most difficult territory of the Lower Vosges and two rivers to cross. To assist McAuliffe's 103rd Division to punch through the German defences, an ad hoc grouping known as Task Force Rhine was formed from the 761st Tank Battalion, infantry and engineer detachments, and the 614th Tank Destroyer Battalion. Of note, both armoured units consisted of African Americans, a rare feature in the still-segregated world of the US Army.[29] The 103rd Division was assigned to take a small town north-west of Hagenau. Lieutenant Paul Fussell recalled that, 'Before that day was over, I was sprayed with the contents of a soldier's torso when I was lying behind him and he knelt to fire at a machine-gun holding us up. He was struck in the heart and out of the holes in the back of his field jacket flew little clouds of blood, tissue and powdered cloth.' He continued, 'Near him another man raised himself to fire, but the machine-gun caught him in the mouth, and as he fell, he looked back at me with surprise, blood and teeth dribbling out onto the leaves.' In the afternoon, the Germans began shelling the area, and Fussell himself was seriously wounded in the back and legs.[30]

On their left flank, over more difficult mountainous terrain, the 42nd 'Rainbow' Division spent three and a half days traversing sixteen miles of hills and forest supported by pack mules before reaching the Siegfried Line. Jimmy Gentry, with Company 'E' of the 222nd Infantry, recalled the advance over this ground as the most arduous of the war. 'They force-marched us all day, all night. I found out something about the human body that first night. You can go to sleep, walking. But you don't worry about it, because when you hit the ground, you wake up, you'd had your nap. We were moving, moving, all the time. We could see the war up ahead of us, and it was just flashes, flashes, flashes in the sky.'[31]

Further to the east, the 36th Texans, who with their attached 753rd Tank Battalion had landed in the Riviera with the Marne Division, struck towards Hagenau and the woods beyond, ground that had already been ceded to the Germans during their *Nordwind* offensive two months earlier. Leading one of the Texans' squads in Company 'B', 143rd Regimental Combat Team, was Jay D. Baxter, who recalled to me his experience of the Hagenau Woods. 'Our regiment led the way with my company just behind the lead company. We had spaced ourselves about ten yards apart to avoid unnecessary casualties from artillery or mortar fire, when our advance stalled. I felt nervous about the woods to my right, though officers reported they had been cleared and declared safe.'

Trusting his instincts, Baxter talked another guy into checking out the area with him, so he unhitched his .45 pistol from his belt, and crept towards the woods. 'Just before we reached the trees, we heard gunfire up ahead. Then there was silence; I couldn't see anything but shadows and tree trunks. All at once thirty Germans stood up with their hands held high and hollered "Kamerad, kamerad". Two German officers lay dead, shot by their own men a few moments before we approached. A German chaplain came forward who spoke English. "We had an argument over whether or not to surrender, and when we saw you headed straight toward us that quickly settled things." They had two of their machine-guns aimed straight at our line of men on the trail. After that I learned to trust my instincts.'[32]

On Seventh Army's eastern flank, Général Guillaume's 3rd Algerian Division, their January days of protecting Strasbourg long gone, slid along the west bank of the Rhine before coming up against the Reich's frontier fortresses. De Lattre had boosted Guillaume's division with a combat command, borrowed from the 5th French Armoured, and two Groupements (Regiments) of Moroccan Goums, and placed the resultant task force under the direction of the II Corps *chef*, Général de Monsabert. This was for a stratagem all of his own, as we shall see.

Ahead lay the Siegfried Line. The very concept intimidated the Allies, just as Nazi Germany intended. Its origins lay in Hitler's experience of the Westfront (Western Front) of the First World War, and particularly the Hindenburg Line of wire entanglements, trenches and pillboxes in which he had served. To the German High Command, the 1917–18 line dug deep into French and Flemish clay was actually the Siegfriedstellung (Siegfried Position), a barrier behind which an army could manoeuvre and attack. Just as Hindenburg's men had done in March 1918.

Back then, much of it had been barely visible, sunk into the earth. In contrast, Hitler's *Westwall* stood proudly above ground, for it was as much a defensive feature to keep the French out as a propaganda symbol of his new Germany. In ancient times the mystique of dark forests, sorcery and dragons had acted as deterrents. Echoing Hitler's Wagnerian obsessions, the real purpose of his *Westwall* was to create a modern equivalent: a series of castles projecting the menace of distant fire and far-off sword.

One of his pet projects before the war, the Führer's inland wall comprised more than 18,000 bunkers and stretched four hundred miles from Holland to the Swiss frontier. When the Reich needed houses, 20 per cent of cement production and 5 per cent of steel output had been lavished on its fortifications: it was thus a military project designed to unite the nation. Between 1936 and 1940, half a million workers, usually six-month conscripts from the Reichsarbeitsdienst (RAD – National Labour Service), 25 per cent of the Fatherland's construction industry, had assembled the defences.[33] In time the propaganda element came to dominate Hitler's thinking and he began to believe his *Westwall* was a continuous, impregnable barrier. In fact, a wall.

However, with the 1940 fall of France, the *Westwall* immediately lost its utility, as the front shifted to the Channel coast and in time another wall grew there. The rhapsody of concrete strewn along French, Belgian, Dutch and Danish cliffs and beaches, known as the *Atlantikwall*, borrowed weapons and ironmongery from Germany's frontier forts that were subsequently lost. Thus, by early 1945 the much-vaunted Siegfried Line was less a wall than a curtain. More to the point, Hitler had misread the utility of fixed defences, which can only delay. They cannot halt an opponent, unless fully manned, and infinitely resourced. In March 1945, Germany had neither the manpower nor the resources for the *Westwall* to do its job.

Having subdued the Colmar Pocket and regained every other last scrap of Alsace, each of Devers' divisions were level with the web of *Westwall* bunkers, whereupon their opponents quickly retreated into their belts of concrete and steel. Not as powerful as they might have been, but still formidable, these were instantly recognisable by their 'dragon's teeth' – several rows of concrete pyramids, three to four feet high, that zigzagged across the countryside. Behind these were two formidable anti-tank ditches, while covering each trackway or on every knoll were mutually supporting concrete pillboxes with interlocking arcs of fire, many disguised as farmhouses or barns, and accessed from tunnels hundreds of yards to the rear. This was what the Cottonbalers had been most nervous about as they prepared to assault Utweiler.

Sometimes there was more than one belt of these defences, each five hundred yards wide, while the whole terrain was laced with barbedwire entanglements and scattered with anti-personnel and anti-tank mines. Mobile artillery and self-propelled guns lurked in camouflaged positions with predetermined shoots overlooking likely approaches. The only proven method of penetration was to drench the terrain with artillery, destroy the wire with Bangalore torpedoes, clear the mines by hand, destroy the dragon's teeth with explosives, bulldoze the ditches, and knock out the bunkers and mobile guns, one by one. This was a task for combat engineers, covered by armour.[34]

Lieutenant Thomas P. Welch of the 601st Tank Destroyer Battalion worried beforehand, 'it's quite a thing, very well fortified and will be pretty rough getting thru'. Yet the armour and infantry were assisted – in the Marne Division's case – by the 10th Engineer Combat Battalion, whose Corporal Joseph F. Borriello recalled, 'We carried extra TNT to blow up pillboxes so the Germans couldn't infiltrate back into them, and bulldozed dirt to fill in the tank traps and cover the dragon's teeth.'[35] Tank units also found that firing their main armament at the dragon's teeth broke them up and loosened their foundations, enabling engineers to finish the job off with explosives. The GIs saw themselves as dentists, pulling out these troublesome military molars.

Thus, when the time of battle came for Robert Lynch of the 15th Infantry, 'before you could blink your eyes, a section of the so-called "indestructible, impregnable" Siegfried Line fortification was breached. Large numbers of surrendering, young German soldiers began to pour in; and deserters and stragglers, likewise, decided that enough was enough.'[36] Yet, in a cautionary note to military historians, Lynch's words come from a letter written home to his parents, which deflected the realities of battling through the Reich's *Westwall*. Every US infantry regiment at some stage had a tough fight, losing experienced men and greenhorns to ambushes, snipers, mortars and machine-gun fire. In the first thirty-six hours alone, Lynch's 15th Infantry, around 3,000 GIs, lost forty-five killed and 175 wounded just getting through the defences.

For the Saar campaign, Eisenhower had suggested Third and Seventh Army headquarters might collocate. It was an argument Devers had made earlier to the Supreme Commander: that Third Army might perform best as part of Sixth Army Group. Patch demurred, observing that any tactical issues could be easily resolved by phone, for he was reluctant to have his predecessor interfering in his day-to-day business. It was Patton who had commanded the Seventh on Sicily. The issue was not raised again.

The first breakthroughs were made by a trio of formations in the same sector, between Saarbrucken and Bitche, initially by 63rd Division on the right of XXI Corps, rapidly followed by 45th and 3rd of XV Corps. To the west and north, Patton's attacks also distracted the defenders, who panicked on finding the Third Army to their rear, blocking their escape routes to the Rhine. After five days of hard combat, on 20 March – the first day of spring – German resistance began to disintegrate, and the defenders started to withdraw eastwards. Patch's armoured divisions lanced through the *Westwall* and started to roll towards the Rhine. Many of the Volksgrenadiers and SS were caught in the constricting terrain of the Pfaelzerwald while Patton's troops were piling in from the west and north. Some of Third Army raced ahead to Kaiserslautern, where they linked up with 6th Armored, cutting off any further escape.

At the very tip of the 6th Armored's advance was eighteen-year-old Private G. Hudson Wirth, newly arrived in Company 'B' of the 50th Armored Infantry Battalion. His job was to spy out 'every spot ahead ideal for an ambush. The first vehicle of our combat recon patrol was a six-wheeled armored car belonging to the 86th Cavalry Squadron. Next in line was a Sherman tank. The third vehicle was my own, a half-track with a squad of armored infantry, meaning twelve soldiers at full complement, which we rarely had because of casualties.'[37]

During the advance north-east of Zweibrücken, 'we were slowly grinding our way up a narrow heavily forested road. Suddenly, the recon car stopped dead in its tracks, screeched into reverse, backing up as fast as possible. As it had poked its nose ahead, the crew saw a German tank on the top loop of the road ahead. The German fired but missed, being unable to depress his gun low enough to catch them backing up.' Quick as a flash, Wirth's squad bailed out to hunt for German troops nearby, for they never left a panzer unprotected by infantry. 'Directly to our front, perhaps no more than twenty feet away, several Germans popped up from their shallow foxholes. We beat them to the draw. All slumped back into the ground, one directly in front of me with half of his skull gone and his brain exposed. It was all over in a matter of a few seconds, but a very frightening skirmish for us.'[38]

Patch's other divisions were advancing from the south, while overhead the dreaded Jabos (a German abbreviation of Jagdbomber, or fighter-bomber) of XII Tactical Air Command roamed at will. Not since the previous autumn had the flying weather been as good, and not since the Falaise Pocket in Normandy of mid-August 1944 had such an array of targets presented themselves. There were so few escape routes that 'fighter pilots had only to aim their bombs, their cannon, and their machine-guns in the general direction of those roads to be assured of hitting some target', noted the official history. 'An acute gasoline shortage added to the German difficulties. Almost every yard became clogged with abandoned, damaged, or wrecked vehicles, guns, and equipment.'[39] Beginning on the 19th, the Germans started to destroy their own bridges over the Rhine, consigning their west-bank comrades to the POW stockade. The last bridge was at Germersheim, blown at 10:20 on 24 March, within sight of task forces from both the 12th and 14th Armored Divisions rushing to seize their prize.

In desperation, on 20 March the Luftwaffe had thrown nearly three hundred aircraft of every kind at their attackers but lost heavily. The *New York Herald Tribune* reported the account of one pilot as he arrived over the triangle. The Luftwaffe 'started dropping their belly tanks and splitting up and running'. I must have killed the pilot with the first burst, because the plane kept going straight and level. I peppered it with lead, and it didn't burn up, so I moved up alongside and saw the pilot slumped over in the cockpit. I gave it another burst and then the ship went down.'[40]

In the centre, 6th Armored passed through the terrain won by the Marne Division, the 50th Armored Infantry Battalion's historian noting, 'The first hours of the advance etched a picture of slow, crawling columns of vehicles picking their way through debris littered streets in the dead of the night. Morning, and exhausted drivers still pushed their vehicles relentlessly. Yet no one was in the least disgruntled because positive results were apparent in the glance at any vehicle odometer; ninety long miles had been pared away from Nazi Germany.'[41] By midnight on 23 March, both 45th and 3rd Divisions were camped on the west bank of the Great Waterway, around Worms, forty miles south of Frankfurt. Pre-Roman in origin and one of the oldest settlements in Northern Europe, the city was famous for its 1521 Diet (assembly) which concluded that Martin Luther was a heretic. Its cowed inhabitants of 1945 had all been fed Nazi propaganda that the Americans would rape, loot and burn every last one of them and were frankly surprised even to be alive.

Some locals remained defiant, as Dean Joy with the 71st Division noted. While driving through Pirmasens, north of Bitche, 'a German family came out of a side street with a cart carrying whatever was left of their belongings. A pitiful-looking old man with a rope over his shoulder was pulling the cart, while several women and small children pushed. We felt especially sorry for one hungry-looking, dirty-faced little girl in a ragged dress, and someone tossed her a pack of chewing gum. But a scowling blonde woman in a kerchief knocked it out of her hand and pushed her roughly on down the cobblestone road, leaving the gum in the gutter. "Ya Nazi bitch!" shouted the GI who had thrown the gum, and several of us added a cacophony of insulting jeers. But the woman never looked back. Those were the first German civilians I had seen.'[42]

The 101st Cavalry Group guarding Milburn's XXI Corps headquarters passed through Pirmasens on 23 March, its historian noting 'the town was practically levelled. German families were huddled together wherever they could find shelter. Others wandered in a daze through still smoking rubble. Broken water mains spouted water and the smell of death was everywhere. We were glad to soon move on.'[43]

However, as Major General Frederick, commander of the Thunderbirds, conceded from his headquarters in nearby Homburg, 'It is difficult to describe the destruction. Scarcely a man-made thing exists in our wake; it is even difficult to find buildings suitable for command posts. This is the scorched earth.'[44] One of his subordinate infantry regiments was equally eloquent in its after action report: 'the Siegfried Line defenses had taken nine years to prepare. The 157th and other Seventh Army units over-ran it in less than a week.'[45]

Devers found his centre of gravity had shifted further north than he had originally intended. It mattered little, as there was no remaining opposition. For all the Hitlerian rhetoric, the Allies were surprised at how quickly the Wehrmacht collapsed, with no defiant stay-behind sniping or sabotage. Haislip's XV Corps immediately started drawing up plans for assault crossings, by the Thunderbirds seven miles to the north of Worms, and by the Marne, the same distance to the south. They would be followed by the 63rd and 44th Divisions.

When Task Force Rhine – the African American armour group in Brooks' VI Corps – paused by their namesake's river, they tallied up their achievements, which included the destruction of 150 vehicles, four self-propelled guns, thirty-one pillboxes, forty-nine machine-gun nests, and twenty-nine anti-tank guns. 'At least 170 of the enemy lay dead and hundreds of horses were killed or left to graze by the road-side,' noted the official history. 'Twelve hundred prisoners were taken. The fire-strength of the task force was such that the 761st Tank Battalion alone used slightly more than fifty tons of ammunition before it halted.'[46] References to horses are often overlooked in accounts by both sides, where the presence of armour tends to blind both the writer and reader. For example, in the earlier *Herbstnebel* Ardennes offensive, the Wehrmacht had deployed 50,000 horses, a ratio of at least fifty equines for every panzer.[47]

The ratio was even greater in these spring battles, where – with little fuel – military units including the SS, relied more than ever on quadrupeds to tow their field artillery, ammunition, and numerous wagons full of supplies and equipment around the battlefield. A Marne Division officer recorded his thoughts on coming across a German horse-drawn column: 'As far as we can see, the road is cluttered with shattered, twisted cars, trucks and wagons. Hundreds of horses have been caught in the barrage. They look at us with puzzled, unblaming eyes, whinnying softly as their torn flesh waits for life to drain from it. We are used to the sight of dead and wounded men, but these shuddering animals affect us strangely.' His GI buddy added, 'I've known horses all my life, and there's not one dirty, mean thing about them. Makes you ashamed to belong to the human race.'[48]

For the first time Germans were on the receiving end of tactical air power over their own country, and for the first time Sixth Army Group GIs advanced through the Reich's own wrecked towns. In Zweibrücken they encountered the soon-to-be-commonplace panorama of 'rubble and craters filling the streets. All officials had long since fled. Thousands of released Allied prisoners and forced workers roamed the place aimlessly, as though terrified of their new-found freedom.' Driving through Homburg, 'dead horses and human corpses littered the business district, where fires still raged. Wholesale looting added to the general chaos.' In Bad Dürkheim 'an estimated 400 civilians still lay unburied beneath the rubble. Dead animals were strewn over the roads leading out of town. The place was overflowing with ex-prisoners and DPs [displaced persons], all of whom had to be fed and temporarily housed by the Seventh Army.'[49]

Hitler's response to the loss of the Saar and his opponents poised all along the Rhine was to issue a proclamation on 19 March calling for German infrastructure in the path of the Allies to be dismantled. 'All military transport and communication facilities, industrial establishments and supply depots, as well as anything else of value within Reich territory, which could in any way be used by our opponents immediately, or within the foreseeable future, for the prosecution of the war, will be destroyed . . . Directives to the contrary are invalid,' he demanded. On 30 March and 4 April, further nihilist decrees clarified what was to be blown up and who was responsible for doing it. Albert Speer dubbed it the 'Nero Decree,' while many regional leaders and the Wehrmacht – who had other more pressing issues to deal with – refused to participate with varying degrees of success. Enforcement was often in the hands of the SS and party faithful, who had little to lose. Those who resisted for the benefit of their communities were shot or hung – if the Allies failed to arrive in time.[50]

Among the first visitors to the region was Captain Marie M. Sieber, entertaining GIs with her USO (United Service Organization) troupe.[51] Better known as Marlene Dietrich, she had just turned forty-three, and as her escorting officer observed: 'She was middle-aged, she was a mother, in fact she was a grandmother, but unlike any grandmother that I'd ever met. She was kind, caring and fun to be with.' On occasion, she worked within a mile of the German front lines. 'When I asked why she took such a risk, with a seven-figure Nazi bounty on her head [for renouncing her German citizenship], she replied, "Aus anstand" – out of decency.'[52]

Clad in a translucent, shimmering blue gown, slit to reveal her famous legs, Dietrich played music on a saw, did magic tricks, and told raunchy jokes. 'She had a pretend mindreading act and told us that she could read minds and asked us to think of whatever came into our heads,' recalled one GI. 'Then she walked over to one dough and told him, "Oh, find something else. I can't possibly talk about that!"' More memorably, Dietrich haunted soldiers with her evocations of pre-war life, singing 'Falling in Love Again' from her 1930 film *The Blue Angel*, other hits from *Destry Rides Again* of 1939, and her version of the maudlin wartime German number, 'Lili Marlene'. Dietrich was in every way the American counterpart to the British siren, Vera Lynn. Both brought a hint of home to the front lines for their audiences.[53]

Before she turned the show over to her fellow musicians and entertainers, Dietrich hiked up her dress and paraded across the stage. Next, she was tossing autographed blue garters to the audience. 'There was pandemonium, bedlam. Men fought each other to capture a prize. You know, Dietrich poured body and soul into the World War Two effort. I heard she never stopped. Lived on cigarettes, coffee, and martinis, working sixteen-hour days every day. Marlene was a hell of a trouper. I know some papers and churches back home complained, but she was our lifeline.'[54]

Dietrich visited XXI Corps area with her troupe on 22 March, entertaining the 254th Infantry of the 63rd 'Blood and Fire' Division. Notably, this was while the campaign was under way, but the tireless singer and actress was keen to set foot in her native Germany to entertain 'her boys', no matter how dangerous the environment. 'I was always impressed by her arrival during the middle of combat,' mused Private Fred C. Clinton, an 81mm mortarman with Company 'D' of the 254th, who saw her near Saarbrucken. 'At the time we had just broken through the Siegfried Line and were pursuing the Germans. Combat lines had not been established; in fact, we were not sure where the German Army was. It took a lot of guts on her part to perform so close to the opposition.' Her presence was one memory GIs treasured long after the war. 'We all loved her and respected her. She was the only USO entertainer who came up, within enemy artillery range, to put on a show.'[55]

Dietrich need not have worried. The German war machine opposite Sixth Army Group was well and truly spent. It had neither the resources nor the will to resist any longer. In fact, so weak was Army Group 'G' that it could do nothing to frustrate the Allied plans. Its two armies, the First and Seventh, had lost 75 per cent of their combined combat strength.

One unit history noted how 'the handling of enemy prisoners became an almost insurmountable task, because every man in a German uniform seemed to be intent on surrendering in the face of this lightning-like onslaught. Harassed MPs started for the overflowing POW cages with three or four Krauts under guard, but before reaching their destination picked up hundreds more straggling along every highway. Roads and towns were jammed with the gray-clad "Supermen", but still they poured in.'[56] The prisoner count was more than 100,000, against which the US Seventh Army suffered 12,000 casualties, of whom 1,000 were killed. Hausser, commanding Army Group 'G', reckoned his command was '15 per cent effective' once it had withdrawn back over the Rhine.[57]

If Colmar had been de Lattre's battle, the Saar belonged to Devers and Patch. Though the pair had Patton's Third Army operating aggressively to their north, they focused on the operational objective of reaching the Rhine, rather than indulging in tactical squabbles about units and boundaries. Both had greatly matured as combat commanders, whatever Eisenhower's estimation of their abilities. The Supreme Commander observed of the Saar-Palatinate Triangle, 'one of the notable features of this late winter campaign was the extraordinary conformity of developments to plans. Normally, in a great operation involving such numbers of troops over such vast fronts, enemy reaction and unforeseen developments compel continuous adjustment of plan. This was one exception.'[58]

Yet there were a couple of anomalies to Eisenhower's claim. Patton's Third Army had advanced so aggressively, and at times out of its boundaries, that at the conclusion of the Saar campaign, Patch wired Patton in jest, 'Congratulations on surrounding the whole of US Seventh Army.'[59] Devers' intent, as directed by Eisenhower, was for Guillaume's reinforced 3rd Algerians, operating the right wing of the VI Corps, to have paused on reaching the German frontier. Thereafter, the First French Army were to remain on the home bank of the Rhine, while Patch's Seventh passed over the Reich's western moat and fought their way into Germany.

Yet Guillaume knew his superiors were determined on something very different. He was to stake out crossing points from which to bridge the great waterway, then go on to carve out an occupation zone in southwestern Germany. Neither was part of Eisenhower's plan. However, from south of Karlsruhe to the Swiss frontier, the Rhine was not traversable, due to the adjacent Siegfried Line defences and the constricting terrain of the Black Forest behind. A crossing needed to lead somewhere, and the only likely places were beyond Guillaume's sector, in the area further north, allocated to Patch's Seventh Army. Which is precisely where Guillaume led his troops.

The Algerian Division pushed hard beyond Hagenau to the German frontier. Arriving before the rest of VI Corps, against orders but with guile, they carried on into the first Reich village to fall to a French Army in World War Two. As de Lattre noted, 'The German soil galvanized our men. The gutted houses were captured with grenades and bazookas. Several were in flames. And when night fell the struggle went on by the light of these fires until 20:30. Scheibenhardt was then in our hands. The 19th of March was a great day for France.'[60] Reinforced by Général Carpentier's 2nd Moroccan Division, the tanks of Combat Command 6, and the two Groupements – six battalions – of Moroccan Goums, the French advanced through the Bienwald, a large wood north of the Franco-German border, and utterly shattered the 257th and 905th Volksgrenadiers garrisoning the *Westwall* in that sector. Again, they overtook the Americans on their left.

By the time these Frenchmen met Combat Command 'A' of the US 14th Armored Division up ahead, they had already cleared a substantial area between the Pfaelzerwald and the Rhine, and Brooks at VI Corps saw no reason to rein them in. The momentum of de Monsabert's II Corps spearhead, which is what Guillaume's force had become, was such that it carried them all the way north to Speyer, thirty miles beyond their allocated front. Devers was fully in agreement with what the French had achieved and declined to displace them, confirming in writing to de Lattre his revised 'elbow room' along the river on 27 March. He knew full well the French were now intending to cross the Rhine. Contrary to Eisenhower's original plan, de Lattre's *outil militaire* (military tool) had been used shamelessly as an *instrument politique* (political instrument) by de Gaulle, in ways the other six Allied armies had not.[61]

However, what mattered to the soldiers on the ground was summed up in a note penned by Major General Ted Brooks to Général Guillaume shortly afterwards. 'It is to you and the troops under your command that has fallen the honour of hurling the very last of the Boche invaders from Alsatian territory. I have long maintained that the command of a division in action is the ultimate reward of every soldier but, in addition, to drive the last invader from his country is an honour and a privilege, which is the prerogative of very few warriors. The US Sixth Army Corps whole-heartedly applauds your victory.'[62]

*

As we have seen, in conjunction with Sixth Army Group's attack from the south, Patton's Third Army simultaneously assaulted the Saar-Palatinate Triangle from the north. At the same moment, further north, Hodges' First Army were crossing the Roer and advancing on Cologne, allowing the Germans no respite to slide reinforcements to where they were most needed – as if they could, with no gas.

In early 1945, Patton was operating with three corps, Troy H. Middleton's VIII, Walton H. Walker's XX and Manton S. Eddy's XII. All three were tremendously experienced general officers. It was Middleton's men, then part of First Army, who had been strung out along the Ardennes when the Germans attacked on 16 December. Although taken by surprise, the unflappable Middleton survived the experience on account of his excellent prior combat experience. By 1944, nearly every US divisional and corps commander in Europe had been a student of his, including Eisenhower, whose mentor he was at Leavenworth. His steel-rimmed spectacles accentuated the college professor look, but Middleton was tough, having led the 45th Infantry Division on Sicily which won him VIII Corps.

Walton H. Walker was two months older than Middleton, had experienced a very good World War One, winning two Silver Stars, had navigated his way through the tricky interwar period of a small army, and by 1942 was at the helm of 3rd Armored Division. Thereafter, he became commander of IV Corps, which morphed into XX Corps, whom he took to England in February 1944 and led to Normandy in July as part of Patton's Third Army. He had soon gained a third Silver Star for personally directing a crossing of the Seine on 23 August under heavy fire.

The bespectacled Manton S. Eddy possessed a similar pedigree to Middleton, with World War One service, when he was wounded but recovered to command a battalion. In the interwar years, he was both student and instructor at Benning and Leavenworth, which is when he first encountered Middleton. He led 9th Infantry Division in North Africa and Sicily, landing at Utah beach on 10 June 1944, D+4. At the end of the month, his men captured Cherbourg, for which Eddy received a Distinguished Service Cross. On 1 August he took over XII Corps, General Bill Simpson's old command in 1942–3, which was most often used by Patton as his spearhead in the march through France.

The idea for the Saar-Palatinate manoeuvre was Bradley's, and he recalled flying down from army group headquarters at the Château de Namur overlooking the Meuse, to brief Patton in Luxembourg. The latter was 'having his hair cut in a home for the aged in which he had established his CP. George called for another barber and we discussed the plan under steaming towels.' Eisenhower, Bradley and Patton could not understand why the substantial German garrison in the Saar had not been withdrawn: military logic would be to pull back militarily exposed troops.[63]

Having been sucked into the relief of Bastogne on 26 December 1944, then clearing the rest of the southern Ardennes throughout January 1945, all three of Third Army's corps spent February occupying terrain, bringing them closer to the Rhine. Middleton advanced beyond Prüm, XII Corps captured Bitburg and XX Corps took Trier. Once a settlement of the Celtic *Treveri* tribe, hence its French name of Trèves, Trier had been conquered by Rome's Tenth Legion. Immediately, the Emperor Augustus chose the site for a sturdy bridge across the Moselle. On 1 March 1945, another tenth legion – Major General William H. Morris' Tenth Armored Division – fought its way to the ancient Kaiserbrücke, built on the piers of Augustus' original structure.

The Roman legacy included not only bridges, but grapes. As Lieutenant Colonel Jack J. Richardson's 20th Armored Infantry Battalion rushed the bridge, a drunken German major stumbled too slowly towards its demolition mechanism. The tanks of the Tenth rolled unhindered across the river, thanks to once-imported Roman grapes. The Tenth Armored, whose call sign was 'Impact', made such an impression on their opponents that they were immediately labelled Gespenst-Abteilung – the 'Ghost Division'. This was praise indeed, for the only other unit that had ever borne that moniker was the German 7th Panzer Division in 1940. It was then led by an officer no one had heard of, Erwin Rommel. As Patton's men left Trier, Bradley radioed him, anxious that battling for the city would cost precious time and men. 'Bypass Trier,' Twelfth Army Group's commander instructed. 'Have already taken Trier,' Patton signalled. 'Should I give it back?'

An officer with XII Corps wrote home (later observing the tone of his reports shocked his family), 'It's a real satisfaction to be on German soil. Terrific destruction, and these babies asked for it! Out of the stagnant lines and rolling across German territory, smashing the opposition as you go. When we take a town, we really shove the civilians around – and it is a pleasure. Oh Boy! The only thing the Krauts respond to are strong-arm tactics, and these are applied with a will. They're a mighty scared bunch these days . . . and white flags fly from all the windows – hot dawg!'[64]

At this stage, Robert S. Allen, the colonel in charge of Patton's war room, noted there were eighty-eight Allied divisions in the west, of which sixty-two were American, ten British, five Canadian and eleven French. Of these, thirty belonged to Twelfth Army Group, and twelve to Third Army. Hodges possessed a similar number and Gerow's Fifteenth Army had five in various stages of training or rear-area security. All were at full strength, with unlimited supplies, spares and fuel flowing through Antwerp.

The day before Third Army's attack into the Saar-Palatinate, Allen attended a command conference, at which his boss characteristically concluded, 'One thing you want to remember. Roads don't matter, terrain doesn't matter, and neither do exposed flanks. The only thing that counts is to come to grips with the Germans and to kill lots of them.'[65] The ensuing advance was not simultaneous, but sequential. Third Army in the north and west began first on the 13th, in an attempt to draw the defenders' attention away from Seventh Army in the south, which is where the Cottonbalers came to grief at Utweiler on 15 March.

Walker's XX Corps hit the nose of the Triangle, coming in from the west, south of Trier, fired in by the impressive total of thirty-one corps and divisional field artillery battalions. At the same moment, to their left, Eddy's XII Corps crossed the lower Moselle. Technically, beyond Trier, the Moselle becomes the Mosel, which 'points a multi-crooked finger north-eastwards to the Rhine and industrial Koblenz'.[66]

Koblenz was another old Roman military outpost on the west bank of the Rhine, whose name was derived from the Latin for confluence. The actual meeting place of the Moselle and Rhine rivers has been known since as 'das Deutsche Eck' (the German corner), where a monument to Kaiser Wilhelm I on horseback was erected by his grandson in 1897. On 16 March 1945, Eisenhower said to Patton, 'George, be sure to take a shot for me at that statue of Kaiser Wilhelm which sticks up in Koblenz.' To which Patton responded, 'Delighted. We'll take care of that for you without trouble.'[67]

Eisenhower recalled the provocative memorial from his time in Germany in 1927–8, when writing his battlefield guidebook for Pershing. This 300-page history of the AEF's battles on the Western Front was researched by walking the ground, which brought the future Supreme Commander detailed knowledge of the terrain his armies would fight over in 1944. The Koblenz statue he so loathed was 120 feet high, with the equestrian figure accounting for fifty of them. On 19 March 1945, when in range, Middleton's artillery duly obliged and blasted the oversized symbol of the First Reich into the river. His VIII Corps then used the moment to warn the Germans by propaganda leaflet 'that for every shell fired across the river at them, ten would be fired back'.[68] The following day, Middleton announced he was 'Mayor of Koblenz', but it took until 1992 for a bronze replica, celebrating German unification, to be erected on the old plinth.

Meanwhile, General Eddy's XII Corps on the Moselle wrong-footed the Germans, who had expected their opponents to strike north-east to Koblenz and join forces with First Army. Instead, XII Corps struck south. In the advance were the 5th and 90th Infantry Divisions, whose job was to cross the Moselle opening the way through the twisting roads and dense terrain for armour to follow. Sergeant Hobart Winebrenner was a young sergeant with the 385th Infantry, a Tough Ombre, as the 90th Division liked to call themselves. The nickname was self-given by its draftees from Texas and Oklahoma, the divisional insignia incorporating the letters 'T' and 'O' in honour of these two states.

Winebrenner remembered the weather on the turn as he entered the Saar campaign. 'Feet of snow melted into a giant mud bog. Roads turned to soup,' yet it was still cold enough for him to be wearing 'a couple of T shirts, a long underwear top, a sweatshirt, a wool GI shirt, one to four stolen sweaters, my field jacket and two or three pairs of field pants'. There was no chance to wash anything, but when time permitted in captured billets, they stripped and cooked their clothing in kitchen ovens to de-bug their attire. He did so in one house occupied by three dead German soldiers and was 'amazed at how uncivilized we had become.

We ate dinner with dead human beings lying at our feet. And perhaps most disturbing, it didn't faze us in the least.'[69]

Patton's Chief Engineer, Colonel John F. Conklin, had squirrelled away enough assault bridging to enable footbridges, then vehicle crossings, to be assembled quickly under cover of smoke. Immediately following was 4th Armored Division, led by Hugh Gaffey, Patton's former Chief of Staff, demonstrating the equal flair he had for staff work and manoeuvre. On being told of the 4th's drive into the Saar, Patton, with tongue in cheek, warned Bradley, 'Tell Devers to get out of the way, or we'll pick him up with the Krauts,' his worry being less the Germans than Patch's Seventh Army (and Patton's old command) beating him to the Rhine.[70] The 4th Armored's call sign, 'Olympic', reflected their busy war and Herculean ability to move great distances at impressive speed. They had been the first to relieve the defenders of Bastogne on Boxing Day 1944.

Stanford University graduate Lieutenant Roger Boas, of the 94th Armored Field Artillery Battalion, was in hospital in January 1945 and found his division's reputation riding high when Patton strode in to visit the wounded. Nearest the door, the general came to him first. Having to answer he was in bed with bronchitis rather than a combat wound, he sensed Patton's eyes narrow as he looked him over. 'What outfit are you in, boy?' asked the general. To which Boas replied, 'Fourth Armored Division, Sir.' 'Patton's attitude changed instantly. He put his hand on my shoulder, flashed me a smile, and said, "Well, you deserve a rest – you've seen a lot." '[71] Boas was back with his division when, on their first day across the Moselle, Gaffey's tanks managed sixteen miles before pausing at dusk. The 89th Infantry Division were soon funnelled into the break-in on the 15th and Brigadier General Holmes E. Dager's 11th Armored, two days later. Dager had just replaced his predecessor, whose performance had been 'disappointing' in Patton's eyes.[72]

This formation, known as 'Thunderbolt', had been bloodied around Bastogne on 30 December, and had been in combat ever since. Once over the Moselle, tank driver Ted Hartman with the 41st Tank Battalion noticed the challenges of the terrain in the melting snow. 'Platoon Sergeant Hugh Wood's tank hit a soft spot in the road and slid over the side of a steep embankment. The tank turned over several times while falling into the valley below. Sergeant Wood, one of the best-loved men in the company, was crushed to death.' The following day the Sherman of Lieutenant Grayson, 'our highly respected company commander, was hit by a bazooka, killing the assistant gunner and injuring Grayson and the gunner.'

A few days later his own tank was attacked by a panzerfaust. 'I opened my hatch and fairly flew out. The bazooka projectile had cut into the track, then melted a hole all the way through the two-and-a-half-inch-thick steel hull and into the water cans stored inside.' The crew were lucky, threw out the damaged jerrycans, pressed the starter button and were soon on their way.[73] Though the Germans were on the run, the cost to those in the American spearhead was high.

Forming the hinge between Eddy's and Walker's two corps was Colonel Charles H. Reed's 2nd Mechanized Cavalry Group, which allowed XII Corps, whose asset they were, to concentrate their combat power and increase their speed, without having to worry about their flanks or rear security. Once Walker's force was level with them, his own 16th Mechanized Cavalry Group, known as the 'Blackhorse', took over the inter-corps liaison duties, and the 2nd Cavalry patrolled the northern edge of XII Corps, along the Moselle and as far as the Rhine.[74]

Piling in from the west, Walker's four infantry divisions – the 26th, 65th, 80th and 94th – spent three days overcoming the concrete-and-steel *Westwall* defences guarding the Fatherland. The latter pair struck eastwards from the Saar river line, while the 26th 'Yankee' Division rolled up the *Westwall*'s pillbox belt laterally, from north to south, with the 65th following later. With the 26th was Staff Sergeant Bruce Egger of Company 'G', 328th Infantry, who recalled the wet, dreary weather that quickly wore men down. He noted just before their attack went in that 'Tony Clemens of the 2nd Squad shot himself in the foot. Clemens was a big man, and it was three miles by trail to the aid station. I heard the two medics made him walk all the way – there was no free ride for those with self-inflicted wounds.'

Even so, Egger himself with remarkable honesty recorded, 'Each attack was becoming more difficult for me to face. I was beginning to wonder how many more I could survive, as I had been in combat longer than any man in the company.' By the time their *Westwall* fight was over, the infantry companies of the 26th had fallen so far behind the other divisions, they were surprised to find on 19 March that even their own divisional headquarters were in front of them. By this time Company 'G' had lost a quarter of their manpower in two weeks; the next day they received fifty-four replacements, an indication of how disproportionately casualties fell on the infantry.[75]

On 16 March, Walker unleashed the 10th Armored Division, who had been lurking in Trier since its capture. From just before daybreak, they thundered past the 94th and 80th on their way to St Wendel, then raced the 80th to Kaiserslautern, 'K-town' to modern American soldiers, and the key logistics base for the First and Seventh Wehrmacht Armies in the Palatinate. To reach the latter on 20 March, they, and other fast-moving American units, had developed night-fighting techniques, including 'using anti-aircraft searchlights on overhanging clouds to illuminate the battlegrounds'[76] Egger and his fellow GIs remembered parts of Kaiserslautern, a city of about 80,000, had been obliterated by aerial bombing. 'Our Air Corps had created havoc with the retreating Germans – judging by the large number of destroyed vehicles we saw along the way. Numerous burned out vehicles and many German prisoners walked unattended, while slave labour refugees were walking west, away from Germany.'[77]

A GI in the 10th Armored's Medical Battalion noted, 'The Tigers were there [Kaiserslautern] first, but credit was given to the 80th who had done the dirty work of mopping up.' Beyond Kaiserslautern, the 10th encountered Major General Robert W. Grow's 'Super Sixth' Armored Division crossing their front from the south. As *Time Magazine* confidently reported, 'Armored divisions sometimes perform feats that would be textbook nightmares. Two Patton armored divisions once crossed each other at a right-angle road junction in the midst of combat, but only the Germans were confused.'[78] The Medical Battalion's diarist recorded, 'All during the Tenth's lightning drive across the Palatinate, the missions of the Division were constantly being changed and each succeeding objective took the Tigers further south. Within gunshot of the Rhine, we found ourselves completely out of the Third Army's boundary and into that of the Seventh [and therefore, on Sixth Army Group's terrain] and made radio contact with the Fifth French Armored Division.'[79]

On 17 March, Walker borrowed Roderick R. Allen's 12th Armored Division, the 'Hellcats', for a week from Seventh Army. He placed them on the north wing of his XX Corps, giving each of Patton's two attacking corps a pair of armoured formations – the 10th and 12th under Walker, with the 4th and 11th under Manton Eddy. With a further three (the 6th and 14th and French 5th) in Devers' Sixth Army Group operating to their south, this made a total of seven armoured divisions employed against the Germans in this operation, or nearly 2,000 tanks.[80]

Meanwhile, Middleton's VIII Corps, stripped bare to support both XII and XX Corps, joined the fray with his remaining troops, the 87th Infantry Division and Colonel Andrew A. Frierson's 11th Mechanized Cavalry Group. The latter, unusually, were responsible for screening both its flanks and rear. As soon as the move to the Rhine was complete and Third Army started to cross, the three Mechanised Cavalry formations embarked on a new task, occupation duties, which was totally new to them.

To watch the progress of the offensive, Eisenhower visited Patton on 17 March. Colonel Allen noted that all non-Third Army 'outfits consider us the brassiest and cockiest on the Continent', so was all the more surprised to hear Ike addressing the headquarters staff: 'If I have one criticism to make, it is you are too modest. You don't boast enough about your great achievements. I want you to talk more about yourselves. Let the world know how good you are. Call in the reporters and feed the right kind of stories to them. We need the right kind of publicity right now.'[81]

This was not aimed at the rest of the US Army, but at Montgomery, who was building up to his set-piece Rhine crossing on 23–24 March. The Americans distrusted the Briton's strategic messaging with good reason. On 7 January 1945, the field marshal all but claimed credit for saving the Bulge and rescuing the US First Army. Bradley had been incensed, complaining loudly to Eisenhower, who passed his protests on to Churchill. Recognising Montgomery's folly, eleven days later, the British Prime Minister addressed Parliament, announcing in no uncertain terms that the Bulge had been an American battle, and an American victory. Clearly Eisenhower feared there would be a repeat and wanted Third Army ready to eclipse his British subordinate.

Patton's cavalry regiments had spent much of the period since September 1944 on defensive security roles along the Saar and Moselle. Once the Saar-Palatinate campaign was under way, they switched to inter-army and inter-corps liaison and offensive tasks with remarkable ease.[82] Manned largely by National Guardsmen during World War Two, US cavalry regiments were doctrinally a combined-arms grouping, usually comprising two mechanised cavalry squadrons which included infantry, armour, engineer, anti-tank and artillery elements. This made them not only very flexible, but open to misuse when corps commanders needed them for duties other than their traditional roles as scouts and flank guards. Historians tend to concentrate on the divisional contributions, but in terms of armour, the United States cavalry are often forgotten. As a former cavalryman, I would be remiss in overlooking another historian's assertion that, 'the cavalry contributed to a huge victory and helped the Third Army destroy twelve German divisions in its drive to the Rhine'.[83]

In the skies, Third and Seventh Armies were greatly aided by the improving weather, which saw the return of Allied air power, so deadly in Normandy the previous summer. The Germans in the Saar-Palatinate were undone as much by General O.P. (Opie) Weyland's XIX Tactical Air Command, with its P-47s and P-51s providing close air support at the front, and air interdiction against their supply lines, as by the lightning thrusts of Patton's armour.

Sergeant Winebrenner of the 90th Division remembered encountering the mobile air defence of Mainz in a suburb that 'our boys up above must have hit with fire bombs. Dozens of 88s lined a city street with barrels pointed to heaven. The scene made me sick. Many German soldiers still sat in position, at their posts to the horrific end. Caught by the phosphorus, most were burned beyond recognition and more resembled ancient mummies than the young men they were only minutes earlier. The intense heat vaporized their uniforms and scorched their skin to the consistency of dried leather.' Other Germans he took captive were 'shells of humanity, mentally and physically stretched to the limit. We did them a huge favour by taking them prisoner. They'd live much better in a POW camp, than in a pile of rubble.'[84]

Yet these victories came at a cost. Taking a single formation, the three casualty clearing stations run by the Tenth Armored Division's medical battalion received 2,741 admissions during March 1945, of whom 355 were returned to duty; most were transferred back to field hospitals, but twenty-three died in the stations.[85] As Patton directed, they were not buried at the roadside, but in cemeteries away from the eyes of GIs marching to their own fates. The Germans had gone to war in 1939 against opponents they could afford to fight. By 1945 they had discovered this maxim no longer held good for the Patton-led force that ran rings around them in the Saar.

Bradley had already warned Patton to 'get that assault stuff [bridging equipment] up closer. I want you to take the Rhine on the run. We're not going to stop and give the other fellow [his name for the Germans] a chance to build up and raise hell when we come across.'[86] However, the Twelfth Army Group commander's real motivation for 'taking the Rhine on the run' was different. He was incensed by Montgomery's boastful antics and determined to beat him across the Rhine. And George Patton would be his instrument of revenge. The latter did not need telling and had in any case already determined to do so.

Meanwhile, Staff Sergeant Egger and his company in the 26th Infantry Division had reached the Rhine, fifteen miles south of Mainz. There they found 'a unit of 4th Armored Division, so we set up an outpost in a field near the town', he recalled. 'Departing Nazis had left signs painted on buildings and walls in English which read "See Germany and Die", "Onward Slaves of Moscow" and "Death Will Give You Peace". The tankers never pulled guard when the infantry was with them, but we made them pay by stealing some of their ten-in-one rations. Since they were mechanized, they usually carried several days' supply.'

Five miles downriver Egger noted the 'gentle rolling hills along the river were covered with vineyards. One GI ran out and gave our truck two bottles of wine. He was from the 5th Division.' Eggers was unaware that Major General Leroy Irwin's 5th Division was that very night preparing to take the Rhine at a run, as Bradley had directed.[87] It was 22 March. The war in the west had forty-seven days to run.

PART TWO

Across the Rhine

(*Above*): 7 March 1945: led by Brigadier General William M. Hoge of Combat Command 'B', the Ludendorff railway bridge over the Rhine at Remagen was seized by the 9th US Armored Division. The pairs of stone towers at each end can be clearly seen, as can the railway tunnel cut into the Erpeler Ley, the hill in the background. The town of Remagen is behind the photographer. (*Below*): It was used for six days, during which time four divisions crossed, but the Ludendorff collapsed on 17 March, killing and wounding 121 engineers repairing the structure. Eventually most of First US Army crossed along this stretch, using additional pontoon bridges and landing craft of the type seen here.

7

The Bridges at Remagen

General Courtney H. Hodges ordered champagne with his roast pork for dinner on 5 March. As the Saar had been cleared by Patton and Devers to his south and Collins had reached the Rhine at Cologne, he proposed a toast 'to an early crossing'. First Army had just moved their tactical headquarters – Master TAC – for the first time in four months, from the Hôtel Britannique in Spa to 'a large chateau high on a hill overlooking Stolberg', east of Aachen, bringing them closer to the front.[1]

The new headquarters had belonged to Hans Prym, scion of an industrial dynasty of gold- and brass-smiths founded in 1530, who for twelve generations had produced haberdashery, copper and other metal products. Amounting to the oldest family-run business in the Fatherland, Prym, known locally as the 'Zipper King', made buttons, zips and other fasteners for the Wehrmacht, and was under arrest.[2] Each formation HQ had a call sign for communications purposes. Eisenhower's 'Liberty'; Montgomery was 'Lion'; Bradley was 'Eagle'; Patton was 'Lucky'; Simpson was 'Conquer'; Hodges was 'Master', hence the new location was Master TAC. Master's air support came from the Ninth Tactical Air Command, 'Football', while Master's three corps were 'Jayhawk' (VII Corps), 'Century' (III Corps) and 'Victory' (V Corps).

With the VII Corps contribution to Operation *Lumberjack* complete, what of the rest of First Army to Collins' south? John Millikin's III Corps had also jumped the Roer at the same time as Collins, but was a slightly larger formation, with John W. Leonard's 9th Armored and four infantry divisions – from north to south, the 1st, 9th, 78th and 2nd. 'A tall officer filled with nervous energy', recently departed from Third

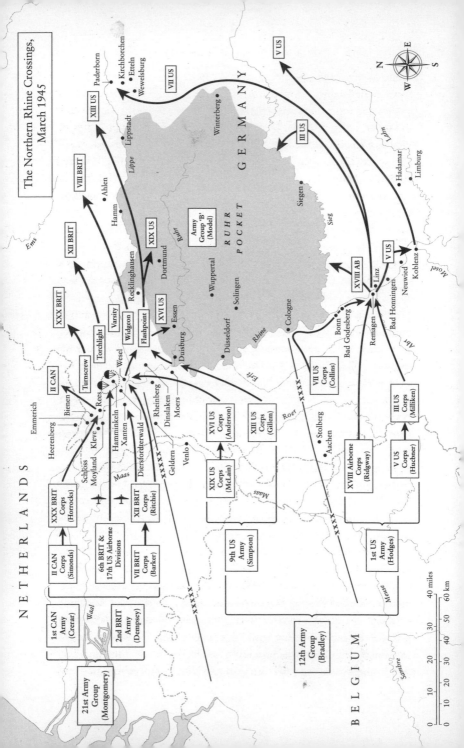

The Northern Rhine Crossings, March 1945

Army, Millikin was a cavalryman like Patton, as were many of his head-quarters staff. However, on transfer to First Army, they assessed Hodges as slow and unimaginative, whereas the latter felt his new subordinates too quick and impulsive. This underlined the different approaches of First and Third Armies, with Millikin favouring Patton's audacious cavalry spirit. The former was well connected; his father-in-law, General Peyton C. March, had been US Army Chief of Staff from 1918 to 1921 and was responsible for redesigning the role subsequently occupied by George C. Marshall, whose ear he had, a series of connections the low-born Hodges resented.[3]

Millikin's subordinates agreed with his ideas. Although commissioned into the infantry, John Leonard shared his corps commander's bold approach to handling tanks. He was a West Point contemporary of Bradley and Eisenhower, another of the famous class of 1915, responsible for so many of the European war's US Army commanders. He had brought his 9th Armored Division to the United Kingdom in September 1944, and immediately deployed with them to France. Also an old friend of Hodges, Leonard was blessed with some extraordinarily able subordinates, such as Brigadier General William M. Hoge, the craggy commander of Combat Command 'B'. Both Leonard and Hoge had won Distinguished Service Crosses during World War One, which prepared them for the hard knocks of combat in the next war. In December 1944, with no real combat experience, Leonard's division suddenly found themselves in the midst of the Bulge, where Hoge put in a very creditable performance defending St Vith. However, the fact that the division was split across the Ardennes front, yet each part fought with distinction, also reflected well on Leonard's training of his men.

The 1st Division, call sign 'Danger', was universally known as the 'Big Red One', after their shoulder flash of a large red '1' on a green background. It had first landed in North Africa, and subsequently on Sicily, then Omaha beach on D-Day. When its popular commander, Clarence Huebner – who had taken over from Terry Allen – had been elevated to V Corps, it was the Big Red One's long-serving head of artillery, Brigadier General Clift Andrus, who took over. He had already led the division through much of the Bulge and had a confident, schoolmasterly look, hence being widely known as Mr Chips, after the popular teacher in the 1939 Hollywood movie, *Goodbye, Mr Chips*.

To their south was the 9th Division, nicknamed the 'Old Reliables', controlled by Louis A. Craig since August. Once overseen by Jake Devers, Craig had taken command of this seasoned outfit who were veterans of both North Africa and Sicily, from Manton Eddy, on the latter's promotion to lead XII Corps. During the war, the 9th was given the radio call sign 'Notorious', with each sub-unit also assigned a name commencing with the letter 'N'. The divisional artillery was 'Noisy', the Recon Troop was 'Nomad', and their towed Tank Destroyer Battalion was 'Nuisance'.[4] Beyond them lay the 78th Division, bearers of the proud moniker 'Lightning', after their divisional insignia. They were led by Edwin P. Parker, who had been chief trainer of artillerymen before activating his own division and taking them to war. Their baptism of fire had been in the northern sector of Ardennes assault.

The final infantry formation was the 2nd Infantry Division, call sign 'Ivanhoe', easily recognisable by their 'Indianhead' shoulder badge, whose first elements had come ashore at Omaha beach on 7 June. They had been in continuous combat under the same commander, Walter M. Robertson, from that day. GIs recollected that in the Bulge their general, recognisable by the two stars on his helmet, was everywhere in their divisional area, directing traffic, calming frayed nerves. He withdrew his men up onto the Elsenborn Ridge, where his artillery had stopped two SS divisions dead in their tracks. Robertson's unflappable leadership was recognised afterwards with a Distinguished Service Cross, an uncommon award for so senior a commander.

In company with VII Corps, Millikin's III Corps had also leapt the Roer on 23 February, experiencing a similar lack of opposition, and capturing up to a thousand prisoners per day. While Millikin was not faced with crossing the River Erft, which entered the Rhine north of Cologne, he was faced with the equally formidable Ahr, which flowed into the bigger river south of Cologne. On 6 March, First Army's war diary noted, 'Tonight Cologne belongs to the First US Army, as tomorrow morning's newspapers will state. If this was big news, the progress made by III and V Corps was almost as good. 9th Armd. Division advanced to within eight miles of the Rhine. They are shooting ahead against light and scattered opposition, and it is possible we may be able to seize bridges before the Germans have a chance to blow them.'[5]

Yet the writer was far removed from front-line life. The men had pushed from the Roer towards the Rhine with little rest and were groggy from lack of sleep. Much of the load fell on the engineers, building endless bridges over icy rivers, usually in the winter drizzle and under German fire. On 7 March, Hoge's Combat Command 'B' of the 9th Armored was tasked with capturing bridges over the Ahr, to cut off a German line of retreat. Others from CCB were ordered to close up to the Rhine at Remagen, and then to make their way down the west bank, meeting Patton's Third Army near Koblenz. Their mission was not to cross the river, but net as many German troops as possible before they could escape across the Rhine. Remagen is a small town of about 10,000, sited at the midway point between Cologne and Koblenz. Originally built as a Roman fort, *Ricomagus*, overlooking a crossing point, like so many other Rhenish settlements, Remagen had grown wealthy through the Middle Ages and Renaissance from the passing river trade, resulting in an impressive range of stone buildings, churches and castles overlooking the Rhine.

For the first time since before the Ardennes, Hodges and his headquarters seemed revitalised. The success of *Lumberjack*, and the occasional bouts of warmer weather helped, and the general himself was recorded as visiting his subordinates – something which had not happened in months. If they had met earlier, it was by being summoned to Hodges, not the other way round. His toast to an 'early crossing' was more an expression of the army commander's change of mood than a realistic expectation. The Germans were past masters at bridge demolitions, and none of the 136 major and minor structures across the Rhine which were standing in 1939 were expected to fall into Allied hands.

Hodges was aware that Bradley had little enthusiasm for a leap across the Rhine on First Army's front. The eastern banks were generally steep, studded with panoramic castles, but offered no easy exits to exploit, with rough terrain and forest beyond. The home bank also had a poor road network that would make any crossing difficult to support or sustain. SHAEF was anticipating a major crossing in Montgomery's sector, and subsidiary ones by Third Army.

The tale of the capture of the Ludendorff railway bridge at Remagen on 7 March 1945 has grown over the years with its retelling. It was born out of the chaos of withdrawal and defeat on the German side and a bold tactical move from an engineer turned armour commander who understood bridges, Hoge, on the other. It was important at the time, but its significance was amplified by Captain Ken Hechler, assigned to the 9th Armored Division as its official US Army historian, and in the vicinity when the bridge was taken.

In the aftermath of the war, he interviewed many of those involved on both sides, eventually publishing the well-received *The Bridge at Remagen* in 1957. It became a bestseller and eventually inspired a movie of the same name in 1969, for which Hechler was the historical advisor. Starring the high-profile George Segal and Robert Vaughan, the film attracted critical acclaim. By then, Hechler was a Democratic Congressman, and former White House assistant to Harry Truman, which indirectly drew even more attention to the 1945 incident. Given that the Remagen crossing was unplanned, and there was daily anxiety – for the first few days – that it might be repulsed, let us stay with 9th Armored Division and III Corps, for the Remagen bridgehead generated as much heat and controversy for the Americans as it did for the Germans, leading to promotions and career downfalls on both sides.

The real truth of the Remagen story was that no one expected to capture a Rhine bridge intact; there was no race to seize one, in fact the opposite. SHAEF *wanted* them destroyed to prevent German forces from withdrawing to fight another day. The previous autumn, Eisenhower had opined that 'as we approached the borders of Germany, we studied the desirability of committing our air force to the destruction of the Rhine bridges, on which the existence of the German forces west of the river depended. If all of them could be destroyed, they would soon have to withdraw. We entertained no hope of saving these bridges for our own use.' The advice from the Allied 'bomber barons' Carl Spaatz and Arthur Harris was that with winter weather approaching, it would 'require more time and bomb tonnage than we could afford to divert from other vitally important purposes' – chief among which was the destruction of Germany's fuel-making, refining and distribution network.[6]

The prevailing gung-ho narrative around Remagen overlooks the fact that Eisenhower intended to use the Rhine as a halt line for his forces. The water obstacle worked both ways: it was the 'Allied Westwall', removing any further threat (however unlikely) of a surprise German counterattack. Pausing along the river would also permit SHAEF to concentrate or thin out forces where needed. Above all, the water represented a secure, defensive line behind which they could shelter while supplies were accumulated via Antwerp. The latter port had been under V-weapon attack since the previous October. For 175 days, during the onslaught, more than 4,000 V-1s and 1,700 V-2s were launched at the city, killing 3,700 and wounding 6,000. Miraculously there were no direct hits on Allied shipping, although twenty ship berths and more than one hundred vessels were damaged, and a 150-ton floating crane sunk.

Until the threat diminished, SHAEF was worried that a single weapon crashing into an ammunition ship might destroy the area. This had happened at Bari, Italy, in December 1943 when a Luftwaffe raid caught the Allied-occupied port off-guard. Hits on two vessels loaded with shells caused widespread damage. Burning fuel spread through the harbour and the eventual bill was twenty-eight merchant ships laden with more than 34,000 tons of supplies sunk or destroyed and the harbour closed for nearly a month. As late as March 1945, eighty-six V-1 flying bombs and forty-two rockets still struck Antwerp, although this was only 30 per cent of those launched, the rest malfunctioning or being shot down. Eisenhower was taking no chances. A logistically balanced force was vital before entering hostile Germany, and there could be no repeat of the stretched supply lines of September–October 1944, which had halted his advance.

In fact, a tactical bridge-cutting programme had begun on 4 September, targeting twenty-two railway bridges across the Rhine, including the Ludendorff bridge at Remagen. Bookended by pairs of castle-like stone towers of steel lattice box-girder construction, it carried a double railway track, with wooden-planked footpaths each side. With a span of 1,069 feet across the water, it led from Remagen in the west into a tunnel on the east bank bored into a 600-foot steep cliff, the Erpeler Ley. The crossing was designed to enhance the flow of personnel and logistics to the Western Front, a role it first fulfilled in the German *Kaiserschlacht* of March 1918, subsequently in May 1940, June 1944 and finally during the Ardennes offensive. One track was generally planked over to allow vehicular traffic.

When the bridge – named after Germany's great World War One hero and later Nazi Reichstag deputy – was opened in 1918, it contained demolition chambers in which explosives could be lodged, a common feature on all important crossings.[7] Those in place under the downriver Cologne–Mülheim bridge blew up in a sympathetic detonation when a night raid by US aircraft on 14–15 October 1944 hit the structure. Hitler was furious and unhelpfully ordered all bridge demolition charges to be removed and stored nearby, for insertion at the last minute. Those at Remagen were piled at the eastern end under the watchful eye of Hauptmann Karl Friesenhahn with 120 combat engineers, and Hauptmann Willi Bratge provided bridge security with thirty-six convalescing soldiers. Above them, on the Erpeler Ley was a Flak detachment of 88mm guns and two hundred men. In order to buy time to reinsert the explosives, Friesenhahn would blow a thirty-foot gap in the road ramp leading up to the structure at its western end when the opposition was seen approaching.

The delay before blowing a bridge (or other obstacle) is a complicated military manoeuvre known today as a 'reserve demolition', whereby destruction is achieved when the opponent is approaching, or on, the object concerned, usually a crossing. Blown too early, friendly troops can be left on the wrong side, destroyed too late and the opposing force might have a chance to rush across. On 7 March, with US troops reportedly a few miles distant, the local 67th Korps commander, General Otto Hitzfeld, sent his personal adjutant, Major Hans Scheller, to oversee the destruction of the Ludendorff bridge.

The day's drama began when Brigadier General Hoge, commanding CCB of the 9th Armored, received the message at 13:00 from Lieutenant Colonel Leonard E. Engeman of the 14th Tank Battalion that the Rhine bridge was still standing. 'I immediately went up to join them, and stood there on the bank and looked down, and there it was,' recollected Hoge. 'The bridge was there right above the town. I couldn't believe it was true. I ordered smoke on the big hill opposite [the Erpeler Ley] so they couldn't see what we were doing. We moved down through the town and got to the bridge. While we were waiting the Germans blew a big crater in the approaches, but we used bulldozers to fill the hole and go over it.'[8] Hoge, who as a combat engineer had erected and destroyed bridges himself, fully expected the Germans to detonate the whole structure as his men were crossing. He could but try.

The cratering puts the time at 15:00, when Hauptmann Friesenhahn destroyed the approach road, right in the faces of Lieutenant Karl H. Timmermann's Company 'A' of the 27th Armored Infantry Battalion. Opposite, Friesenhahn had re-laid the explosives, but received only 660 pounds (300 kilograms), half of what he considered necessary, and they were of inferior commercial type, used for quarrying. Major Scheller, meanwhile, had ordered the bridge be blown at 16:00. It was nearby civilians boasting to the GIs that the Ludendorff bridge would be destroyed at that hour that alerted Hoge to the necessity of capturing the structure forthwith. He had no time to lose.

Seeing that several of the new Pershings in Engeman's tank unit (a sister outfit to the one with 3rd Armored Division that did so well in Cologne) had driven up to the Ludendorff bridge, Hoge ordered suppressive fire from their 90mm guns onto the defenders, while Timmermann's company stormed the crossing. With the weight of incoming fire, including that from small arms, Scheller, in the tunnel under the Erpeler Ley cliff, realised the bridge itself was under attack and at 15:20 ordered the structure blown. With Bratge's defenders engaging the GIs with machine-gun fire from the stone towers, Friesenhahn turned his key in the clockwork firing mechanism and – nothing happened. After three attempts, he realised the circuit must have been severed, almost certainly by a tank shell, and called for a volunteer to rush halfway across to trigger a backup mechanism. Unteroffizier Faust volunteered, ran across, lit the fuse and was on his way back when there was a huge roar, piles of smoke and dust, while girders and timbers flew sky-high.

'As we started to go across the bridge, an explosion went off about midstream and blew out one big panel, but all the charges had failed to go off for some reason,' remembered Hoge. Both sides paused. Probably only seconds passed, but they seemed like minutes. Parts of the bridge were seen to topple into the fast-flowing Rhine below. Yet when the smoke cleared, the vast Ludendorff railway bridge, weakened by two earlier air raids, tank fire and a huge demolition charge, was still standing. The construction company, Grün and Bilfinger of Cologne, had spent two years building it and had done their job well. Hauptmann Friesenhahn was vindicated also. His calculations were correct: he had been sent too few explosives of inferior quality to do the job properly, and not all of them had exploded.

'I sent my armored infantry across and with them a squad of engineers to remove any more charges,' Hoge continued. 'We found maybe 1,000 pounds underneath. [It must have been far less than this.] They cut those loose and dropped them into the river. Then we put a company of tanks across, in the meantime, I got some pontoon bridges there; they diverted everything to me once I reported the bridge captured.'[9]

The first of Timmermann's men across the bridge – and thus the first Allied soldier to reach the east bank of the Rhine – was Sergeant Alexander A. Drabik, whose background and that of his company commander, Timmermann, neatly illustrated the chaotic story of the many European migrants to America who formed the GI generation. Born in 1910, Drabik's parents had emigrated from what was then Eastern Germany, later Poland, and Timmermann, born in 1922 and raised in Nebraska, was the son of a US soldier of German ancestry on postwar occupation duty, and his German war bride. Both GIs had been wounded in the Bulge and since returned to duty. These two former Europeans were able to turn the tables on their tormentors in spectacular fashion at Remagen, which brought both men Distinguished Service Crosses.

Almost immediately, there emerged indecision at higher levels about what to do with the Remagen bridgehead. Brigadier General Hoge observed, 'While I was started across the bridge, I got orders to abandon my mission and head southwards to Koblenz. Well, as I was already half across, I decided to wait and see whether the bridge survived. Then I'd report back what was happening. I disobeyed the order, but my decision was the correct one.'[10] The following day, 8 March, the First Army's war diarist revealed, 'To what extent our crossing will be permitted to become a major one remains to be seen. Apparently, no decision as yet has been reached in SHAEF or Twelfth Army Group headquarters as to whether full exploitation will be made. Or whether III Corps will simply make the bridgehead secure and then halt. The [future] show of Monty's up north opposite the Ruhr is still apparently the big thing. Gen. Hodges was in touch with Gen. Bradley 4 or 5 times during the day. From their conversations no clues were received as to our future directions.'[11]

Instantly, Remagen acted as a magnet for war correspondents, including *Stars and Stripes* reporter Andy Rooney, who arrived on the scene and encountered 'German artillery shells plopping into the river all around the bridge. It was an event in progress and the 9th were jamming across as many men and vehicles as possible. It looked like George Washington Bridge across the Hudson at rush hour. German artillerymen were firing blind from behind the hills on the other side of the river, but there was always a chance they'd get lucky, and we were plenty nervous running across the bridge, stepping on the wooden ties with six-inch gaps between them.'[12]

In his *Crusade in Europe*, Eisenhower reported that he 'fairly shouted into the telephone "Go ahead and shove over at least five divisions instantly, and anything else that is certain to make sure of our hold". This was completely unforeseen. We were across the Rhine, on a permanent bridge. The final defeat of Germany was suddenly now, in our minds, just around the corner.'[13]

Bradley, too, gushed about Remagen in *A Soldier's Story*: ' "Hot dog, Courtney," I said, "this will bust him right open. Are you getting your stuff across? Shove everything you can across it." ' Major General Harold R. 'Pinky' Bull, Eisenhower's G-3 at SHAEF, visiting Bradley's headquarters, 'blinked back through his rimless glasses. He sat down before the map and shrugged his shoulders. "Sure, you've got a bridge, Brad, but what good is it going to do you. You're not going anywhere down there at Remagen. It just doesn't fit into *the* plan."

"Plan – hell," I retorted. "A bridge is a bridge and mighty damned good anywhere across the Rhine."

"You're not going anywhere down there at Remagen. You've got a bridge, but it's in the wrong place. It just doesn't fit in with the plan."

"What the hell do you want us to do, pull back and blow it up?" '

Bradley continued, 'I phoned Eisenhower at Rheims to confirm the order I had given Hodges. Ike was delighted with news of the bridge.

"Get across whatever you need – but make certain you hold that bridgehead." [14]

However, these popular memoirs of Eisenhower and Bradley (mostly ghosted by their respective aides, Harry C. Butcher and Chester C. 'Chet' Hansen) are at variance with the historical record. Bradley and Hodges had a more reserved and respectful relationship towards one another than the 'Hot dog, Courtney' suggested here. On 9 March, Hodges received orders to hold the bridgehead but limit it to an area five divisions could defend, and units in the perimeter were to advance no more than 1,000 yards per day.' [15] More significantly, on 11 March the First Army's war diarist observed, 'No word from Group whether this bridgehead is to be expanded and made a main effort, or whether SHAEF is still placing its money on the yet-to-be-won bridgehead north of us in Monty's sector.'

This was despite the 9th Armored having crossed at Remagen 'three infantry divisions [9th, 78th and 99th], plus, two battalions of III Corps artillery, and the loan of additional cannon from V and VII Corps'. By 13 March, this totalled nine field artillery battalions, while around the bridgehead, seventeen anti-aircraft battalions 'four of 40mm guns and thirteen of quadruple Brownings' had deployed and were daily shooting down dozens of Luftwaffe aircraft trying to hit the bridge. On this date, the air defence around Remagen reached its peak of 672 anti-aircraft artillery pieces in sixteen gun and thirty-three automatic weapons batteries. The concentration accomplished its mission, for no German aircraft managed to hit the bridge in ten days of attacks. First Army's Anti-Aircraft Advisor, Colonel Charles G. Patterson, had 'never seen so many anti-aircraft units in one place. They were so numerous that rounds were landing on friendly troops and causing casualties.' It later emerged this was the heaviest concentration of AAA units for the US Army during World War Two. [16]

The German sorties began at dusk on 8 March when 'at 17:00, the crews of 413 Auto Anti-Aircraft Weapons Battery watched in amazement as eight Junkers-87s [Stukas], out of the Luftwaffe scrap heap, flew down the river valley at 3,000 feet, refusing to take evasive action as they came under fire; none of them survived.' [17] Realising that only the fastest aircraft would even get near to the bridge, Reichsmarschall Göring requested volunteers to sacrifice their lives by crashing bomb-carrying Messerschmitt-262 jets into the Ludendorff. Two stepped forward but were dissuaded by their squadron commanders. A special Luftwaffe jet strike force of around thirty Me-262s and forty Arado-234s was formed to destroy the structure, using an autobahn as its operational base between 13 March and 20 April, but utterly failed to even damage their target. Additionally, 974 Squadron of the Royal Auxiliary Air Force were deployed to fly barrage balloons at selected points along the approaches, canalising flight paths towards the waiting American guns.[18]

Typical of the rush to get troops across the Ludendorff bridge was the story of Major General Walter E. Lauer's 99th Division, in Collins' VII Corps, who were miles to the north, opposite Cologne. Suddenly ordered into trucks on 9 March, most had no idea where they were heading or why, but were happy to be riding instead of walking. Only when a GI going the opposite way flung a copy of *Stars and Stripes* at John Hendricks of Company 'G', 394th Infantry, did his platoon learn about a captured bridge. Time was urgent and there were no stops during the bumpy sixty-mile ride south to Remagen, so men urinated or defecated over the tailgate as their 6x6 truck alternately crawled and sped along for nine hours.

By day, GIs could see the knocked-out tanks and bodies of the recent battlefield, and after dark, the eastern horizon was lit up by a 'big wall of flame', which was Cologne burning. In Remagen, the 394th Infantry stumbled their way to the bridge along cobblestoned streets, their faces lit by burning vehicles and buildings. Guy Duren spotted a sign declaring 'This street subject to enemy shell fire', as he sped through the ruins in his Jeep. He noticed that Adolf Hitler-Strasse had already been renamed Yank-Strasse. His buddy, B.C. Henderson in the same regiment, watched a chunk of hot metal skidding along the street, clanging and throwing off sparks, and thought to himself, 'if that shell fragment didn't immediately slice you in half, they'd have to use a mattress as a dressing', for the wound would be so huge.[19] During the night of 9–10 March, the 394th, with the rest of the 99ers, nervously picked their way across, staring at the icy torrent racing past fifty feet below, as German fire lit the sky and geysers of water shot skywards from rogue shells.

On 13 March, Allen noted that Lieutenant General 'Beetle' Bedell Smith, Eisenhower's Chief of Staff, had paid First Army a visit, 'his first since last August. He had no news to give Genls. Hodges or Kean [First Army Chief of Staff] about the bridgehead or future plans.' Similarly, on the 15th, Bradley, 'still wearing three stars although his fourth was given to him yesterday, flew in by Cub [spotter plane] to see Gen. Hodges, still of the view that there should be no major effort on the far bank of the Rhine until all resistance was cleared from the west, a policy with which Gen. Hodges disagrees.'[20] In other words, far from encouraging the breakthrough, SHAEF and Twelfth Army Group applied brakes to its exploitation. The reason was principally not to distract from Operation *Plunder*, Montgomery's long-planned Rhine crossing due to take place on 23–24 March, 125 miles further north.

Meanwhile, 367 Luftwaffe planes attacked Remagen in the first nine days, of which 106 were claimed as destroyed. As well as under near-continuous German artillery fire over this period, a tracked 'Karl' 540mm mortar was brought up to fire 1½-ton shells at the bridge, all of which missed. Eleven V-2 rockets were also loosed at the site on 12 March, followed with an attempt by six frogmen five days later. On the first night a tank destroyer fell through the hole caused by the failed demolition, taking three hours to be towed free. A shell hit an ammunition truck driving across on 9 March, and a gasoline tanker the following day, both of which had to be bulldozed away, causing damage to the structure.

By this time, a sign had been erected, 'Cross the Rhine With Dry Feet, Courtesy of the 9th Armored Division'. Six days after capture, First Army had ceased to use the railway bridge and commenced repairs to strengthen it and to make it two-way. Instead, First Army and III Corps engineers constructed two pontoon bridges and later a Bailey bridge capable of taking various weights of vehicle, supplemented by a ferry service using Bailey bridging pontoons with motors, DUKWs, and twenty-four navy LCVPs (landing craft, vehicle, personnel), transported from the coast on giant trailers.

While the Ludendorff bridge itself was the enabler of this dramatic turn of events, becoming a metaphor for America's forcing of the Rhine, it was the US Army Corps of Engineers, in building additional floating roadways, and maintaining them under fire, that made the bridgehead viable. Thus, this episode is better understood as the 'bridges at Remagen', for the majority of First Army's men, machinery and supplies crossed by the *eight* engineer treadway and Bailey bridges, eventually assembled along a twenty-mile stretch of the Rhine between Bonn and Bad Hönningen, rather than using the stone-and-steel structure towering above them, used by traffic for only six days.

Seven of these were open by 22 March, the eighth at Bad Godesberg on 5 April. A ninth pile trestle bridge, capable of taking up to seventy tons, upriver at Neuwied, was opened post-war, on 15 May.[21] A tank driver described the experience of crossing one of these floating roadways: 'As far as we could see, there were countless pontoons lying side by side across the broad expanse of the Rhine. They were long, airtight metal drums. Both ends were attached to steel cables strung across the river and solidly anchored to each shore. Treadways were placed on the pontoons for vehicles to drive on. I was a bit nervous about driving a thirty-three-ton vehicle onto a bridge that floated on water. As we drove onto the bridge, we were spaced by military policemen to minimize the undulations caused by the heavy tanks, one vehicle at a time.'[22]

Andy Rooney remembered the pontoon bridge two hundred yards upstream, 'pushed by the flow of the river into a long, graceful loop'. He crossed it twice, 'as shells continued to drop into the Rhine around us. They fell like huge raindrops into still water, exploding as they struck.'[23] This took the strain off the Ludendorff, and eventually all of III, V and VII Corps crossed at this point, using the combat engineer bridging and waterborne craft. The latter could cross in under ten minutes and on 15 March transported 2,200 infantrymen in three hours.[24]

Meanwhile, persuaded he was surrounded by traitors, a vengeful Hitler summoned a loyal general to Berlin, giving him complete powers to court-martial and execute any he could deem responsible. Corps, division and regimental commanders came under the Nazi gaze, and there was much finger-pointing until six local commanders at Remagen were tried as scapegoats. The Wehrmacht engineer responsible for blowing the bridge, Friesenhahn, and security officer, Bratge, escaped death because they were prisoners in American hands, but four other officers, including Major Scheller, who had left the scene to summon reinforcements on 7 March, were executed for no more than being in the wrong place at the wrong time. Generalmajor Richard von Both-mer, last of a long line of Saxon nobles, and commander of Bonn and Remagen, was immediately arrested but managed to grab the pistol of a court official and commit suicide on 10 March. A German 1967 legal review exonerated them all.[25]

I have often visited this stretch of the Rhine, and enjoyed the company of a former Bundeswehr colonel, the late Hans-Joachim Krug, commissioned into the Wehrmacht in 1944, who lived in Linz on the east bank, opposite Remagen. His father was a resourceful and distinguished Wehrmacht Oberst who had commanded a bunker behind a British beach on D-Day, and his son another Bundeswehr officer with whom I have served.[26] Hans-Joachim built his delightful retirement home amid some of the former gun positions overlooking the river and each year had unearthed cartridges from the battle when digging in his roses. He knew the story of the bridge in intimate detail. 'It's all about leadership,' he mused one day to me when discussing Timmer-mann, surrounded by military history books and hunting trophies. 'The junior leader can still make a difference in a big war. You call such a man "the strategic corporal". It is good that individuals can still make a difference.'[27]

Krug was right. Soldiers need to know they can influence events by their determination and professionalism. Brigadier General Hoge, senior commander on the spot, was perhaps even more important in turning the course of the war at that moment. 'I knew it was right,' Hoge wrote later, of storming the bridge without orders. 'I just had to make a try for it. Here was the chance of a lifetime, and it had to be grasped immediately. If I had waited, the moment would have gone. That was the greatest turning point in my whole career as a soldier – capturing it. Otherwise, I'd have retired as a colonel. If it hadn't been for the bridge at Remagen.' Hoge would eventually reach the four-star rank of General and Commander-in-Chief of United States Army Europe.[28]

While Hoge's star was in the ascendant because of Remagen, that of Generalfeldmarschall Gerd von Rundstedt, Wehrmacht Commander-in-Chief in the West, was fast waning. He had long fallen out of favour with his Führer, and the loss of the Ludendorff railway bridge was the final nail in the coffin of their relationship. On 9 March Hitler phoned Rundstedt from Berlin to reveal he had assigned Albert Kesselring, formerly supreme commander in Italy, to replace him as Oberbefehlshaber West. This amounted to little more than shuffling the deckchairs on the *Titanic*, but Rundstedt was probably happy enough to hang up his field marshal's baton after a military career of fifty-two years.

There was a final audience with Hitler on 11 March whereupon he turned his back on the 'Bohemian Corporal' whom he loathed so much, and retreated to a sanatorium in Bad Tölz, south of Munich and in Sixth Army Group's area, becoming a prisoner of the 36th Texas Division on 1 May.[29] Kesselring inherited three army groups ('H' under Blaskowitz in the north, Model's 'B' in the centre, and SS-Oberst-Gruppenführer Paul Hausser's Army Group 'G' to the south), all three amounting to no more than twenty-six divisions. At the same time the number of German divisions fighting the Russians had risen to an estimated 214, though many were divisions in name only. 'Whenever two or three of you gather together in my name, you shall be called a division,' observed a Wehrmacht pastor, only half joking.

We have already witnessed the despondency of the First Army diarist on 15 March, a week after the Ludendorff bridge was captured. Before signing off for the day, he again spelled out his headquarters' disappointment with SHAEF. 'We learned pretty definitely that SHAEF does not wish the bridgehead expanded, and as a matter of fact, were almost disappointed when they learned the news we were across the river, since it upset their previously made calculations. Gen. Hodges also discussed with Gen. Bradley the possibility of replacing Gen. Millikin with another corps commander. Both agreed he was good officer but too timid.'[30] This was at odds with Hodges' earlier impression that his subordinate was too hot-headed, and rings hollow as a fair excuse. The real problem here was a personality clash, which Hodges' own temperament and First Army's confrontational environment did little to dissipate.

Though Hodges claimed Millikin had also clashed with Patton, recent research suggests this was not so; after all, it was Millikin's corps that had executed the impressive ninety-degree turn northwards into the Bulge. He may not have possessed the forceful character Hodges wanted, but he responded better to the direction of his fellow cavalry-man, Patton. As a staff officer in Third Army's headquarters noted at the time, 'Am certain [Millikin's seizure of Remagen] threw SHAEF, and Dear Old Monty, into a terrible flap. Patton would have decorated Mil-likin, SHAEF busts him.'[31] Unravelling the controversy about Rema-gen is challenging, not least because Hodges left no papers of his own.

Eisenhower at SHAEF appeared to be in favour of exploiting the Remagen bridgehead, but his staff were not. Bradley did what SHAEF instructed. Hodges had backed Millikin's quick exploitation of Leon-ard's and Hoge's initiative. However, Hodges may have interpreted his superiors' reluctance as a judgement on his III Corps commander, which in turn reflected poorly his own leadership of First Army. Millikin's chief problem lay in the fact that he was not Collins. The latter was well aware of his popularity with his army commander, to the extent that when Collins called into Eagle TAC on 12 March, he boasted, 'What a shame it was that VII Corps did not establish the bridgehead.'[32]

The jibe at Millikin's expense reflected Hodges' own thinking, as well Collins knew. The VII Corps commander went on to state that had he captured Remagen, 'by the end of the first day he'd have been on the Bonn–Limburg autobahn', which was fifteen miles distant, though this was only reached and cut by the 309th Infantry (General Parker's 78th Division) on 16 March.[33] With Bradley's five-division limitation imposed on the size of the bridgehead and its expansion limited to a thousand yards a day, Millikin was hardly 'timid', but merely the inheri-tor of SHAEF and army group uncertainty as to what to do with the Remagen bridgehead. Collins could not have expanded any faster with the same orders even had he wished to do so.

Millikin may not have been J. Lawton Collins, but he was no fail-ure, either. As one author has observed, 'The case of Millikin's relief does not reflect well on the First Army headquarters,' and an element of Hodges' own petty-mindedness trickles down when examining the rele-vant papers today.[34] Three further points are worth illuminating. First, Hodges was not a great personnel manager, for he had already relieved Charles H. Corlett, of XIX Corps, in October 1944. Although the imme-diate trigger was a breakdown in Corlett's health from service in the Pacific and an infection contracted in Normandy, Hodges noted on the former's report his dissatisfaction with XIX Corps' progress through the Siegfried Line, with which others disagreed.[35]

Second, at this late stage in the European campaign, with victory in sight, it was strange for such a major change in command to take place. It was not Eisenhower's place to intervene, but Bradley may have deferred to Hodges so as not to undermine his former deputy, whom he still regarded highly. On 16 March, Major General James A. Van Fleet, another Eisenhower and Bradley contemporary from West Point and then commanding the 90th 'Tough Hombres' Division, was alerted to succeed John Millikin at III Corps. As First Army noted, 'his rise in this war has been spectacular. He landed on D-Day as a regimental commander in the 4th Division. Now he has won himself a Corps.'[36]

Third, Millikin's departure was sweetened by the award of a Silver Star for his valour in forcing the bridgehead in the absence of orders. Pleasingly, he was back in his cavalry saddle within the month, leading the 13th Armored Division whose commander, Major General John B. Wogan, had been seriously wounded on 16 April. Clearly Millikin's command was not that bad. Thus, it fell to his successor, Van Fleet, along with Collins and Huebner, to hear the good news from Hodges on 20 March that Bradley had assented to a build-up of nine divisions in the Remagen bridgehead, in preparation for a breakout on the 23rd, in tandem with the Montgomery assault to the north.

Far from the rapid exploitation the senior commanders claimed in their memoirs and in many popular narratives, SHAEF had been stricken with nearly two weeks of operational indecision and paralysis about what to do with Remagen. Hardly the dynamic direction handed down in public memory. Meanwhile, Hodges, reticent about a face-to-face meeting with Millikin, had called his subordinate at 14:50 on 17 March. 'I have some bad news for you,' he began, and told him he was being replaced. When his army commander had finished, Millikin was able to respond, 'And, Sir, I have some bad news for you, too. The railroad bridge has just collapsed.'

Rather absurdly, it was SHAEF's own indecision that helped the demise of the Ludendorff crossing. An instant determination to reinforce the bridgehead would have led to the immediate construction of numerous other pontoon spans. Instead, the railway bridge was kept in heavy use for six days bearing the wheeled and tracked traffic of four divisions, while engineer ferries, DUKWs and LCVPs conveyed most manpower.

Weakened by earlier Allied air strikes, the failed detonation and an estimated 600 near misses from artillery fire, Luftwaffe raids and V-2 rockets, the Ludendorff buckled into the icy Rhine exactly ten days after its capture. Historian Ken Hechler, two war artists, several reporters and newsreel camera crew were present. All reported hearing a sound like a rifle shot, or a rivet popping; then a second. 'The entire deck of the bridge started to tremble,' recalled Lieutenant Colonel Clayton A. Rust, of the 276th Engineer Combat Battalion whose men were repairing the structure. Men dropped their tools and started to run. 'The whole deck was vibrating, and dust was rising from the surface.'

Sergeant Henry Giles of the 291st Combat Engineers was working a hundred yards downstream and wrote of hearing a 'screeching, cracking, splintering noise. I looked over at the bridge, and right before my eyes it began buckling and caving in. It just collapsed. Sort of slow motion at first, the way you'd run a movie at the very slowest speed possible, then it began settling very fast. There were a hell of a lot of men working on it and I could see them running toward both ends. But they began to slide back down into the river as the middle caved in. My God! To see something like that. I'll not forget it until the day I die.'[37]

Those on the treadway pontoons witnessed 'the centre span of the bridge twisting counter-clockwise and buckling, then it fell into the river and the adjacent spans with it'.[38] Colonel Rust started to race to the Remagen side but in a few seconds found himself running uphill as the structure collapsed around him, shedding girders into the waters below. Rust was dragged under but swept downriver to one of the pontoon bridges and survived.[39] Troops he had spoken to minutes earlier were less fortunate. Of the engineers present, 121 were killed or wounded.

Just as General Erich Ludendorff had fought the Americans during 1918, another Ludendorff had conducted a final offensive against the same Western Allies, thirty-seven years later.

Ironically, despite the hostility of SHAEF and Twelfth Army Group to exploiting the Remagen bridgehead, it became Hodges' main, indeed only, access to the far side of the waterway. Through this funnel the entire First Army would trickle over the Rhine and break out into German plains beyond, enabled by eight 1,000-foot bridges of various types, mostly resting on pontoons, supplemented by a ninth completed just after the war's end.

They were protected by Colonel William F. Damon's 14th Cavalry, who provided all the wireless liaison between units in Millikin's III Corps (to whom they were assigned) and were responsible for traffic control, no mean feat on both sides of the congested bridgehead area and illustrative of the flexibility of the cavalry arm. Until 23 March, the cavalrymen pushed troops and their equipment across the engineer bridges along a thirty-mile stretch of the Rhine. DUKWs and landing craft augmented the spans, which indicated the rapid expansion of the far bank, giving new landing sites daily.[40]

On 25 March, Hodges attacked along a forty-mile front with all of his corps in line, fed by the multitude of bridges, between Bonn in the north and Koblenz. He had moved his headquarters to Bad Godesberg, a smart spa town overlooking the Rhine, a few miles south of Bonn. The Germans, who had been trying to chip away at the Remagen perimeter with too few panzers, no fuel and worn-out infantry, gave way almost immediately. At the same moment, the 49th Anti-Aircraft Brigade assumed responsibility for the close defence of the bridgehead, coordinating the numerous air defence battalions, artillery, radar, engineer, chemical smoke, searchlight and balloon barrage units, naval landing craft dropping depth charges, and special searchlight-mounted tanks. With IX Tactical Air Command, they established an air exclusion zone around the site, inside which air defenders had an exclusive 'weapons-free' policy against any attackers.

This stretch of river became First Army's critical weakness, its centre of gravity in modern terminology, without which it could not function. Had the V-2 rockets aimed at the bridges been more accurate, and the Germans been able to equip their warheads with poison gas, then – as weapons of mass destruction – the Reich might have been able to halt First Army in its tracks. Hence the largest concentration of air defence ever assembled by the US Army.

Thirty miles beyond, near Limburg, surrounded by high fences on a hill overlooking the town of Hadamar, Walter M. Robertson's 2nd

Infantry Division, with V Corps, made a shocking discovery. They had captured a mental institution. Yet many of its over seven hundred inmates, crammed into accommodation designed for half that number, seemed remarkably sane and lucid. Very soon GI investigators learned the reason for the huge quantities of Veronal and Luminal barbiturates found in its pharmacy.

From 1939 the Nazi regime had embarked on the enforced sterilisation of 'children unfit to reproduce'. These included mixed-race infants of the 24,000 African-Germans then living in the Reich, many the progeny of white German mothers and French colonial soldiers born during the occupation after 1918, and derogatorily called 'Rhineland Bastards'. However, the policy soon progressed from sterilisation of these children to outright murder. As the Nazis grew bolder, the euthanasia programme was extended to adults. Hadamar's meticulous records, kept in two safes blown open by the V Corps War Crimes Team, revealed that from January to August 1941 alone, over 10,000 men, women and children were asphyxiated by carbon monoxide and interred locally.[41] Texan Johnnie M. Marino with the 2nd Division remembered a ravine full of the dead whom the guards hadn't time to cremate or bury. 'Thousands of people just laying there, their eyes open, staring up at the sky. I thought I had seen war, death, Omaha beach, Battle of the Bulge, but I never, *never* was prepared to witness something like Hadamar . . . I see them today as I saw them then, especially the children.'[42]

When news leaked out to the wider German public in 1941, the programme – concealed by its bland operational title of 'T-4', after its Berlin headquarters address, No.4, Tiergarten Strasse – was suspended. But the Nazis lied. Transferred to SS control, the murders soon recommenced, with another 5,000 lethal doses of barbiturates administered at Hadamar to those who could not serve the Reich. US War Crimes interpreter Private George Jaeger recalled learning that the 'victims arrived in trucks once or twice a week, usually at night, having been told that they were going to a hospital for rest and treatment. They were then actually put into nice, clean beds in a tidy ward, where the chief nurse, Irmgard Huber, a motherly, pink-cheeked woman, would give them a heavy injection of scopolamine which killed them in two hours.'[43]

Jaeger recollected that 'there was a deep, glowering anger and moral outrage at all we had seen. In my case, it broke through on several occasions. Once when I was billeted in an especially comfortable upper-middle class German house, undoubtedly belonging to well-to-do Nazis, I got massively drunk and then, single-handedly, and systematically, smashed and broke every bit of furniture, glassware, bric-a-brac and what-have-you in the entire house. My major gave me a bit of a talking-to, but clearly understood.'[44]

Huebner's V Corps initially followed the Rhine south to Ehrenbreitstein, outside Koblenz, where the last American flag of occupation flew over Germany in 1923. This was also behind Patton's future crossing areas, whose defenders V Corps was now isolating. Many senior officers in First Army remembered the original flag-lowering and held a ceremony on 6 April 1945 at the twelfth-century Ehrenbreitstein fortress to raise it again, using the same companies of the 8th Infantry who had participated in the earlier event. This was a moment full of significance, for the date marked the twenty-eighth anniversary of America declaring war on Germany in 1917, and – as Bradley observed to the parade – it was US Army Day as well. All present would have been heartened to know their war would be over in thirty-two days.

Third US Army's crossing of the Rhine, beginning on the night of 22–23 March, was designed as a spoiler to Montgomery's set-piece Operation *Plunder*, launched a day later. It was presented at the time, and has been since by historians, as an improvised leap across the river, with none of 21st Army Group's extensive preparations. In fact, the opposite was true. Since the previous autumn, Patton's engineers had carefully rehearsed the manoeuvre. They assembled huge quantities of bridging pontoons and equipment (*above*) and even landing craft (the LCVP Higgins boats, *below*). The date was brought forward, but it was methodical logistical planning that yielded success, not spontaneity.

8

Third Army

Exactly a year after the Third US Army's headquarters had landed in Scotland, they stood contemplating the dark, oily waters of the Rhine. It was 22 March 1945. Over the preceding nine days, George Patton's 320,000-strong force had lanced through the Saar-Palatinate, scrubbing it clean of their opponents, and taking around 90,000 prisoners.

The mighty river, full of winter rain and debris, flowed past at 7.3 feet per second.[1] There had been a total of twenty-two major road and twenty-five railroad bridges spanning the waterway before the war, but all except for Remagen had been destroyed. With no dry crossings left, reaching the far bank would have to be by wet means. The considerable engineering challenge that lay ahead for Third Army, of spanning the water obstacle, was complicated enough, without the added factor of the Germans firing at them.[2]

At the time, Patton's army looked like this. Troy Middleton, the self-styled 'Mayor of Koblenz', sat in the north with his VIII Corps of two infantry formations (87th and 89th Divisions), having just toppled the Kaiser Wilhelm statue at Eisenhower's request.[3] Battling their way from Trier to line the river opposite Mainz, a combat journey of over one hundred miles, was Walton Walker's enlarged XX Corps (65th, 80th and 94th Infantry, plus 6th and 11th Armored). Manton Eddy's XII Corps (5th, 26th, 76th and 90th Infantry, and Gaffey's 4th Armored) had fought their way to the Rhine's west bank, south of Mainz.

We may recall that Major General Leroy Irwin's 5th Division, closely followed by the 90th (both XII Corps), were preparing to 'take the Rhine at a run' from an area ten miles south of Mainz.[4] Such phraseology implies an ad hoc leap across the mighty river wherever the opportunity presented itself. The initiative to do so may have been Bradley's, but Patton needed no encouragement. The timing was triggered by Montgomery's set-piece assault in the north, Operation *Plunder*, planned for the night of 23–24 March, but Bradley was keen for political and personal reasons to get American troops over in advance, as a spoiler. Simpson's Ninth Army headquarters, too, usually so cordial towards Twenty-First Army Group, was incensed by Montgomery's refusal to let them cross before him. If Bradley and Patton had harboured a simmering resentment of Montgomery's lordly style during the previous year, it was made worse by the latter's 7 January press conference, and subsequently his insistence that he dominate the Rhine crossings.

However, there was nothing incautious or hasty about Third Army's plans to leap the Rhine. Over the previous weeks while fighting through the Saar, Patton's chief artillery advisor, Colonel Edward T. 'Molly' Williams, had already devised a 'Third Army Troop Carrier Command', an ingenious plan to concentrate all their artillery spotter and liaison planes, which could each take one passenger. There were enough aircraft to ferry a battalion across the river in about ninety minutes, and on 21 March, they conducted a dry test run.[5] More significantly, since the previous November, three naval units had been stationed in Belgium equipped with seventy-two LCVPs, the acclaimed thirty-six-foot D-Day Higgins boats.[6]

They had been brought across the Channel by landing ship, transported overland on huge trailers to be stationed on the Meuse, Moselle and Maas rivers, supporting First, Third and Ninth Armies, respectively. Each unit comprised two hundred US Navy and Coast Guard personnel and twenty-four boats. The early-seeming deployment was because the Rhine crossings were initially planned for December, before the Ardennes campaign intervened. In the winter months units were augmented by fifty-four LCMs (landing craft, mechanised) which sailed from England to Antwerp under their own power and thence down the Albert Canal. These were fifty feet long and capable of taking a single tank. The assorted landing craft first proved their worth at Remagen, easily outperforming the army's amphibious vehicles. LCVP crews ferried 2,200 troops of the 1st Infantry Division to the far shore in three hours, each boat taking thirty-six GIs for a seven-minute round trip, as well as supporting the construction of pontoon bridges.

On 19 March, Bradley agreed that Third Army would cross the Rhine in the near future; three days later Hodges would break out of Remagen, head south, and the two armies would meet around Limburg. The same day, Third Army counted 17,000 prisoners processed, a sure sign of the disintegration of their opponents, and Colonel Robert S. Allen noted in his diary, 'Bradley remarked that Gen. Marshall was very anxious to get a lot of publicity for ETO. Wonder what this is about? Must be a lot of heat over something – it's clearly big topside inner politics.'[7] Allen speculated this was a MacArthur versus Marshall, Pacific theatre versus European, confrontation for American hearts and minds. Yet Bradley's comments were actually preparations to outmanoeuvre Montgomery in the forthcoming battle for news of the Rhine crossings. How much the Allied bonhomie reigning before D-Day had unravelled.

Behind the scenes, Patton was incensed at SHAEF's insistence that the main effort of spanning the Rhine lay with Twenty-First Army Group. The Third Army commander determined that he would *precede* Montgomery with a crossing of his own. Yet with his own history of speaking and acting out of turn – the slapping incidents in Sicily had cost him an army command – Patton had to be careful not to move too soon or draw too much attention to his proposed illegal move. He knew that timing was the issue, not intent. However, according to headquarters staff in the know, Patton acted with 'Bradley's full blessing and knowledge', but secretly from SHAEF.[8]

Thus, unaware that Major General Leroy Irwin of the 5th Infantry had just discussed with his own formation's leadership plans for the division's well-earned rest, the Third Army commander stormed into his morning Ultra briefing on 22 March, according to the recollection of Colonel Allen, and announced, 'We've got to get a bridgehead. Every day we save doing that means saving hundreds of American lives. The Germans are smashed and in chaos now on our front.' Patton continued, knowing that Montgomery was about to cross on the 23rd further north, 'If we delay, seventy-two hours from now they [the Germans, though the language was more profane] will have reorganized. We must not give them that chance – and I don't give a goddamn what other plans there may be. I don't propose to give the sons-of-bitches a chance to recover from the killing we gave them in the Palatinate. We are going to make a crossing immediately. I don't care where or how we get the necessary equipment but get it. Steal it, beg it, or make it. We are going to cross the Rhine and do it today.'[9] Furthermore, Patton ordered there was to be a paperwork 'blackout for twenty-four to forty-eight hours. No mention of assault to be in any reports, nor to be shown on any maps.'[10]

However, this was *not* a thrown-together operation. Third Army plans for the crossing of the Rhine were initiated as early as August 1944, shortly after the formation reached France, in expectation of crossings that autumn. In September, a special staff section was established to estimate and order engineering equipment and assess which stretch of river might lie within their zone of advance. Dossiers on specific bridge sites were compiled, and distributed to corps, divisions and engineer combat groups. By October, Brigadier General Conklin, Third Army Chief Engineer, had established a school for all units in anticipation of traversing the Rhine, where each engineer combat battalion spent three days training with all the bridging equipment they would use. At the same time, they were given 1:10,000 scale models of each proposed crossing site, to study and plan.[11]

An engineer depot had also been initiated on the Moselle, where all equipment was evaluated and totals computed for every section of bridging needed for a series of Rhine crossings, originally expected in December 1944. By the following March, Conklin had squirrelled away 1,500 assault boats, 300 storm boats, 15,000 paddles, 910 outboard motors, 11,000 feet of treadway bridge, 7,000-feet of floating Bailey bridge and 2,200 feet of heavy pontoon bridge in readiness for the Rhine, whenever it was to be attacked. The Corps of Engineers understood that just bringing forward thousands of tons of heavy equipment, in the right sequence, a circuitous 300-mile round trip, over a very poor road network, made even worse by rain, snow and the constant pounding of traffic, where wreckers would have to drag each truck and trailer through the mud, might prove an engineering triumph in itself.[12]

Thus, the Rhine had long been the goal of the 1135th Engineer Combat Group, attached to Eddy's XII Corps, an organisation 7,000-strong, almost the combat infantry strength of an average division.

PERSONAL MESSAGE
FROM THE C-IN-C

(To be read out to all Troops)

1. On the 7th February I told you we were going into the ring for the final and last round, there would be no time limit: we would continue fighting until our opponent was knocked out. The last round is going very well on both sides of the ring—and overhead.

2. In the WEST, the enemy has lost the Rhineland, and with it the flower of at least four armies—the Parachute Army, Fifth Panzer Army, Fifteenth Army, and Seventh Army: the First Army, further to the south, is now being added to the list.

   In the Rhineland battles, the enemy has lost about 150,000 prisoners, and there are many more to come; his total casualties amount to about 250,000 since 8th February.

3. In the EAST, the enemy has lost all POMERANIA east of the ODER, an area as large as the Rhineland; and three more German armies have been routed. The Russian armies are within about 35 miles of BERLIN.

4. Overhead, the Allied Air Forces are pounding Germany day and night. It will be interesting to see how much longer the Germans can stand it.

5. The enemy has in fact been driven into a corner, and he cannot escape.

   Events are moving rapidly.

   The complete and decisive defeat of the Germans is certain; there is no possibility of doubt on this matter.

6. 21 ARMY GROUP WILL NOW CROSS THE RHINE.

   The enemy possibly thinks he is safe behind this great river obstacle. We all agree that it is a great obstacle; but we will show the enemy that he is far from safe behind it. This great Allied fighting machine, composed of integrated land and air forces, will deal with the problem in no uncertain manner.

7. And having crossed the RHINE, we will crack about in the plains of Northern Germany, chasing the enemy from pillar to post. The swifter and the more energetic our action the sooner the war will be over, and that is what we all desire: to get on with the job and finish off the German war as soon as possible.

8. Over the RHINE, then, let us go. And good hunting to you all on the other side.

9. May "the Lord mighty in battle" give us the victory in this our latest undertaking, as He has done in all our battles since we landed in Normandy on D-day.

B. L. Montgomery

Germany,
March, 1945.

Field-Marshal,
C.-in-C.,
21 Army Group

As he had done prior to all his major battles, most notably Alamein and D-Day, Montgomery issued an order of the day for the forces under his command: 'The complete and decisive defeat of the Germans is now certain: there is no possibility of doubt on this matter.'

Eisenhower (*seated, centre*) with some of his US command team in 1945. Seated, left to right, are Simpson (9th Army); Patton (3rd Army); Spaatz (Strategic Air Forces); Bradley (12th Army Group); Hodges (1st Army); and Gerow (15th Army). Standing, left to right: Stearley (IX Tactical Air Command); Vandenberg (9th Air Force); Bedell Smith (SHAEF Chief of Staff); Weyland (XIX Tactical Air Command); Nugent (XXIX Tactical Air Command).

Churchill, amidst the 'dragon's teeth' of the Siegfried Line, stands with Field Marshals Brooke and Montgomery, with General Bill Simpson of the 9th US Army.

Field Marshal Albert Kesselring (1885–1960), commander of all three German army groups.

The monocled Field Marshal Walter Model (1891–1945) of Army Group B.

SS-Oberst-Gruppenführer Paul Hausser (1880–1972), who presided over Army Group 'G' in the south.

Generaloberst Johannes Blaskowitz (1883–1948), who led Army Group 'H' Holland. He loathed the excesses of the Nazi regime.

In Montgomery's 21st Army Group sector, the Rhine crossings were preceded by an intense barrage involving weapons from heavy artillery, anti-aircraft guns firing in flat trajectory, to Vickers medium machine-guns.

Before the Rhine could be crossed, the 9th and 1st US Armies had to storm the River Roer. Here, ten GIs rehearse in an overloaded craft, coached by four engineers.

It was the 3rd US Infantry Division who attacked Utweiler in the German Saarland on 15 March 1945. They were known as the 'Blue and White devils', after their divisional insignia.

All the Allied combatant armies supplied their own medical vehicles, but additional help came from the American Field Service. The AFS was an all-volunteer ambulance service, first raised in 1915.

A French soldier, clutching a hand grenade and his Browning Automatic Rifle (a light machine-gun of 1918 vintage), has paid the ultimate price on the battlefield.

The Allies benefitted from an extraordinary range of specialised military vehicles. Shown here is the versatile Studebaker M29 'Weasel'.

Some British Churchill tanks, manned by Royal Engineers, carried short lengths of combat bridging, which allowed gaps, such as this crater, to be bridged in minutes, if necessary under fire.

The Germans used these multiple 20mm rapid-fire anti-aircraft cannons mounted on a turntable with devastating effect. Known as 'flak wagons', they were also deployed against American ground forces.

A pair of US Army half-tracks, mounting quadruple .50-inch Browning machine-guns, guard the approaches to the Ludendorff railway bridge at Remagen.

Crossing the Rhine. The US 89th Division attacked at Sankt Goar in the picturesque Rhine Gorge, overlooked by high cliffs and the Lorelei statue.

The US 87th Division had an easier time crossing at Boppard where the defenders were weaker, even if equipped with mobile 20mm 'flak wagons'.

By the end of 26 March, Patch's Seventh Army had erected a 1000-foot pontoon bridge over the Rhine at Worms. Haislip's XV Corps are seen here thundering across. In the background stands the wreck of the sabotaged Nibelungen bridge, whose 200-foot tower still stands today.

On 10 December 1944, engineering and naval staff had been called to a conference at Third Army HQ, then in Nancy, in anticipation of crossings in the next couple of weeks. Ferry and bridging positions had been selected from aerial photographs, though without time to confirm them on the ground. Detailed terrain analysis had already indicated the Nierstein-Oppenheim area had a good network of approach roads, with hills and towns masking assembly areas, landing sites that would require no engineer work, and excellent potential observation posts of the German-held far bank. These were the 'gentle rolling hills along the river covered with vineyards' that Staff Sergeant Eggers of the 26th Infantry Division had noted earlier while his men stole ration packs from the tankers of the 4th Armored, billeted along the banks.[13] Thereafter, Hitler's Ardennes offensive intervened to delay the Rhine operations by three months.

Of his March 1945 crossing, the local US Navy commander, Lieutenant Commander William Leide, observed, 'We had not been briefed, and the reconnaissance of the river itself for launching, embarkation and debarkation sites [was] not complete.'[14] The 5th Division recorded the equally short notice. 'With no artillery preparation or air cover, this kind of came as a surprise, but everything was so well prepared. There was no pause to get organized, they brought up a row of trucks filled with assault boats. It was really a simple thing, just like basic training. The GIs were surprised the Navy was there, and the Navy was surprised they were so far away from the ocean. They did a lot of grumbling.'[15] Nevertheless, Leide managed to get twelve LCVPs delivered by truck to Oppenheim and lifted into the waters after dark, using their own mobile crane.

A substantial XII Corps artillery preparation was available, with guns dug in and ammunition dumped, but it was decided to try for a silent approach to gain tactical surprise. Besides the spotter planes, which due to the Luftwaffe, but to the disappointment of all, were not used, army chemical units equipped with smoke were alerted for action. Bridging units – the 150th Engineer Combat Battalion, with a dump truck company, the 995th and 996th Treadway Bridge Companies and platoon of the 1301st Engineer General Service Regiment attached, specially trained in protective boom construction – were ordered forward.[16] Of the twelve LCVPs available, ten were to assist in the build-up on the far shore and the others in bridging work. Although XII Corps had not worked with the US Navy before, it had conducted numerous assault crossings under fire in recent weeks, while the 5th Division was the veteran of twenty-two since arriving in Normandy.

Receiving Patton's directive for instant activity, Eddy immediately ordered Irwin's 5th to make the crossing that evening, the 22nd, 'a balmy springish night with brilliant moonlight'. Irwin, expecting to move back for rest, not forward into battle, responded 'that it would be extremely difficult to conduct a deliberate crossing at such short notice, but 5th Division would establish some sort of bridgehead using Colonel Paul J. Black's 11th Infantry'. The LCVPs were not used for the first wave, which was ferried across the 1,000-foot expanse by engineer assault rafts and DUKWs, accompanied by Company 'B's swimming Sherman DD (Duplex Drive) vehicles of the 748th Tank Battalion.

Launching at 22:30, the first men from Third Army to cross the Rhine from Nierstein was an assault boat containing ten men from the 11th Infantry's Company 'K', led by Lieutenants Irven H. Jacobs and John A. Mannow. At once, they came upon seven Germans who promptly surrendered. Crossing behind them were Companies 'I' and 'L' with Major Alexander C. Stiller, Patton's aide who had served with him in 1918, and an air force observer. The surprise was complete. Initially not a single shot was fired.

However, Companies 'A' and 'B' of the 11th Infantry's First Battalion, crossing seven hundred yards upstream at Oppenheim, were caught by machine-gun crossfire, alerting the Germans right across the front. The staccato gradually increased, catching Third Battalion in the flank at the Nierstein site. When First Battalion's assault boats beached, hostile fire, including panzerfäuste, increased to the extent that they were faced with their own Omaha beach moment, as commanders fell. Staff Sergeant Foster Ferguson, for example, rallied his leaderless platoon and punched a hole in his opponents' defences using rifle fire and grenades alone. They were fortunate their adversaries were in open, sandbagged machine-gun nests, and not in concrete pillboxes in this sector, which they had no means of overcoming.

When his M-1 rifle jammed, PFC Paul Conn Jr of Company 'B' threw caution to the wind, pulled out a hand grenade and rose before the opposition. Transfixed at the sight of a weaponless, but menacing, lone American advancing towards them clutching a grenade, the seven-man crew of one machine-gun nest threw up their hands and surrendered. The sector had quietened down somewhat when Company 'C' arrived with Mexican-born Private Edgar N. Valderrama, who remembered, 'By the time my boat reached the far side, our first sergeant, a young hillbilly from Tennessee, was standing on the levee with a little note-book in one hand and a flashlight in the other, taking roll call. I could see tracer bullets flying over his head and shoulders. The heavy artil-lery fire made me nervous enough to jump ship a few yards before we reached the shore. I didn't want to be branded a coward, so instead of dashing for cover, I heroically yanked the boat the last few feet to shore, and then dashed for cover.'[17]

Realising how important the supporting arms were to the infantry beachhead, artillery forward observers soon followed, with armour of the 737th Tank and 403rd Tank Destroyer Battalions arriving on motor barges, nosed across by the landing craft, to render direct help, along-side the amphibious tanks of the 748th. Like the well-oiled machine the 5th Division had become, by 07:00 on the 23rd, the last battalion of the following 10th Infantry was completely across, the first ferry was work-ing, and the Higgins boats were scuttling back with forth with heavy equipment, field guns and vital supplies.

German guns started to search the waters with puzzling accuracy. A platoon commander on the far bank heard guttural voices barking out fire control orders rather too loudly, investigated, then found and captured a hastily built dugout containing seventeen Germans direct-ing artillery by field telephone. Smoke cover was initiated which soon masked the operation, and within hours the 5th Division had won themselves a beachhead seven miles wide by six deep.[18] Into it, Gen-eral Manton Eddy's XII Corps poured their own field artillery, ready to repel German counter-attacks. By midnight on the 23rd, seventeen artillery battalions were on hand to destroy the first one of any size, mounted by students from an officer candidate school in Wiesbaden, who tried to make up for their lack of numbers with belief and pat-riotic cries. Daylight soon dispersed their attempts and encouraged their surrender.[19]

Indicative of low morale within the defending 159th and 559th Volks-grenadier Divisions manning the sector, three Company 'I' runners were escorting forty-one prisoners back to the river when they tripped over a bypassed Wehrmacht platoon. The uncaptured Germans, full of fight, quickly set up their machine-guns. The three American guards, PFC Conn Connewalt, T/4 Frank McArdle and Private Paul Bonwits, reminded their prisoners that 'Alles Kaput', who in turn shouted emotional pleas to their comrades. The upshot was an additional, fully equipped German platoon joining the procession back to the POW cage, ushered along by the intrepid GI trio.[20]

The Third Army's commander noted his gamble eventually cost 'twenty-eight men killed and wounded', a tragedy for their next of kin, but 'remarkably small change for a rushed major military operation of operational significance'. He praised Leide, the US Navy commander, for 'this superior work accomplished by your units', whose craft had carried more than 15,000 troops across the river, returning with German prisoners of war and casualties.[21] Within twenty hours, the first 972-foot bridge capable of handling tanks was thrown across, a second during the next day and a third soon after. When daylight came, the Luftwaffe attacked but the air defenders were ready and waiting, claiming eighteen aircraft brought down. Five divisions from XII and XX Corps with supporting troops and supplies soon thundered over the three engineer bridges erected at Nierstein and a single one at Oppenheim. Following the 5th came the 90th then 4th Armored; on 25 March, the entire 6th Armored Division crossed in sixteen hours and forty-five minutes. During the period of 24–31 March, a total of 60,000 vehicles passed over the pontoons.

Patton's first 'hasty' venture across the Rhine had thus long been planned, but for a different date. There was nothing impromptu about it: what had happened was the assault day had secretly been brought forward. The Third Army crossings were described as 'improvised' to contrast with those of Twenty-First Army Group, which had taken as long to plan, were just as detailed, but were more lavishly supported, and widely publicised.

This was the real reason for Eisenhower's earlier insistence on Third Army's increased self-promotion – to be able to talk up Patton's understanding of tempo and gut instinct, in contrast to the Britishers' more 'studious and plodding approach' further north – and it worked. Building on Patton's reputation for swift manoeuvre, most recently his no-notice, ninety-degree shift of axis towards Bastogne during the Ardennes crisis, US Secretary of War Henry L. Stimson (who had held Patton's fate in his hands after the 1943 slapping incidents), announced, 'We gave Monty everything he asked for – paratroopers, assault boats and even the Navy, and by God, Patton has crossed the Rhine!'[22]

At Twelfth Army Group's morning briefing on 23 March, Lieutenant Colonel Richard R. Stillman, Patton's liaison officer, announced proudly to Bradley and his staff, 'Without benefit of aerial bombing, ground smoke, artillery preparation or airborne assistance, the Third Army at 22:00 hours, Thursday evening, 22 March, crossed the Rhine River.' His twenty-five words amounted to a seamless dig at Montgomery's exhaustive preparations for his crossings that very evening. Bradley in his 1951 memoirs played up the mythology of Patton 'crashing the Rhine', allegedly receiving a phone call on the evening of the 23rd.

' "Brad, don't tell anyone, but I'm across."

"Well, I'll be damned – you mean across the Rhine?"

"Sure am," he replied. "I sneaked a division over last night. But there are so few Krauts around here they don't know it yet. So don't make any announcement – we'll keep it secret until we see how it goes." '

Later, Patton changed his mind and phoned Bradley back.

' "Brad," he shouted, and his treble voice trembled, "for God's sake tell the world we're across. I want the world to know Third Army made it before Monty starts across." '[23]

Over the next few days Patton's air support, the P-47s and P-51s of XIX Tactical Air Command, slaughtered the Luftwaffe trying to attack his bridges. One of Patton's staff recorded, 'In one encounter, eight P-51s pounced on fifty Junkers-88s and got eleven. In another, P-47s jumped a flock of Focke-Wulf-190s and downed eight out of nine. These German planes are as good if not better than ours, but pilots are apparently untrained and unfit to equal our by-now battle-tested youngsters.'[24] The killing power of American aircraft was considerable and illustrated the quick advances in aeronautical design. In 1940 the maximum load of most twin-engined bombers ranged between 2,000 and 4,000 pounds, yet five years later each single-engined P-47 was capable of delivering up to 2,500 pounds of destruction over Germany. However, it is also worth observing that American aircraft 'kill' claims of the era were wildly exaggerated when compared with Luftwaffe archives and are more accurate when *halved*. Yet the point about the German inexperienced pilots was accurate.

Subsequently, Third Army would make five more runs at the Rhine. Before daylight on Palm Sunday, 25 March, Middleton's VIII Corps arranged for the 87th 'Golden Acorn' Division to cross at two sites, six and twelve miles upriver from Koblenz. Both were in the Rhine gorge, with its picturesque castles, and 300- to 400-foot cliffs overlooking swift, tumbling water. At Rhens, alert German observers launched flares and brought down a torrent of fire from machine-guns, mortars, 20mm flak guns, and artillery on two of the 347th Infantry's launch sites. The defenders may have been alerted to a future crossing by the testimony of John C. Schweitzer, Third Platoon, Company 'A' of the 35th Combat Engineers, who on reaching the far bank saw that 'Some crazy SOB had already crossed the river and painted "Kilroy Was Here" on the cement wall'. [25] Aware that the division's simultaneous effort upriver at Boppard was successful and seeing the damp morning air in the gorge was preventing his smokescreen from rising above the water, John L. McKee, the 87th's assistant division commander, ordered abandonment at Rhens, which had cost seven killed and 110 wounded.

At the 87th's other crossing site of Boppard, the terrain remained challenging with its high cliffs, but the defenders were weaker, even if equipped with mobile 20mm flak-wagons, whose bark turned out to be worse than their bite. Richard Manchester, of Company 'K', who carried a wireless set for his company commander, recollected, 'We began to cautiously filter down through the moonlit streets toward the shingled beach. Around midnight, we climbed into small metal boats. With no explanation, engineers handed paddles to men with no training in how to use them. We set out to cross in bright moonlight. We were on the river without cover or concealment. Nothing happened. We were not fired on. Apparently the 20mm guns could not be depressed enough to fire on our boats.' Manchester continued, 'We landed in some confusion, separated by current and timing. An embankment gave us cover. I saw one dead GI lying on his side, his face covered with a film of dust. I didn't recognize him. Dead Germans didn't bother me, but I never wanted to look at our own men.'[26] This would have been the only man from Colonel Douglas Sugg's 345th Infantry recorded killed on that day, while seventeen were wounded. Six LCVPs operated here, moving 5,000 men and four hundred vehicles into action.

The following day was the turn of Middleton's other division, Thomas D. Finley's 89th, which had only entered combat at the beginning of the Saar campaign. This action would mark their fourteenth day of combat. Designating the 89th his main effort, Middleton augmented Finley with a group of three artillery battalions, and placed the 1107th Engineer Combat Group under his command, along with the 748th Tank, 811th Tank Destroyer and 550th Anti-Aircraft Battalions. Altogether, Finley's force numbered well over 23,000 men. He had watched the 87th's progress at Boppard, whose site he hoped to use, but seeing the congestion and continued German fire, concluded he would have to make his own assault crossing, the division's first. Still within the Rhine gorge, Finley had been allocated two sites, one at Sankt Goar, twenty miles upstream from Koblenz, the other at Oberwesel, another ten miles beyond. This sector finds the Rhine at its most attractive, overlooked by romantic castles perched on high cliffs, and the destination of every river cruise. The waters narrow to 275 yards, as the torrent twists and turns where it has found flaws in the natural rock.

From their battlements, feudal river barons once exacted tolls from merchants forced to sail beneath their gaze. They belonged to the days of *Ritterlichkeit*, the medieval ideals of chivalry, unthinkingly emulated by their descendants under the Third Reich, but chivalrous no longer. The 89th would launch in the middle of the night, with two regiments in the assault, the 354th from Sankt Goar, their immediate objective being its sister town, Sankt Goarshausen, directly across the river. The latter is dominated by heights reaching up to six hundred feet and its twin Renaissance castles, literally named *Katz* and *Maus*, home to many an artillery observer and machine-gunner. The 353rd would put in the second attack upriver at Oberwesel, with Finley keeping his remaining regiment, the 355th, in reserve.

For some, the discomfort started long before reaching Sankt Goar. Phil Leveque of the 354th Infantry remembered coming under fire on the march up. 'The day before there was scuttlebutt [rumour] whether the Krauts would use poison gas on us. That thought was chilling enough. We marched about twenty miles, the last five through a fir forest with trees about thirty feet tall. German Artillery fired tree bursts where the shrapnel exploded downwards on us. This kept up for about two hours. When we got to the last ridge overlooking the Rhine, they shelled our mess tent at suppertime. That was a bad day, but the next was even worse.'[27]

From Burg Rheinfels, Sankt Goar's own medieval schloss, General Finley had observed his own infantry tramp down steep, twisting trails to the river's edge, and noted his division's trucks, bumper to bumper, creep along the narrow, winding roads transporting pontoons, bridge components and assault boats through the town. After dark, crews put blackout hoods over their headlamps and drove in the light of narrow slits, called 'cat's eyes', but flow of men and machines remained unabated. When they heard their own 155mm 'Long Tom' cannon, hurling ninety-pound shells to some distant spot fourteen miles away, GIs knew they were nearing the river.

In the small hours, Finley watched helplessly as Colonel Robert C. Aloe's 354th Infantry had an even rougher time than those at Rhens. From 02:00 his men came under intense fire even before launching their boats. Flames flickered through the night from a barge full of oil-soaked straw anchored midstream and ignited by German tracer. Riddled with gunfire, assault boats sank, while others were swept away in the cascade that raced through the ravine. Company 'E' lost its commander, Paul O. Wofford, and his first sergeant, when flak targeted their boat. 'An eighty-eight shell wiped out three boats and an engineer launching crew on the beach at Sankt Goar,' noted the division's history.[28]

Oscar Friedensohn, with Company 'C', 168th Combat Engineers, had already unlaced his boots for ease of kicking off, likewise shedding his heavy equipment and cartridge belt in case of capsize. 'Squad by squad, the infantry came down the steep hill onto the street,' he remembered. 'Each stopped at our stack of boats and lifted the uppermost one down. They carried them to the edge of the water. I dropped my equipment and rifle in the bottom, right under me.' His boatload of three engineers and twelve infantrymen cast off, battling with the current and trying to avoid the tracers they saw lashing out from the German side. Then they were hit.

'Seconds after the explosive force ripped into us, an unworldly silence covered the boat,' Friedensohn recalled. 'The firing continued, along with the deadly light-streams. We barely heard the noise; it came from a distant world. Our world had shrunk once again to the few still left aboard this small boat.' They drifted onto the far shore. 'We all lay there – three uninjured infantrymen, including a lieutenant, and two wounded engineers. Ten of the thirteen doughs who had piled into my boat and one of three engineers were gone. Some bodies were in the boat, but most had been blown away by the hellish fire or had drowned in the river, to be listed as missing. We, however, were temporarily safe, at least from the guns above us.'[29]

The 89th Division's history picked up the story. 'As frail craft slipped into midstream, German flares floodlit the gorge from shore to shore. Camouflaged 20mms slammed shells at the oncoming boats, tore paddles from the men's hands, blew one boat to bits and tossed the doughs into the water. Somehow, the assault craft kept coming. Men swam or waded ashore. Reorganizing quickly on the waterfront, they crawled up the stone embankments, carved out a toe-hold and hung on. Boatload after boatload fought their way across the open water, battling drift as well as Nazis. When one of the leading vessels was sunk by machine-gun fire, Private Joseph Martin swam through the bullet-sprayed water, applying tourniquets to the wounded, his action saving the lives of several marooned for six hours on the German side. Yet, by noon, approximately five battalions were across.'[30]

One battalion peeled left (north) to Wellmich, but bitter fighting raged in Sankt Goarshausen itself, the Germans resisting with furious determination to hold this key bridge site. Smoke generators could not be used to screen operations because the wind was in the wrong direction. It was the Second Battalion of the 354th Infantry who braved the storm of shot and shell, then methodically went to work flushing snipers and panzerfaust-men from battered buildings. Watching all from the highest point on the far side as the Rhine gleamed under a faint moon was the fabled Lorelei, a little bit of Greek mythology repackaged for the nineteenth century Germans. Allegedly a beautiful maiden who, jilted by her lover, threw herself into the narrowest and fiercest part of the Rhine, her angry spirit remained, singing her siren songs and luring watermen to their deaths on the rocks below.[31]

The bridgehead was only deemed secure when the Stars and Stripes fluttered the next day over Lorelei's rock, overlooking the most dangerous bend of the whole Rhine. Perhaps not best pleased by the air strike executed by a squadron of P-51 Mustangs aimed at Germans in her vicinity, Lorelei exacted a heavy toll. Most of the 89th's casualties (twenty-nine killed, 146 missing, 102 wounded) were suffered by the 354th Regiment beneath her gaze.

Eventually Friedensohn recalled being rescued by a DUKW which bore him back to safety. His commander reported that 'eight boats landed at the far shore. The fate of the balance will never be correctly known. At 08:00, when it was relieved, Company 'C' consisted of six men, three wounded.'[32] As soon as Sankt Goarshausen was cleared, the 1107th Engineer Combat Group worked through the night and following day under artillery fire to erect a bridge. By 23:00 on 27 March, the span was completed, and an unstoppable snake of men, vehicles and supplies slithered across to exploit the bridgehead and spearhead the 89th's drive beyond the Rhine.

Upriver at the other crossing site, Oberwesel, on another right-angled bend in the river, amid more Gothic castles and vineyards, the 89th launched their twin assault, using the 353rd Infantry. Although the resistance was determined, it was not as fierce as at Sankt Goar, and the flow of assault craft never stumbled. Soon after, fifty DUKWs of the 453rd Amphibious Truck Company ferried successive waves over, even though the river remained under small arms fire, lethal for the un-armoured amphibious trucks.

Each packed with eighteen fully loaded infantrymen, the DUKWs helped shift the rest of the 89th across the Rhine within forty-eight hours, some working at Sankt Goar also. They proved a popular ride with GIs, coping with the current and often moving faster than the German gunners' aim. Although there was no opportunity to use landing craft at Sankt Goar, six were transported to Oberwesel, shuttling all the 89th's vehicles across, as Ed Quick, with Battery 'B' of the 340th Field Artillery, recorded. 'As we reached the crest of a hill and looked down into the valley, I saw a crudely whitewashed sign on the side of a building. "See the Rhine and Leave Your Skull There," with a skull and cross bones beneath to magnify the unsettling message. We passed several gray-painted landing craft beside the road on large flatbed trucks, accompanied by Navy personnel in blue dungarees and hats. We shouted jibes at the sailors, pointing out to them the general direction of the ocean and asking them if they were lost.'

Quick's battalion queued to load their vehicles and 105mm howitzers. 'The current was very swift and carried us rapidly downstream as our propellers churned the muddy water, driving us forward to the paved sloping bank on the far side. Our landing was without incident, but as we climbed the ramp to the village, we saw a 20 mm gun, just silenced, emplaced in a railroad tunnel, and passed a dead German soldier, lying on his back at the top of the slope. We could see the black and white cylinders of riverboat steamship funnels rising out of the water, sunk by the Germans to deny us their use.'[33]

From Oberwesel the lead battalion had soon taken the heights opposite, and a second had swung right (south) to wrest Kaub, on the Rhine, from German control. By 15:00 the 353rd's reserves and combat supplies had landed at Kaub, expanding the beachhead by five miles. As was so often the case, the German defences proved to be a thin crust that, once penetrated, had nothing behind them in the way of fixed defences or reserves. This was illustrated by General Finley's wisdom in forming an all-arms mobile grouping, Task Force Johnson, using the reserves VIII Corps had given him. It included an infantry battalion, two companies of tanks, two of tank destroyers, a cannon company, with platoons of engineers, air defence and mortars. On 26 March, by prior arrangement, he sent it across the 87th's bridge at Boppard, after which it turned right, passed through Sankt Goar, then struck eastwards, and by noon on 29 March, Task Force Johnson had entered Bad Schwalbach, thirty miles away.

The front had burst wide open, Finley handling his division extraordinarily well in his first major independent action. It drew Patton's praise, with Middleton, VIII Corps Commander, noting that 'For a green outfit, many of whose men were under fire for the first time, this was a tough assignment'. He continued, 'The almost insurmountable obstacles of terrain would have tested a veteran outfit. It was all the more outstanding when executed by a new division, relatively untried in combat.'[34] By 2 April these two divisions, the 87th and 89th, had cleared the area between Koblenz and Wiesbaden, a fifty-mile front, and taken 3,000 prisoners.[35]

Patton's third corps, Walker's XX, also made an assault over the water. In this case it was Horace L. McBride's 80th 'Blue Ridge' Division who were alerted on 26 March 'to force crossings of the Rhine and Main rivers and seize bridgeheads, and this being accomplished, to continue the attack to the North and Northeast'.[36] The division, which had been in action since early August 1944, 'jumped off', in the terminology of the day, two days later at 01:00, when Colonel Henry G. Fisher's 317th Infantry paddled the Rhine from Mainz to the far shore suburbs of Kastel and Kostheim. The initial wave in twenty assault boats took heavy casualties from small arms and flak detachments. At 03:30, Fisher suspended operations due to the heavy incoming fire destroying his boats. However, Naval Reserve Ensign Oscar Miller did not get the suspension order and sent his first Higgins boat (LCVP) across.

As luck would have it, the craft landed five hundred yards downriver and met no resistance. Other boats followed and within three hours, the entire 317th Infantry – some 3,500 men – had leapt ashore without casualties. With daylight, German artillery soon found its mark on the launch site, scoring a direct hit on a bulldozer, demolishing several trucks, and killing US Navy Lieutenant Vincent Avallone, the navy's only fatality during the entire Third Army crossing. Thereafter, the ferocity of the opposition ebbed during the morning and Colonel James S. Luckett's 318th Regiment, acting as divisional reserve, also crossed via LCVPs and LCMs, into the bridgehead established by their colleagues.[37] The 80th Divisional War Diary noted 7,556 prisoners captured during the crossing period of 23–31 March.[38]

Apart from the assault waves, the reality for those traversing the river was often far less dramatic, as Roy Altenbach, a soldier from a German-speaking family in Sheboygan, Wisconsin, recollected. He had crossed on 27 March, as part of Third Army's large 'tail', supporting its 'teeth', assigned to the 47th Medium Maintenance Company, 22nd Ordnance Battalion, a XII Corps unit. Unsung heroes of the war, his company maintained vehicles, from jeeps and staff cars to trucks and tanks, but also weapons, ranging from pistols, machine-guns and mortars to 155mm field pieces, watches, binoculars and optical sights.[39] Altenbach observed 'the landing boats on the sides of the road, on big trailers, with US Navy sailors. For a long time, we had looked forward to seeing the Rhine, but all we glimpsed were barrels spewing out white smoke that hid everything, save the back of the vehicle ahead of us and the water between the pontoons.'[40]

Patton had earlier traversed the bridge at Nierstein with his aides, Charles Codman and Alexander Stiller. Halfway over, he halted his command car and, as Codman recorded, ordered, 'Time out for a short halt.' The general exited the vehicle, surveyed the current, unbuttoned his fly, and stated, 'I have been looking forward to this for a long time.' Two official photographs were taken of 'Old Blood and Guts' adding to the water level of the Rhine before continuing on his way.[41] Meanwhile, Altenbach, the ordnance battalion GI, had continued on to Darmstadt, arriving about noon. 'We stayed in the Locomotive Works and slept in the office building,' he recollected. 'There were locomotives in the shop, and most of them were shot up. At the railyard, hundreds of civilians were looting boxcars on the tracks; I don't know what they were taking, but they looked like a bunch of ants moving all over the place.'[42]

After consolidating on the east bank, XX Corps secured Mainz, where Patton's logisticians had decided to construct a railway bridge, because of the pre-existing, if badly damaged, railway arteries that coincided with Third Army's main supply route.[43] Due to the excellent undamaged road network heading east, Third Army engineers assembled five spans at Mainz, of which the largest was a 2,223-foot structure, named after the late President, who had died two days earlier. The President Roosevelt Bridge was opened by the Third Army commander on 14 April, twenty-two days before the end. When offered a pair of scissors to cut the ceremonial ribbon, the response was pure Patton:

'What d'you take me for? A goddamned tailor? Goddammit, give me a bayonet!'

(*Above*): In Operation *Varsity*, the 6th British and 17th US airborne divisions landed early on 24 March. Here a British glider passes over American paratroops, illustrating the perfect cohesion of the two forces. (*Below*): Winston Churchill arrived to witness the spectacle personally. The following day he crossed to the far side of the Rhine with General Bill Simpson of the 9th US Army. As he clambered across the ruined Büderich bridge at Wesel, aged seventy, he came under hostile fire. He was furious when Simpson curtailed the visit.

9

Montgomery

The first thing the twenty-six officers and 590 other ranks of Lieutenant Colonel Jeff Nicklin's 1st Canadian Parachute Battalion, based in England, knew of 'bouncing the Rhine' was after they had returned from seven days of leave on 7 March 1945. Then they were told the mission of 6th British Airborne Division – to seize the town of Hamminkeln, five miles east of the river, and bridges in the vicinity. Additionally, they were to take the Diersfordterwald, a wooded ridge overlooking the assault crossing routes. With the American 17th Airborne, they would land north and south of this high ground, deny its use to their opponents, and enable their colleagues in the assault divisions to lunge eastwards.

Major General Eric Bols' 6th Airborne Division were detailed to land on five zones. On one of them, measuring 800 by 1,000 yards, Brigadier James Hill's 3rd Parachute Brigade, including the Canadians, would arrive during a six-minute drop. They were to secure the northern end of the Diersfordterwald, a vital role, they were told, to ensure the ground troops were not confined to a sliver of muddy riverbank and there annihilated. The Canucks were also warned the area was well defended by their opposite numbers, the 7th Fallschirmjäger Division.

They were wakened at two in the morning, enplaned in thirty-five C-47s, crewed by the American IX Troop Carrier Command, and by 07:30 had left from Chipping Ongar airfield in Essex, twenty miles northeast of London, for their two-hour flight to Germany. 'They were the scruffiest looking guys, with baseball hats and cigars,' recalled Major Richard Hilborn of his US aircrew, 'but they were awfully good. They radiated matter-of-fact confidence, well suited to the fleeting but vital relationship between parachutists and aircrew.' Their journey across the Channel and to the Rhine was undramatic; many recalled the clear, blue sky just before the drop.[1]

Eisenhower had long promised Montgomery that his, the northernmost crossings of the Rhine, would be SHAEF's main effort. The Supreme Commander later observed that Montgomery's force for this task, including its airborne component and Simpson's Ninth Army, totalled twenty-nine divisions and seven separate brigades, of which fifteen formations would be in the assault: more than the victor of El Alamein had ever led before. Although the outline planning for Operation *Plunder*, the amphibious assault, and *Varsity*, its airborne counterpart, had begun in October 1944, the process was interrupted by the Ardennes, and only concluded on 21 February 1945 by Dempsey and his chief, while Crerar was busy with *Veritable*.

To call the operation elaborate would be an understatement. Second only in ambition and scale to D-Day, as well as its substantial multinational airborne element, *Plunder* included Canadian ground forces on the left and Americans on the right. Devised as the final stepping stone to victory, after which his command would dissolve, Montgomery intended it to encapsulate every tactical and operational technique and lesson that his Twenty-First Army Group had learned since D-Day. With a recorded 1,020,581 personnel under his command, Montgomery could do whatever he wished to leap the Rhine and vanquish his foe.[2]

Reflecting the fact that his was SHAEF's main effort over the Rhine, he emptied his entire 'toy cupboard' and used everything, because he could. The undertaking was also designed to be a showcase of Montgomery's operational technique, crafted and developed since before El Alamein in 1942. *Plunder* and *Varsity* were also to be Monty's swansong. With the end of the war in sight and at the age of fifty-eight, his days of command in the field would soon be over. He intended the Rhine, rather than the desert or D-Day, to linger in the minds of post-war soldiers, politicians, allies – and historians – as a vindication of his, and the British, way of conducting war.

Due to the 'Shadow of the Somme', a commonly held interwar view that any future conflict would kill another generation of British youth, Montgomery's way of doing battle was extremely risk-averse.

The Bible-reading son of a bishop sincerely wished to inflict on his own men as few casualties as possible, though he had his own future reputation in mind as much as the impact on his nation. He saw how former premier Lloyd George in his memoirs had cast Field Marshal Sir Douglas Haig as the butcher of the 1914–18 generation and had no wish to be perceived in a similar light. This in turn would give rise to Montgomery's many post-war writings justifying his actions, for he was also aware Haig left no literary legacy in his own defence.

Yet Allied assessments after *Veritable* indicated that the forces opposing Montgomery's army group had already lost around 50,000 prisoners, as a result of the Canadian-run campaign and excluding the switch of reserves to meet the threat at Remagen. Along with the 185,000 captured by Twelfth Army Group and the 47,000 taken by Devers' GIs and Frenchmen, the Germans in the West had suffered 282,000 captured and 100,000 killed and wounded just defending forward of the Rhine in 1945. All were avoidable, had Hitler permitted his forces to withdraw to the eastern bank. In the light of these German losses, Bradley, Hodges and Patton derided the overcautious nature of British planning, but Montgomery was wedded to the techniques which had worked for him before and would not, probably could not, adapt to changed circumstances. The Allied casualties suffered during the mudfest of *Veritable*, totalling 10,348 Britons and 5,303 Canadians, plus 7,300 American losses in *Grenade*, also shaped his thinking.[3]

For the Anglo-Canadian operation, Second Army assembled 32,000 vehicles, including 2,000 tanks and 400 tank transporters, to move their armour forward.[4] The latter belonged to British and Canadian armoured delivery regiments who fought an unsung war, shifting Sherman and Churchill tanks to the front with their Scammell Pioneer and American-built Diamond-T fifty-foot-long tractor-and-trailer combinations. This was in contrast to the Germans, whose panzers clattered everywhere under their own steam, their normal method of conveyance, by rail, made impossible by Allied air attack. Hence the remarkable post-war conclusion that more German armour was lost through mechanical breakdown, abandonment or sabotage, than in field combat. This was especially true of the later models, Tigers and Panthers, not designed for long road journeys, whose engines struggled with poor-quality spare parts and synthetic fuel, and whose crews were less well trained in maintenance.

However, that Horrocks' XXX Corps was augmented for *Plunder* with the addition of 8,000 sappers led by his Chief Engineer, Brigadier C.B. 'Splosh' Jones, should alert us to the fact that Second British Army's preparations were really no more elaborate than their counterparts at US First, Third and Ninth Armies, for whom similar numbers of engineers had been assembled to support each assaulting corps. The 118,000 tons of stores and thirty-six Royal Navy landing craft assembled by Second Army compares favourably with the 138,000 tons and LCVPs assembled by Ninth Army, whose two assaulting divisions were each supported by 9,000 combat engineers. Additionally, Dempsey stockpiled 22,000 tons of bridging stores, including 25,000 wooden pontoons, 2,000 assault boats, 650 storm boats, 260 miles of steel-wire rope and eighty miles of cable along with 60,000 tons of ammunition, beyond normal daily usage.

Captain George G. Blackburn of the 4th Field Regiment, Royal Canadian Artillery, noted in his sector that, 'due to the far bank of the Rhine being somewhat higher than ours, exposing most of the rolling open country to German observation, it is necessary to lay down, right up until D-day on 24 March, a dawn-to-dusk smokescreen along a thirty-mile stretch of river. Our smoke generators use two hundred tons of zinc chloride and fog oil per day to mask our preparations, which require constant adjustments for wind and atmospheric conditions.'

Before the operation, Lieutenant Peter White with the 4th King's Own Scottish Borderers, an infantry battalion of the 52nd Lowland Division, recalled special 'noise' parties on his side of the river 'had done their level best to tempt the Germans into firing and giving away their gun locations and strongpoints'.[5] Artillery commanders had complained that an airborne operation before the crossing would hamstring the 3,411 British and Canadian guns, plus 2,070 cannon belonging to Ninth Army, supporting the ground assault.[6] Hence *Varsity* being triggered *after* the amphibious attacks, on the morning of the 24th, when paratroopers and glider forces could use wireless to correct and avoid the fall of shot from Allied guns on the west bank.

Plunder's artillery support began at 17:00 on the 23rd, using every conceivable weapon in British and Canadian arsenals. These included super-heavy 9.5-inch, heavy 8-inch and 7.2-inch guns, medium 5.5-inch and 4.5-inch howitzers, 3.7-inch and 40mm anti-aircraft guns, American 155mm 'Long Tom' cannon, 25-pounder field and 17-pounder anti-tank guns, the innovative 3-inch 'Land Mattress' rocket batteries mounted on trailers, 75mm and 76mm guns mounted on tanks and tank destroyers, 4.2-inch mortars and Vickers .303-inch medium machine-guns.[7]

The schedule was precise with a list of targets to be worked over at various times and rates of fire. Ranges varied, Captain Blackburn noting 'the 9.5s throwing their 360-pound missiles 25,000 yards (fourteen miles) into the Reich; 8-inch guns unloading 240-pound shells up to 18,000 yards (ten miles) away; right down to Land Mattress rockets saturating small areas 7,000 yards (four miles) distant; 4.2-inch mortars dropping high explosive shells onto positions 4,400 yards (2.5 miles) across the river; and the Cameron Highlanders of Ottawa Machine Gun Regiment, with their powerful Vickers machine-guns, chattering with their two-mile range'.[8]

Predesignated ground targets included German bunkers dug in on the riverbank, the 4th Canadian Light Anti-Aircraft Regiment alone firing 13,896 rounds in flat trajectory and their sister 8th Light Ack-Ack wearing out forty-three barrels in expending 2,400 rounds per gun. Equally wearing on their gun barrels, tank battalions were employed in a role for which they were never designed, loosing off intermittent salvoes reaching a rate of two and a half rounds per minute, totalling 1,600 shells per tank.[9]

Voice communication was impossible, Private Glen Tomlin, with the Highland Light Infantry of Canada, a battalion with the 3rd Canuck Division, observing the 'awful noise, the ground just shook, everything shook. The guns started off and then you heard the shells come over, and they whistle different sounds for different shells. As the guns increased their tempo, the sound became a continuous roar.'[10] So rapid was the fire that Bombardier John Foster of the 33rd Field Regiment, whose job was to manually load 25-pounder shells into the breech of his weapon, proudly recalled being stopped by a passing German prisoner who 'asked me in fluent English if our guns were automatic.'[11]

The 13th Royal Horse Artillery, whose members were City of London volunteers from the Honourable Artillery Company (HAC), Britain's oldest regiment, had a ten-hour schedule of uninterrupted firing, recording 16,800 rounds fired from their Sexton 25-pounder self-propelled guns; 'the noise and pressure on the gun position was unbelievable. A normal regimental target might last twenty minutes, but from dawn to dusk non-stop was a really tough programme. The two gun position officers alternated one hour on, one off as the need to sustain pinpoint accuracy required acute concentration.'[12] A 52nd Lowland officer remembered the aftermath of 'a lovely dawn that greeted the tired eyes of the gunners and glinted its first light off thousands of hot, smoking gun barrels which had so out-thundered the mythical German Rhine gods'.[13]

This was the largest Montgomery-signature bombardment of the war and reflected his understanding of the mass use of artillery from his days on the planning staff of Alexander Hamilton-Gordon's IX Corps at Messines and Ypres in 1917, another legacy of the First World War. Since then, accuracy had improved immeasurably, aided by well-trained Forward Observation Officers with tactical wirelesses, who could initiate and switch off various kinds of shoots at a moment's notice. Under their eyes, and those of Air Observation Officers in their spotter planes, gunfire could be 'walked onto targets' providing instant destruction, against which the Germans had little defence.

Montgomery also concentrated extra guns in six British and two Canadian AGRAs (Army Group, Royal Artillery), which were switched to wherever Montgomery, Crerar and Dempsey wished. They controlled all non-divisional artillery, normally supported a single corps, possessed their own workshops and had been devised by Brooke, a former gunner, in the months before D-Day. Of these, five AGRAs were used for *Plunder*, which exceeded all of Montgomery's previous opening bombardments. At El Alamein he had used 980 guns, while 1,060 had supported his Eighth Army in the Liri Valley in Italy at the opening of the fourth Cassino battle. Weeks earlier for *Veritable*, he had directed Crerar to muster 1,034 guns (excluding anti-tank and light anti-aircraft guns) for the opening cannonade.[14]

Additionally, Allied heavy bombers scattered 1,100 tons of munitions over Wesel, freezing all movement of German reserves, hampering their ability to communicate, and destroying twenty-three flak positions near the drop zones and all known headquarters. Before the first Allied soldier crossed the river, the ferocious air and ground bombardment had 'shocked many Germans in the vicinity into incontinence'.[15] For the city of Rees, this had been their eighteenth raid since 1 February, where *Veritable* and *Blockbuster* had been fought just over the river.

From the Commando headquarters opposite, Alan Moorehead, the Australian-born war correspondent for the *Daily Express*, watched the bombing of Wesel by 201 Lancasters at 22:30. 'As we watched the pathfinder came in, a single hurrying black moth in the air, and he shot his clusters of red flares into the centre of the town, which meant – how acutely one felt it – that Wesel had about ten minutes to live. Then the Lancasters filled the air with roaring and great black stretches of the skyline simply detached themselves from the earth and mounted slowly upwards. The uncontrolled savagery of the bombing went on until the sky to the east was lit with a red glow, spattered here and there with the chandelier light of flares and puff of anti-aircraft shells'.[16] The raid lasted just fifteen minutes, synchronised to coincide with the arrival of Commandos, who recalled being 'lifted bodily by the shock waves and thudded back, winded by the violence'.[17] Peter White of the King's Own Scottish Borderers sensed the 'electric feeling of excitement and confidence in the air, symbolized by a throbbing stream of our bombers which had sailed over to empty an avalanche of bombs on Wesel'.[18]

Plunder's assault phase was subdivided into three sequential missions. To the north, from 21:00 on the 23rd, in Operation *Turnscrew*, Horrocks' XXX Corps (Guards Armoured, 3rd British, 3rd Canadian, 43rd Wessex and 51st Highland Divisions, 8th Armoured Brigade, 4 and 5 AGRAs) was to assault Rees, with 3rd Canadian securing the home bank. They would be spearheaded by Major General Tom Rennie's Highlanders with 9th Canadian Brigade under command, and the rest of 3rd British, the Wessex and the Guards Armoured waiting behind to exploit.

In the centre, at 02:00 on the 24th, Neil Ritchie's XII Corps (7th Armoured, 15th Scottish, 52nd Lowland, 53rd Welsh Divisions, 4th and 34th Armoured and 1st Commando Brigades, 3, 8 and 9 AGRAs) would assault in Operation *Torchlight*, with Major General 'Tiny' Barber's 15th Division in the lead. With the Lowlanders in possession of the home bank, they would cross from Xanten, midway between Rees and Wesel.

As soon as a Class 40 Bailey bridge had spanned the Rhine, the 7th Armored Division would clatter their way over the steel box girder components all capable of being lifted by six men, whence its armoured vehicles would punch their way out of the bridgehead.

On Dempsey's right boundary in Operation *Widgeon*, 1,600 men from Brigadier Derek Mills-Roberts' 1st Commando Brigade (landing from north to south, 6 and 3 Army Commandos, 46 and 45 Royal Marine Commandos) would jab at the important communications and anti-aircraft centre of Wesel from 22:00 on the 23rd. Though its pre-war bridges were at the bottom of the Rhine, attention was focused on Wesel, because its road and rail network offered unique access into Germany. To the south lay 30th and 79th Divisions of Ninth Army, from 02:00 staging *Flashpoint*, examined shortly.

Intended as the southernmost of three separate prongs in Dempsey's chase across the north German plain, the 11th Armoured Division and 6th Guards Tank Brigade of General Evelyn Barker's VIII Corps would play no part in the assault, waiting instead to lead the breakout. It was to advance on the right of Ritchie's XII Corps and collect 6th Airborne Division and the Commando Brigade as it passed by. Major General 'Pip' Roberts' 11th Armoured Division had just been equipped with the 32-ton Comet cruiser tank, mounting a 17-pounder gun, which proved a good match for heavy German tanks, being adequately armoured, and sporting a far lower profile than the Sherman.

To the north, other units in the First Canadian Army would advance over the Dutch border and clear northern Holland, including Stanisław Maczek's 1st Polish and the 5th Canadian Armoured Divisions, and 1st Canadian, 5th British and 49th West Riding Infantry Divisions, and 1st Canadian Armoured Brigade.

First over the Rhine in *Turnscrew* were the four assault battalions of the Highland Division, comprising the 5th/7th Gordons of 153rd Brigade, and 7th Black Watch, 7th Argylls and 1st Black Watch of 154th Brigade. Though the follow-on battalions had to manage with the puny, much-despised storm boats, the first wave crossed in 150 Buffaloes, crewed by 4th Royal Tank Regiment and the Northamptonshire Yeomanry, which illustrated the flexibility of the Royal Armoured Corps, for both regiments had manned tanks earlier in the war. They were supported by swimming tanks of the Staffordshire Yeomanry, whose armour had last swum in the clearing of the Scheldt supporting the Lowland Division. Three of 'C' Squadron's tanks, whose canvas side screens were pierced by shrapnel, sank like stones, their crews escaping. There was almost no opposition to the crossing by 153rd and 154th Brigades, or during its immediate landfall, but the 8th Fallschirmjäger Division contested nearby Rees and the vicinity for over twenty-four hours.

By 26 March, XXX Corps' first bridge was complete, whereupon the 3rd Canadian Division surged across. However, earlier on the first morning, Major General Rennie had driven down to the river to assess the progress of his Highland Division. As air whistled with the noise of incoming mortar rounds, everyone bent down to shield their bodies. As the dust cleared, Rennie's ADC saw his boss still hunched over in his Jeep and shook him. 'Are you all right, Sir?' There was no response. The invincible Rennie, taken prisoner with his division at St Valéry in 1940, but escaping nine days later, who had fought under Montgomery at Alamein, on Sicily, and commanded the latter's old formation, 3rd Division, on D-Day, was dead. His passing profoundly shocked Dempsey, his beloved Highlanders and Montgomery. He died as many would wish to go, in his hour of victory, felled by the most common killer of the final campaign, a mortar round.

In the south, as Alan Moorehead was looking across to Wesel, the guns suddenly lifted their bombardment at 22:00 and 'the Commandos had launched their armoured Buffaloes.'[19] Here the Rhine narrows to around three hundred yards, and the first across were swimmers from No. 5 Combined Operations Pilotage Party (COPP), who had earlier reconnoitred the east bank for landing positions in the bright moonlight. On their advice, Mills-Roberts chose seemingly unsuitable sites to land, confident the element of surprise would be worth the inconvenience, sending his men off with the rousing 'Never in the history of warfare have so many guns supported so few men. When you go in tonight, cut hell out of them!'[20]

After blacking their faces and receiving the traditional issue of rum and biscuits, No. 6 Commando were taken over by amphibious Buffaloes, crewed by the Royal Engineers' 77th Assault Squadron. The crossing took only three and a half minutes, but much of the brigade had to rely on the tiny wooden storm boats that carried five or six fully equipped men and two crew, manned by the engineers' 84th Field Company. Among the sixty-five prisoners taken in the first few moments, one recalled, 'We couldn't see anything properly. The noise was terrible, and we were blinded by the flashes. We thought you had landed tanks and couldn't understand where all the men had come from.'[21]

Both forms of transport hit problems. Of twenty-four employed, one Buffalo was struck, with flames shooting fifteen feet into the air killing nine men. Dave Morris of 45 RM Commando recalled it 'got a direct hit that lit up the river like a beacon.'[22] One storm boat was overladen and sank, spilling men into the current. Those with rucksacks on their backs instead of carrying them while on board, drowned with the weight. The Second-in-Command of 6 Commando survived and swam across. Given to occasionally wearing a monocle, the *Daily Mirror* duly reported 'Monocled Major Swims the Rhine'. In the aftermath of the recent air raid, Mills-Roberts wrote that his maps were useless. 'Wesel had been *over-bombed*, the streets were unrecognizable. Many of the buildings were mere mounds of rubble. Huge craters abounded and into these flowed water mains and sewers, accompanied by escapes of flaming gas.' Lieutenant Colonel A.D. Lewis of 6 Commando observed, 'Luckily the opposition was fairly feeble. The Germans were stunned. All the fight had been taken out of them by the aerial attack. I can remember going down to a cellar to establish my HQ and finding seventeen German soldiers, all lying in their bunks.'[23]

However, not all the defenders had taken cover or been killed by the bombs and shelling. At one stage, Mills-Roberts paused to talk with Lieutenant Colonel Nicol Gray of 45 Royal Marine Commando, 'when a "dead" SS soldier came to life and fired a panzerfaust at the officers. The blast knocked everyone off their feet, wounding Gray, and killing two others. There was a chatter of Stens as several magazines were emptied into the German, and thereafter every corpse was given an extra squirt of lead just to make sure.'[24] Colonel Lewis discovered his headquarters was adjacent to that of the German Kommandant, Generalmajor Friedrich Deutsch, also leading the 16th Flak Division. Trapped in his bunker, 'Deutsch became very aggressive, and quite dangerous,' Lewis recalled. 'He had to be shot,' and Sergeant Major Woodcock felled him at ten yards.[25]

In *Torchlight*, the four leading battalions of 'Tiny' Barber's 15th Scottish were the last to be flung across the Rhine by Buffalo and storm boat at 02:00 on the 24th. Barber deployed 227th Brigade on his left, 44th Brigade on his right. While the 6th Royal Scots Fusiliers and 8th Royal Scots on the right attacked according to plan, elements of the 7th Fallschirmjägers put up a much tougher fight lasting into the morning, delaying Barber's left-hand pair of battalions, the 2nd Argylls and 10th Highland Light Infantry. Major B.A. Fargus, adjutant of the 8th Royal Scots, summed up the whole *Plunder* operation with his observation that its success 'was the result of detailed and competent planning and the two rehearsals, one by day, this other at night, we had all undertaken on the Maas.'[26] The 44th Brigade history thought the picture at daylight on the 24th resembled 'Henley or Oxford in Eights Week. The storm boats, rafts and Buffaloes plied back and forth with their loads, every moment landing more stuff on the east bank. The Staffordshire Yeomanry's amphibious tanks, like strange canvas boxes, dived into the water and swam slowly across, emerged on the far bank, shook themselves, deflated, and then miraculously appeared as Sherman tanks again.'[27]

The Rhine saw the first mass use of the 'Alligator/Buffalo' landing vehicles.[28] The five British regiments operating them for *Plunder*, the same number for the Americans, certainly proved their value. The correspondent Alan Moorehead acknowledged their importance, noting, 'The Buffaloes lay about in the fields in the sunshine like prehistoric monsters, their exhausted crews spreadeagled out on the grass asleep after the night's work.'[29] By early morning, before the airborne element arrived, five infantry brigades – around 15,000 men – had established themselves on the eastern shore, supported by swimming tanks, while engineers immediately set to work on the construction of three bridges, the first of which was complete before midnight that evening, with the 53rd Welsh crossing on the 26th and 7th Armoured Division the day after.

Soon, twelve pontoon bridges had been strung across the Second Army sector, including five named after the Thames spans of Lambeth, Westminster, Waterloo, Blackfriars and London, several the handiwork of Royal Canadian Engineers. The London suburbs of Tilbury, Poplar, Gravesend and Barking featured in the names of four additional ferry rafts, constructed from Bailey components. These crossings became the centre of gravity for Second Army, with three anti-aircraft brigades, 100th, 106th and 107th, defending them, as one infantry officer observed. 'Several times as we stood on watch listening to the squeak of the bridge straining against the 3½-knot stream, and the clatter of Royal Engineers working on it in the chill night air, groups of Bofors guns burst into deafening life, spitting fountains of red tracer.'[30] The durability of these spans, and a later twin-carriageway bridge at Rees, called Tyne-Tees, was such that they lasted into the 1950s, reinforced by the plentiful rubble available in Rees and Wesel.

'From a pilot's point of vantage, the Rhine must have appeared to be alive with busy water beetles, running up and down the banks and churning through the water,' thought an officer in the King's Own Scottish Borderers.[31] Soon those pilots, crewing transport aircraft and gliders, were overhead. 'Looking out the window my impression was of a very wide lake,' noted Sergeant Anderson of the Canadian Parachute Battalion. 'I have no idea what I expected, but the river was massive, cold and uninviting.' However, the remaining flak emplacements, untouched by the bombing and for three years dedicated to protecting the Ruhr, came alive.

Some gun crews had been in place so long that Allied paratroopers reported window boxes filled with flowers and vegetable patches adorning some positions. All the while, the aerial transports and tugs, mindful of the need for accuracy, flew straight and level, taking no evasive action. Major Fraser Eadie, second in command of the Canadians, observed, 'I have never been on a better drop, training or operational.' Yet the price was heavy, as his colleague Lieutenant William Jenkins recalled. 'Lying on the ground, looking up taking off my chute, I could see these things [Douglas C-47s, the twin-engined troop carrier, known as the Dakota or Skytrain] blasted all over the sky. I couldn't help but admire those guys.'[32]

Aware that most farmsteads and houses in the vicinity had been converted into small fortresses, Brigadier James Hill had advised his paratroops before the mission, 'If by chance you should happen to meet one of these Huns in person, you will treat him, gentlemen, with extreme disfavour.' However, their Fallschirmjäger opponents heeded the same advice, and during the first two hours around Hamminkeln and the Diersfordterwald both sides mauled each other. The clash was brief but exceptionally bloody, the Canadian battalion losing sixty-seven out of 475 soldiers, including its commander, Jeff Nicklin. Fate dictated that the six-foot-three football champion from Winnipeg, veteran of D-Day and the Bulge, landed atop a German position, and he was found hanging from his parachute in the upper branches of a tree, riddled with bullets. Once the fighting had died down, Alan Moorehead 'climbed into a tracked Bren carrier to contact the airborne troops. All round us, bright red and yellow parachutes lie over the fields like enormous poppies.'[33]

The German opposition across the *Plunder* and *Varsity* sector had amounted to three weak infantry divisions, although three under-strength Fallschirmjäger formations were regarded as a tougher proposition. After the war, Generalleutnant Gustav Hoehne of the 2nd Fallschirmjäger Division asserted that the morale of his men 'was fairly high and this was especially true in our Fallschirm Divisions.'[34] Apart from the German parachute arm, trained to expect unpleasant shocks, Generalmajor Heinz Fiebig's 84th Infantry Division 'had been badly surprised by the sudden advent of two complete divisions in his area,' and his command promptly dissolved under the 'shattering effect of such immensely superior forces on my already badly depleted troops.'[35] However, within two and a half hours all troops from both airborne divisions had arrived and had reached their objectives. The British 6th Airborne had delivered two brigades of paratroops and a brigade of glider troops. They brought with them 109 tons of ammunition, 695 vehicles and 113 artillery pieces, but the price was 1,297 killed, wounded or missing.[36]

It was really the airborne drop that differentiated Montgomery's Rhine operation from those of the US armies, which, as we have seen, were equally well prepared and resourced. Huge concentrations of artillery were on call in the American sectors, even if they were not used. The criticisms, that *Plunder* was over-insured by the projection of paratroopers onto the high ground east of the river, were made because Allied land and air forces joined together within hours. Such objections are valid only because the Germans were so weak in that sector.

Had there been any delay on the river, whether by effective use of the Luftwaffe in bombing or mass mining operations; panzer counter attacks; well-directed artillery concentrations; the sudden and efficient use of reserves; unexpected use of poison gas along the river front; or other unpredicted misfortune, which would have led to a slaughter on the Rhine, then few could have protested at the employment of the two airborne divisions operating in the hinterland. Yet the fundamental reasons for the objections that Montgomery attracted were due to his own abrasive personality and the nationalistic drum he was encouraged to beat by Churchill and Brooke.

The switch away from Berlin announced by Eisenhower soon afterwards (and examined shortly) seemed to reinforce this antipathy towards Americans. By extension this included the Britons who held senior SHAEF positions.[37] On 29 March, Montgomery wrote in his diary, 'With victory in sight, the violent pro-American element at SHAEF is pressing for a set-up which will clip the wings of the British group of amies and relegate it to an unimportant role on the flank; then the Americans then finish off the business alone.'[38] Brooke's private diary echoes the same narrow-minded belief, that an American nationalistic clique dominated SHAEF, determined to belittle Britain's wartime effort. Yet there was no clique, whether 'violently pro-American' or anti-British; those at SHAEF were pro-Allied. Montgomery was blind to this. Thus, some historians argue that the Twenty-First Army Group commander did more than Hitler and Goebbels combined to attempt to wreck the Anglo–American coalition. It is to Eisenhower's credit that he managed to hold the alliance together at this stage.

Churchill himself, with Brooke in tow, had arrived on the evening of 23 March to watch *Varsity*, staying at Montgomery's TAC HQ at Venlo. Clad in the uniform of an Honorary Colonel of the Royal Sussex Regiment, his old regiment, Churchill and Brooke found a vantage point south of Wesel to watch the airborne armada for two hours, visited the spot where Tom Rennie had died hours earlier, then lunched at General 'Bolo' Whistler's 3rd Division's headquarters at Schloss Moyland on the west bank. Now Baron von Steingracht's world-class museum, a pug dog carved into the main staircase commemorates Churchill's visitation. The fourteenth century turreted and moated castle later served as Montgomery's HQ. That evening, the British premier watched Monty's liaison officers report to the chief. 'I thought the system admirable,' he wrote, 'indeed the only way in which a modern Commander in Chief could see as well as read what was going on in every part of the front.'[39]

The next day Churchill visited Ninth Army's sector and insisted on clambering across the twisted ironwork of the former Büderich road bridge into Wesel. Many pictures were taken, but soon his party was bracketed by German shells plunging into the river, and hearing sniper fire, Simpson insisted they depart. 'The look on Winston's face,' wrote Brooke, 'was just like that of a small boy being called away from his sand-castles on the beach by his nurse! He put both arms round one of the twisted girders and looked over his shoulder at Simpson with angry eyes. It was a sad wrench for him; he had been enjoying himself immensely.'[40] On 26 March, Churchill, then aged seventy, flew back to London, having achieved his main aim of coming under hostile fire for the final time in his life, a feat first achieved on his twenty-first birthday in 1895.

The same evening Alan Moorehead recorded Second Army's senior intelligence officer announcing, 'This is the collapse. The German line is broken. They no longer have a coherent system of defence between the Rhine and the Elbe. It is difficult to see what there is to stop us now.' Yet, the assembled correspondents were wary. 'Could it really be the end? So many people had cried *Wolf* so often before.'[41]

While there is little evidence left of the fighting along the Rhine, some of the older brick buildings in Bienen still bear the scars of shot and shell. On 1 April, the Highland Light Infantry of Canada liberated the Dutch frontier town of Heerenberg, a couple of miles north of the river, near Emmerich, to the sight of joyous faces. 'The roads were lined with waving, cheering people,' remembered the battalion commander. 'Old men in blue caps with knobbly sticks, their wives in laundered, white bonnets of linen; pretty girls with orange bows in their hair, and children with orange flowers, symbolic of the Royal House of Orange. And above the roar of vehicles passing by, the happy shouts of "Hallo, Tommy!"'

To the Dutch, the uniforms of the Canadians and British were indistinguishable, and the Maple Leaf as yet meant little to them.[42] A 25-pounder in the town square forms a memorial to the 29,000 Royal Canadian Artillery personnel who manned 1,100 guns of thirty-eight

RCA regiments, of whom nine hundred lost their lives. Although April 1945 is remembered by the Dutch as their month of liberation, for the 1st Canadian Army it was the cruellest month. Another 1,191 Canucks would be killed ejecting the Germans over the next thirty days.[43]

Turning now to Simpson's Ninth Army, plans were being finalised for them to cross the lower Rhine while they were still shedding blood clearing the approaches to it during *Grenade*. Flexing his muscles as the army group commander, Montgomery had initially tried to ensure that while Ninth Army secured the crossing points, it would be the Canadians and British who used them as stepping stones to victory. Simpson and his staff were 'flabbergasted' when Montgomery's planning directive of 21 January stipulated that one corps of two American infantry divisions should be transferred to his control and that US engineers build the bridges Montgomery's troops would use. Of Ninth Army itself, there was no mention.

The directive was hotly contested, not least by SHAEF, when it became apparent that not only was Montgomery short of engineers and bridging components, but he lacked the combat strength to sustain an advance the other side. At some stage, he would have to allow Ninth Army a share in the battle ahead. Eventually a compromise was hammered out whereby Montgomery's Rhine crossings became a simultaneous three-army assault: Crerar's Canadians in the north, Dempsey's Britons centre, and Simpson's GIs to the south.

At further meetings the field marshal conceded more spans were needed, and on 4 February – grudgingly, it seemed to Simpson and his staff – he authorised Ninth Army bridging sites for two American corps either side of Rheinberg. This was a small, left-bank town between Moers and Wesel, once walled and fortified, but so excessively fought over in the sixteenth and seventeenth centuries that it became known as 'the whore of war'. By the time Simpson's GIs reached the area, its many stone and brick buildings were smashed beyond repair from the air, and fit only for hardcore for bridging sites.

In addition to Rheinberg, once the British had secured a bridgehead at Wesel, using four American-built trestle spans, Simpson could put his third corps across in the direction of the Ruhr. Ninth Army would also construct bridges over the Maas at Venlo for supply purposes and protect the British bridgehead at Wesel, as well as their own at Rheinberg. Simpson decided to allocate the assault roles to a pair of veteran formations in Anderson's XVI Corps. Leland S. Hobbs' 30th Division would make a simultaneous crossing with the British in the corps' northern sector, followed by Ira T. Wyche's 79th Division, one hour later to their south. Hobbs had graduated with Eisenhower, Bradley, Van Fleet and many others from West Point in 1915 and had taken over the 30th, a National Guard formation, in 1942 from Bill Simpson, his future army commander.

The 30th had the moniker 'Old Hickory', recognising their origins in Andrew Jackson's home state of Tennessee. Hobbs landed with them on Omaha beach during D+5 and had led them through 313 days of combat since. Son of a Methodist pastor, small, wiry, intense but popular with his men, Wyche's story was similar. From the West Point class of 1911, he had started his military career as an artillery officer in the 30th and had likewise taken over his division, the 79th, in 1942, landing in Normandy on D+8. Wyche's division wore the Cross of Lorraine as their shoulder patch in honour of their successes in France during the final months of World War One. The 79th would also cross the Rhine with several hundred secret weapons, which they had tested and distributed to each assault battalion. These were panzerfäuste, captured in prodigious quantities earlier and now turned on their former owners. Both the 30th and 79th had been deployed in the final stages of *Grenade*, were combat-hardened, in good shape, and up to strength. They would be supported by Anderson's 35th and 75th Infantry and 8th Armored Divisions later. Once across, the 30th were to meet Mills-Roberts' Commando brigade, and with them envelop and capture Wesel.

For *Flashpoint*, Ninth Army issued more than 800,000 maps and assembled 138,000 tons of technical stores for the 31,120 non-divisional US Army engineers who would participate. On 9 March, Major Edward P. Ludington of the 313th Infantry (79th Division) noted his regiment was issued M29 Weasel tracked amphibious vehicles and had started training packages at the 'Ninth Army Stream Crossing School', set up on the Maas River near Roermond by Simpson's Chief Engineer, Brigadier General Richard U. Nicholas. The school, supervised by the 1143rd

Engineer Combat Group, opened in November 1944, ran for five months and trained GIs in day and night river crossings, street and village fighting, conduct in Germany, chemical warfare, mine and booby traps, and engineer familiarisation.[44]

After extensive 'dry' training on land and 'wet' rehearsals on the Maas, the 30th and 79th Divisions had the 1153rd and 1148th Engineer Combat Groups respectively, of 9,000 men each, assigned to them. Working day and night, under fire, they would be responsible for all aspects of bridge-building, operating and maintaining the storm boats, rafts, pontoons, anchors and winches. Additionally, booms of floats and nets were to be constructed as protection against swimming saboteurs and debris carried in the river; ramps to crossing sites had to be made across water meadows; and hardcore found for roads, trackways and assembly areas. Hard standings were created for heavier loads, such as the cranes that would lift landing craft into the water. Strengthened entry points were made for the LVTs, DUKWs and swimming tanks that would shuttle across the water.[45]

Despite the huge stockpiles of equipment and their combat experience to date, Simpson's engineers knew they had the most challenging task of their careers, erecting several treadway bridges, of between 1,100 and 1,500 feet within nine hours of the first boats reaching the far shore. The timing was not of their choosing, but sequenced with the British attack further north, and could not be altered. None could plead that the first successful bridging of the mighty Rhine by Julius Caesar in 55 BC had taken ten days.[46]

In addition to Anderson's own XVI Corps artillery, the 34th Field Artillery Brigade were attached with thirteen battalions of medium, heavy and super-heavy pieces, plus the XIX Corps' artillery with eleven further battalions, all overseen by Ninth Army's Chief of Artillery, Colonel Lawrence H. Hanley. A tank destroyer group of six battalions added to this already impressive firepower, along with six separate armour battalions, two anti-aircraft artillery groups, a smoke generator battalion, and another of chemical mortars, whose 4.2-inch weapons acted as short-range artillery. With the assigned USN landing craft flotilla, these enhancements brought Anderson's strength to that of a small army, at 120,000 men, including fifty-four artillery battalions on call.[47]

The confluence of the Lippe and the Rhine marked the northern boundary of Anderson's eleven-mile sector in which he would attack. To his south, Gillem's XIII Corps (84th and 102nd Infantry, 5th Armored) would hold the river and conduct decoy operations in Operation *Exploit*. They were assisted by the obscurely named 23rd Headquarters Special Troops, whose tactical speciality was inflating rubber vehicles, tanks and artillery, and moving them around at night, to suggest activity. Their business was deception, even though their name may have implied a Commando/Rangers-type unit to the Wehrmacht.[48] In front of both corps the water was 'slow of current, with ideal launching and landing sites, in which a mass of assault craft could be employed', read one of Simpson's G-2 estimates.[49]

McLain's XIX Corps (83rd and 95th Infantry and 8th Armored Divisions) were assembled behind, ready to plunge east towards Düsseldorf. The 29th Division was retained as Ninth Army reserve. Security was paramount, with radio silence imposed for Anderson's corps, but false radio chatter scripted for Gillem's men to broadcast. The latter also built fake engineer dumps of equipment, which were twice attacked by the Luftwaffe. Finally, Anderson's troops were ordered to remove shoulder patches and signposts, and paint over unit identification codes on vehicles, so that no villagers might warn their friends on the opposite bank of the assembled and incoming units.

At 01:00 on 24 March, Eisenhower and Simpson moved to a vantage point in an old church tower from which to witness the gunfire. 'Every flash could be seen. The din was incessant. Meanwhile infantry assault troops were marching up to the water's edge to get into their boats. We joined some and found them remarkably eager to finish the job.'[50] What the generals saw was the hour-long barrage, during which 40,000 US artillerymen fired a total of 65,261 rounds from 2,070 guns. Within the next four hours, this figure had doubled to 131,450 rounds, every bit as spectacular as Montgomery's set-piece preparation for his attack further north. At the same time 1,500 heavy bombers were attacking a dozen airfields within range of the crossing sites.

Beginning at 02:00, each regiment of the 30th Division – 119th in the north, 117th centre, 120th right – committed a battalion to the assault wave, equipped with fifty-four storm boats and thirty double assault boats. Friendly machine-guns firing tracer guided the first waves. Only when the boats were midstream did a few German mortar rounds find a target, hitting two storm boats, killing one man and wounding three.[51] Private Ralph Albert of the 119th recalled 'a panorama of red tracer, smoke, and small boats motoring across the river. We all got as low as we could because there was a lot of enemy fire coming across, as well as water spraying over us which made it difficult to see. A boat alongside us was hit by a burst of gunfire, which killed the engineer steering it, and slammed into us, almost capsizing our own boat, before it rocked away and turned over. I think it was hit by a cannon shell.'[52]

'It was the artillery that did the job for us,' thought Lieutenant Colonel Whitney O. Refvem, leading the 117th Infantry's Company 'B'. 'The artillery preparation was timed perfectly, lifting moments before our boats reached the eastern bank.'[53] Within two hours, the first line of settlements east of the river had fallen, all three regiments had at least two battalions across, and a platoon of DD (Duplex Drive, able to operate on land or water) Shermans from the 736th Tank Battalion had arrived, in company with the 747th Tank Battalion, operating LVTs.

The second assault, on a two-regiment front, by the 79th Division south of Rheinberg, launched at 03:00, landing on the far bank around fifteen minutes later. Each of the two attacking battalions from the 313th and 315th Regiments had companies of engineers, medics, armour, tank destroyers and chemical mortars attached to them. Their arrival was preceded by an hour's bombardment, with mortars adding to the din, detonating minefields on the eastern bank, of which Major Ludington, the 313th's Motor Officer, remembered, 'As far as anyone could see, up and down the river, the west bank was ablaze with flashes from the artillery. The thunderous crashes on the far bank were terrific. The Divisional artillery, supported by Army and Corps, actually fired 300,000 rounds beginning at 02:00 until 03:00.' As the 299,999th shell flew through the air, Sergeant William L. McBride of the 311th Field Artillery Battalion took time to scrawl '300,000' on the next one. 'It was,' thought Ludington, 'the greatest bombardment of all time.'[54]

Most of the 315th's casualties were caused by men falling overboard into the icy water. Captain John E. Potts, an S-3 (operations officer), was one, plucked from the river after his overloaded boat sank, by Lieutenant

Colonel Earl F. Holton, a battalion commander, who exclaimed, 'Well, I'll be damned. What's my S-3 doing swimming out here when we have work to do?'[55] The main challenge for the 313th Regiment turned out not to be the German defenders but fog and smoke drifting in from the attacks downriver. Embarrassingly, at least one boat in the fourth wave, launching at 04:00, became disorientated in the smoke and mist. Its men leapt ashore – only to meet other GIs coming down to the water to load. As an indicator of the slickness of their drills, and effectiveness of their training, the 313th managed to get their 57mm anti-tank guns and ammunition across by M29 Weasel, which provided 'a good morale factor for the troops', and within 150 minutes, the Division Signal Company had an underwater cable, laid by DUKW, and weighted with anchors, across the river providing instant communication.[56]

Still in the small hours, using the night as cover, the first vehicle, a Sherman tank-dozer, was loaded onto a Bailey raft, and floated over, rapidly followed by towed anti-tank guns, more Shermans and tank destroyers. This was more than an expression of confidence by its crew, for Allied tanks were still disinclined to operate by night in 1945, let alone sail on a wobbling raft in the midst of an icy river. Five DUKWs shuttled supplies of food, water and ammunition across, with the regimental surgeon having priority on all vehicles returning to the near shore. In the event, they were hardly used, with Eisenhower later writing of his pleasure that Ninth Army's casualties during the assault amounted to only thirty-one. Major Ludington recorded at his crossing site, 'There were six different Army branches and the US Navy working as one unit. Some of these men had never heard German gun fire before, while the 461st Amphibious Truck Company had been in action since D-Day in Normandy.'[57]

A little after noon on 24 March, Major General Wyche of the 79th arrived at the 313th's crossing point. Ludington observed a German shell 'exploded right next to our general, knocking him down, but luckily he was not injured'. A United Press war correspondent, Clinton Conyer, who crossed with the division, wrote that their operation 'had been carried out with ferryboat precision'.[58] Later, a maintenance section of the 717th Tank Battalion, who had never been in combat before, landed, 'got confused and instead of turning right, headed left into German territory.

They could be seen going up the road and toward the German lines. On order of the commander of Tank Company 'A', a warning shot was fired in front of its leading Jeep. This, however, just made them go faster, so the order was given to hit their maintenance tank on its track. This was done and the vehicle burst into flames, but personnel were seen to jump from the burning vehicle and Jeep and disappear. However, that was the end of the maintenance section.'[59]

Although neither division had much intelligence knowledge of their opponents nor were able to carry out detailed reconnaissance beforehand, it was the element of surprise, aided by the huge deception effort and artillery barrage, that propelled both over the Rhine with minimal casualties. By the end of the month, a week later, Anderson's XVI Corps had killed or wounded seven hundred of their opponents and processed 1,896 prisoners, for losses of thirty-eight killed, 426 wounded and three missing.[60]

Hard on their heels came the 134th Infantry of 35th US Division. We last met them linking US and British troops on 3 March, at the end of *Blockbuster* and *Grenade*, in Geldern. Then, James Graff's squad had nearly opened fire on a column of British troops approaching his barn, but now on 24 March, Graff recollected that the sight beyond Rheinberg resembled the D-Day beaches. 'Barrage balloons were moored; anti-aircraft batteries were dug in, and scores of artillery battalions were firing in support of the men across the river. Getting ready to move out, we were strafed by German aircraft trying to knock out the bridge. Anti-aircraft guns knocked down three of them and all they got was one barrage balloon that went up in a ball of flames. Engineers had completed a big pontoon bridge in less than twenty-four hours which was quite a feat, as the Rhine was almost a half-mile wide here. Searchlights lit up the site and we walked across accompanied by vehicles, tanks and trucks.'

'That was my most apprehensive moment of the war, as I can't swim,' observed Graff. 'On the other side, we walked all night, occupied some buildings, and stayed until morning. As we were resting, the order came to move out. I told another GI and he said something to the one sitting beside him. I looked at his companion – he was a dead German. I just pushed him with my foot, and he fell over. The GI wondered why his sitting companion hadn't answered back when he spoke to him.'[61] Graff and his buddies had traversed one of ten bridges and four floating Bailey ferries assembled mostly within the first two days, the quickest built in seven hours, forty-five minutes. Most spans were clustered opposite Wesel as Montgomery had directed, the remainder spread between the assault sites of the 30th and 79th Divisions.

Once they had cleared the area of mines and booby traps, the 1117th Engineer Group constructed four bridges at Wesel, to be used initially by the British Second Army, before they reverted back to the Ninth. They flanked a handsome 1874 trestle railway bridge, 'collapsed in sections like a children's toy', the result of sabotage by the Germans on their withdrawal from the west bank. A fourth Engineer Group, the 1146th, assembled a pile trestle for the heaviest transport, and eventually a replacement railway bridge at Wesel. All were overwatched by Ninth Army's 55th Anti-Aircraft Brigade while tracked and wheeled traffic on each averaged 8,000 per day, rising to 10,000 on 2 April. These were staggering quantities of vehicles, given that all the Western Allies had been operating with horsed cavalry only five years before. By 1945, the era of boots and saddles had truly come to an end, only no one had told the Germans, who, with no gas, were reliant on their quadrupeds.[62]

As the 79th Division was clearing Dinslaken, a once proud town of 10,000 but now mostly in ruins, shortly before 10:00 on 24 March they heard the steady hum of aircraft engines coming from the west. For reasons of security, most ground troops had not been given any details of the two-division airborne assault about to take place to their front. This was *Varsity*, the counterpart to *Plunder* and *Flashpoint*, the airborne operation whose Anglo-Canadian element we examined earlier. For the next two and a half hours, a vast carpet of aircraft stretching as far as the eye could see swept over them, as paratroops tumbled out of 1,696 transports, mostly C-47s, but including seventy-two of the new Curtiss Commando C-46s, descending to nearby drop zones. The C-46 could carry double the number of men, or tonnage, of a C-47, was faster, and had doors on both sides of the fuselage, allowing troops to deploy more rapidly.[63]

The air assault, of which Montgomery was the principal proponent, was the result of airborne, air force and high command politics, for

Bradley and many US officers regarded it as totally unnecessary. They were suspicious of Monty's demands for a 'big show', whereas the Allied airborne fraternity, excluding its chief, Major General Matthew Ridgway, were anxious for a final mass deployment before the war's end. A Virginian born into a military family, Ridgway was a West Point contemporary of 'Lightning Joe' Collins and Mark Clark, and had taken over the 82nd Division from Omar Bradley, converting it into its airborne role. He had led them in Sicily and Normandy, before taking command of the newly formed XVIII Airborne Corps in August 1944. As a regular officer with a military pedigree, Ridgway had his eyes fixed on a post-war future as a senior US land forces chief, and did his best to get *Varsity* cancelled. To him, it was a high-risk venture, with limited operational significance, but career-threatening in the event of failure, as *Market Garden* had been for some British officers.

In the event, William M. Miley's US 17th, coming from airfields around Paris, floated down over Diersfordt, five miles north of Wesel. Some 1,348 gliders headed for their landing zones, followed by 240 four-engine Liberators of the Eighth Air Force dropping 582 tons of supplies. The gliders, some double-towed, had a bumpy ride in the turbulence of so many aircraft. The 680th Glider Artillery Battalion recorded that control of their aircraft was so difficult that pilots and co-pilots had to rotate positions every fifteen minutes.[64]

Shepherded by 889 escorting fighters, this vast armada brought 21,680 parachutists and glider troops to the eastern banks of the Rhine, of whom 9,577 were Americans, stupefying friend and foe alike as the 'sky literally turned black with planes, gliders and parachutes', in the words of one German civilian caught in the battle. Eisenhower watched the spectacle, writing, 'a number of our aircraft were hit by anti-aircraft [fire], however only after they had dropped their loads of paratroopers. Generally, those that were struck fell inside our own lines, and in most cases the crews succeeded in saving themselves by taking to their parachutes. Even so, our loss in planes was far lighter than we had calculated.'[65]

As Private Robert Vannatter of the 513th Parachute Infantry was descending silently by parachute, he saw a lone German soldier kneeling on the ground thirty feet below him, unaware of his presence. As

he landed, his opponent turned round in surprise, but the quick thinking Vannatter beat him to the draw. He levelled his carbine and the
German surrendered, unaware that the young GI's weapon was without a magazine, and empty.[66] Airborne losses included nineteen C-46s,
twelve C-47s and thirteen gliders, though many more were damaged.[67]
The aircraft of PFC Vitautas Thomas with the 194th Glider Infantry was
written off when it slammed into an embankment. Under machine-gun
fire he tumbled out and into a ditch but left behind his helmet and rifle.
When he crawled back to retrieve them, he found 'a German round had
passed through my helmet, leaving two gaping holes'.[68]

Elsewhere, another 2,153 fighters formed a protective umbrella over
the target area or sought out Luftwaffe aircraft that might try to inter-
fere, though none did. Additionally, 2,596 heavy bombers (660 of them
of the Fifteenth Air Force, flying from Italy) and 821 medium bombers
attacked airfields, bridges, marshalling areas and other targets in Germany. This was a much larger effort than the first day of *Market Garden*
the previous September, and the 9,743 Allied airframes on duty that day
were only exceeded by those in the air on 6 June 1944.[69]

James Graff of the 35th Division recalled the scene soon after the
paratroopers had descended. 'The area was littered with airborne equipment. All kinds of abandoned ordnance and supplies attached to parachutes were scattered over a huge area. Different coloured parachutes
meant different supplies, green for medical and red for ammunition.
German soldiers and civilians had dumped large amounts into canals
and streams. We found one dead paratrooper whose chute had failed to
open, a sad sight. It seemed there were many wrecked gliders and several C-47's, and we thought the airborne show completely unnecessary.
To us, it wasted a lot of supplies and resulted in a larger number of casualties than a straight infantry attack.'[70]

Graff was reflecting on the nearness of the drop zones to the Rhine,
a distance of five miles. This was partly the result of lessons learned
from previous missions. Normandy had taught that large-scale airborne
assaults worked best in daylight – the 5–6 June 1944 missions were made
at night, scattered and unable to concentrate. *Market Garden* had indicated that sky warriors should not be dropped too far away from ground
forces. Operation *Varsity* was the corrective to both, but because the

Germans were so weak, the ground forces, Graff's included, arrived within hours.

It was at 14:58 that patrols from the British 1st Commando Brigade marching out of Wesel reached elements of the 17th Airborne, marking the first juncture of airborne and amphibious units. The speed of this union, five hours, far exceeding SHAEF's planning, caused many to think that *Varsity* was an elaborate irrelevance. Just in case the airborne invasion ran into trouble, a small Jeep-borne reinforcement of three hundred Special Forces troops known as 'Frankforce' was also deployed. Named after Brian Franks, CO of 2nd SAS, it comprised two squadrons, one each from 1st and 2nd SAS, and mounted in seventy-five of their signature Jeeps, bristling with machine-guns, radios, supplies for long-range activities, self-sealing fuel tanks and armoured glass windshields, some with 3-inch mortars. Padre John Kent, chaplain to the 2nd SAS, asked if he could accompany the mission, dubbed Operation *Archway*. While the Royal Army Chaplain's Department refused permission, taking a very dim view of the SAS's piratical and often murderous activities, Franks allowed Kent to assume the rank of Private and drive one of his Jeeps into battle.

Varsity had originally been larger, and would have included the 13th US Airborne Division, but was scaled back due to the lack of extra transport aircraft and the objections of Ridgway, commanding XVIII Airborne Corps, who insisted that the paratroops must land together in a single drop. He was aware that *Market Garden* had also failed due to its chronologically separated waves. Ridgway wisely, but to the derision of some, also deployed by LVT, refusing to repeat the error of Browning, the British Airborne Corps commander, who arrived during *Market Garden* using up valuable glider space, and was unable to contribute to the September 1944 battle in any meaningful way.

One US airborne innovation was the training of 875 glider pilots and co-pilots in rudimentary battlefield tactics in the weeks before *Varsity*, organising them into a provisional battalion of four companies. This echoed the role of the British Glider Pilot Regiment, whose personnel fought as ground troops once they had landed. By contrast, American glider crews had previously waited for evacuation. This immediately paid dividends, with one company of pilots repulsing a German counter-attack on the night of 24 March.[71]

Ridgway was soon touring the area in a three-Jeep convoy, visiting all the airborne units he could, but at around midnight, his party ran into a German patrol and a sharp gun battle ensued. A German grenade exploded under his vehicle lodging a fragment in Ridgway's shoulder. He received a Purple Heart but ignored medical advice to have the fragment removed and carried it for the rest of his life. James Graff recorded a similar incident on 26 March when a German tank to his front opened fire. 'My friend Bob Landrum and I were near a big oak tree when we heard this shell coming right at us. We didn't have time to get down when it hit. I was kinda bent over when it exploded. I saw the leaves move by my left foot and Bob remarked, "What was that?" as he saw it too. I stayed in position and with my trench knife dug a piece of shrapnel six or seven inches long and one and a half inches wide out of the ground by my foot. I had missed death or serious injury by a scant few inches.'[72]

Despite the politics, *Varsity* was the most successful Allied airborne operation of the war and its targeting of the Wesel area, with its pre-war population of 25,000, destroyed the considerable anti-aircraft defences deployed against bomber streams heading towards the Ruhr. Without the deployment of these two airborne divisions, the vast array of flak guns would have been turned against the ground troops crossing the Rhine. However, this success came at a cost of forty-one aircrew, 346 British (including glider pilots) and 393 American airborne personnel killed and 1,802 wounded from all units. To Montgomery, *Plunder* and *Varsity* were all about hunting and killing the German forces. Thus, his message, issued as a paper leaflet to all troops, was a morale-boosting technique he had used before Alamein and Normandy. It concluded, 'Over the Rhine, then let us go. And good hunting to you all on the other side. May The Lord mighty in battle give us victory in this our latest undertaking, as He has done in all our battles since D-Day.'[73]

The French Army relied completely on the USA for its material support. (*Above*): Général de Lattre inspects M4 Shermans of the 1st Régiment de Cuirassiers (5th Armoured Division) in Colmar, prior to the battles that would bring them to the banks of the Rhine. (*Below*): Plans to cross into Germany were advanced by Général de Gaulle, who demanded a crossing on 30 March. He was suspicious of the US Army stealing his proposed French occupation zone. This was despite Generals Patch (*nearest the camera*) and Devers (*beyond*), supporting de Lattre's men with bridging, ammunition, fuel and rations far beyond their official remit. Behind Patch and Devers stands Lieutenant Colonel Henry Cabot Lodge, former Senator for Massachusetts, who played an important role in furthering Franco–American relations.

10

Sixth Army Group

Let us now travel two hundred miles south of Bill Simpson's Ninth Army Rhine crossings to those of 'Sandy' Patch's Seventh. Here, we left the XV Corps of Eisenhower's old friend, Major General Wade H. Haislip, staring at the frothy, coffee-coloured water next to the ancient city of Worms. 'Ham' Haislip provided an extra, unofficial communication channel between the Supreme Commander, Patch and Devers, for it was he who had introduced Second Lieutenant Eisenhower to his future wife, Mamie, in 1915. From September 1944 until the war's end, he acted as the Supreme Commander's eyes and ears in Sixth Army Group and Seventh Army. As a graduate of the two-year course at the *École Supérieure de Guerre*, Haislip with his fluent French, also saw eye-to-eye with de Lattre.

Full of winter snowmelt, broken tree limbs and other detritus, here the Rhine was a thousand feet wide, an average of seventeen icy feet deep, and moved at the disheartening speed of eight feet per second, comparable with the non-tidal sections of the Thames or Hudson. Seventh Army would be just three days behind Patton's Third in its Rhine leap, on 25 March 1945, Palm Sunday. Haislip had alerted two divisions to cross, his 45th 'Thunderbird' Division at Hamm, a few miles to the north of Worms, the 3rd 'Marne' further south at Frankenthal.[1] All were apprehensive, for along this length of the river, wide marshy flood plains existed on both sides, affording no cover. The US Army Corps of Engineers observed, 'With the possible exception of the Normandy beaches, the river presented the most formidable natural obstacle in Western Europe.'[2]

Intelligence was poor as to the state of the opposition who had recently tumbled out of the Saar-Palatinate Triangle in disorder. Most German units who had survived the recent battles were reassembling and attempting to re-equip. Noted an intelligence summary, 'Remnants of twenty-two divisions were believed to have escaped across the river in the XV Corps zone, but effective strength of the divisions could not be estimated.'³ Seventh Army G-2 reckoned that their opponents were capable of defending 'with fifty men per river front kilometre', or around thirty per mile. Although the situation maps in Berlin at the moment alleged seventy-two divisions along the entire German *Westfront* in March 1945, with 173 in the East, none anywhere were at full strength. On average, most hovered at one-third of their authorised establishment. Military structure had broken down, and divisional symbols appeared on maps for the benefit of one man only – Hitler.⁴

Crude barricades and other defensive positions in towns were manned by the enthusiastic Hitlerjugend (Hitler Youth), supplemented by stragglers collected by Feldgendarmes (military police) and Volkssturm. The latter organisation crops up continually in the narrative of 1945, and it is worth examining them for a moment. Back in the fall of 1944, Hitler's Secretary Martin Bormann and Propaganda Chief Josef Goebbels had lobbied for the raising of a people's militia. The resultant 'home guard' embraced civilian males between sixteen and sixty, not already in military uniform, and was dubbed the Volkssturm (People's Storm). Poorly armed, to the malevolent duo, its military value was of secondary importance. To them the Volkssturm was a vehicle to radicalise the German people. When the militia were sworn in on 18 October, Goebbels, as detached from reality as Hitler, broadcast 'We know that an idea lives on, even if all its bearers have fallen. An opponent will eventually capitulate before the massed strength of a fanatically fighting people.'⁵

This was precisely the reception that Hitler, Bormann and Goebbels expected the Reich to give to their invaders. Similar proclamations emphasised a heroic future of self-sacrifice, reminiscent of Wagnerian operas. Berlin journalist Ursula von Kardorff secretly noted of the occasion, 'The last round-up of the halt and the lame, the children and the dotards. This New Guard, most of them pressed into service against their will, will not save us from defeat.'⁶ Bernard L. Kahn, a Thunderbird GI with the 157th Infantry, observed: 'Their only common uniform was a black-and-white armband with the word *Volkssturm* embroidered on it. The old men rapidly learned that the GI was much more interested in their armband as a souvenir, and the clever Volkssturmer could be on his way home, unmolested, and usually with several cigarettes. All he had to do was give up his armband in exchange.'[7]

Where possible, trenches and crude bunkers had been fashioned by slave labourers along the Rhine's banks, but the most effective defence would come from batteries of roving anti-aircraft guns, normally on the look-out for Allied aircraft. Guarding bunkers and other fixed defences along Germany's frontiers were Fortress Battalions, a concept created by Guderian after the 1944 collapse in France to make the best use of the pre-existing field fortifications along the Reich's western borders.

However, to speak of Fortress 'battalions' and 'companies' was meaningless military terminology. In terms of numbers and equipment they bore no relation to their Volksgrenadier equivalent battalions of companies. Fortress units differed from ordinary units in having no heavy weapons, limited mobility (a few commandeered horses or bicycles at best) and no logistics of their own, and were formed around specific locations and the weapons therein. Thus, leaving manoeuvre to others, fortress battalions absorbed older, less fit men and convalescing veterans (usually from Russia) with frostbite, stomach or hearing complaints. Alternatively known as the 'Bread Battalions', on account of their strict diets, they were not unusually led by officers missing a limb, fingers, toes or an eye.

To young men, everyone senior to them is 'old', but many GI accounts of this time, official and private, frequently noted the advanced age of some of their prisoners. This was found through examination of a prisoner's Soldbuch, the key identity document all Wehrmacht, SS, police and Volkssturm personnel were obliged to carry in their tunic pockets. It gave many personal and unit details, with promotions, training courses, decorations, qualifications, theatre service and medical issues all highlighted, thus providing vital information for US intelligence personnel. From their dates of birth, the CIC (Counter Intelligence Corps) folk were shocked to learn that some of their opponents were in their mid-to-late fifties.

Increasingly, the Western Allies also began to seize the very young. Adolescents, often in Luftwaffe uniform, formerly serving in air defence who had volunteered or been conscripted for combat duty, started to be captured within the Fatherland. American cameramen lingered on those who, according to their Soldbuch, were in their young teens. GIs echoed this revelation in their letters home. As one MP (prisoner handling and guarding was the job of military policemen) put it, 'The Germans are surrendering by hundreds. Some of these soldiers are old, old men with one eye gone or have a wooden leg. Others are so young; they haven't learned to use a razor. Their ages run from twelve to fifty, but as far as we're concerned, they are Nazis and can shoot a gun if given a chance. The SS troops are the worst and deserve no mercy. I have no compassion for any of them.'[8]

Along the banks of the Rhine, Seventh Army's two assaulting American divisions were preparing to throw their men across the water. The Marne's attack at Frankenthal would be preceded by a barrage of 10,000 rounds in a thirty-eight-minute period, though in the north at Hamm, the Thunderbirds' guns would stay silent to preserve surprise. As GIs in the Marne Division received and wrote letters, relaxing after their ordeals in the Saar, Lieutenant Clayton H. Moore Jr with Company 'F', 30th Infantry, observed their three rifle platoons ranged in strength from seventeen to twenty-two. Each was established at one officer and forty-five men, but casualties had been heavy in the Vosges and Colmar, and in breaking the Siegfried Line.

The Saar campaign alone had cost Company 'F', established at 6 officers and 187 other ranks, some nine killed and twenty-two wounded. However, morale was good because all understood the significance of storming the great river. Furthermore, they had recently completed opposed river crossings in Colmar and the Saar, and amphibious exercises with engineers on a lake at Nancy.[9] Faced with little idea of the German defences opposite, an intrepid four-man patrol, led by a US battalion CO from the 180th Infantry, 45th Division, had earlier paddled across in a rubber dinghy to discover there were no visible wire obstacles, mines or emplacements.

In the north, the doughs were assembled under darkness and crossed in five waves of storm boats, beginning at 02:30 on 25 March, Palm Sunday. Their plywood assault craft were equipped with a fifty-five-horsepower outboard motor which allowed the engineer crew of two, plus six infantrymen with all their fighting kit (though more troops were often carried) to rush the far shore. However, the throb of a hundred little engines carried through the silence of the night and the Germans soon realised what was afoot.

The first wave of the 45th were unmolested, but the second had a hard time, losing half its craft, their occupants swept away and drowned in the speedy current. PFC Vincent Presutti with Company 'M' of the 179th Infantry recollected, 'It was small compared to the Hudson. Nonetheless it was no picnic because we had no cover as we crossed.'[10] Enough made it; there was a glint of bayonets in the moonlight and the closest German positions fell. For the Marne Division, the southern crossing proved much less dangerous, but all four regiments, from north to south, the 179th, 180th, 30th and 7th, had to fight hard to establish a foothold on the far bank and nearby villages.[11]

Both divisions had been allotted fourteen DD swimming tanks, last used in anger in southern France on 15 August.[12] All in the north were able to cross and provide immediate fire support, but the 756th Tank Battalion (who had fought all the way through Italy, southern France and Colmar with the Marne Division) lost four of theirs. When bridging was in place on the following day they were bolstered by conventional armour. Having carried their boats four miles to the river, paddled across and fought for thirty-six hours without relief, the first wave of GIs was soon exhausted. They operated for the first day in the absence of supporting arms, though with artillery on call, and the few DD tanks on which the men rode. One platoon commander reported his men 'suffering from extreme fatigue. Most of them were so tired they found walking difficult, many merely hung on the sides of the tanks and were literally dragged along. Company 'F', including the officers, was so physically exhausted that any further action seemed impossible.'[13]

Extensively trained and rehearsed, two US Engineer Combat Groups were in support, the 40th behind the Thunderbirds, while the 540th accompanied the Marne Division. Although the men of Brigadier General Garrison H. Davidson, Patch's Chief Engineer, were by now hugely experienced in building bridges, all recognised – as the US Corps of Engineers later put it – this was 'The Big One', the ultimate test of almost every aspect of field engineering.[14] In both sectors within the first twenty-four hours, pontoon bridges and rafts, able to bear the weight of tanks, and infantry treadway bridges were constructed. All the while they were protected by a dense pall of artificial smoke which blotted out the area.

Huge numbers of half-tracks bearing quadruple .50-inch anti-aircraft mounts and towed 40mm guns collected on both riverbanks, ready for the anticipated German reaction. 'As the tail of our column crossed, the night was streaked by stabs of tracers as individual units of the Luftwaffe made futile attempts to delay the operation,' noted one GI from the back of his truck. 'Call that thing a river?' said another. 'Why, we've got mill streams bigger than that back home!'[15]

By the end of 26 March, eight battalions of field artillery, two of Shermans and two of tank destroyers had crossed. Additionally, another thousand vehicles had traversed by raft, with casualties and POWs returning by DUKW, for the bridge traffic was one-way, ever eastwards, deeper into Germany. In the centre, following the main road out of central Worms and across the Rhine, the 85th Combat Engineer Battalion had soon constructed the thousand-foot 'Alexander Patch' heavy pontoon bridge, and within five days Haislip's entire XV Corps of six divisions were across, through the Odenwald Hills and advancing to the River Main beyond. Sergeant Carl Erickson driving a Sherman with Company 'A', 43rd Tank Battalion of the 12th Armored, crossed at night on 30 March. 'The tank rose as it approached each pontoon and dipped as it rolled off. If I had seen that [terrifying sight] in daylight,' he joked, 'I would have gone AWOL.'[16]

Marvel B. Rowland with Company 'B', 56th Armored Infantry, Combat Command 'B', followed the same night. 'It was dark, I was asleep in the half-track when someone woke me up and said that we were crossing the Rhine. I looked over the sides of the half-track and could only see water. Since I could not see the pontoons, I thought that the half-track was floating on the water.'[17] First Sergeant Joe Cotten with Company 'D', 47th Tank Battalion, found crossing the following morning just as scary. He had to walk out front, guiding each driver, as they could only cross one at a time. 'Each pontoon sank a few inches as the tank slowly rolled over it. I was so happy when we got all five tanks of my platoon to the other side.'[18]

On their right, meanwhile, Général de Monsabert's II French Corps were celebrating the luck that brought them – against all expectations – a springboard for their own Rhine crossing. Alas, they possessed little combat bridging of their own, and American generosity did not run to spare 1,000-foot lengths, but General Robert Dromard, de Lattre's Chief Engineer, had been locating older military pontoons hidden during the occupation, and salvaging American and German spans, abandoned or damaged during their advance from the Riviera. Additionally, he had other items copied and manufactured in French factories. Though short of the trucks to even carry these items forward, Dromard had squir-relled away enough material for one 1,000-foot, ten-ton bridge, suit-able for infantry and trucks, but not armour. Reconnaissance indicated a suitable site at Germersheim, and earth-moving equipment to prepare both banks was readied.

Brooks' VI Corps – though under no obligation to do so – had offered to loan bridging pontoons and storm boats. Using it and the French equipment, de Monsabert directed his II Corps to cross at two sites – Speyer and Germersheim – on 31 March, with regiments from two divisions. At this moment, de Gaulle entered the fray, irritated by the pace of Rhine crossings by his Anglo-American Allies elsewhere. He was also concerned that the Seventh Army, crossing earlier, were already marching south and out of their bridgehead opposite Worms, to Karlsruhe and Stuttgart, which he considered to be French objec-tives. Accordingly, the French leader sent de Lattre a note on the 29th: 'My Dear Général, you must cross the Rhine even if the Americans are not agreeable, and even if you have to cross it in boats. It is a matter of the greatest national interest. Karlsruhe and Stuttgart await you, even if they do not want you!'[19]

Under pressure from de Gaulle, II French Corps thus crossed twenty hours early, forgoing rehearsals, and with none of their bridging equip-ment in place. In the north, the 3rd Algerian Division set out from Speyer the following evening, 30 March, using the single pneumatic rubber dinghy that had arrived. In a very surreal image, initially, Sergent

Bertout and ten men with paddles from the 3rd Régiment de Tirailleurs Algériens (3rd RTA) climbed aboard at 02:30 and represented the *sole* French contingent invading Baden. By daybreak, three more dinghies then seven American storm boats had arrived, but the Wehrmacht were alerted to their presence and shrapnel rained down.

Some of the invaders had been stationed at Sedan in May 1940 and recalled the dinghy-borne German assault pioneers similarly crossing the Meuse with horrendous losses, but sufficient determination to make their costly attack a success. This sense of settling old scores, and French national pride, spurred the Tirailleurs on. By nightfall, a whole battalion of the 3rd RTA were across, and by 22:00 that night Dromard's ten-ton bridge was in place, whereupon all in the Algerian Division, save heavier vehicles and armour, started to pour onto the east bank.

However, using two more regiments – the 4th RTA and the 151st Régiment d'Infanterie of Carpentier's 2nd Division d'Infanterie Marocaine – de Lattre had ordered a second crossing further south at Germersheim. The west bank settlement had only just fallen to the US 5th Infantry (71st Division), whom we met earlier manoeuvring around Bitche. Mortar squad commander Sergeant Dean Joy on his sixteenth day in combat was caught in the vicious Palm Sunday fight for the area which cost his Company 'G' eleven killed (mostly officers and NCOs) and twenty wounded, to snipers and machine-guns, and observed this was 'sixteen percent of the full-strength company of 187 men'. These men were friends with whom he had trained over the previous twelve months. As Joy wrote home of this encounter, 'As you can imagine, this combat business isn't easy to talk about . . . the infantryman's war is without the slightest doubt the dirtiest, roughest job of them all. The thing that keeps us going, through it all, is just each other. We're all in it together, and we're all buddies.'[20] Their replacements were not and had a hard time integrating.

Of course, as the GIs withdrew, the Germans had remembered the layout of Germersheim, so when the French occupied the area, likely assembly areas remained under intermittent mortar and artillery fire. Colonel Gandoët's 151st Régiment, a distinguished old Napoleonic unit that had also fought at Verdun, had been commanded by Colonel de Lattre in the 1930s but was disbanded after the 1940 Armistice. De Lattre had just re-formed it with young recruits, formerly with the Resistance, in tribute to his old command. Yet at Germersheim disaster threatened, for the various assault craft were late in assembling and missed the suppressive artillery barrage that would have taken them to the far shore, with the result that they started in daylight. Initially only three out of ten boats made the far bank, under withering fire from German machine-guns which knifed into the plywood and rubber craft. It took several hours just to get a company across, and they were swiftly eroded by four German counter-attacks.

Boats and their occupants trickled across throughout the day, determined to hang on to their hard-won beachhead – a sliver of German soil, which measured a mere fifteen hundred by five hundred yards. With de Gaulle breathing down their necks, no one was counting the cost. One battalion of the 151st, which days earlier had been a ragtag unit of Resistance volunteers, lost eighty-eight killed and fifty-one wounded (out of five hundred), while fifty-four boat crewmen out of ninety from the 211st French Engineer Battalion became casualties, losing three-quarters of their craft.

Dromard's ten-ton bridge had originally been earmarked for Germersheim, but because of the ferocious German response was sent upriver to Speyer instead. Gradually the 4th RTA and 151st built up strength on the hostile shore, reinforced solely by American storm boats which were now arriving in quantity, and the following morning, 1 April – Easter Day – the French burst out of their confined perimeter, and welded the separate beachheads together the same afternoon. Yet, with a single ten-ton bridge in operation, how were the French to expand their gains? The solution proved remarkably simple, as de Lattre observed: 'A perfect comrade-in-arms, Brooks agreed to the passage of twenty vehicles and the right to use the blanks in American convoys over his pontoon bridge at Mannheim.'[21]

The blanks must have been numerous since the 3rd Régiment de Spahis Algériens de Reconnaissance and the 7th Chasseurs d'Afrique – both armoured battalions, the former armed with M5 Stuart light tanks and M8 armoured cars, the latter with thirty-six M10 tank destroyers – were able to trundle across the same day, turn right and soon make contact with their fellow countrymen. The rest of de Monsabert's armour followed, and with the 9th Division d'Infanterie Coloniale leaping the Rhine at Leimersheim on 2 April, his combat power soon amounted to 130,000 personnel in three infantry divisions and one of armour, plus all the other assets of II French Corps.

De Lattre immediately moved his army headquarters across to Karlsruhe, accepting the surrender of its Kommandant, Generalmajor Walther Hossfeld, on 4 April, and ordered the 9th Colonial and 2nd Moroccan Divisions to sweep south along the banks of the Rhine. They overcame strong opposition at Rastatt – where Eisenhower had abruptly vetoed the US XV Corps crossing four months earlier – and by mid-month had taken Baden-Baden and Kehl. In the latter town, a north-eastern suburb of Strasbourg, stood a demolished bridge at whose western end French troops had first lingered on 23 November 1944. The Volksgrenadiers in the vicinity offered such feeble defence that in the final Allied storming of the Rhine, the 23rd Régiment d'Infanterie of Béthouart's I Corps swept all before them.

'The Rhine is swift as the Rhône, as wide as the Loire, deeply embanked like the Meuse, winding as the Seine, limpid and green as the Somme, historic as the Tiber, royal as the Danube, mysterious as the Nile, spangled with gold like a river of America, and covered with fables and phantoms like a river of Asia', wrote Victor Hugo of the waterway his countrymen had just crossed. The Reich's western moat, a corner-stone of the German psyche, whose crossing Eisenhower expected to be as bloody an affair as traversing the English Channel in June 1944, had proved to be a gentler experience than Devers' Sixth Army Group had any right to expect.[22]

The French Army was now complete on the far bank of the river, something it had taken five and a half years to achieve since the lack-lustre Saar offensive of September 1939. Since then, France had changed beyond all recognition. So had her forces. Several factors had made all the difference from 1939–40 and included political will, in the person of de Gaulle, so lacking at the beginning of the war. Then there was the training and combat experience that de Lattre's force had gained. Vitally important, too, was their American equipment and logistics network, vastly superior to anything previously possessed. Finally, air power, which in the hands of the Luftwaffe had undone France in 1940, but now in turn was the undoing of the Reich. Above them, twelve British-equipped French squadrons were operating with the RAF, while others in American fighters flew with the XII Tactical Air Command, whose headquarters was collocated with Sixth Army Group at Vittel.[23] The Rhine crossing at Kehl on 15 April, made by the sons of France following in Napoleon's footsteps, was the last of the war, and undertaken just twenty-three days before the cessation of hostilities.

PART THREE

Beyond the Rhine

(*Above*): Major General Wade Haislip, commander of XV US Corps, is decorated by Général Philippe Leclerc. French-speaking, 'Ham' Haislip had introduced Second Lieutenant Eisenhower to his future wife in Texas. He acted as Ike's unofficial eyes and ears throughout 6th Army Group. (*Below*): These French colonial troops, who went to take Karslruhe, Stuttgart and Ulm, are demonstrating their US Thompson submachine-guns, webbing and uniforms, worn with French helmets.

11

Tensions with the French

Allied intelligence officers routinely monitored German news programmes. On the night of 1 April, they were stunned by Deutschlandsender's instructions to their loyal listeners. All German men, women, and children were summoned to become *Werewolves*. 'You will sabotage the Allied armies and murder its soldiers, and wreak vengeance on defeatist Germans,' the broadcaster ordered.

The announcer stated, 'Those towns in the western Reich which have been destroyed by Allied terror raids have taught us to hate our opponents. The blood and tears of our brutally murdered men, of our despoiled women and of our children cry out for retribution. Those who have banded together in the *Werewolf* proclaim their determined, irrevocable oath, never to bow to their will, but rather to offer resistance, and to go out facing death proudly and defiantly to wreak revenge by killing them.' The broadcast was aimed at the listening Allies, rather than the population of the Reich, and amounted to a classic example of psychological operations. It warned, 'Every means is justified to strike a blow. The *Werewolf* will decide their life and death, as well as those traitors in our own people. Our foes should know that in those areas of the Reich they occupy, they will meet an opponent more dangerous, who is not tied by limitations of bourgeois methods of warfare. From now on, every Bolshevik, every Britischer, every American on Reich soil, is fair game. Hate is our prayer. Revenge is our battle cry.'[1]

The was the first public affirmation of an idea senior Nazis had first mooted the previous autumn. The terminology drew on an ancient tradition of residents bonding together as vigilantes to defend themselves

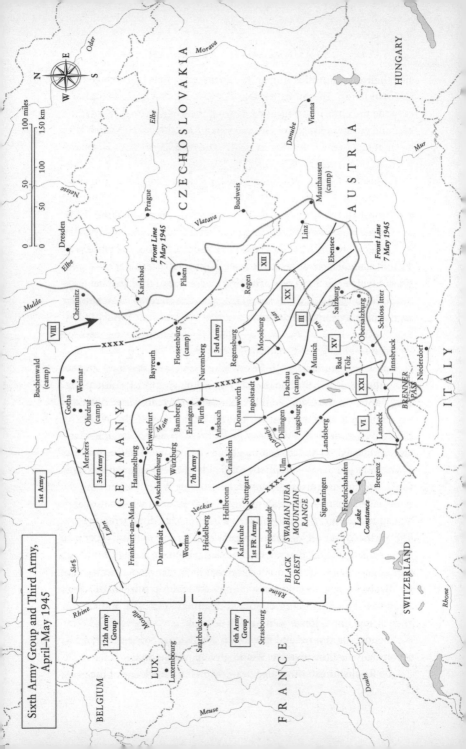

Sixth Army Group and Third Army, April–May 1945

and their communities during the many wars that had ravaged the German lands. The more terrible the invader, the more brutal and extreme the citizens' vengeance. During the Thirty Years' War (1618–48), one group in northern Germany had used this precise label, later brought to national attention in 1910 by the popular novelist, Hermann Löns. Its title was *Der Wehrwolf* (The War-wolf).

Dr Josef Goebbels, presiding over the Reichsministerium für Volksaufklärung und Propaganda (Reich Ministry for Public Enlightenment and Propaganda), was particularly entranced by the blend of the *Wehrwolf* novel, which he had reprinted and serialised in Nazi newspapers, with older Werewolf legends. People who appeared as normal citizens by day, but at night were driven to acts of extreme violence under the moon. It was a typical witches' brew of history and fiction of the kind that drew the Nazis to Wagner, Aryan super-race theory and Nordic mythology.

Goebbels had been disappointed by the Wehrmacht's military inability to halt the western invaders. As April 1945 dawned, Berlin was recording sixty-seven alleged divisions assigned to the West (by now, divisions in name only), with 163 in the East. Those in the West included 150,000 fully equipped personnel uselessly bottled up in four Atlantic ports, the Channel Islands and Dunkirk. In addition, twenty-three divisions were still contesting Italy against Mark Clark's Fifteenth Army Group, with eleven pointlessly lurking in Norway and twelve operating in the Balkans and Eastern Mediterranean.[2] Facing the Western Reich alone, Eisenhower at the same moment was fielding ninety-one full-strength divisions, including twenty-five armoured.[3]

To supplement Germany's uniformed defenders, what better way to inspire the Nazi faithful and strike fear into his opponents than to reignite the Werewolf legend among the civilian community? Goebbels was a sufficiently skilled and shrewd manipulator of human minds to understand this policy did not have to work. The mere concern that Nazi Werewolves might abound would be enough to tie up substantial Allied resources in looking for an opponent that might not exist. Either way, he surmised, the Nazis would win. In fact, Goebbels hoped that Werewolf bands would form and exact such a high price for the occupation of Germany that the invaders would give up and go home.

The Reichsminister was also drawing on his knowledge of the great anxiety caused by English-speaking SS commandos who had operated behind American lines during the Battle of the Bulge. No more than a few dozen hand-picked soldiers, dressed in American uniforms, had a massively disproportionate impact in slowing Allied tactical movements for over a month. Goebbels would not have known that this extended as far as Eisenhower in Paris and commanders elsewhere, who were layered in suffocating security against a threat that was a figment of their own imagination.[4]

To aid his psychological warfare, a wireless station, Radio Werewolf, was allegedly set up, endlessly quoted in other Nazi media, and picked up by foreign news services. Typical of one of its venomous broadcasts was this chant: 'We must become the flames to lick and burn our enemies. We must become the dynamite to blow up our foes. We must become the toxin to poison the invaders. We must become knives to cut them up. We must continue the fight until the last foreign soldier has been driven from the Reich or the last attacker has been buried in a mass grave in Germany.' However, such rhetoric was merely an adjunct of Goebbels' broadcast media with no direct link to any Werewolves. Airing such Gothic nonsense rather than practical advice soon gave the game away that this was another Hitlerian fantasy rather than a real menace.[5]

It was all far too late. No thought had been given to raising any Werewolf guerrilla units until after the fall of Aachen – the first German city to fall to the Allies – in October 1944. Then a senior SS officer, Obergruppenführer Hans-Adolf Prützmann, was appointed to investigate raising a cohort of stay-behind assassins and saboteurs, in the event of more Reich territory being overrun. When not hunting Jews in Latvia and Ukraine, Prützmann and his staff had analysed guerrilla tactics used by Russian partisans behind the lines, and the structure of the Polish Home Army, recently overwhelmed in the 1944 Warsaw Uprising.

He was completely the wrong man for the job, for numerous SS and Gestapo officers were experts on the hierarchy and operations of resistance movements in France, Belgium and Holland, and could have replicated what they knew in the Fatherland. They were ignored and in early 1945 Prützmann initiated training camps for selected SS volunteers. However, in typical, chaotic Third Reich fashion, the Hitlerjugend had also initiated their own Werewolf programme. As all 'defeatist' talk was forbidden, their chief, Reichsjugendführer Artur Axmann, told no one, and even when the SS revealed their hand, was reluctant to cooperate. Few by March–April 1945 were persuaded that Werewolfism was a viable policy. The moment had passed to win acceptance, and no preparations had been made. One of their rare successes was the assassination of the Allied-appointed Bürgermeister (Mayor) of Aachen on 25 March 1945. As the wife of one SS instructor recounted after the war, her husband's job 'was to form a group of Werewolves and continue the struggle behind the lines. He said the whole thing was pointless. His Werewolves were nothing more than a bunch of hormonal Hitlerjugend adolescents.'[6]

Echoing his experience of Bandenkampf (bandit warfare, the Nazi term for anti-partisan operations), Prützmann set out his doctrine in a training pamphlet: 'Your opponent will be obliged to deprive his front lines of troops, which must instead be employed for the security of his rear areas. He will lose vital material and cannot employ it against our soldiers. Everything that handicaps the opposition helps our troops.'[7] Also on Prützmann's reading list was the *Wehrwolf* novel by Hermann Löns.

Isolated confrontations with snipers left behind after their comrades had withdrawn; the discovery of weapons caches abandoned by the Volkssturm, rather than hidden by fanatics; firefights with regular Wehrmacht forces behind the lines trying to break out; and accidents with weapons and munitions were attributed to Werewolves by the Allies and Germans, but with little evidence. Thereafter Allied troops remained on their guard against even the friendliest of natives. If offered something to eat or drink, civilians were ordered to taste whatever was on offer first, to demonstrate it was not poisoned.[8] Urban legends abounded, most of them certainly untrue, of Germans expiring from deadly cakes or schnapps they had first offered GIs.

Having crossed the Rhine on 24 March and taken Heidelberg on 31 March, Patch's Seventh Army was soon battling their way further east along the Neckar Valley. On 2 April, they came across a network of labour camps that supplied labour to armaments factories tunnelled into the hillside at Obrigheim, twenty-five miles south-east of Heidelberg. The largest belonged to Daimler-Benz, bombed out of Berlin in March 1944 and relocated to this quieter corner of the Fatherland. The SS brought in five hundred slave labourers from Dachau to expand an old gypsum mine and build production line facilities. Messerschmitt 109 aero engines left the factory, code-named *Goldfisch*, from that October. By then, various subterranean projects in the vicinity employed around 10,000 inmates, who were based in seven Neckar camps, and suffered numerous deaths from overwork, typhus and the collapse of one of the tunnels. Those too sick to work were executed on the spot.[9]

When the US 63rd 'Blood and Fire' Division liberated the area, they discovered at least 250 graves, and a trainload of female detainees burned to death, their wagons sabotaged by SS guards who then bolted. The French- and German-speaking CIC officer with the division's HQ, Second Lieutenant J. Glenn Gray, already a veteran of Italy and France, recorded a similar scene on 3 April. 'Last Saturday the German guards loaded the inmates onto freight trains and tried to haul them away. When they discovered the trains could not proceed [due to Allied bombing] they left them. We found them there this afternoon, some 880, half-dead, horribly starved people, among them three hundred French Maquis, political prisoners . . . To see these living dead, their striped suits in rags, dragging their feet, was a sight I could have done without. To add to its gruesomeness, there was a dead German soldier deserter, who had been hanged, lying by the road under a tree with a rope around his neck and his feet tied.'[10]

The German soldier's crime was *Wehrkraftzersetzung*, an offence invented by the Nazis, which meant 'negatively affecting the fighting forces', or 'defeatism'. Those expressing doubts of the Reich's ability to win the war or concerns about Hitler's leadership could be sentenced by passing Feldjägerkorps personnel, a special force set up in 1943 to curb desertion and maintain discipline. Small patrols, which had the authority of a field judge, could hold an instant *Fliegendes Standgericht* (flying court martial) for any soldier, officer or civilian on the flimsiest of evidence, and within minutes convict and execute anyone suspected of cowardice, lowering morale, malingering or desertion, however so defined. Here is stark evidence that the Third Reich was at war with itself, for at least 18,000 Wehrmacht personnel were executed during the war, mostly for alleged desertion or 'defeatism', of whom 8,000 (plus countless thousands of undocumented civilians, refugees and slave workers) perished at the hands of flying courts martial in the last four months of the war.[11] By contrast, for military crimes such as desertion, the United States executed one (on 31 January, Private Eddie Slovik, at the height of the Battle of the Bulge), and the United Kingdom, none.[12]

From Heidelberg, Major General Withers A. Burress' Century Division recorded an 'unmolested drive' before coming to an abrupt halt at Heilbronn on 4 April, another forty miles along the Neckar. Here, elements of five German divisions had dug in, determined to slug it out. An industrial centre of 100,000, Heilbronn's Communist workers and ancient Jewish communities were heavily persecuted under the Nazis, not a few of them fleeing to the United States and returning as conquering GIs. Eric Levi was one, forced out of his *gymnasium* (high school) in 1935, his family leaving for New York three years later. Levi returned as a medic with Company 'D', 399th Infantry, and able to speak the local *Schwäbisch* dialect, helped interrogate residents, some of whom he knew, and discover where the defenders were lurking.[13]

Heidelberg, Heilbronn and upriver Stuttgart had developed as inland ports, handling wood floated down the Neckar from its catchment areas in the high ground of the Black Forest. They grew wealthy from the trade that passed into the Rhine and as far as the North Sea, with Heilbronn also exploiting nearby coal and salt deposits, whose caverns were used for storing Nazi loot and housing displaced industries. Heilbronn had benefitted from massive investment and expansion in the Nazi era and one of the first autobahns, completed in 1936, ran south to Stuttgart. Thus, the National Socialists in Heilbronn led by Kreisleiter (County Leader, the political rank below Gauleiter) Richard Drauz, were particularly ardent.[14] After a major air raid in December 1944 destroyed much of the old city centre and killed 6,500, he ordered the execution of aircrew parachuting to safety. Labelling them *Luftgangster* (air gangsters), he personally shot an American aviator on 24 March, encouraging others to do the same.

Drauz, an early Nazi Party member and protégé of the regional Gauleiter and Reich Defence Commissar Wilhelm Murr, was one of the nastier fanatics around in the dying days of the Reich. He was an enthusiastic enforcer of Hitler's recent 'Nero Decree', demanding that all be reduced to scorched earth. As the GIs approached, all four bridges over the Neckar were blown, but Drauz also destroyed local factories, disbanded fire brigades, ordered every nearby village turned into a bastion, and executed colleagues who failed to match his zeal. On 3 April, 57-year-old Ortsgruppenleiter (Local Group Leader, the rank below Kreisleiter) Karl Taubenberger was shot for failing to prevent residents from removing a tank barrier.[15] The unfortunate official's remains were left on display with the obligatory sign around his neck, '*Ich bin ein Reichsverräter*' (I am a national traitor).[16]

Assessing that the rim of high ground on the Neckar's eastern bank would prove ideal for defence, with all the other intelligence collected by VI Corps' G-2 cell, General Brooks concluded that Heilbronn, already in ruins, would hold out to the last. On 3 April, two regiments of the Century Division were gathered up, briefed on their mission, and given three days' rations. They struck at dawn the next day, crossing the Neckar at two points in assault boats. Both bridgeheads were immediately hit by impassioned Hitlerjugend, whom Drauz had mobilised, indoctrinated and armed. When the youngsters broke, screaming under an intense mortar counter-barrage, they rushed forward to surrender, or back to their own lines, but were mown down by their own officers. 'These were fourteen- to seventeen-year-olds, who fought like demons until subjected to the intense fire of our mortars,' recorded one GI.[17]

Alongside them were Volkssturm grandfathers, Luftwaffe air-gunners, Kriegsmarine sailors on leave and Afrika Korps veterans, as well as Volksgrenadier draftees, many with little motivation to fight, save the threat of execution from Drauz and his henchmen. Rufus Dalton of Company 'H', 397th Infantry, recalled that Heilbronn 'was like stumbling into a beehive'.[18] German gun positions in the eastern hills interrupted all bridging efforts for several days, while the Neckar's steep banks prevented the 824th Tank Destroyer Battalion, newly equipped with M18 Hellcat armoured vehicles mounting a 76mm gun, or the 781st Tank Battalion's Shermans (the 'Red Raiders' we met in Bitche), from closing to give direct support. Handfuls of GIs and their equipment trickled onto the eastern bank by boat, and occasionally by bridges – which were invariably destroyed as quickly as they were assembled.[19]

To starve the defenders of reinforcements and supplies, the 10th Armored Division sent two combat commands thirty miles behind German lines to take Crailsheim, on the Nuremberg–Heilbronn main supply route, and sever the lifeline into the latter city. With Nuremberg, home to the pre-war rallies and a cradle of National Socialism, only another forty miles up the highway to the east, it was a move the defenders had anticipated. 'The Germans reacted quickly,' noted the 10th Armored's history, 'and threw in planes and ground forces in their biggest display of strength since the Ardennes, to halt this dangerous threat to their rear.'[20] 'Bastogne No. 2' reported some newspapers, as soon it was the 10th's GIs in Crailsheim who were surrounded, not the Germans. 'A fading Wehrmacht and dying Luftwaffe suddenly were rejuvenated in demoniacal fury reminiscent of 1939–40,' claimed one journalist.[21]

On 9 April, A.I. Goldberg of Associated Press accompanied a relief column bringing supplies along the 'Bowling Alley' to the hard-pressed attackers of Crailsheim, themselves surrounded by tank-hunting teams of SS. 'An eighty-eight boomed out from the corner of woods four hundred yards away and scored a direct hit on the convoy. We rolled into a protective ditch and watched exploding gas cans sail over our heads and into the fields on either side of the road,' he reported.[22] During 9–10 April, evoking the earlier drama of Bastogne, the gradually-isolated and surrounded task force had their accompanying engineers prepare Crailsheim's captured airfield to fly in 20,000 gallons of gas, 1,000 rounds of 105mm shells, 7,000 rations and other ammunition. 'Escorted by dozens of blunt-nosed P-47s, fifty C-47s troop carriers then took our casualties out.'[23]

One GI remembered, 'after they had finished unloading the five-gallon jerricans, the inside reeked of raw gasoline. When all had boarded, the pilot got aboard smoking a cigarette, none too careful where the ashes or sparks fell. I remember thinking that would be one Hell of a way to die, but they started the engines and flew off.'[24] Such was the ferocity of the constant attacks by the 17th SS Panzergrenadiers, as well as SS-Kampfgruppe Dirnagel, a battlegroup of 2,500 combat troops stationed in Munich, that after four days the little Allied island of Crailsheim was abandoned. The cost to the 10th Armored was fifty-six killed and over two hundred wounded, though over 1,000 Germans had been 'silenced' and 2,000 made prisoner.[25] Later, when the 141st Infantry of the 36th Texas Division passed through Crailsheim, they saw that 'war had lingered here for a moment – long enough to leave it as hollow and gutted as the scorched-earth towns of France.'[26]

However, when the 10th Armored approached Brettheim ten miles to the north, the villagers refused to show white flags of surrender. Incensed, GIs hit the settlement with a brief but intense wave of shell-fire, killing seventeen. Then it transpired they had all wanted to capitulate but did nothing through fear. When assured the Nazis would not return, the doughboys were led to the village cemetery where they found three men hanging from trees. Then the story came out. Days earlier, Johann Rössler, a member of the local Volkssturm detachment, had quit, while others disarmed four Hitlerjugend intent on making Brettheim a battleground, throwing their weapons into the village pond. The youths ran off, reported this to Nazi officials, and the same evening, several SS men arrived to investigate.

Rössler was immediately found guilty of *Wehrkraftzersetzung* (undermining military morale) and shot, while farmer Friedrich Hanselmann was assessed as being involved and condemned to death. When two local officials, Bürgermeister Gackstatter and Ortsgruppenleiter Leonhard Wolfmeyer, refused to endorse the sentence, they too were sentenced to death. On 10 April, all three had been hanged as a warning to others. 'The German *Volk* are determined to wipe out such cowardly, selfish, and disloyal traitors, and will not shrink from also expunging their families from the community of those who fight with honour,' ranted SS-Gruppenführer Max Simon, chief of the local XII SS Korps, headquartered in the nearby Schloss Schillingsfürst. He had signed the death warrant with a handwritten annotation: 'Hang the bastards, leave bodies on display.' It was his anger that cowed the residents of Brettheim into inactivity when the GIs arrived, who promptly shelled them. SS zeal had caused the needless deaths of twenty-one civilians. Consequently, the survivors welcomed the Americans not as occupiers, but as liberators.[27]

This was a story oft-repeated throughout small-town Germany, the 101st Cavalry Group recording the army-wide procedures when occupying each new settlement. 'We would summon the Bürgermeister and have him direct all citizens to turn in their weapons, binoculars and cameras. If we were to remain overnight, he was told to arrange for billets in private homes, a *Gasthaus* or school. The Group's interpreter, a German-speaking sergeant, was eventually wounded, and evacuated, so our Catholic Chaplain, Father Powers, sometimes had to converse in Latin with the local priest. The reaction of the Germans varied from sullenness to friendliness but rarely outright belligerence. Most were glad that Americans had come and not Russians.'[28]

'Crailsheim was wrecked,' recalled Staff Sergeant Donald R. Jerge, a New Yorker with Company 'A', 54th Armored Infantry Battalion. 'The Germans had bombed, strafed and shelled it so much that it looked like Saint-Lo and other badly-damaged French towns.'[29] The weather, so often overlooked in these accounts, made a difference here, for the drizzle of spring still softened everything apart from metalled roads, forcing the American vehicles to keep to the highways, where they were targeted by panzerfaust-wielding, rifle-grenade-bearing Volksgrenadiers, Hitlerjugend and SS. Despite the intermittent overcast, Messerschmitt-109s and jet-propelled 262s swooped on US units at every turn. 'At no time, except when the Germans controlled the air in [North] Africa, have I ever seen so many German planes as over the Crailsheim area,' reported Brigadier General Edwin W. Piburn, then leading the 10th's Combat Command 'A'.[30]

Abandoning Crailsheim entailed 'a miserable trip back through the woods at night, as we foundered in ditches a couple of times', remembered Staff Sergeant Jerge of his half-track. 'We used a white cloth so the tank behind could avoid ramming into us, and the pitch blackness was filled with sparks, the roar of tanks and clink of half-tracks as we rolled past knocked-out German and American vehicles on both sides of the road, where we had fought only a few days before.'[31] Leaving Crailsheim on 11 April, the 10th immediately shifted its combat weight back to Heilbronn, where all three regiments of the 100th Division were slowly dissolving Drauz's defenders.

For all the Century men, Heilbronn was their first experience of urban combat. As the 397th Infantry made for a factory and warehouse area, Second Lieutenant Erle Theimer, with Company 'H', and just in

receipt of a battlefield commission, mused, 'Getting down to the pontoon boats and in them with all our gear was nerve-wracking. We paddled across, racing as fast as we could. From the boats to the [factory
complex] wall seemed like a couple of football fields. Going over the
wall beyond seemed to take forever.'[32] For Corporal Clarence Rincker, a
radioman with Company 'H', his baptism of fire came at the same wall.
'A sniper's bullet snapped past my head with such a loud crack that I
just about jerked my head off in reflex. I took off immediately and had
no trouble clearing the five-foot stone wall in front of me in one big
jump.'[33] Most men made it into the various factory buildings but were
pinned down over the next twenty-four hours by its German defenders
and friendly artillery fire.

Several men of the 397th's Company 'E' had ruptured eardrums as
a result, and one of the Company's medics, Joe Cosby, recollected a GI
'in horrible shell shock after our building had been hit. He was screaming and I had to hush him up. It really was the only chance of saving
him because he couldn't just run from the building. I put my hand forcibly over his mouth and ushered him down to a coal cellar where he
stayed for three days.'[34] Ken Siebe, in the same company, remembered
his opponents firing through windows at the GIs inside. 'They were
firing tracer – at night you could see the paths of bullets as they came
through the windows. The Germans started shooting their panzerfäuste
at the building, which dislodged concrete on the inside, creating missiles
as deadly as the bullets they were shooting. Lieutenant Petracco took a
position a little bit behind and to the right of me, and I remember when
he took a bullet to the neck or to the head – Captain Law held him in
his lap on the floor as he died.'[35]

Both sides had met on an equal footing, but the 100th Division were
better resourced and had air support (when it could fly) on their side.
Slowly, their opponents began to run out of energy, enthusiasm – and
men. After four days of relentless combat in the factory and beyond,
the Century's two bridgeheads managed to unite and push the Germans back, but it still took another four days and the arrival of the 10th
Armored, attacking from the rear, before Heilbronn was subdued on
12 April, and its 1,500 remaining defenders marched into captivity.

Two weeks later, Heilbronn resident Robert Bauer wrote in his diary,

'Severe battle damage everywhere. All major factories totally destroyed. On the corner of Wilhelmstrasse black and white American soldiers are playing handball with two German boys. Russian and Polish workers harassing women. The Bismarck statue is undamaged. Unmoved, the Old Man looks out over the bombed city and ruined bridge. One might think his gaze is even harsher and gloomier because of the terrible effects of a policy that deviated his path of keeping and securing peace with the Russians.'[36]

On 15 April, worried about the German Nineteenth Army in the Schwartzwald (Black Forest) withdrawing to an Alpine redoubt, SHAEF directed Devers to isolate this threat by taking Stuttgart, to the east and thirty miles south of Heilbronn. Capital of the former kingdom of Württemberg and the Fatherland's sixth largest metropolis at 500,000, Stuttgart sits in a bowl surrounded by high ridges and vine-covered hills on all sides except in the north which opens onto the Neckar. Consequently, Allied bombers found it easy to locate and in fifty-three raids dropped 27,000 tons of munitions on its railway yards, as well as Bosch, Daimler-Benz, and other factories.

At a cost of around three hundred Allied aircraft and 2,400 aircrew, 68 per cent of residential buildings and 75 per cent of industrial plant lay in ruins by the time the GIs arrived on 22 April. Stuttgart was no longer a city, but a moonscape: rubble totalling 6.4 million cubic yards greeted them. City records found in the Stuttgarter Politzeipräsidium (the old city hall, but by then the Gestapo headquarters), revealed that 4,562 Württembergers had perished with 8,908 injured. The area was less easy to defend than Heilbronn, and by the second half of April 1945, even the most ardent of Nazis found their enthusiasm for dying in a stinking ruin fast evaporating. Preceded by their friends of the 10th Armored, the Century Division, with McAuliffe's 103rd on their left, and the 44th beyond them, circled round to the south-east, closing the door on any fleeing Wehrmacht units. They entered the city along the Alte Weinsteige (Old Wine Road), meeting little opposition – but were puzzled to find the French Army already in possession.

General Devers had directed that the capture of the Schwarzwald and Stuttgart area be conducted by de Lattre's force. They had been operating all this while on Patch's right. Post-war Anglo-American writers have consistently struck an anti-French note, if mentioning them at all. Frequent claims were that their fellow combatants were 'weak', 'forever lagging behind', implying they were slow, bumbling and incompetent.[37] None of this was true. It is worth recalling that although the Frenchmen crossed the Rhine slightly later, they had their own logistics challenges; and though there had been political disagreements, liaison and cooperation at the tactical and operational levels were excellent. However, at Stuttgart the common Allied cause was tested to its limit.

Unknown to Devers, de Lattre was under huge pressure from his political master to gain as large an area of Catholic south-west Germany as possible. De Gaulle was fully aware of Anglo-American-Soviet plans to carve up the Reich discussed at Yalta in February, from which he was absent. He had thus determined, as part of his plan for France to once again become a world power, to have his fair share of the aggressor's terrain. De Lattre noted, 'For a Frenchman the problem did not exist; to take part in the invasion of Germany was for our country a duty and a right. Yet the plans of the Supreme Allied Command did not answer to our wishes in the least.'[38]

Devers, as directed by SHAEF, foresaw no such ambitious plans for an expansive French occupation zone, if anything a modest bridgehead around forty miles deep, opposite Strasbourg. His Chief G-3 (Operations), Brigadier General Reuben Jenkins, summarised the anticipated role of the French: 'The initial effort by First French Army would be more in the nature of a holding effort which would indicate weakness and encourage the Germans to stay in their position [in the Black Forest] until our VI Corps was in proper position [to sweep round to their rear] . . . which was explained in considerable detail to General de Lattre personally at a conference in his office on the afternoon of 17 April.'[39]

Yet when de Lattre summoned his two corps commanders to his headquarters in Karlsruhe in the early hours of 18 April, he envisaged far more. He now had nine divisions across the Rhine, in compliance with de Gaulle's wishes, but not Devers', who had cautioned 'against a premature advance of the First French Army'. First, de Lattre directed his formations to envelop the Black Forest. De Monsabert's II Corps, who had jumped the Rhine first, was already clearing its northern fringe and advancing to Freudenstadt, on its eastern edge. Béthouart's I Corps was to drive from their assembly area east of the Rhine, through the central Schwarzwald, likewise meeting in Freudenstadt, a town of 20,000, some forty miles from the Rhine and equidistant between Strasbourg and Stuttgart. Founded in 1599 as a refuge for Protestants fleeing Catholic Salzburg, Freudenstadt, meaning 'town of joy', was exactly the sort of occupation headquarters Devers had in mind for the French.

However, de Lattre also ordered Béthouart, 'From Freudenstadt you will then exploit southward, encircle the Black Forest from the east, cross the Danube on 22 April, take Ulm with your left, and push on into Austria with your right.'[40] He also directed them to take Sigmaringen, a midpoint between Freudenstadt and Ulm. Inside the Hohenzollern-owned Gothic Schloss Sigmaringen, perched on a rocky outcrop overlooking the town, Vichy survived in a bizarre mini-state, having fled France. Pretty much as hostages, from 7 September 1944, Pétain and his fellow *collabos* had established a government-in-exile with ambassadorial presence from the German, Italian and Japanese governments. Hundreds of Fascist fellow travellers who faced execution in France had arrived as well.

Here is evidence that French operations were being swayed by emotion as well as military concerns, for the passion of de Lattre's written orders to de Monsabert is evident: 'Go full throttle for Sigmaringen, shut up everything, hold it in force, put in a master, firm and hard, someone who locks up the collaborators and will keep silent until I arrive.' However, when the 1st French Armoured Division arrived on 22 April, Général Sudre's men found 'what only the day before had the pretension of being the picturesque but ridiculous capital of a "French Government". *Hélas!* The collaborators had cleared out some hours before.'[41]

At the same time, de Lattre ordered his II Corps to charge another fifty miles north-east into Stuttgart. If both corps moved quickly, these manoeuvres, although grossly exceeding Devers' expectations, and poaching on Seventh Army's territory, would fulfil the overall aim of cutting off the retreat of all hostile units in Baden and Württemberg, for to the south lay neutral Switzerland.[42] This would bring de Lattre not only a springboard into Austria, but an occupation zone to meet de Gaulle's aspirations.

On 21 April, at the precise moment Béthouart's 1st Armoured Division was crossing the Danube a day early, de Monsabert's II Corps was infiltrating Stuttgart. Guillaume's 3rd Algerians took the north of the city, while the 5th French Armoured and 2nd Moroccan Divisions occupied the south, capturing 28,000 prisoners and splitting in two the Wehrmacht's 64th Korps, with whom they had battled all through the Vosges and Colmar. Now arose a question of boundaries, for the French had entered Patch's territory. De Lattre reasoned his rights to the city were unquestionable since his soldiers were the ones to have captured it, a day ahead of the Century Division. De Lattre attempted to keep the mood sweet with his opposite number, Patch, and wrote of the double-stemmed flower they had shared eight months earlier. 'I am happy, *mon Général*, that our two Armies, side by side, should be delivering the final *coup de grâce*. The little flower gathered in August has brought luck to our armies. I still keep it.'[43]

Stuttgart was ringed with slave labour sites, which had included many concentration camp inmates from Natzweiler-Struthof, near Strasbourg, whose discovery we noted earlier. Natzweiler had administered up to seventy satellites in Alsace, Lorraine, Baden and Württemberg. On 8 April, Colonel Jacques de la Boisse's 3rd Régiment de Tirailleurs Algériens arrived at Vaihingen-an-der-Enz, fifteen miles north-west of Stuttgart. 'We sort of fell on it quite by accident,' recorded the war correspondent Evelyn Irons, attached to the parent Algerian Division. 'Inside the enclosure, clinging to the trellis-wired cage were men in rough prison suits. They included French, Czechs, Hungarians, Lithuanians, Russians, Poles. Some were so weak they could hardly stand. Their cropped heads were scarred and verminous. Their hands outstretched towards us were like claws.'[44]

De Lattre remembered the inmates as 'spectres, animated skeletons wandering about in convicts' clothes. Haggard, incapable of smiling, these deportees had been ending their lives in a camp where the SS had abandoned only the moribund and the dead.[45] Days earlier, 515 prisoners had been taken to Dachau by the SS; these were the 650 detainees left behind. First established as a labour camp then transformed into a stockade for the seriously ill, Vaihingen was the site of 1,700 deaths, including eighty-four after liberation, who were beyond help. Irons concluded, 'its discovery suddenly gave our [French] soldiers a new and implacable motive for fighting.'[46]

Another work site was the Luftwaffe night-fighter airbase at Stuttgart-Echterdingen, six miles south of the city centre. Air raids in the summer of 1944 prompted the Organisation Todt, the Luftwaffe and Air Ministry to request six hundred workers from Natzweiler to clear the runway of rubble and fill in bomb craters. All Jewish, they hailed from a wide range of countries,[47] were billeted in Hangar Thirteen, penned in by barbed wire, and observed by four watchtowers. To rebuild the runway, they had to quarry stone from two nearby sites, overseen by Luftwaffe guards, but directed by a brutal Alsatian SS officer, Untersturmführer René Romann.

The heavy physical work and poor nutrition soon led to a minimum of 119 recorded deaths. In January 1945, an outbreak of typhus forced the closure of Echterdingen, and the survivors were marched elsewhere. In a scene repeated all over Germany, when the arriving French troops liberated an empty site on 20 April, there was no sign of the inmates. It was only in September 2005, when building work at the location, by then a US airbase, uncovered the remains of thirty-four Jewish forced labourers, that the area's dark past was revealed.[48]

As Devers had anticipated using Stuttgart as a logistical base for Patch in his drive further into Germany, he ordered de Lattre's men out of the city and Brooks' VI Corps to occupy it in their place. This difference of views prompted an exchange of responses that eventually rose to the national level. Wisely, to resolve the situation, both Devers and de Lattre exchanged correspondence with one another while simultaneously appealing to their higher headquarters. The Frenchman immediately contacted de Gaulle, whose response was direct: de Lattre's presence in Stuttgart was to continue; military government teams sent from Paris were to begin their work of communicating French policy to the occupied Germans, while the Allies thrashed out the details of a French zone of occupation. Furthermore, by way of those diplomatic sweeteners that often solve crises, de Lattre was to let Devers know that 'Stuttgart was available to meet the needs of the Sixth Army Group, but would remain under French occupation'.[49]

However, complicating the situation were newspaper stories of mass rape and looting in Stuttgart itself. The reported North African perpetrators of these abuses had initiated similar outrages in Italy the previous year, where 12,000 victims were eventually identified, causing Pope Pius XII to complain to Général Juin. Eventually his Corps Expéditionnaire Français had been withdrawn and absorbed into de Lattre's force before invading the Riviera. Such sexual violence – in Italy, the victims had also included men and livestock – was a Moroccan tradition of asserting status over the conquered which de Lattre's officers ought to have foreseen. In fact, it turned out that the rapes and looting were largely undertaken by released slave labourers, and not de Monsabert's colonials.

Devers was sufficiently concerned to visit the city on 27 April to investigate. As he noted in his diary, 'I immediately contacted Generals Patch and Burress [of the Century Division]. I had with me Colonel Lodge [his liaison officer]. I verified facts and found them to be substantially as stated . . . but greatly exaggerated.' Devers with Lodge visited a local divisional commander, announcing, 'Look, I didn't come here to accuse your troops of rape. I came to protect you. Do you want it spread all over the press that this great and glorious division did these things in Stuttgart?' He said much the same to de Lattre, observing, 'I desired very much in the interest of the French nation that he take immediate steps to correct these excesses.' The French commander 'shot an officer and a couple of enlisted men and that stopped all the foolishness'. At SHAEF's behest, Devers was forced to accept the Francophone occupation, changing the army boundaries to give Stuttgart to de Lattre – but he left Lodge in Stuttgart for several days to ensure the French restored order.[50]

However, there was another aspect to the American reaction to France overstepping the mark in Stuttgart, which few historians have unravelled. The Alsos Mission was the name given by Brigadier General Leslie Groves, in charge of the Manhattan Project (America's operation to develop atomic weapons), to a top-secret task force sent to Europe to track down German research on nuclear fission, seize uranium ore, capture scientists and destroy their facilities. Cooperating with the equally shadowy T-Force (an Anglo-American military mission to secure German scientific and industrial technology before it could be destroyed or fall into Russian hands), this intelligence arm of the Manhattan Project eventually comprised over one hundred counter-intelligence officers, linguists and scientists.[51]

Operating across Europe in the vanguard of the advancing Allies, Alsos personnel chased shipments of fissionable materials, scientists and documents from Italy, Belgium and Holland to France and Germany. In March, intelligence indicated that the German atomic project had relocated to several small towns south of Stuttgart centred on Hechingen, midway between the city and the Swiss border. So sensitive was the matter that Devers and the SHAEF Chief of Staff, Bedell Smith, authorised Operation *Effective* for 22 April. This was to be a desant by the entire US 13th Airborne Division, then in SHAEF reserve, who were to occupy the area, capture an airfield and fly out seized material and scientists. Thus, we now know there was another reason for Devers to retain control of the Stuttgart area – to deny fission research and scientists from falling into French hands, where Communist sympathisers, it was felt, would pass the findings on to Stalin.[52]

Due to the pace of de Lattre's sudden advance, *Effective* was cancelled on 19 April and Operation *Big* substituted. This was a ground-based force comprising forty Alsos military officers and scientists, grafted on to the US 1269th Engineer Combat Battalion, lent by Brooks' VI Corps. Led by Lieutenant Colonel Boris Pash, a Manhattan Project Counter Intelligence Corps expert, and obscurely known as Task Force 'A', a column of trucks and Jeeps, armed to the teeth, set off behind German lines on 20 April. At times they came under hostile fire but managed to locate the missing scientists in several locations, dismantle a small experimental nuclear reactor, retrieve three drums of heavy water and one and a half tons of uranium ingots, load what they could into trucks and destroy the rest. All this was done under the noses of the French, who had no idea what had just occurred.[53]

Devers and de Lattre might have buried the hatchet had not French intransigence resurfaced almost immediately. This time the bone of contention was the city of Ulm on the Danube, whose capture de Lattre had ordered on 18 April. The original army boundaries, drawn by Devers and agreed by de Lattre, put Ulm inside Seventh Army territory by a full forty miles, in the path of the US 44th Division. This infantry division by now had learned to travel the quickest way, by clinging to hulls of their Shermans and tank destroyer units. Indiana University graduate Walter McElvain, with the 44th Divisional Signals Company, recalled this swift advance and the transition from 'those early Spring days we spent lazily in the green hills of Alsace. Instead, we are rumbling around in a rugged terrain and surrounded by a mute, hostile people. They stare at you sullenly, insolently, or just look the other way. Some of the kids, unable to cover their fiercer emotions, stick out their tongues, spit at you, or take mock pistol shots at you.'[54]

However, for many GIs at this time of chase, the last couple of months of the war went by in a blur. As Dean M. White, also 44th Division, observed with a ring of honesty, 'As a replacement rifleman, I knew which Division I was in. We had a badge of two fours, back-to-back. I forget which regiment. All I needed to know was that I was in Company 'B', First Battalion; I knew my sergeants, but not the officers who came and went, often shot by snipers. I couldn't tell you exactly where I fought. It didn't matter: April 1945 was a never-ending series of smashed towns and dusty roads, some were mined, sometimes we were ambushed. I knew the names of some big cities, but none of the small towns, they were all the same. All I wanted was a house with a roof, or basement, as I hated having to dig a foxhole to escape those mortars – and there were few of those.'[55] Another GI noted, 'The scenes of destruction have perhaps never before been surpassed anywhere in the world. Town after town had completely lost its identity, smashed by our air corps, and torn by our artillery and infantry. People lived in the ruins of their once immaculate homes, a drab contrast to the proud people who were set to rule the world.'[56]

Despite being warned that the US 44th Infantry and 10th Armored were racing to Ulm, de Lattre nevertheless instructed his 1st French Armoured Division to drive hard for the same city. They arrived on 23 April, simultaneously with the 10th Armored who were surprised to find the French in their area. Its commander, Major General William H. Morris, seemed to sense de Lattre's aim and made no difficulties, instead exclaiming, 'We cavalrymen will always understand each other.' Again, it was the French who ended up in possession, de Lattre proud it was the *tricolore* that flew over Ulm, as it had done in 1805 when

Napoleon bested an Austrian force of 23,000 outside the city, effectively ending the War of the Third Coalition.

Aware there would again be fireworks, de Lattre – at his diplomatic best – sent Patch a carefully worded signal, which, at the tactical level, appears to have worked. 'It is my desire to express to you the joy we feel in returning, in brotherly union with your army, to Ulm which is so full of historical memories particularly precious to French soldiers. I wish to express my feelings at this moment, when armored detachments of First French Army, in liaison with their Seventh Army comrades, are reaching this town. It is my wish to renew the expression of my most friendly and faithful combat comradeship to you.'[57]

Full of his sense of history but completely unaware of the Franco-American tensions, Winston Churchill unhelpfully waded in with a telegram addressed to de Gaulle. 'Please accept my congratulations on the capture of Ulm by French arms. I should be grateful if you would convey to General de Lattre and his brave soldiers my admiration for their prowess and success.' The Frenchman craftily used this to legitimise his actions, and flatteringly responded, 'The French soldiers are very grateful for these words from the fighter and leader that you are.'[58]

On the ground, the Sixth Army Group commander was predictably furious. When Général André Demetz, de Lattre's new chief of staff, was summoned to Devers' presence to explain, he bore from his boss an evasive letter which illustrated the predicament in which the French Army commander found himself. 'In view of the fact that my head of government has given me, in precise terms, my actions to be taken, I can exert no initiative of my own on the matter.' Demetz recorded, 'Devers – that good and upright Devers – was angrier than I had ever seen him'.[59]

Devers correctly appealed to Eisenhower, stating he could not tolerate 'such interference with [Sixth Army Group's] tactical operations by the chief of the French Government and the Commanding General'. Ike was so alarmed at the threat to Allied cohesion that he warned de Gaulle on 28 April, 'As you are aware, orders were issued by Gen. Devers to Gen. de Lattre to evacuate Stuttgart. I regret to learn that because of instructions received direct from you, Gen. de Lattre has declined to obey the orders of his Army Group Commander. Under the circumstances, I must of course accept the situation, as I myself am unwilling to take action which would reduce the effectiveness of the military effort against Germany. I can do nothing else than fully inform the Combined Chiefs of Staff of this development, and to point out that I can no longer count with certainty upon the operational use of any French forces they may contemplate equipping in the future.'[60]

As Devers would later observe, 'De Lattre was a great student of Napoleon, and although times, people and weapons have changed, the names of rivers and towns had not. This caused General de Lattre to be naughty. He had a feeling – not justified – that I gave him roles sometimes not in keeping with French tradition.'[61] Devers' forbearance and the tone of his comments was admirable; Eisenhower's other two army group commanders, Bradley and Montgomery, would have been far more hawkish and less forgiving.

On 25 April Captain Charles F. Marshall, one of Brooks' VI Corps intelligence officers, visited Lucie, wife of the late Generalfeldmarschall Rommel, at the family home in the Ulm suburb of Herrlingen. The purpose was to request any useful documents she might have, but during a pleasant chat, Frau Rommel had broken down and revealed that 'her husband had not died of a heart attack but had been poisoned by two generals sent to Herrlingen by Hitler [on 14 October 1944] for that purpose. Since she still had a son in the army, she begged us to say nothing until the boy was killed or captured.'[62] Two days later, French forces captured Manfred Rommel in Luftwaffe uniform in nearby Reidlingen. That same evening, the sixteen-year-old was interrogated by de Lattre himself and swore in a witnessed deposition how 'his father had been forced to take poison by two of Hitler's generals in response to the 20 July 1944 plot, and that the murder had been concealed by the regime'. The story would be smothered by other war news, and it was not until January 1950 that some of the true story of the life and death of the acclaimed Desert Fox emerged.[63]

Christabel Bielenberg, an Englishwoman whose German husband was on the run from the authorities because of his friendship with some of those connected to the same 20 July plot against Hitler's life led by Count von Stauffenberg, had fled Berlin for the rural sanctuary of Rohrbach, a pretty hamlet in the Black Forest near Furtwangen. While her community waited for liberation, the commanders of three retreating

German divisions were billeted in Rohrbach until moving out on the night of 24–25 April. As they scurried away southwards, elements of the 1st Spahis Brigade and Groupement Bourgund (task forces of the 9th Colonial Infantry Division) were hard on their heels. 'By morning, the muddy green river was flowing down the winding road to Schönenbach,' she wrote, referring to the French uniforms.[64]

Bielenberg noticed how the Wehrmacht's military transport had been reduced to oxen, horses, bicycles, farm carts and Alsatian-drawn dog sledges. 'All the motor transport had been pushed into the fields, tipped up and abandoned, since the last drop of petrol had to be saved for the [generals'] Mercedes.' The last soldiers to leave 'flung hand grenades and lighted torches into the abandoned motor transport'. That night the village was a hive of industry. 'There was so much to scavenge. Provisions, cigarettes, fine leather straps, axles, tyres, and wheels, so much that could come in useful was stored beneath the hay. The next morning spotless white drapery fluttered and flapped from every farmhouse, as if we had all taken part in some stupendous communal washing day.'

Bielenberg later walked into the village mayor's office and immediately noticed the usual portrait of the Führer was missing. On being told it was already in the room's central heating stove, she felt emboldened to ask him, 'Did you ever hear the story of Hitler looking at his portrait and saying, "I wonder what will happen to you and me after the war's over," and the picture answering back, "You will be hung, and I will be unhung – *aufgehängt, abgehängt*."' In earlier times, her witticism would have got her shot; now the mayor and his clerk burst out laughing. 'It wasn't a funny story really, but God, how we laughed! It was as if some spring within us, tense and taut over the years, had all of a sudden been released. We were instinctively, impulsively bent on hurling to the winds the deception, the evasion, the cant, the dreadful pressure, in one convulsive storm of near-hysteria.'[65]

The Berlin journalist Ursula von Kardorff had likewise relocated, in her case to the small Württemberg town of Jettingen, near Ulm, and recorded the French arrival. On 24 April, she noted, 'SS troops are reported to have set fire to farms around Ulm, and all the bridges are blown. I do not mean to be a victim of such mad destruction.' The following day, to the sound of 'shells and mortars bursting around us, the last scene of a dreadful drama', she dropped into the local River Mindel 'a handful of [Nazi] Party badges handed over to me in secret', something she had 'longed to do for many years past'. She noticed others burying uniforms, all the while to 'distant gunfire and dull explosions'.

Then a friend arrived with the shocking news: 'We cheered too soon. We have to take the flags down.' Von Kardorff recorded 'the parson, the mayor and the Orstgruppenleiter have been arrested by the SS and taken away. The SS are now our most dangerous enemies, worse than the Americans [in fact, it was the French] who are overrunning us.' Then finally, on 26 April, salvation. 'They are here. Their tanks are rumbling through the main street of the village. Men in khaki everywhere. Some of them smile at one in quite a friendly manner.'[66] In fact, true salvation from the war was a mere twelve days distant.

In *Crusade in Europe*, Eisenhower looked back at the difference in French and Anglo-American war aims. 'When inspired, the French are great fighters,' he wrote with a touch of cynicism. 'I personally like de Gaulle, as I recognized in him many fine qualities. We felt, however, that these qualities were marred by hypersensitiveness and an extraordinary stubbornness in matters that appeared inconsequential to us.'[67] However, Eisenhower (and his ghost-writer and personal aide Harry C. Butcher) was commenting when the Cold War was at its height when France was seen as a key European ally, and was thus restrained in his comments. He probably admired de Gaulle's tenacity, rather than liking him as an individual.

The contretemps over Stuttgart and Ulm induced the Western Allies, as de Gaulle hoped, to agree a large zone of French occupation. Recognising the direction in which the French wind was blowing, Devers sensibly set future objectives for de Lattre in southern Germany rather than in the east. It is a testament to his ability as a coalition commander that he bore no malice. Three weeks later, he expressed a wish to join in the French celebration of the Festival of Joan of Arc, held in Stuttgart, where he exclaimed publicly and with tongue in cheek, 'For many months we have fought together – often on the same side!'[68] A similar crack from Bradley or Montgomery would have been beyond the wit of either man.

De Lattre's men remained in Stuttgart until the Allied occupation zones were finally agreed on 8 July 1945, then withdrew. In the 1950s, with no regard for its pre-war historic splendour, but reflecting the urgent need for mass housing, huge chunks of the city were torn down and rebuilt to a new street plan. The resultant modernist concrete blocks confused veterans returning to trace their war and few were able to identify a single landmark. In 1948 the city applied to become the new West German capital; although eclipsed by Bonn, Stuttgart did become a major centre of US military activity in post-war Germany, since 1952 hosting US European Command (EUCOM), appropriately in Patch Barracks. Over the years, their generosity has enabled me to explore the April 1945 battlefields in considerable detail.

In 1974, Manfred Rommel was elected Oberbürgermeister (Lord Mayor) of Stuttgart, a post he held for twenty-two years. He did much to restore good relations with America, Britain and France, forming personal friendships with Major General George S. Patton IV, and David Montgomery, Second Viscount, the sons of his wartime adversaries. As big a man politically as his father was militarily, he was the recipient of an honorary CBE from Her Majesty the Queen in 1990 for improving Anglo–German relations. When I met him in Westminster Abbey at a service to commemorate the sixtieth anniversary of Alamein, he confided that the most intimidating individual he ever met was – Général de Lattre. 'He was the same height as my late father but had a piercing gaze that never left you.'[69]

(*Above*): Overlooking the Main river, this is Schloss Johannisburg at Aschaffenburg, dating to 1605, and HQ of its Kommandant. Beyond lie the stone and brick buildings of the old town. All were gutted by US aircraft and 45th 'Thunderbird' Division artillery, during the battle of 28 March–3 April 1945. (*Below*): The struggle for Würzburg followed during 3–5 April. These German prisoners march in front of the sabotaged 1543 bridge. The Heil Hitler slogan on the 1640s Marienburg fortress was soon replaced by one reading '42nd Rainbow Division'.

12

Aschaffenburg, Würzburg and Schweinfurt

Patch's Seventh Army were chasing the Germans hard. They could smell victory. Operating north of the French, let us follow Haislip's XV Corps, which had encountered little opposition since the Rhine. Until, fifty miles due east, they arrived at the River Main. There, at Aschaffenburg, their opponents were dug in and waiting. For the Thunderbird Division the ensuing struggle came as an unwelcome surprise. They had been lulled into a false sense of security over the preceding days and were assured the area had already been cleared by Combat Command 'B' of the 4th Armored Division. The latter belonged to Patton's Third Army, whose southern boundary lay on their left flank. After four months of tough fighting through the Vosges, during *Nordwind*, in Colmar and the Saar, Haislip's GIs were expecting a moment to draw breath.

It is worth dwelling on the fight for Aschaffenburg, as it represents so many similar struggles, large and small, in the towns and cities of western Germany at this time. Perched on an outcrop of high ground, the settlement of 30,000 had been an important military centre overlooking a bend of the River Main since Roman days. Two Germanic armies had clashed there in the Austro–Prussian War of 1866. A fortified waypoint on the Frankfurt–Nuremberg road, it also sat in the middle of a seventy-mile defensive line of three hundred bunkers linking Wetter, Main and Tauber river valleys. Work on these fortifications was abandoned after the Rhineland was occupied in 1936 and the Siegfried Line constructed further west. However, in March 1945 they were reoccupied and strengthened, when the phrase *nach dem Sieg graben* (dig for victory) took on an ominous, new meaning. Equally drawn into the struggle was the nearby settlement of Schweinheim; flanking Volksgren-adier divisions manned the home bank of the Main, north and south, with each written down to a strength of 3,000–5,000 men.[1]

Apart from a sizeable tank repair workshop full of half-assembled but immobile Panthers, there were five *Kasernen* (military barracks) in town, one of which was the domain of Major Emil Lamberth, a World War One veteran and reserve officer, who since July 1944 had com-manded the local engineer training battalion in this backwater.[2] Greying and bespectacled, he had been a college teacher before the war, and was a dedicated Nazi. By early 1945 his base housed an Ersatzheer (Reserve Army) officer school, whose training area around the town took advan-tage of the pre-existing web of defensive pillboxes linked by trenches. When the Thunderbirds' 157th Regiment arrived, Lamberth's six hun-dred students, well drilled in classroom exercises of how to defend Aschaffenburg, put their scholarly studies into practice.

Lamberth also rounded up an eclectic mix of Volksgrenadiers, Waffen-SS, police, Hungarian volunteers, Luftwaffe stragglers, Hitler Youth and Volkssturm. Totalling around 5,000, they were designated *Kampfkommando* (Combat Command) *Aschaffenburg*. Initially, they had no heavy artillery or panzers, and the Volkssturm possessed only old rifles, the odd machine-gun and panzerfäuste. Yet numbers do not tell the full story: many of Lamberth's 5,000 were 'battle babes', who had seen little or no action. Others were convalescents turned out of hos-pitals, their average age around forty. Generally, the defenders were far older when compared to the mid-twenties of the GIs, each of whom was fitter, and had experienced at least a year of boot camp in America or combat in Europe. All these the Major commanded from his headquar-ters, which he relocated into the Schloss Johannisburg, a huge castel-lated Renaissance palace dating from 1614, built over several preceding forts stretching back to Roman times, which dominates both town and river from the eastern bank.[3]

Typical of the Hitlerjugend was fifteen-year-old local resident Man-fred Baunach, who first dug anti-tank ditches alongside slave labour-ers, was then posted as an observer in the towers of the schloss, and finally delivered messages by motorcycle. He remembered his training to operate a panzerfaust. 'It was quite easy to use, and I fired several on exercises. I saw the Volkssturm use them, too. However, operating it made deep demands of our courage. We were issued bicycles and straps to carry two panzerfäuste.[4] Then we trained to lie in wait, maybe by the side of a road. When a tank or other vehicle rolled past at point-blank range, we were to rise suddenly, fire, throw it away and use the other.'

Baunach recollected his instructor ordering him to take a deep breath, then say '*Sieg Heil*' silently to himself, which steadied the body for a better aim, before firing. 'In truth, you would fire the thing and bolt for safety like a startled deer. At night we practised a stealthy crawl toward an American *laager*, like Red Indians. All the time we must avoid being seen or heard. It was an effective weapon, we saw that. But at the same time, it was a suicide job. We were trained to be prepared to die, just for the chance of disabling a Yankee panzer.'[5]

Hitler was convinced that the defence of urban areas acted as a force multiplier at the operational level of war. The Russian defence of Stalingrad still obsessed and haunted him, and in creating fortresses across the shrinking Fatherland, he aimed to impose extortionate casualties he felt the Western Allies could not afford and would not tolerate. The first city in the west to fall had been Aachen, which had held out for five days when surrounded in October, but the wider impact on US First Army was a huge casualty bill and the end of their 'Home for Christmas' hopes for 1944.

Closely scrutinised by Kreisleiter Heinmuth Wohlgemuth, the regional Nazi administrator who was also the Oberbürgermeister, Lamberth was assessed as having the necessary fanaticism to be promoted to Festung Kommandant (fortress commander) on 5 March, over the heads of other higher-ranking colleagues who ran the district's military replacement barracks and convalescent centres. On 23 April, Major Lamberth had received the code word *Gneisenau* and readied the town for combat. They had already suffered eight major air raids. On 28–29 March, civilians who wished were permitted by Wohlgemuth to leave. The estimated 3,500 residents who remained hid in basements or a nearby quarry, subject to martial law. On pain of death, Lamberth's word was the new authority over everyone – all civilians as well as those in uniform.[6]

As if they were a class of delinquent schoolboys, he addressed his garrison in uncompromising terms: 'Soldiers, Men of the Volkssturm, Comrades – the Fortress of Aschaffenburg will be defended to the last man. As of today, everyone is to give to his last. I order that no one shall rest more than three hours out of twenty. I forbid anyone sitting around or loafing. Our belief is that it is our mission to give the cursed enemy the greatest resistance and to send as many of them as possible to the Devil.'[7] In his words, Lamberth was echoing the stand-and-fight mentality handed down on 26 February by SS-Oberst-Gruppenführer Hausser of Army Group 'G', that 'He who gives up the fight is not only a coward, but he also betrays our women and children. All soldiers separated from their units who are found loitering on roads, in towns, with the trains, claiming to be stragglers, are to be executed on the spot.'[8]

Kreisleiter Wohlgemuth also weighed in with his own lines: 'Whoever remains in the city belongs to a battlegroup which will not know any selfishness, but only unlimited hatred for this cursed opponent of ours. They will know only complete sacrifice for the Führer and Reich. Day and night we will work. We will commit all our power to do the opposition the greatest possible damage, because we know that Germany will live if we are prepared to give our lives.' The point about these missives was less that they all parroted each other's surreal language, but more that they were issued for their superiors to read as much as their subordinates. At a time of shifting loyalties in the crumbling Reich, printed words were cheap, and no one wanted to be blamed for a lack of zeal. Indeed, a two-man SS commission visited Aschaffenburg to check on Lamberth's preparations for defence; his plans met with their approval.

These were the days of endless such exhortations and orders from military officers, Nazi officials and anyone in public office. Given the overall strategic situation, few of these lines make sense, but all in Germany felt that Hitler still had a very long reach through his loyal minions. Indeed, on 29 March, during the battle, Lamberth received a teletype message direct from OKW ordering 'Festung Aschaffenburg will fight to the last cartridge', a reminder that Berlin was watching.

Major Lamberth and Kreisleiter Wohlgemuth went further than most, and in recognising the potential of fighting words, published the *Aschaffenburger Soldatenzeitung* (Aschaffenburg Soldiers' Newspaper), a daily troops' newsletter, laced with Hitlerian quotes, Nazi rhetoric from other newspapers and radio bulletins, and advice on how the civilian population could assist in the struggle, moving water, rations and ammunition around in baby carriages. Perhaps Lamberth and Wohlgemuth also felt under acute pressure because of the loss of the nearby railroad bridge, though not even in their area of responsibility. Thus, outnumbered in every possible way, Hitler, through his faithful followers, was inciting the Reich to use the only real strength they had left. The same quality that had brought him to office and kept him there. Willpower.

Their opponents were Colonel Walter P. O'Brien's three battalions of the 157th Infantry, a Thunderbird outfit who, despite having fought on Sicily, at Salerno and Anzio, and having stormed the Riviera during Operation *Dragoon*, were newcomers to urban warfare. To their south was the Marne Division; beyond them, the 12th Armored; and to the rear of all three lay the 44th. Since leaving the Rhine, all four US formations were probably over-optimistic, having encountered nothing but flags of surrender fluttering from each dwelling, and civilians and stragglers turning themselves in. On 29 March Bob Lynch with the Marne Division's 15th Infantry, wrote home, 'as we push through German cities, one can't help noticing that just about everyone has a white sheet or towel hanging from an upstairs window. When we arrive all the windows and doors are closed tight, and the Nazi's insignias and flags are gone for good.'[9]

There was a misunderstanding that the Third Army had taken the town. This lay in the fact that its 4th Armored Division had, indeed, secured their objective, which was the capture of an intact railroad bridge over the Main, just to the south. As the Thunderbird Division arrived in the area on 27 March and took over the captured bridge from the 4th Armored, the inter-army boundary shifted slightly north, and Aschaffenburg suddenly became a Seventh Army responsibility.[10] The crossing points over the Main, not the town itself, were the Americans' principal interest, but as the defenders overlooked the river, the town had to be captured.

Major Lamberth's aim was to attrit US forces and buy time. A disciple of Nazi Aryan superman ideology, he assessed the German soldier, man-for-man, to be morally superior to his foes. If the Americans could be stripped of their armour and air support, using the complex terrain of the town, he felt he might prevail.[11] Neither US division fought hard for the town initially, uncertain of the flanking support of their friendly neighbours. On 26 March, the 4th Armored focused on another task completely, which we shall examine later, of sending a 57-vehicle, 300-man task force on a special mission fifty miles beyond Aschaffenburg, deep behind German lines.

Such is the nature of inter-unit boundaries that even today conflicts over responsibility arise, and these are sectors an opponent always seeks to exploit. For Aschaffenburg lay not only on a boundary between two divisions, two corps and two armies, but this was where the army groups of Bradley and Devers also met. Given his support for Eisenhower and antipathy towards Sixth Army Group, Bradley was disinclined to commit any of his units to an urban brawl in a town beyond his southern flank. For the Thunderbirds, this meant that officers at all levels had to grapple with issues of morale: their GIs expressed increasing bitterness and resentment that 'they had been lied to by the 4th Armored of Patton's Army', which was not actually the case.

When battle commenced on 28 March, the Thunderbirds' 157th Regiment, though better resourced, was outnumbered by Lamberth's scratch force, but unaware of the imbalance as they were drawn deeper into the town. The attackers, ill-prepared to fight a miniature Stalingrad, found their officer school opponents had laid out killing zones for mortar fire, and arcs for their machine-guns with great care and precision. Whereas many small German towns consisted of medieval wooden houses, the *Altstadt* (old town centre) of Aschaffenburg had been rebuilt as a Renaissance showcase of stone and brick, which greatly aided its defence, the structures virtually impenetrable to direct and indirect fire.

Lamberth's inner defence was based on the five thick-walled *Kasernen* which ringed the town. Using intimate knowledge of their home terrain, the officer school instructors had studied the notional defence of the town as a textbook exercise for ten months, and the Thunderbirds essentially walked into a series of urban ambushes without warning. As combat intensified on the 29th, the fighting was such that Company 'L' of the 157th Infantry suffered fifty-nine casualties, three of them killed – a staggering revision of the usual expectation of one killed for every four wounded.

This is where the supporting armour of the 191st Tank and 645th Tank Destroyer Battalions acted as a force multiplier in systematically reducing each resisting building. Some of the former equipped their Shermans with dozer blades to force their way through the rubble-congested streets. However, on the second day of fighting, three Shermans were destroyed, two by panzerfäuste and one to a mine. Nevertheless, as the defenders had minimal anti-tank capability, even M5 light tanks armed with a puny 37mm cannon were found to increase the pace of advance.[12] Eventually, Lamberth's force fielded a panzer from the workshop and a captured Sherman, though both were soon destroyed by an M10 tank destroyer, the latter clash a unique engagement on 31 March between two American-made armoured vehicles.

The Thunderbirds' field artillery (three battalions of 105mm and one of 155mm), augmented by the guns of the 44th Infantry Division (four similar battalions), plus the 194th and 173rd Field Artillery Groups (XV Corps formations totalling five battalions of guns) and the 2nd Chemical Mortar Battalion (thirty-six 4.2-inch weapons firing white phosphorus shells), poured massed indirect fire into Aschaffenburg. Over 5,000 artillery rounds of all calibres were fired on 29 March alone. Eventually several tracked M12 155mm 'Long Toms' and eight-inch howitzers were brought up and used at point-blank range to subdue particularly troublesome resistance nests. However, aerial support proved problematic as the weather was often poor and the front lines too close. Meteorological conditions improved sufficiently on 31 March for a rare use of napalm against the defenders, while on 1–2 April, P-47s of the 64th Fighter Wing, flying from bases just inside France, released over 100 tons of bombs and fired thousands of rockets into the town, but they could do little in direct support of the infantry.[13]

As the Thunderbirds' official narrative of the next few days summarised, 'All day long, planes swooped over the town as heavy demolition and fragmentation bombs mushroomed below. Great artillery pieces pounded the town. Rubble and debris showered into the air. Houses crumbled and the factory's steel beams were twisted with the concussion . . . But the resistance in the town, fired by the threat of death at the hands of the SS, went on.' The account continued, 'Thunderbird troops forced a wedge into the southern tip of the town. From room to room, they fought into the town. It wasn't a case of cleaning one room and having the rest of the house surrender. Each room had to be cleared in a separate operation. As the 45th Division troops inched ahead, German snipers infiltrated through the heaps of debris and harassed the dough-boys from every possible vantage point. In some cases, civilians sniped at our troops.'[14]

Staff Sergeant Albert R. Panebianco was a mortar squad leader in Company 'K' of the Thunderbirds' 157th Infantry. He recalled that just before the assault their 60mm mortars were taken away and replaced with bazookas. However, in attacking the officer school itself, the new weapon 'did not prove successful. Company 'K' spent an entire day pinned down by German fire. As soon as one of our men raised his head to fire into the barracks, he was picked off by snipers from behind. From our squad of nine men, only three of us survived. Finally, at 15:30, our tanks arrived, and the barracks were taken.'[15] They would have been better off keeping their mortars, which were soon returned to them.

It took several days for the balance of forces to swing in the Americans' favour. Having begun with inferior numbers, they only attained a 1:1 ratio towards the end, still far short of the traditional 3:1 an attacker seeks over his opponents. However, after action reports of the 157th and other regiments also show their numbers were constantly eroded by the necessity to process and guard the steady trickle of prisoners – hundreds each day. On 30 March, the Rainbow's divisional commander, General Frederick, criticised Colonel O'Brien for attacking on too narrow a front, limiting the number of troops who could be deployed. The immediate result was that the town was gradually enveloped by all three Thunderbird regiments plus the 324th Infantry, borrowed from the 44th Division. Cut off from resupply or reinforcement, after six days of hand-to-hand fighting in the rubble, Aschaffenburg was finally prized from Lamberth's fanatical army on 3 April. The mad major did not commit suicide, but surrendered to Lieutenant Colonel Felix Sparks, command-ing the Third Battalion of the 157th Infantry, and who had directed much of the fighting.[16]

Sparks forced the 'loathsome Nazi fanatic in his polished boots' to perch on the front of a Jeep which was driven around for him to per-suade the remaining pockets of diehard defenders to capitulate. GIs and reporters meandered through the smoking piles of bricks to find bodies swinging from lamp posts: from their necks hung the sign *Tod allen Verrätern* (Death to all Traitors). The German commander had personally hanged at least one of his fellow officers, Leutnant Friedl Heymann, and shot many others. Groups attempting to surrender were mown down by their own side.[17]

Lamberth, described in an after action report as 'a firm believer in the principles of Nazism, and one of the most noteworthy adversaries ever encountered', was not released from the Jeep until all had surrendered, and to his disgust found most of his men who survived had turned themselves in during the battle, in defiance of his orders, rather than afterwards. The defence of what the 45th described as 'Cassino-on-the-Main' cost the defenders 1,600 killed or wounded, plus 3,500 POWs. The 157th Infantry had suffered.[18]

Such an expensive defence of a minor German town sent shock-waves throughout the Allied armies. Such was the confusion over the part civilians (male and female) and the very young had played in Lamberth's obstinate defence that SHAEF briefly considered ordering that 'any German soldier found in civilian clothes will be considered a spy and shot'.[19] De Lattre went as far as to transmit a directive that required 'all German military personnel within the zone occupied by his army to surrender, or they would be designated a partisan, without regard to clothing, open carriage of arms or other circumstances, and shot'. Devers was uncomfortable enough to demand de Lattre rescind these instructions, drawing his attention to the far more lenient treatment of all Germans, pre-agreed for Sixth Army Group's military governance of the southern Reich.[20]

Roosevelt's Secretary of War, Henry L. Stimson, was worried this 'stubborn Cassino-defence' would be repeated throughout the conquest of Germany, exclaiming during his 7 April news conference, 'There is a lesson with respect to Aschaffenburg. Nazi fanatics used the visible threat of hangings to compel German soldiers and civilians to fight. After a week, during which the city was reduced to rubble and many Germans lost their lives, the inevitable took place and the fanatics ran up the white flag and surrendered to our veteran 45th Infantry Division.'[21]

Could Aschaffenburg have been bypassed? Indeed, but SHAEF's

attention was focused on the single objective of the destruction of the enemy's forces, not the occupation of terrain (which was de Gaulle's ambition for the French, and Stalin's in seizing Berlin). This followed the directive Eisenhower had received from the Combined Chiefs of Staff on 14 February 1944 which ordered him to 'undertake operations aimed at the heart of Germany and the destruction of her armed forces', and at Aschaffenburg there was a concentration of military capability led by a dangerous fanatic.[22] The German aim was to buy time and destroy American combat capability, neither of which they achieved. The 45th regarded the fight for the town as their hardest task of the war, and in May 1945 compiled a selection of news reports, radio stories and press releases into a small booklet *The Story of Aschaffenburg*, for troops to send home.

Even after the war, Aschaffenburg remained a military town. Its various *Kasernen* were initially patched up to house refugees and displaced persons until 1949, then taken over as a major US Army headquarters along with its training area, closing only in 2007. I was lucky enough in 2001 to have spent a few rewarding days tracing the battles, each evening hosted in the old-world charm of the US Officers' Club, and meeting locals who remembered the contest of 1945. It took over sixty years to repair the red sandstone Schloss Johannisburg, originally the seat of the Prince-Bishops of Mainz, one of the many small German statelets in the Holy Roman Empire swept away by Napoleon. Because of its prominent position, the schloss was targeted by aircraft and artillery and totally gutted, but has risen again from the ashes as the region's main tourist attraction.

The Western Allies would encounter many Aschaffenburgs in March and April 1945, each led by a Lamberth. Although none of the defending fanatics had any hope of victory, it is a tribute to their leadership that they put up such a spirited defence based on the accumulated combat experience of ten years in two world wars. Some Germans fought on in such places because they had no alternative, facing death not only from their opponents but their own side. Others were true believers, still expecting *Endsieg* (final victory), or were tainted with the regime's criminal activities, so that surrender was not an option.

For the faithful, but faint of heart, there was always the promise that awesome new armaments would tilt the balance in Germany's favour once again. Alas, V-1 flying bombs and V-2 rockets turned out to be area weapons, not the tactical devices needed for victory, while Messerschmitt-163 rocket fighters and 262 jet aircraft appeared too late and in such small numbers that they made no difference in the air. Revolutionary new Type XXI U-boats were mostly captured under construction, as was the V-3 supergun aimed at London. Even Generalfeldmarschall Albert Kesselring found black humour in the *Vergeltungswaffen* (Vengeance weapons). 'Well, gentlemen, I am the new V-3,' he had told his new staff on 10 March, when appointed Commander-in-Chief West after Rundstedt. Ironically, the man who believed in the new *Wunderwaffen* (wonder weapons) most, in effect a dupe of his own propaganda, was Hitler.

Ignoring such hollow promises and (to them) fairy-tale gobbledygook, a substantial minority of the old professional Wehrmacht fought on because it never occurred to them not to. These warriors were not Nazis but included men who had seen great adversity during 1914–18 and in Russia. Some were pre-war volunteers who joined for the same purpose that in times of peace young men around the world have always enlisted: for adventure, employment, lust for military glory, and the age-old attraction of a medal ribbon or glint of a sabre. Others came from long lines of aristocrats and Prussians, Hessians, Saxons, Bavarians and Württembergers, in which each generation had fought for their monarchs, and for whom military service was in the blood. Knowing only loyalty to their overlords, these veterans, who had served both the earlier *Kaiserreich* and the Reichswehr of the Weimar state, did not – or could not – distinguish between the criminal National Socialist regime and previous rulers. For them, capitulation was seen not only as a betrayal of their own profession, and Germany, but of their ancestors.[23]

Although initiative in junior officers had once been encouraged, the Wehrmacht was a hidebound organisation, obsessed with hierarchy, its oath to the head of state, and following orders. Senior German officers were heard to exclaim they could not surrender because they had no orders to do so; others would only capitulate to an officer of equivalent rank. For them, the very concept of voluntarily conceding in battle was not within their military lexicon. All of these fought at Aschaffenburg, which thus represents the last few months of the North West European campaign, in microcosm.

*

Elsewhere in Sixth Army Group, Lieutenant General Frank W. Milburn's XXI Corps had followed the rest of Seventh Army over the Rhine at Worms. He had pushed on due east to the city of Würzburg, sitting astride the Main, fifty miles upriver from Aschaffenburg. This is firmly in the heart of Franconia, an ancient ethnic region of Old Germany, centred on Würzburg, Schweinfurt, Bamberg and Nuremberg, and defined by its culture and dialect. When Napoleon abolished the old Duchy of Franconia in 1803, it was absorbed by the state of Bavaria.

Folk memory looked back to several devastations of the area, during both the Thirty Years' War and the Napoleonic Era, and there was no desire for history to come full circle. By April 1945, the region was thus torn between its loyalty to Hitler, as seen at Aschaffenburg in western Franconia, and conflict. Sicherheitsdienst (SD – Security Service of the SS) monitored the private views of its German citizenry. In Franconia, the locals, they reported, thought last-ditch resistance would only lead to catastrophe, and that the purpose of the war was solely to promote the selfish interests of the leadership.[24]

This brought many *Fränkisch* (Franconians) into conflict with their regime, whose agents – unable to stop the Americans – seemed capable only of killing their own troops and citizens. National Socialism had begun by cleansing the Reich of 'undesirables': criminals, the mentally ill, Roma, homosexuals, Communists, Jews, Freemasons and the rest. Yet by 1945 ordinary Germans disillusioned with the conflict had also become a threat to the Reich, in need of disciplining or elimination by the faithful. Indeed, by April 1945 many citizens had come to see their own Nazi officials and the SS as a greater danger than the Allies.

Ursula von Kardorff noted in her diary the 'dreadful reports of how the Russians are treating people who stayed behind in Silesia – children being beaten to death, women raped, farms set on fire, and peasants shot. Goebbels' propaganda machine is obviously working at full blast. Or perhaps it is true, after all? I no longer believe anything I have not witnessed with my own eyes.'[25] The general consensus was the Russian reports were accurate. Based on this, Goebbels tried to persuade the Reich that GIs were the same. American soldiers, he claimed, were former criminals, emptied from jails, who would rape, torture, plunder and murder their way through Germany. Had not their bomber crews, he argued, already demonstrated their inhumanity?

However, German citizens were soon perplexed and amazed as word spread of GI generosity, handing out chocolate, rations and coffee to children and families. Thus, Seventh Army's advance was challenging, having no way of anticipating which town or village would contest their advance and which would surrender. The difference was usually predicated by the presence of a fanatical military commander, but there could only be one outcome. As Sixth Army Group's Weekly Intelligence Summary of 8 April surmised, 'The German is completely restricted to a single capacity: to delay his defeat.'[26]

Villagers frequently took matters into their own hands, displaying white flags of surrender, and dismantling the tank barriers and roadblocks every settlement had been obliged to erect. Trouble usually began when Nazi officials or the SS heard what had happened and arrived to exact revenge before the Americans intervened. There are countless US reports from this time of advancing on settlements showing the white flag of surrender, only to be fired on by 'treacherous' locals. Unaware of the tensions within the Third Reich, if attacked in this way, GI rough justice was often to shoot anyone in uniform and teenaged males, out of hand, even if in the act of surrender.

The front – there was never a front line, as in Normandy or elsewhere in France and Belgium – was best described as 'fluid'. Patch's Seventh Army in Bavaria faced isolated opponents, scattered and disorganised, fighting with varying degrees of motivation. Centres that were defended bore no resemblance to their importance, and merely reflected the availability of local forces, for there was little transport and no fuel. The result was American spearheads needling their way deep into German terrain, with GIs riding on tanks and following in half-tracks to mop up bypassed strongholds as best they could. A 10th Armored Division G-2 put it rather well when describing the front as having 'the appearance of an irresistible molten mass spreading southward over the maps. Armored rivulets moved ahead suddenly, were slowed, and outdistanced by other rivulets, with which they joined. Pockets of resistance were left in the armored wake and overrun.'[27]

Some of these rivulets comprised the Shermans, half-tracks and other vehicles of Roderick R. Allen's 12th Armored Division, XXI Corps, who met no significant opposition until they reached the much-bombed city limits of Würzburg on 2 April. This industrial centre and regional capital of around 80,000, though half had fled, had been governed by another line of Prince-Bishops, similar to those in Aschaffenburg. Their old seat of the Marienberg fortress, an ancient, walled stronghold overlooking the western bank, and their rococo *Residenz* palace were both daubed with *Heil Hitler!* slogans, the doors and windows barricaded with sandbags, behind which lurked determined snipers, machine-gunners and grenadiers wielding panzerfäuste.

Würzburg had escaped serious bombing, until an RAF raid on 16 March 1945 carpeted the area with 1,000 tons of high-explosive and incendiary bombs, destroying as much as 90 per cent of the old city. Officials were still assessing the casualty bill, thought to have been between 3,000 and 5,000, when the GIs arrived.[28] Perhaps because of this, there was a resolve to contest every yard of the ruins, hence GIs recalling Nazi graffiti on every wall and building. Nineteen-year-old Robert Limpert, a local university student with a heart condition that excluded him from military service, was caught in the Würzburg blitz. Panicked and dazed, he stumbled home to nearby Ansbach. There, he was caught posting flyers urging *Tod der Nationalsozialist-Henker* (Death to the Nazi hangmen) and calling on his fellow citizens to surrender. With GIs spotted in the vicinity it would have been easy to let him go. Yet the Ansbach military commander, Luftwaffe Oberst Ernst Meyer, insisted on convening a flying court martial, finding Limpert guilty, then personally hanging him – not once, but twice because the first rope snapped – from Ansbach town hall, then pedalling off on a bicycle minutes before the first American patrols arrived.[29]

In Würzburg, many of the local Volkssturm and Hitlerjugend had once burned books in the *Residenzplatz*, the square in front of the palace, led by their local Gauleiter.[30] Now, armed with an assortment of muskets, hunting rifles and World War One-era weaponry, they had to defend the consequences of their handiwork. On first seeing the Americans, the city Kommandant Oberst Richard Wolff ordered all three stone bridges across the Main to be blown, obliging the leading regiments to cross by rubber boats. On 3 April, the infantrymen attacked under the watchful eyes of machine-gunners in the 431st Anti-Aircraft Battalion, equipped with half-track mounted, quadruple Brownings. Divisional artillery fired salvoes in support, while engineers assembled pontoon bridges.

In the vanguard of the 42nd Rainbow Division, which had been assigned to XXI Corps on 25 March, was Jimmy Gentry. We last met him walking while asleep when advancing in the Saar. He observed that his buddies of Company 'E', 222nd Infantry, 'had a hard time in Würzburg'. As they approached on foot, he saw flashes up ahead, and thought, 'Boy, we're going into the worst thunderstorm that's ever been. Then I heard "boom, boom" and realised, "That ain't no thunder." When we got there, the buildings were still burning. They were all rubble except the churches. You'd leave the church – it was a reference point for us to tell artillery or mortar men what we wanted. We always liked to see a church steeple.'[31]

Opposite the 222nd Infantry was seventeen-year-old Rudolf Decker, a former bank clerk, studying to be a junior leader. In response to a Berlin order 'to defend every house and street of Würzburg to the last man', his training company had been moved from his NCO school at Garmisch into the city. Decker recollected 'when marching into the ruins of Würzburg, the bricks of the burnt and collapsed houses were still warm from the allied bombing ten days earlier. As we approached the city cemetery near the *Residenz*, we ran into heavy machine-gun fire and suffered our first wounded. Suddenly a Jeep came into our area. We exchanged shots; the driver was killed, his passengers taken prisoner. The chocolate and cigarettes we found in it were like a present for us, as we had not had any food in the past two days.'[32]

On the first day he noted, 'We lost some men to snipers and machine-gun fire, secured the area, then I spent the worst night of my life in a bombed-out house, up on the second floor. I remember the Venetian blinds and shutters were just hanging down, glass everywhere, but we still had a roof somehow, and the buildings around it were burning. There were shadows of Germans in the street, and you could hear their hobnailed boots. We didn't have hobnails. You couldn't hear our rubber soles, but you could hear theirs.' The next day Gentry survived being knocked unconscious by a bullet or shrapnel that dented but did not penetrate his helmet. He took a replacement from 'a guy to my right who didn't make it'. His second night in Würzburg was spent in 'the basement of a gutted villa. We were on a pile of coal, and it felt like a feather mattress to me. Just laid down and went straight to sleep.'[33]

His unit was supported by the 232nd Infantry, who crossed the Main on 4 April, moved into the area cleared by their buddies, then turned left towards the north-western portion of the city. They cleared fifty-five city blocks with suppressive fire from the 692nd Tank Destroyer Battalion, and Shermans mounting dozer blades. The following day this combination cleared another forty-five blocks. However, the urban strife rapidly eroded their junior leaders. Clemson University alumnus Sergeant Randolph B. McDavid, with Company 'E' of the 232nd, was one such victim, sniped while observing the fire of his machine-gun squad. However, as the citation for his posthumous Bronzer Star read, 'the gun position chosen by him was so effective that a rifle platoon was able to advance under the fire of his gun and clear out a nest of snipers'.[34]

Another in the 232nd Infantry was Corporal Donald J. Carner, with Company 'C', the Pearl Harbor survivor we met earlier. Leading his machine-gun squad through the ruins, he witnessed the attrition of his rifle platoon. With his commander, Lieutenant Alvin White, Carner saw the platoon scout ahead hit by a sniper's bullet and fall dead. 'While we were discussing where the firing was coming from, I saw the lieutenant's helmet go spinning around the top of his head then fly off behind him. He stood there rubbing the top of his head. He was OK, and bending forward, I saw the bullet had just skinned the top and made it bleed. I picked up his helmet and liner, but he was pale, sick, and looked bad. Platoon Sergeant Henry Andrechuk came forward to take over but was soon hit. Soon Thomas Booth, a rifle squad leader, came up, and also fell. In the end I was in charge of the platoon; as we pulled back someone asked where Nick Diminico, our ammo-carrier, was. Burns, the assistant gunner, answered, "Dead. Hit between the eyes." Later on, I found a flag with the swastika and eagle on; I took it because it represented who we were fighting and mailed it home.'[35]

Meanwhile, Rudolf Decker observed a US spotter plane droning overhead, directing accurate fire at their every movement. 'Our medical officer was killed rescuing the wounded. At dawn we received orders to launch a counter attack; we took about half the street opposite before being forced back to our starting position by American tanks.' His assault was part of a larger 200-man effort aimed at the two engineer bridges over which US armour and infantry were pouring. As in Aschaffenburg and elsewhere, it was American combined arms tactics that undid the defenders' efforts. Decker continued, 'In the afternoon of the next day, I carried one of our wounded to the field hospital. In the entrance hall lay twenty unattended American and German soldiers. After delivering our comrade, hospital nurses suggested that I stay and surrender to the Americans. Since I was only seventeen, I struggled over what I should do. I thought what would happen to me as a prisoner of war – or if the SS came.' In the end Decker joined another company, before changing into civilian clothes and melting away to his parents' home near Munich.[36]

As the fighting concluded, emotions ran high, with the not uncommon consequence of prisoner abuse. Don Carner never forgot the moment 'those up in front sent a prisoner back. The next thing, a mortarman came running up behind him, gave him a hard kick in the rear, then put a machine-pistol to his back and pulled the trigger. "That's for my brother," he said – his sibling had been shot down over Germany. I told him that wouldn't help his brother at all.' This was the exact corollary of the mistreatment, sometimes execution, of those US airmen termed *Teufelsflieger* (devil flyers) by the bombed. 'Next, they brought up five prisoners. A lieutenant gave 4th Platoon orders to shoot them. When a tank commander nearby saw what was taking place, he yelled "No, no, not that way." With my high school German, I could understand one was asking for mercy as he had a wife and three children at home. My squad did not take part in this, I am proud to say. Burns felt something hit him and it turned out to be part of a skull bone.'[37]

Defiance collapsed when the defence ran out of ammunition – and defenders. There was no formal surrender. German intransigence at Würzburg cost the lives of around a thousand, a third of its garrison. By the time they moved on eastwards, the Rainbow Division had left behind thirty-six infantrymen, two engineers, plus five tankers from the 12th Armored killed, and at least 150 wounded.[38] The imbalance of deaths is not explained by unauthorised executions – they were actually few in number – but the extensive use of artillery on the defenders, who

mostly died at their posts, and the professionalism and combat awareness of the GIs, which kept their casualties low. One of the occupiers'
first acts was to repaint the *Heil Hitler!* graffiti on the Marienberg's walls
to reflect its new owners: *42nd Rainbow Infantry Division.*[39]

The 42nd did not linger in Würzburg and other units soon took over
the city's military complexes. The principal *Kaserne* was soon renamed
Leighton Barracks after a 4th Armored Division officer killed in combat
in 1944, and later became the home of the US 1st Infantry Division for
many years, until the keys were handed back to the Bundeswehr in 2008.
The city itself has been totally rebuilt, but sharp eyes will notice nicks
from bullets and shells in the stonework of older structures, such as
the river bridges, the Marienberg and the *Residenz.* After the Germans
surrendered, mail finally caught up with the Rainbow men and Jimmy
Gentry received six letters. 'We had one guy in our squad from Missouri,
and he'd never gotten a letter. We felt so sorry for him. He just never got
any. He didn't have anything to look forward to. And I remember that
morning as I sat there, he said, "Hey Gentry. Do you mind if I read one
of your letters?" I said, "No, Jack. You read three and I'll read three, and
then we'll swap." We did that for the rest of the war.'[40]

It took the Rainbow Division nearly a week to reach their next objective, Schweinfurt. Named for a place where pigs once forded the River
Main, this north Bavarian medieval settlement had grown into a city
of 50,000. Despite the supportive firepower of Combat Command 'A'
in the 12th Armored Division, endless pockets of resistance meant the
Rainbow Division took nearly a week to advance the next twenty-five
miles along the river from Würzburg to Schweinfurt.

By the 1940s, the city was a centre of ball-bearing manufacture. To
make these vital components in most German weapons of war, 17,000
worked at five major sites. As the Allies sought to flatten these factories,
the name of Schweinfurt had already become associated with the great
air battles over the Reich, fought through 1943–4 between the Eighth
Air Force, then based in England, and the Luftwaffe. The US Army Air
Force lost scores of four-engined bombers and hundreds of aircrew on
Schweinfurt missions. In the first major raid of August 1943, thirty-six B-
17s were shot down and 118 damaged, another sixty were lost in October,

and sixteen more in February 1944.[41] As one of the most-bombed German cities, it was hit by major raids on twenty-two occasions over eighteen months, and by the time the 42nd Division men arrived, 8,000 tons of munitions – 592,598 individual bombs, including countless small (six-pound) and medium (thirty-pound) incendiaries – had been released, wrecking its factories and destroying the city.

However, the air battles meant that Schweinfurt grew to be ringed with nine searchlight and 140 flak positions, ranging from light 20mm and 37mm, for use against low-flying fighter-bombers, to fixed 88mm and mobile 105mm and 128mm, mounted on rail cars, intended for high-altitude bombers. These were rapidly redeployed against ground targets as XXI Corps approached. Flak emplacements at nearby Ettle-ben (eighteen 88mm guns), Hambach (twelve guns) and Schwebheim (another twelve) delayed the Rainbow Division's advance for three days, exhausting their ammunition, before the teenaged crews disabled their guns and fell back into the city. They were led by officers like Ober-leutnant Hans Hellmut Kirst, later a popular novelist, whose wartime service was in anti-aircraft artillery, in his case as a *Nationalsozialis-tischer Führungsoffizier* (National Socialist Guidance Officer), responsi-ble for corrupting the minds of his young charges with Nazi ideology.[42]

These schoolboys of the Luftwaffe, like Manfred Rommel and other youngsters we met earlier, were usually Flakhelfer personnel. They were only supposed to man searchlights and range-finding equipment, but often ended up in uniform, carrying ammunition and cleaning, load-ing and firing the guns. Flakhelferinnen, their female equivalents, and Blitz Mädels (signals girls) also operated weapons and manned the air defence communications networks. In January 1943, the German gov-ernment had ordered all secondary school males born in 1926–8 to be drafted as Flakhelfer personnel to release more adults for the front. In February 1945 the net was extended to those born in 1929–30.

All would serve a year with the flak guns, then six months in the labour service (RAD) before time in the armed forces, and in all about 200,000 schoolboys (who were meant to continue their classes on the gunlines) were affected. Most were aged sixteen, but at fifteen, Karl Schlesier was one of the youngest. He noted, 'During the day we saw the vapour trails of American bombers and fighter planes criss-crossing the sky . . . I think there was not one amongst us kids, those in our battalion were generally seventeen years old, who believed that the war could still be won. I was not sure whether the officers and non-coms thought otherwise. I doubted it. They were caught with us in the same trap.'[43]

Other youths joined the RLB (Reichsluftschutzbund – National Air Raid Protection League) as air-raid wardens. In addition to guiding civilians to shelters, they were stationed on rooftops to extinguish incendiary bombs and fight fires. As was the Nazi way, each of these organisations had their own uniforms, insignia and ranks. It gave everyone the feeling of being involved, playing their part, but imposed additional strain on the already overstretched German war economy. Britons on their home front, by contrast, usually made do with a simple armband or unobtrusive badge: no uniforms, daggers, ornate belt buckles or exotic headgear.

Around Schweinfurt, as elsewhere, bomber crews had perfected the technique of first dropping high explosives, to blow off roof tiles, then incendiary devices to set fire to the exposed wooden beams and joists. Thus, streets were littered with debris and unexploded ordnance, especially the small incendiaries. One GI recalled, 'as we drove along the road to Schweinfurt the highways were scattered with mangled bodies of animals and disabled or abandoned German equipment that had been caught by our artillery or air support'.[44] About half the population had fled, but the city's thirteen large concrete shelters kept the death toll down to 1,079 of those who remained.

On 10 April, Jimmy Gentry reached the outskirts with the rest of the 222nd Infantry, surrounded the city, and watched an artillery and tactical air strike on Schweinfurt. 'It was unusual for us infantry to see a bombing raid. From on top of a high hill the city was down below us. All of a sudden, we heard this roar, and those planes came right over us. They bombed the daylights out of that place. They bombed, and those tall smokestacks gave a big shake, and "Woom," down they came! Dust and smoke everywhere.' Gentry recollected the people coming out of the city after the raid: 'the first two were US air crew held as prisoners. They came up the hill to us and said, "Hey, anybody got a cigarette?"' [45]

This last raid disheartened the defenders so much that resistance simply melted away. Bürgermeister Ludwig Pösl, a young businessman

whose rule was more tolerant than many, nevertheless committed suicide, and by nightfall on 11 April, the city was in American hands. The
Rainbow's commander, Harry J. Collins, directed that one captured Nazi
flag be sent to the Eighth Air Force's 305th Bomb Group for its cata-
strophic losses in various raids on Schweinfurt. Another went to the
42nd Bomb Wing of the Ninth Air Force, for their help in softening up
the city on 10 April.

Three days later, as the Century Division left Schweinfurt, Captain Thomas H. Garahan, whom we last met unfurling the Stars and
Stripes in Bitche, wrote home of gossip that had swept through his regiment. 'The rumor at breakfast this morning is that Roosevelt had died
yesterday, but no one believed it. It wasn't until the eight o'clock news
broadcast that the shocking news was confirmed. I think, regardless
of political beliefs or personal prejudices, most people will agree that
Roosevelt's death at this time is quite a blow to America . . . And what
of Harry Truman? No one knows. I doubt that even his closest associates can foresee what kind of President he'll make. Rising to an occasion
like this is little short of expecting a miracle from the man. I only hope
and pray that he surprises all of us. All I can say is that personally this
is a sad day for me, because I firmly believe that history will prove that
Roosevelt was one of the greatest statesmen that ever lived.'[46]

Most Americans were unaware their President had suffered from
polio since 1921, being photographed only from the waist up. In March
1944, he had been diagnosed with hypertension and heart disease, but
with the connivance of the press – in a manner impossible today – his
various ailments were kept secret throughout his life.[47] Thus, his death
was met with great shock and grief by his GIs serving around the world,
whom he had brought through the Great Depression. Many had barely
known another president within their lifetimes. Hardened to combat,
some nevertheless broke down in tears. Exhausted by the war, Roosevelt
had travelled to the 'Little White House', his cottage in Warm Springs,
Georgia, for a fortnight of relaxation. At 13:00 on 12 April he was in
the living room surrounded by friends and family, having his portrait
painted. The conversation was lively, the atmosphere congenial. The
President turned to the artist and, having reminded her that they had
only fifteen minutes left, suddenly announced 'I have a terrific pain in

the back of my head.' He slumped forward unconscious and died very shortly afterwards of a massive cerebral haemorrhage.

Roosevelt's declining health had not been obvious, and his relative youth made the event more tragic – he was only sixty-three. He liked to boast he had 'been in the job longer than Hitler', having been elected to the White House in November 1932, two months before Hitler came to power in Germany, when 13 million Americans were unemployed. After twelve years in office, several of them under the added stress of steering his nation through a world conflict, Roosevelt was simply worn out. Harry Truman immediately acceded to the White House, but more to the point, the thirty-second President was cheated of seeing victory in Europe by twenty-six days.

(*Above*): On 12 April, Eisenhower, Bradley and Patton inspected looted art treasures and gold stored 2,000 feet underground in a salt mine at Merkers-Kieselbach, in the Thuringian hills, captured by the 90th US Division. (*Below*): After lunch with General Manton Eddy at XII Corps HQ, the generals drove to XX Corps headquarters in Gotha, from where General Walton Walker took them to Ohrdruf, the first 'death camp' uncovered by the 4th Armored and 89th Infantry Divisions eight days earlier. Here a grim-faced Eisenhower (1) and Eddy (2) accompanied by Bradley (3) and Patton (4) tour the camp, where the dead still lay unburied.

13

Patton's April

Let us re-join Third Army, now across the Rhine and nearing Aschaffenburg, the battle we have just examined. Before moving on, Patton has some personal, family business to conclude. He ordered a raid behind German lines on a POW camp, Oflag XIII-B, a mile south of Hammelburg, where his son-in-law was detained.[1] Captured in Tunisia in 1943, Lieutenant Colonel John K. Waters, who had married Patton's daughter Beatrice in 1934, was one of many officers interned there. Initially occupied by Yugoslav officers until expanded to cope with an influx of Americans captured in the Bulge, an earlier internee at Hammelburg was another important son, Yakov Dzhugashvili – eldest son of Josef Stalin, taken in July 1941. On hearing of Hitler's offer to exchange him for Friedrich Paulus, taken at Stalingrad, the Russian leader allegedly replied, 'You have millions of my sons. Free all of them or Yakov will share their fate.' The son duly obliged by throwing himself at the electrified fence surrounding Sachsenhausen concentration camp.[2]

Yakov was long gone when, in March 1945, a group of about four hundred Americans arrived from Poland, having marched hundreds of miles in snow and extreme cold. One of them was Waters. On 9 March, prior to crossing the Rhine, Patton received intelligence that his son-in-law had arrived at Hammelburg camp, fifty miles to the east. With the US Army across the mighty river, he worried that the Germans would execute their prisoners rather than let them be liberated. To prevent this, the Third Army commander conceived of a daring swoop by an armoured force to rescue the men, penetrating deep behind the German lines and bringing them back. On 24 March, in his command post at Undenheim, south-west of Frankfurt, Manton Eddy at XII Corps received Patton's personal orders to mount the operation, which he argued against, assessing it as a wild goose chase.

Patton was not to be deterred; on 26 March he arrived by plane at Eddy's headquarters and – in the corps commander's absence – directly ordered Brigadier General William M. Hoge, commander of the 4th Armored Division, to undertake the mission. Hoge, the fiery, determined veteran of D-Day and the Bulge, hero of Remagen, and appointed divisional commander only five days earlier, was sceptical. Under pressure, Hoge allocated the mission to Lieutenant Colonel Creighton Abrams with the whole of his Combat Command 'B' (one-third of the 4th's combat power). This commitment was in turn overruled by Eddy, who deemed it too high-risk. In the event, Patton's vision was scaled back to an ad hoc task force, consisting of a company each of Shermans and armoured infantry, and a platoon of M5 Stuarts – totalling eleven officers, 303 men, sixteen tanks, twenty-eight half-tracks and thirteen other vehicles, led by Captain Abraham Baum. They charged into the night on 26 March. One of Patton's liaison officers, Major Alexander Stiller, who knew John Waters personally, was ordered to tag along.

It is perplexing to try to understand what the tiny force was supposed to achieve, for they had too little transport to evacuate the entire prison camp, holding 'an estimated 900 American POWs', although the reality was double that.[3] They were not even sure where the Oflag (Offizierslager, officers' camp) was located, and would have to ask locals when they arrived in the little town, seemingly unaffected by war until now. Nor did they have aerial photographs, and only fifteen maps for fifty-seven vehicles. Baum was also unaware that Hammelburg housed an infantry combat school; his chosen route passed through the assembly area of Generalleutnant Freiherr von Schaky's 413th Infantry Division; and a Panzerausbildungsverband (armoured training unit) had by chance been directed to the area by train.

It is difficult to conceive of any offensive operation at this stage of the war, however minor, with so little intelligence of the terrain and threats ranged against them. The organisation was hasty: Baum noted in his after action report that 'The only briefing prior to the mission was the actual telling of the men the purpose of the mission'.[4] None were told of

Waters, just the rescue of prisoners. The men who comprised the force had slept just one night in the four days prior to the mission. Before even penetrating German lines, the forces took losses passing Aschaffenburg on 26 March. Task Force Baum were wrongly briefed that it had been subdued by other Third Army units, and so suffered unnecessary casualties there before punching through German lines the following morning under cover of artillery fire at Schweinheim.

Puzzled, the Luftwaffe sent a spotter plane to shadow Baum's army. The latter ran into trouble first at Gemünden, where a bridge was destroyed, then survived an ambush by seven *Hetzer* tank destroyers mounting 75mm guns. Under direction of Hauptmann Heinrich Köhl, this German armoured unit immobilised five half-tracks and three Jeeps for a loss of three of their own vehicles. The depleted task force arrived at their destination around 18:30, six hours behind schedule. Meanwhile, Oberfeldwebel Eugen Zöller had found a marked map in a knocked-out US tank, highlighting the route to Hammelburg, confirming the purpose of the American troops.

Unaware that the camp also housed prisoners from the Royal Yugoslav Army who wore similar grey uniforms to the Germans, the task force mistakenly opened fire on their Allies, and as Waters moved forward to explain the situation and negotiate a truce, he was shot by one of the few German guards not to have fled. Only two-thirds of the rescue squad had survived to reach Hammelburg, and Baum was soon overwhelmed by over a thousand GIs wanting a quick ride to freedom. Euphoria turned to anger, and morale slumped when it was decided to take back only senior officers, led by Colonel Goode, the senior American prisoner. Most GIs, malnourished and barely able to walk after their forced marches from the east, chose to remain where they were, though scores did set out on the return leg, clinging to vehicles. The one individual key to the operation – Waters – was too badly wounded to move and was left in the camp.

With the whole sector alert, what was left of Baum's force departed for the American lines, fifty miles distant in the evening of the 27th. Unaware they were in the midst of a Wehrmacht training area, almost immediately they bounced off several roadblocks before being ambushed in nearby Höllrich by veteran instructors of the local infantry combat school. Losing four Sherman tanks, the task force was surrounded during the night and attacked at 09:15 on the 28th. Goode and Stiller were captured, and Baum shot in the groin, joining Waters in the Yugoslav-administered hospital back at Hammelburg camp, where they were liberated days later. As Patton's Third Army advanced, the Germans were panicked into moving those POWs able to travel, taking them by rail to a large POW facility at Moosburg, where we shall meet them later.

With every vehicle lost and all but thirty-five members of Task Force Baum killed or captured (a 90 per cent casualty rate), and its principal focus – Waters – still in captivity and wounded, the mission had been a complete disaster. None of this was Baum's fault – the mission was always a long shot, with fuel and ammunition levels constant concerns. Its only chance of success would have been to deploy Abrams' entire Combat Command 'B', but this would have drawn official attention to what amounted to a private Patton family rescue attempt. Officially, the general claimed the manoeuvre was to distract German attention from his forces advancing to the north of Hammelburg, by offering the Wehrmacht a matador's cloak in the form of the task force, coming from the east. In his defence, at least one military writer has noted, 'The effect of the diversion of those [German] units on the subsequent advance of the Third Army was evidenced by the fact that the 4th Armored Division didn't fire a single shot for the first 90–100 miles of its subsequent attack.'5

Monitoring the airwaves for news of their task force, at 20:00 during the evening of 29 March, Third Army headquarters was surprised to hear Radio Berlin announce 'a great victory had been achieved by the German army near Hammelburg, with the annihilation of the entire 4th Armored Division, known as *Roosevelt's Butchers*'. This cannot have been confusion on the Germans' part and more reflected desperate Nazi propaganda. On Baum's liberation from Hammelburg hospital and return to duty on 10 April, the 24-year-old was promoted to major, and awarded a Distinguished Service Cross and seven days' leave on the French Riviera; twenty-six others received Silver Stars. Baum was further warned, 'Patton has classified this mission Top Secret. Speak to no one about it until it has been declassified.' Silence, bought with medals, leave and promotion, was to be the order of the day.

Eisenhower was furious and reprimanded his unflustered subordinate, who insisted he was unaware of his son-in-law's presence (a bizarre claim he later made to Waters himself), and merely intent on rescuing the POWs. Bradley wrote in his memoirs, 'I did not learn of the expedition until it had been on the road for two days. Certainly, had George consulted me on the mission, I would have forbidden him to stage it.'[6] Although the Third Army's leader conceded in his posthumous memoirs 'I know of no error I made except that of failing to send a combat command to Hammelburg', he wrote privately to his wife, 'I sent a column to a place forty miles east of where John [Waters] and some 900 prisoners are said to be. I have been nervous as a cat . . . as everyone but me thought it too great a risk. If I lose that column, it will possibly be a new incident [for reprimand]. But I won't lose it.'[7]

Having driven the route today, the countryside is challenging. There are endless ambush sites along the route which follows winding valleys, dominated by the thickly wooded Spessart Forest, a river crossing and twenty small towns or settlements along the old Reichsstraße 26. The Lager Hammelburg is still in business, as a Bundeswehr camp; Task Force Baum finally came to grief in part of its wider training area. Several hard targets, peppered with holes from modern weaponry, have been identified as armoured vehicles once belonging to Baum's army. The assessment is that Combat Command 'B', led by Creighton Abrams (a future Chief of Staff of the US Army), would have succeeded, but the expedition would then have become a major offensive, requiring resupply, with little point in subsequently returning. Task Force Baum was not *Kelly's Heroes*, although the 1970 movie was clearly inspired by the 1945 mission, albeit with a bank heist rather than a prison breakout as its objective.[8]

In late March, Bradley had submitted to Eisenhower an estimate by his staff that the capture of Berlin would cost 100,000 Allied casualties. Twelfth Army Group feared that the city's population, halved due to Allied bombing raids from its pre-war total of 4.3 million, would themselves impose a significant delay on their attackers and would need considerable management after twelve years under the swastika. As Aschaffenburg had just demonstrated, and Stalingrad, Ortona and

Monte Cassino had earlier, urban warfare was not only an expensive business, but one in which the West's air supremacy was of limited value. At the same time, Marshall back in Washington DC further worried about how and where Western and Soviet forces, in ignorance of each other's language, tactics and intentions, would meet, with the possibility of friendly fire casualties highly likely.

As Berlin lay within the proposed future Soviet occupation zone, agreed at the highest levels by Roosevelt, Churchill and Stalin, the Supreme Commander saw no point in taking an objective at high price, only to later hand it to Stalin. Furthermore, Ike was becoming increasingly anxious to seize the Bavarian Alps in southern Germany, the location of Hitler's famed Berchtesgaden retreat and the reputed site of the National Redoubt, the rumours of which we shall explore later. Accordingly, on the 28th of the month, on his own authority, he had telegraphed Stalin to alter the Western Allies' plans. For these reasons, the Berlin metropolis was no longer in his sights.

As Bradley recounted, 'After studying the map, Eisenhower and I agreed the Elbe offered the likeliest bet [for a line of demarcation]. Not only did it run north and south, but it represented the last major obstacle between the Rhine and the Oder [which the Russians had reached]. South of Magdeburg, where the Elbe bent to the east, the meeting line could be extended along the Mulde all the way to the Czech border.'[9]

First informed by phone of the decision on 28 March, Montgomery, furious at being denied his chance of taking Berlin, and at the lack of consultation, complained over Eisenhower's head to Churchill. The latter telegrammed Roosevelt that Eisenhower was exceeding his authority. Clearly under political pressure, on 30 and 31 March, Marshall asked for clarification. In his final telegram back to Ike, Marshall wrote that Eisenhower's new directive was justified as an 'operational necessity', that it was 'in accord with agreed strategy' and that it 'was up to the Supreme Commander to judge the measures which should be taken. He should continue to communicate freely with the Commander-in-Chief of the Soviet Army.'[10]

On 31 March, Eisenhower confirmed his new instructions to Twenty-First Army Group, concluding: 'You will notice that in none of this do I mention Berlin. That place has become, so far as I am concerned, nothing but a geographical location, and I have never been interested in these. My purpose is to destroy the opposition's ground forces and his powers to resist.'[11] In Eisenhower's eyes, Berlin had become a political objective, not a military one. To reach the Elbe and the Soviets as swiftly as possible, Simpson's Ninth Army would now swing south of Berlin, and return to Bradley's Twelfth Army Group. Montgomery tersely responded, 'It is quite clear to me what you want. I will crack along on the northern flank one hundred percent and will do all I can to draw the Germans away from the main effort being made by Bradley.'[12] Montgomery's careful wording acknowledged that he was no longer SHAEF's effort, a bitter pill to swallow. The decision to halt at the Elbe was probably the most controversial of Eisenhower's career. At the time, Britain's political and military establishment was furious and never quite forgave their American Allies. For patriotic reasons Churchill had wanted Montgomery to make every effort to reach Berlin before the Soviets, and his political antennae correctly sensed trouble ahead.

The Supreme Commander, at Marshall's behest, also realised the necessity of keeping his armies intact, for after Europe, loomed Japan. However, until his decision had been accepted by the Soviets with his proposed demarcation line of the Elbe, Eisenhower and Bradley kept the change of mission to themselves. The notoriously secretive Stalin and his Stavka (high command) took their time in responding. They were waiting for Königsberg, capital of East Prussia and today's Kaliningrad, to fall to Marshal Konstantin Rokossovsky's Second Belorussian Front. On 9 April that city fell, allowing Stalin to move the extra troops he needed to the east bank of the Oder facing Berlin, joining the additional Fronts (Soviet Army Groups) of Zhukov and Konev ready to envelop the German capital.

Thus, Eisenhower through Bradley only formally announced the change of objectives once he received word the Soviet Oder campaign was about to begin. On its eve, 15 April, he briefed his army commanders although the press had already picked up rumours of the new plan. Montgomery's Twenty-First Army Group would head for Hamburg, the Baltic coast and Denmark. Ninth Army, re-joining Bradley's Twelfth Army Group, was to aim for Magdeburg on the Elbe. First Army's destination was to be Leipzig. The mission of Patton's Third was to reach the Czech border and eastern Austria, while Devers' Sixth Army Group would take Munich, south-western Germany and western Austria. Simpson, slated to take the German capital, was disappointed. Patton, from his command post at Bad Hersfeld in central Germany, disagreed in open discussion with Eisenhower but abided with his decision.

Since then, the issue has been debated and distorted largely through the lens of the Cold War. James M. Gavin of the 82nd, who had planned to drop into the city with his airborne division, was never convinced, arguing several times in public, and in his provocatively titled 1979 autobiography, *On to Berlin*, 'I have never been able to satisfy myself as to why we did not seize it.' To seize the city SHAEF had a detailed plan, involving an Anglo-American force of two US airborne divisions and the British 1st Airborne (with the SAS and 1st Polish Parachute Brigade). The 82nd was to take Tempelhof airfield, the 101st, Tegel, while the British would land at Gatow. Once the airhead was secured, Western Allied armored and infantry divisions would race to the German capital in another *Market Garden*-style lunge.[13] Charles Whiting was typical of many historians active during the Cold War in his assertion that lingering to reduce 'the Ruhr pocket was one of Eisenhower's major strategic blunders and should never have been fought', for it robbed the West of their only chance to seize Berlin.[14]

We shall examine the Ruhr aspect of this military equation in the next chapter, but the wheel has since turned on the wisdom of capturing Berlin. Stephen Ambrose, among many others, has argued that avoiding the German capital was the correct decision. Abandoning the marathon sprint for the city prevented an accidental east–west confrontation that would have fuelled Stalin's suspicions, and acknowledged that the Soviets, already on the Oder and thirty miles from the heart of Berlin, were always going to win any race to the capital.[15] Even Churchill, who had protested loudly at the switch, soon saw the wisdom, as he cabled Foreign Minister Anthony Eden, 'it would seem that the Western Allies are not immediately in a position to force their way into Berlin. The Russians have two and a half million troops opposite that city. The Americans have only their spearheads, say twenty-five divisions, which are covering an immense front and are at many points engaged with the Germans.'[16]

The day after Eisenhower's initial missive to Stalin about Berlin, he directed Devers' Sixth Army Group to arc south-east, protecting Bradley's southern flank, preventing the escape of German forces and – anxious about the Nazi National Redoubt threat – lunging towards Austria and Bavaria. On 15 April, the day after Eisenhower had given Patton his fourth star, elevating him to full general, he ordered Third Army to pursue the same course, on the outside of Devers' arc, attacking south-east down the valley of the Danube River into Austria and Salzburg, for an eventual link-up with the Red Army. They began their move towards General Rodion Malinovsky's Second Ukrainian Front on 22 April, sweeping the Germans before them.

From this time forward, Third Army divisions were less fixed in Patton's various corps and moved between formations as boundaries changed in what became a very fluid advance during April and early May, corps even being traded between armies, as necessary. Momentum became the key, and as the armoured divisions lunged far ahead, centres of resistance were bypassed for the infantry divisions behind to subdue, their flanks protected by the mechanised cavalry troops and squadrons. Patton always operated with three corps, each of which functioned as miniature armies, completely self-sustaining, with separate axes of advance.

First Army's boundary was moved south to include Middleton's VIII Corps. It had once been a part of First Army until the Bulge, and thereafter under Patton's stewardship; now it returned to its old home under Hodges. This made sense, operating on Patton's northern flank, at a time when the rest of Third Army was being deflected south-east into Bavaria and Austria. In exchange for giving up VIII Corps, Third Army gained Major General James A. Van Fleet's III Corps from First Army (7th Armored, plus 5th and 99th Infantry Divisions), which had been left on the Rhine attacking the Ruhr Pocket. At the same time, Devers was given two divisions earmarked as SHAEF reserve, plus the use of the First Allied Airborne Army should he need them, which explains how the 101st Airborne came to rest in Berchtesgaden, as we shall discover.

By chance, Third Army's initial advance would take them first through central Germany, close to the Buchenwald network of concentration camps. Subsequently, they were ordered to the Bavarian and Austrian fringes of the Fatherland, where they encountered many more. After the Rhine crossings, the abiding memory of Third Army GIs ceased to be of battling with the Germans, but of encountering the results of Nazi racial policies, both slave workers toiling in factories and the inmates of camps. During the first two weeks of April, the First, Third and Ninth US Armies steamrollered their way through 150 miles of central Germany, not, as Stalin accused Roosevelt on 3 April, because of some deal with the Reich to open the Western Front to the Allies, but because the Germans who might have defended the region had been caught in the Ruhr Pocket, which we will examine shortly.

From the logistics lessons learned the previous autumn, Allied supply lines were taut, but nowhere near breaking point, with maximum use made of captured airfields to fly forward essentials such as ammunition, food and fuel, the aircraft returning with casualties. Patton noted that in a single day, 'C-47s carried 526,000 gallons of gas and 150,000 rations forward', assessing that these aircraft and the 2½ truck were 'our secret weapons'.[17] Eisenhower likewise observed that his logistics were strong enough to be able to move 2,000 tons of supplies daily by air. Initially, Hoge's 4th Armored Division (XX Corps) headed for Darmstadt which it captured without a fight on 25 March, while Major General Robert Grow's 6th Armored (also XX) aimed for Frankfurt. At this time, the Third Army prisoner count topped 300,000 since arriving in Normandy. The fiercely competitive Third Army staff, who briefed Patton on the cumulative total each day, noted this was '1,000 more than First US Army, although we became operational fifty-five days later'.[18]

On 29 March, Generalmajor Friedrich Stemmermann, Kommandant of Germany's third largest city, Frankfurt-am-Main, downriver from Aschaffenburg, surrendered to Irwin's 5th Infantry and Grow's 6th Armored Divisions. Along the way they freed 25,000 forced labourers who worked and died making components for Tiger tanks.[19]

'Frankfurt is the size of Baltimore,' noted Robert S. Allen, head of Patton's war room, 'heart of town completely destroyed. Yet, streets cleaner than most of our towns. Debris piled neatly on sidewalks behind walls made of more debris.'[20] GI journalist Meyer Levin hunted for the remnants of Frankfurt's 40,000-strong pre-war Jewish population, which had included the Frank family, whose daughter Anne (of the famous diary) had been born there in 1929. The community had shrunk to 106 by March 1945, all of them chronically ill, or over seventy. Several had relatives in the US Army. 'Even Solly Strauss, a former prominent fish monger, was assigned to cemetery labour,' reported Levin.[21] Their status was equal to that of the city's slave workers. Their survival was equally miraculous, not least because they were refused access to food rations and air-raid shelters. One of the huge concrete shelters, built by slave labour, remains at No. 5, Friedberger Anlage. It was constructed on the site of Frankfurt's principal synagogue, razed to the ground by the Nazis.

The city was also the headquarters of I.G. Farben, a major backer of the pre-war Nazi Party, the fourth largest corporation in the world, and the largest in Europe in 1939. It was the industrial cornerstone of the Reich, with half its 330,000-strong workforce made up of Eastern slave labourers or forced conscripts from the West toiling at 334 sites across occupied Europe. It manufactured all of Germany's synthetic oil and rubber, 84 per cent of the Reich's explosives, and 50 per cent of all pharmaceuticals. One of its synthetic rubber plants was at Auschwitz, which used 30,000 slaves leased to the company by the SS. Elsewhere, another I.G. Farben subsidiary made the Zyklon-B poison gas that would kill them.

Understanding their war guilt, before the end I.G. Farben's executives burned fifteen tons of paperwork in their Frankfurt headquarters building.[22] The sprawling complex was sufficiently undamaged to become Eisenhower's first post-war headquarters. Patton had initially set up his command post in Frankfurt on 3 April, finding the seven-storey I.G. Farben *Hochhaus*, then the largest administration building in the world, being used to house 'thousands of Displaced Persons. Cross-section of the dispossessed of Europe, living in their own dirt and squalor.' His 'Lucky' headquarters had crossed the Rhine that morning, staff officers observing, 'Road packed with displaced persons, hundreds of them, all heading west; walking, riding horses, bicycles, pulling carts – soldiers, men, women, children, the chaff of Europe, tragic, homeless, helpless.'[23]

On 4 April advance elements of Hoge's 4th Armored Division arrived at the illustrious city of Weimar, a name known to many, for it was where the constitution of the 1919–33 Republic had been drafted. With Berlin considered too dangerous for politicians to meet, after the bloody rioting of the Communist-inspired 1918–19 Revolution, the small but influential centre of culture, already capital of Thuringia and in the middle of Germany, was chosen as the leading city of the new nation. Nearby is the smaller burg of Gotha, incorporated into the surname of the British royal family, when Queen Victoria married Prince Albert of Saxe-Coburg-Gotha in 1840.[24] Like some other small-town chiefs in 1945, Gotha's Kommandant, Oberstleutnant Josef Ritter von Gadolla, on his own initiative declared Gotha an 'open city' at the beginning of April and sent his Volkssturm home. Unluckily, as he drove in search of the US Army, Gadolla's car with its white flag was intercepted by an SS patrol. After a court martial in Weimar, he was shot on 5 April. Local lore has it that his last words were, 'So that Gotha can live, I have to die!'[25]

Thirty miles west of Weimar and ten miles south of Gotha, the 4th Armored and 89th Infantry following them, arrived at Ohrdruf, a tiny town where Johann Sebastian Bach had once attended school, and which later became a centre of toy-making. Its name meant nothing to anyone. However, it was here that the full immorality of the Reich hit the Allies for the first time. One mile south, in an old Wehrmacht training camp, they uncovered their first concentration camp with inmates. The shock of discovery was all the greater because they were not looking for such a place. No one was. Few had seen one or even knew what one was. Dark comments about the fate of Europe's Jews were assumed by many to be wild exaggerations.

The unveiling of extermination camps in Poland by Soviet troops the previous summer, all empty and partly dismantled, had not registered. The reporting of mass graves, piles of shoes, spectacles, wedding rings, suitcases and Zyklon-B canisters failed to alert Eisenhower's SHAEF staff of what to expect. Perhaps the liberation of Auschwitz-Birkenau on 27 January 1945, or Gross-Rosen in Western Poland, another oft-forgotten principal camp, freed on 13 February, both by Soviet forces, should have warned the West, but somehow the scale of slaughter within the wire failed to alert them. It was beyond anyone's comprehension.[26]

Colonel Hayden Sears' Combat Command 'A' of the 4th Armored was actually looking for a Wehrmacht emergency communications centre, being chiselled into the rock under Ohrdruf's Mühlberg castle. The work camp, not technically a concentration camp, had been established in

1944 as much to connect the site to the Reich's main railway network, via tunnels in the nearby mountains, as to work the camp inmates to death. The discovery was accidental and came as a huge, life-changing shock for those GIs who witnessed the moment. David Cohen, a New York City native and radio operator, recollected: 'as we got there, we saw thirty to forty bodies just lying around . . . you could see the bullet holes in their backs. I saw many buildings with bodies stacked in them. The first time I went in and walked out. I couldn't take it; I was sick; I wanted to throw up.'[27] Sergeant Joseph Kushlis remembered 'nothing but dark holes in their skull and face' of the two barely alive survivors he encountered.[28]

Meyer Levin, attached to the 4th, was immediately confronted with the piles of the dead, still clad in their striped prison clothes. 'The corpses were fleshless, and at the back of each skull was a bullet hole. The bodies were flat and yellow as lumber.'[29] Levin perceptively mused, 'We had known. The world had vaguely heard. But until now not one of us had looked on this. It was as though we had penetrated at last to the center of the black heart. This was the source of fear and the guilt in every human who remained alive. For human beings had had it in them to do this, and we were of the same species.'[30]

Leon Tulper was in the 3rd Battalion, 260th Regiment (65th Division, VIII Corps), which visited shortly after the liberating units had moved on. 'We thought it was a work camp,' said Tulper of Ohrdruf. 'I was in the second Jeep because I was the XO's radio operator and followed the colonel in the first Jeep.' He saw 'a skeleton in a prison uniform'. As he remembered, 'Everybody's looking at this guy thinking, "What the hell is this?" I was the one that radioed headquarters and told them, "This place is unbelievable; you can't even begin to describe it." They were like one of those statues, where they have a person broken down to just bones. Their faces – nothing there hardly. Their hands were out: "We need food." There was one of our fellows – this gets me. He had a Hershey bar; he gave it to a guy who took two bites and fell over dead. We didn't know what the hell happened. A medic comes running up, checked him, and he was dead. We found out because he was so emaciated that the chocolate just tore up his insides.'[31]

The previous month, Ohrdruf had held 11,700 inmates, about 6,000 of whom were Jewish, but in early April the SS evacuated most on death marches to Buchenwald, thirty miles north-east. SS guards attempted to kill many of the remaining prisoners too ill to walk and burn evidence of their crimes but fled before finishing. A.C. Boyd, with the 89th Division, recollected the bodies of those recently shot lying on the ground near the entrance. 'I still have vivid memories of what I saw, but I try not to dwell on it. There were so many dead, and some so starved all they could do was gape open their mouths, feebly move their arms and murmur. There were ditches dug out in the compound and we could see torsos, lots of arms, and severed legs sticking out.'[32] President Barak Obama remembered hearing stories of this camp from his great-uncle Charles Payne, a GI in Company 'K', 355th Infantry of the 89th.

Eight days after its liberation, Eisenhower, Bradley and Patton stopped by. They were unaware that the site, technically Ohrdruf-Nord, was merely an outstation of Buchenwald main camp. Its slaves had toiled not only at building the underground signals centre but some assembled Messerschmitt-109s and 210s in twelve-hour shifts for the Gothaer-Waggon-Fabrik factory, where they were subject to Allied bombing. Flying overhead in February 1944 had been the actor turned aviator Major Jimmy Stewart in a B-24 Liberator named 'Nine Yanks and a Jerk'. Over Gotha the cockpit of his bomber was hit by radar-directed guns, which blew a huge hole in the fuselage, inches from his seat. Stewart piloted his damaged plane back to England, all the while gazing down at enemy territory, with the sub-zero wind whistling through, but had nearly perished near the town.[33]

On 12 April, the Supreme Commander had already visited the scene of one Nazi crime in the morning, when XII Corps' Manton Eddy showed him a site captured earlier by the 90th Division.[34] One hundred miles north-east of Frankfurt, his men liberated the small town of Merkers-Kieselbach, in the Thuringian hills. Of significance was not the above-ground settlement, but the below-ground salt mines that riddled the area. In one, some 2,000 feet underground, in crystal-encrusted caves, lay Germany's and other nations' stolen financial reserves – endless bags and crates of paper money, gold coin and bullion – together with looted jewellery and paintings.[35] In all, there was over a hundred tons of gold, twenty-seven Rembrandts, other works by Botticelli and Rubens, an ancient Egyptian bust of Queen Nefertiti in richly painted limestone, and other treasures from the fifteen state museums of Berlin. Hobart Winebrenner, with the 90th, marvelled at the 'sensational photo opportunity', and recollected 'the countless containers full of personal property seized, ranging from dinnerware and jewellery to gold teeth.'[36]

After lunch, Eisenhower, Bradley and Patton drove an hour north-east to XX Corps headquarters in Gotha, from where Walton Walker took them to Ohrdruf, accompanied by members of the Signal Corps who shot 80,000 feet of film and took numerous photographs. Everything had been left intact because Walker wanted as many GIs as possible to view the scene. Soldiers and the press were bussed in from miles around to understand the evil of the Third Reich. This was the first time Eisenhower, Bradley or Patton had been confronted with the Holocaust. It left them poleaxed.

Ike's immediate response was to cable Marshall in Washington DC that same night. 'The most interesting – although horrible – sight that I encountered during the trip was a visit to a German internment camp near Gotha. The things I saw beggar description. The visual evidence and the verbal testimony of starvation, cruelty and bestiality were so overpowering as to leave me a bit sick. In one room, where there were piled up twenty or thirty naked men, killed by starvation, George Patton would not even enter. He said that he would get sick if he did so. I made the visit deliberately, in order to be in a position to give first-hand evidence of these things if ever, in the future, there develops a tendency to charge these allegations merely to propaganda.'[37] Eisenhower would write to his wife, Mamie, 'I never dreamed that such cruelty, bestiality, and savagery could really exist in this world.'

In fact Patton, nicknamed 'Old Blood and Guts', vomited several times at Ohrdruf, writing in his diary the next day, 'It was the most appalling sight imaginable. In a shed . . . was a pile of about forty completely naked human bodies in the last stages of emaciation. These bodies were lightly sprinkled with lime, not for the purposes of destroying them, but for the purpose of removing the stench. When the shed was full – I presume its capacity to be about two hundred . . . The bodies were taken to a pit a mile from the camp where they were buried. The inmates claimed that

3,000 men, who had been either shot in the head or who had died of starvation, had been so buried since the first of January.[38]

Patton's aide, Charles R. Codman, noted that every nearby unit and those not at the front was ordered to tour Ohrdruf: 'We are told that the American soldier does not know what he is fighting for. Now, at least, he will know what he is fighting against.'[39] In 1948, Eisenhower reflected on his afternoon at Ohrdruf in his memoir *Crusade in Europe*. 'I saw my first horror camp. It was near the town of Gotha. I have never felt able to describe my emotional reactions when I first came face to face with indisputable evidence of Nazi brutality and ruthless disregard of every shred of decency. Up to that time I had known about it only generally or through secondary sources. I am certain, however, that I have never at any other time experienced an equal sense of shock.'[40] Bradley also pondered the same moment in his *A Soldier's Story* of 1951. 'The smell of death overwhelmed us even before we passed through the stockade.' Noting the naked dead, he recorded, 'Lice crawled over the yellowed skin of their sharp, bony frames.'[41]

Eisenhower directed Ohrdruf should receive the widest coverage in the print media of the day, and later in newsreels. In Britain, the front cover of the 28 April issue of the *Illustrated London News* read: 'The usually genial General Eisenhower shows by his grim aspect his horror of German brutality: the macabre scene of victims murdered by SS guards at Ohrdruf camp.' It was followed by six pages of photos describing the 'torture camps'. In November 1945, the first film about German war crimes to be shown in American cinemas would describe the camp as a 'murder mill'.[42] Thus, Gotha, once the noble surname of the British royals, became sullied with the Holocaust. As if Ohrdruf wasn't enough, this was the evening that Eisenhower, Bradley and Patton learned that President Roosevelt had died that afternoon. It was the worst of all days.

Widespread news reporting subsequently brought Ohrdruf, and later Buchenwald, Dachau and Belsen, to international awareness – and the attention of the liberating troops. However, after Ohrdruf, it was the scale of horror that merited reporters' attention, rather than the fact that it had happened. In pondering the fate of the luckless nobleman Ritter von Gadolla of nearby Gotha, it becomes apparent that modern accounts of his honourable martyrdom have evolved as a necessary counterweight to the horror of Ohrdruf, about which he must have known or at least suspected.

However, Ohrdruf paled in comparison to nearby Buchenwald, uncovered on 11 April at 15:15; today, its clock remains frozen at that time. It was Captain Frederic Keffer's Combat Team 9 of the 6th Armored and later the 80th 'Blue Ridge' Divisions which brought the slaughter to a close. One of the original concentration camps, since its first inmates had arrived on 15 July 1937, around 240,000 had passed through its gates, of whom 56,545 were murdered, an execution rate of 24 per cent. Patton, like all US commanders, was ignorant of the typology of Nazi detention facilities, and recorded it as the discovery of 'another slave camp north of Weimar, which was apparently much worse than the one at Ohrdruf'.[43] Despite his nausea at the latter, Patton took time to visit Buchenwald on 15 April, whereas Ohrdruf was Eisenhower's only camp visit.

Buchenwald's pastoral name, meaning 'beech wood' – allegedly chosen by Himmler himself – emphasised how the business of the SS was conducted by euphemism. Blatant slaughter and brutality were never mentioned in conversation or official documents. Victims were not tortured but 'intensely interrogated', then 'processed'. Ghettoes and homesteads were 'cleansed' and communities 'sent east', the whole project being the *Endlösung* ('Final Solution'). The beech forest – largely destroyed to build Buchenwald – was associated with Goethe, where he allegedly composed many of his finest works. A single tree was left standing in the camp and summed up the contradiction of Nazi Germany. For the SS it represented continuity with the old nation of Goethe. For the prisoners it reminded them of the opposite: that Hitler's Reich was a break with their nobler past.

In time, Buchenwald became the hub of 174 sub camps, one of which was Ohrdruf. Its discovery was given as much publicity as Ohrdruf, with Sir Alan 'Tommy' Lascelles, Private Secretary to King George VI, noting on 15 April that Ed Murrow, the CBS London bureau chief, had broadcast 'on the wireless this evening, giving a terrible account of a concentration camp at Buchenwald, near Weimar, which he visited on Thursday last'. Murrow's ten-minute report stunned listeners with a matter-of-fact description of the piles of dead bodies so emaciated, that those shot through the head had barely bled, and of children tattooed with numbers, 'which they will carry until they die'. Their ribs showed through their thin shirts. 'I pray you believe what I have said about Buchenwald,' he asked listeners. 'I have reported what I saw and heard, but only part of it; for most of it I have no words. If I have offended you by this rather mild account of Buchenwald, I am not in the least sorry.'[44]

New Yorker Nathan Futterman was serving with the 10th Infantry (5th Division) when they approached Buchenwald. 'Let me tell you something about the average GI, the grunt soldier,' he said, his recall crystal clear more than sixty years after the event. 'We didn't know where the hell we were, what we were doing, where we were going. One day this officer shows up and asks who can operate a radio. So stupidly I raise my hand and he tells me to come with him in his Jeep. And we drive and drive. I don't know where the hell we are. Then, all of a sudden, you could smell that something was wrong. The thing that got me was when I looked at the leaves. I asked myself what the hell is the matter with them? The leaves were gray. I rubbed one and it was covered with ash.'[45]

Meyer Levin wrote several communiqués for the Overseas News Agency, delivering horrific details of the site. 'There were two Buchenwalds, the upper and the lower, separated by a high barbed-wire fence. The upper camp meant possible life, and the lower camp was death,' he recorded. 'As we entered one swarming barrack, I unthinkingly brought out a handful of chocolate bars; the creatures were upon me, shrieking, tearing at each other and at me, and I was shocked at the power, the tenacity of their fleshless limbs.' He reported the story of Mordecai Strigler, a Polish Jew who in 1940 received from a Nazi with a razor, 'neat swastikas on his cheeks and forehead just deep enough for the blood to trace the lines. The marks are still there.'[46]

Then there was the tale of 'a German officer attentively lining up a number of Jewish children, patting their heads until they were precisely one behind the other, then putting a single bullet through the line'. Nevertheless, Meyer managed to conclude in upbeat tone: 'The liberated Russian workers had already seized a quantity of the black leather SS jackets worn by their former guards, and formed up a column, marching through the camp, singing Red Army songs.'[47]

Leon Tulper, who had liberated Ohrdruf, reflected, 'I was an "armpit-smeller" when we captured the German soldiers. If they came in with their hands up and had the SS tattoo [on the underside of the left arm, usually near the armpit, which identified their blood group], we took them round the back. You know what happened to them. That's what we did. We eliminated a lot of SS guys, and they deserved it.'[48] Hobart Winebrenner also pondered the changing attitudes towards the Germans after finding the camps. 'Older locals, realizing that only formalities remained, cooperated fully. But the Hitler Youth provided some of the stiffest resistance. Those aspiring young terrorists refused to quit. There was nothing quite like losing three or four friends to a kid with a rifle on a rooftop. Then the rosy-cheeked, peach-fuzzed-faced freaks had the nerve to smile at us, laugh and ask for a cigarette. Let me say that some of those cocky little assassins needed extensive dental work by the time they made it back to the POW cage.'[49]

The discovery of Ohrdruf and other sites prompted Eisenhower to send a cable on 19 April to Marshall: 'We continue to uncover German concentration camps for political prisoners in which conditions of indescribable horror prevail. I have visited one of these myself and I assure you that whatever has been printed on them to date has been understatement. If you could see any advantage in asking about a dozen leaders of Congress and a dozen prominent editors to make a short visit to this theater in a couple of C-54s [four-engined, long-range passenger and transport aircraft], I will arrange to have them conducted to one of these places where the evidence of bestiality and cruelty is so overpowering as to leave no doubt in their minds about the normal practices of the Germans in these camps. I am hopeful that some British individuals in similar categories will visit the northern area to witness similar evidence of atrocity.'[50]

Marshall received immediate assent from Truman and Stimson. Churchill instantly agreed and announced his decision to the House of Commons the same day. A multi-party delegation of ten lords and Members of Parliament departed straight away, with Lascelles telling George VI that the British delegation had flown out on 21 April 'to see the horrors of Buchenwald and Belsen camps, which the Americans have publicised widely. The revelations from these camps will do more to kill Isolationism in [the] USA than would years of inspired instruction.'[51]

Churchill telegraphed his wife, Clementine, who was in Russia, with the words, 'Intense horror has been caused by the revelations of German brutalities in the concentration camps. They did not have time to cover up their traces.'[52] Later, the editor of the *St Louis Post-Dispatch*, Joseph Pulitzer, leading the team of senior newspapermen to inspect the camps, wrote home, 'I came here in a suspicious frame of mind, feeling that I would find many of the terrible reports printed in the United States before I left were exaggerations, and largely propaganda. They have been understatements.'[53]

Patton's Third Army continued its march through central Germany, gyrating now to the south-east. On 19 April, Major General Manton Eddy, the rock of XII Corps since August 1944 and a combat commander before that in North Africa and leader of 9th Division from D-Day, was obliged to give up his beloved corps due to extreme hypertension. Evacuated home, Eddy eventually recovered, but meanwhile was replaced by Stafford LeRoy Irwin of the 5th Division. At this time, XII Corps was fighting its way through south-east Bavaria, almost to the Czech border.

Sixty miles east of Nuremberg, Ted Hartman, a Sherman commander with 41st Tank Battalion in Combat Command 'B', 11th Armored Division, noticed 'a number of brown-skinned people crawling in the woods. At first, we thought they were Krauts, but they were wearing odd-looking suits. It turned out they had been prisoners at the Flossenbürg and Buchenwald concentration camps, were really holding up our progress, and would not get out of the way before they had expressed their thanks in one way or another.' These were some of the 16,000 detainees his division recorded liberating along the roadside on 20 April alone. Hartman – later a surgeon – recorded, 'Their teeth were black and crumbling. All of them were starving. They were almost ghostlike in appearance, and they just kept coming. Some would kneel in front of the tank and pray. Others would stand smartly and give a salute or bend over and kiss the front of the tank. It was the most emotional scene I ever witnessed.'[54] Despite the war having eighteen days left to run, the 11th would experience more than their fair share of both shock and action.

As their journey progressed, Hartman and the other tankers of the 11th's CCB observed the 'countless wounded and dead concentration camp prisoners. The Germans had fired at them forcing them to get in the way, thus delaying our advance. I couldn't but help cry a little as I saw some of them standing silently by the bodies of their buddies who had been wounded or killed.' Retribution, however, was swift. Standing in the turret of *Eloise II* with his 0.5-inch Browning, Hartman later 'came upon some of those guards wearing SS uniforms trying to hide in the village of Posing. Believe me, we gave no mercy. Hoppie Langer [the Sherman's gunner] and I shot at masses of them. The doughboys on the rear deck were also popping the SS soldiers off with their rifles . . . Never in my life have I felt so sorry for one group of people, while gaining such disrespect for another.'[55]

In mid-April, all Third Army units started encountering some of the ninety-four sub camps of Flossenbürg. Most were concentrated around the armaments factories of south-eastern Germany and the western Czech lands, although one *Arbeitskommando* (work group) tended the agricultural estate of Lina Heydrich, widow of the SS general assassinated in Prague in June 1942. The main camp of Flossenbürg itself, another innocuous-sounding name chosen by Himmler, was established in May 1938 to supply labour for nearby quarries operated by the SS-owned Deutsche Erd-und Steinwerke (usually abbreviated to DESt – German Earth and Stone Works). The showcase architecture of Nazi cities like Munich and Nuremberg rested on huge limestone blocks, hewn and blasted by DESt's Jewish labour.

Flossenbürg fell to the 90th 'Tough Ombres' Division of XII Corps on 23 April. Winebrenner, with its 358th Regiment, pondered, 'After witnessing the carnage at Flossenbürg, I raged with hate. I still find myself at a loss for words to describe it. Terms like "war crimes" or "atrocities" fall short. They're too sterile, too bookish when compared to the ghastly sights, sounds and smells of that place. Although words must suffice, they'll never do it justice. Words don't make you retch or reel away or cover your nose and mouth, but Flossenbürg did.'[56]

Born in the Carpathian Mountains of Transylvania in 1920 and arriving in New York aged ten months, former Harvard Law School graduate, Sergeant Benjamin B. Ferencz, had just transferred from his anti-aircraft battalion to the newly created War Crimes Branch of the US Army. He remembered the road to Flossenbürg. 'At regular intervals along the way were small mounds, under which lay two or three bodies. There must have been between two and three thousand murdered people lying along this road.' Of arriving at Flossenbürg, the future prosecutor of Nazi war criminals recollected, 'Even today, when I close my eyes, I witness a deadly vision I can never forget: the mounds of emaciated corpses stacked like cordwood waiting to be burned . . . I had peered into Hell.'[57] Further along the route of the trek, Captain James C. McNamara noted 'on one pine-studded knoll lay the battered bodies of 161 Polish Jews, shot and beaten to death by SS guards for faltering along the way. The bodies crumpled in the roadside mud bore unmistakable signs of clubbing and shooting.'[58]

The following day, 24 April, saw XII Corps, now under Irwin, advancing down a corridor between the Danube and the Czech border. Preceded by the 11th Armored, they formed Third Army's left wing. Irwin's other flank was guarded by the 26th Infantry Division, whose right coat sleeves brushed the River Danube. At the same moment in Third Army's centre, Walker's XX Corps – augmented by John Millikin's 13th Armored Division, who had arrived on 22 April – pushed forward its 3rd Cavalry Group.[59] They reached the banks of the Danube south-west of Regensburg, opening the way for assault crossings by the 65th and 71st Divisions the following night. On Third Army's right, around Ingolstadt, three divisions of Van Fleet's III Corps, 14th Armored, 86th and 99th, had also come level with the Danube.

On Third Army's eastern flank, Hartman and the rest of 11th Armored's CCB were nearing the small town of Regen, where one in five of the local population were conscript workers toiling in local factories, relocated from the bigger cities. Some laboured on farms, others manufactured glass lenses for tank periscopes and gunsights. In a story repeated many times over in April–May 1945, the town's elders met and decided to surrender to the approaching Americans, whose artillery they could already hear. As they did so, Knight's Cross holder Oberst Dr

Fritz Bingemer arrived with two hundred officer cadets and SS troops, determined to resist. They blew several bridges and hit some of the 11th's tanks with panzerfäuste, inflicting casualties. GIs took one prisoner and ordered him 'down to the river to wash the blood from his face. When he leaned over to wash his face, shots were heard, and he toppled into the stream. I played no part, but felt no remorse,' remembered Hartman.[60]

The townsfolk, afraid of last-minute execution by their own countrymen, could not dissuade the would-be defenders. A four-hour battle ensued, destroying thirty-six buildings, and killing fifty. As shots were still being traded, Hartman recalled, 'a woman came over to one of our tanks and asked if we supplied fire-fighting equipment, as her home was next door to a burning building'. The tank crew were amazed to be asked to put out a fire in the middle of combat. Hartman observed that their interpreter 'really told her off. He took her up the street and showed her American blood and said he didn't care if her home did burn down.'[61]

On Third Army's right flank, one of the largest POW camps in southern Germany, Stalag VII-A at Moosburg, twenty miles northeast of Munich, lay in the path of Van Fleet's newly arrived III Corps. As Allied military internees were transferred west, away from the Russians, and large numbers of aircrew continued to be shot down, the Stalag's series of single storey military shacks, designed to accommodate 10,000 *Kriegsgefangene* (prisoners of war, often abbreviated by the incarcerated to *Kriegies*), swelled to housing 110,000, including 40,000 Russians. Aware of friendly forces drawing near, the POWs watched streams of aircraft attack Munich. US aviator Frank Murphy recollected, 'On virtually every clear day in April 1945, we heard and saw P-47 and P-51s strafing targets in and around Moosburg. Every so often one of the American pilots on these missions would indicate his awareness of us by swooping low over the camp and wagging his wings.'[62]

By 27 April they could hear the tell-tale thump of far-off artillery, then US armour was glimpsed in the distance. These were from Charles H. Karlstad's Combat Command 'A' of the 14th Armored, part of III Corps. Hearing he would soon receive orders to remove or massacre his prisoners, the Kommandant, Oberst Otto Burger, decided to defy the local Nazi authorities. He authorised a staff car containing the two senior Allied officers, Group Captain Alfred Willetts, RAF, and Colonel

Paul Goode, US Army, escorted by a Red Cross official and SS major, to find the nearest friendly troops and alert them to the camp.[63] We have met Goode before, for he was the senior US officer at Hammelburg where Task Force Baum came to grief. He and most of the former camp had since been moved to Moosburg. The Germans proposed a truce – creating a neutral zone around Moosburg, which would have been to their advantage – which was rejected by Karlstad, incidentally an old friend of Goode's, and his force prepared to seize the camp immediately.

As the staff car returned to the Stalag, Karlstad's 47th Tank Battalion started to occupy the town, aware that an SS unit were digging in to resist. Later that morning, local Moosburgers were obliged to halt their church services and rush for cover as the Allied POWs witnessed the SS fight.[64] Murphy remembered, 'The first shots rang out about 09:00. In the beginning there was only the sporadic rattling of small arms fire coming from somewhere in the woods just outside the fence. Within minutes, however, the noise from the incessant firing of hundreds of small arms and heavy automatic weapons was deafening. Kriegies were everywhere scrambling for cover or attempting to burrow into the hard ground like moles. Some were climbing on top of the buildings and guard towers to watch the excitement. I flattened myself as best as I could on the ground next to my barracks. Bullets were ricocheting over the compound. Several kriegies were hit, none seriously.'

Thomas J. Flynn, a captain with the 110th Infantry, captured in the Bulge with many others of the 28th and 106th Divisions, saw the firefight, but interpreted it differently. 'With the advancing American Army near, SS troops began to fire their weapons into the camp in a last-ditch attempt to carry out Hitler's orders. Shots even came from those positioned on the roof of a cheese factory nearby. The POWs were told by the guards to stay inside with their heads down,' while the garrison 'fought off the Gestapo and SS and saved all the prisoners'. Flynn's scenario was unlikely, as the SS were fighting for their lives, and if captured were unlikely to last long if they had just executed defenceless American POWs. However, Flynn always remembered 'the vibration of Sherman tanks heading in their direction, and the sounds of euphoria erupting from every able-bodied man in Stalag VII-A'.[65]

Murphy recollected the firefight being over by 10:30. 'The silence that followed was an almost deathly quiet, too quiet, strange and unnatural.' Unknown to the POWs, the SS had managed to blow a river bridge in Moosburg, and the pause before liberation reflected the need to deploy an engineer bridge to replace the demolished span. Three Jeeps of the 68th Armored Infantry Battalion, one mounting a machine-gun, quickly crossed and made their way up to the camp. As 240 German guards surrendered to five Jeep-borne GIs, Murphy reminisced, 'We heard the unmistakable rumble and clanking of heavy armour approaching the camp from somewhere outside our perimeter fences. Suddenly, without fanfare or warning, three Shermans came crashing through the fence near the front gate. Amid the shouting, screaming, and cheering of the newly freed prisoners, the tanks drove a short distance down the main street of Stalag VII-A and halted. Kriegies immediately swarmed all over them.'[66]

Floyd C. Mahoney of Company 'C' in the 47th Tanks found himself freeing his own son, a lieutenant in the air force. Another airman kissed a tank. 'Goddamn, do I love the ground forces,' he cheered. 'You damned bloody Yanks, I love you,' shouted a six-foot-four Australian. A weary, bearded American paratrooper climbed on a Sherman and kissed its commander, tears streaming down his cheeks. Frank Murphy's most vivid impression of the day came later. 'The true end of our captivity came about 12:30 when the American flag, *Old Glory*, was seen being hoisted to the top of the church steeple in the town of Moosburg only a short distance away. As one, 8,000 American kriegies faced the church, came to attention, and saluted, all with tears of pride in our country and pent-up emotion trickling down our cheeks.'[67]

Two days after liberation, the Third Army commander himself arrived at Moosburg, with James Van Fleet of III Corps and Albert C. Smith leading the 14th Armored Division. They strode through the camp exchanging words with small groups of American prisoners. Murphy recalled that when Patton approached his group, 'the General paused, looked at us, shook his head in disgust at the sight of the thin, unkempt scarecrows standing before him and said in a low voice, "I'm going to kill these sons of bitches for this."'[68]

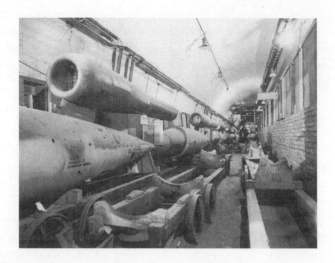

(*Above*): On the southern edge of the Harz mountains, during First US Army's advance to Leipzig, the 3rd Armored and 104th Infantry Divisions of Collins' VII Corps found underground factories around Nordhausen, where V-weapons and jet aircraft were assembled. Discovered on 11 April, the main site was code-named Mittelbau (Central Construction). By 1945, some 26 per cent of Germany's workforce were slaves, usually kept in conditions of appalling cruelty. At Nordhausen, 60,000 inmates passed through a network of thirty-eight above-ground camps, the largest named Dora. (*Below*): Clad in their striped woollen prison garb, these reluctant workers had little incentive to make such complicated weapons as jets, V-1 flying bombs and V-2 rockets.

14

First and Ninth Armies:
From the Ruhr to the Elbe

We will leave Patton's Third Army for now and return north to Hodges' First. Here, safely across the Rhine at Remagen, Collins' VII Corps had been ordered to stride north-east and link up with Simpson's Ninth Army beyond Paderborn.

In the lead of Collins' corps was 3rd Armored Division, advancing an unprecedented ninety miles on 29 March. Tank gunner John P. Irwin remembered the day as 'warm for the month. The concrete highway we were travelling was cluttered with rubber from tank treads. We stopped only to refuel. When nature made its requirements known, spectators were treated to the spectacle of men urinating from their tanks or dumping into their helmets (one of the most versatile of army implements) and tossing it away as they travelled.' As usual, Maurice Rose, its commander, was right up at the front, Irwin noted. During their mammoth advance, a Jeep came alongside his tank. A helmetless officer with 'a crew cut, stiff, graying hair, a serious handsome face and a big frame, looked up at us, touched a forefinger to his brow in salute and said, "My helmet's off to you men – keep it up!"' It was General Rose, 'Just the best f**king officer in the whole goddamn US Army. He was a GI just like the rest of us. Always up front.'[1]

The 104th Infantry Division, Terry Allen's Timberwolves, were struggling to keep up with them, clinging on to every vehicle they could find, but frequently halting due to mines laid across their routes. 'We were assigned the task of clearing the road,' recalled Timberwolf engineer Art Diamond. However, at a junction and under fire, his unit took casualties

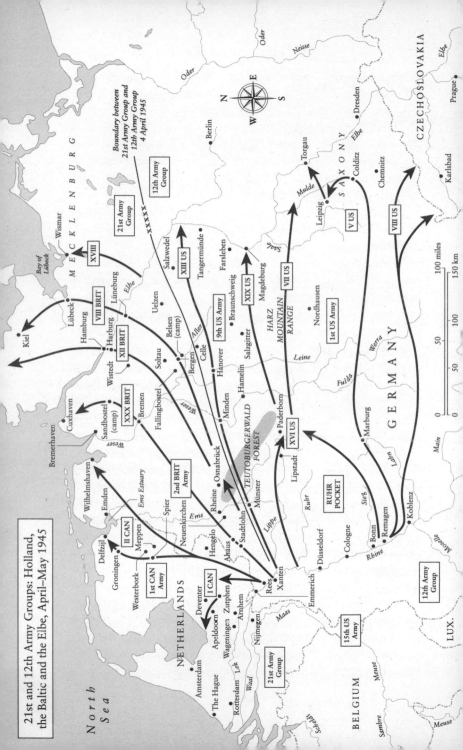

21st and 12th Army Groups: Holland, the Baltic and the Elbe, April–May 1945

in removing mines ahead of some 3rd Armored elements coming up from behind. 'Around 03:00, tanks began making their way up our road,' Diamond recollected. 'The first tank passed; the second and a third. The fourth vehicle turned out to be an open half-track. It pulled over to the side, stopped, someone hopped out and went directly over to the wounded, sharing words of encouragement with them. I asked the driver, "Who in the world is that?" He responded, "Oh, that's General Rose. He's our guy. Whenever the tanks are rolling, he's up front. We call him our point man, our spearhead man."' Diamond had an iconic divisional leader in Terry Allen, but he never forgot the general who stopped his vehicle to comfort the wounded.[2]

Allen and Rose were a well-matched pair of divisional commanders who relished being at the front, close to their men, when most preferred to be further back, hand on the tiller, with better situational awareness. However, soldiers appreciate the proximity of their superiors, seeing them share the same risks. Hence the popularity of figures like Patton and Rommel: the great battle captains from history were always those seen by their troops. This is still the case today and will always remain so.

German resistance at Paderborn proved unexpectedly fierce. Unknown to Rose, the Germans had created a new formation, SS-Panzerbrigade-Westfalen, combining all the various military schools in the Paderborn–Sennelager area into two improvised SS-led infantry regiments comprising training personnel – hardened veterans all – officer cadets and Hitlerjugend. To them were added a core of toughened steel, the Army's Schwere-Panzer-Abteilung (Heavy Panzer Battalion) 507, with two companies of King Tiger tanks. As was usual, Rose's 3rd Armored deployed as six task forces, two per combat command. During the morning of 30 March, those moving down two axes, Task Forces Richardson and Welborn, drove straight into a wall of German armour they were not expecting. They may have been lulled into a false sense of security by their unopposed marathon of the previous day.

After one of the most impressive armoured advances of the war, the Spearhead Division were tired, logistically stretched and off their guard when they slammed into the disciplined, motivated and well-equipped Westfalen Brigade deployed five miles south-east of Paderborn. Task Force Richardson triggered the first unpleasant surprise when companies of its 36th Armored Infantry Regiment drove into Kirchborchen. The small town was defended in textbook fashion by more than two hundred Hitlerjugend and SS, equipped with thousands of panzerfäuste and larger 88mm reusable Panzerschreck rocket launchers. German tactical doctrine taught at the Paderborn battle schools directed that oncoming armour should face simultaneous anti-tank fire from multiple directions, at a distance of no more than two hundred feet, and that is exactly what they delivered. The impenetrable barrier of missiles met Task Force Richardson from every angle – attic windows, cellar hideouts and piles of rubble. They caused immediate casualties and forced the GIs back, pursued by projectiles used as indirect artillery. By the time the Americans had reorganised and attacked at night, their opponents had melted away. In the Spearhead's memory, Kirchborchen became 'Bazooka-Town'.

Meanwhile, Task Force Welborn had hit a similar barrier of opposition in Etteln, a couple of miles south-east. Feeling the pressure of a future rendezvous with Ninth Army, keen to seal the huge German force in the Ruhr Pocket (examined shortly), and puzzled at this sudden brake on his success, Rose drove forward to see for himself the nature of the problem. He was as tired as his men from their Olympian sprint the previous day. In his account of the Spearhead's war, former general Daniel P. Bolger makes the astute observation that Rose, in near-continuous action since North Africa, had begun to make rash judgements as he played with danger on a daily basis. His insistence on always being at the front of his division, invariably with his command group, may have indicated undiagnosed PTSD. Rose was a private man, and though respectful and caring of his men, did not easily wind down with his staff.[3]

In what was certainly an imprudent act, at 19:30 Rose set off towards Etteln in a Jeep with his aide, Major Bob Bellinger, following another containing the divisional artillery commander, Colonel Frederic J. Brown. Behind them in an M20 wheeled armoured car, was the Division's G-3, Lieutenant Colonel Wesley Sweat. Almost immediately, they were caught up in the remains of an ambush that had destroyed the vanguard of Task Force Welborn – seventeen Shermans, seventeen half tracks, a tank destroyer and other vehicles had been knocked out by panzers and panzerfäuste. Assessing the situation, they sheltered in a roadside ditch before remounting, turning right and racing cross-country to join the safety of an oncoming column of four Pershing tanks they could see silhouetted ahead. Reaching the armour, the command team realised they were among not Pershings, but King Tigers from Schwere-Panzer-Abteilung 507.

Colonel Brown in the first Jeep squeezed past the German column at breakneck speed, but the second-to-last tank swung sideways, blocking the other vehicles. As Brown escaped, the cupola of the stationary King Tiger opened and its commander shouted a series of orders in German, and motioned for the general, his aide and their driver to surrender. The latter pair dropped their pistols, but as Rose struggled with his own side arm, the tank commander put four separate bursts from his Schmeisser machine pistol into him. When his body was recovered the next day, the divisional surgeon counted wounds from fourteen 9mm rounds across his head and body. The first burst had knocked the general's helmet off his head and into the air. Other rounds struck him on the left side of the head, killing him instantly.

When his helmet was later retrieved, it was seen that two rounds had struck it from the rear, exiting through the front near his two general's stars.[4] The aide and driver escaped, though Lieutenant Colonel Sweat and his G-3 staff were captured and held for a month. The mood within the Spearhead Division was immediately ugly as they learned of their general's 'execution' at the hands of the SS. Speculation grew that Rose was killed because he was Jewish, or because he was a general. Neither was true. The King Tigers were manned by German Army personnel, not SS. According to his companions, Rose was recognised neither as Jewish nor as a general. The maps and codes in his Jeep were not even touched.[5] The episode characterised the night-time panic, fear and confusion that is the fog of war. His deputy, Doyle O. Hickey, immediately took over and would lead the Spearhead for the rest of the war, but, in the eyes of many, the US Army had been robbed of a talent that would have taken Maurice Rose, then forty-five, to the very top.

The young tanker, John Irwin, of Rose's division, recalled his captain immediately afterwards briefing that their opponents were 'completely nuts and would commit any atrocity for the Führer. "We really don't want any more prisoners than necessary," ' he concluded. In fairness,

Irwin's superior also ordered, 'I'm *not* telling you to shoot men who are surrendering. Just because the Krauts have no consciences doesn't mean that we don't either.'[6]

The battle for Paderborn would continue until 17:00 on Easter Sunday, 1 April, when the much-depleted Westfalen Brigade withdrew across the River Weser, pursued by the 3rd Armored and 104th Timberwolves. The Spearhead Division had taken a hard blow, losing, besides their commander, 125 killed, 504 wounded, forty-two Shermans and numerous other vehicles. The anger over General Rose's death was magnified when, on 2 April, Lieutenant Colonel Mike Yeomans' 83rd Armored Reconnaissance Battalion occupied nearby Wewelsburg, an unusual, triangular Renaissance castle.

Built on a slight hill and once home to the Prince-Bishops of Paderborn, it had been taken over by Heinrich Himmler as an ideological training centre in 1934. For over a decade, the SS leader had spared no expense in creating a high-walled and turreted fantasy castle and giving free rein to his 'ersatz religion' incorporating notions of an ancient Nordic race, Viking sagas, assorted pagan nonsense and the Knights of the Round Table. Pretentiously, he named the project *Das Zentrum der Neuen Welt* (Centre of the New World). The Reichsführer-SS held leadership seminars there, and envisioned the castle as a reborn Templar estate, the focus of an Aryan settlement.

For his 'ideological cathedral of the SS', Himmler planned an eternal flame for his dead warriors, had Schutzstaffel insignia and runes set in marble and oak throughout, and named various rooms after King Arthur and his knights. Abandoned when the Spearhead's Reconnaissance Battalion arrived, Captain Theodore M. Black of the US Counter Intelligence Corps was soon rifling through the sabotaged ruins, and in addition to SS honour rings and many other souvenirs, he discovered that 3,900 Jews, Russian and Poles had toiled there, of whom 1,855 died from ill-treatment or execution – a 47 per cent death rate.[7] The massive blocks of stone carved for the organisation that worshipped Germanic *Blut und Boden* (blood and soil) were the result of Jewish blood and sweat.

Beyond Wewelsburg, Collins' VII Corps HQ directed a Spearhead detachment to the town of Lippstadt. There, the previous afternoon,

3rd Armored's Task Force Kane had made contact with elements of the 41st Armored Infantry, 2nd Armored Division, belonging to Simpson's Ninth Army. Although the Ruhr Pocket, encountered soon, would linger for another eighteen days, while the Allies tightened their grip, the vast majority of Field Marshal Model's Army Group 'B', numbering well over 300,000, who should have been halting First Army, were caught between the forces of Montgomery and Bradley.

For the first time, SHAEF allocated strategic objectives to its armies, where it anticipated they would meet the Russians. Prior to this, directives had concerned operational movement through France, the Rhineland and crossing the river. As we have noted, Eisenhower's instructions would change over Berlin before the month was out, but on 3 April the Ninth Army was still told to head for Berlin, the First for Leipzig, and the Seventh for Munich. Gerow's Fifteenth would look after First Army's rear west of the Rhine, train incoming units and reinforcements, and commence occupation duties. For Hodges, Bradley passed on an ultimate objective of the Mulde River, fifteen miles on the far side of Leipzig, which was the farthest distance he felt he could operate without railroads, and the first time the Mulde began to feature in operational orders. The Elbe, where they would eventually meet the Russians, lay another fifteen miles beyond it.

At the same time, First Army gained Matthew Ridgway's XVIII Airborne Corps, containing Bryant E Moore's 8th Infantry Division, veterans since Normandy, and Edwin P. Parker's 78th, which had arrived just before the Ardennes offensive. With the latter was Melvin Kaminsky, a young corporal in an engineer combat battalion assigned to the 78th. One of his tasks was to defuse landmines, but as he reminisced, 'You thought about how you were going to stay warm each night, how you were going to get from one hedgerow to another without some German sniper taking you out. You didn't worry about tomorrow. I was a Combat Engineer. Isn't that ridiculous? The two things I hate most in the world are combat and engineering.' The eighteen-year-old corporal is better known by his later stage name, Mel Brooks.[8]

With the 8th and 78th were the 86th and 97th Infantry, who would be new to battle, but Ridgway's airborne corps was shorn of its sky warriors. The latter were still retained as SHAEF reserves, of which the

82nd eventually made its way to Ninth Army, with the 101st ultimately joining the Seventh. This now allowed Hodges to take on two separate missions. Initially, XVIII and III Corps were to stay and reduce the Ruhr Pocket from the south, a few miles each day, while VII and V Corps raced due east towards Leipzig, sandwiched between Montgomery's troops on their left and Patton's GIs to their right.

Ridgway's corps would line the southern edge of the Ruhr area, controlling five divisions, including the 13th Armored, loaned for the purpose. On their right, the whole of Van Fleet's III Corps – 99th Infantry, 7th Armored and 5th Infantry Divisions – continued the ring of steel around Model's Army Group 'B'. Beyond them, 1st Division of VII Corps also helped seal the German enclave for the first few days, before rushing off eastwards to join the rest of First Army. To the north of the pocket, six of Ninth Army's divisions likewise prevented any escape, while the German forces slowly lost ground, were split in two, and eventually surrendered. Once XVIII and III Corps had completed their work in eradicating the Ruhr Pocket, Van Fleet's divisions would join the Third Army for the south-east push into Austria, and Ridgway's men in the last days would operate with several different armies, in the manner of a well-drilled fire brigade.

Meanwhile, with his armoured divisions in the lead, Hodges unleashed VII and V Corps eastwards, Collins aiming for the north of Leipzig and beyond to the River Mulde, with Huebner's V Corps expected to take its southern approaches and up to the river. In the interests of speed, both corps were obliged to leave their outside flanks in the hands of their armoured cavalry regiments (4th and 102nd), taking risks unthinkable the previous month. The route of Collins' VII Corps lay through the challenging terrain of the Harz mountains, and as William B. Kean, Hodges' Chief of Staff, lamented, it was free of the four-lane autobahns that criss-crossed the rest of Germany. All recognised that the pace and nature of warfare had changed.

By 11 April, VII Corps had reached the western edge of the Harz, and 3rd Armored, now under Hickey, had cleared the road and rail centre of Nordhausen on the southern edge 'where a terrific fight had been expected but did not materialize'. That evening, noted First Army staff, 'Gen. Collins called up a justifiable rage to tell Gen. Kean that his troops had discovered a concentration/slave labour camp (he used both terms), still spread with the bodies of workers literally starved to death.'[9] In fact, the Spearhead's Combat Command 'B' and the 104th Timberwolves had tripped over not one, but a network of *thirty-eight* camps in and around the town of Nordhausen, which housed nearly 25,000 skeletal inmates working on a top-secret project nearby.

Gypsum mining in the local Kohnstein hill had left tunnels, which were taken over by the SS for V-1 flying bomb and V-2 rocket assembly, after the RAF had attacked their facilities at Peenemünde in 1943. Labourers at the underground sites – obscurely code-named Mittelbau (Central Construction) – were housed in thirty-eight above-ground *Arbeitslager* (work camps). The largest was dubbed 'Dora'; another – the Boelcke-Kaserne (Boelcke Barracks, named after a Great War air ace) – was a couple of miles distant in Nordhausen town itself, with others in the vicinity.[10] Nazi officials destroyed many records from the National Socialist era, but those of Nordhausen somehow escaped. We know that at the beginning of March 1945, in addition to some 42,207 inhabitants, there were 23,697 'non-local' people (36 per cent of the total) registered with the authorities, most of them foreign workers.[11]

The many reports made on 11–12 April by the Spearhead and 104th Infantry Divisions, plus the 9th Division of III Corps, referring to Nordhausen or Dora-Mittelbau, thus refer to the same, linked complex. One local German teenager, later a naturalised American, recollected, 'I saw trucks loaded with what we now know were concentration camp inmates, wearing those striped suits. Emaciated people. I could actually see the tunnel entrance from my aunt's window. Nobody appeared to pay any attention. If you acted too nosey, you ran the risk of getting your head chopped off.'[12]

Initially accommodated inside the warren of dank tunnels, the workforce suffered some of the highest death rates for slave labour in the Reich. Those forced to stay underground were kept in chambers up to two storeys high, with little food, sanitation or heating, and slept on bunks four-high. The rock walls oozed water, while tuberculosis, typhus, pneumonia and toxic dust felled them in droves. Few managed to sleep because of the constant noise. Without protective clothing or masks, they worked with picks, dynamite and bare hands to enlarge the caverns. The vibrations of explosions and the small subterranean railway allowed no rest. The sick and weak were evacuated to the Boelcke in Nordhausen and simply locked up to starve to death. VII Corps CIC personnel saved all the records they could, which revealed that the complex was run by the SS for I.G. Farben, whose corporate headquarters in Frankfurt we have already noted.

Some 60,000 passed through the Mittelbau camps between August 1943 and March 1945, of whom 12,000 died – some claim a higher total of 20,000 – with 350 hanged for 'sabotage'. Quizzing the surviving inmates, GIs found that sabotage could amount to talking among themselves when instructed to work in silence; not working fast enough through illness or malnutrition; or making faulty components, usually due to the poor quality of materials and metals provided. Yet it was the Germans who sabotaged their own secret weapons programme by using unmotivated slave labour. The prisoners had no interest in quality control and post-war it was found that 25 per cent of all V-1 airframes had failed before reaching their targets due to poor components.

Overall, detainees in their rough prison garb, and dying like flies, assembled over 13,000 V-1 flying bombs and V-2 rockets, as well as jet engines for Messerschmitt-262 and Arado-234 aircraft. Mittelbau eventually became the sole site for V-2 production, using some components manufactured elsewhere. The first rocket was launched in anger on 6 September 1944, the last on 27 March 1945 against London, and later the port of Antwerp, and Remagen bridge.[13] The complex was equipped with a crematorium, which was not large, but kept busy. Still full of ashes, it was illustrated in the 18 May edition of *Yank*.[14]

'The first thing we saw was cordwood stacks, but as we got closer, we saw they were human beings, totally emaciated, many of them naked. Just bones,' remembered Malachowsky, with the 329th Medical Battalion, a Timberwolf unit. 'Then we saw movement, three bodies down, an arm was moving, and realised there were living people in these piles of the dead. When I got back to the States, I had one heck of a job convincing people, who should have known better, that the Germans were capable of doing just what we said they were doing.'[15]

One of many GIs deeply affected by the experience of Nordhausen was Captain Reuben Levinson, a D-Day veteran who had seen it all with the 42nd Field Hospital – Utah beach, Saint-Lô, Aachen, Bastogne. As a surgeon at Nordhausen he spent two weeks caring for those that were left. Then 'he had a nervous breakdown after seeing that place. When he lost it, the Army sent him to the Riviera for some R&R. That's why it took him so long to return to the States. We couldn't understand why, six months after all the other boys were back, Reuben was still over there,' a relative explained to his daughter.[16] Earlier, Levinson had written home, 'I am deep in the heart of the Rhineland, and it is very pretty country . . . It is difficult to comprehend why people with many virtues should have gone berserk and raving mad.'[17] But Levinson was then raging at the Germans waging war; it was eight days before the full horror of the Holocaust was revealed to him.

PFC John M. Galione, also with the 104th, recalled, 'We thought nothing could hurt us. We were hard from war. But, when we walked in there, we couldn't help getting choked up. Some of the soldiers turned aside and threw up by the fence.'[18] Decades later, a 3rd Armored man, Sherman tank driver Lou 'Louch' Baczewski with CCB, would still be overcome whenever recounting those moments at Nordhausen to his grandson. 'It was a bad sight. A bad sight. Something terrible,' he would repeat over and over while rubbing his forehead.[19] Nordhausen also left its mark on Technical Sergeant Harold Bruce Welch, another Timberwolf. His daughter often asked her father about his war, but 'he couldn't bear to tell his child about the evil out there in the world,' mused the girl, later First Lady of the United States, Laura Bush.[20]

Of 1,500 sick inmates locked into the nearby Boelcke barracks, in central Nordhausen, around half were killed in an RAF air raid on 3–4 April, just days before their liberation. Bombs ripped out the heart of the old half-timbered medieval centre but destroyed none of the weapons factories. Although the targets were military, the nature and technology of night-time bombing in the mid-1940s meant that in reality the whole settlement became a target, causing 8,800 civilian casualties and leaving 20,000 homeless. On arrival, GIs freed several hundred near-dead prisoners at Boelcke and discovered the already dead strewn about.

'Only a few could stand on rickety, pipe-stem legs. Their eyes were sunk deeply into their skulls and their skins under thick dirt were a ghastly yellow, noted journalist Al Newman in *Newsweek* on 23 April.[21] Due to the unusual nature of the subterranean sites and partially assembled rockets, war correspondents wrote, snapped pictures, and made films of the dead and dying which were soon circulated around the globe. All the secret weapons and documents fell into American hands and were immediately sent by road and rail to Erfurt. This was part of Operation *Paperclip*, hastily concluded before the Soviets – as agreed at Yalta – took over the area on 1 July.

A Timberwolf chaplain, Father Edward P. Doyle, was one of those who encountered the 'sight beyond description of mutilated, beaten, starved skeletons. One thousand were "living" in various stages of decay, merely breathing among the already dead.' Doyle, later professor at Providence College, Rhode Island, continued, 'I had seen as many as 125 wounded a night in our combat area of Belgium and Holland, and assisted in prepping the wounded for surgery, but never had I seen such suffering and anguish. The gun and the pursuit of the enemy was dropped, and all hands turned to the job here and now, helping the helpless. We were in the area five to six days and after doing all that could be done for the survivors, the attention had to be given to the dead. The war continued and the command was given to move on.'

Many sensed the anguish felt by the 104th's divisional commander, Terry Allen, at having to follow the war, rather than linger and tend to the living.[22] The liberators made the city's surviving residents dig graves and bury 4,000 broken and skeletal camp victims on 13 April. 'I was put in charge of the burials and insisted that the local Germans came for the occasion in their Sunday best,' recounted W. Gunther Plaut, a Jewish chaplain with the Timberwolves. 'Of course, we didn't have enough tools to do the work. But in my anger mixed with revenge, I told the burghers to use the knives, forks and spoons from their own homes.'[23]

We need to step back in time by a couple of weeks and focus on the Ruhr Pocket. The Rhine River crossings had been fixed on two prizes. First was racing on to Berlin, 375 miles distant. The second goal, and a more nuanced approach to defeating the Third Reich, was capturing the Ruhr area and destroying Germany's heavy industry. Most iron and steel, transported elsewhere to thousands of manufacturers across the Reich, which made or assembled everything from cutlery, helmets, cannon and engines, to locomotives, aircraft, U-boats and machine-guns, came from the Ruhr. The ore-rich region is defined by the layers of coal on which it sits and proximity to its river waters, giving rise to multiple industries and becoming the most urbanised area of Germany. It is a rectangle, bounded by the Lippe River in the north, from Duisburg, where it flows into the Rhine, via Hamm, to Lippstadt.

Its lower boundary lies beyond the Ruhr River, and in 1945 was taken to reach as far south as the Sieg, which flows into the Rhine opposite Bonn. An eastern border traced a line via Siegen as far as Winterberg, then north to Lippstadt. The western boundary is formed by the Rhine. The whole area, eighty miles from west to east, and sixty from north to south, comprised 4,800 square miles, encompassing the great industrial centres of Duisburg, Essen – home to the Krupp Steelworks – Dortmund, Düsseldorf and Solingen. The Germans were determined to defend the area's cities, factories and millions of civilians. Hitler had visions of turning the region into a super-Stalingrad, an urban battle on an unimaginable scale.

The barrier to the Allies' route to the Ruhr was a pair of German armies consisting of the 400,000 men of Generalfeldmarschall Walter Model's Army Group 'B'. Generaloberst Josef Harpe's Fifth Panzer Army was closest to the Rhine, General der Infanterie Gustav von Zangen's Fifteenth beyond it. These totalled nineteen divisions plus some 100,000 anti-aircraft personnel, manning belts of flak artillery defending the Ruhr's numerous factories. Both armies had contested Normandy and had been steadily pushed back into their Fatherland over the subsequent nine months.

Instead of a head-on assault, Eisenhower envisaged a double envelopment of his opponents. Every officer at every staff college in the world had been taught the rudiments of this manoeuvre, first recorded during the Second Punic War at Cannae in 216 BC and regarded as the most perfect of military stratagems. As Model's group was firmly anchored to the Ruhr area and showed little sign of moving, SHAEF devised a classic pincer manoeuvre, an indirect approach deploying two armies to envelop Model's vast garrison. Hodges' First Army, forming the lower jaw, had already broken out of the Remagen bridgehead and driven east along the southern boundary of the Ruhr. The upper jaw, ninety miles to the north, would be formed by Simpson's Ninth Army along the axis of the Lippe River. They had two tasks – to help surround and destroy the Ruhr Pocket, then advance towards the Elbe River.

Speed was essential, for the moment Model realised Army Group 'B' was not being attacked from the west, but encircled, he could deploy reserves to meet the threat, as he had done countless times in his great defensive battles in Russia. There he was known as the *Feuerwehrmann des Führers* (the Führer's fireman), for the way he speedily dealt with crises, while Basil Liddell Hart described his 'amazing capability to collect reserves from an almost empty battlefield', and his dexterity as 'a patchwork-quilt artist of the first order', for the way he strung together quite disparate units to keep the semblance of a continuous front.[24]

Part of the underlying logic of the *Varsity* airborne operation had been to help fix Army Group 'B's armoured reserves, and prevent them from being deployed elsewhere, and in that the airborne operation was highly successful. In the week after *Plunder* and *Varsity*, Ninth Army was impatient to break out eastwards, but it took a full week to chew through the German defensive crust, assisted by US artillery fire stationed on the west bank and attacks from Richard E. Nugent's XXIX Tactical Air Command, Simpson's attached air power. Nugent had been commissioned into the tank arm before transferring to the Air Corps in 1929, so well understood the principles of close air support to ground forces.

Once across the Rhine, Simpson recognised his infantry-heavy bridgehead south of Wesel was not large enough to hold the armoured combat power at his disposal, and that tanks would be the key to breaking clean. On 27 March at the risk of congestion, he decided to send Devine's 8th and Rose's 2nd Armored Divisions (both with McLain's XIX Corps), with infantry regiments from the 75th and 95th Divisions riding on their hulls, over the river to punch their way through and break out, and on the 28th, the German defences began to crumble as what was left of the German 47th Panzer Korps limped away. On 30 March the Wesel bridges reverted to Simpson's use, instantly expanding his bridgehead area.

As we have seen, it was at Lippstadt on 1 April, Easter Sunday, just after noon, when the pincers around the Ruhr snapped shut. Isaac

White's 2nd Armored of Simpson's Ninth met Doyle Hickey's 3rd Armored of Hodges' First. Maurice Rose narrowly missed living to see the triumph of his 'Spearhead' formation. The result was that Model's Army Group 'B', the Fifth Panzer and Fifteenth Armies, seven corps and nineteen divisions, with all their various headquarters elements and the Luftwaffe flak detachments, had been surrounded, trapped in an oval enclosure, roughly thirty by seventy-five miles in size. Within were twenty-six generals and one admiral, Werner Scheer, commander of Defence District I in Essen. Thereafter, the Ruhr Pocket would shrink like a slowly deflating balloon, pushed on all sides by the five US corps placed around its perimeter.

However, the speed of the encirclement, particularly to German civilians, seemed nothing short of miraculous. On the far eastern side of the pocket, as the villagers of Gesseln, a suburb of Paderborn, were attending their delayed Easter Mass on 3 April, they heard tanks clattering down the main street. One peeped out and warned, '*Pastor, sie sind da*' (Pastor, they're here), as an American tank passed, backed up and nosed its main gun through the church door. Yet the GIs had come in peace; they knelt and prayed with the shocked burghers, who had been told by Goebbels to expect looting, rape and death.[25]

Model's several requests to withdraw or break out from the Ruhr *Kessel* (cauldron) were denied by Hitler, who immediately designated the region *Festung-Ruhr* (Fortress Ruhr), which he expected to resist for months, tying down thousands of Allied troops. Instead, it would take First and Ninth Armies just fourteen days to tighten their noose around Model's neck. Anderson's XVI (17th Airborne, 35th, 75th and 79th Infantry Divisions) sealed the north-west, McLain's XIX (8th Armored and 95th Infantry) the north-east, with Ridgway's XVIII Airborne (13th Armored, 8th, 78th, 86th and 97th Infantry) to the south-west, Van Fleet's III Corps (7th Armored, 5th, 9th, and 99th) to the south and a single division of Collins' VII Corps (1st Infantry Division), deployed briefly, to the east. These sixteen formations, at full strength, supported by air, with unlimited reserves of fuel and ammunition to hand, easily outnumbered the wreck of Model's command.

On 10 April, Colonel Edson D. Raff's 507th Parachute Infantry of the 17th Airborne Division forced the surrender of Generalmajor Werner von Raesfeld, Kommandant of the vast conurbation of Essen. Wyche's 79th 'Cross of Lorraine' Division was in at the kill, taking as one of its last prisoners Alfried Krupp von Bohlen und Halbach, the last of a 400-year-old dynasty that had first produced cannon in the Thirty Years' War. His factories employed 5,000 from concentration camps, 23,000 prisoners of war, and 70,000 foreign civilians, including children between ten and fourteen; all were regularly beaten. Of the 168 hours in each week, the arms manufacturer required 41 per cent, or sixty-nine hours, of heavy physical labour from all. Solitary confinement of recalcitrant workers in a small steel box for two-day periods without food was common. German employees who tried to help were punished. 'Any sympathy is false pity, which the courts will not accept as an excuse,' they were warned.

Babies born to forced labourers were taken from their mothers at six weeks and placed in the nearby Krupp-Voerde-Westkinderlager children's camp, where eighty-eight died 'of illnesses' between the autumn of 1944 and early 1945. After the war, Alfried Krupp and his fellow directors were found guilty of failing to provide shelter for their workforce. 'Quite apart from the fact that it was illegal to employ them at all for war work, and to employ them in so dangerous an area, it was the duty of the employers to see that these prisoners were properly housed and furnished with adequate air raid protection' read part of the verdict.[26]

The 2,500 paratroopers of the 507th – nicknamed 'Raff's Ruffians' after their 37-year-old commander – needed all their ingenuity to subdue and police Essen, home to more than one million Germans and slave workers, the latter spread across 350 sites. Apart from Krupp, the largest *Arbeitserziehungslager* ('labour education camp', in reality for enslaved workers) was at Essen-Müllheim airfield, where 8,000 foreign captives built reinforced hangars, extended runways, and cleared bomb damage under conditions of extreme privation. When the Luftwaffe ordered the area evacuated and destroyed on 24 March, these same workers undertook the destruction. They barely had the strength to lift a pick or shovel. GIs noted the irony of labourers from France, Belgium and Holland killed by aerial bombs dropped by their comrades-in-arms in two big raids of 24 December and 20 March, unaware of the nature of the conscript workforce below.

Around the Ruhr, the Americans began, like sheepdogs, to herd the flock of their opponents into smaller concentrations, and the number of US divisions in the Ruhr gradually lowered, through sheer lack of manoeuvre space. By 11 April, the pocket was half its original size; three days later it had broken into two. Most of the Wehrmacht were by then in despair; as Feldwebel Otto Henning with Panzer Lehr's 130th Reconnaissance Battalion observed, 'Survival was what mattered to us. We spent a good deal of time speculating about what we might have to face, imprisonment, that sort of thing. How can life go on, what will happen? Our towns were in ruins.'[27]

When the 95th 'Victory' Division of McLain's XIX Corps captured the Hanseatic city of Dortmund on 13 April, they found 98 per cent of the city centre and 65 per cent of the metropolitan area in ruins. This was the result of 106 raids on its oil and coking plants from May 1943 to March 1945, and the release of 22,242 tons of bombs, making it the most heavily attacked city in the Reich. Its factories had been run via hydroelectric power from the Ruhr dams, first attacked with bouncing bombs in May 1943. Ironically – according to German records – the principal victims of the RAF's Operation *Chastise* were around 1,500 prisoners of war and slaves, swept away in the ensuing floodwaters.[28]

The 95th's GIs discovered 45,000 foreign workers in Dortmund's work camps, who had struggled to exist in local arms industries and mines. Due to the city's extensive air-raid-shelter network, the number of residents who died was relatively low at 6,341, a total far eclipsed by the captives who had no access to such protection. When the American forces neared, Dortmund's Nazi officials began a round-up of political dissidents and forced labourers, taking them to Gestapo prisons on the Benninghofer Strasse and at Steinwache.[29]

More than 66,000 people passed through the latter facility in the Third Reich era, giving it the nickname of *die Hölle von Westdeutschland* (the hell of western Germany). The Victory Division's GIs were unaware they were in a race against time: the longer they took to advance, the more innocent lives would be snuffed out by fanatical Nazis. Some three hundred were murdered by guillotine in the Lübecker Hof, Dortmund's court prison, but most suffered at the hands of a 150-strong Gestapo squad. They began executing their victims on 7 March and ceased only on 12 April, the day before the Victory men arrived.[30]

Ever since the Americans had arrived at the opposite bank on 3 March, Düsseldorf had been a *Frontstadt* (front-line city) and under shellfire for the subsequent six weeks, losing many of its church spires and towers, presumed to be observation posts. Its Gauleiter, the rabid Nazi Friedrich Karl Florian, wanted to expel the population and turn his domain into scorched earth, which aroused the ire of its citizenry. Thus, as Milton B. Halsey's 97th Division of XVIII Corps were poised to strike from the east, architect Aloys Odenthal and lawyer August Wiedenhofen put *Aktion Rheinland* into play on 16 April 1945. This amounted to a rare German Resistance group of nine senior figures in the city's hierarchy agreeing to surrender their city. Although the plan was betrayed and five of the plotters were executed by Florian's diehard fanatics, Wiedenhofen and Odenthal reached the American lines, and were subsequently able to ride on Halsey's tanks to Düsseldorf's police headquarters on 17 April and negotiate the fall of Germany's seventh largest city and home to half a million, including 35,000 slave labourers in four hundred camps. Florian fled with his police chief, the sinister SS-Brigadeführer August Korreng.[31]

Anderson's XVI Corps artillery in the north-western corner of the Ruhr alone fired 259,061 rounds in fourteen days, suggesting that Army Group 'B' were on the receiving end of a million shells, besides other ordnance, during the two-week battle. Simpson's Ninth Army was also lent a squadron of the 1st Fife and Forfar Yeomanry, a Scottish tank unit whose 'Crocodile' Churchill tanks specialised in propelling liquid flame at particularly stubborn defenders, whose will to resist usually subsided within seconds. As the single pocket became two smaller ones, surrenders began. However, the German prisoners did not include the monocled Field Marshal Model, whom Ridgway called upon to capitulate on the 15th.

In his headquarters at Sonnborn, midway between Wuppertal and Solingen, and still angry at being bombed on 13 April, Model replied he still considered himself bound by his oath to Hitler and his sense of honour as a German field marshal. Thus, a formal surrender was out of the question. On the 16th, Model had received authorisation from Berlin to break out, but as usual Hitler had dithered too long, and the order had arrived far too late. Rolf Munninger, a *Gefechtsschreiber* (combat clerk), formerly on Rommel's staff and inherited by Model, witnessed the signal's arrival. 'It was a *Führerbefehl* – a personal order from Hitler. We were to fight our way out and go to Berlin. We were supposed to grab our supplies from the civilian population and start reprisal actions. These might include setting fire to the homes of those who refused.'[32]

Instead, Model recognised the inevitable and began to dissolve his army group. First, the oldest and youngest soldiers were discharged from military service with orders to return home; later, the remaining men were allowed the choice of surrender or an attempt to escape. Rolf Munninger recalled being given his release papers, then 'Model said to us, "Gentlemen, it's over, there's nothing more we can do. It is up to you what you do from here. There will be no more orders." '[33] Few made it through American lines, and the total prisoner count exceeded 317,000 men, twice the US intelligence estimate. The exchange rate was an extraordinarily low 2,000 killed and 8,000 Allied wounded of whom 462 killed or missing and 2,000 wounded were Ninth Army GIs. On 17 April, when Fifth Panzer Army surrendered, two days after the Fifteenth, Model's own future became clear from a conversation with his chief of staff, General Carl Wagener, when the marshal speculated, 'What is left for a defeated general? In ancient times they took poison.'[34]

What finally opened his eyes was the radio broadcast from Berlin on 20 April, Hitler's birthday, when Goebbels publicly denounced Army Group 'B' and its commander as traitors to the Reich, an act of self-harm that Model utterly failed to comprehend, having faithfully served the Reich until the end. The following day, the loyal Generalfeldmarschall, holder of the Knights Cross with Oak leaves, Swords and Diamonds (the highest German war decoration, awarded only twenty-seven times), took leave of his aides in woods outside Duisburg. A single shot from his 6.35 mm service pistol did the job. He had followed his field marshal predecessors, Hans von Kluge and Erwin Rommel, who were both pressured into suicide by the Reich. Commanding Army Group 'B' for all three had been, literally, a poisoned chalice.[35]

Model's son, Hans-Georg (later a brigadier general in the Bundeswehr) told me that it was only in 1955 that he was led to his father's lonely grave by Oberst Anton Staubwasser, former Army Group 'B' Chief of Intelligence. Together, they had the Marshal reburied in the Vossenack

Soldatenfriedhof (war cemetery). Today, Model shares a random plot with one of his men, Hermann Henschke, south-east of Aachen in the Hürtgen Forest.

At this stage Eisenhower, commanding the equivalent of ninety full-strength divisions, had contacted Stalin with his decision to eschew the costly street fighting that would be needed to take Berlin, though had yet to communicate this to his field armies. Meanwhile he ordered his armies to 'move their armour forward at once and get to the Elbe with the utmost speed and drive'. As the tank forces of McLain's XIX Corps became Simpson's shock troops, they forced their way out of the bridgehead and slid along the north bank of the Lippe, the northern edge of the Ruhr Pocket. From then on, German opposition would be unpredictable and patchy.

At Recklinghausen, Devine's 8th Armored encountered part of the 116th Panzer Division, led by a 'fanatical Nazi leader who exacted an oath from his men to die rather than surrender,' and fought for six days until they had not a single working panzer or serviceable gun to their name.[36] Another fierce firefight with more of the same unit, known as *die Windhunde* (the greyhounds), followed at Hamm, thirty miles east, but at Ahlen, a further ten miles beyond, the town's elders proved wise to the changing fortunes of the Reich; German police turned out to guide the 2nd Armored through their town, while the local population looked on, dutifully waving.

With his formations on the north-eastern tip of the Ruhr, Simpson was obliged to split the Ninth Army in two. While under Montgomery's Twenty-First Army Group, Simpson had been directed to head for the Elbe, and to 'hold Second Army's right flank facing the Ruhr and as far east as Paderborn, and to assist Twelfth Army Group in mopping up the Ruhr'.[37] On 4 April, Ninth Army at last re-joined their compatriots in Twelfth Army Group, though initially Simpson's instructions were the same: 'Keep in contact with the British on the left and First Army on the right.' Leaving Anderson's XVI Corps to help destroy the remnants of Army Group 'B' and with no direction yet to leave Berlin alone, Ninth Army commenced their drive to the Elbe and, in their minds, to the capital of the Reich.

Most of McLain's XIX Corps headed due east, with 2nd Armored Division in the lead, aiming for Magdeburg and brushing their right sleeves with Collins' corps of First Army, who were picking their way through the Harz mountains. Meanwhile, Gillem's XIII Corps (84th and 102nd Infantry, 5th Armored, plus the 11th Cavalry) crossed the Rhine at Wesel and raced north-east, initially to Münster and thence to Hanover and Celle. They traced their boundary with Dempsey's Second Army, and guarded the British southern flank, which would take them to the Elbe north of Magdeburg.

Meanwhile, the 84th 'Railsplitters' and 5th Armored Divisions of XIII Corps progressed beyond Münster to cross the River Weser and capture Hamelin. Once known as the 'Gibraltar of the North' for its fortifications, this was where the Treaty of Westphalia had been signed, ending Europe's Thirty Years' War. Napoleon had its walls pulled down and an Allied bombing raid further damaged the place in October 1944; however, enough remains to convey a sense of how picturesque this old town once looked. It was taken on 8 April 1945 by troops of both divisions, hurrying eastwards. Some 202 Nazi war criminals condemned by British courts would be executed in its jail during 1946–9, a fitting riposte for the 220 murdered there by the Third Reich.

The town is chiefly known to my generation and our predecessors for its Pied Piper, and I can recall endless recitations of Robert Browning's poem at school, where 'The river Weser, deep and wide / Washes its wall on the southern side'.[38] This is where the British Army came to settle after the war, its final bases closing after seventy years' continuous use only in 2015. The area is deeply ingrained in British history, with Minden, site of a 1759 victory over the French, nearby, and the region ruled over by the British Crown from 1714 to 1837.

Two days after Hamelin, the city of Hanover, capital of Lower Saxony, fell to the same divisions. The House of Hanover was associated with six British monarchs, from George I to Victoria, but in 1945 the city was found to have played host to many odious labour camps. Most were empty, but at Hanover-Ahlem, the slave labourers were still present. 'Having gone through the war, my emotions were numbed, but I couldn't believe what I saw. It doesn't fade, doesn't go away. Even when I look at a photograph, I can smell it,' observed Railsplitter John O'Malley.[39] A doctor in the 335th Infantry, Captain William J. Hagood Jr, wrote home to his wife requesting lipstick for the girls found at Ahlem, because, he reported, 'up to ten women would share one tube, collectively reclaiming their femininity. All the grisly scenes I'd witnessed in four years of combat paled as I viewed the higgledy-piggledy stack of cadavers. You have to see it, and you are so stunned, you only say it was "horrible". You cannot think of adjectives.' George Chornesky in the same unit, recalled, 'When we overran Ahlem, the medics were sent in to see what could be done. I was among them. We entered the barracks to find emaciated people lying sick on bunks of straw. I was so upset at the time; I felt a sense of incredulity and anger.'[40]

By 11 April, Combat Command 'R' of the 5th Armored had moved through Hanover and fifteen miles further east reached Kirchhorst, home to the distinguished German writer Ernst Jünger. Famed for *Storm of Steel*, his meticulous observations of the Western Front in 1917–18, as the commander of the local Volkssturm, Jünger had ordered his men to guard the village's tank barrier but 'open it as soon as the [American] point unit comes into view . . .' He recorded, 'at the moment the first tank with its five-pointed star appears' a bystander 'releases the safety catch on his pistol and shoots himself in the head.' The chief of a local artillery battery had already done likewise.

Jünger went on, 'Following the first tank in close formation come armoured vehicles – myriads of them pass by for hours and hours. Small aircraft hover overhead. The pageant makes an impression of a highly coordinated effort in its military and mechanical uniformity.' Jünger, who had accompanied the panzers into France in 1940, thought the US tank commanders in their turrets like 'a procession of dolls rolling past'. When the vehicle columns halted 'the marionettes bend forward then backward, as if jerked on their strings'. He noted 'the radio antennae that sway above the tanks and their escort vehicles: they give me the impression of an enchanted fishing expedition.'[41]

Shortly afterwards, more Railsplitters arrived at Salzwedel, to the north of Magdeburg and fifteen miles east of the Elbe, where they found a complex of wooden huts occupied exclusively by women prisoners. Originally housing a thousand internees from Hungary, Poland and Greece, who made small arms and anti-aircraft ammunition, in 1945 it held three times that number. They were supervised by sixty SS men and women and forced to work in two twelve-hour shifts. Ninety corpses of those who had died of typhus, dysentery and malaria littered the site when the Railsplitters arrived. Lieutenant Kenneth Ayers with Company 'A' of the 333rd Infantry recalled, 'I saw the guards on the gate shot and killed. I was behind, maybe, hundred yards away, with no idea I was going to come across this kind of place. How did it affect my attitude toward the Germans? Shoot 'em in a minute. Couldn't bear to think about 'em. After we saw the camps, we didn't take any prisoners.'[42]

One incident, which brought Gillem's XIII Corps closer to the mechanism of the Holocaust, occurred on 13 April, when the European war had just twenty-five days left to run. Major Clarence L. Benjamin with Company 'D' of the 743rd Tank Battalion – an outfit that had landed on D-Day – encountered a train halted at Farsleben on a line that ran parallel to the Elbe and ten miles north of Magdeburg. It was standing in a siding, with steam up, and some of its occupants had been allowed to stretch their legs under the eyes of their guards. According to infantrymen of the 119th Regiment riding on the tanks, the passengers were clearly starving, in great distress, and convinced of their imminent demise.[43]

Several photographs of the moment exist, showing the row of forty-five cattle cars containing 2,500 unfortunates, hemmed in 'like sardines', who had been shipped out of Bergen-Belsen camp on 7 April, but, with the swift Allied advance, had been abandoned by their driver. He had disagreed with his orders to take the train onto a damaged bridge that spanned the Elbe and shunt it over the edge drowning the occupants. Their Landesschützen (reserve militia) guards melted away as soon as the American tanks appeared.[44] 'The victims received some badly needed food that night, were promised more food to be gotten from the German farms and homes near the area, and efforts were begun by the [local] government to find quarters to which they could be moved away from the filthy, jammed, evil-smelling railroad cars. So, the day was indeed a very joyful one for those who had been living for so long without hope,' wrote Major Benjamin in his after action report.[45]

Meanwhile, McLain's XIX Corps were keeping pace to the south. On 10 April, forty miles east of Hanover, Combat Command 'A' of the

2nd Armored stormed through Salzgitter, an iron-and-steel town established as part of the Third Reich's Four-Year Plan of 1936–40 to smelt low-grade ore in what had been an agricultural area. Their report highlighted the challenges of manoeuvring through 'the usual urban obstacles of blocked streets and rubble'. CCA then fought a pitched battle with 'sixty-seven big anti-aircraft guns, grouped to protect the Hermann-Göring-Stahlwerk [Steel Works] and able to fire against ground targets with devastating effect, because the level terrain gave superb observation and fields of fire'.[46] Within hours, 2nd Armored were then confronted with 'the vast problems of feeding thousands of displaced persons; reinstituting law and order; investigating known Nazis and other suspicious persons. The problem was complicated by a serious shortage of food. It became necessary to divert troops to police duty to ensure that military arteries remained unimpeded by civilian traffic. Main supply routes were banned to civilians and all refugees were forced to travel across fields or on secondary roads'.[47]

Meyer Levin noted the scene, common right across the Reich during its twilight moments, writing of 'liberated slaves and prisoners of war, a ragged yet cheerful human flood surging across Germany. They were on every road; walking, pushing their few belongings in go-carts, lugging their wrecks of suitcases, their packs swollen with a little retribution collected from German households. Clothes, an ornamental clock, souvenirs'.[48] For many the sight was medieval, or like something out of the Thirty Years' War, which these same roads would have witnessed.

The next day, 11 April, elements of the 2nd Armored raced fifty-two miles east in thirteen hours. At 20:00 hours, Brigadier General Sidney R. Hinds' Combat Command 'B' sent a four-word message to division headquarters. 'We're on the Elbe.' They had arrived at Schönbeck, ten miles south of Magdeburg. On the 12th, while negotiations were attempted with the defenders of the city, Hinds tasked the 17th Armored Engineer Battalion with forcing a river crossing downriver at Westerhüsen, a Magdeburg suburb, three miles south of the centre. By 23:00 the same day, three infantry battalions were landed by DUKW, unopposed on the east bank, while engineers assembled a bridge behind them.

Westerhüsen was soon bracketed by German artillery. The armored engineers got to within twenty-five feet of the far shore before the weight of fire, which punctured floats and damaged treadways, forced them to abandon work. By 14:00 when the job was called off, they had laid 560 feet. Attempts to get tanks and guns across by ferry were likewise nullified by hostile fire, and without anti-tank support, the battalions were forced to withdraw, losing two of their three DUKWs to German armour. GI prisoners were taken and placed in front of panzers as human shields.[49] The Battalion Surgeon of the 17th Engineers, Captain James F. Mills, set up an aid post on the west bank, and operated on casualties for thirty continuous hours during the action. His valour brought him a Distinguished Service Cross, which he added to the Bronze Star and the Belgian Croix de Guerre won elsewhere. Thoughtfully, Patton – a previous commander of the 2nd Armored – sent him a letter of congratulation, while Mills himself commented, 'It was really the Jeep that was Hitler's secret weapon. I recall one hospital I visited had half its beds filled with victims of Jeep accidents.'[50]

However, in the wake of the 2nd Armored, Robert C. Macon's 83rd 'Thunderbolt' Division had also arrived at the waterline at Barby, twenty miles upriver, and lunged beyond in their own amphibious assault. They had kept pace because of the transfer to them of XIX Corps artillery trucks and captured German vehicles, the latter hastily daubed with olive-drab paint and white stars, earning them the moniker of the 'Rag-Tag Circus'.[51] 'We pressed into service every conceivable means of transportation we encountered,' reported Colonel Edwin 'Buckshot' Crabill commanding the 329th Infantry, and author of the division's history. 'If it had wheels, we used it. It was not unusual to see thirty or more riflemen clinging to a single tank, or a whole platoon riding down the street in a dilapidated German jalopy. Such was our momentum, we called ourselves the 83rd Armored Division'. This had its advantages, not least when 'a staff car filled with senior Kraut officers, joined a column thinking it was one of theirs, only to learn to their dismay that it was not, and were swiftly apprehended'.[52]

Two regiments of the Thunderbolt's infantry immediately fought their way through Barby, and masked by smoke, crossed in assault boats. Colonel Crabill strode around the bridgehead balling, 'Don't waste the opportunity of a lifetime. You're on your way to Berlin.' He had yet to find out otherwise. Unlike Westerhüsen, at this site battalions of Shermans and tank destroyers had been ferried across to provide a strong back-bone of protection, while the 295th Engineers built a bridge and the 113th Cavalry and 453rd Anti-Aircraft Battalion watched the home bank. Despite German shelling and sabotage attempts, the 'Truman Bridge' remained intact, to which Brigadier General Hinds soon sent the rest of 2nd Armored's Combat Command 'B' after their failed attempt ten miles downriver.

By the end of 12 April, McLain's XIX Corps was on the Elbe with, from north to south, the 35th Infantry, 2nd Armored and 83rd Divisions, with an aggressive bridgehead at Barby. Forty miles north at Tanger-münde, the 5th Armored and 102nd Infantry of Gillem's XIII Corps were approaching the waterline, with the 30th fighting its way past flak batteries at Braunschweig (Brunswick) and its 84th Division in contact with the British at Celle, north-east of Hanover. Thus Simpson, with two corps on the Elbe, was poised to strike at Berlin, a mere fifty miles from his men at Tangermünde.

Simpson and his Chief-of-Staff, Major General James E. Moore, flew to Bradley's headquarters on 15 April to discuss the coming Berlin offen-sive and were poleaxed to be told 'You must stop on the Elbe. You are not to advance any further in the direction of Berlin. I'm sorry, Simp., but there it is.' Ninth Army's commander wrote later, 'All I remember is that I was heartbroken, and I got back on the plane in a kind of daze. All I could think of was, how am I going to tell my staff, my corps com-manders. Above all, how am I going to tell my troops?' Simpson found Hinds moving more men across the Elbe and told him, 'Keep some of your men on the east bank if you want to. But they are not to go any fur-ther. Sid, this is as far as we're going.' Hinds at first did not understand and retorted, 'No sir, that's not right. We're going to Berlin.' Struggling to control his feelings, Simpson replied, 'We're not going to Berlin, Sid. This is the end of the war for us.'[53]

Despite this shocking news, a substantial hostile garrison needed subduing at Magdeburg. A ninth century fortress founded by Charl-emagne, with bitter memories of its sacking in the Thirty Years' War, and surrender to Napoleon in 1806, Magdeburg readied itself to do battle with a regiment of Leland Hobbs' 30th 'Old Hickory' Division. The city had been declared a *Festung* (fortress) on 7 April, since when anti-tank barriers and 88mm guns had been placed along all arterial roads to the south, west and north, as well as in the city centre. The Festung Kommandant had the usual orders from the Reich leadership: 'Fight to the last cartridge: if you disobey, you face the death penalty.' Its defenders had built a detailed system of roadblocks, tank traps and fortified houses. Since the 12th the city had been on high alert, when the long wail of a siren heralded the arrival of their opponents. Fifteen- and sixteen-year-old Hitlerjugend, who had been called up earlier in February, and had all received fourteen-day courses on MP-44 assault rifles and panzerfäuste, readied themselves for battle.[54]

At 12:00 on 16 April, the 120th Infantry sent its regimental intelligence officer to demand the city's surrender. Blindfolded and taken to the Kommandant, he sensed a willingness to comply, were it not for the SS troops stationed at every point. Accordingly, in Field Order No. 70, Hobbs changed his plans from an attack by one regiment to one by two divisions. First, he ordered an aerial assault for the 17th when Magdeburg was blitzed for three and a half hours by 360 medium bombers. Some 775 tons of munitions, supported by corps artillery, rained down.

The moment the bombs stopped falling, the 30th attacked from the north, and the 2nd Armored from the south and west. They were greeted by 8 million cubic yards of debris, the city being the third most damaged by bombing after Dresden and Cologne. Earlier RAF raids had targeted the Krupp-Gruson-Werke and Junkers-Aerowerke, both heavy users of slave labour, but had also hit the *Gründerzeit*-era (post-1871) suburbs, and the *alte Stadt* with its baroque buildings. Ninety per cent of the once-beautiful centre which straddled the Elbe and 60 per cent of the wider city lay in ruins. Fatalities were estimated at 3,000, but forced workers suffered disproportionately.

Four major industrial sites around Magdeburg belonging to Maschinen-Fabrik-Polte, Germany's largest ammunition producer since the days of the *Kaiserreich*, were destroyed. Half their 30,000 workers were forced labourers, 3,000 of whom were penned in at the Neue Welt stadium, inadvertently targeted by the Old Hickory's artillery during the ground assault. Two American shells hit the prisoners' camp, resulting in a stampede to escape. The SS guards panicked and opened fire, causing an uncounted death toll running into hundreds. On the eve of the war, Magdeburg had boasted a civilian population of 330,000. As those not killed in raids had escaped to the surrounding countryside, a mere 90,000 were left when the GIs arrived. 'Battalions had difficulty in navigating their way round the shells of ruined apartment blocks, having to clear such dwellings room by room,' reported the 30th's narrative of the battle. Artillery strikes 'were not significant and armor was of limited benefit. Both 81mm and 60mm mortars were found to be the best close support weapons. Civilians stayed most in cellars or air raid shelters, however curiosity brought many out, where they interfered with fields of fire.'[55]

The struggle paused at 23:00 for the night, until both sides renewed the fighting at 06:30 on 18 April. The clash continued through the city and down to the river, when at 12:45 the Germans blew their last span over the Elbe. Magdeburg had fallen to McLain's XIX Corps. Combat cameramen pictured a smiling Generalleutnant Kurt Dittmar surrendering the ruins of his hometown, together with his aide, Major Werner Pluskat. The latter's military career was notable from his previous posting to an artillery regiment in Normandy. Stationed in a bunker overlooking Omaha beach on the eve of D-Day, Pluskat was the first recorded Wehrmacht officer to spot the Allied invasion fleet (which won his character a significant moment in the D-Day movie *The Longest Day*). He was one of the very few to have reached the Elbe alive, with twenty days left before the war's end.[56]

Foreshadowing the massive civil administration challenges that lay ahead, Anderson's XVI Corps was to the rear, starting to process some of the 124,618 German prisoners of war, 924,500 refugees and displaced people, and 204,379 Allied liberated prisoners within Ninth Army's area of responsibility. Two days later, 120 miles downriver at Neu Darchau twenty miles east of Lüneburg, Lunsford E. Oliver's 5th Armored Division of XIII Corps had contacted the British Second Army. The front line was continuous.

Nine days later at 13:30, patrols from the US 113th Cavalry, attached to XIX Corps, discovered their Soviet counterparts of the 121st Rifle Division, at Zerbst, twenty-five miles south-east of Magdeburg. Holbrook Bradley, war correspondent with the *Baltimore Sun*, watched them: 'the great surge of Soviet humanity that crawled across the land had none of the Jeep-led motorization of our army. They were a greater mass who had walked from Kiev, Minsk and Novgorod, hauling ancient Gatling guns, mortars, and equipment from another era. We passed Red soldiers pedalling captured bicycles or riding decrepit animals. We had a sense of awe that nothing could halt this human wave as it surged west, consuming everything in its path.'[57] East had met West. The advance of Ninth Army, then numbering 480,000, had come to an end.[58] Within days, Simpson had met his Russian counterpart, Colonel General Dmitri Tsvetaev of the 33rd Soviet Army, for a celebratory lunch and obligatory exchange of pistols.

Meanwhile, Joseph C. Harsch, the *Christian Science Monitor*'s correspondent with the Ninth Army, was alert to every nuance and mood among Simpson's men. 'I was traveling along the Allied front with a group of war correspondents,' he recorded. 'In the middle of the night, I was awakened and saw the bearded face of NBC correspondent John Vandercook standing at the foot of my bed. "The President is dead," he said. My first thought was, "What will this do to the war?" I dressed and went outside. An American GI passed by. I asked, "Have you heard the news about the president?" I could see tears in his eyes. He said, "I feel like my father has died." Just then, slits of light from nearly blacked-out headlights came around the corner: a convoy of "dragon wagons" – tank transporters. There was a long line of them moving to the front. I knew then that Roosevelt's passing would not change the war. FDR's death was a tragedy, but the vast machine of war rolled on.'[59]

(*Above*): As 21st Army Group entered Germany, on 15 April, VIII British Corps captured Belsen concentration camp, where a typhus epidemic was raging amongst its 60,000 detainees. It was the only concentration camp taken in working order with its staff still present. Most of the structures were subsequently dismantled and burned, and this sign erected in their place. (*Below*): When the Allies crossed the Rhine, they began to encounter millions of civilians they designated DPs (displaced persons). Most were former slave labourers, including this group bearing the letters 'S.U.', meaning they were from the Soviet Union.

15

April: Northern Flank

In the aftermath of *Plunder* and *Varsity*, Montgomery's various bridgeheads had merged on 28 March to an area thirty-five miles wide and twenty deep. The Canadian 3rd and 4th Divisions crossed Germany's moat at Rees, then turned left and followed the Rhine north to Emmerich and then over the border into northern Holland. Even when loaned 'Crocodiles', the flame-throwing armoured vehicles, based on a Churchill tank, which could project jets of flame at targets 150 yards distant, the Canadians found Emmerich a tough proposition.[1] Their 7th Brigade recorded, 'Defences consisted mainly of fortified houses, and as each house and building had to be searched, progress was slow. Our tanks in support found it almost impossible to maneuver due to well-sited road blocks and rubble.'[2]

While also guarding Second Army's left flank, the Canadians would have to battle with the remnants of General von Schlemm's First Parachute Army, who, though depleted in numbers, could withdraw from one Dutch water-line to the next in an infinite delaying action, in an attempt to deny Montgomery the north German ports and naval bases. The Canadian campaign in the north Netherlands was foretold when the German 346th Infantry and 6th Fallschirmjäger Divisions sold themselves dearly, inflicting 173 Canuck casualties over three days, before even reaching the Dutch frontier.

On Second Army's right, Simpson's Ninth had slid along the north of the Ruhr Pocket to protect Dempsey's flank. The British central axis, from Wesel via Bremen to Hamburg, the Reich's second largest city sitting astride the Elbe, lay open. Accordingly, Montgomery ordered

Crerar's Canadian Army to isolate the Germans in north-western Holland and clear the Frisian coast, while Dempsey's Second was to drive hard for the line of the River Elbe and gain quick possession of the plains of northern Germany.

With Simpson's Ninth Army returning to Bradley's control on 4 April, for the final month, Twenty-First Army Group would advance with Simonds' II Canadian Corps on its extreme left. The latter would cross the German frontier and were bound for the north of Holland and the German cities of Emden and Wilhelmshaven on the coast. As an unwelcome reminder of what they were fighting for, on 11 April, 'D' Squadron of the 18th Armoured Car Regiment (XII Manitoba Dragoons) and the 1st Black Watch of Canada, both II Corps units, liberated Kamp Erika, situated in a forest ninety miles east of Amsterdam, near the Dutch-German border.[3] Its particularly brutal guard force of the Dutch SS killed around 170 at Erika and another 150 in one of its two satellites.[4]

In the vicinity, 700 Frenchmen of 3rd and 4th SAS, led by the former Chindit Brigadier Mike Calvert, were parachuted into the province of Drenthe to conduct hit and run attacks on the withdrawing Germans. Operation *Amherst* was generally successful, but one group was discovered in the early hours of 8 April and a vicious firefight broke out. Canadian troops of the 8th Reconnaissance Regiment soon relieved the French, but in nearby Spier, the 14th Canadian Hussars 'were shown the corpses of fourteen Dutchmen murdered by more Dutch SS. Their heads were beaten to a pulp, their wrists were burnt, and when they had been tortured sufficiently enough to satisfy the lowbrow bastards that had done it, they had been shot through the back of the neck.'[5]

With four divisions moving north along parallel axes, resistance was spasmodic. On the left, 3rd Canadian Division ran into a Fallschirmjäger training battalion made up of teenagers, resulting in a hard fight to take Zutphen, but by 15 April, they had reached Leeuwarden, ninety miles north-east, and only ten miles from the North Sea. 'Canadian soldiers rate the boyish defenders of Zutphen among the most fanatical troops they have encountered,' wrote Douglas Amaron, a Canadian Free Press correspondent who had earlier covered the Canucks' war in Italy. 'The SS had some sense, but these Hitler Youths were absolutely mad. Nazis to the core.'

The river line between Deventer and Zutphen was crossed in Operation *Cannonshot*, where Captain Syd Frost of Princess Patricia's Canadian Light Infantry noted, 'On the east side of the river, it never looked like a war, or that an attack was in progress. People were sitting in their gardens, and everything seemed awfully peaceful. The Germans hardly reacted.'[6] Nearby Zutphen was liberated by two other Canadian battalions, the North Shore Regiment and the Régiment de la Chaudière, who likewise asserted, 'For the first time there was evidence that the enemy's attitude was gradually changing and although he fought well at times, the old tenacity was lacking.'[7]

On their right, the 2nd Canadian Division reached the outskirts of the medieval city of Groningen on 12 April, where 7,000 Dutch and Belgian SS as well as Luftwaffe flak-gunners, Naval marines and Wehrmacht snipers slowed down its capture for four days. This was to cover the retreat of their forces to the Ems River and port of Emden, still used by U-boats and surface vessels. Major General Bruce Matthews banned the use of field artillery to protect the city-dwellers, deploying it only to halt the eastwards retreat of the garrison. It took good infantry-armour drills to clear Groningen, house by house, though the owners were usually in residence, having nowhere else to go. Private Frank Holm of 'B' Company, Calgary Highlanders (5 Brigade), watched a Bren gunner set up his weapon on an antique table while firing from a bay window. 'The lady of the house, seeing him in the process of ruining her little table, handed him a cushion which she asked him to put under the legs of the gun, then handed him a cup of coffee as he continued to fire down the street.'[8]

Groningen cost the Canadians 200 killed and wounded; there were fears of a much higher total from four days of urban slogging, but the low body count emphasised how skilled they had become. The German garrison was ejected, 5,000 prisoners being taken. Kurt Herdina, the wounded Fallschirmjäger NCO we last met being felled by shrapnel near Goch during Operation *Veritable*, was being treated in a city hospital. Medical orderlies exaggerated his wounds, enabling him to stay and be captured, as further evacuation would have killed him. Herdina recollected Dutch Resistance fighters roaming through his hospital ward with pistols drawn. They hauled away all the Dutch nurses and paraded them through Groningen with shorn heads, at which point the Canadians mounted a guard to prevent further such incidents.[9]

Next to them, Maczek's 1st Polish Armoured Division snaked north along the Dutch-German border, while the 4th Canadian Armoured Division advanced on II Corps' right flank, through Meppen on the German side of the border. On 12 April, the Canadian 2nd Division encountered Westerbork, thirty miles south of Groningen, which had served as a transit centre for Dutch Jews, including Anne Frank. From here a recorded ninety-eight trains had transported over 100,000 to their deaths further east. As the Royal Hamilton Light Infantry (the 'Rileys') approached the camp, the Germans fled leaving 876 inmates barely alive and the graves of another 750 who had perished there.[10] Liberating the oppressed in the midst of trading shots with the 6th Fallschirmjägers proved challenging, as Lance Corporal John Lisson remembered. 'The Jews came running out of the place yelling "Tommy, Tommy" because of our pisspot-style helmets. Those that got to us began to throw their arms around our necks and hung on. We had to shake them off. After all, we were right in the middle of a battle.'[11]

Behind them, Lieutenant General Charles Foulkes' I Corps – which had re-joined the Canadian Army on 15 March after leaving Italy – moved down the Rhine, headed due east towards Arnhem, thirty miles from Rees and scene of bitter memories from *Market Garden* the previous September. In Operation *Quick Anger*, with the 49th British Division – the 'Polar Bears' – under command, they cleared the Arnhem area over 14–16 April, and Apeldoorn, twenty miles beyond. Riding on a Sherman of the 1st Canadian Armoured Brigade, Kenneth J. West with the 11th Royal Scots Fusiliers (with the Polar Bears) remembered having to debus as the head of his column was attacked. 'Crack, crump. There was a sound of heavy metal objects hitting heavy metal targets. We dug in and formed a protective screen around the Sherman with its maple leaf emblem, and waited. Almost as I finished digging, so did the argument to our front between a Spandau and a couple of Brens. We sat with the men of the Ontario Regiment and talked quietly and dispassionately, as fighting men do, about friends who had just been killed. They had lost Charlie, a well-liked Lieutenant, together with his driver, to two well-aimed anti-tank shells.'[12]

After *Market Garden*, Arnhem had been forcibly evacuated of civilians by order of the Germans who then systematically looted the town. All furnishings and even doors and windows had been removed to towns in the Saar and Ruhr to repair and replace damage caused by the Allied air forces. As they advanced, I Canadian Corps troops noted the malnutrition of Dutch civilians, following their horrendous *Hongerwinter* of 1944–5. This had resulted in 18,000 civilian deaths, and to avoid a worse humanitarian crisis, the corps paused on April 22 to negotiate a truce. Foreshadowing the Berlin airlift of two years later, the RAF, RCAF and USAAF mounted Operations *Manna* and *Chowhound* from 29 April to 8 May. Over 11,000 tons of food floated down by parachute into the yet-to-be-liberated western Netherlands – with German consent. On land, in Operation *Faust*, two hundred Allied trucks were also allowed through Wehrmacht lines, bringing succour to starving civilians, who were reduced to eating tulip bulbs and sugar beets. The occupiers, who clearly saw surrender just around the corner, were disinclined to intervene, and in any case, militarily impotent. Post-war brides would make wedding dresses from the discarded parachute silk – an acknowledgement both to surviving the war, and to the Allied aircrews who switched from conveying death, to bringing life during the last aerial hurrah of the European war.

Next in line, Horrocks' XXX Corps (Guards Armoured, 3rd British, 43rd Wessex and 51st Highland Divisions, 8th Armoured Brigade) were the first to break out of the bridgehead, aiming towards Bremen astride the Weser, and Bremerhaven at its mouth. The armoured brigade noted their use of 'tank loud-hailers', giant speakers mounted on armoured vehicles, used by German linguists to induce their opponents to capitulate.[13] These, and the widespread use of surrender leaflets dropped by air, reflected Montgomery's attempts to use every available means to keep casualties to a minimum. This was because they had some of the toughest opposition ahead of them, in the 6th and 7th Fallschirmjägers, as Brigadier Walter Kempster (9th Brigade, 3rd Division) asserted: 'These para boys will have to be exterminated; they do not surrender easily.'[14]

To their south, Ritchie's XII Corps (7th Armoured, 52nd Lowland, 53rd Welsh Divisions, plus thirty-year-old Brigadier Mike Carver's 4th Armoured Brigade) headed for Hamburg. In 9th Royal Tank Regiment was Sergeant Trevor Greenwood, whom we met long ago, commanding a Churchill, and skating in Holland. He crossed at Rees, observing, 'Completely battered, mass of ruins. Did not halt. Beyond Rees country very flat with much evidence of recent fighting. In Bocholt, ten miles from the Rhine, hardly a building was left, only gaunt, and blackened walls and heaps of rubble. Civilians searching among the wreckage. Now the Heerenvolk (literally Army people, but a British expression more generally meaning Germans) are having a taste of war with a vengeance.'[15] A Lowland officer recalled his advance. 'Boarding a handful of trucks, we swayed, clattering and squeaking, over a floating bridge and into the countryside beyond. So, this was what the artillery had been steam-rolling so heavily. Everywhere were scenes of indescribable desolation: dead cattle, shattered orchards, houses, fields, farms, villages. Many buildings were still smouldering. The few civilians about wore dazed, vacant expressions as though they had not yet dared to face the implications of their broken surroundings.'[16]

On their right flank, Barker's VIII Corps (11th Armoured, 6th Airborne and 15th Scottish Divisions, and 1st Commando and 6th Guards Tank Brigades) struck out for Osnabrück, Uelzen and beyond for the Elbe. With the armoured cars and half-tracks of the divisional reconnaissance unit, the Inns of Court Regiment, out in front, the 11th's move began in heavy rain with 8th Rifle Brigade (an infantry battalion) advancing with the armour of 3rd Royal Tanks close behind. 'There was no question of fraternization on anyone's part,' wrote Noel Bell of the Rifle Brigade. 'Any friendly gestures by the Germans were met by frigid British stares.'[17] And no doubt, vice versa. Such was the need for infantry in the fast-moving advance that the 75th Anti-Tank Regiment was ordered to quit their guns and take up rifles, while the 6th Airborne commandeered any available transport to keep up, from perambulators and bicycles to fire trucks, and at one stage, a steam traction-engine.

On 30 March, for the first time 11th Armoured's war diary recorded, 'first hundreds, then thousands of DPs [Displaced Persons], plodding sadly, gratefully accepting cigarettes and biscuits on their way'.[18] Alan Moorehead wrote that 'All the Nazi flags and parades and conquests in the end were based on one thing – millions upon millions of semi-slave workers'. The further the Allies advanced into Germany, the more numerous they became: 'little groups of Frenchmen, then Dutch, then

Belgians and Czechs and Poles and Italians, and finally, in overwhelming majority, the Russians in their bright green uniforms with "S.U." – Soviet Union – painted in white on their backs. All moving blindly westwards along the roads, feeling their way by some common instinct.'[19]

Estimated at Nuremberg as reaching 12.5 million in total, the former slaves were observed by Moorehead thus: 'These millions lived a vagabond existence. At every bend of the road, you came on another group, bundles on their shoulders. And still that vast moving human frieze kept pouring down the roads. What we were seeing was something from the dark ages, the breaking up of a medieval slave state.'[20] A US officer, Lieutenant Jesse Glenn Gray, precisely echoed this: 'More and more, this problem of displaced persons is becoming tremendous. Germany really was a slave state on a giant scale. Almost all of these foreign workers are on the road a few hours after their liberation, going they know not where, but away from the front and towards home – though thousands must know they no longer have a home.'[21]

For the British, 15 April marked the day they discovered the worst atrocity witnessed by Twenty-First Army Group. As the 11th Armoured Division approached Lüneburg, word arrived at Barker's VIII Corps headquarters that the Wehrmacht were asking for a local truce. On the 12th, two German medical officers in a staff car bearing a white flag had explained that typhus had broken out in a nearby camp, forty-five miles south of Hamburg. Their commander urged avoidance of any actions that might allow the inmates to escape and spread disease to the troops of either side or local civilians.

It was Jeep patrols comprising men from the old 'L' Patrol, the original special forces detachment founded in July 1941 that grew into the 1st Special Air Service (SAS), who verified the site's presence. They were part of 'Frankforce', the 300-strong SAS contingent that had crossed the Rhine earlier and were now operating forward of Second Army's three corps. A ceasefire was arranged, and on 12 April a twenty-square-mile exclusion zone agreed around the facility, which included three sub-camps. Reg Seekings of the SAS recalled, 'We'd been coming up through this forest and for a day or so we'd had this horrible stink.'[22] As with facilities discovered by the Americans, it was the stench that betrayed Belsen. Even had the Germans not asked for a parley, the reek was already alerting the British to a tragedy of apocalyptic proportions. SAS Lieutenant

John Randall was struck by the obscenity of 'neatly tended flowerbeds on either side of the gate and gleaming whitewashed kerbstones' in contrast to the malodorous dead and dying wretches who lay just yards beyond. The hard-as-leather, tough-as-steel SAS men vomited.[23]

Three days later British troops found the Germans had massively understated the real truth. Intelligence officer Major Derrick Sington, equipped with a loudspeaker, and Jack Bailey with the 43rd Reconnaissance Regiment were the first to arrive. 'Two tanks were in front of our armoured car. As we approached, I saw a wrought iron gate with the German Eagle on it. As a blacksmith in civilian life, I stopped to look at the fine workmanship,' Bailey remembered. 'The complex went much further than people usually imagine. After around six miles there was a terrible smell. In the distance we saw cattle wagons. We couldn't make out clearly what was in them. The stench now was vile, vile. We could make out something like heaps of flesh. We guessed that they were sheep carcasses left to rot.'[24]

Built to hold 7,500 prisoners, Belsen had eight times that crammed into its huts. The Kommandant, Josef Krämer, and Dr Fritz Klein, camp doctor, were simply overwhelmed by additional detainees arriving from the east, on foot and by train, swelling numbers to around 60,000 skin-and-bones inmates of twenty different nationalities. Disease had broken out; there was no medical support, little food and inadequate drinking water. Among the Dutch Jews sent there was Anne Frank and her sister Margot, both of whom died of typhus sometime in February 1945. The fact that we know neither of their dates of death alerts us to the chaotic conditions prevailing at the time. Around five hundred were dying per day when the Allies arrived. The crematoria could not keep pace, with the result that unburied corpses lay around the site. Additionally, there was a Soviet prisoner-of-war camp attached, whose inmates were also in a catatonic or near-death state. Aiding the living was a major task: all were in desperate need of sustenance and medical attention.[25]

So far, even though details of the 'Final Solution' – the camps, the railway journeys, the slavery and mass murders – had been circulated, they were not widely known. It was not even understood to be specifically anti-Jewish. When No. 5 Army Film and Photographic Unit arrived at Belsen, they shot not just images of emaciated or dead bodies, but the perpetrators – who, uniquely, were still present due to the military truce. SS guards had not generally been caught elsewhere, but at Belsen the fully functioning camp administration fell into the hands of 11th Armoured Division. SS-Hauptsturmführer Josef Krämer, the only Kommandant not to flee, and his henchmen were detained. For the first time the barbarity could be linked to individuals, whose faces were caught for posterity.

Welsh-born Leslie Hardman, a Jewish army chaplain, later mused, 'If all the trees in the world turned into pens, all the waters in the oceans turned into ink and the heavens turned into paper, it would still be insufficient material to describe the horrors these people suffered under the SS.' He described first walking into Belsen: 'Towards me came what seemed to be the remnants of a holocaust – a staggering mass of blackened skin and bones, held together somehow with filthy rags.' He was equally horrified when witnessing Krämer's interrogation: 'He was without the slightest regret or remorse.'[26] Doon Campbell of Reuters recalled 'Krämer sitting, brooding, on a short-legged stool, when I met him. The inmates would have torn him limb from limb but for his British guards.'[27]

Over 15,000 dead lay unburied. The Hungarian and SS guards and German prisoners of war were made to load the remains onto carts by hand then cover them with spoil. No one shed tears when they caught typhus and died. Local civilians, including the town council of nearby Celle, were forced to witness the mass graves being filled. Still-distressing newsreel footage showed a tumble of torsos and limbs being bulldozed into pits, the military driver holding a handkerchief over his nose to ward off the smell.

With many openly questioning, and subsequently losing, their Christian faith, that a Higher Being could allow such systemic mass murder, responsibility fell heavily on military padres for spiritual guidance to make sense of it all. Understandably the Royal Army Chaplain's Department had not foreseen the need to prepare its evangelists for scenes that exceeded the worst torments depicted in the Bible or Torah. The leap from his parish at Holy Trinity, Aberystwyth, to Belsen was vast, as the Reverend Thomas Stretch acknowledged to a British *Movietone News* camera, standing in front of a mass burial pit. 'Never in my life have I seen such damnable ghastliness. This morning we buried over 5,000 bodies. We don't know who they are. Behind me you can see a pit which will contain another 5,000. Two others like it are in preparation.'[28]

Listowel-born Father Michael Morrison, an Irish Jesuit priest attached to British forces, remained undeterred. When his work of anointing the sick and the dead began to lessen, he decided to hold the first Mass to be said in Belsen. The weather was so bad on the appointed day that he felt that no one would come, but Morrison was stunned to see hundreds of people of many faiths and none patiently waiting in front of his makeshift altar in the pouring rain. He looked back on this as one of the most significant moments of his life and began to say Mass every day. However, his private diary revealed the grim reality of Belsen. 'What we saw within the first few days is utterly beyond description. People crawling on their hands and knees because they have not got the strength to walk – harrowing.'[29]

Brigadier Hugh Glyn Hughes, Chief Medical Officer for Second British Army, told Reuters, 'No photograph, no description, could bring home the horrors I saw. The huts overflowed with inmates in every state of emaciation and disease. They were suffering from starvation, gastro-enteritis, typhus, typhoid, tuberculosis. There were dead everywhere, some in the same bunks as the living. In my thirty years as a doctor, I had never seen anything like it.'[30] The lasting effect on the British liberators was identical to those experienced by their American and Canadian counterparts who freed other camps.

Joy Taverner, a member of Queen Alexandra's Imperial Military Nursing Service with 29th General Hospital arrived at Belsen two days after its liberation. 'We had been through the war, but this was something so terrible that it took some time for us to come to terms with what we saw,' she recounted. 'It was so terrible we cried ourselves to sleep for many nights in our tents two miles away. We had no-one to talk to, we just had to keep going. Two of our sisters started drinking heavily and were sent home. I don't really know how we survived – we all supported each other and cried every night with our arms around each other.'[31]

As well as appearing over the airwaves and in the national press, Belsen was covered in *Soldier*, the newly established magazine for British Liberation Army troops, printed fortnightly in Brussels. As the house journal of Montgomery's Twenty-First Army Group, its wide circulation among British, Canadian and Polish forces brought it a stamp of authority and lent moral clarity for the war against the Third Reich, just as Buchenwald (liberated on 11 April) and Ohrdruf (visited by Eisenhower the next day) had done for Twelfth Army Group. While Montgomery's men might have expressed sympathy for the plight of ordinary Germans as they fought through their shattered towns and broken cities, that sentiment evaporated after Belsen.

In April 1945, Montgomery's army group was best pictured as a right hand poking into Germany, its wrist on the Rhine crossing sites, the thumb representing Charles Foulkes' I Corps heading east to Arnhem and eventually Amsterdam, Rotterdam and The Hague. Positioned as the index finger was Guy Simonds' II Canadian Corps, heading north to the German border, with four divisions moving along parallel axes, 3rd Canadian closest to the coast, followed by 2nd Canadian, Maczek's 1st Polish Armoured and 4th Canadian Armoured, the last two weaving their way back and forth over the Dutch-German frontier.

As the middle finger, Brian Horrocks' XXX Corps was driving hard for Bremen, Cuxhaven and the North Sea coast, with the Guards Armoured forging ahead of the 3rd British, 43rd Wessex and 51st Highland Divisions. Each of the latter infantry formations was supported by one regiment (a tank battalion) of Brigadier Erroll Prior-Palmer's 8th Armoured Brigade. The brigadier 'owned' the 4th/7th Royal Dragoon Guards, Sherwood Rangers Yeomanry and 13th/18th Royal Hussars, each equipped with around sixty Shermans. Their axis (named Route Club) would be peppered each day by short, vicious actions from determined defenders, the casualties from which no one could predict. On 28 March, Lieutenant Bob Boscawen, a Coldstream tank commander in the Guards Armoured, whom we met attending a regimental history lecture before *Veritable*, penned in his diary, 'The whole front is crumbling. It is a terrific feeling. Really, after six years is it coming to an end? My God, how wonderful! The Germans are collapsing. Roll on victory.'

Four days later he was in his tank, about to seize a canal bridge fifty miles from Rees. Along his route, he passed 'a number of Germans showing no fight, while a few Dutch civilians waved and cheered'. As he reached the bridge, it blew. 'I found myself broadside on looking down the barrels of four 88mm flak guns. I hit one with my seventy-five straight away, saw the other eighty-eight shots flying up at me, there was a woof, and the turret was engulfed from below in a whirlwind of flame.' Badly wounded and requiring over a year's treatment for his burns, three of his crew perished in the canal-side action at Enschede.[32]

On 3 April, Julius Neave, adjutant of the Sherman-equipped 13th/18th Hussars, noted in his diary, 'Although we have had a relatively smooth passage so far since crossing the Rhine, ten killed, eighteen wounded and five tanks knocked out, some people have had stiff fighting. Bill Deedes' company had a bad do losing twenty men and two of his best young officers.'[33] We met Deedes in the Introduction, angry with the newspapers prematurely foreseeing victory while there were 'lots of sixteen-year-olds keen to die for Hitler.'[34]

The day before, 'B' Company of the 12th King's Royal Rifle Corps, around 130 infantrymen, including four other officers, led by Deedes, had attempted to secure a crossing over the Twente Canal south of the Dutch town of Hengelo. Met with concentrated machine-gun and mortar fire, his men were ambushed while on the bridge. With his reserve platoon all but destroyed by another mortar concentration, from the middle of the bridge Deedes skilfully manoeuvred what was left of his company back to the home side. It cost him almost half his command: in addition to twenty-two men killed, plus two officers, a third officer was wounded with another twenty men. Although the action brought Deedes – a future Member of Parliament, Cabinet minister, editor of the *Daily Telegraph*, and peer of the Realm – a Military Cross, he refused to ever discuss the incident, haunted by the loss of so many so near to the war's end, for there were just thirty-six days left to go.[35]

As they closed up to Bremen, the twenty-five pounders of 33rd Field Regiment in 3rd Division fired five hundred rounds into the city. They contained not phosphorus, nor high explosive, but propaganda leaflets. A taste of the response was noted in the artillery regiment's history. 'We had two Nazi schoolmistresses in our custody who were behaving very aggressively. On being told their Führer was a prisoner of the British, they demanded to be shot forthwith. Instead, we locked them up in a farmhouse. Next morning, we discovered them dead, having taken poison.'[36] Five decades later while touring the route from the Rhine to

Bremen with me, Sydney Jary, an infantry officer with the Wessex Division, recounted the pointless fanaticism of his opponents at this stage of the war.

As he wrote in his seminal autobiography, *Eighteen Platoon*, 'I heard the cry. "Sir, they're charging at us." Sure enough, from 150 yards ahead, a well spread-out line of about twenty Germans were putting in a bayonet charge. Brave lads, they didn't stand a chance. I gave no orders except "Cease Fire!" Not one got within seventy yards of us.'[37] Noel Bell of the 8th Rifle Brigade experienced an identical situation, when infantry were reported advancing in waves towards his company's positions. 'Hundreds of 'em,' warned his colleague, Lieutenant Clark. A defensive fire programme from neighbourhood twenty-five pounders brought down 'an almighty stonk [concentration] in the midst of them. The attacking force was written off,' recorded Bell laconically. 'First class. That'll teach the bloody Boche.'[38]

Within range of British bombers since the beginning of the war and dominated by its access to the North Sea, Bremen was a city of 300,000 with many dockyards and factories, including Focke-Wulf-Aerowerke, and two airfields defended by batteries of flak guns. Its associated port of Bremerhaven, forty miles down the Weser, was the premier military port of both the Second and Third Reich, though tenth the size of Bremen. The two cities received over thirty major Allied air raids, beginning on 17–18 May 1940, and including the RAF's third thousand-bomber attack of 25–26 June 1942.

Among the dozens of formations humbling Bremen was 305 (Polish) Squadron, flying Wellingtons under RAF command, who regularly took their canine mascot *Ciapek* ('Spotty') on missions. He was the only dog in the world who could claim to have also bombed Berlin, Hamburg, Cologne and Stettin.[39] The final bombs of the 12,831 dropped on the city fell on 30 March 1945, as XXX Corps approached. Taking no chances, Horrocks slowly ringed Bremen with 'Bolo' Whistler's 3rd British, Ivor Thomas' 43rd Wessex, and Edmund Hakewill-Smith's 52nd Lowland Divisions, borrowed from XII Corps. They reduced the pocket in two phases, during 13–19 April when the outlying villages to the south-west were cleared, then the city itself during 25–27 of the month.

Whistler's 3rd Division began grinding their way through the suburbs from 13 April, plunging through waterlogged areas in Buffaloes of the 4th Royal Tank Regiment, and protected by flail mine-clearing tanks of the 22nd Dragoons. On the same return to the battlefields as Sydney Jary, Captain Ian Hammerton, whom we last encountered in the mud of *Veritable*, recalled the fanatics of an SS training battalion 'leaping out of their foxholes yelling "Heil Hitler" as our spiders advanced with guns blazing'. I was puzzled that he called his flail tank a 'spider'. He responded, 'That was how a Hitler Youth told me we looked when driving towards him – like a giant spider.'[40] Later, Hammerton found himself following a Churchill AVRE, an engineer tank, approaching a roadblock in the Hamburg suburbs. 'There was a colossal explosion and forty tons of Churchill just rose into the air, shattered. A Jeep which had nipped in behind it simply vanished. The road had been sabotaged with a naval mine which had also set off the explosives carried inside the AVRE.'[41]

Their opponents also included flak crews, reluctant Volkssturm, ill-trained Bremen police officers, and U-boat and R-boat (minesweeper) crews taken from their immobile naval vessels. Werner Ellebeck was among them, observing, 'We had military training, although it didn't always make sense to us. However, one thing we were drilled in very thoroughly was the use of panzerfäuste – our task was to destroy tanks. We were provided with few other weapons. The order was "find them yourselves," which we were happy to do. We managed to get hold of a lot from abandoned camps and flak batteries, so that most of the company possessed a panzerfaust, carbines, hand grenades, and a few machine-guns. Armed with these, we had great confidence.'[42]

However, Ellebeck and his comrades were up against the 3rd Division, which was not only Montgomery's old command from 1940, but the most experienced in Second Army, having landed on D-Day, fought through the Falaise Pocket, *Market Garden*, the Rhineland and *Plunder*. Their drills were slick and confidence unmatched as they attacked from the south, in mixed groups of infantry and Crocodile flame-throwers from 7th Royal Tank Regiment. However, on 18 April, the 2nd East Yorkshires, a battalion with 8th Brigade, lost their Second-in-Command, Major C.K. 'Bangor' King, blown up on a mine at Gross Mackenstedt, a village six miles south west of Bremen. In receipt of two DSOs, well known and liked throughout 3rd Division, while approaching Sword beach on D-Day, King had addressed his company with extracts from Shakespeare's *Henry V* on the landing ship's tannoy.[43] One of their number noted, 'the whole Division was proud of Major King and saw him as a representative of all that was best in themselves'.[44] King had nearly made it, perishing just twenty days before the war's end.

It was in the early morning drizzle of 21 April, just as XXX Corps were dealing with Bremen, that Sherman tanks of the 2nd Irish Guards arrived in the village of Wistedt, with a blocking mission to prevent reinforcements arriving to relieve the defenders of Bremen. With no one in sight, the tankmen of Brigadier Norman Gwatkin's 5th Guards Brigade, with Grenadier infantry riding on the back, dismounted and started to make breakfast. Suddenly all hell let loose, as shells, mortars and machine-gun fire rained down on the guardsmen. Lieutenant Quinan, watching through binoculars, had an armour-piercing shell pass so close that it blew his beret off before hitting the house behind. German officer cadets led by experienced instructors from the 115th Panzer Grenadier Regiment, supported by self-propelled guns, were trying to punch their way through to Bremen.[45] 'The Micks', as the Irish Guardsmen were known, were in their way.

Guardsman Bill Ashley, buttoned down in a Sherman also under attack in a neighbouring Elsdorf recalled, 'We were right down on ammo and to our surprise we saw three lorries racing into our orchard. Their drivers were amazed when we told them that they had just come through Jerry lines. We soon had our ammunition on board and straightaway Jerry started to let us have it from Wistedt church. A tank shot soon put a stop to that. Later, when the weather started to change and we could see blue sky appearing, the German shelling stopped. We opened our hatches to see where the RAF were. With targets located, the Typhoons peeled off into a steep dive and we saw rockets leave the planes.'[46]

However, back in Wistedt, with three of four Shermans disabled in the maelstrom and seeing his colleagues in danger of being overrun, Quinan's driver, Guardsman Eddie Charlton, realised they would have to fight it out. He quickly removed the turret machine-gun and, firing the weapon from his hip, caused such heavy casualties that the leading German company paused, allowing the Guards time to re-organise and withdraw. Charlton stayed behind, and when wounded in his left arm, carried on firing his gun from a fence before being hit again. A final wound caused his collapse, but the one-man army had single-handedly saved his troop and their accompanying infantry.

Although he died later of his wounds, Charlton would be awarded a posthumous Victoria Cross. Eyewitness accounts supporting the citation unusually included that of Leutnant Hans-Jürgen von Bülow, commanding the German assault, himself awarded an Iron Cross First Class at Wistedt. Charlton's medal would be the last VC of the European War, won seventeen days before the finish.[47] The village today has largely been rebuilt, but in the 1980s it was possible to identify where Charlton's troop of tanks had been surprised from slivers of mortar shell still embedded in walls and woodwork.

By the evening of 25 April, as organised resistance in Bremen was disintegrating, Major Glyn Gilbert of the 2nd Lincolns, with 9th Brigade of 3rd Division, found himself standing beside a German U-boat commander outside the shattered control tower of Bremen-Neustadt *Flughafen* (airbase), just captured by his company. 'It was about 17:30 and I watched as, under a Petty Officer, the Germans fell in and marched past us, carrying their wounded. Their Commander called out the equivalent of "Well done" and received a spontaneous and tremendous cheer from his seamen. We saluted each other and he followed them into captivity. The officer and his men provided a perfect example of leadership and high morale when their country was in ruins and their future quite unknown. My Company Sergeant Major observed, "That's about it, then. Japan next, I suppose." We had fired our last shots in Europe.'[48]

Bremen, 'sullied and humbled by bombs', fell after four divisions of Horrocks' XXX Corps had encircled the city on 26 April. As the 13th/18th Hussars moved into Bremen on 27 April, Captain Neave confided to his diary, 'In the evening we went round rather ghoulishly to see a most remarkable sight in a real Somerset Maugham setting. The chief Nazi and his wife both shot dead, suicide, in their chairs upstairs in the office of the Bremen Stormtroopers HQ! It was worth seeing and just like a play. Apparently, a doctor's sizing-up of the situation is that first they drank a bottle of brandy, then she shot him, then herself. It was nevertheless rather beastly, but a sign of the times.' Hard on Neave's heels was Private Bob Thornburrow of the Somerset Light Infantry. He saw the blood-soaked carpet, empty spirit bottle and pistol. Naturally he pocketed the Luger.[49]

As Bremen's Kommandant, Generalleutnant Fritz Becker, was surrendering the city from his five-storey bunker in the central Bürgerpark, American and Russian generals were shaking hands and back-slapping on the banks of the River Elbe at Torgau. The Reich had been torn in two. While the high-ups shuffled papers and agreed terms, the 4th/5th Battalion Royal Scots Fusiliers, an infantry battalion of the Lowland Division, saw scores of shoeless, teenaged Hungarian, Polish and Russian girls, all forced labourers, calmly pulling each other to safety through the rubble, clutching looted clothes and foodstuffs, undeterred by sniper fire.

The Fusiliers noted the 'utterly demoralised displaced persons from internment camps in the surrounding countryside' who 'were looting and shooting in a first, fine, careless rapture of liberation' and proved 'rather more troublesome' to subdue than the minimal resistance offered by the Wehrmacht. Having earlier observed 'the terrible pathos of a four-year-old German child by the roadside solemnly giving the Nazi salute', the division witnessed the chaotic twilight of the Reich. The civilian residents of Bremen 'were in a physical sense bomb happy, and had gone wild, looting, drinking, fighting among each other, with a shocking inability to accept the consequences of their own political stupidity'.[50]

Another Royal Scots Fusilier was Captain Peter Reynier, who later wrote home to his wine-merchant father: 'We were the first to break into the suburbs of Bremen and once again my guardian angel has been with me all the way. My own carrier got a direct hit from an anti-tank gun at about 700 yards. With it went my new pair of spectacles and all my personal kit. Bremen is a fine testimonial of the accuracy of the RAF. Those areas that have been military targets are well and truly flattened into bricks and rubble. Hats off to Bomber Command, they have done a great job and their last raid, the night before we attacked, was a magnificent if terrifying sight. Amongst my souvenirs, I liberated a dozen bottles of Chateau Cheval Blanc 1920; a couple of dozen Piesporter Grafenburg 1937; a bottle of Chateau Margaux 1911; and a miscellaneous selection of port and liqueurs. With the aid of the above life has almost become bearable.'[51]

A week later, in an illustration that Allied summary justice could be just as violent and instant as that of their opponents, Neave wrote of 'a frightful thug who walked in saying he was a refugee. He denied anything else till he was given a little rough justice, when a pistol was found on him, and he admitted to being a German Marine. He also had on a Red Cross armband and was a thoroughly bad lot. After a certain amount of argument, we decided he was a proper wrong 'un and he was duly despatched by firing squad in the garage.'[52]

However, Bremen had one nasty surprise up its sleeve for XXX Corps. As the Guards Armoured streamed beyond Bremen and towards the coast at Cuxhaven, it tripped over Stalag X-B at Sandbostel. This was an 85-acre site with 150 buildings lined up on either side of a central road, which turned out to contain around 15,000 military inmates, plus at least 10,000 civilians. It was overcrowded, being used as an overflow for inmates evacuated from concentration and POW camps further east. In the military part of the camp, half the detainees were British and American POWs; amongst this throng the liberators found men from their own regiments, soldiers of the Rifle Brigade taken at Dunkirk, and 11th Hussars captured in North Africa.

Dr H.O. Engel of the 10th Casualty Clearing Station later reported of Sandbostel that 'most civilians had been without food or water for over a week. Many had severe infections; 3,000 had died and were lying unburied in the open; the survivors were crammed into huts, but our rescue work was much better organised than that in Belsen, because the DDMS [Deputy Director Medical Services] had had two weeks' experience in the relief of that camp, and the liberation of British prisoners of war freed up Red Cross supplies and medical personnel, who were rapidly diverted.'[53]

Some of the prisoners were Polish fighters who had fought in the Warsaw Uprising, like Bohdan Dembiński. Just sixteen when his country was invaded in 1939, his life was one of unutterable suffering, pain and hardship for nearly six years until his final liberation by the British on 29 April. He and many of his generation of young Poles would eventually settle in England.[54] The 168th (City of London) Light Field Ambulance witnessed 2,000 dying in Sandbostel after liberation, at a rate of two hundred per day. Some seven hundred American POWs were recorded as 'undernourished, sleeping on bare wooden floors without a mattress and only half had blankets'. Less well remembered than it should be, Sandbostel was soon dubbed by its liberators 'Little Belsen'. Lieutenant F.W. Gordon remembered the head British doctor regarding a hut full of victims and confiding that all 'were going to die, he was sure of it, and he couldn't do a damn thing about it'.[55]

The next digit of our right hand was represented by Neil Ritchie's XII Corps, thrusting to Hamburg, spearheaded by 7th Armoured, with 52nd Lowland and 53rd Welsh Divisions, plus 4th Armoured Brigade. Crossing near Xanten, 1st Royal Tank Regiment of Major General Lou Lyne's 7th Armoured were soon in Stadtlohn, thirty miles east, where 'three hundred dead German soldiers were counted in the rubble'. They then made 'a real cavalry charge in the night to Ahaus, ten miles beyond, and got through hordes of panzerfaust-men with amazingly light casualties'.[56] Thirty miles beyond Ahaus lay Neuenkirchen, first encountered by Richard Brett-Smith of the 11th Hussars. His was an original Desert Rats formation, who in their distant past had picked up the nickname of 'Cherrypickers' and had since exchanged their horses for armoured cars. He noted in his diary, 'In the narrow streets, the rumble and rattle of our vehicles and the explosive coughing of their exhausts sounded forbidding. A group of Luftwaffe pilots, with either no aircraft or no fuel, stared sourly out of a café.'

Five miles further found the 11th Hussars as the divisional reconnaissance regiment, exploring Rheine, where 'On the faces of most of the civilians was a look of blank wonder and incredulity. To them it did not seem possible there were so many tanks, guns, and cars in the world, for by this time our whole column was nose to tail.'[57] The Germans had long been used to seeing their Wehrmacht towed by horses. By decree in August 1943, citizens of the Reich were even forbidden the use of farm horses and carts, except in the interests of the Fatherland. On their way, 'tough, unruly Gunner Jones of 3rd Royal Horse Artillery (with 7th Armoured) spied a jeweller's shop in a relatively unscathed German village. He persuaded the owners that a strong German counter-attack was imminent and advised them to return to their cellars for safety. The haul was two watches per head per wrist for his troop.'[58]

Loot, excitement, revenge – these were a heady mix of emotions for young men to carry as they charged into the Reich with no restraints, a law unto themselves. Lieutenant Colonel Martin Lindsay, commanding the 1st Gordons, a battalion in the Highland Division, observed that looting was 'so hard to define. We have agreed to take only what is necessary to make ourselves more comfortable, such as bedding or furniture; luxuries that the Huns can well do without, like eggs and fruit, but not meat or poultry; forbidden articles we want for our own personal use, such as shot-guns, cartridges, cameras and field-glasses; and wine.'[59]

The next 150 miles, from Rheine to Hamburg, were covered by XII Corps at between twenty and fifty miles per day, keeping their infantry close, trying to seize bridges as they went, but the Germans could now only delay, rather than prevent. The 2nd Devonshires, an infantry unit with 7th Armoured Division, spent most of their time in March–April riding on the back of tanks, as platoon commander Robert Davies remembered. 'The only snag was that you couldn't hear anyone firing at you due to the noise of the engines and tracks. I had my back to the turret and one man was speaking to me, and the next moment he fell dead. When we met resistance, we got down and went on with or without armour, depending on the terrain.' The weather had turned warm, bringing out much-needed close air support in the form of Hawker Typhoons and Tempests, called down onto quite small targets, such as individual flak guns. The deep roots of Nazism inculcated into the very young were discovered by the 11th Hussars when they overran a school in Harsfeld, twenty miles west of Hamburg, and found from blackboard illustrations a lesson on the use of panzerfäuste had been in progress.

Via Tostedt, the 7th Armoured thundered towards Harburg, ten miles across the Elbe from Hamburg, from where intact bridges and ferries allowed the German First Parachute Army and others to retreat eastwards. Meanwhile, to the south and east, a cordon was drawn around the city as the 53rd Welsh acted as a row of beaters in a pheasant drive. By 20 April, artillery forward observation officers were on the Elbe and able to direct fire on targets in the city. The net had closed around the city and the assaulting units paused for five days to tighten their perimeter, rest, and prepare for a bout of vicious urban warfare. Mathilde Wolf-Mönckeberg, anti-Nazi daughter of a former Oberbürgermeister, and married to a professor of English at Hamburg University, observed on 26 April, 'Days and nights drag on in their weary way. We are now besieged by the British. Every now and again, we can hear their artillery fire, a hollow, angry sound. While the Americans have conquered most of the middle and south Germany – there is hardly a big town not yet occupied by them – the British have come to a stop around Bremen and Hamburg. Our torment of waiting goes on.'[60]

That the Germans were still capable of unpleasant surprises was evidenced by the sally out of Harburg at 02:30 on 26 April by elements of the 12th SS Hitlerjugend Training and Reinforcement Regiment, supported by flak guns firing from the city centre. Known as the Kampfgruppe Panzerteufel (Armoured Devils Battlegroup), two companies and other volunteers attacked Vahrendorf, three miles to the west. Fighting continued all day and only abated after twenty-four hours with the arrival of Allied armour. Klaus Möller, then serving in a 120-strong Panzerteufel company, remembered their three-pronged advance. 'We surprised the British in their sleep, took twenty-one prisoners and occupied Vahrendorf – but only for a short time. We were adolescents, still in training and poorly equipped, fighting an opponent who was superior in every respect, both personally and materially. The English did not back down; on the contrary: they received reinforcements and counterattacked with tank support.

'It was a hopeless fight as our company commander, SS-Untersturmführer Heinz Früh, soon recognised. After a few hours and threatened with total annihilation, he gave the order to retreat, but the order only reached part of our company. Around sixty stayed behind and one after the other, lost their lives, including fifteen-year-old Henry Erdmann and Martin Muskowitz, just sixteen.' With them perished Stefan Silvestero, a Serbian prisoner who was ordered to carry ammunition up to the front and was caught in crossfire. 'It was just a massacre,' recalled Wolfgang Buchwald, another survivor. After the war the locals set up a special cemetery on the Krähenberg hill, west of Vahrendorf, for forty-four of the German youths, and Maria and Georg Muskowitz moved from Pomerania to tend the grave of their only child and the others around it. Post-war forensic examination of the remains as they were reburied refuted rumours spread by unrepentant Nazis that nineteen of the SS had been shot in the back of the head as they surrendered.[61]

Two days later, the British began their assault on the city, attacking from Harburg, and navigating their way around great chunks of the autobahn which fed into Hamburg from the south and had been blown up. Here was testimony that Hitler's 'Nero Decree' was fully implemented. The final defence was 'conducted by ships' crews, stevedores from the docks, policemen and firemen from Hamburg, submarine crews, with a sprinkling of SS, parachutists, Hitler Youth and Volkssturm'. The result was a foregone conclusion, as their training – if any – was uneven, weaponry too diverse, communications non-existent and leadership patchy, even if their motivation was not in doubt. Language was a challenge for some with the presence of a Hungarian SS unit.

Already much bombed, particularly on 27–28 July 1943 in Operation *Gomorrah*, which killed an estimated 37,000 and wounded 180,000, Hamburg had received 187 air raids by the war's end. Bomber Command reported 183 large factories destroyed out of 524 in the city and 4,118 smaller ones out of 9,068. Among Hamburg's industries was the headquarters of Tesch & Stabenow, a market leader in pest control chemicals, whose director, Dr Bruno Tesch, suggested to the SS they might like to purchase his Zyklon-B pesticide. From 1942, he also sold them small, brass screw-top cylinders containing a cyanide capsule, widely used in the last days of the war.

'The city's labour force,' stated RAF Bomber Command's official history, 'was reduced by ten percent and food supplies ran out', without noting that these workers were predominantly slaves.[62] State records of the numbers of workers in Hamburg's war industries have survived and indicate that in June 1943 10.5 per cent of the city's workforce of 634,000 were forced labourers.[63] The BBC reporter, Wynford Vaughan-Thomas, who accompanied an earlier raid in a Lancaster, memorably described the experience as the 'most beautifully horrible sight I have ever seen. It was like watching someone throwing jewellery on black velvet. Winking rubies, sparkling diamonds, all coming up at you.'[64]

Most heavy raids by the RAF had stopped by April 1945, the last and most notorious being several mounted by the RAF and USAAF in quick succession against Dresden, capital of Saxony, over 13 and 15 February. Although the wider area included at least 110 factories producing military equipment, where 50,000 slave workers propped up the German war effort, Dresden was also a key transportation hub for personnel and weapons heading east. The raid also appears to have been a subliminal attempt to demonstrate to Stalin what the Western air forces could achieve, if ever necessary. These collective assaults killed between 20,000 and 40,000, including many refugees.

Since the early 1960s, Nazi apologists have claimed higher death tolls of up to 250,000, since widely discredited. We will never know the precise number, which was due to the lack of air-raid shelters and the little understood phenomenon of a firestorm. Extraordinarily high temperatures were generated, which sucked out oxygen. Air rushing into the resultant vacuum created fierce winds. Everything in their path was vapourised or melted, including the inhabitants. As a result, Churchill revised his bombing policy on 1 April, observing 'the question of the so-called area bombing of German cities should be reviewed from the point of view of our own interests. If we come into control of an entirely ruined land, there will be a great shortage of accommodation for ourselves and our allies. We must see to it that our attacks do no more harm to ourselves in the long run, than they do to the Nazi war effort.'[65] On the ground, Allied troops had no awareness of the destruction of Dresden, the city eventually falling to the Red Army, though the effect on the Germans was profound.

In Hamburg, Wolf-Mönckeberg noted, 'One cannot plan anything. Terror raids occur in all weathers, sometimes just warnings but then bombardments five times a day, and always for hours at a time.'[66] The inhabitants spent hours each day queuing for food; domestic gas and electricity was rationed, and water came only from street standpipes. Terrified as to who their new masters might be – Americans or Russians – Hamburgers subsisted for the last few months of the war on 'table scraps for a dog – soup that tasted like rainwater and bread made from animal feed, sawdust and salt. The bread was baked in the morning and if you didn't consume it by late afternoon, a green mould would burrow its way to the crust.' City dwellers were exchanging their silver cutlery and Persian rugs with farmers for eggs and turnips.[67]

The final advance, that of the little finger on our right hand, saw General Evelyn 'Bubbles' Barker's VIII Corps stabbing its way to Osnabrück, Lüneburg and as far as the banks of the Elbe, with 11th Armoured, 6th Airborne and 15th Scottish Divisions, and 1st Commando and 6th

Guards Tank Brigades.[68] With the airborne division on the extreme right flank, beyond lay Simpson's Ninth Army, the inter-army group boundary running from Wesel to Münster and beyond to south of Osnabrück. Twelve miles west of Osnabrück, an ancient city of 100,000, runs a long, narrow strip of dense forest, the Teutoburgerwald. Today an unremarkable feature, three miles wide and thirty long, in ancient times it was a huge, forbidding affair of closely spaced trees, poor tracks wending their way between hills and valleys, of the kind that inspired the Grimm Brothers' tales.

More significantly, it was in AD 9 that Arminius, unifier of several Germanic tribes, turned traitor on the Romans who had trained him in military tactics, and destroyed three legions, cavalry detachments and cohorts of auxiliaries in the Teutoburg. The annihilation of 20,000 well-drilled legionaries was regarded as 'Rome's greatest defeat'. By the nineteenth century, Arminius had evolved into a folk hero, before being appropriated by the Nazis who sought to cast Hitler as his successor, as a unifier of the German peoples and destroyer of foreign invaders. In 1945, Arminius' forest was still a formidable defensive position and, as it dominated the VIII Corps main axis, had to be cleared. For ideological reasons, it was inevitably going to be contested by true-believers. These turned out to be 3,000 war-school trainees – seven companies with their instructors from the Hanover Kriegsschule (war school), where NCOs were prepared to become officers.

Dr Wolf Berlin was one, then a young soldier stationed at Bergen, north of Hanover, who marched only at night for 120 miles, from 24 March to 1 April 1945, with weapons, food and ammunition. They followed forest paths and dug in on the high ground of the Ibbenbüren Ridge, among the Teutoberg's ivy-clad beech and silver birch trees, and stubbornly refused to be shifted from their positions. When their sergeant major was pulled, badly wounded, from a demolished building, the cadets asked anxiously when he thought the war would end. 'When we win,' was his defiant response. This was less fanaticism than the reply of a professional veteran of an earlier world war, as most instructors were.

From 31 March, the 1st Herefordshires, 3rd Monmouthshires and 4th King's Shropshire Light Infantry, all battalions with the 11th Armoured, were among those tasked to clear the terrain ahead. Ray Griffiths of 'C' Company, 1st Herefords, recollected that 'communication by radio was difficult, and telephone lines had to be run out behind the attackers, while visibility was so severely restricted, in places limited to a few yards, that our advance was easily stopped by a few snipers, bayonet charges and machine-guns'.[69]

Reg Worton, also of the Herefords, noted, 'We saw some stragglers, very young boys, and if they did not put their hands up empty, we shot them,' while Private Roy Nash of the Monmouths recorded 'the murderous machine-gun fire was the worst I had experienced in ten months of action'.[70] At one stage, both sides agreed a truce, when a young German officer cadet approached the British lines with a 3rd Monmouths prisoner, both waving white handkerchiefs. The guns fell silent, medical staff and stretcher-bearers collected the wounded, the German then returned to his unit and the shooting started again. The award of Victoria Cross to Corporal Ted Chapman, for rescuing his company commander under heavy fire and manning a Bren gun 'in a one-man island of khaki amidst an ocean of field grey', indicated the savagery of the Second Battle of the Teutoburgerwald. So high were the casualties sustained by the 3rd Monmouths during six days in the wood, that the 3rd Monmouths had to be permanently withdrawn from operations and replaced by another battalion.[71] Chapman, who survived, was awarded his VC for bravery on 2 April, nineteen days ahead of Eddie Charlton's, whose story we have just examined.

This battle typified the last month, as too often the 11th Armoured Division's new Comet tanks and other armour tended to charge ahead, leaving their infantry behind. Yet, as Bill Close of the 3rd Royal Tank Regiment asserted, 'No one wanted to take any risks anymore. The men in lead tanks knew they would be the first to get it if they bumped into a last-ditch battle-group. People were reluctant to drive around corners. I gave orders that no chances were to be taken with the bazooka merchants'.[72] The main threat was not from other German armour, but, as Close observed, panzerfäuste and anti-tank guns, for whom the only remedy was infantry. Outrunning his infantry support is what happened to Bob Boscawen at Enschede, and the 15th/19th Hussars, of the 7th Armoured Division, encountered a similar challenge in having to run a gauntlet of anti-tank weapons in the close terrain of the southern Teutoburgerwald.[73] Eventually the German defence sold itself dearly, sucking in not only the 11th Armoured but elements of the 52nd Lowland, 43rd Wessex and 7th Armoured, and the woods were not cleared until 6 April.

Derek Mills-Roberts' 1st Commando Brigade led the way into Osnabrück early on 4 April. The Teutoburgerwald had robbed the local garrison of any further fighting spirit, and his brigade's war diary noted German casualties in Osnabrück as fifty killed and wounded, 450 prisoners, for no losses of their own. The town had fallen by 10:00, with the local Gestapo chief shot dead in his office by 1st Commando's Field Security Officer, Major Viscount de Jonghe, a Belgian noble in British service. After the war, VIII Corps settled there and Osnabrück evolved into the British Army's largest garrison outside the UK, and home to 4th Armoured Brigade for several decades.

Another sixty miles north-east, as they neared the town of Uelzen, an old Hanseatic brick-and-timber town that had escaped Allied air raids, a brigade of the 15th Scottish Division and Churchill tanks of the 4th Coldstream Guards, part of 6th Guards Tank Brigade we met with Robert Runcie in Winnekendonk, ran into some determined opposition on the night of 14–15 April. This turned out to be Generalleutnant Martin Unrein's Clausewitz Panzer Division, another impressive map pin for Hitler's situation room, though in reality a ragtag grouping of armoured sub-units, hastily assembled in early April from the remains of units like *Feldherrnhalle*, whom we met in Cologne, and Hitlerjugend teenagers. Some were experienced and equipped with almost every known type of panzer from Jagdpanthers, Jagdpanzer IVs and Sturmgeschütze assault guns to Panthers and even a few Tigers. Elements of its 106th Panzer Brigade surprised a battalion of Glasgow Highlanders, halted overnight in the village of Stadensen, who suffered seven killed and forty-seven wounded or missing in the confusing night-time encounter.

Coldstream losses amounted to a pair of Churchills, a fuel bowser and two M10 tracked tank destroyers, but the Highlanders' transport lines were overrun, and flames from twenty-two carriers, ten half-tracks and thirty-one other vehicles, including the battalion signals truck and command vehicles, plus two 17-pounder guns, lit up the night sky, mostly dispatched by infantrymen wielding panzerfäuste. However, daylight revealed twelve Clausewitz panzers and seven half-tracks damaged or abandoned around Stadensen, 150 dead Panzergrenadiers with another 150 rounded up as prisoners.

Major Peter Earle, one of Montgomery's liaison officers, was caught up in the action, noting, 'The woods were ablaze, the noise of tanks, the bark of anti-tank guns, sweet stench of dead cows. The air filled with smoke and impenetrable dust; the special silence that means danger, shattered lorries and tanks, with clothing and litter [meaning human remains] on the trees as though they were Christmas tree decorations.'[74] The town itself was a ruin, and civilian casualties heavy, but after the war the inhabitants and the British were amused to discover the Clausewitz panzermen had claimed twenty-two British tanks destroyed, for which Major Gustav Walle, Leutnant Friedrich Anding and Obergefreiter Stütz-le were awarded Knight's Crosses, almost the last of the war.

Later on, military historians became equally confused, some claiming the Clausewitz success was due to the German use of infrared searchlights on their Panther tanks. Careful scrutiny of the surviving records suggests this was highly unlikely, but demonstrates that for both sides, night-time battle remains extremely difficult to assess, and can result in false claims for technology – and medals.[75] In the same 6th Guards Tank Brigade, the 4th Grenadier Guards, who had landed in France with fifty-two Church-ill tanks, calculated they 'had 104 of them replaced between Normandy and the Elbe', a not untypical exchange rate for British armoured units.[76]

Also in the region lay another future British Army of the Rhine garrison town and home to 7th Armoured Brigade, Fallingbostel. It was on 16 April 1945 that the antecedent of this brigade, 7th Armoured Division, liberated a large prisoner-of-war complex in the small town, adjacent to the Bergen-Höhne Training Area, a pre-war Wehrmacht facility. They knew in advance of Stalag XI-B but were unaware that many of its inhabitants had just been marched there from prison camps in Poland, to escape the Russians.

Thrusting far ahead, armoured cars of the divisional reconnaissance regiment, the 8th Hussars, arrived at Fallingbostel early on 16 April. War artist Edward Ardizzone was with them. 'Up at 05:30. Very cold but fine. Breakfasted in the half-light by my tank on a fried egg between pieces of bread and a mug of tea. Off almost immediately afterwards. Dawn light very beautiful, with the brew fires of the tanks seen here and there among the trees. Travel some miles eastward, through the usual alternating forest country and open land. Halt by a clearing and am sent on ahead in a Dingo [armoured car] to 'C' Squadron, which was reaching the big POW camp, in which over 15,000 of various nationalities were kept.'[77]

At Fallingbostel the Hussars observed the inmates wore smarter, cleaner uniforms than themselves. Ardizzone, with his artist's eye, noted, 'When I arrived, the scene was orderly and quiet, with troops of Airborne Division captured at Arnhem acting as guards. Many of them had only been prisoners for six to twelve months. Paratroops with red armlets, dull pink berets and clean battledress, gaiters, very smart.' This was the work of the extraordinary Regimental Sergeant Major John Lord. Months earlier, on his arrival as a captive, Lord had taken control of the prisoners' morning *Appell*, turning it into a dapper muster parade. Even behind the wire, he insisted on the neatest possible dress, and soon inmates outshone their guards in turnout. Morning physical training was introduced, and under Lord's tutelage, the disheartened captives became proud soldiers once more, so much so that German officers were seen to berate their own guards for their slovenly appearance, embarrassed by RSM Lord's reforms throughout the camp.[78]

The same applied to the officers. 'We were all dirty and unshaven and in various stages of dress and undress,' recollected Major Frank Lindley. 'The door opened and in came RSM John Lord, also a POW. He was dressed in immaculate battledress, trousers creased, and he had an arm supported in a snow-white sling. Without a word he turned his head slowly to look at each individual in turn and then said in his brisk voice "Gentlemen, I think you should all shave!" He then turned about, stamped his foot, and marched out of the room. The effect was electric.'[79] By the time it was liberated, the British had taken over the running of the camp.

Arriving with Ardizzone, Major Ralph Cobbold of the Coldstream Guards remembered, 'At the gate was an impressive guard in maroon berets. We thought that the 6th Airborne Division must somehow have got there first, but when I asked the guard commander when he had arrived his answer was, "Just after Arnhem, Sir". It was faultlessly turned out, that guard. It could have gone on duty at Buckingham Palace and done credit to the Corps. Then a majestic figure appeared, the RSM himself, with gleaming brass, immaculate webbing, razor-edged trouser creases, dazzling boots, a spectacular salute.'[80] A six-foot-two former Grenadier Guardsman, Lord of the 3rd Parachute Regiment had also fought in Tunisia and Sicily and after the war would take up an appointment as Regimental Sergeant of the Royal Military Academy Sandhurst, serving for fifteen years. Such was his spell that, during my time there, he was still referred to in hushed, almost reverent tones, as though still present, which his spirit undoubtedly was, and continues to be.

Ardizzone carried on with his story of Fallingbostel, 'There were POWs who had been there for years, and we were the first British soldiers to arrive. They were almost crazy with delight, mobbing our Dingos [scout cars], asking questions about old friends and all demanding autographs, a very moving scene.'[81] Reuters man Doon Campbell reported freeing 'men who had fought at Dunkirk and Alamein, commandos who had assaulted beaches in Italy and Normandy, troops captured at Arnhem, or overrun in the German offensive in the Ardennes.'[82]

Yet, with their slight frames and ribs showing, the photographic record shows that many of the British military prisoners resembled concentration camp victims. Although conditions varied greatly, by the end their meagre diet was almost non-existent. As the Reich shrank in January–March 1945, around 80,000 POWs were subject to forced marches westwards, from their camps in Poland, Czechoslovakia and East Prussia, as the malevolent Nazi beast seemed to draw its luckless internees closer to its heart. Enduring a 600-mile footslog through snowdrifts, often in wooden clogs, up to 3,500 of them died.[83]

Lord's counterpart in every way was RAF Sergeant Jimmy 'Dixie' Deans who had been shot down in 1940 and elected Allied representative in several POW camps as well as gathering intelligence which he passed back to London in coded letters. In March–April 1945, he had taken charge of over 2,000 Allied POWs during their month-long westwards trek through Poland and Germany. Deans ensured that rations were fairly distributed, the sick cared for and prisoners sheltered overnight. Later, he bullied his German Kommandant into allowing him to slip through the lines and contact the approaching British Army, then return to await rescue with his men, meanwhile accepting his guards' surrender.[84] Both Lord and Deans would be decorated for their leadership while POWs.

Sergeant George Guderley, waist gunner in *Queen of the Skies*, a B-17 with the 774th Bomb Squadron, watched the first British tanks arrive at Fallingbostel. 'They drove right through the front gate, followed by a couple of Bren-gun carriers. Everyone started hollering, and the soldiers were throwing out rations and cigarettes. Then the reality of the situation sank in, and it was like New Year's Eve, the Fourth of July, your birthday, and the wildest bacchanal you've ever been to, all rolled into one.'[85] Another liberated was Corporal Frank Yarosh, whom we last met being captured in a Maginot Line bunker during Operation *Nordwind*. He recalled the British tanks arriving and that during three months of captivity he had lost sixty-five pounds and afterwards needed a special diet 'because they didn't want American people to see how thin we were, how the Germans had treated us. As a prisoner it was a constant battle of thinking positively. You must have the will to live, otherwise you're not going to make it.'[86]

Private Les Allan, Oxfordshire & Buckinghamshire Light Infantry, captured at Dunkirk, was lying down on the ground when liberated. 'So were lots of others. We were so weak we could not get up and move. I was in such a dreadful state I had to have food brought to me. He continued, 'After the war, people wanted to know about my experiences as a prisoner of war, but I wouldn't tell them. Why? Because I had a feeling that they wouldn't believe it, so consequently I just bottled it up. It might also have been because of a sense of shame about being a prisoner of war – people might ask why I hadn't escaped. But it was also because I got the impression that people believed we had, in effect, been in holiday camps, having a cushy time. That's why we didn't want to talk about it. Those who didn't know said we'd had a good time, that we were lucky to have been prisoners when so many other fellows had been killed.'[87]

All the while, the VIII Corps advance was shadowed by Montgomery's TAC which operated independently. Its small size allowed it to move eight times during April 1945 alone. At the beginning of the month, they had driven through the chaotic labyrinth of ancient Münster, where their 'tyres and tank tracks crunched and pulverized the carved stone faces of mediaeval statues.'[88] When encountered, Germans at this stage either surrendered with alacrity or rabidly fought on, though it was impossible to predict which. On 21 April, two of the TAC liaison officers, Majors John Poston and Peter Earle, had just visited VIII Corps HQ and were driving back through woods near Soltau when their Jeep was suddenly ambushed by Hitlerjugend. Bullets tore into the engine and windscreen. They both fired their Sten guns until the magazines were empty.

Wounded himself, Earle remembered the Germans closing in on Poston. 'I heard John cry out in an urgent and desperate voice, "N-No – stop-stop." These were his last words, and spoken as a bayonet thrust above the heart killed him instantaneously.'[89] Earle survived, but Montgomery was inconsolable over Poston's death, wrote an obituary for *The Times*, and informed Churchill and King George VI, who had both met him. The latter pair wrote letters of condolence, while the Field Marshal 'wept unashamedly' at Poston's funeral a few days later. He was the longest serving of Montgomery's various liaison officers, in fact since Alamein thirty months earlier. Breezy and light-hearted by nature, he was considered the jester of TAC, cruelly taken with the end in sight, for there were just seventeen days to go.

(*Above*): On 20 April, Leipzig fell. Many war photographers caught the suicide by cyanide of its Oberbürgermeister Alfred Freyberg and his family in the city hall. Countless senior Nazis chose this personal route to Valhalla rather than surrender. (*Below*): By 26 April, Major General Emil F. Reinhardt of the 69th US Infantry Division was greeting his opposite number, Major General Vladimir Rusakov of the 58th Guards Infantry Division, at Torgau on the River Elbe. The meetings were spontaneous, with neither side quite sure how to react to the other.

16

First Army: To Leipzig and the Elbe

In mid-April, we left elements of First Army in disbelief at the inhumanity on display at Nordhausen, in the southern Harz mountains. This was their first major exposure to the Holocaust, a week after Patton's men uncovered the horrors of Ohrdruf, and the same day that his Third Army liberated Buchenwald. These discoveries, with the uncovering of Belsen by Twenty-First Army Group, hardened the Allies against their opponents. Prisoners were less likely to be taken, and those captured more likely to be roughed up on their way to POW compounds.

However, the main business of First Army was the race towards Leipzig of its two corps, Joe Collins' VII Corps in the north, with Colonel John C. MacDonald's 4th Cavalry guarding its left flank, 3rd Armored in the lead, and five infantry formations – the 1st, 8th, 78th, 86th and Terry Allen's 104th. To their south, was Clarence Huebner's V Corps. He put the 9th Armored in the vanguard, followed by the 2nd, 28th and 69th Infantry Divisions. Colonel Cyrus Dolph's 102nd Cavalry, mostly National Guardsmen from New Jersey, covered their open right flank. The pace of advance – three hundred miles in the twenty-five days from the 25 March Remagen breakout to 19 April when Leipzig surrendered to V Corps – was underlined by the issuing of one million gallons of fuel to First Army formations on a single day, 11 April. This was made possible by up to three hundred C-47s per day flying into a midpoint captured airstrip.

Occasionally there were losses to flak detachments not yet destroyed. On 3 April, a C-47 of the 316th Troop Carrying Group took a burst of 20mm anti-aircraft fire fifteen miles south-east of Cologne. 'Aircraft was loaded with 114 five-gallon cans of gasoline,' read the official report. 'C-47 immediately caught fire. Pilot put the plane down in a pasture, gear up, and got it down so quickly that all on board were able to exit to safety.' Excluding the pilot, Colonel Harvey A. Berger, whose 'cockpit had turned into an inferno, though he could be seen silhouetted through the flames'. The only casualty that day, Berger made the flight because his mother had been born in Cologne and he wanted to see the city for himself. This popular officer, an ex-civilian airline pilot who had flown in Sicily, Normandy and Varsity, was the CO of the 316th TC Group.[1]

However, only two of Hodges' corps were heading east, while the other pair, Ridgway's XVIII and Van Fleet's III, were still reducing the Ruhr Pocket. This meant that while a task force of the 3rd Armored Division, 'the very tip of the Spearhead', had reached the Elbe on 14 April, as the army's war diary observed, XVIII Corps still had elements of the 97th Infantry and 13th Armored Divisions anchored on the Rhine, confining the Germans in the Ruhr Pocket, some three hundred miles to the west.[2] Needing to be equidistant between their strung-out forces, First Army headquarters moved to the university town of Marburg, capital of Hesse, and 120 miles east of Cologne, and location of the C-47 airstrip. Hodges and his headquarters found their main challenge was not controlling their forces but staying in touch with them.

Hodges' headquarters noted that the seventy-five minutes' flying time to their units furthest east 'was testimony to the great space that separates us from the front line'.[3] The distance played against the command team's tendency to micro-manage, and disinclination to travel far. They were happier in a static situation and found themselves uncomfortable in this final pursuit. As a result, Signal Information and Monitoring (SIAM) Companies were introduced, in imitation of Montgomery's Phantom Regiment. Ike's son, Lieutenant John D. Eisenhower, was attached to the one at First Army's headquarters on 10 April, but the innovation was far too late to ease Hodges' communications burden, which remained First Army's principal challenge.

Logistically, they were never embarrassed. Learning lessons from the previous autumn and the Bulge, First Army had pre-stocked enough ammunition of all types, rations and medical supplies. The V-2 threat to Antwerp was over, traffic was flowing unimpeded. In fact, the only shortages proved to be related to such a swift advance – tank bogie wheels, tracks, jerrycans and spare engines. These were met by cannibalising other disabled vehicles, so that the main administrative problem became a shortage of wagons with which to move everything forward. However, a lower use of artillery in the chase across Germany and the dwindling Luftwaffe threat meant artillery and air defence vehicles could be commandeered for use by truck companies of the Quartermaster Corps to meet their transportation needs.

Fuel – as in the previous September – might have proved a limiting factor, but so much had been decanted into jerrycans at fuel distribution points – hence the ability to issue a million gallons in a single day – that First Army was never threatened with a lack of mobility. Their opponents suffered exactly the opposite problem. As with Third Army, pipelines were also laid across Rhine engineer bridges to bring fuel closer to the battlefront. Additionally, the C-47 fleet of IX Troop Carrier Command was not only used to bring POL (petrol, oil and lubricants) forward but evacuate casualties on the return leg, which required learning new skills. Regulations stating that patients had to be fitted with Mae West life jackets when flying over water were studiously ignored, as were instructions that medevac flights were not to bank more than twenty degrees, or fly above 3,000 feet, because the thinner air made patients breathe harder.

'Landing on small fields was like landing on an aircraft carrier. When the grass was slippery, you didn't dare to brake the plane,' recalled pilot Rex Selbe. The 81st Troop Carrier and 806th Medical Air Evacuation Squadrons noted that each medevac C-47 carried one nurse and a medical technician, and up to twenty-four litter patients. In April these units alone evacuated 17,287 casualties from nine forward airfields back to hospitals west of the Rhine, in Paris and the United Kingdom. 'I can still smell the odor of rotten flesh,' remembered crew chief Jerome Loving. 'I will never forget the sight of some of those boys on litters covered with bandages and what great morale boosters the flight nurses were, as they went from one GI to another.'[4]

As V Corps sped on another hundred miles to the Elbe, VII Corps to their north was slowed down by the Harz mountains which took nearly three weeks to clear.[5] Germany's most northerly mountain range stretches for sixty miles between the Weser and the Elbe, with peaks rising to 4,000 feet, dense forests, rushing streams and plunging valleys. It was the origin of much Germanic folklore collected by the Brothers Grimm but, militarily, this stunning scenery was an attacker's nightmare, where the mechanisation of the US Army mattered little. However, such a large area, seething with armed and dangerous troops, could not be ignored and had to be stripped of its defenders.

With Collins' corps was Captain Felder L. Fair, commanding Company 'B' with the 26th Infantry of the 'Big Red One', who was briefed that their opponents included battlegroups formed from soldiers who had drifted into the region, plus a core of experienced staff from divisions no longer in existence. In the north-west of the Harz lies the old garrison town of Goslar, which had trained generations mountain soldiers. Both Guderian and Rommel had at one time commanded the Goslar-Jäger-Battalion, though by 1945 the barracks had been taken over by the 6th SS Mountain Division. There was great anxiety that the area would be a particularly tough nut to crack, if it could be subdued at all. 'It was believed there were about 100,000 fairly well-organized men, enough to make the reduction of the Harz a difficult task.'[6] The oft-overlooked campaign, 'while short, was a tough grind for the infantry' echoed a 1st Division after action report.[7]

Of the terrain, Fair recalled that 'it was forbidding to an attacker. The road net was more limited than in the Ardennes, and rougher than the Hürtgen Forest, because the woods were thicker and the ground more broken by ravines, hills and draws. The winding roads could be cratered at a moment's notice and were easy to block; the number of trees that could be felled was limited only by the number of men available to handle saws.' In the vicinity of Elend, twenty miles north of Nordhausen, Company 'B' had to advance with a bulldozer in the vanguard, being the only way to speedily remove the all-too-frequent roadblocks. Captain Fair found the mid-April weather 'of strong winds and heavy rainstorms which completely blotted out all vision, and masked all attempts with our radio sets, made control of my company extremely difficult. I had to use messengers for all communications.'[8]

During his 17 April advance on Elend, 'which turned out to be full of hospitals containing convalescing soldiers, a patrol captured a horse-drawn cannon, whose five horses were ridden back by my men, which eased mobility problems'. Eventually, for a cost of one killed and five wounded, Fair's company captured five hundred on 17–18 April. 'Next day, five hundred more were rounded up, including one major general. During the reduction of the Harz Mountains, our First Division captured 50,343 Germans who, when added to those taken by the adjacent units, made a grand total of 73,490 taken in the area. I felt this operation would have been far more difficult had our opponents made a greater effort in their defence.'[9]

Fair thought that 'The Germans were very low in spirits and morale, knowing the end was not far off and their cause in the Harz was hopeless. Only SS troops could keep the Wehrmacht in line and resisting, and a single SS man in the rear was an excellent incentive to fight on.' By contrast, he found his own company's 'morale and esprit de corps was high. They were in an excellent frame of mind. All could see the early end of the war and themselves as the conquerors. Many of our seasoned veterans had returned from hospital; a large percentage of them had been fighting the Germans since Africa and were happy to be back for the kill, the finish of it all,' which must reflect the experience of VII Corps and First Army as a whole.[10]

To ease his task in the Harz, Collins' flank guard, the 4th Cavalry, formed Task Force Macdonald, named after its commander, which included the 24th Cavalry Reconnaissance Squadron, a battalion of infantry, another of light tanks and a third of self-propelled artillery. This force spent the rest of their war supporting the 1st Division and then the 83rd in chasing isolated units, hunting for stragglers, rounding up war criminals, and supplementing their rations by hunting deer throughout the idyllic, still snow-capped Harz.[11]

Technical Sergeant Gil Blum was aboard an M5 light tank with the 4th Cavalry as it thundered through the Harz, which he found 'grim and eerie. Dark, full of trees all over. Gingerbread houses with tiny windows and narrow, cobblestone streets, castles with turrets. I thought of childhood stories: wicked witches, Red Riding Hood, dwarves counting gold in caverns and poor woodcutters in lonely cottages.' Blum continued, 'We're coming around this bend, and out from behind a tree comes this young boy. Couldn't be more than ten. And he's screaming at the top of his lungs "*Ich bin jüdisch*" (I'm Jewish). Obviously, someone had told him: when the Americans come, just tell them you're Jewish and they'll take care of you. So, we stopped and said to him, "You stay right here. In a little bit, Headquarters Company is gonna come along. They'll look after you." And he stood by that tree, looking so forlorn. I can still see now, him getting smaller and smaller, and I just wonder whatever happened to that kid, or what his story was."[12]

To Collins' south, Huebner's V Corps had a much easier axis heading east. Apart from a series of minor rivers flowing at right angles to their advance, they had the advantage of a natural route corridor all the way to Leipzig. Seated at the confluence of several rivers that gave access to the North Sea, and numerous ancient roads, Leipzig had long been a centre of Germanic culture, education, trade and industry. The largest conurbation in Saxony, with a pre-war population of 750,000, it was Germany's fifth largest city, and beyond the range of Allied bombers until 1943. It housed over two hundred munitions-related factories, employing 150,000, one-third of whom were slave labourers. However, as Allied aircraft technology improved, the city had been bombed twenty-four times by April 1945, killing 5,000, and reducing many of its oldest buildings to rubble.

It is a city easy to like, with wide-ranging architectural styles, broad avenues, parks and many open spaces. Martin Luther had preached there; Johann Sebastian Bach was organist at St Thomas' Church for twenty-five years; Felix Mendelssohn founded the Leipzig Conservatoire; and Richard Wagner was born in the city. Its south-eastern edge had also witnessed the largest battle fought in Europe before the First World War, where over 400,000 clashed between 16–19 October 1813 at the Battle of the Nations. It heralded the end of Napoleon's dominance of the Germanic states and led to his first exile on Elba. For the centenary in 1913, Kaiser Wilhelm II unveiled the 300-foot-high *Völkerschlachtdenkmal* (Monument to the Battle of the Nations), with a viewing platform on top, which became the focus for many ceremonies, including those of the Nazis, and would feature in the coming battle.

On 12 April, as V Corps approached the Saale River, about thirty miles to the west, Leonard's 9th Armored Division came under fire from a wide belt of flak artillery, protecting the city and nearby synthetic oil refineries, in an arc from Halle, Merseburg and Weissenfels to Zeitz. The opposition comprised several hundred Luftwaffe-manned anti-aircraft guns of the 14th Flak Division, ranging from 75mm to 128mm. The area was well known to Allied aircrew as 'flak alley' – though no one had thought to warn First Army of this threat to their ground forces. Immediately, the batteries of between twelve and thirty-six guns with their excellent fields of fire accounted for nine American tanks.

Huebner therefore ordered the Ninth to work their way round to the south and reach the Mulde River, while Walter M. Robertson's 2nd Indianheads advanced on Leipzig from the west, with Emil F. Reinhardt's 69th Division following Leonard's armour, to assault the city from the east. Robertson was a West Pointer, class of 1912, who had seen action in 1918 and subsequently occupied the same Rhineland through which he had just fought. In June 1944 he led the 2nd ashore at Omaha beach on D+2, and for his leadership in the Bulge had recently received a Distinguished Service Cross. Reinhardt was a second-generation American, whose grandfather hailed from Braunschweig, 120 miles north-west of Leipzig. The younger man graduated from West Point in 1910 with John Millikin and had led the 'Fighting 69th' since September 1944, taking it into battle the following February.

The Mulde was reached by Lieutenant Colonel Lee Shaughnessy's CCR of the 9th Armored, when it arrived at a small town, dominated by an ancient schloss overlooking the river, on 16 April. Some thirty miles south-east of Leipzig, the eleventh century castle, sited on a steep hill, housed a *Sonderlager*, a maximum-security prison for around five hundred Allied officers. This was Colditz – home to many persistent escapers, sent to Oflag IV-C (in German nomenclature), as a punishment.[13] Others were *Prominenten* – celebrity hostages the Nazis hoped to use as bargaining chips. Among them were Giles Romilly, nephew of Churchill's wife Clementine; Earl Haig, son of Britain's Great War commander-in-chief; Battle of Britain pilot Douglas Bader; David Stirling, founder of the Special Air Service; New Zealander Charles Upham, twice awarded a VC; Lieutenant John G. Winant, son of the US Ambassador to Britain; and the exotically named Lieutenant Colonel Florimund Duke, at forty-nine, the oldest American paratrooper of the war. Duke was one of a trio of OSS operatives parachuted into Hungary to prevent it joining forces with Germany.

'Although space was at a premium, we were constantly hungry and the stone walls made it bitterly cold, I thought it was the best POW camp in Germany,' said Flight Lieutenant Walter Morison, the sole survivor of his Wellington bomber, shot down in June 1942. With a comrade, Morison had earlier escaped from Stalag Luft III in home-made Luftwaffe uniforms and narrowly missed flying to Sweden from a military airbase in a two-seat trainer. Their punishment was Colditz, of which the resourceful officer observed, 'There were benefits. If you get together a group of intelligent, well-educated young men, they will always find interesting things to do, besides escaping. There was a theatre, books, music, and we managed to hide a radio, meaning we could listen to the BBC. Crucial to our morale, as we realised the Germans were certain to be defeated.'[14]

Captured in 1940, one of their comrades was Second Lieutenant Desmond Llewellyn of the Royal Welch Fusiliers, who put his wide knowledge of making escape equipment from mundane items to good use in the role of 'Q', the British secret service quartermaster in seventeen of the James Bond movies. Supposedly escape-proof, Colditz witnessed 186 Allied breakout attempts before the camp was liberated, with twelve Frenchmen, eleven Britons, seven Dutch and one Pole making 'home runs'.

Apart from numerous tunnels dug with drinking cups and soup spoons, elaborate disguises and home-made ropes, 'type-written' documents painstakingly crafted by hand and authenticated by official-looking rubber stamps made from floor linoleum, the resourceful POWs secretly constructed a glider from looted floorboards, cotton sheets stiffened with porridge and control wires fashioned from electric cables. Alas, the Americans arrived before the 'Colditz Cock' was able to fly. As the 9th Armored in concert with the 69th Infantry neared, the Kommandant, Oberstleutnant Gerhard Prawitt, was ordered to remove his prisoners by local SS officers. The POWs refused and the castle itself came under fire from US artillery who were initially unaware of their incarcerated colleagues. Eventually an American inmate crept out, linked up with his attackers and ushered GIs into the schloss.[15]

Those inside observed their first liberator, a single GI, 'his belt and straps festooned with ammunition clips and grenades', step gingerly into the courtyard. An Allied officer grasped his hand, as the American asked, 'Any doughboys here?' Suddenly, 'a mob was rushing towards him, shouting, and cheering and struggling madly to reach him, to make sure that he was alive, to touch him, and from that touch know again the miracle of living . . . Men wept, unable to restrain themselves. They kissed the GI, they kissed everyone within range. The storm of emotion burst. Home and country beckoned. Wives, sweethearts, mothers, fathers, and children never seen were calling across the gulf of the absent years.'[16]

Once the city of Leipzig was firmly invested, Huebner relieved the 102nd Cavalry of their southern flank security duty, giving them free rein for the rest of April to sweep the corps rear area south of the Harz for German stragglers, a textbook cavalry role, for which its high mobility and excellent communications equipment was ideally suited.[17] Initially approaching Leipzig from the west and south-west, the 2nd and 69th Divisions attacked the various towns along the flak belt, crossed the Saale in small boats, radioed coordinates of the German guns to their own artillery, brought accurate fire on the positions, and so eliminated the menace.

During 14–15 April, the history of Colonel Walter D. Buie's 272nd Infantry (69th Division) noted, 'In those two days, we accounted for seventy-two 88-mm guns, and the complete garrisons manning these positions, which were stubbornly defended. Because of the timing and coordination of the attack with the artillery, tanks, and tank destroyers, practically no casualties were suffered. The fire, which was so effective, was directed by both liaison plane and a ground observer. The ground observer did such excellent work that many direct hits were scored on the well-dug-in guns and on individuals. After the action, the troops, in their enthusiasm for the fine work of the artillery, cheered and embraced him.'[18]

By the morning of 18 April, both divisions had reached the outer suburbs and were ready to assault Leipzig itself. They had been broken down into task forces earlier in their dash across Germany, as they would remain during the fight for the city. For example, to the 1st Battalion of 272nd Infantry was added a company each of tanks and tank destroyers, and platoons of engineers and chemical mortarmen, the latter for making instant smokescreens.[19] Other battalions had at least a platoon of tanks and tank destroyers attached. With Simpson's Ninth Army already on the Elbe to the north, Patton's Third reaching towards the Czech border to the south, and the Russians closing in from the east, Leipzig was cut off and would have to defend itself with its own resources.

Few German troops were available apart from those youngsters of the 14th Flak Division, who had lost their anti-aircraft guns and were now serving as infantry, some Hitlerjugend, and several battalions of Volkssturm. There soon emerged a difference of opinion between the city's highly decorated Kampfkommandant, Oberst Hans von Poncet, and Volkssturm Bataillonsführer Major Walter Dönicke, on the one hand, and Oberbürgermeister Alfred Freyberg and Generalmajor der Polizei Wilhelm von Grolman on the other. Ordering the Volkssturm to create roadblocks by packing tramcars with rubble, Poncet and Dönicke were determined to fight to the last bullet.

However, Freyberg and Grolman were hostile to destroying the city's infrastructure and felt sending the Hitlerjugend into battle was 'blatant child murder'. Though his personal history, as a former SA and SS official who had taken part in the 1923 Munich putsch with Hitler, suggested he was an ardent Nazi, Grolman refused to release his 2,500-strong police force for combat duty, whereupon Dönicke barricaded himself into the *Neues Rathaus* (New City Hall), a castle-like structure of stone walls and tall turrets built in 1899, with five hundred Volkssturm. Poncet chose to make his symbolic last stand with three hundred of the faithful in the Völkerschlachtdenkmal monument, with its twenty-foot-thick walls.

The 272nd Infantry noted that 'Friendly civilians reported that during the night, SS troopers had cruised the outskirts, forcing townspeople to take down the white flags and to organize resistance. They had expected us to attack on the seventeenth, when air raid sirens were sounded to warn that hostile tanks were approaching.' The 1st Battalion of Colonel Buie's regiment heard them, observing, 'The night air was suddenly cut by the weird sounds of sirens from the city of Leipzig and all surrounding villages. If the troops had had no reason to be apprehensive prior to that time, the sinister wailing of the sirens was enough to make them so.'[20]

On the morning of 18 April, patrols from the 272nd ran into heavy resistance on the south-eastern outskirts from machine-gun, sniper and panzerfäuste fire as they swung around the outskirts anti-clockwise, to attack the city from the east. To their left, the task forces of Colonel Charles M. Adams' 273rd Regiment advanced in tandem, and both formations were to meet the 2nd Division in the city centre, where a series of bridges crossed over the Elsterbecken Canal. The 69th's remaining regiment, Henry B. Margeson's 271st Infantry, was further south, and in reserve.

The 2nd Division's three regiments in their various task forces advanced from the west, supported by sub-units of the 741st Tank and 612th Tank Destroyer Battalions. Colonel Jay B. Loveless' 23rd Infantry Regiment aimed towards the city centre, that of P.D. Grinder's 9th was to their right, with Francis H. Boos's 38th Infantry further south still, beyond the city limits. In certain quarters there was resistance; in others, white flags fluttered, with civilians out in large numbers, lining the streets, some even waving and offering flowers and drinks.

In the city centre and around the Neues Rathaus, Dönicke's men resisted fiercely, destroying at least one Sherman. A group of about 150 defended the Hauptbahnhof (Main Railway Station) throughout the day and night, and although there was some moonlight, in the blackout it was too dark to root out the opposition. The 272nd noted the station, the largest in Germany, seemed immune to their shellfire. 'Artillery of available calibre had little or no effect on its heavy masonry. The tanks and tank destroyers fired at it, but their shells bounced off, as an unchalked cue would slide over a billiard ball.'[21] After dark, in a novel approach to urban warfare, a Sherman actually drove into the huge railway station, firing into rooms with its main gun, in an attempt to drive snipers out into the streets. However, the firefight was abandoned after two hours, as the armour withdrew to bypass the Hauptbahnhof until daybreak, by which time the defenders had vanished.

With Company 'F' of the 23rd Infantry was the acclaimed war photographer Robert Capa, one of the world's best-known cameramen who had already covered the Spanish Civil War and much of World War Two. He followed the GIs in their attack on the Zeppelin bridge over the Elsterbecken Canal and climbed up to the top floor of an apartment block to record a four-man machine-gun crew setting up their weapon and tripod on a balcony. As his camera clicked a young corporal at the gun was hit by a sniper and fell back, a growing pool of blood issuing from his head. The sequence of images, with the soldier's face masked, appeared in the 14 May edition of *Life* magazine, symbolically captioned 'the last soldier to be killed in the war'. This was technically incorrect by nineteen days, as we shall discover.[22]

That evening, Captain Charles B. MacDonald, leading Company 'G' in the same 23rd Infantry, reported that emissaries from Grolman had arrived at his command post to negotiate a surrender. MacDonald, later a US Army official historian, and whose seminal autobiography *Company Commander* (1947) has been reprinted many times, wrote of a surreal evening. He was chauffeured in a luxurious Mercedes-Benz 'with two Germans as travelling companions, their jaunty caps silhouetted against the dark windshield', to meet senior police officers. They discussed surrender terms over 'cocktail glasses on a silver tray filled with cognac. I decided I must be quite mad. My wildest dreams had never envisioned a social hour with a group of German officers as hosts.'[23]

In the police headquarters, he found more Germans, 'immaculately groomed, their uniforms stiffly pressed, and their boots brilliantly shined. Their officer caps sat at rakish angles on their heads, their smoothly shaven faces shining beneath them. I was suddenly conscious of my own shabby appearance. I felt my beard, unshaven in at least a week, my face and hands unwashed for two days, my uniform a dirty, ill-fitting combination, and my combat boots covered with dust. I stopped a few paces from the major, tried my best to make my rough heels click and found myself imitating their stiff stance and flinging up a sharp salute that I hope showed no sign of subservience.'

MacDonald found General Grolman 'even more immaculately dressed than the others, a long row of military decorations across his chest. His face was round, red, and cleanly shaven. A monocle in his right eye gave him an appearance that made me want to congratulate Hollywood on its movie interpretations of high-ranking Nazis.' As it transpired that Grolman could only surrender his own police force and had no authority over Dönicke and his Volkssturm or Poncet's Wehrmacht, MacDonald's eccentric evening's entertainment was a 'noble, but fruitless' diversion.

Aware that there were fanatics deeply dug into some of the city buildings, the 69th Division had formed a special grouping based on the 777th Tank Battalion, of two hundred personnel and twenty vehicles, including Shermans, M10 tank destroyers, half-tracks and 105mm self-propelled guns, named Task Force Zweibel after its commander, Lieutenant Colonel David T. Zweibel. It kept the Neues Rathaus under observation and periodic fire through the night, then from 07:30 on 19 April, opened an attack with sustained fire for one hour and forty minutes at point-blank range. Zweibel then sent in a POW to demand an immediate surrender, or the task force would attack with heavy artillery and flame-throwers, neither of which they actually possessed. The bluff worked and minutes later the edifice disgorged nearly 200 personnel.[24]

Of Dönicke there was no sign until BBC reporter Edward Ward, guarded by 'two American soldiers who carried tommy guns at the ready, since we were the first to explore the inside of the building', obtained the keys from a caretaker to Oberbürgermeister Freyberg's office and that of his deputy, Dr Kurt Lisso. The two officials had taken poison with their spouses and children, as had Dönicke, clutching a picture of Hitler. Ward noted 'three Volkssturmers lay sprawled, dead, over tables, with pools of blood on the floor – they had committed suicide. By the side of one was a bottle of cognac, and a half-empty glass. He'd evidently needed courage.'[25]

At noon, Major General Emil Reinhardt of the 69th Division arrived and was handed a swastika flag from the Neues Rathaus by Zweibel. The battle for central Leipzig was almost over, but there remained Oberst von Poncet and his garrison holed up in the granite Völkerschlachtdenkmal memorial, sitting on the hill from where the victors had directed their forces against Napoleon 132 years earlier. West Point, Sandhurst, Saint-Cyr, Kingston and all the great military colleges had taught their cadets about the October 1813 clash at Leipzig, when the Coalition armies of Austria, Prussia, Sweden and Russia defeated the *Grande Armée* of Napoleon (which also contained Poles and Italians). In 1945, slave labour from most of those nations had been forced to dig anti-tank ditches and field defences on the former battleground against the approaching Americans. Crates of documents on the earlier Battle of Leipzig lay in the monument's basement with the city's other cultural treasures.

All through 19 April, dust rained down on the priceless artefacts as thirteen US artillery battalions chipped away with little effect at the massive tower during the Second Battle of Leipzig. An assault by a US battalion made no headway against a structure that seemed designed for defence. Except that it controlled nothing; it had no military utility, but a dangerous bunch of fanatics behind American lines could not be ignored. Eventually Captain Hans L. Trefousse, a Leipzig-born naturalised GI with the 273rd Infantry, volunteered to try and negotiate with Poncet, who was holding seventeen GIs prisoner. After nine hours of discussions, Poncet agreed to go into captivity alone if his men – and their hostages – were allowed to go free, and on that basis fifteen officers and 275 other ranks trickled out of the memorial, hands held high, in the small hours of 20 April. Despite the deal, the defenders soon found themselves rounded up and herded into a prisoner-of-war stockade. The Second Battle of Leipzig was over. Within days, both the 2nd and 69th Divisions had caught up with the rest of V Corps lining the banks of the Mulde, fifteen miles further east.

Reinhardt's 69th Division summarised their part: 'The resistance encountered, while determined, was of comparatively short duration because of our effective fire and maneuver placed against it. Some of our casualties resulted when the civilians formed a shield for snipers. As our troops approached, the civilian shield would disappear, and weapons would fire on our troops. The attack was remarkable in that the troops did not get lost. The directional control by the troop commanders was worthy of note. The battle of Leipzig and the events surrounding it were linked with experiences that will long live in the memories of all the troops involved.'[26] Some of those experiences were not related to fighting, but the discovery of around five hundred slave labour camps in Leipzig, where over 50,000 were crammed into fenced-off dance halls, gymnasiums, schools, restaurants, hotels and barracks.

While their colleagues were busy clearing the city centre, other elements of the 2nd Division arrived at Zöschen labour camp, twelve miles

During the clearing of the approaches to the River Rhine and in the assault itself, all seven Allied armies drenched the German defenders with millions of surrender leaflets like this. They were highly effective, prompting the capitulation of hundreds of thousands, many of whom hoped that possession of a leaflet would guarantee their safety.

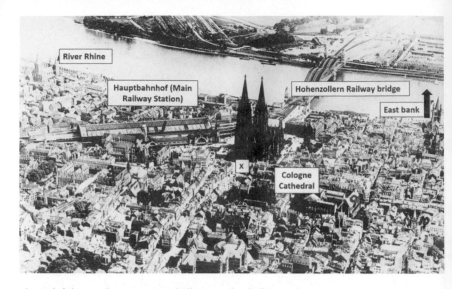

The tank fight in Cologne on 6 March illustrates the challenges of urban combat facing the Allies in 1945. This pre-war aerial photograph of the city illustrates the proximity of the railway station and its bridge to the cathedral. The bridge had been sabotaged before the Americans arrived. 'X' marks the spot where a lone Panther tank awaited the 3rd US Armored Division.

The main 75mm gun of the German tank has just hit two Shermans, killing several crewmen. However, a brand-new M26 Pershing, behind the cameraman, is about to destroy the panzer, using its 90mm cannon. The cathedral can be seen at the end of the street.

On 20 April, the 69th US Infantry Division subdued the last defenders of Leipzig. Here a GI picks his way through the interior of the Völkerschlachtdenkmal, the monument to the battle of Leipzig, fought in 1813 against Napoleon, and where the die-hard Germans stood their ground in 1945.

The ancient city of Münster was taken on 2–3 April by the 17th US Airborne Division with the 6th Guards Tank Brigade in support. They found the area already battered by a series of air raids, the last being on 25 March, when these railway yards were destroyed.

To defend local villages and towns, the Germans had mobilised the Volkssturm, a civilian home guard, the previous autumn. It was armed principally with rifles and panzerfaust anti-tank weapons (as seen here).

Nazi officials forced local residents to build wood-and-brick roadblocks. Allied armour, such as this M10 tank destroyer, had little difficulty in bulldozing their way through in minutes.

When they crossed into Germany, the Allies were initially hostile to the local population. Fraternisation, even with children, was frowned upon, but the ban ultimately proved impossible to maintain.

Across Germany, forced labourers and prisoners of war were liberated by the Allies. Here, to the evident delight of the inmates, some of whom had been incarcerated since 1940, Stalag XI-B at Fallingbostel is liberated on 16 April. Their rescuers were units of 7th (Desert Rats) Armoured Division.

On 29 April, Dachau camp outside Munich was liberated by the 42nd and 45th US Infantry Divisions. Most of the 32,000 inmates were barely alive, and many died after their rescue of typhus and other afflictions. Days earlier, SS guards had marched another 7,000 away to their deaths.

On 8 May 1945, the German armed forces formally ceased to be a fighting arm of the Nazi state. All soldiers, including these bicycle-mounted Hitlerjugend equipped with panzerfäuste, were disarmed and crammed into vast encampments holding tens of thousands.

All of those who surrendered had to be 'denazified', and many would not emerge from captivity for two years. Amongst most, there was a sense of relief that it was all over. Very few kept the embers of National Socialism alight.

For long after the surrender, various German military police forces, in uniform and wearing side arms, were used to keep order amongst their own fellow countrymen.

On 4 May 1945, a German delegation, led by Generaladmiral Hans-Georg von Friedeburg, head of the Reich's navy (leather coat, clutching papers), meets Montgomery before the surrender ceremony. Next to their field marshal, intelligence officer Lt Colonel Joe Ewart and interpreter, Captain Derek Knee (back to camera), look on.

Generaloberst Hans-Jürgen Stümpff of the Luftwaffe and Generalfeldmarschall Wilhelm Keitel, Armed Forces Chief of Staff, arrive at the Russian-organised surrender ceremony in Berlin on 8–9 May. Keitel completely misread the moment, pompously turning up in full dress uniform, flourishing his marshal's baton and angrily signing the capitulation documents.

After Air Chief Marshal Sir Arthur Tedder had signed for SHAEF, and Marshal Zhukov for the Soviet Union, General Carl Spaatz (*left*, head of the Strategic Air Forces in Europe) signed for America, and Général Jean de Lattre (*right*) for France.

west of Leipzig. The occupants lived in wooden huts with earthen floors covered with straw, surrounded by a barbed-wire fence, and watch-towers set at intervals along the perimeter. They walked to the Leuna-Werke chemical factory or cleared streets of rubble from air raids, filled bomb craters and removed unexploded bombs. A typhus epidemic had been raging in Zöschen since January 1945. Of the 5,019 prisoners later found to have passed through, 1,000 were liberated; the remainder were transported to camps elsewhere, or had died at Zöschen. In theory this was a re-education camp, where slave labourers could earn their release, but to every GI this smelled and looked like a death camp.[27]

In Böhlen, ten miles south of Leipzig, eight hundred toiled at Braunkohle-Benzin, distilling synthetic fuel from coal. Others made weaponry at factories including Hugo-Schneider-Aktiengesellschaft, where 10,000 slaves produced small arms ammunition and panzer-faust anti-tank weapons. At the Mitteldeutsche-Motorenwerke 4,000 foreign workers assembled aircraft engines, and more made parts for Junkers at Allgemeine-Transportanlagen, but the biggest plant was Erla-Maschinenwerke, which manufactured 32 per cent of all Messerschmitt-109 fighters, with four major sites in the north-eastern sector of the city alone.[28]

By 1943 64 per cent of Erla's Leipzig workforce – around 16,000 people – were unwilling guests of the Reich. Their numbers were swelled by 2,000 concentration camp inmates from Buchenwald, who under-took the final assembly of wing sections, control systems and landing gear, working twelve-hour days with little rest or food, under the watch-ful eye of German foremen. In 1944 at Erla's Leipzig-Heiterblick aero components factory, 450 slave workers were recorded as killed during a single air raid. Taking shelter was forbidden. Their comrades had to salvage machine tools and other equipment from the bombed-out and twisted wreckage, and physically remove all unexploded ordnance.

Others were fenced in at Leipzig-Thekla barracks, where more than one hundred succumbed to illness or malnutrition. On 13 April, 1,500 were evacuated on a death march, leaving behind over three hundred too ill to walk. As the Americans battled through the suburbs, a dozen SS guards set fire to a building at Thekla containing their immobile prisoners. Most perished, but in the dense smoke some managed to escape. With their bodies aflame, they were machine-gunned by guards, impaled on the electric fence, or beaten to death by civilian residents in the vicinity. GIs who arrived only a few hours later documented and filmed the crime scene.[29]

On the eve of Hitler's fifty-sixth birthday, photographer Margaret Bourke-White captured the atrocity at Thekla before rummaging through the city's ruins with her camera. As Dr Goebbels was preaching that 'the perverse coalition between Bolshevism and Plutocracy is about to break up, and that it is "our Hitler" who will still turn back the tide and save Europe', Bourke-White climbed into the city's town hall and snapped the suicides in the Neues Rathaus. She had been told by a colleague, 'Hurry there before they clean it out. The whole inside of it is like a Madame Tussaud's waxworks.' Bourke-White and *Life* magazine's Bill Walton 'rushed in the jeep over the Zeppelin bridge, past street cars filled with rocks and drew up before the City Hall. Here the siege had been intense, and the deeper carvings of artillery were added to the ancient outlines of the fine old Rathaus.'[30]

She struggled to make sense of the wave of suicides she encountered there and elsewhere, of the violence the Germans seemed to turn against themselves. 'Death seemed their only escape,' she surmised. Her images of Oberbürgermeister Freyberg and his family in the Neues Rathaus are remarkable. Immaculately attired in a civilian suit, the lord mayor is slumped forward on his desk. Opposite are his wife and daughter slouched in leather chairs. There is no disorder; nothing is out of place. The scene is tranquil, as though a spell has cast all three to sleep. Except that they are dead.

Bourke-White also snapped a ruined office. A smashed typewriter sits in the rubble, the name of its manufacturer, 'Triumph', clearly visible. Alongside it lies a severed human hand, reaching for the machine it will no longer use.[31] Another well-known photo-journalist, Lee Miller, covering the war for *Vogue* magazine, had photographed the same Neues Rathaus tableau and came to a similar conclusion. 'Germany's beautiful landscape, dotted with jewel-like villages, was marred by its ruined cities and inhabited by schizophrenics. The love of death, which is the under-pattern of the German living, caught up with the high officials of the regime. They gave a great party, toasted death, and Hitler, and poisoned themselves.'[32]

In Leipzig, as elsewhere, there was no way out for senior Nazis. For them, the choice was simple: pistols or poison. In Berlin alone, 7,000 took their lives. At least 20,000 of the Party faithful must have died by their own hand across the Reich in April–May 1945. From the earliest days of the Nazi rise to power, its followers had been wedded to a 'victory or death' ideology. Now, with defeat staring them in the face, the Party machinery handed out cyanide capsules made by Tesch & Stabenow of Hamburg, with detailed instructions on how to terminate one's life. Whole families chose to die together. Underlining the total indoctrination of the country, suicide was promoted by the regime as a Wagnerian, heroic sacrifice. Hence, eight out of forty-one Gauleiters, eight out of forty-seven senior police and SS leaders, fifty-three out of 554 army generals, fourteen out of ninety-eight Luftwaffe commanders and eleven of out fifty-three admirals, choosing this quick route to Valhalla in the dying days of Greater Germany.[33]

Later, Major Richard J. Eaton of the American Military Government reported on the funeral procession he insisted the new Oberbürgermeister of Leipzig organise for the dead of Thekla, led by a GI guard of honour. '[Then came] the *Burgo* and his hundred leading citizens in morning dress and silk hats. In addition, 1,000 others were present to represent a cross-section of the population. I think the people of the city were shocked by the tragedy. One wonders how much they knew of the horrors of the Hitler regime.'[34]

For most V Corps GIs, the fighting was over. They moved forward to the Mulde River, fifteen miles east of Leipzig. Another fifteen miles further lay the Elbe, which Stalin, Churchill and Roosevelt had agreed would be the initial Allied demarcation line between East and West. Simpson's Ninth had already reached it. Beyond the Mulde, a tributary of the Elbe, Eisenhower and Bradley imposed a no man's land for First and Third Armies, to prevent incidents of friendly fire. Opposite lay General Gleb Baklanov's 34th Corps of the Fifth Guards Tank Army, whose various divisions were sending forward reconnaissance units, often horse-mounted, to look for the Americans. Slowly both sides began to patrol this dead zone, which is where the first contacts were made between US forces and the Soviets, although the secretive Red Army refused to pass details of their dispositions to their Allies. On 22 April, Collins was forced to spend 'the afternoon aloft in a Cub [artillery spotting aircraft] trying to spot the Reds. Although I saw shell bursts, presumably Russian, I could not locate their guns or positions.'[35]

Although the town of Torgau on the Elbe is best known as the site where the two sides joined hands, smaller meetings had already taken place. On 25 April, a small team led by Lieutenant Albert Kotzebue with Company 'G' of the 273rd Infantry had been ordered to reconnoitre beyond the Mulde. They met a lone Russian on horseback, Aitkalia Alibekov from Kazakhstan, at 11:30 in the tiny hamlet of Lechwitz, two miles west of the Elbe. This was the first encounter of the armies.

Later, at 12:05, Kotzebue spotted a group of Russians across the Elbe, crossed, and was entertained by a series of officers from the 175th Rifle Regiment, including its commander, Lieutenant Colonel Alexandr Gordeyev, Major General Vladimir Rusakov of the 58th Guards Infantry Division, and his superior, Gleb Baklanov, of the 34th Corps. On the same day, at 16:45, a second US patrol led by Major Frederick W. Craig, Executive Officer of the Second Battalion, 273rd, encountered a horsed column from the 1st Guards Cavalry Regiment in the same area. Craig's larger group also traversed the Elbe and were met by the same Russian officers who had entertained Kotzebue.

A third exploratory Jeep patrol had also set off from the 273rd's headquarters led by the First Battalion's S-2 (intelligence officer), Lieutenant William D. Robertson, and arrived in Torgau at 14:00. The small town, eighty-five miles south of Berlin, is dominated by its turreted schloss on the banks of the Elbe. Seeing Russians on the far bank shooting at him, Robertson broke into an apothecary's shop, found red and blue powders and using an old white bedsheet, ingeniously made a Stars and Stripes flag. He climbed the stairs of the castle's watchtower facing east and at 15:15 began waving his symbol of the West. The Red Army were at first suspicious, until Robertson brought up a former Russian prisoner to shout across the river to his comrades. With that, the firing stopped. Men from both sides ran towards a twisted box-girder bridge that lay before the castle, washed by the Elbe. At 16:00, clambering over the sabotaged bridge, Robertson met his opposite number, Sergeant Nikolei Andreyev, in the centre of a broken metal joist. Robertson returned to his headquarters with four Russians, led by Major Anafrim Larionov, to arrange a formal meeting of their commanders for the following day.

However, Robertson's superiors, Colonel Adams of the 273rd, Reinhardt commanding the 69th and Huebner of V Corps, were furious. Robertson and the other patrols had disobeyed their instructions not to stray five miles beyond the Mulde. Despite the presence of the Russians in his headquarters and every correspondent within a wide radius descending on him at this news of world significance, Reinhardt toyed with the idea of court-martialling the officers. Yet, when Huebner phoned the news through to Hodges at First Army, that the unauthorised patrol had delivered the required contact with the Red Army, the latter pronounced himself 'delighted'. Bradley, too, was happy, with the result that the chain of command had to hastily reverse their displeasure. Reinhardt and Adams were obliged to congratulate Robertson, to whom they had just given a dressing-down.

The controversy neatly illustrates the military concept of mission command. The overall intent was to make contact with the Soviets. How local commanders achieved this should have been up to them. Instead, the chain of leadership became blinded by their five-mile rule, imposed at the expense of the overarching aim. Common sense only prevailed when the First Army commander indicated his approval. Yet, without Kotzebue, Craig and Robertson using their initiative and exceeding orders, the overall mission would not have been achieved.

The following day, with Robertson leading the way to Torgau, Adams and Reinhardt met their opposite numbers, Colonel J. Rogov of the 173rd Rifle Regiment, and Major General Rusakov. Allied reporters were flown in by artillery liaison aircraft, the Russians bringing correspondents, including five uniformed women reporters from the Tass News Agency, to record the scene, and at 16:00 the two divisional commanders formally shook hands. The V Corps historian Forrest Pogue was present and recorded swapping his K rations for 'black bread, sardines, figs, cookies and vodka, which we undertook to drink in one gulp as they told us to'.

Later he chuckled when General Reinhardt, somewhat the worse for wear, 'tottered uneasily as he tried to get into a rowing shell [racing boat with oars], to be propelled across the Elbe by a tipsy Russian soldier who almost let us be swept downriver before beginning to row'.[36] The following day, 27 April, the two corps commanders, Huebner and Baklanov, met and sat down to an open-air feast with Russian musicians. Area security was provided jointly by Russian sabred-and-horsed cavalry and the mechanised US 102nd Cavalry, whose New Jersey Guardsmen admired the hardy little Steppe ponies of their opposite numbers.

Three days later, on 30 April, General Hodges flew from First Army headquarters, now relocated to Weimar, to meet his opposite number, Colonel General Zhadov of the Fifth Guards Army, at Graditz Castle, home to a 300-year-old stud farm. After an elaborate banquet, 'staged in an alcoholic haze of epic proportions', American largesse permitted Hodges to present Zhadov with a brand-new Jeep, while, in Soviet style, Hodges received an engraved Russian 7.62mm Tokarev pistol – the favourite weapon of the NKVD. The final meeting of opposite numbers occurred on 5 May, when Bradley journeyed from Twelfth Army Group at Verdun to meet Marshal Konev of the 1st Ukrainian Front. Bradley's staff noted, 'as usual, the Russians did their best to outdo the Americans in drinking and succeeded in doing so. Correspondents were flat on the floor before the ceremony had broken up at 16:30.'[37]

At all of these meetings, apart from spectacular vodka-drinking sessions initiated by the Russians and the exchange of gifts (Bradley received a Don stallion, Konev a Jeep, its tool compartments stuffed with American cigarettes) and medals, dispositions on maps were discussed. At the last Bradley offered Konev help in capturing Prague, which was 'declined with a friendly smile', and indicated Stalin's continued suspicion of the West. Elbe Day, 25 April, is an anniversary particularly observed in Eastern Europe and throughout Russia, although its significance has declined with the end of the Warsaw Pact and the Cold War. However, Stalin's anti-Western paranoia soon dominated his thinking, and post-war, many of the personalities and units associated with Torgau and other encounters with the Western armies were demoted, downgraded, or exiled to Siberia. They were 'infected', in the dictator's mind, by anti-Soviet imperialism and capitalism.

When I last visited Torgau, it was in the company of staff from the National World War Two Museum of New Orleans, Louisiana and their guests, who included those whose forebears had liberated the area in

1945. This pretty town, with its imposing Hartenfels Castle dating to 1544, brown bears resident in its dry moat, timber houses and pointed roofs, has changed little since the war. I climbed to the window from where Robertson waved his home-made flag. Eisenhower later requested to meet him and view it, on the spot promoting the young man to captain. One can sense the emotion of the moment, for on the western bank, adjacent to the new bridge spanning the Elbe, is a striking memorial to the East–West encounter by Avram Miletsky, a Red Army captain and architect, who had lost much of his own family in the war.

Unveiled in September 1945 and reflecting the pre-Cold War 'Spirit of the Elbe', the monument is far from the usual Soviet triumphalist style. At its crown are the lowered flags of the Soviet Union and America, with stacked rifles flanking a wreath, symbolising the end of hostilities. Opposite is an uglier, more recent East German version in concrete, featuring Communist soldiers liberating the oppressed of Germany, for on 1 July the whole region including Leipzig became part of the Russian occupation zone. It reads 'Glory to the Soviet People – Gratitude for our Deliverance', but typically for the former Communist German Democratic Republic, it fails to mention the Americans at all.[38]

(*Above*): Nuremberg fell on 20 April, Hitler's birthday. After a bloody four-day battle, it was taken by the 3rd and 45th US Divisions who are seen inspecting the Zeppelin Stadium, the huge arena to the city's south-east, which hosted pre-war Nazi rallies. (*Below*): After Nuremberg, river crossings over the Danube beckoned. Here, the 157th Infantry (a 45th Division outfit) cross in a DUKW with their 57mm anti-tank gun.

17

Southern Flank: Nuremberg and Augsburg

We left General Sandy Patch's three corps battling their way through southern Germany. Wade Haislip's XV Corps, having conquered Aschaffenburg, were on the left, adjoining Third Army. In the centre, Frank Milburn's men of XXI Corps were fighting their way through Würzburg and Schweinfurt, and Ted Brooks' VI, fresh from their adventures in Heidelberg, Heilbronn, Stuttgart and Ulm, were advancing with the French on the right. By mid-April there was no German defensive line as such, but Allied intelligence at every level detected a drift of men and resources into the south-east of the country.

Although Franco–American tensions had distracted Devers, his Sixth Army Group's new objective, using Patch's GIs to his left and de Lattre's Frenchmen on his right, was to halt the German withdrawal. It made sense for the more numerous Seventh Army to seize the eastern edge of this funnel through which the defenders were flowing towards the mountainous terrain of southern Bavaria and Austria. The prize Devers had in mind for Patch was Nürnberg (Nuremberg). As well as a military objective, with its road and railway network connecting all the main cities of the Fatherland – especially Munich and Berlin – to German minds, the city was the shrine of National Socialism.

To reach this Nazi altar, the 3rd, 44th and 45th Infantry and 14th Armored Divisions of Haislip's XV Corps, preceded by the Illinois National Guardsmen of the 106th Cavalry Group, manoeuvred from Schweinfurt via Bamberg round to the north of Nuremberg. As elsewhere, ten-foot-high barricades had been built across many roads, usually consisting of two separate walls of wooden telegraph poles or tree trunks. The inner void was filled with rubble – cobblestones, brick, whatever was to hand. Taking days to build according to Volkssturm specifications, these obstacles were bulletproof and appeared formidable. However, US formations had learned to put combat engineers in their vanguard, and the combination of engineers armed with power saws and Sherman dozer tanks meant these barriers rarely lasted more than ten minutes. Bob Lynch of the 3rd Division observed of them, 'The Germans spent weeks constructing these road blocks to halt our advance, but they were useless. For thirty-nine minutes we Americans would stand and scrutinize the obstruction and laugh. The next minute we would crush it.'[1]

Just forty miles away from the heart of National Socialism, Bamberg today appears as every German town and city would have done prior to Allied bombing. Some damage was done by field artillery, but it is a rare survivor of 1945. Spread across seven hills and packed with medieval architecture and narrow cobbled streets, and still in possession of its city walls, Bamberg contained nothing of military note and fell after a brief firefight. The two military hospitals were found to be packed with German and American wounded. Its last fifty defenders – the worse for wear on account of the schnapps with which they had armed themselves – lurked in the Old Town Hall, which sits on a small island in the middle of the Regnitz River, and capitulated to the Thunderbirds' 180th Infantry on 14 April.

With a long history of religious tolerance, the city's flirtations with National Socialism were more ambiguous than elsewhere, although equidistant from Schweinfurt to the west, Bayreuth to the east and Nuremberg to the south, and thus close to the Nazi core. Bamberg was for centuries the home of the aristocratic von Stauffenbergs, and its most famous son, Count Claus, author of the 20 July 1944 bomb plot, had joined the 17th Bavarian Cavalry Regiment, based in the local *Kaserne*. Renamed Warner Barracks in 1945, US forces only relinquished the site sixty-nine years later in 2014.[2]

The day after Bamberg surrendered, Erlangen, twenty-five miles south, fell without a fight. Oberstleutnant Werner Lorleberg surrendered the town against orders; later, he was found dead. Nazi radio claimed the World War One veteran had committed suicide through dishonour.

His friends insisted he had been murdered by diehard fanatics. Soon, Nuremberg's north-eastern suburbs came under attack. During 17–18 April, Rainbow GIs of the 222nd Infantry were sucked into the unexpectedly stiff fight for Fürth, a neighbouring city of 100,000 to the north-east of Nuremberg. They adjoin, but Fürth has forever asserted independence from its larger neighbour. Perhaps urged on by folk memories of the Thirty Years' War, when, like so many others, the settlement was destroyed, diehard Nazis in Fürth put up a fanatical resistance in response to a decree of 12 April that 'The city will be resisted brick by brick in a one-centimetre war. Fürth must never be declared a free city, but defended to the last metre.' Karl Holz, Gauleiter of the region and responsible for civil defence, demanded, 'Fighting for honour and freedom is never a hopeless thing. I am Reich Defence Commissioner, not Reich Submission Commissioner.'[3]

The Rainbow Division advanced under a heavy protective screen of artillery fire. 'All but the centre of Fürth had been heavily bombed because of a factory making fighter airplanes,' remembered Pete Hardy, a GI switchboard operator. This was the Bachmann-Blumenthal-Werke, recessed into the side of a hill and protected by heavy steel doors, where thousands of foreign workers assembled Messerschmitt-110 nightfighters. 'While the residents hunkered down in three huge concrete shelters, the slave workers had to stay outside, enduring the bombing. I recall seeing their dead bodies being used by the Germans for a footbridge over a little bitty river, and women snipers shooting at American soldiers. Death was just everywhere – terrible. You'd see horses and cattle all dead from artillery. I guess because you're so used to death in war, you try to keep it out of your mind. That's the only thing you can do because the war goes on,' he pondered. Fürth capitulated at around 11:00 on the 19th, as the battle for next-door Nuremberg reached its height.[4]

Master Sergeant Charles Senteney with the 144th Field Artillery Group, who supported XV Corps, remembered driving through the ruins of Fürth shortly after its fall, with its 'torn buildings and street car cables hanging down, when we found the 42nd's entire band, who were playing us through the town just like on parade. It made us feel good.'[5] It was a reminder that there were many ways to lift morale, and the timeless lure of military music has always been one of them. However, the fall of Bamberg, Erlangen and Fürth had left the door open to Nuremberg.

It was challenging terrain, lying in a broad valley veined with natural and artificial waterways and 'at the centre of a spiderweb of roads and railroads', but Nuremberg's capture was a political necessity and would be achieved by tactical envelopment.[6] The characterful medieval city had been an administrative centre of the Holy Roman Empire and had a long history of anti-Semitism, which made it a perfect anchor for Hitler's ideology and Goebbels' propaganda. Consulting nineteenth-century newspapers from Bavaria, Württemberg and Franconia proves that many towns and cities in this region had long been tainted by a rejection of their Jewish communities, who were more commonly excluded than persecuted. Such attitudes went unquestioned in many families and institutions, but only under the Nazis did this find political expression and lack of restraint, with awful consequences. Nuremberg's dominant political figure in the early days of Nazism had been the rabid 'Jew-baiter', Julius Streicher, editor of the notorious *Der Stürmer* newspaper, and known for striding through the streets with a bullwhip and inciting what became the Holocaust. Cast from the same mould was Gauleiter Holz, an ambitious and ruthless party functionary.

From 1923, Nuremberg had hosted fifteen years of pre-war rallies, which grew each year into mass gatherings of hundreds of thousands of the faithful, recorded on films distributed throughout Germany and the wider world. Most famous were the trio of documentaries made by Leni Riefenstahl, recording the *Reichsparteitage* (Reich Party Conventions) of 1933 (*Der Sieg des Glaubens* – Victory of Faith), 1934 (*Triumph des Willens* – Triumph of the Will) and 1935 (*Tag der Freiheit: Unsere Wehrmacht* – Day of Freedom: Our Armed Forces). Extracts from them usually amounted to the total knowledge of the wartime generation about Hitler and his Reich. Meanwhile, National Socialism brought an era of prosperity and prestige to the 900-year-old city, as tourists and journalists from all over the world visited the rallies, putting Nuremberg on the international stage – all of which was welcomed by residents.

In 1934, CBS journalist William Shirer wrote of 'tens of thousands of Swastika flags blotting out the Gothic beauties of the place, the faces of the old houses, the gabled roofs. The streets, hardly wider than alleys, are a sea of brown and black uniforms'.[7] This pre-war prominence led to twenty-six major air raids on the city, targeting not just the rally grounds but the railway marshalling yards and factories such as MAN-Diesel and Zündapp motorcycles in the southern outskirts. Easily the most destructive was Operation *Grayling*, the RAF raid of 2 January 1945, which caused 5,000 dead and injured, 100,000 homeless, and the devastation of around 120,000 dwellings. However, the sword was double-edged in that the attacker suffered as much as the attacked. *Grayling* cost Air Chief Marshal Sir Arthur Harris 108 aircraft, or 13 per cent of the total force committed, and 545 aircrew – more than had perished in the Battle of Britain – a rate which almost broke the back of his Bomber Command.[8]

While aerial bombing had dispersed some of the population, many more fled as XV Corps approached, reducing by half the number of its 400,000 pre-war inhabitants. In the first week of April many of those who stayed were given steel helmets, armbands and weapons. Some panicked as the reality struck home that they were expected to resist to the last bullet. Goebbels was broadcasting *Endsieg* – final victory – but the omens did not look good. Due to their unabashed embrace of Nazism from the earliest days, Nürnbergers knew they were unlikely to find any sympathy from the GIs. The defenders could rely on 150 anti-aircraft artillery pieces encircling the city, which – as at Schweinfurt – were instantly commandeered for use against ground troops. Apart from scattered Volksgrenadier regiments and battalions – the time of formed German divisions was long past – the defenders included the usual Volkssturm and Hitlerjugend, as well as 140 police officers and even city firemen who fought as infantry. Their numbers were supplemented by SS-Kampfgruppe Dirnagel, whom we met in Crailsheim, and Kampfgruppe Rienow, composed of Luftwaffe officer cadets, both named after their commanders.

There was also the grandly termed 38th 'Nibelungen' SS Panzergrenadier Division. Borrowing their title from a Wagner opera, the Nibelungen was hardly a division, but a group of Hitler Youth volunteers, the staff and students of the Bad Tölz SS-Junkerschule (Officers' School) and other fanatics totalling no more than 3,000 – two full-strength battalions, with five more considerably weaker. First alerted for duty on 7 April 1945 and given a name of which the Reichsführer would approve, the 38th was a typical Nazi sham. As with so many other new units scattered around Germany in the dying days, it made for an impressive map symbol pinned to the daily situation charts in Berlin; its grenadiers would fight like demons, but their numbers would be too few to make a difference.[9]

The plan was simple: Gauleiter Holz expected an attack from the west, but having completely enveloped the city, the men of the Marne Division instead closed in from the east with responsibility for everything north of the Pegnitz River, while the Thunderbirds took the terrain to its south and south-east. Rubble choked most areas as the two divisions felt their way through the outskirts of Nuremberg on the evening of 15 April, while the 106th Cavalry (south and south-east) and 14th Armored (south-west) screened fifteen miles out, to prevent a sudden German bolt for the mountains.[10] The 36th Texans cleared further south, beyond the two armoured formations, acting as a further backstop.

The same night, the clearly deranged Holz, gripped by the language of the now in-vogue Werewolves, vowed to Berlin that he would 'rather die fighting than abandon the most German of all cities. Even if we have no weapons, we will spring at the Americans and tear their throats open. No matter how superior our opponents' strength may be, eventually it will break.'[11] The first two flak batteries in Heroldsberg were taken by outfits from each division: Company 'L', 7th Infantry, led by Lieutenant Sherman Pratt, a first sergeant, only four months previously, the other by the 179th Infantry. Over the next thirty-six hours, some forty-five anti-aircraft guns were taken in hand-to-hand fights with their crews.

Having subdivided the city into sectors, at 07:00 on 16 April, both divisions plunged into the curious blend of medieval sandstone and Third Reich concrete that was modern Nuremberg. The 45th attacked with its three regimental combat teams abreast, the divisional artillery having just fired its millionth round in combat. In a report written after the war, Captain Paul L. Peterson, leading Company 'E', 180th Infantry, noted that of his four officers, fifteen NCOs and 115 privates, '95 per cent were replacements. The company had turned over eight times since landing in Sicily in 1943 in twenty-two months.' Yet, he observed,

'Morale was generally excellent. The individual soldier was proud of his unit. It was no trouble to keep a division patch on any man in the company.'[12]

Shermans of the two divisions' attached tank battalions, the 191st and 656th, ground their way through the debris, along with the two tank destroyer units, the 645th and 601st. Fortunately, both the latter had just replaced their M10s with brand-new M36s, which combined the Sherman's reliable engine, suspension and chassis, with a new turret mounting a 90mm gun – packing far more punch in urban combat. In an illustration of how manpower-intensive the city assault would become, by 09:45, Peterson's company had liberated a POW camp containing 13,000 inmates, including 250 Americans and 450 British, and 'before the company could be extricated, it was necessary to request other troops', he wrote.

Peterson had a brand-new second lieutenant whom he deployed into his first day of combat. In the middle of his first assault, the latter 'Suddenly stopped and stood looking at a very dead German soldier. The lieutenant then kept repeating "I killed him, I killed him."' Peterson was fortunately just behind and assisted the greenhorn with the advice that 'his place was now with the platoon, who were continuing to clear the position and his men should never be forgotten'. By the day's end, Company 'E' was sufficiently organised to be fed a hot meal while under fire; and had captured 175 Germans at a cost of one killed and seven wounded, but three of these were NCOs. Morale remained high, Peterson felt, because he constantly rotated sub-units, leaving none overexposed to danger for a prolonged period. He also made sure that his GIs remained properly fed, at least ensuring 'hamburger sandwiches were sent forward from the company kitchen'.[13]

On 17 April, the battle diary of the 645th Tank Destroyer Battalion noted the 'stiff resistance' met by all its sub-units: Company 'A' supporting the 157th Regiment fired seventy rounds of high explosive and armor piercing at houses and personnel. Company 'B' shot down a German 'Cub' [meaning a Fieseler-156 'Storch' reconnaissance plane], mounting three panzerfäuste under each wing.'[14] By this time, the attackers had fought their way through the rail marshalling yards and captured the city's airport in the north, and artillery was close enough to target the ancient centre with direct fire, destroying those buildings RAF's bombers had not already ruined. 'Now and then we could see a building with some outer walls gone, the inner floors still suspended in mid-air with furniture, rugs, and bedding intact, looking like a huge doll's house,' recalled George Wilson, a lieutenant with the 4th Division who passed through shortly afterwards. 'The rail yards were a mess of shattered boxcars, steam engines, and roundhouses. Heavy rails were bent like wires, some twisted into giant corkscrew spirals thirty or forty feet into the air. Wooden ties were splintered or burned, and even heavy steel supports under boxcars were melted so they sagged to the ground.'[15]

On this day, the battalion transport officer of the First Battalion, 15th Infantry – not a job that should have put him at the front – spotted and repelled a German ambush, then led a counter-attack that felled his opponents in droves. It brought the Marne Division's Lieutenant Frank Burke a Medal of Honor. Meanwhile the Thunderbirds' 180th Infantry acquired a former South African POW officer, Lieutenant James W. Low of Johannesburg, who spoke German, knew the city, and insisted on fighting with Company 'E', although told 'it was strictly forbidden, and he had surely carried his share of the burden by spending three years in a prison camp. On each of the four days fighting it was mentioned he should leave, but he always managed to spend "one more day" and rendered valuable service, especially after the loss of some leaders, constantly assisting wherever possible.'[16]

Gradually pushing back the defenders, who were using 'civilian men and boys to walk about, observe, and move on, after which accurate shellfire arrived on American positions,' by the end of the second day Captain Peterson's company had killed thirty-five and taken 130 prisoners, but at a cost of two officers and three privates killed, and seven enlisted men wounded. The drain on manpower, especially junior leaders – his friends – was intense. He thought later that it was the judicious use of tank support and phosphorus grenades which most subdued his opponents into surrendering, and prevented him from sustaining more losses, but the 'inability of certain officers and NCOs to read a map' was almost as life-threatening.

The third day of combat, 19 April, saw the remaining defenders withdraw inside the ancient citadel that was the heart of Charlemagne's

First Reich. Once the castle keep of the Holy Roman Emperor, where the imperial regalia and jewels were kept, it sported twenty-foot-thick masonry walls studded with battlements, turrets and watchtowers. While Captain Peterson's Thunderbird unit were withdrawn into battalion reserve, enabling them to lick their wounds, in the north of the city, leading his men of Company 'A', 15th Infantry, Captain Michael Daly had the busiest of days. He first dealt with a German sniper, then spotted and silenced a panzerfaust-equipped patrol lurking in ambush, before attacking and destroying three machine-gun nests in quick succession.

The one-man army 'performed the combat duties normally done by a full company', read some of the supporting paperwork that brought Daly a Medal of Honor, the second for the 15th Infantry. He almost failed to receive it, for the following day while leading his men over the turreted walls into the old city he was shot in the head by a sniper, only narrowly surviving. Daly had flunked West Point but went on to enlist as a private. His father, a regular army colonel and close friend of General Patch, persuaded the latter to take the younger Daly under his wing. Their confidence was not misplaced; in addition to a battlefield commission, Daly had already won three Silver Stars and a Bronze Star before receiving the ultimate accolade of an American warrior.[17]

The attackers used loudspeakers in efforts to bring about a surrender, but the urban slugfest turned medieval, as defenders poured fire from arrow slits and battlements onto the Blue and White Devils and the Thunderbirds. The siege only ended when bazookas were used instead of rifles, and self-propelled 155mm M12 guns from the 144th Field Artillery, which had also supported the street fighting in Aschaffenburg and Schweinfurt, began gouging out great chunks of the stonework and stout wooden gates. 'Twenty rounds of the hard-hitting big stuff were fired point-blank. But the old wall stood up under the terrific pounding with huge chips flying everywhere,' noted an artilleryman.[18] Snipers abounded, and when 120 Germans in the main *Laufer* tower surrendered, the remainder of the Marne Division rushed in through holes made by cannon-fire and snaked up scaling ladders, probing their way through the maze of narrow alleyways that made up the old town, towards the main square. This was the old Hauptmarkt, renamed the Adolf-Hitler-Platz on 25 March 1933.

Gauleiter Holz had already retreated to the Palmenhofbunker underneath the main police station and Gestapo HQ, with the Oberbürgermeister, Willy Liebel. The pair were ardent Nazis who loathed one another yet refused to concede. Echoing Berlin's last wireless exchanges with Friedrich Paulus in Stalingrad two years before, early on 20 April, Holz and his leader traded their own *Alice in Wonderland* compliments: 'My Führer: The final struggle for the town of the party rallies has begun. The soldiers are fighting bravely, and the population is proud and strong. I shall remain in this most German of all towns to fight and to die. In these hours, my heart beats more than ever in Love and Faith for the wonderful German Reich and its people. The National Socialist idea shall win and conquer all diabolic schemes. Greetings from the National Socialists of the *Gau Franconia* who are faithful to Germany. Holz.'

Hitler shot straight back: 'I wish to thank you for your exemplary conduct. You are thereby bolstering the spirit not only of the people in your own *Gau*, to whom you are such a familiar figure, but also of millions of Germans. Now starts that fervent struggle which recalls our original struggle for power. However great the enemy's superiority may be at the present moment, it will still crumble in the end – just as it has done before. I wish to show my appreciation and my sincere gratitude for your heroic actions by awarding you the Golden Cross of the German Order. Adolf Hitler.' He would never receive it. With the city about to fall, and the fighting all but over, both must have known they were lying to themselves and to each other, but in his last days Hitler sprinkled decorations and promotions around like confetti, hoping such trinkets would somehow turn the tide.[19]

Declining offers to surrender or escape, both Holz and Liebel, presumably still detesting one another, ended their own lives in the police station bunker on Hitler's birthday. Their offices – in a four-storey underground complex, accessed by heavy metal doors – came as a great surprise when they were discovered by Captain Peterson's Company 'E'. Back in action from battalion reserve, on this, their final day of combat, Peterson's men killed around forty-five defenders, at a cost of three of their own wounded, and netted 750 prisoners (for whom only two privates could be spared to act as guards).[20] Meanwhile, around them,

90 per cent of the *alte Stadt* (old town) had been reduced to ashes, piles of stone and brick dust.

The Holy Roman Emperor's jewels had earlier been hidden by the SS eighty feet below the citadel walls in a bricked-up alcove inside one of the city's bunkers. Among the treasures were the imperial crown, sword, orb and sceptre, and the Holy Lance, a sacred object associated with the crucifixion of Christ. In the unreal world of Nazi myth, creed and fascination with the past, there is evidence that these baubles mattered to Hitler, as they legitimised his links and succession to the First Reich. Bizarrely the Lance, an intensely Christian relic, was hidden by the most un-Christian of regimes in hope of its use as a symbol in an eventual return to power.[21]

The four-day battle had cost the lives of more than a thousand defenders, 371 civilians, while 17,000 marched into captivity. The Marne and Thunderbird Divisions buried 150 GIs before they moved on. Oberst Richard Wolf, the military commander, gave orders for the remaining garrison to surrender at 11:00, then fled, aware he had committed a crime punishable by death. Fortunately for him, it was GIs who apprehended him later that day, not the SS. At roughly the same hour, a scout from the Second Battalion, 7th Infantry, reached one side of the Adolf-Hitler-Platz and met some of their opposite numbers from the 30th Infantry. The former unit belonged to Lieutenant Colonel Jack Duncan, whom we first met at Utweiler, his battalion in pieces around him. It was fitting retribution.

Within hours, engineer bulldozers had cleared rubble from the Platz, then erected a flagpole at one end of it. That evening, General 'Iron Mike' O'Daniel briefly spoke to representative units of his division, commending their hard work in capturing the city and noting that 'the twilight of Nazism was approaching total blackout'. By then, the square had already been rechristened 'Iron Mike Place'. O'Daniel ordered it renamed the 'Roosevelt Place', in honour of the deceased president, though in time it has reverted to being the Hauptmarkt.

At this point, we will let the Cottonbalers' April 1945 daily combat narrative take over, for its wartime author had worked hard on his prose: 'It was thus that Hitler's Nuremberg, the pulse, and nerve centre of the Nazi Party, was entered by the 7th Infantry. Nuremberg was a gigantic ruin – hardly a house remained that was not destroyed or damaged by the heavy bombing and shelling. Most of the famous landmarks were erased. No longer would it be a cauldron of war and a center of distribution of Nazi Laws and Propaganda. At 18:30 hours in the now barren and deserted Adolf-Hitler-Plaza, where many a flaming torch burned in the Fuehrer's honour, to the lilting tune of the National Anthem, Colonel Heintges and a rifle platoon participated in an American flag raising ceremony.'[22]

The same venue played host to a review the next day when the victors commemorated their capture of Nuremberg with a ceremony. 'Representative units of XV Corps, including infantry, artillery, engineers, tanks, and tank destroyers, paraded before Generals Patch and Haislip. Fighter-bombers joined the review by covering the formation from the air.'[23] The final act in Nuremberg took place two days later at the Zeppelin Stadium, the huge arena to the city's south-east, designed by Hitler's architect, Albert Speer, to host the Nazi rallies.[24]

Built to resemble the huge Pergamon Altar, dating to the second century BC, Speer's creation was topped by a twenty-foot gilt, wreathed swastika. Hitler's rostrum was placed dead centre from where he reviewed his masses. As the original altar, over 100 feet wide and fifty tall, had been removed and reconstructed in its own Berlin museum in 1901, the architectural echo in Nuremberg was one many Germans would have recognised. On 22 April, 'in a snow, hail, rain and wind storm', GIs tore down the hated symbols of Fascism and unfurled the Stars and Stripes on the poles that lined the complex. Designed to hold 200,000 stormtroopers, a more modest 3,000 Marne and Thunderbird GIs stood at attention while several of their number received the Congressional Medal of Honor from General Patch.[25]

'As soon as the ceremony was over, Lieutenant Colonel Petherick, CO of the 10th Engineer Battalion, had been given permission to blow the hefty bronze *Hakenkreuz* from its plinth. He suggested anyone taking pictures would get a better view from across the stadium. I went with Father Ralph Smith, 3rd Divisional Senior Chaplain, to the other side,' remembered Engineer Corporal Joseph M. Borriello. His comrades ignited a 200-pound TNT charge, the offending insignia rose into the air wreathed in smoke, but 'unfortunately a piece of shrapnel flew across and hit Father Smith. Medics arrived immediately and I thought he had just been knocked down. I found out later Smitty was seriously injured, but he survived.'[26] It remains a striking newsreel image. Although the men destroying the swastika had once worn the same crooked cross symbol on their left shoulders, the Führer had had the final word.

At the end of the third week of April 1945, Jacob Devers had much to celebrate with the fall of big cities like Stuttgart and Nuremberg, and much of his army group poised to cross the River Danube. To his left, Patton's Third Army, which had been driving due east towards Prague and Dresden, had just been switched south-east to follow the Danube to meet the Russians, and take Salzburg. Accordingly, Devers – on the inside of this great wheeling movement – was manoeuvring his two armies round to the right, reorientating them from an eastwards axis to one facing south-east.

Military historians have long been besotted by Patton's reorienta-tion of a corps through ninety degrees in December 1944 during the Battle of the Bulge. Yet Devers redirected two whole armies – *five* corps (de Lattre's pair, plus Patch's three) – through a similar ninety degrees, at equally short notice, after the fall of Schweinfurt in mid-April 1945.

Such a fluid battlefield played to his strengths, as his G-3, Brigadier General Reuben Jenkins, opined. 'Devers was more adept at handling troops on the go, than in a stabilized situation. He really was a mobile fighting man.'[27] For the last five weeks of the war, he was constantly obliged to shift his corps and army boundaries, mostly to help de Lattre. Yet, Devers was also accommodating Patton's Third Army, which was essentially operating as part of Sixth Army Group, in his southwards lunge, though remaining under Bradley's command. Devers knew not to raise the issue of Third Army's subordination to him with either Bradley or Eisenhower, such was the anti-Devers mood in both headquarters, but it would have made much sense.

For Sixth Army Group, this change of axis reflected as much the pol-itical realities of the French carving out their own occupation zone – whatever Eisenhower and Devers thought about it – as the fear that their opponents were withdrawing into an Alpine *Festung*. Such a mountain fortress was calculated to possibly stretch from Bregenz in the west to

Salzburg in the east. Centred on Innsbruck, if true, militarily it would be almost impossible to winkle out determined defenders from this range of heights and valleys. The race was on to overtake the fleeing Germans and deny them an opportunity to set up and man final defensive lines in southern Bavaria and northern Austria.

The whole 'Final Redoubt' concept, encompassing the Bavarian Alps and Austrian Tyrol, and reaching as far south as the Brenner Pass and Bolzano in northern Italy, was assessed as being 150 by 100 miles, or 15,000 square miles, and would have contained enough infrastructure to sustain an army of over 100,000 and the local population for several years. We now know there was no serious planning or preparations made for any historic last stand. The concept appeared to have arisen from French and American intelligence misassumptions, in part fed by German prisoner interrogations. They in turn had been the victims of Nazi domestic propaganda, which suggested that all was in hand to continue the struggle from an *Alpenstellung* (Alpine position), as a way of reviving hope and raising morale. The drift of German formations towards Austria was simply units fleeing before their aggressors to the relatively safety of high ground.

Yet there was logic to the Allied deliberations, in that the region was the most ferociously National Socialist area of the Reich, and the terrain was in the defenders' favour. The Allies would no doubt have soon concluded this was another Wagnerian fairy story but for one reason. In December 1944, SHAEF had reached a similar understanding that the German war machine was at its last gasp, when the Ardennes winter campaign erupted. The combat indicators had been present but were missed at the time.[28] Allied intelligence at every level had lost face and was not going to be caught out again.

Although distanced from the oversights of Twelfth Army Group and the Ardennes, Sixth Army Group's Chief G-2 (Intelligence), Brigadier General Eugene Harrison, who had worked under Devers for two years and had his absolute trust, was inclined to dismiss the Alpenstellung as propaganda. Yet he was obliged to be wary. Thus, from February until April, the concept of a Final Redoubt was embraced by the entire Allied G-2 chain, and with nothing to lose, peddled as fact rather than possibility. Leaning heavily on the advice of Major General Kenneth

Strong, SHAEF's British Assistant Chief of Staff for Intelligence, who had worked for Eisenhower since March 1943 and whose counsel he greatly respected, the Supreme Commander felt he had to listen, and exercise extreme caution. Such fears had earlier reached the House of Commons, where the British parliamentarian Harold Nicolson noted concerns on 15 March 1945 that the Nazis 'may retire to their Alpine redoubt and seek in some way to stage a Götterdämmerung to prolong their own invincible legend. Others do not share this idea and believe there will be a series of large-scale capitulations. All of which boils down to the fact that the war may last till Christmas, but it may end by June. Nobody can tell.'[29]

Reichsleiter Martin Bormann, gatekeeper to the Führer by virtue of being his personal secretary, and thus regarded as the second most influential person in Germany, had indeed planned for the Nazi leadership and their staff to escape Berlin by air and fly down to Berchtesgaden. From there they would continue the war from the deep bunker network under the Obersalzburg complex, close to the east Bavarian–Austrian frontier. Some zealots shared the Goebbels vision of the propagandised Alpenstellung, but there were no defensive positions built, or supplies of ammunition, fuel, food, vehicles or anything else in place.

However, on 22 April, in the depressing aftermath of his fifty-sixth birthday, when Russian field artillery could be heard from the grounds of the Reichskanzlei, Hitler was brought news that a relief army had failed to break through to Soviet-encircled Berlin. Thereupon, the Führer exploded with all the pent-up rage he had been stifling, in fact ever since returning to Berlin on 16 January after overseeing the Ardennes campaign. He lashed out at everyone, never once acknowledging his own part in the drama. Then, his passion spent, he appeared to accept defeat and decided to remain in the Führerbunker.[30]

There is nothing in the job description of world leaders, or dictators, that requires them to live in underground bunkers. Neither Stalin nor Mussolini, for example, expressed this proclivity. In Hitler's case, it was a hangover from his troglodyte life in the trenches of the First World War. His Führerbunker was built fifty-five feet under the garden of the Old Reich Chancellery at 77, Wilhelmstrasse. It contained eighteen claustrophobic rooms and was fully self-sufficient, with its own air conditioning, water and electrical supply. With a small staff of aides and secretaries, cooks and chauffeurs, his intimate circle, including the Goebbels family, Eva Braun and his Alsatian, *Blondi*, had been waiting for the order to bolt for the Bavarian Alps.

Those in the Berlin headquarters noted, 'The Führer has collapsed; he considers further resistance useless, refuses to leave. All present (Keitel, Jodl, Bormann, Himmler, Goebbels, and the Grand Admiral [Dönitz] over the phone) have tried to sway the Führer. Everything was in vain. He now speaks of treason from all sides, of failure, corruption, and that the SS is now lying to him . . . the troops are not fighting, the roadblocks are opened and are not being defended . . . soon we will have no ammunition and gasoline. The Führer has given no orders, he only said the others should go wherever they please.'[31]

A week earlier, SHAEF's assessment had reached a similar conclusion, that 'From every viewpoint it is only a matter of time before the organized resistance in Hitlerite Germany collapses completely. Nothing can alter the inescapable fact that the opposition is on the verge of a defeat. Nothing now can rectify the mistakes of Hitler and his staff officers in order to prolong the war or even partially retrieve the situation. Their capabilities are in fact, nil. No steps he can take with the present means of conducting warfare are such that they will influence, or hardly delay, the outcome.'[32] This was tempered by the knowledge that even if the German military could not go over to the offence, the Allies could not afford to let up pressure: the Wehrmacht and SS would still punish any lack of professionalism. 'Always, you had to be at the very top of your game, any lapse, any gap, any unguarded pause, and you paid the price. The best analogy I can draw is fencing. No matter how good you are, you have an opponent who is always seeking to get past your defences,' remembered one junior staff officer.[33]

Eisenhower, rigidly fixed on destroying the German military machine, grew ever more concerned lest his opponents retreat into the Alpine regions where, even if they did not fight, it would be difficult to prevent them from dispersing. This played into SHAEF's additional concern. After 1918, the Kaiser's Army would claim it had not been defeated in the field but was 'stabbed in the back' by Bolshevik uprisings at home. Many in the Fatherland bought into this myth, aided by the sight of troops marching home with bands playing and banners flying after the Armistice. It was a cornerstone Nazi lie, although by November 1918 the *Kaiserreich* had been fought to a standstill. Eisenhower understood that Hitler's military machine had to be seen to be utterly defeated, disarmed and neutered by battle, so there could be no future claims they had not 'lost'.

Within Sixth Army Group, Monsabert's French II Corps was consolidating its hold around Stuttgart and the Swabian Jura mountains north of Ulm. Béthouart's I Corps was racing for the northern shores of Lake Constance, Bregenz and the Tyrol region of western Austria, trying to turn the flank of their fleeing foes. Next to them lay Brooks' VI Corps, preceded by two combat commands of the 10th Armored, with the 36th, 63rd, 100th and 103rd Divisions clinging to the hulls of their tanks or squeezed into any and every available vehicle. Hence the surreal sight of amphibious DUKWs making their way through the rural Bavarian pasturelands, as part of long columns of trucks, half-tracks and Jeeps struggling to keep up with the armour ahead. From General Brooks came the instruction, 'Push on and push hard. This is a pursuit, not an attack.'[34]

'Some of us were riding on tanks, some of us on trucks, anything that would move, and full speed ahead with lights on overnight,' recollected Frank J. Waldeck of the 103rd Division.[35] At up to speeds of 30mph, they were chasing the remnants of the German Nineteenth Army who had escaped from Stuttgart and fled across the Danube at Ulm, where the French left had met Brooks' right – though the two had collided for political rather than tactical reasons, as we have discovered. Brooks, meanwhile, had gained an extra division, the 101st Airborne, for the possibilities of using any Allied sky warriors in these days of fast-moving warfare were over. Many VI Corps units noted the discovery of the Luftwaffe, its aircraft camouflaged under treelines, parked by the roadsides, which they were using as makeshift runways.

On 26 April, McAuliffe's 103rd 'Cactus' Division entered Landsberg-am-Lech, taking the surrender of its thousand-strong Hungarian garrison, discovered by a single platoon. 'These guys had strange uniforms and didn't speak German. I was amazed to find we were even at war with Hungary. Could have fooled me,' observed Ohio-born Richard H. McCullough with the 409th Infantry. 'The guys were really worried we'd open fire, so had already stacked their rifles, with all the ammo separately in boxes. An ancient, supply sergeant-type showed us some heavy, leather-bound books and papers covered with signatures and stamps. They told him, now us, stuff like how many rifles and bayonets and field dressings and flashlamps they had issued, and how many spare horseshoes for their four horse-drawn field kitchens. Like a scene in a movie, their commander, flashing a sword and medals, I believe from Austrian Empire days, with a huge moustache to match, called his guys to attention, did an about-face, saluted us, and with tears running down his cheeks, surrendered.'[36]

Every loyal Nazi knew of the town, for Cell No. 7 of the local prison had accommodated Hitler in 1924 after his failed Munich putsch of the previous year. It was here that he wrote *Mein Kampf*. A visit to Landsberg, with its pretty bridge over the River Lech, cobbled square, walls and medieval gateways, was a near-obligatory pilgrimage for the pre-war Nazi Party faithful. Apart from snipers, there was little resistance, but the 411th Infantry's souvenir hunters were more than satisfied by the huge array of Nazi kitsch on display in the prison, and throughout the town. PFC Wendell H. Hall remembered going to 'have a look at Hitler's room. Just a plain unadorned downstairs cell, with a commemorative plaque, a cot, a washstand with a water jar and a porcelain wash basin on it. A large, framed photo of der Führer on one wall, and a first edition of *Mein Kampf* on another stand.' Echoing the common practice of the moment, he continued, 'Despite Eisenhower's instruction of *No Looting*, do you think that Private First Class Hall took even one of those terrific German officer caps? Our Colonel, Donovan P. Yuell, seized Hitler's flag, and added it to the regiment's trophies.'[37]

The charm of Landsberg contrasted greatly with the tragedy of eleven labour camps hidden in the Bavarian landscape around Kaufering, which began to be liberated by Seventh Army formations from 27 April. The US Army labelled them all as 'Landsberg', the nearest large town, forty miles west of Munich. The Germans knew them as 'Kaufering' sites, after the local railhead – emphasising the system's reliance on Deutsche Reichsbahn. The Kaufering camps, all between five and twenty miles from Landsberg, reflected a decision taken in March 1944 by the Luftwaffe, Air Ministry, commercial manufacturers and the Organisation

Todt, to establish bomb-proof production sites for the assembly of fighter aircraft. One result was Operation *Ringeltaube* (wood pigeon), giant bombproof concrete hangars, in which Messerschmitt-262 jets and other equipment were to be manufactured, free from Allied aerial interference.[38]

Construction of three huge structures around Kaufering began in June 1944 and eventually employed a 30,000-strong Jewish workforce, including 4,200 women and 850 children. Some of their accommodation sites were named in US Army reports for the nearest village; thus Hurlach, Obermeitingen, Seestall, Türkheim and Utting 'death camps' all refer to Kaufering sites. Most inmates came from Dachau, thirty-five miles to the west, but their inhumane living and working conditions resulted in the death of around half their number. With the hangars incomplete, prisoners in some Kaufering satellites were marched away by the SS as the Americans arrived, others were simply abandoned. For example, Kaufering IV – designated as the sick camp where prisoners too weak were sent to die – was freed by the 12th 'Hellcats' Armored Division with the 506th Parachute Infantry.[39]

Staff Sergeant T-5 Carold W. Bland was one of those 'Hellcats' who arrived that day. Serving with Company 'F' in the 92nd Cavalry Reconnaissance Squadron, he reckoned he was a tough veteran by April 1945, but Kaufering 'we could not handle. There's no way on earth you could exaggerate what happened there. *That* they didn't train us for.' In the following decades, Bland suffered nightmares and depression from the experience. 'No photograph can represent my memories because a photo only reveals so much. It can't enable you to smell, to hear. No photo has ever shown what the soldiers encountered when they walked through the camp gates.'[40]

However, a film-maker's approximation of the truth was captured in episode nine of *Band of Brothers*. 'The memory of the starved, dazed men,' remembered Major Richard Winters of the Second Battalion, 506th Parachute Infantry, 'who dropped their eyes and heads when we looked at them through the chain-link fence, in the same manner that a beaten, mistreated dog would cringe, leaves feelings that cannot be described and will never be forgotten. The impact of seeing those people behind that fence left me saying, only to myself, "Now I know why I am here!"'[41] He and the rest of Easy Company witnessed the adult population of nearby Hurlach, who disclaimed all knowledge of the site, report for gravedigging duties, at least giving the inmates dignity in death that had been denied them in life.

Charles P. Larson, a US Army doctor, examined 258 corpses at Kaufering IV, noting that 189 had died of typhus or starvation, eighty-six had been burned to death, seventeen had been shot outside the camp and eleven gunned down inside.[42] Sergeant Louis 'Lou' Vecchi with Company 'H' of the 506th observed, 'When we got there, the people were practically dead from starvation. I know there are people who say the Holocaust didn't happen, but that's bull. I saw it.'[43] His colleague Eugene 'Gene' Cook of Company 'A' recollected, 'I didn't even know what we were looking at. It took me a while to realize it was a pile of dead bodies. The prisoners came out of their quarters, emaciated, filthy and disoriented. It was awful, some walked around like zombies. Some were so feeble they couldn't even stand. That was a bad day, I never want to see anything like that again.'[44]

These thoughts were echoed by another Kaufering IV liberator, Staff Sergeant Jerry D. Salinger, a German-speaking Jew and D-Day veteran, whose job was to interrogate captured German soldiers. 'You never really get the smell of burning flesh out of your nose entirely, no matter how long you live,' he later told his daughter Margaret. Soon after, he checked himself into a psychiatric clinic in Nuremberg, his experience of Kaufering triggering a form of nervous breakdown. The future author of *Catcher in the Rye* later penned an autobiographical short story, which recorded Staff Sergeant X of the Twelfth Infantry Regiment, 4th Division (Salinger's unit), sitting on a bed, vomiting into a waste bucket, and feeling 'his mind dislodge itself and teeter, like insecure luggage on an overhead rack'.[45]

It is thought that 4,300 died at the various sites, and many more back at Dachau. All the barracks have now disappeared, save for a couple of accommodation blocks and a memorial at Kaufering VII outside Erpfting. The 10th Armored and 36th, 63rd and 103rd Infantry Divisions (all Seventh Army) participated in the liberation of the various camps, as did the 522nd Field Artillery Battalion, which consisted entirely of Japanese Americans. The latter found themselves freeing prisoners of the Nazis while their own families were interned back home.

Lieutenant Susumu Ito, later a Harvard Medical School professor, whose relatives were behind wire at Rohwer, Arkansas, recalled finding 5,000 prisoners marching through the countryside. 'They were heading south into Bavaria. It snowed a day or two after. There would be lumps in the snow. It was something we were totally unprepared for. It was really shocking to have these walking skeletons come by. And even worse to see them trying to salvage the food we threw away in garbage pits.'[46]

Norman Brody, a 'T-Patcher' with the 36th Texas Division, who had fought at Salerno, Cassino and in southern France, had 'vaguely heard that something was happening to Jews, but I didn't know what until we arrived at Landsberg. I couldn't believe what I saw. Human beings, or what used to be human beings, were lying in piles in the centre of the place. This experience made me more aware of my Jewishness.' John W. Malone, with the 103rd 'Cactus' Division, was severely wounded just hours after he left one of the Kaufering sites. He concluded, 'It was the ones who were alive that I felt most sorry for; the dead were dead. Those sights bothered me more than getting hurt.'[47]

Landsberg remains charming, a fairy-tale old town, were it not for the knowledge of its sinister recent past. Since 1945, the town's fathers have been at pains to find something other than the Holocaust and Hitler to commemorate. They have arrived at the happy solution of recalling that the singer-songwriter Johnny Cash was billeted here in the early 1950s when serving as a staff sergeant, monitoring Soviet radio signals for the US Air Force.

Brooks' GIs resumed their advance immediately after Landsburg, being ordered due south by one hundred miles to Innsbruck in Austria. This slowed their pace of march as the land turned mountainous, and in the Germans' favour. The roads twisted and double-backed, while craters, minefields, blown bridges and rockfalls all conspired to almost bring VI Corps to a halt. Eventually the 44th requested the supporting vehicles of the 10th Armored Division be removed from their front, as it was slowing them down. A few well-placed snipers, anti-tank guns and cleverly sited artillery held up units for hours; these were tasks best suited to infantry, not tanks. To add to Seventh Army's woes, the excessive terrain meant that elements of 44th Division ran out of fuel. Nevertheless, by 30 April the division had somehow managed to crawl over the border into what until 1938 had been Austria, or 'Ostmark' as the Nazis had renamed it.

In the centre of Seventh Army's advance on 22 April, the US 12th Armored, vanguard of Milburn's XXI Corps, reached Dillingen on the Danube. Captain William Riddell of the 43rd Tank Battalion had discovered – through finding the phone lines still worked and calling the Bürgermeister – that its two-lane, 600-foot concrete bridge remained intact, though wired for demolition. Dillingen resident Karl Baumann recollected the calm of a lazy Sunday morning, the Hitlerjugend Sunday roll call ending, when 'suddenly around midday a powerful blast shook the entire town. Almost immediately came the first rifle shots and the rattle of machine-guns. The Americans were here.'[48] While Lieutenant Ippolito's Company 'A' stormed the town, Captain Riddell led Sergeants J. Houston and Robert Welch across the bridge cutting wires to the explosives the mayor had told him about. They were the first three Americans to cross the famed waterway.

'Led by Lieutenant Charles J. Ippolito, the force swept into the town with guns blazing,' boasted *Beachhead News*, the Sixth Army Group's newspaper, 'routing more than 1,000 disorganized defenders and shooting up a retreating mechanized column.'[49] In Riddell's company was Sergeant Carl Erickson, last met gingerly crossing pontoons over the Rhine, who observed, 'We caught them by surprise.' Erickson recalled firing across the river while the 66th Armored Infantry Battalion followed Riddell onto the bridge and flowed across to the other side. *Hellcat News*, the division's newspaper, reported: 'Great Blow at Dillingen: It was at the Danube bridge at Dillingen that the 12th struck one of the great blows of the war by seizing the span, cutting wires to nine 500-pound aerial bombs and much dynamite, then pouring troops across to rob the enemy in the redoubt area of vitally needed time.' *Hellcat News* with much justification boasted the Dillingen bridgehead was second in importance only to Remagen.'[50]

'Surging on to the bridge,' continued the newspaper, 'the unit captured a handful of demolition men and drove other Nazis away with tank fire before the span could be blown.' Engineers of the 549th Engineer Light Pontoon Company, a unit of African Americans with white NCOs and officers, were on hand to remove the explosives, check for damage and throw across an additional pontoon treadway to speed up the advance. Attached to XXI Corps, they had been present throughout the Seventh Army's advance, bridging the Saar at Saarbrucken, the Main at Würzburg, as well as the Danube. The span at Dillingen was the only one left intact over the Danube, and the 549th swiftly erected a sign for their followers to read: 'You are crossing the beautiful blue Danube through the courtesy of the 12th Armored Division.'

German counter-attacks at Dillingen were incompetent and disorganised; one truckload of defenders perished when driving into their own minefield. The fanatical local commander, Leutnant Schneider, drowned while attempting to swim the Danube and detonate the bridge charges by hand. The Luftwaffe failed to destroy the structure, losing six aircraft on 23 April, and three more the following day to the anti-aircraft weapons of the 441st (borrowed from the Marne Division) and 572nd Anti-Aircraft Artillery Battalions. Both units contained four batteries of eight half-tracks with 37mm and 0.5-inch guns.

The presence of sixty-four gun-crews around the bridge was an indication of its importance. A GI casualty of the second air raid was Texan Corporal Clarence J. Miculka with Battery 'C' of the 441st, whose vehicle was attacked by two Messerschmitts in a strafing run. Engaged in a deadly duel, Miculka brought down one with his 37mm cannon, but had himself been hit and his half-track riddled with shrapnel. In the exchange, his right leg was severed, and he bled to death minutes later. A rare victim of a German fighter managing to hit a 'flak-wagon', killing the gunner at his post, Miculka was later awarded a posthumous Distinguished Service Cross. The 572nd, a 12th Armored Division outfit, also lost vehicles and personnel in the second raid, indicating the potency, when it had fuel, of the Luftwaffe – and despite the terrific air defence concentration.[51]

Nine miles downriver, the 45th Division crossed the Danube at Marxheim, while seventeen miles upriver, midway between Dillingen and Ulm, the 63rd Infantry Division bounced the waterline at Günzburg. The Thunderbirds of the 45th began their journey over at 03:00 in dozens of small assault boats, as at the Rhine, their engines humming like a swarm of mosquitoes. In the lead was Company 'B' of the 179th Infantry, under Captain William Robertson and his executive officer, Lieutenant Ira Palm; they had crossed the Rhine together and were firm friends. To supplement their numbers, they had picked up a young Polish volunteer along the way. He begged them to let him fight the Germans and at this stage, because of casualties and the shortage of replacements, all units were low on numbers, and the Pole was given a set of combat gear, olive drabs and a rifle.

Opposite Marxheim, the defenders withheld their fire until the Thunderbirds' assault boats grounded on the far side. First out was Robertson, who almost immediately was felled by a fatal sniper's shot. There was no further firing and shortly afterwards a gaggle of Germans surrendered. Palm ordered an NCO to inspect the Germans' rifles to see who had fired the single shot that killed his friend. Sniffing the gun barrels for the tell-tale scent of burnt powder, the sergeant picked out the offender. Palm nodded towards the young Pole, who ordered the German into the river. Seconds later, the sniper lay in the shallows, his body, dancing in the current, had taken all eight rounds from a single clip of the Pole's Garand M1 rifle.[52]

Meanwhile, the 12th Armored, 63rd and 3rd Infantry Divisions – the last temporarily under Milburn's XXI Corps – pressed on towards Augsburg, thirty miles distant. Upriver from Landsburg, it is Germany's third-oldest city, founded in 15 BC and named after the Roman Emperor Augustus. It sits on the Lech, at the confluence of two other Alpine rivers, and dominates routes into Italy. As an Imperial Free City of the Holy Roman Empire, Augsburg grew wealthy from passing trade, became a centre of rococo architecture and culture – it was where Mozart's father had been born – industrialised early, and by the 1930s was the head-quarters of the Messerschmitt-Aerowerke corporation, several associated airfields and three military barracks.

With the Organisation Todt constructing underground facilities in the nearby hills, and the Dynamit powder factory also employing large numbers, the city's population had swelled to 200,000 by 1945. Throughout the United Kingdom, due to aerial bombing the British had long since learned to disperse their manufacturing, but the Germans only followed suit once the Allied air campaign began to bite, and there were still many assembly plants in the area. Three heavy air raids had already destroyed 25 per cent of the city and killed several hundred, with forced labourers summoned to clear up the mess with their bare hands. Few city dwellers had fled, as the surrounding geography largely restricted any natural direction of travel.

Both sides squared up for a vicious fight, but as XXI Corps neared, a local resistance movement, led by Georg Achatz, Franz Hesse and Dr Rudolf Lang, senior physician at the city's main hospital, sprang into action. On 27 April, they contacted the advancing Marne Division in the name of the self-styled Freedom Party of Augsburg, offering to assist in surrendering the city. They had also approached Bürgermeister Josef Mayer who was not unsympathetic to saving his city and its inhabitants, although the military commander, Generalmajor Franz Fehn, remained deaf to the idea. The message was reinforced by XXI Corps Psychological Operations (Psyops) troops who arranged for Augsburg to be leaflet-bombed. The text read: 'Soldiers and civilians of the city of Augsburg! Large numbers of allied troops are on their way and threaten your city with total annihilation. They are ready to blanket you with thousands of tons of steel. Save your city and its inhabitants from total devastation! As a sign of acceptance, hoist white flags on every building. Every member of the Wehrmacht must leave the city limits. Augsburg will not be destroyed if these proofs of acceptance are given: No German soldiers and no weapons can be allowed to remain. Save your old city and its inhabitants from the rain of steel which threatens to destroy Augsburg!'[53]

The psychological intimidation largely worked, and by the morning of 28 April, anti-tank guns and roadblocks were found abandoned, and the defenders had shrunk in numbers from one thousand to around eighty. Although a substantial SS detachment lurked ten miles to the south, they were unaware of the change of heart. Fearing a ruse, the Marne Division's Major John O'Connell, commander of the Third Battalion, 15th Infantry, and a strong patrol, accompanied Achatz, Hesse and Lang to Fehn's headquarters in the main Riedingerbunker (air-raid shelter) to negotiate a surrender. The Generalmajor could see no sense in Hitler's 'Nero Decree' of 19 March and had refused to sanction demolishing bridges and over-passes, also ordering hundreds of tons of military rations distributed to Augsburg's civilian population. Yet Fehn, like so many, tried to appease both sides. Considering his humanitarian duty to the city and its inhabitants done, 'being of the old school with forty-one years of military service', he then played for time and tried to contact the SS.[54]

To the south, the Luftwaffe airbase of Lechfeld, home to a swarm of Messerschmitt-262 jet fighters, fell at the same time, removing further threat of the strafing raids that many American convoys in the vicinity had received. This was from where Deputy Führer Rudolf Hess had flown to Scotland in his bizarre May 1941 peace bid. Almost exactly four years later, Company 'A' of the US 70th Tank Battalion, supporting the 4th Infantry Division, celebrated 'the capture of eighty grounded aircraft, twelve anti-aircraft guns, 362 prisoners of war and innumerable vehicles' at Fliegerhorst Lechfeld.

Back in Augsburg's central air-raid shelter, O'Connell immediately sensed Fehn's duplicity and seized both the general's telephone and pistol, arresting him. There was a loud retort that echoed through the concrete rooms as the deputy Bürgermeister standing at Fehn's side shot himself, but soon white flags were seen everywhere and fluttering from the Abbey Church of St Ulrich and St Afra, the highest point in the city.[55] Fehn was hastily relieved of anything with which he could commit suicide, and packed off to XXI Corps' POW cage. Local teenager Hermann Winter noted in his diary seeing his 'neighbours hastily incinerating their paintings and busts of Hitler, party badges, medals, and flags. Also, jewellery and other precious items are buried in the garden. We are afraid of looting, especially by the former forced labourers.' Ten days before final victory, Augsburg, where all feared another bloodbath, fell without a shot being fired.[56]

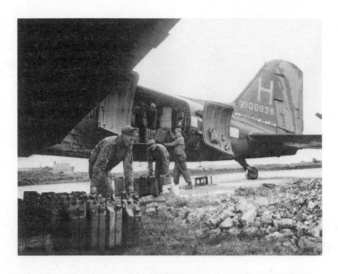

(*Above*): It was Douglas C-47 transport aircraft, each capable of carrying over 500 gallons of fuel in jerrycans, as here, that enabled all US formations to range far into Germany. (*Below*): On 30 April, elements of the 42nd and 45th Infantry Divisions (XV Corps) liberated Dachau then fought their way into Munich, ten miles south. Here GIs exhibit a souvenir of the occasion, a road sign announcing Munich as the Hauptstadt der Bewegung – the Capital of the Movement.

18

'The bloody dog is dead.'

Like a magnet, München (Munich) now drew Patch's Seventh Army towards its towers and spires. It was the city most entwined with the Nazi story, even more than Nuremberg. In May 1913, Hitler had fled there to avoid arrest for evading military service in his native Austria. The next year, on 2 August, now enthused with a cause, he was photographed in the city's central Odeonsplatz welcoming the declaration of war, shortly afterwards enlisting in the 16th Bavarian Reserve Infantry Regiment of King Ludwig III's Royal Army.

It was also a city of coups. In April 1919, Munich had witnessed the proclamation of the Bavarian Soviet Republic, and its brutal suppression by the army and *Freikorps* a month later, which saw the deaths of over a thousand Communists and the arrest of as many more. This backlash led to the formation of many small right-wing political parties, and on 12 September 1919, in a beer hall, Hitler attended a meeting of one of them – the German Workers' Party – whose membership could be counted on a couple of hands.

On 8 November 1923, the city witnessed another attempted coup, this time by Hitler and the restyled National Socialist German Workers' Party (NSDAP), who tried to seize power by marching from the Odeonsplatz, but their putsch failed, defeated by the city police in a hail of gunfire. Hence the Führer's eventual detention in Landsberg's prison. Many of his supporters were by then in rudimentary uniforms, having effortlessly morphed from already right-wing, anti-Communist *Freikorps* units into SA (*Sturmabteilung*, or Storm detachment) gangs, the Nazi brownshirt brigades who specialised in street brawls. Additionally,

Hitler had his own bodyguard and security service, only a few dozen strong, who wore black shirts, the *Schutzstaffel* (protection squad) – the future SS. The 1923 putsch also gave the Nazis their most venerated object – the *Blutfahne* or 'blood banner', allegedly splashed with the blood of its sixteen martyrs, those who fell in the failed coup. Thereafter kept in Munich, the flag was brought out for display at meetings, parades, and rallies of the faithful. Like a medieval saint's relic, oaths of loyalty were sworn on it, and one function of the nascent SS was to guard it.

Never comfortable in Berlin with its Prussians, plutocrats and swarms of 'red' workers, Munich was Hitler's and the Nazi Party's home, and der Hauptstadt der Bewegung – the Capital of the Movement. In the 1920s, a small local journal, the *Münchener Beobachter* (Munich Observer), was taken over by the NSDAP, becoming the party's daily organ, and retitled the *Völkischer Beobachter* (People's Observer). Although its national circulation rose to around 2 million copies daily, it remained based at 11–17, Thierschstrasse, in Munich. Additionally, the city bore the stain of the September 1938 Accords, which – with the connivance of Britain, France and Italy – dismembered Czechoslovakia and put Europe on the road to war.

Munich was also a natural military target, the home of Bayerische Motoren Werke (BMW) from 1922, making aero engines, motorcycles, vehicles and, later, aircraft. Another revered Munich corporation, Krauss-Maffei, manufactured locomotives, trolleybuses, buses and half-track artillery tractors. Lodenfrey turned out huge volumes of Wehrmacht uniforms, while the city housed one of the largest rail centres in the Reich. Without its fiercely nationalistic residents, and their right-wing nostalgia for the old Catholic monarchy, their xenophobia and hatred of Communism, there would have been no Nazi Party – and no Hitler. Although hit by seventy-four air raids during the war, damaging 50 per cent of the wider metropolis and 90 per cent of its centre, rendering 300,000 homeless, Munich had to be taken rather than bypassed. This was the only way to forever extinguish the dying embers of National Socialism.

The prize of capturing this massive urban area fell to Haislip's XV Corps, on Patch's left flank. The 42nd Rainbow Division, which had fought its way through Fürth then followed the 3rd and 45th Infantry Divisions through Nuremberg, was transferred into XV Corps on 25 April, adding more muscle for the assault on Munich. Side by side, Rainbow and Thunderbird GIs had then raced south to the Danube, crossing at Donauwörth on 27 April. Due to its ancient importance at a junction of two rivers, and as a crossing place over the Danube, Donauwörth had been much fought over during the Thirty Years' War, by Marlborough in 1704, and by Napoleon in 1805, and its railway yards had been devastated by US bombers on 11 April 1945. 'It took a vicious six-hour battle by the Rainbowmen,' using the language of the day, 'to disinfect Donauwörth of its SS defenders, house by house,' of whom only sixteen out of seven hundred surrendered.[1]

This gritty disinfection was undertaken by a combined arms task force led by Lieutenant Colonel Downard, comprising the 27th Tank battalion, two of Rainbow infantry, plus engineers and tank destroyers, whose swift advance on tracks caught the Germans by surprise; they had been expecting a slower infantry assault. However, the SS were sufficiently organised to blow all the bridges in the vicinity before Downard's men could reach them. The arrestingly low number of prisoners was due to a combination of loyal Nazis fighting to the end (and the fact that they had no exit with the crossings destroyed), and GIs refusing to take prisoners, for this was the moment when word was spreading of the discovery of the first concentration camps.[2]

After their first combat action, Downard's 27th Tank Battalion then held the riverbanks, while assault craft, engineer pontoons and rafts shuttled both the 42nd and 45th Divisions to the far shores. Thunderbird Sergeant Dan Dougherty with Company 'C', 157th Infantry, wrote home, 'Well, here I am humming the Blue Danube Waltz while looking at the actual river. Not supposed to tell you where I am, but our lieutenant never reads our mail . . . While crossing the river, the engine conked out in our DUKW, and we quite literally became a sitting duck as we floated deeper into hostile territory on the swiftly flowing Danube. The engineer eventually restarted the engine and got us across, but we had coasted quite aways downstream and were lucky not to have encountered German troops.'[3]

A certain amount of musical chairs followed, shuffling formations into place for the task ahead. The 3rd Division, whom we saw temporarily seconded to Milburn's XXI Corps, raced from the west, 'barrelling down the big highway [autobahn] direct from Augsburg'. As Patton's Third Army had moved into Nuremberg immediately behind XV Corps, the 14th Armored Division, which for so long had led Haislip's advance on Patch's extreme left, now fell into Third Army's area. Thus, they reverted to Patton's control, to be replaced by Major General Orlando Ward's 20th Armored, who had arrived in continental Europe only in February and been training under the US Fifteenth Army before entering combat on 24 April.

At various times, the 4th, 36th, 44th and 103rd Infantry, 101st Airborne and 10th Armored had all been designated SHAEF reserve formations, overseen by Fifteenth Army, with predicted future roles of 'occupation duties' – which none welcomed. During March and April, all had trickled into Seventh Army, giving it 'greater hitting power and greater depth for its offensive, becoming less of an adjunct to Third Army and freer to strike out independently in its own zone'.[4] This was how they saw themselves in the final months. Long overshadowed by their illustrious neighbour, whose leader had once commanded them in Sicily, only in the last three weeks did the Seventh attain the force density General Sandy Patch had long requested.

Until October 1944, when the 20th Armored was alerted for overseas duty, its mission had been to train soldiers as individual replacements for armored units, but such was the casualty rate that they found themselves shipped into theatre as a formed unit. It was their 27th Tank Battalion that had done so well in seizing crossing places at Donauwörth. Among their complement of GIs was Staff Sergeant 'Sparky' Schulz, serving with Company 'B', 8th Armored Infantry Battalion, who rode in a half-track with his lifelong nickname painted on the door. Although his unit would serve in combat for less than two weeks before the war's end, the sights that Charles M. Schulz encountered gave the future creator of *Peanuts*, Charlie Brown and Snoopy much to ponder.

To give them more 'muscle' in the forthcoming fight for Munich, the 20th Armored integrated with the two infantry divisions; their CCB operated with the 45th Infantry Division as Task Force 20, and other elements with the 42nd. The Marne Division, likewise, formed Task Force

Horton, a similar all-arms grouping, utilising part of the 601st Tank Destroyer and 756th Tank Battalions, which gave them 'tremendous firepower and powerful hitting force'.[5] Ever since D-Day, the Allies had evolved continuously, learning to make the best use of their resources to better their opponents, a process which continued right up to the final days.

All these units needed fuel. Colonel Adriel N. Williams' 436th Troop Carrier Group flew in 400,000 gallons for the four attacking divisions; this may sound a lot, but their consumption rates were prodigious. Travelling a notional fifty miles in a 24-hour period, 14,037-strong US infantry divisions (with a bayonet strength of 9,204) were calculated to use 5,000 gallons per day, with 25,000 gallons a day for armoured divisions. The latter, at 12,697 men, assumed eight US gallons per wheeled vehicle, twenty-four for its 450 half-tracks and fifty-two for its 350 fully tracked light and medium tanks, self-propelled guns and recovery vehicles. Though fuel consumption varied enormously with usage, Shermans generally used between one and two gallons per mile, a rate that was often tripled by the heavier German tanks.[6]

Within Munich, the most Nazi of German cities, lay a nest of ardent, hard-core anti-Nazis. In June 1942, a group of university students and professors formed the Weisse Rose (White Rose) resistance movement, which indulged in an anonymous leaflet and graffiti campaign opposing the regime. Given that they staged their activities in the heart of the wasp's nest, their bravery was beyond compare – and their fate inevitable. Three, including brother and sister Hans and Sophie Scholl, were arrested in February 1943, immediately found guilty and guillotined four days later. Twenty others were sentenced at other hearings. Yet, even in 1945, sceptics of the benefits of National Socialism remained in the city.

Aware that an anti-Nazi movement had helped liberate Augsburg, Patch's chief of staff, Major General 'Doc' White, agreed to receive a deputation from the well-organised FAB – Freiheitsaktion Bayern (Freedom Action Bavaria) resistance group. White cautioned his advancing formations to let the FAB, if possible, surrender their city. The FAB captured the Bavarian governor, Ritter von Epp, a much-bemedalled World War One hero who had led the *Freikorps* revolt against the Munich Soviet back in 1919. FAB activists also assassinated several Nazi elders and seized the city's radio station. From there, they broadcast a call to arms and code words which brought their supporters onto the streets.

Journalist Ursula von Kardorff heard the coup in progress over the airwaves. 'There seems to have been a revolution in Munich,' she noted. 'They now have two [wireless] stations. On one, a captain issues stirring orders, and then from time to time the voice of the Gauleiter is heard.' Three days earlier, as we saw, the Württemberg village to which she had fled was occupied by the French, and she concluded, 'we're damned lucky to be in Allied hands'.[7] However, the Munich plotters had moved too soon. The Gauleiter, Paul Geisler, eluded his assailants, led a loyal-ist fight back, and the coup failed. Yet some of the movement, wearing FAB armbands, frustrated the sabotage of Munich's bridges, and attack-ing GIs reported 'the putschists were of considerable help'.[8]

Timing was everything. Some settlements ran up white flags and surrendered as the GIs appeared. Others were premature. Eleven days before the war's end, on 27 April, aware the Americans were closing in, at Penzberg, twenty miles to the south, a group led by the town's pre-war Bürgermeister tried to save their settlement, halting the sabotage of local infrastructure, and throwing the Nazi mayor out of his office. White sheets and towels soon hung from every balcony to show the advancing Americans there would be no resistance. Alas, a group of diehards, from the nearby SS officer school at Bad Tölz, arrived and shot the former Bürgermeister and six others. The 36th Texas Division found another nine, including two women, hanging from the town hall balcony and nearby trees. Maria Wallertshauser recalled the moment the SS departed and finding her father: 'I counted twenty-six shots in his breast. All he wanted to do was to stop the destruction of our town when we knew the war would end in a few days.'[9]

The following day, Father Josef Grimm, the Catholic priest of Götting (thirty miles south-west of Munich), and local teacher Georg Hangl, heard the FAB broadcast, lowered the swastika from the village church and replaced it with the old white-and-blue flag of Bavaria. Within the day, three Belgian SS NCOs stationed in the village had executed the pair.[10] This was the rationale behind 7th Army's alliance with the FAB in Munich: it was obvious that the European war would very soon end.

Few wanted to run the risk of being one of the last to die, hence the idea of giving Munich's surrender a sporting chance. Communications in the Fatherland still worked, and residents were aware of their range of options, from the contrasting fates of Nuremberg and Augsburg.

In their race to capture the capital of Bavaria, Patch's Seventh Army unexpectedly started to find satellites of the Reich's first concentration camp, twelve miles to the north-west. Dachau was not a name that had meant anything to the US Army. To the British, it was a Renaissance town with a castle, home to many Bavarian painters, and the birthplace of Ritter von Thoma, the first German general captured in battle, at Alamein in 1942. By contrast, the average German reacted with excessive and immediate fear at any mention of the name. It had first opened its gates on 22 March 1933, intended as the new regime's model detention centre for political prisoners. By the time its murderous business had ceased, 4,421 days later, nearly 200,000 had passed through the gates, of whom at least 22 per cent had died. Dachau was the prototype of the whole detention camp network. Many aspects of its design and activities were copied elsewhere; it was first to display the cynical sign above its entrance reading *Arbeit macht frei* ('Work will make you free'), widely imitated at other sites.

Seventh Army knew none of this, but the horrors of distant Ohrdruf and Buchenwald, 220 miles from Dachau, had focused American minds on the conditions that might be found in the Reich's first *Konzentration-slager*. Sixth Army Group intelligence knew of its existence, for in its early years, Dachau's first purpose as a prison for detaining Communist and Social Democrat politicians and activists was widely publicised. Those who were suitably submissive were indeed released, but from the late 1930s, the Jewish community and others the Reich desired off its streets were interned, without prospect of release, and eventually murdered. Haislip's XV Corps was directed to form a special 'Dachau affairs group' from members of its G-5 (civil affairs) section with others from G-4 responsible for sanitation, food and medical support, plus two batteries of the 601st Field Artillery Battalion to act as guards. Its chief, Colonel Kenneth E. Strong, anticipated his group might find 'an unknown number of prisoners, reports vary from 12,000 to 30,000. Conditions will probably be bad, insofar as food, health and sanitation are concerned,

[with] danger from typhus and other diseases.'[11] The wide range of XV Corps' estimate of Dachau's occupants illustrated how little they understood of its murderous activities.

From 1943, many Dachau inmates had been farmed out to its 123 sub-camps, where huge numbers, usually working in mines, and armaments factories, expired through cruelty and neglect. Their overseers were encouraged to be brutal, with fresh inmates exchanged for the dead on a one-for-one basis. In the sub-camp at Allach, a north-west suburb of Munich, GIs discovered twenty-three nationalities of Jews amounting to 10,000 prisoners, a tenth of whom were women, repairing BMW aircraft engines or manufacturing porcelain for SS mess halls. Other sites, all containing starving inmates in a pitiful state, were also freed by the 4th and 99th Infantry, and 12th and 14th Armoured Divisions, with no hint that more lay ahead.[12]

Just before the Americans arrived at the main site of Dachau, the SS managed to spirit 7,000 souls away on a march southwards, from which a mere tenth survived. On 29 April elements of both the 157th Infantry (45th Division) and 222nd Infantry (42nd Division) simultaneously arrived at the camp. None had any inkling of what they would discover. 'I went away a twenty-year-old boy and came home four years later a forty-year-old,' explained Captain Maurice Paper, a US Army interpreter. All he had been told was to find a prison full of typhus in a wood ten miles outside Munich. 'I didn't know what I was going to face. We thought they were internment camps. When I saw it, this completely changed my life. I was very affected by it.'[13] 'We'd been to Anzio, Sicily, Salerno, southern France, the Battle of the Bulge, but we'd never, ever, seen anything like this,' said Staff Sergeant Edward Fitzgerald, of the 157th Infantry. 'We were a combat unit. Our men cried. If we'd known anything like this was going on, the war would have ended six months earlier.'[14]

As a prelude to the Hell all were about to encounter, a train of the dead – eventually counted as 2,310 – still in their freight cars and yet to be unloaded, lay adjacent to the front gates. Most had died of starvation and neglect, but some had perished en route from a strafing run by Allied aircraft, attacking what appeared to be a military transport. After all, why would the Reich waste valuable resources in its dying days shuttling civilian detainees around? The 42nd Division was accompanied by Marguerite Higgins and other correspondents who made the camp front-page news across the world. Several photographs exist of the moment of freedom, and of the unauthorised execution of several dozen of the SS guard force, both by GIs and the prisoners themselves.[15] Ironically, most of the long-term guard force, who had committed most of the crimes, had departed to shepherd their prisoners on death marches elsewhere. Those who bore the brunt of the GIs' anger had only been there a few days.

The veteran war reporter Martha Gellhorn later noted, 'Behind one pile of dead lay the clothed healthy bodies of the German soldiers who had been found in this camp. And for the first time anywhere one could look at a dead man with gladness.'[16] Beyond the death train, bewildered GIs were confronted by more than 30,000 inmates, of whom one-third were near death. Many were too far gone for the Americans to help. The 2,000 on the train, together with 7,000 prisoners evacuated in a forced march on 26 April, and the 30,000 living, far exceeded the '12–30,000' inmates anticipated by XV Corps.

As Rabbi Eli A. Bohnen, chaplain with the 42nd Division, later wrote to his wife of the day, 'Nothing you can put in words would adequately describe what I saw there. The human mind refuses to believe what the eyes see. All the stories of Nazi horrors are underestimated rather than exaggerated. We saw freight cars with bodies in them. The people had been transported from one camp to another, and it had taken about a month for the train to make the trip. In all that time they had not been fed. They were lying in grotesque positions, just as they had died. Many were naked, others in thin clothing. But all were horrible to see.'

Bohnen, not unaccustomed to death, continued, 'We entered the camp itself and saw the living. Many of them looked worse than the dead. They cried as they saw us. They were emaciated, diseased, beaten, miserable caricatures of human beings. I shall never forget what I saw, and in my nightmares the scenes recur. When I got back, I couldn't eat, and I couldn't even muster up enough energy to write you. No possible punishment would ever repay the ones who were responsible.'[17]

His assistant, Eli Heimberg, recalled, 'I had heard of concentration camps but thought they would be similar to the internment camps the United States had to incarcerate Japanese civilians. I never expected to see what we saw at Dachau. Before we crossed the moat leading into the camp, we encountered a stench that permeated the air. As we entered, we saw pyramids of clothing and shoes piled fifteen-feet high – the victims' belongings. When we turned around the corner, we saw opened railroad box cars with people who had perished. When we entered, we saw emaciated people whose skin was so close to their bones, it looked as if silk stockings were pulled over skeletons. We stood there for a moment, unsuccessfully trying to control our emotions as the victims, who were able to, surged forward to kiss our feet and hug our hands. We took their names and messages to send to their families who were in the United States. I wept unashamedly.'[18]

Born in Poland, Sergeant Morris Eisenstein grew up in Chicago. 'I wanted to prove a Jew can fight; that's what motivated me.' He arrived at Dachau with the Rainbow Division. 'What struck me was the bleakness of everything and the grotesque uniforms of the survivors milling around. That's when I saw a little Jewish fellow in a corner weeping and wailing. I told him, "I am an American Jewish soldier!" I had a pile of money in my pocket captured from the SS two days before, about 15–20,000 marks in a large wad and I handed it to him. He grabbed my hand and said in Yiddish: "I have nothing to give you but my yellow Jewish star." I never heard from him again. But I still have the yellow star. How did my comrades feel about what they saw? The truth was, they were more upset than I was. They couldn't believe it. Some of those guys broke down.'[19]

Martha Gellhorn arrived at Dachau on 7 May, nine days after its liberation, but before the dead had been removed: the focus had been on saving the living. Hardened to conflict, she had covered the Spanish Civil War with Ernest Hemingway, whom she married in 1940 and divorced five years later. In her 23 June piece for *Collier's* magazine she observed, 'Behind the barbed wire and electric fence, the skeletons sat in the sun and searched themselves for lice. They have no age and no faces; they all look alike and like nothing you will ever see if you are lucky. In their joy to be free and longing to see their friends who had come at last, many prisoners rushed to the fence and died, electrocuted. There were those who died cheering, because that effort of happiness was more than their bodies could endure. There were those who died because now they had food, and they ate before they could be stopped, and it killed them.' Gellhorn was in Dachau when the Germans surrendered: it seemed to her the most suitable place in Europe to hear the news of victory. 'For surely this war was made to abolish Dachau, and all the other places like Dachau, and everything that Dachau stood for, and to abolish it for ever.'[20]

However, the effect of liberating the camp on Sunday 29 April had a profound effect on every GI, Seventh Army-wide, who henceforth was far less inclined to treat German civilians with courtesy, their soldiers with respect, and the SS and Nazi loyalists with anything other than total abhorrence. Unsurprisingly, instances of the execution of prisoners, even wounded, rose in retaliation for the barbarity GIs had witnessed or heard of, at Dachau. Never again would Dachau be 'just another anonymous town in the vicinity of Munich'.

At 06:30 in a sleet that turned to snow on the morning of 30 April, the three American divisions started moving into Munich. The weather made artillery observation difficult and ruled out air strikes, but the 3rd and 42nd – rivals, and racing to be first into the city – were puzzled to find they were greeted by groups of cheering civilians, waving the blue-and-white flag of old Bavaria. The FAB's revolt had, in fact, yielded results. The Marne Division noted that 'resistance in Munich was weird – some of the troops meeting fanatical and last ditch fighting as they pushed thru the southern suburbs – others were given the "liberator" treatment. Some of the troops were met by German forces holding hands overhead, ready, eager and almost too willing to be captured.'[21]

By contrast, in the north of the city lay the München-Freimannan Kaserne, a huge SS barracks on Neuherbergstrasse and Ingolstädterstrasse which housed the SS-Standarte Deutschland (Deutschland SS-Regiment). They furnished ceremonial squads for all the guard details of the various party memorials and buildings throughout the city. By 1945 many of the Kaserne's occupants were Flemish SS volunteers, for whom a return home was impossible, so they had no other option than to fight to the last cartridge. Not short of weapons, ammunition or courage, few ever surrendered, having dug in around their Kaserne and sparred like demons. It took most of the day to 'purge the SS college of its inhabitants, window by window, and wall by wall'.[22]

The fanatics were generally in their teens, for – as in every culture – the young rarely have close experience of death, which in their eyes strikes only at old people and pets. With few personal responsibilities such as businesses, partners or children, they tend to assume they are invincible; fate will kill someone else, never them. When that set of assumptions is broken, having no life experience to fall back on, they often revert to being the children they are. In the south-eastern Munich suburb of Pullach, 'resistance came from a group of juvenile soldiers, belonging to the Hitlerjugend, who abandoned their flak guns after destroying them, to resume the fight with small arms. Only one hundred of these youths were captured after a battle lasting for several hours.'[23]

At this time, 29-year-old Chaplain William Boice was serving with the nearby 22nd Regiment of 4th Infantry Division. Ministering to his own flock, many barely older than the German teens they were fighting, he was perhaps better qualified than most to comment on the opposition. 'They were young, from fifteen to nineteen, but fought with a fanaticism of which we had read, but seldom met. One had a wound in his leg which prevented his crawling away. One of our medics started toward the wounded German, when the boy picked up a "potato masher" stick grenade. The medic stopped and pointed to his red cross armband. The German stared at him stonily, and as the medic again moved to approach him, unscrewed the cap of his grenade. The lad held it immediately under his chin until it went off, blowing his head cleanly from his body. Such was their fanaticism.'[24]

This was emotionally and physically tiring work. Alternating between joyous welcomes and firefights as it manoeuvred, one of 3rd Division's battalions 'marched, tactically, by foot and covered twenty-five miles in one day, cleared eighteen towns and villages' in the Munich suburbs, its first day's haul of prisoners amounting to thirty officers and 1,210 enlisted men.[25] This was a war only for the young and fit. The sterile-sounding phrase of 'clearing an area' invariably meant killing a lot of the opposition. Weapons and equipment were taken by GIs before they moved on, while American Graves Registration units swiftly buried their own. The German dead, of whatever age, in whichever uniform, or none, were left for local civilians to inter, if there was anyone about. With the weather slowly warming, Padre Boice remembered, 'the German dead lay piled like cord wood over every conceivable defensive terrain feature. Some of them had been dead for several days, and their skin was turning black, and the blood-clotted clothing swarmed with flies. There was a foul stench of death in the atmosphere.'[26]

This was the insanitary environment in which GIs had to operate during the last weeks of the war in Europe. Veterans in their memoirs and historians by their analysis tend to gloss over the unpleasantness of a recently fought-over battlefield. In the spring of 1945, Germany was littered with them, surrounding most towns and cities, each as grim as the aftermath of Waterloo or Gettysburg. Bodies were located by the stench and often relieved of their shoes, even clothes, by the living, before being covered with earth. When the *Volksbund Deutsche Kriegsgräberfürsorge* (German War Graves Commission) were retrieving the dead in the 1950s for reburial, they found that few, if any, possessed footwear.

Elsewhere, eyewitnesses remembered the immediate aftermath of combat with Seventh Army troops: 'I saw lots of dead Germans, all dressed, but when I went back a couple of hours later, they had nothing left on them: no more boots, no more weapons, nothing, they were naked.' Another observed an elderly man eyeing a dead German officer's footwear, among a group of putrefying grenadiers. 'The older man said, "Damn, look at the boots on that one over there. I am barefoot and he has those nice boots. I'm going to take them." They had been dead for two or three days and already huge hornets were taking meat off the bodies. They were completely swollen, with their belts pressing into their stomachs. He went to pull off the boots, but the legs came off too. In the end he left them.'[27]

Master Sergeant Wolfgang F. Robinow, a Hamburg Jew who had emigrated to Pennsylvania in 1938, remembered arriving in Munich, in the central Marienplatz with the rest of his Intelligence and Reconnaissance Platoon of the 42nd. Two weeks earlier his team had been ambushed, but Robinow's quick thinking had saved the group, and he went on to direct the fire of three tanks in a counter-attack. He was then unaware that he had already been nominated for a Silver Star.[28] 'We never knew what was hiding around the next corner. We didn't have tanks or anything like that. Just the Jeeps. My soldiers had rifles. I had a pistol. That was it.' On that cold morning of 30 April, his men began to encounter more and more waving residents and by early afternoon, he and his troops were surrounded by a happy throng. 'Most of them were the very old, too elderly even for the Volkssturm. We were greeted as the great liberators of the city, which, to be honest, really made me angry at the time. This was, after all, where the Nazi party got its start.'

Robinow met his first armed Germans when he marched into an adjacent police station to confiscate their weapons. He was surprised to be greeted with salutes, and to discover the weapons already boxed up ready for him to take away. Shortly afterwards he found himself interrogating Leni Riefenstahl, film-maker of the pre-war Nuremberg rallies ('it was only because the commanding officer wanted her autograph'), and a sinister SS officer. On asking the latter how many people he had killed, the chilling response was 'Are you in the habit of counting the number of slices of bread you have for breakfast in a year?'[29]

Thunderbird Sergeant Dan Dougherty, last encountered adrift in his DUKW on the Danube, had been involved in the liberation of Dachau and Allach camps, and arrived in Munich on 30 April. He wrote home, 'We walked the eleven miles from outside of Dachau to Munich and I never once took my gun off my shoulder. We assumed Munich would be another Nuremberg and approached with great apprehension. So, we were delighted to learn the early units of the 45th and 42nd Divisions had met only scattered resistance that morning. At one point we walked on a boulevard with a wide median strip that was strewn with German military paraphernalia. It seems that when the Wehrmacht and SS troops learned they would not have to defend the city, they changed clothes and threw their uniforms and gear into the streets.'[30]

On 1 May Eisenhower issued a special Order of the Day, stating, 'The whole Allied Expeditionary Force congratulates the Seventh Army on the seizure of Munich, the cradle of the Nazi beast.' The conurbation had simply given up. As soon as it fell, the GI souvenir hunters were out in force. Eleven Thunderbird field artillery officers from the 45th Division snaffled a red leather presentation copy of *Mein Kampf* from a second-floor apartment at 16, Prinzregentenplatz. Captain Daniel Allen wrote on the flyleaf 'From Adolf Hitler's apartment in Munich', followed by the signatures of his ten friends.[31]

The address's first visitors had been GIs from Company 'B' of the 179th Infantry, a Thunderbird outfit led by Lieutenant Ira Palm. The seasoned warrior, whom we met losing his friend when crossing the Danube, had already been awarded Silver and Bronze Stars for his leadership and valour, and was assigned the special mission to kill or capture the German leader. Of course, we now know he was in his bunker in Berlin, but with the talk of Alpine redoubts in Bavaria and Austria, at the time there was reason to think he might have returned to his spiritual home.

Guided by an FAB insurgent, Palm and his men had burst in during the pre-dawn hours of 29 April. The nine-room apartment, Hitler's residence since 1929, was deserted. In the top-right drawer of the Führer's oak desk, Palm found a 7.65mm gold-plated PPK pistol, a personal gift from its creator Carl Walther. A fiftieth birthday present, it was decorated with the intertwined initials A.H. inlaid in gold on the ivory pistol grips. The American trousered it and departed; within hours he was wounded in a firefight but hung on to his prize as he passed through a series of hospitals and eventually back home.[32]

From the same place, stacks of off-white notepaper, with the Führer's name engraved top left below a gilt swastika, were also in high demand. Sergeant Danny Jacobson, a Jewish Oklahoman serving as a clerk with the 179th Infantry, used about twenty sheets, beginning one letter to his wife: 'And so, Hitler's treasured stationery has come to this. Imagine how many times he would turn in his grave if he knew a Jew was writing on his precious personal stationery.' He observed the 'Supermen of the world were a very defeated and broken people', and that Hitler's personal quarters were relatively untouched in a city that had been 'bombed beyond repair'.[33]

Photographer Lee Miller also visited the Prinzregentenplatz residence on 30 April, acquiring Eva Braun's vanity set as part of her well-deserved loot. 'It was an ordinary semi-corner, old fashioned building on a platz, and there were no signs that anyone more pretentious than merchants or retired clergy lived there, or rather, had lived there. Now it was obviously a command post. The signs said that it belonged to the 179th Regiment of the 45th Division.' Miller found it guarded by GIs, but they let the attractive blonde, and her photojournalist colleague and sometime lover David Scherman, in to snoop around. It was he who propped a portrait of Hitler on the rim of the bathtub, set Miller's dirty combat boots on the bathroom rug and took a discreet photograph of her bathing. Left unsaid was the symbolism of her washing away the dirt of Dachau, just visited, in Hitler's own tub. She recorded the 'snow-sprinkled Jeeps on the sidewalk, wires falling out of the windows and an inconspicuous sentry guard on the door. Lieutenant Colonel William P. Grace Jr was checking reports at his field desk, parked on top of a table. His military telephone lay on a chair which Hitler's bottom had warmed, and the rest of the staff were carrying out their various duties around the place as if they weren't living in a museum.'[34]

Thus, Sixth Army Group had seized both Nuremberg and Munich, ironically deemed by SHAEF the previous autumn as 'not especially worthwhile objectives'. Whether the GIs knew it or not, of far more interest to the victors was the Munich *Reinheitsgebot* (purity order) law of 23 April 1516, which outlined the correct ingredients of beer. This in turn had given rise to Munich's Oktoberfest, instituted in 1810, which became so important that Bavaria insisted on the application of both throughout Germany as a precondition of unification in 1871. Somehow America has never quite forgotten its acquaintanceship with German beer, initiated on an industrial scale in 1945.

Unlike the Lance and other treasures of the Holy Roman Emperor recovered in Nuremberg, the Nazi *Blutfahne*, last seen at the swearing in of the Volkssturm on 18 October 1944, seems to have disappeared in the ash and rubble of its Munich home. There remains the intriguing possibility – with a nod to *Raiders of the Lost Ark* – that the blood banner sits anonymously among the souvenirs of a returning GI, unwittingly looted in the chaos of capture or subsequent occupation. More likely, however, was its destruction when the Braunes Haus – the Nazi Party's headquarters at 45, Briennerstrasse – was flattened in an Allied air raid. None of this mattered, for between 15:00 and 16:00 on 30 April, Hitler had shot himself in his Berlin bunker. With a line from Shakespeare's *Richard III*, the BBC Home Service announced, 'The day is ours. The bloody dog is dead.'[35]

*

On 25 April, Marshals Zhukov and Konev had closed their ring of Soviet steel around Berlin: there was no way out. For many German and Russian soldiers this would be a fight to the death. There are many conspiracy theories as to what finally happened to the German leader, but we now know, beyond doubt, that as the security situation deteriorated, Hitler and his entourage withdrew into the Führerbunker complex beneath the Chancellery. With the nearest Russian troops about two hundred yards away, after midnight on 29 April, Hitler married his long-term mistress Eva Braun in a small civil ceremony and the following day at about 15:30 the pair committed suicide, Hitler by gunshot, his new wife by poison.

There was no last-minute flight by plane, armoured vehicle or subterranean passage. The pair did not resurface in Switzerland, the Vatican or South America. Their remains were inexpertly cremated in a shell-hole in the Chancellery garden. Since then, much unwarranted debate has continued about Hitler's last days, the torch relit in recent years by a new generation of conspiracy theorists. Forensic research of every archive by Luke Daly-Groves in his *Hitler's Death: The Case Against Conspiracy* has proven to the satisfaction of modern scholars that the uncertainty was engineered by Stalin as a means of confusing the West.

The Führer's manner of death was determined by the fate of his fellow dictator, Benito Mussolini. Il Duce had been captured near Lake Como by partisans on 27 April and shot with his mistress the following day. Their bodies were dumped in central Milan for a large and angry crowd to abuse, then strung up, feet first, from a metal girder like two medieval bandits. Hitler wanted no such humiliation and ordered his remains and those of his wife to be burned, then buried. His remaining staff surrendered on 2 May 1945, a day which also saw Soviet war photographer Yevgeny Khaldei taking his iconic images of Russian soldiers unfurling a huge Red Army flag from the roof of the Reichstag. Below lay a smoking city of dead cars and tanks, gun barrels split like celery, arranged on a canvas of corpses and rubble. Berlin had fallen.

(*Above*): Generalmajor Alwin Wolz, Kampfkommandant of Hamburg, at the moment of his surrender on 3 May to Brigadier John Spurling of 7th British Armoured Division. Both sides exhibit faultless military discipline, while the German officers appear to be delighted that their ordeal is over. (*Below*): After their liberation on 5 May by Staff Sergeant Albert J. Kosiek's squad of the 41st US Cavalry Reconnaissance Squadron, former inmates of Mauthausen concentration camp pull down the hated insignia of the Third Reich.

19

Eight Days of Agony and Ecstasy

It was on Tuesday 1 May, at 21:30, that Hamburg – one of the last Nazi stations still broadcasting – warned the German people of 'a grave and important announcement' about to be made. Half guessing the importance, Allied intelligence officers as well as those Germans still possessing wireless sets, and the electricity to run them, tuned in. The solemn mood was exacerbated by several gloomy Wagnerian opera excerpts and the slow movement of Bruckner's Seventh Symphony.

Then, at 22:20, came the voice of Grossadmiral Karl Dönitz, whom most knew as commander of the regime's U-boats. 'German men and women, soldiers of the German Wehrmacht, our Führer, Adolf Hitler, has fallen. He recognised the terrible danger of Bolshevism at an early date and dedicated his existence to this struggle. The end of this, his struggle, and of his unswerving straight path of life, is marked by his hero's death in the capital of the Reich.' The 56-year-old Führer's cowardly suicide was not mentioned. By implying Hitler had died fighting at the head of his troops, the Reich, built on untruths, continued to lie after its leader's death.

The admiral then announced his own appointment as the new Führer but, to the astonishment of his listeners, avoided any mention of surrender. He intoned, 'It is my first task to save Germany from destruction by the advancing Bolshevist enemy. For this aim alone, the military struggle continues. So long as achievement of this aim is impeded by the British and the Americans, we shall be forced to carry on our defensive fight against them as well. Under such conditions, however, the Anglo-Americans will continue the war not for their own peoples but solely for the spreading of Bolshevism in Europe.' He ordered, 'Maintain order and discipline in town and country. Let everybody do his duty at his own post. Only thus shall we mitigate the sufferings that the coming time will bring to each of us; only thus shall we be able to prevent a collapse. If we do all that is in our power, God will not forsake us after so much suffering and sacrifice.'[1]

The killing would continue. This announcement was especially important for Devers' Sixth Army Group, for within its orbit lay not only the heartland of Nazi support, but all of National Socialism's principal towns and cities. While Munich marked the end of any meaningful defence by large-scale forces, the question that remained for Devers was what would bring about a German surrender? His formations were now pursuing their opponents who rarely stood and fought, capitulating or not as local commanders saw fit, otherwise melting away. Sixth Army Group's war diary noted the situation 'fluid'. Yet this bureaucratic shorthand concealed the fact that it was not only frustrating, but potentially still dangerous.

Patch's Seventh Army, now headquartered in Augsburg, began to chase the Germans across a hundred-mile front. He detailed the 45th Division to garrison Munich, then little more than a collection of smoking ruins. Habitable buildings were few and limited to government properties that needed repair. Displaced people – former forced labourers from every conceivable country – and locals rendered homeless all needed help. On 1 May Seventh Army faced opponents scattered from Innsbruck to Salzburg, everywhere in an arc of confusion. Although there was a widespread feeling that the war was almost over, this only gained traction on 2 May, once news of Hitler's death spread. Yet as the campaign against Germany drew to a close, the Seventh Army G-3 noted, 'there is a growing need for maps of the Pacific area.'[2]

GIs were covering enormous distances. *Hellcat News* of the 12th Armored Division observed that its 17th Armored Infantry Battalion set a Sixth Army Group record of fifty-nine miles in a seven-hour advance from 08:00 to 15:00 on 2 May. 'At times two half-tracks were moving abreast at top speed down Hitler's super four-lane highway. Bypassing destroyed bridges and underpasses, the tracks sped along the highway, firing at the startled and surprised Germans who were trying to escape the assault by driving away in their vehicles, running across open fields, or by trying to hide in brush piles, wooded areas, or foxholes. They captured 5,000 prisoners, including five generals, numerous vehicles, and acres of supplies and equipment. During the entire operation, no casualties or equipment was lost to German fire. Tactically, the drive was a huge success because the opposition was taken completely by surprise and was not given a chance to prepare defensive positions.'[3]

Working with the French in the west, Dean's 44th and McAuliffe's 103rd Infantry Divisions of VI Corps were confronted with a panorama of knuckled mountains – the need to storm Innsbruck and Landeck, and the challenge of taking the Brenner Pass, deep in Austria. Their passage, surprisingly, was made easier by the appearance of Austrian partisans, who guided them around German roadblocks, enabling the Yanks to take the defenders from the rear. Innsbruck fell to McAuliffe on 3 May unopposed, the Austrians having already negotiated its surrender. To Seventh Army's south, hurrying through the Italian Alps, was the US Fifth Army. Since December 1944 it had been led by General Lucian K. Truscott Jr, a former commander of both the 3rd Marne Division and Brooks' VI Corps. Truscott's scouts, patrolling north to meet them, were encountered mid-morning on 4 May.

In the centre, Milburn's XXI Corps entered the Inn River Valley with 4th and 36th Divisions. This feature, running north-east to south-west, was sandwiched between two great mountain ranges, which isolated it from Bavaria in the north and Italy to the south. On 2 May, with the 12th Armored Division and 106th Cavalry Group ranging far along the road network of the Inn, both units took the surrender of General Ferenc-Lozak and 8,000 of his Hungarian soldiers. The latter had remained loyal to Hitler only to help keep the Soviets out of their country.

In the east, Haislip's XV Corps was reorientated from the south, to face Salzburg in the south-east. Originally a Third Army objective, Patch had more combat power, and was closer, so army boundaries were changed and the Austrian city, Mozart's birthplace, was allocated to the 20th Armored and 3rd, 42nd and 86th Infantry Divisions. The distances covered by the armoured formations often exceeded their notional fifty miles per day fuel allocation. This was made possible not only by airlifted supplies but using Devers' reach-back to Marseilles and Toulon. Some

575,000 tons of cargo was landed in March 1945 alone and brought forward by road and rail via an endless merry-go-round of trucks and rail wagons. Fuel pipes were constructed across the Rhine to ease the pressure on that vital commodity, but the nature of the pursuit kept ammunition consumption low, where a shortage of 105mm artillery shells had been a severe challenge for the previous six months. As ammunition needs decreased, the Army Group's requirements for fuel, vehicle spares and vehicles themselves went up dramatically, and even DUKWs were diverted to troop-carrying duties.

At this juncture, many supporting artillery battalions found themselves underemployed, whereupon their infantry buddies commandeered their trucks. Speed, as well as mobility, was everything. This relieved some of the burden from the Quartermaster Corps truck fleets that transported men around, whose vehicle loss rates from collisions, accidents and combat ran as high as 30 per cent. Generally, DUKWs were assigned to units, such as paratroopers and glider infantry, who had minimal transport of their own. With their outsized rubber tyres, carrying twenty-five GIs with all their equipment, the spacious DUKWs were a popular ride in the 101st Airborne, having none of 'the bounce of the deuce-and-a-half, or the springless jarring of the Jeep'.[4]

The wider operational picture was also being driven by events further south on the Italian front, a separate theatre for both the Germans and the Allies. Since February, the two sides had been engaged in tentative, highly secretive negotiations in Switzerland, initiated by SS-Obergruppenführer Karl Wolff, Higher SS and Police Leader in Italy. A dedicated Nazi and former adjutant of Himmler, Wolff worked through Italian colleagues to contact Swiss Army intelligence and, via them, Allen Dulles, the chief of the Office of Strategic Services (OSS). The meetings were dubbed Operation *Sunrise*.

Wolff's initial motivation was strategic – he envisaged an Allied–German alliance against the Soviets – but also personal, for he had overseen the deportation of Polish, Russian and Italian Jews for extermination and wanted to mitigate the future hand of justice. Initially working without the knowledge of Field Marshal Albert Kesselring, military commander in Italy, after many weeks' hard bargaining a Wehrmacht–SS delegation agreed terms. They signed a document with the British Field

Marshal Sir Harold Alexander on 29 April in the former royal palace at Caserta – the Allied HQ in Italy – and were given two days to implement the act, by 14:00 on 2 May.

At some stage Kesselring was made aware of the situation, but to protect himself, did not tell his staff, and the negotiations proceeded with his tacit approval. Later, after replacing Rundstedt as Oberbefehlshaber West (Supreme Commander West), he worried about the potential domino effect of a surrender in Italy on the rest of the Western Front. Farcically, with the ink dry on the surrender document, he then tried to renege and halt the proceedings. Orders and arrest warrants flew between headquarters until Kesselring phoned Wolff at 02:00 on 2 May and harangued him for two hours. The call degenerated into a slanging match of increasingly obscene expletives. Apparently, staff officers at both ends of the line were embarrassed and impressed by the endless range of profanities employed by their two superiors.

Wolff stood his ground, arguing there was nothing to be gained from fighting on, cleverly suggesting that surrender would give the Anglo-Americans time to stop the Soviets, who were advancing with the help of Tito's partisans. The alternative might be a pro-Communist uprising in northern Italy, which Wolff could not prevent. The Oberbefehlshaber West rang off at 04:00, and half an hour later a staff officer rang back to say that Kesselring had reluctantly agreed. Radio messages were sent out to all formations in clear, and at 14:00, in an air of chaos and confusion, German forces in Italy ceased all hostilities, robbing those Axis formations further north of an entire flank. Devers and his subordinates were only warned on 29 April of the intended German surrender to their south. The intervening period until the final act was effectively an armistice in Italy, but not in Austria or southern Germany.

As the war in Europe was ending, two great prizes remained. The first, Berlin, was already smothered by the Red Army and about to fall. The second, Berchtesgaden, home to Adolf Hitler's famous mountain retreat, seventy-five miles south-east of Munich, remained to be captured. It was in 1923 that Hitler first visited the area, staying in an Alpine log cabin in Obersalzburg, on the heights overlooking Berchtesgaden. Later he acquired a house there, the Berghof ('Mountain Court'), and soon his retinue, cronies and SS bodyguards had bought up the surrounding properties. Party Secretary Bormann created security zones in the vicinity, and Berchtesgaden itself was given a makeover to receive the many dignitaries who arrived there by rail or air. Above the Obersalzburg complex was the Kehlsteinhaus, since known as the Adlerhorst (Eagle's Nest), sitting on the peak of a 6,000-foot mountain.

Basically a huge dining room with wonderful views – though no overnight accommodation – it was reached by an elevator carved into the heart of the Kehlstein mountain. It runs still, silently ascending four hundred feet to the buildings above, the polished brass fittings exuding the style and wealth of the era. Bormann, the great organiser, and gatekeeper to Hitler, was the one responsible for the construction of the Kehlsteinhaus, and its presentation to Hitler on behalf of the German people in 1939. It was not to Hitler's taste, for although he loved being in the mountains, he disliked being on top of them; most were unaware the Führer suffered from vertigo.

The Berghof was where Hitler had welcomed the former British Prime Minister, David Lloyd George, in 1936, the former king, the Duke of Windsor, in 1937, and the serving Prime Minister, Neville Chamberlain, the following year. It was where he had learned of the D-Day landings. The Führer felt safe in the remote location, although the endless military complexes and subterranean tunnels drastically altered the rustic setting that had originally drawn him there. Beyond the range of most Allied aircraft, the area remained untouched by war, until a massive air raid by 359 RAF Lancasters and sixteen Mosquitoes on 25 April 1945 destroyed many of the buildings. It would still be smoking when the Allies arrived.

Nevertheless, it struck many in Devers' army group that whoever seized the Berchtesgaden-Obersalzburg complex would earn themselves a place in the history books as captors of the crown jewel of the Third Reich. This alternative seat of government to Berlin suddenly became a key objective. There was a second motivation. Loot. It was reasoned – correctly as it turned out – that at Berchtesgaden the Nazis ate and drank well, surrounding themselves with, well – crown jewels and other fine things. To the victor the spoils. The race was on.

Several units would arrive almost simultaneously, but in the vanguard was the 7th Infantry, the 'Cottonbalers', with whom we started our story at Utweiler. On 2 May, they had moved on from Munich and taken Salzburg, over the border in Austria, which fell with no opposition. Looking at his campaign maps, 'Iron Mike' O'Daniel realised his Marne Division was in perfect position to make a dash for Berchtesgaden, just fifteen miles away to the south. With the German surrender in Italy confirmed, it was unlikely there would be much opposition. He felt his men deserved the honour, and thus O'Daniel privately resolved to try and reach the area. 'By that time, the prize of Berchtesgaden was so radiant, it was obvious that considerable fame and renown would come to the unit that was first to reach Hitler's Eagle's Nest,' noted Major William B. Rosson, a battalion CO in the 30th Infantry, one of the Marne Division's regiments. 'We were resolved to be the first into Berchtesgaden.'[5]

O'Daniel requested a move towards Hitler's headquarters which was denied. Patch had felt that US 3rd Division would encounter a stiff fight for Salzburg and would thus be too busy to even consider making a play for Berchtesgaden. Besides, for understandable political reasons, Devers had already offered the French, in the form of Philippe Leclerc's 2nd Division Blindée, the liberators of Paris, the supreme accolade of taking Hitler's mountain lair. The French had been busy subduing the German-held Royan pocket on the Atlantic coast, but, alive to the publicity that would ensue, de Gaulle had them rapidly transported across France by rail. As Leclerc still refused to join the 'former-Vichyites' of de Lattre's French Army, in Germany his division was attached to Patch's Seventh Army. They operated for the last days of the war with Major General Roderick R. Allen's US 12th Armored Division.

However, at the same time, Maxwell Taylor's 101st Airborne – who had been operating alongside Leclerc's Frenchmen during the previous week – also had their eyes on Hitler's former headquarters – and perhaps because they were more nimble than a heavy armoured division slogging through the mountains, felt they could beat their opponents to the finish. With US and British troops also coming up from Italy, the potential for casualties, especially from friendly fire, was huge. Released slave labourers and camp inmates, Austrian partisans, German soldiers trying to return home, staff officers trying to retrieve possessions from the area, Russians who had fought for the Reich drifting westwards to escape their avenging countrymen, and fanatical SS rearguards determined to forfeit their lives expensively, all added to the potential confusion.

At about 10:00 on 4 May, O'Daniel confided in the German-born Colonel John A. Heintges, commander of the Cottonbalers: 'I did not get permission to go into Berchtesgaden.' Iron Mike then asked, 'Do you think you can do it?' Just two words came back: 'Yes, sir.' O'Daniel flung Heintges a couple of words in return: 'Well, go.'[6] At the same hour, similar orders were being cascaded down other divisional chains of command by Generals Leclerc and Taylor, though the Marne Division was better placed, and started sooner.

Fortunately for O'Daniel, the Saalach River flows south-west out of Salzburg, dominating the quickest route to the Nazi stronghold, and his men controlled the remaining two crossing points. Initially, Iron Mike left most of his division guarding Salzburg, and sent Heintges out to Hitler's headquarters with his First and Third Battalions. Probing forward, one Marne sub-unit headed through Bad Reichenhall to approach from the north-west, while another used the autobahn to come in from the north-east, as two arms of a tactical pincer. Blown bridges elsewhere meant these were the only two viable routes, Berchtesgaden being shielded by high mountains to the west and south. Knowing he had competitors following in his wake, O'Daniel then set up heavily manned roadblocks, with orders to let no other units through.

Taking the north-east route along the autobahn, first into Berchtesgaden that afternoon was Lieutenant W. Sherman Pratt. Cut from the same cloth as Earl Swanson, Michael Daly and Audie Murphy, Pratt had joined the Cottonbalers in 1939, was a sergeant in North Africa, received a battlefield commission, and by 1945 was a company commander. He recalled, 'Berchtesgaden looked like a village from a fairy tale. Its houses were of Alpine architecture and design. Some had gingerbread decorations.' Other Marne units trickled into the town over the next few hours, capturing around 2,000 troops, among them Hermann Göring's nephew, Fritz. Photographs and personal testimony show the German prisoners clad in greatcoats, the wintry weather of the previous days having subsided, but there was still snow on the ground. Even in early May this was unsurprising, given the town lies at 2,000 feet.[7]

Meanwhile, Pratt mounted one of his platoons on tanks and led them

up to Hitler's Obersalzburg complex, another 1,500 feet above Berchtesgaden, and inspected the ruins of his Berghof home. In his 1992 memoir,
he wrote, 'We were winding our way up the steep and winding mountain road. The air was clear and crisp with almost unlimited visibility.
We rounded a bend and there before us in a broad opening lay the ruins
of what had once been Hitler's house and the SS barracks. Everyone in
my group was struck into silence . . . by the significance of the time and
place. After all the years of struggle and destruction, the killing, pain,
and suffering . . . here, for sure, was the end of it.'[8]

Some of his men walked to the ornate entrance of the elevator shaft
that led to the still-intact Kehlsteinhaus sitting on top of the 6,000-
foot Kehlstein mountain, but did not ascend, and soon Pratt and his
men returned to Berchtesgaden. Few Cottonbalers thus saw the Berghof, and most of Heintges' men stayed in the lower town, trousering the
many souvenirs they found, from flags, pistols and silverware to dress
uniforms, wine and foodstuffs. Arriving shortly after, the Australian
war correspondent Oscar White recalled the 'once beautiful little village
strangled by a cancer of concrete and steel ostentation'. His colleague
observed, 'I'm damned glad Adolf didn't decide to shack up here with
a survival kit. It would have taken another six months to crack him.'[9]

In the meantime, the French armoured division had come up
against the Marne's roadblocks and were denied passage. At 17:00, Général Leclerc himself arrived, incandescent with rage. 'He was standing upright in his vehicle with authority and great assertiveness,' Major
Rosson recalled. There was a delay while O'Daniel checked that Heintges
had reached his destination, and only then did he allow the French to
pass. The 101st, too, had been rebuffed but were allowed through with the
French. However, Leclerc was in no mood to cooperate with a second
American formation, insisted his vehicles take priority, and raced for
Berchtesgaden, arriving at 20:00. The airborne troops trickled in early
the following morning.

Wallowing in the unaccustomed luxury of a Berchtesgaden hotel,
Heintges was soon visited by an old military friend, his opposite number
of the 506th Parachute Infantry, Colonel Robert Sink. The latter had
come to warn his friend. 'My regiment is on the way up here to relieve
you.' Heintges was stunned, expecting to be in occupation for a week or

more. He checked with O'Daniel and found the 7th Infantry had indeed been ordered to return to their official occupation zone, in Salzburg. The top brass were uneasy at Iron Mike's unofficial manoeuvre, however much it was deserved.

Before they left, Colonel Heintges determined that he needed to record the 3rd Division's presence at Obersalzburg and led a small posse of trucks and Jeeps up to the complex. However, the French division had now staked this out as their occupation zone, and their sentries denied him access. Uncaring that his men had captured the area the day before, the two sides bickered and argued, accompanied, apparently, by pushing and shoving. Ironically, dissolution of the great coalition ranged against him that Hitler had long sought, looked like happening on his doorstep, though he had been dead for less than five days. In view of their treatment less than twenty-four hours earlier, the Leclerc's Division Blindée were trenchant in their 'Non!'

That wise old leader of men, Heintges, came up with a solution acceptable to all. There would be a joint Franco-US flag-raising ceremony at Obersalzburg. A selection of battalion commanders and enlisted men saluted as the Stars and Stripes was raised, war correspondents took photographs, and then the Marne Division drove back down the hill. As the historian John C. McManus observed, 'They left behind no billboards or signs to mark their feat nor any indicator that the 7th Infantry had been the first ones there. Heintges should have made sure this was done. By not doing so, he left open the possibility that other Allied soldiers would believe themselves to be the conquerors of the Berghof.'[10]

Yet another race also developed. Among the first French tanks at the Berghof was a Sherman commanded by Sergent-Chef Bernard de Nonancourt, a former Resistance fighter and member of the Lanson champagne house, which also owned Laurent-Perrier. On 5 May de Nonancourt and his crew climbed to the Kehlsteinhaus and blew off its steel doors to discover Hitler's wine cellar. 'I saw every great wine I had ever heard of, every legendary vintage. All that had been made by the Rothschilds was there, the Lafites, the Moutons. As well as rare ports and cognacs dating from the nineteenth century, there were outstanding Burgundies, while the Bordeaux were just extraordinary. There were 500,000 bottles, many of them magnums.'

His orders were to rescue it for France ahead of the Americans. With the elevator shaft sabotaged by the SS, de Nonancourt directed over two hundred Alpine soldiers and their mountain rescue stretchers to manoeuvre the great wines down the mountainside. Filling every vehicle the Division Leclerc possessed, even ambulances, over the next few days his men worked with their canteens full of 'such legendary greats as Latour '29, Mouton '34 and Lafite '37, de Nonancourt's own tipple being Salon '28 champagne'. They were unmolested by the GIs, few of whom understood the French system of vintages and chateaux. In any case, the Americans were distracted by Hermann Göring's own 10,000-bottle cellar. The doyen of post-war champagne-makers and head of Laurent-Perrier for fifty years, de Nonancourt was proudest of his Croix de Guerre, awarded by Général Philippe Leclerc de Hauteclocque, for his 'service in action to French wine'.[11]

Apart from the French, those other Allied soldiers who believed themselves first into Obersalzburg included Easy Company of Colonel Sink's 506th Parachute Infantry, which arrived on 5 May and did not encounter the 7th Infantry. They had taken their time, for during the previous afternoon had come under fire from SS fanatics using mortars and machine-guns defending a broken bridge across a ravine. When the Second Battalion's commander, Major Dick Winters, had proposed taking aggressive action, Sink had demurred, stating, 'No. I don't want anybody to get hurt.' The sense that the war was about to end and further bloodshed would be pointless was uppermost in the minds of all.

As the 101st Airborne Division occupied the Berchtesgaden until the end of July, it became the accepted history that they had arrived first, something the Screaming Eagles did nothing to discourage. An error made by a recent historian has reinforced this myth. Writing in 1992, Stephen E. Ambrose – normally scrupulously correct – erred when he claimed that 'Easy Company got there first' in his seminal *Band of Brothers*. However, it was the airborne soldiers who picked the area clean of souvenirs, were extensively recorded on camera posing in front of various landmarks with their mementos, and left a forest of Screaming Eagles signboards and graffiti throughout Berchtesgaden, Obersalzburg and the Kehlsteinhaus.

Such details of history matter as surely as political parties claiming credit for introducing a piece of influential legislation. When defence cuts are mooted, the victors' laurels of units are put under the magnifying glass and considered. The historian will observe the 101st Airborne, who had fought long and hard since jumping into Normandy on the night of 5–6 June 1944, certainly deserved their moment in the sun. Yet, so too did the 7th Infantry Regiment, who had made four amphibious assaults since November 1942, and taken even more casualties. I was once with a tourist searching for a signature of his GI uncle, scratched into the great marble fireplace at the Kehlsteinhaus in May 1945. There are hundreds, for there was no better way for victorious GIs to personalise their conquest, just as countless Red Army soldiers left their mark in the Berlin Reichstag. Amazingly, we found it. Exactly where the nephew was told it would be.[12]

The French, having arrived in Berchtesgaden, had other issues on their minds. On 4 May, once through the Marne Division's roadblocks, they had driven to Bad Reichenhall, ten miles south-west of Salzburg, where some of Leclerc's men had stayed overnight in the numerous well-appointed hotels the spa town had to offer. They found there a German military hospital full of convalescing soldiers. The attention of Lieutenant Maurice Ferrano of the 4th Company, Régiment de Marche du Tchad, was drawn to thirteen Germans trying to escape. Ferrano's half-tracked mechanised infantry company comprised Communist Spaniards who had fled Franco's Spain after the Civil War and operated with the Maquis in south-western France until joining the Division-Leclerc.

Why, with the war all but over, would a few wounded soldiers try to escape from a hospital, where they were safe and well? His men soon discovered the answer. They were French, either anti-Communists or members of the former Vichy Army, who had donned field grey and served with the 33rd 'Charlemagne' Division of the Waffen-SS. Leclerc himself came to inspect the turncoats and found to his horror that one was the son of a Free French officer friend of his. The young man was discreetly removed and clandestinely sent back to his father. Leclerc ranted at the remaining dozen for serving in a foreign uniform. Yet one of them was courageous enough to retort, 'Sir, you too are wearing a foreign uniform: an American one!' Three photographs exist of Leclerc glowering at the men, his face distorted with contempt.

Angered, Leclerc demanded their immediate execution. Two Catholic chaplains of the division, Fathers Fouquet and Giaume, interceded and demanded the accused be given confession. With Leclerc and his G-2, Major Lebec, watching, Lieutenant Ferrano was then ordered to assemble a firing squad, who dispatched them in groups of four. Each refused an eye covering and cried 'Vive la France' as they died. Leclerc ordered their remains to be left unburied, and it was GIs who interred them after the French had moved on. A stone plaque in Bad Reichenhall cemetery marks their resting place today. The pain of collaboration and stain of Vichy ran deep; they would take years to expunge. There were countless similar examples of summary justice. Most, unlike this one, went undocumented.

Other Frenchmen in de Lattre's army had reached the Swiss frontier and shores of Lake Constance, deep in south-western Germany. Racing through the Alpine towns and villages, German units were too shocked by the sudden appearance of the French, and their North African Berbers – about whom terrible rumours circulated – to offer resistance. All the French formations could afford to break down into much smaller task forces to round up their opponents. Général Schlesser's 5th Division Blindée, like their American colleagues, split into three combat commands during this advance. Philip Moulton Mayer with part of his American Field Service Ambulance Company was attached to the 14th Medical Battalion with Colonel Lecoq's Combat Command 4. Their war ended on 30 April with the surrender and guarding of hundreds of Gebirgsjäger – mountain troops – at Primisweiler, near Friedrichshafen. Evidently the surrender went well, as townsfolk kept in touch with the young Harvard graduate for decades afterwards.[13]

The twelve Frenchmen shot by Leclerc's men died on 8 May. Their demise went unnoticed for it was the day when Europe exploded into relief at the cessation of the European war. Yet, as springlike days of late April had given way to a final winter flourish, with snow and sleet falling, and low clouds in Bavaria 'feeling like the ceiling of a room', the Germans opposite Devers' Sixth Army Group had already surrendered three days earlier.

It was the surrender in Italy on 2 May that had caused General Friedrich Schulz, commander of the German Army Group 'G' since 2 April, to reach out to Jake Devers. He had been authorised to do so by Kesselring, who – having let go Army Group 'C' in Italy – saw no reason to prolong the agony of Army Group 'G' in Bavaria. Yet to talk of German army groups, armies, corps or even divisions was, by early May 1945, a misnomer. Very few had any transport, or rations, and some divisions numbered as few as five hundred combat effectives.

Thus, one reason why Devers took little interest in who was first into Berchtesgaden, and denied O'Daniel's Marne Division their little foray, was because – in the middle of surrender negotiations – he wanted no more casualties in his two armies. After three days of consulting maps and confirming where the Axis forces were located and would be collected, the final act of their disbandment took place, at Baldham, in the Haar suburb of eastern Munich, five miles from the centre. The venue was a huge studio workshop, built by Hitler's architect Albert Speer. In peacetime it had been the lair of the 'official' Nazi sculptor, Josef Thorak, responsible for many of the regime's giant human and equine bronzes. Thorak, son of an Austrian potter, only accepted giant-sized commissions; his studio was the largest in the world at the time. Typical in its Third Reich art deco, minimalist style, tall and imposing – and still standing today – it was a fitting place to end the Nazi regime in Bavaria.

US and German Army delegates, all driven to and from the venue in 3rd Division military staff cars, had met over several days in its 55-foot-high central hall to confirm details, before a small table was laid on 5 May. The delegates sat shoulder to shoulder around it, heads craning to see the maps laid out, and shivering with cold. The air, common for the era, was thick with cigarette smoke. After an adjournment at 14:30, General Hermann Foertsch of the Wehrmacht's First Army, his Knight's Cross glinting in the arc lights, picked up a fountain pen to agree the 'unconditional surrender of all forces between the Bohemian mountains and the Upper Inn River', including his troops, with those of General Erich Brandenberger's Nineteenth and Hans Schmidt's Twenty-Fourth Armies – all by then paper formations.

Lieutenant Colonel Henry Cabot Lodge, the senator turned liaison officer, was present and described how 'Foertsch sat stiffly to attention. A full minute passed before he said anything. He was clearly suffering from violent emotion. Finally, he broke the silence, bowed his head slightly, flushed a little, and replied, "I understand. I have no choice. I have no power to do otherwise." [14] The document was counter-signed by Devers, Patch and Haislip, with O'Daniel and Haislip's XV Corps chief of staff, Brigadier General Pearson Menoher, looking on. It took effect the following day, 6 May. Elsewhere, General Brandenberger signed a similar document at the same hour, surrendering his Nineteenth Army to Generals Brooks of VI Corps, with Dean of the 44th, McAuliffe of the 103rd and Morris of the 10th Armored, looking on. Officers and military police could retain their sidearms, prisoners were to be released, weapons dumped at set locations, minefield maps provided, and Nazi badges, flags and pennants removed from display.

US Army photographers and a newsreel camera crew caught the moment of surrender at the Munich venue. The dozen German delegates entered the surrender room, clicked their heels and bowed their heads in Prussian style to Devers, before resuming their seats.[15] Interestingly, several of the junior officers on both sides in the room would later serve together in NATO forces based in West Germany, facing a different opponent.

Neither Devers nor Patch were as adept at publicity as their contemporaries. As Montgomery's surrender ceremony in north-western Germany had taken place on 4 May, it scooped the news, and Devers' triumph was lost amid the other document signings at 16:00 that same afternoon to the Canadians in Holland, at Rheims on the 7th and in Berlin on 8 May. Jake Devers' and his Sixth Army Group's finest moment had come and gone. Yet it was a significant one. That day, the Reich shrank by the 100,000 square miles it conceded to Sixth Army Group.

In its death throes, the Fatherland became more dysfunctional than ever. Having just signed the act of surrender, General Foertsch's motorcade was ambushed by SS fanatics while driving away from the Thorak estate. He managed to get through, but his staff officers were obliged to turn back and shelter at the Marne Division's headquarters. Meanwhile, sixty miles south of the city, in XXI Corps' territory, occurred one of the more bizarre incidents of the war, which underlined just how broken Nazi Germany had become. Sherman tanks of the US 12th Armored Division's 23rd Tank Battalion liberated the idyllic drawbridged, battlemented and turreted Austrian castle, Schloss Itter, in the north Tyrol. Resembling a huge baroque church, its inhabitants were more of the

Prominenten hostages, including former French prime ministers Paul Reynaud and Eduard Daladier, a sister of de Gaulle, and Generals Weygand and Gamelin.

Their reverie of freedom was soon interrupted when diehard crazies of the 17th SS Panzergrenadier Division arrived to execute the prisoners. As the Frenchmen and GIs prepared to fight for their lives, they were joined by a squad of German guards, led by two German officers, Major Gangl of the Wehrmacht, and Hauptsturmführer Schrader of the SS, who took up arms with their inmates against their former colleagues. The motley coalition only narrowly prevailed against their would-be executioners with the help of local Austrian partisans and a relief column of the 36th Texan Division, to whom war correspondent Mayer Levin was attached. He reported, 'While the SS, attacking from the valley below, fired their last shots at the towers, weary GIs climbed out of their tanks and found things to eat in the kitchen. Referring to the hostages, they asked, "Who are all these old geezers anyway?"'[16]

Their rescue was preceded by the escape of another 139 *Prominenten*, from seventeen nations – among them fourteen Britons and six French, including four survivors of the Great Escape, and the former Prime Minister Léon Blum and his wife. The rest numbered journalists, military commanders, clergymen and politicians – the former Austrian chancellor, Kurt Schuschnigg; commander-in-chief of the Greek Army, Alexandros Papagos; Miklós Horthy, son of Hungary's ruler; and Mario Badoglio, son of Italy's field marshal. The most numerous were sixty-six Germans: aristocrats, diplomats and officers who had fallen out of favour with Hitler, or those connected with the 1944 Stauffenberg plot and their relatives. They had been arrested under a medieval legal code called *Sippenhaft*. Resurrected after the July 1944 plot and applied retrospectively by the Nazi judicial system, *Sippenhaft* determined kin liability for a crime or act committed by one of its family members. Wives, parents and cousins of the plotters were arrested, and their children placed in orphanages.[17]

Beginning on 27 April, on Hitler's direct orders, this group were taken to the south Tyrol town of Niederdorf, near the Austro-Italian border, where it was discovered their SS guards were to execute them. The German officers managed to get word through to Wehrmacht colleagues who eventually arrived to face off with the SS in the town square. The latter surrendered and made themselves scarce. Meanwhile one of the Britons was able to contact the 339th Infantry, with the 85th Division of the US Fifth Army, and an American patrol reached the *Prominenten* at dawn on 4 May, to whom the Wehrmacht guards surrendered in turn. It had been a close-run affair, with the Tyrol valleys crawling with trigger-happy Nazi and Fascist diehards, Italian partisans, an Austrian Resistance movement, a former Wehrmacht Russian legion fleeing the approaching Soviets, besides regular German and American soldiers from separate armies of the European and Italian fronts.[18]

At the same moment, German-speaking officers of the US 106th Cavalry Group, driving a six-wheeled Mercedes staff car previously owned by Foreign Minister von Ribbentrop, bluffed their way into the Villa Sartori, at Strobl, on Lake Wolfgang. There, they liberated Leopold III, King of the Belgians, and his second wife Princess Lilian, disarming his seventeen SS jailers, then acted as his royal honour guard. Alas for him, Leopold was soon confronted by his brother Prince Charles with allegations of having surrendered the Belgian Army without consultation in May 1940 and subsequent collaboration with the Nazi occupation in its early stages. The Americans ended up conveying Leopold not to Belgium but to exile near Geneva.

Sixth Army Group had fired its last shots on its epic journey from the Riviera to Austria. Its success was down to Jacob Devers. His excellence had been recognised by Marshall in March 1945, when he elevated Devers to full General. This promotion was dated to 8 March 1945, two days ahead of Mark Clark and four ahead of Omar Bradley, giving Devers seniority in Europe second only to Eisenhower. Marshall understood it was Devers who faced challenges of language and culture not faced by the other two army group commanders, Bradley and Montgomery, who operated in English. In difficult terrain and weather, Devers coaxed his two armies to extraordinary achievements, reaching the Rhine River first in November 1944, a mere ninety-five days from landing on the Riviera, compared with the 277 days Bradley and Montgomery needed to get there from Normandy.

Churchill once observed that the heaviest cross he had to bear during the war was the Cross of Lorraine, by which he meant de Gaulle.[19] Yet it was Devers who really carried that Cross throughout the 1944–5 campaign. He bore it particularly well during the three major contretemps with his French Allies, at Strasbourg, Stuttgart and Ulm. Despite the Cross, and aided by Senator Lodge, it was Devers who let his French troops know that he was their friend, sometimes relying on his smile and gestures to make up for his difficulties with the language. Their good fortune was to serve under him.

On Devers' left flank, we have left the Third Army strung along the Germano-Czech frontier and battling their way through southern Austria. By then, Patton was operating with four corps, totalling eighteen divisions, making it the largest single American army commanded in battle, with a strength of 540,000 men.[20] In the north-west confines of the Czech lands, he was fielding the newcomers, Huebner's V Corps. With the 1st, 2nd and 97th Infantry and 9th Armored Divisions, they had transferred from First Army at the beginning of May.[21] Next, also poised on the Czech border, was Irwin's XII Corps, who had earlier discovered the vast treasures stored in the Merkers salt mines, and later, Flossenbürg camp. Walker's XX Corps was thrusting along the line of the Danube for Linz while, to their right, Van Fleet's III Corps was plunging deep into south-east Austria.

With the Germans stubbornly resisting in eastern Bohemia, forcing the Red Army to fight for every yard, Patton had been lobbying Bradley for permission to liberate Prague. On 4 May he was ordered to advance as far as Pilsen, sixty miles west of the Czech capital, for which XII Corps, with 5th, 26th and 90th Infantry and 11th Armored Divisions, set off the next morning, with V Corps on their left.[22] Bradley was wary of Third Army – now spread out in a semicircle stretching some 150 miles, with axes of advance to the east, south-east and south – overstretching their logistics, and demanded to know 'Why does everyone in Third Army want to liberate the Czechs?' Swallowing his barely contained repugnance of Communism, and throwing up a smokescreen as to his true motives, Patton responded, 'Oh Brad, can't you see? The Czechs are our allies. On to Czechoslovakia and fraternization,' which was forbidden in Germany.[23]

Bradley hinted that Patton 'could and should reconnoitre vigorously as far as Prague'. Third Army's headquarters took that to mean *capture* Prague, and by 5 May an OSS team had already entered the city, which had begun a general uprising against their hated occupiers that very day. However, when Eisenhower contacted the Soviet High Command with an offer to liberate the western Czech lands, the Red Army chief of staff, General Alexei Antonov, insisted US forces advance no further than a line between Karlsbad to Pilsen and Budweis. The Allies were as yet unaware of Stalin's determination to occupy Czechoslovakia, and other central European nations, and remain there after the war. On the morning of 6 May, Patton in V Corps headquarters near Pilsen received a phone call from Bradley: 'The halt line is mandatory. Ike does not want any international complications.'[24] The same day in Pilsen the suicidal urge among senior German officers persisted when Generalmajor Georg Majewski surrendered his garrison of 8,000 at a brief ceremony which he concluded by shooting himself in front of his astonished wife, his staff and Lieutenant Colonel Percy H. Perkins Jr of the 16th Armored Division.

None were aware that every hour counted for the prisoners in the Reich Protectorate of Bohemia and Moravia, as the Czech lands had been renamed. At Holleischen (today Holyšov), around 1,000 French, Czech, Dutch, Hungarian and Polish women were digging field defences, overseen by SS and Luftwaffe guards including SS-Aufseherinnen (female staff). On 3 May Polish partisans of the Holy Cross Brigade operating in the area heard rumours the prisoners were soon to be executed and the facility burned to the ground. Rushing there, they surprised the guards, and discovered jerrycans of fuel outside each locked barracks.

The Holy Cross partisan commander, Colonel Antoni Skarbek, recalled, 'Emaciated faces appeared from little windows, and there were loud screams for help. The Kommandant told me that prisoners of Jewish origin were locked up here on Hitler's orders. The buildings, along with the women, were to be doused with gasoline and burnt the moment [the Americans] approached. From the darkness of the buildings there was emerging a horrible stench of human waste mixed with the smell of rotting cadavers. From the depths the surviving women crawled out with great tears of joy'.[25] Two days later the Poles handed the site over to the 2nd Indianhead Division and 741st Tank Battalion, who adopted the brigade, enrolling the Polish guerrillas in US-guard companies, to prevent them being returned to Soviet-occupied Poland.[26]

Not far away, Sergeant Raymond Gantter's platoon with the 16th Regiment (1st Division) had arrived in Bukovany, where one of his men hollered, 'Hey Sarge, there's something funny up ahead – some big buildings, with a wire fence around, and a bunch of guys inside yelling their heads off!' They found 'several buildings, iron-barred, and faces pressing against them; scores of faces, a clotted mass of bearded, howling faces' surrounded by a twelve-foot barbed-wire stockade that resembled 'a zoo; here were cages and animals; I smelled the place, the foul breath of it'.[27]

The tiny village, known to their German settlers as Buckwa, accommodated slave workers 'who had no rights, no privileges, no hope of deliverance except death'. Gantter inspected their 'four-decker bunks, the gallows, and the coal mines where they worked fourteen to eighteen hours a day' and immediately regretted his men had saved any of the guards from being beaten to death. Gantter, a thirty-year-old graduate of Syracuse University, was uncomfortable with the demi-god status bestowed on him by the now ex-prisoners, finding their welcome 'a pagan scene, a Pan-ic revel, with emotions too raw, too unashamedly naked, to be contained in the cool syllables of dignity'. This was accentuated when the former slaves started searching for their guards.

'The manhunt that followed was a frightening thing to witness: the hunting pack of ragged, foul, wolfish men creeping upon a suspected hiding place, moving with a cushioned stealth that stirred dim, atavistic terrors and made the hair on the back of your neck suddenly bristle. The howl of the pack, the animal howl of feast and delight. We had to fight to save one guard. A higher note of hysteria from the crowd, and more piercing screams of agony warned us that this must be a special case and we'd have to move fast. We had to use our rifle butts roughly before we reached the skinny wretch in SS uniform who writhed on the ground. His face was covered with blood, his nose had been broken, and the slaves were jumping on him with savage intent. [They] were angry at our interference and explained he had been the officer in charge of their food rations.[28]

Rarely so explicitly described in print, this was the fate of countless thousands of SS men when found by their former inmates. Most often

GIs stood aside and let 'the bitter spit of hate' run its course. Gantter also noted 'a new turbulence arose when the slaves broke into the kitchen and storehouses [and] began to gorge. I tried to halt this insane banquet, but only half-heartedly. There would be many sick men before the night was out, but I could not find it in my heart to take the food from them.'[29]

Some of Gantter's buddies in the 16th Infantry found yet another camp at Falkenau (today's Sokolov). It was where 1,200 female slaves had toiled making Luftwaffe equipment, many expiring from malnutrition and mistreatment. On 8 May, the call went out to the entire regiment to cease all forward movement. The war was over. In 443 days of combat, the Sixteenth alone had lost 1,250 officers and men killed in combat. An additional 6,278 were wounded or missing in action, a turnover of roughly 300 per cent. Its GIs had earned an astonishing four Medals of Honor, eighty-seven Distinguished Service Crosses, and 1,926 Silver Stars. They had fought their way through North Africa, Sicily, Omaha beach, and Nuremburg.

The dead of Falkenau were recorded in amateur footage by Sam Fuller, a Hollywood filmmaker-turned-infantryman and veteran of Omaha beach on D-Day.[30] With the war just ended, and already looking towards resuming his film career, on 9 May Fuller privately shot twenty-two minutes of 16mm film, having 'one hell of an opportunity to cover the biggest crime story of the century', as he wrote in his autobiography, 'and nothing was going to stop me from being an eyewitness'. He documented the emaciated bodies, 'thrown on top of each other like newspaper'. Spectating in Fuller's film were the barely-alive inmates who 'raised their bald heads and looked at us, eyes sunken in anguish, their mouths agape, a hand here and there reaching out, grasping for anything, begging us for assistance in helpless silence.'

Fuller recorded Falkenau's former inmates, both the living and the dead, and local Germans being forced to witness the camp's conditions and the fate of their victims. His Falkenau footage is a rare item, being a personal documentary but produced by a Hollywood professional, who had fought through the war as a foot soldier. He later wrote of the need to archive such scenes which remained 'imprinted on my mind like a leaf in a fossil, never to fade away'.[31]

Third Army would go no further, for on 7 May Patton received a secret signal from SHAEF warning of the impending German surrender. There was much surprise that the senior Wehrmacht officer in Czechoslovakia and last commander of Army Group Centre, the brutal *Generalfeldmarschall* Ferdinand Schörner, did not practise what he preached and end his own life. Widely despised by his fellow Germans for executing thousands of his own men on the flimsiest of pretexts, on 8 May Schörner discarded his uniform, deserted and escaped to Austria in his personal aircraft, dressed in Bavarian hunting rig.[32]

For Lieutenant Colonel Charles W. Goodwin's 803rd Tank Destroyer Battalion, with the prophetic radio call sign of 'Victim', the news of surrender would come too late. Operating with M36 Jacksons and attached to the 5th Infantry Division (XII Corps), on 7 May Company 'C' had advanced just five miles over the Czech frontier to Volary in the southwest of the country. In the vanguard an M8 armoured car came under fire from several panzerfäuste; the second vehicle was an unarmoured Jeep driven by PFC Charley Havlat. His parents were Czechs who had migrated to Nebraska in 1910. A Czech speaker, proud to be liberating his homeland, his job was to liaise with the locals.

According to his brother Adolph, in the ambush Havlat 'fired once at the Germans and then ducked down behind the hood of the Jeep. But when he peeked back up from the same position, a bullet struck him directly in the forehead, killing him instantly.' Tragically, the ceasefire had taken effect nine minutes before Havlat died. The German officer from the 11th Panzer Division who led the ambush was captured soon after. He was unaware of the cessation of hostilities until thirty minutes later and apologised for the death. Havlat would be the last GI to die in combat in Europe.[33] Buried back in the American military cemetery in Metz, a roadside plaque near Volary now marks the precise spot of his demise.

In early May, the 3rd Cavalry, forward reconnaissance element of Walker's XX Corps, arrived at Ebensee, fifty miles south-west of Linz, and a satellite of Mauthausen concentration camp. One of the most beautiful spots in Austria, *The Sound of Music* would later be filmed in the area. Here 20,000 slaves working in shifts, twenty-four hours a day, were hollowing out enormous underground caverns for armaments factories and a petroleum refinery. In its sixteen months of operation, around half the workforce perished, though continuous drafts had kept their numbers up to strength. Not even permitted to see daylight and almost without food, the tragedy was that while some clung to life long enough to be liberated, they were too weak ultimately to survive.

The 3rd Cavalry took 4,500 prisoners in local towns, while 'SS troopers each day would filter down and give themselves up to us, mainly, I think, for protection against the liberated prisoners from the camp,' noted 'B' Troop's history.[34] The more numerous 80th 'Blue Ridge' Division arrived soon after to take over medical relief. 'I went through a barbed wire gate and everybody in our outfit was literally stunned; no one talked,' wrote Corporal Kenneth Colvin, a surgical technician in the 515th Medical Clearing Company. His unit of twelve GIs and four doctors attended various camps as they were liberated, giving emergency medical attention; separating the living from the dead; and feeding and medicating those still alive, who were mostly malnourished and had tuberculosis. 'In front of me I could see the crematoria, these huge chimneys reaching up into the sky, covering the countryside with horrible ash. People who had not yet been cremated were naked, stripped of their hair. The survivors looked bewildered in their striped uniforms and had staring faces.' Another liberator recalled seeing a cadaverous inmate take a shower only to collapse from the shock of the water.[35]

Communications Sergeant Samuel S. Klein with Company 'F', 3rd Cavalry, observed people 'eating coal to get nutrients from it, that's how desperate they were. One man asked for a cigarette. He took two puffs and passed out. A nameless survivor painted my portrait. When I look at it, I think how fortunate I was.'[36] Corporal Colvin wrote a letter that night about how this experience had 'given his whole life definition'. Years later he mused, 'Looking at the emaciated survivors, it was impossible to allow ourselves to feel, because we would have all crashed. I contained those feelings many, many years. We had no forewarning of what we were going to see; we had only heard that such things existed. I still, to this day, dream about it.'[37] After liberation, at least 735 prisoners died, and were buried locally with over 3,000 earlier victims.

'To describe this camp is an impossibility. Words alone cannot begin to tell of the stink of decaying human flesh, or of the miserable condition of the hungry, living mummies who were confined there,' recorded the

3rd Cavalry's History. 'The camp, operating on a principle of planned starvation, worked on the assembly line basis. Opponents of the Reich entered in comparative good health; were passed from barrack to barrack in successive stages of hunger, and finally, too weak to move, were carried to the crematorium. The remaining inmates, resigned to their fate of gnawing pain, milled about the vehicles of the liberating 3rd Cavalry. No man will forget that concentration camp. They will not soon forgive the dainty frauleins and sedate burghers who comprised the progressive, educated, *nice* German people, and who lived so close to the camp, yet pretended ignorance of its existence.'[38]

Decades later, Sergeant Klein reflected on his painful memories of that place. 'We were never informed about concentration camps. We were completely surprised and horrified . . . You started talking about it and then you'd start crying . . . What we went through was worse than any battle, injuries, anything else we saw during the war . . . Our men just broke down crying. Just couldn't believe what they saw or what they smelled. The worse part of it was that the camp smelled like death.'[39]

Alan Moskin, an eighteen-year-old American soldier with the 66th Regiment, 71st 'Red Circle' Division (Walker's XX Corps), recollected discovering several detention camps near Lambach on 4–5 May. These were fifteen miles south-west of Linz, the capital of upper Austria. First, he stumbled on a POW camp, holding mostly Royal Air Force aircrew; the British airmen told them they had heard of a different kind of camp, for Jews, at Gunskirchen, a few miles distant. 'I remember my buddies and I looked at each other. We knew Hitler wasn't fond of Jews, but we hadn't heard anything about concentration camps.'

Moskin and his fellow GIs followed a forest trail, baffled by a sickening stench. 'We tried to cover our mouths and noses with a bandana, then I remember looking through some trees at a tall, barbed wire fence guarding a compound,' he recounted. 'There were dead bodies on the left, piles of dead bodies on the right – and their arms and legs looked like broomsticks covered with no flesh.' As Moskin's unit entered, they handed out all the rations they carried. 'Many of them would start biting and chewing so fast they started to grab their oesophagus, and I remember they would start choking and falling to the ground. We got frightened. We didn't know what was happening. And then the medics started screaming at us, "No solid food, damn it!" '[40]

PFC Ralph Talanian, also with the 71st, recalled, 'I had never seen anybody so emaciated, just literally breathing skeletons.' Due to their malnutrition, Talanian frequently failed to determine their sex, asking himself, 'Is this a man or a woman I'm speaking to?' He concluded, 'The only similarity to humans is, they were standing . . . A few of them knew English and were able to converse, though mentally they weren't rational.'[41]

On Patton's left flank, the 26th Infantry and 11th Armored Divisions, both XII Corps, occupied Sankt Georgen an der Gusen on 5 May. The original Gusen camp dated back to 1938 and was chosen for its proximity to a quarry where prisoners produced granite blocks for sale by DESt (Deutsche Erd- und Steinwerke – German Earth and Stone Works), the innocent-sounding SS front company for all concentration camp quarrying, ceramics and brick-making industries using slave labour from 1938.[42] In 1943, DESt – conveniently headquartered in Sankt Georgen – switched to underground arms manufacture. Three camps, Gusen I, II and III, evolved, from which prisoners trekked to nearby mountains to chisel out a tunnel system code-named Kellerbau (basement construction), where rifles, machine pistols and aircraft motors were assembled for Messerschmitt-Aerowerke and Steyr-Daimler-Puch, who had relocated from Regensburg after Allied bombing.

A larger underground project nearby was code-named B-8 Bergkristall (rock crystal) for the mass production of Messerschmitt-262 jet fighters, where nearly one thousand fuselages had been made by the war's end. GIs discovered that prisoners spent over twelve hours a day in the fourteen miles of rock chambers, where the dust and lack of oxygen killed thousands; their remains were reduced to ashes in the camp crematorium.[43] Although the SS planned to murder all the 40,000 inmates at Gusen, by herding them into the caverns and dynamiting the entrances with twenty-four tons of explosives, already laid and fused, the sheer speed of the 11th Armored Division nullified such plans.[44]

Staff Sergeant Albert J. Kosiek's task was to check whether the local bridges around Gusen would bear the weight of CCB's tanks. By the day's end, the twenty-three men of his 1st Platoon, Troop 'D', 41st Cavalry

Reconnaissance Squadron, had achieved something quite different, which reflected the extraordinary circumstances of those dying days of the European war. It was all due to the intervention of a Zurich bank clerk turned Red Cross official, Louis Häfliger, who had earlier led a convoy of nineteen trucks carrying food to the area. From local people the Swiss learned the true conditions at Gusen, and from the SS, their plans to blow up the inmates in the tunnels.

A few weeks earlier, the International Committee of the Red Cross (ICRC) in Geneva had received permission from SS-General Ernst Kaltenbrunner, in charge of Reich security forces, for its delegates to visit concentration camps with vehicle convoys bearing aid and food parcels. The change of heart was motivated, no doubt, by an understanding that the fighting would eventually cease. However, the Swiss officials would have to stay until the war's end. Häfliger was among ten delegates who volunteered for the hazardous mission, arriving at nearby Mauthausen camp on 28 April.

Aware of the Reich's rapidly changing fortunes, and the intent of the SS to slaughter all their inmates, on 5 May Häfliger decided to exceed his responsibilities as a Red Cross official and prevent the pointless act of defiance the Nazis intended for their slaves. He persuaded the SS to lend him a car, repainted it white with red crosses, identifying it as an ICRC vehicle, and flying a white flag, set off to look for the advancing Americans. With the military situation fluid, Häfliger equipped himself with two junior SS officers and a motorcycle escort in case of trouble from local Nazis. The SS, concerned about their own skins in the immediate future, played along. Thus, when they encountered Kosiek's reconnaissance patrol, GIs initially regarded the car as an SS ruse.

The Americans had already freed the small Gusen III camp containing three hundred inmates and were aware of more ahead. Häfliger was convincing enough to persuade the M8 armoured cars of the 41st Cavalry to follow him next to Gusen I and II, after Kosiek had received permission from Combat Command 'B' to amend his mission. The patrol sped on to the main Gusen I camp, where they found elderly Volkssturm and Viennese Firemen in control, as most SS had fled. According to Gusen's official records, 27,842 people died at the three Gusen sites before liberation on 5 May. The cavalrymen freed the 20,487 who were left.[45] A

US Army photographer was on hand to record the moment. The GIs accepted the surrender of the guardforce, though the newly liberated inmates literally tore other jailers apart, while more committed suicide. Freedom was a messy business, with around five hundred guards killed that day. Conditions at Gusen were so bad that the GIs were powerless to prevent another 2,000 ex-prisoners dying in the immediate aftermath of their liberty.[46]

Kosiek's armoured vehicles finally came up to Mauthausen camp, still following Häfliger in his white-painted automobile. This was the mother camp, perched on the highest ground in the area, flanked on one side by the Danube. It resembled a castle, with huge granite walls and a gatehouse with stone towers. The Polish-American later reported, 'The situation was ticklish, for there was no guarantee that the roads were undefended, in spite of assurances we would not run into trouble. The camp had been taken over by an international prisoners' committee in the absence of their warders, who had fled.'[47] Hanging from the walls of the Mauthausen gatehouse, Kosiek noted home-made flags of the thirty-one nationalities incarcerated, and banners erected by the prisoners' committee. The latter – with the agreement of the Volkssturm and Fire Brigade, who had been left to patrol the camp fence – had imposed a form of self-government at Mauthausen as soon as the regular SS guards had melted away.

Kosiek learned that Mauthausen had been built next to the Wiener Graben quarry, another DESt enterprise, from which 186 narrow, uneven stone steps led up to the camp. This was the *Todesstiege* (stairway of death), which captives had to climb carrying quarried stone blocks. To stumble was to invite instant death. SS guards amused themselves by placing prisoners at the edge of a 150-foot cliff known as *die Fallschirmspringerwand* (the parachutist's wall), from which each inmate had the option of jumping to certain death, pushing the man in front or being shot. Over one hundred died every day. Nearby, Kosiek was shown the sports fields where, when relaxing from mass murder, the SS played football. The ordinariness of their leisure activities, something Kosiek and his buddies would do, somehow made the Germans' crimes against humanity more grotesque. 'How could you,' he wondered, 'play ball one moment and put to death fellow humans the next?'

Edgar Edelsack, a 91st Armored Field Artillery Battalion gun crewman, was also part of the 11th Armored's entry to Mauthausen. Over sixty years later he looked back to 5 May 1945 when he was twenty-one. He had seen colleagues blown up as they tried to de-arm German mines and had loaded bodies of frozen GIs onto trucks, 'so I was a very hardened soldier. But to see Mauthausen was something very, very emotionally . . . something to this day I haven't made peace with.'[48] Staff Sergeant Kosiek recalled, 'Behind that gate hundreds of prisoners were in formation and when I walked in, they were so happy to see an American soldier that they all started yelling, screaming, and crying. To these people my appearance was freedom from all torture and horror. As I stood there looking out at the mob, I realized what this meant to them, and I was glad we had made the effort to free the camp.' Once the 2,000-volt electric stockade wire was turned off and the elderly guards had surrendered, 'behind that fence were hundreds of people who went wild with joy when they first saw us. It's a sight I'll never forget,' Kosiek recorded. 'Some had just blankets covering them, and others were completely nude, men and women combined. I still shake my head in disbelief when that picture comes before me, for they hardly resembled human beings.'[49]

The 41st Cavalrymen disarmed and rounded up the elderly guards from Mauthausen and guided them back to the divisional prison cage at Gallneukirchen, where one of the interrogators was Staff Sergeant Salinger. On the way the 41st collected those at Gusen; the total swelled to over 1,800. Other ad hoc units also surrendered by the roadside, happy to enter American captivity rather than that of the Soviet Army, rumoured to be in the vicinity. From their vehicles, the two dozen GIs shepherded their long marching column, and it was not until 01:30 on 6 May that the Germans arrived at their new home, a large field. As Kosiek observed, 'The major in charge of the PW cage said he would not believe the fact that we had brought in so many prisoners, if he had not seen it with his own eyes.'

They had captured around 2,000 Germans and rescued a minimum of 32,000 inmates, for at Mauthausen, First Platoon freed another 12,000 in addition to 20,000 in the three Gusen camps, acting fast enough to prevent their massacre by the SS. Among those released was Simon Wiesenthal, an Austrian Jew who would spend the rest of his life hunting Nazi war criminals. Mauthausen was one of the most brutal of all camps.

From the first wagonload of inmates in 1938 to Kosiek's arrival in 1945, between 123,000 and 320,000 died during the tenure of Mauthausen's Kommandant, SS-Standartenführer Franz Ziereis. As one detainee recollected, 'the guards would tell us, "Above me is only God." And it really was like that. You cannot imagine the power these people had. They could do whatever they wanted. There were no limits.'[50]

Of Mauthausen's other eighty-eight sub-camps, there were several in Linz itself, taken by other units of the 11th Armored on the same day. At one, No. 16, Hauptstrasse, 250 prisoners had to build a concrete air-raid shelter. When they and their fellow slaves were too weak to work, they were simply thrown into the River Danube by their overseers. The total Mauthausen death count remains uncertain due to the destruction of most records. However, seven volumes bound in tooled red leather survived, recording the camp number, name, sex, age, nationality, cause of death and 'death number' of 35,318 men, women and children murdered in 1945.[51] It was cited in evidence by the Prosecution at Nuremberg and in two special Mauthausen trials of 1946–7. 'The names of the dead are all carefully listed; the victims are all recorded as having died of the same ailment, heart failure. They died at brief intervals. In alphabetical order.'[52]

Tanker Ted Hartman recalled that his divisional commander, Major General Holmes E. Dager, ordered 'all men in each unit to be taken to see Mauthausen. Once out of the truck we noticed a haze in the air and an awful stench. The townspeople insisted that they had not known what was going on.[53] After Mauthausen, the 11th sped on to Linz, where they met the Soviet 7th Guards Airborne Division. 'The nearest troops to us were miles behind and nothing on either flank. Our determined armor "paid the rent" and pulled the infantry along. We were the farthest east of all American units when the war ended and itching to go further,' he observed.

Perhaps the 11th Armored's Staff Sergeant Dale V. Olson best summed up what the liberation process meant to him and all Western Allied troops in uniform. 'I do not have words to express how horrible it was. Sometimes I wondered while in the Army why I was there, but after viewing these camps I had no question why, and felt grateful that I had done my little part to stop these atrocities.'[54]

*

Up on the northern flank, under Montgomery's direction, we left Neil Ritchie's XII British Corps besieging Hamburg. However, both sides were negotiating hard. Originally businessman Albert Schäfer, Leutnant Otto von Laun and medical officer Dr Hermann Burchard had approached British lines with a request for the attackers to stop shelling a hospital. Schäfer was sent back with a surrender demand from Major General Lewis Lyne of 7th Armoured Division hidden in his shoe. The Gestapo would have taken a dim view of any attempt to capitulate. Over 29–30 April, with secret approval of Generalmajor Alwin Wolz, Kampfkommandant of Hamburg, the trio, plus a German speaker for General Lyne, hammered out an agreement, while closeted in the Hotel Hoheluft in Buchholz, outside the city.[55]

The defenders were exhausted by a week of accurate shellfire, running out of ammunition, manpower and willpower, and on Hitler's death, requested permission from Dönitz, their new Führer, to surrender. Hamburg had never been an ardent Nazi city, with support for left-wing parties high among its pre-war population of 1.7 million; even in 1944 there lurked underground Communist cells. It was rarely visited by Hitler on account of its political ambivalence, and by the time of its surrender, two-thirds of the population had already fled.

On 2 May, the large white flag fluttering from a black Mercedes staff car announced the arrival of two staff officers from Wolz's headquarters at British lines. Blindfold, they were led to Brigadier John Spurling, commanding 131st Brigade of 7th Armoured Division. After confirming the capitulation terms, the senior Wehrmacht officer asked to speak to Spurling alone. 'As soldier to soldier,' the German began, 'I ask your advice on whether the staff and I should commit suicide on our return.' The question again emphasised how the concept of surrender was unknown to professional Wehrmacht officers. Spurling replied, 'That's entirely up to you.' An Oxford-educated British colonel pointed to the other Wehrmacht officer's blindfold. 'Isn't that a Brasenose scarf?' In perfect English, the other responded, 'No, Christ Church. I was there studying your House of Lords.'[56]

There was much saluting on both sides as cameras clicked the next day when Wolz formally surrendered the city outside the Rathaus. 'Suddenly British soldiers are everywhere,' recorded Mathilde Wolf-Mönckeberg. 'They creep like ants through the streets, and soon motor vehicles, motor bikes, tanks and armoured cars follow. They settle in, bringing wooden posts with notice boards: Army Post Office, Tailor, Leave Centre. We are bursting with curiosity, standing on our balconies all day long to watch what is happening.'[57]

Squadron Leader Edgar Venning, a dental officer with the Second Tactical Air Force, found he had little call for his services so joined No. 83 Group's 'Official Observer' in a blue-painted RAF Jeep. 'It was an amazing drive. There was no resistance at all. In fact, in Hamburg's outskirts the Germans were lining the streets, wide-eyed with relief, and undoubtedly pleased that for them it was all over. Many were waving, if a little self-consciously. The centre was like a city of the dead. We drove through a desolate, devastated and deserted landscape, with piles of rubble and twisted steel on either side of the road. The road was lined on both sides by German military police, every hundred yards, in long green greatcoats and impressive helmets. Many saluted as the convoy went by – no Nazi Heil, but a deferential cap salute.'[58]

Hamburg turned out to possess its own concentration camp, Neuengamme, a name almost unknown today, although it also administered a labyrinth of at least ninety-nine sub-camps in north-west Germany. It had first opened its gates on 13 December 1938, as another SS-run enterprise supplying bricks for Reich building projects. Established fifteen miles south-east of Hamburg, it evolved into a huge complex. Over 100,000 passed through its gates, and as the war ground on, the satellites came to employ three times more than the main site. During the winter of 1944 nearly 2,000 a month were dying of abuse or neglect, but there were still 13,000 in the main site with another 30,000 in sub-camps during March 1945.[59]

Many of Neuengamme's work sites were in Bremen and Wilhelmshaven, where two huge ammunition bunkers were being built for the Kriegsmarine, code-named *Hornisse* (Hornet) and *Wespe* (Wasp). Another giant reinforced concrete structure was erected on the River Weser north of Bremen. *Valentin* was a giant submarine factory, constructed by 10,000 slave workers who lived in seven nearby camps, 10 per cent dying of overwork and malnutrition. The inmates included thirty-two seamen from (theoretically neutral) Ireland, who revealed that the highest mortality rates came from the Zementtrupp (cement squad) – carrying and emptying heavy, dusty bags of cement – or the Eisenbahnkommando, shouldering and laying rail tracks or iron and steel girders. With a fatalistic air, the detainees dubbed both details Himmelfahrtskommandos (suicide squads).[60] The jailers were recalled by the Rev. Iain Wilson, padre of the 1st King's Own Scottish Borderers in 3rd Division, as 'many SS, some weary old men and young boys, a sadistic labour camp Kommandant and a large proportion of the Bremen Police Force.'[61]

Valentin was 90 per cent complete when, during March 1945, it was heavily damaged by RAF Grand Slam earthquake bombs and abandoned. The vast bunker was designed to shelter manufacture of the latest Type XXI diesel-electric U-boats, that were quieter, and could stay underwater far longer than earlier models. Several Type XXIs, plus all relevant technical drawings, were captured in Bremen by 30 Assault Unit, a British specialist outfit that operated with front-line troops to 'seize intelligence, in the form of German codes, documents, equipment or personnel'. Before he could depart from Bremen docks with his loot, Lieutenant Commander Patrick Dalzel-Job found his way barred by a pen-pushing British staff officer, insistent he sign a receipt for sixteen U-boats. Their details soon ended up in the hands of 30 AU's creator and leader, Commander Ian Fleming.[62]

In mid-April, Neuengamme began to be emptied. Over 9,000 inmates, including *Valentin* workers, with others from Nordhausen and the Berlin camp of Sachsenhausen, were loaded onto four prison ships at anchor in the Bay of Lübeck: *Cap Arcona*, a luxury liner and former flagship of the Hamburg-Sudamerikanische shipping line (27,500 tons, 5,000 prisoners), *Deutschland*, a liner belonging to the Hamburg-Amerikanische line (21,000 tons, 2,000 prisoners), and two merchantmen, *Thielbek* (2,815 tons, 2,800 prisoners) and *Athen* (4,450 tons, 2,300 prisoners). Post-war testimony suggested the regional Gauleiter, Karl Kaufmann, had ordered these ships scuttled with their human cargoes, to remove all trace of the camps' victims.

RAF Typhoons beat him to it on 3 May, when Allied intelligence wrongly concluded the vessels contained fleeing Nazi officials bound for Norway. Three vessels were struck, left burning and later capsized; the *Athen* escaped, still in harbour. Those who jumped into the water were either strafed by RAF Typhoons or shot by the SS. Phillip Jackson, a Briton on board *Thielbek*, recalled, 'I managed to reach one of the three lifeboats. I was rescued before [the Germans] knew we were prisoners. After that, they only rescued seamen and their own soldiers and simply let several thousand prisoners drown. The first 150 to reach the shore were shot by the SS.'[63]

Lining the coast, British troops could just make out the still-smouldering wrecks under the grey skies of early May. The heads and shoulders of thousands of floating corpses were visible like a latter-day *Titanic* disaster. It was only on seeing their emaciated frames, and finding the victims clad in the blue-and-white-striped woollen garments of the camps, that the significance of what had just taken place hit XII Corps. Only 450 survived, discovered by No. 6 Commando and 11th Armoured Division, washed up on local beaches, half dead, while around 9,000 died. One soldier never forgot the girl of about seven he found, still clutching the hand of a woman, presumably her mother, their vice-like grip inseparable in death. Just before British troops appeared at Neuengamme itself, six hundred prisoners had been retained on 29 and 30 April by the remaining SS guards to burn all archives, dismantle the main camp crematorium, scrub barrack floors and windows, and even whitewash the walls – as if a lick of paint could cover years of obscenity. Thus, when the British 4th Armoured Brigade arrived on 3 May, it was reported 'clean' in more than one sense of the word.

SHAEF soon realised that strictly adhering to their pre-agreed River Elbe meeting line with the Stavka (Soviet High Command) would leave the northern Reich states of Mecklenburg and Schleswig-Holstein, including the key port of Kiel and its canal leading to the North Sea, and the whole of Denmark open to the Red Army. Nearby Bremerhaven, earmarked by the US Army as their future port of entry into North West Europe, would also be vulnerable to any Soviet aggression. Thus, it was in order to contain the mass of Germans, military and civilians, from pouring out of Mecklenburg ahead of the Russian Army, but mainly to stop a Communist advance into Denmark, that Eisenhower directed Montgomery to advance to the ports of Lübeck and Wismar on the Baltic coast and halt the Red Army in its tracks. Stalin's presence in Denmark would have upset any future European balance of power in allowing him to seal off the entire Baltic and control the sea trade of every country around its rim. With the Soviets focused entirely on their battle for Berlin, on 30 April Eisenhower secured the Stavka's agreement for Montgomery to temporarily move beyond the Elbe to occupy western Mecklenburg and up to the Baltic coast.

In Operation *Enterprise*, during the early hours of 29 April, Barker's VIII Corps made an assault over the Elbe, with bridges thrown across the river by sappers of 11 AGRE (Army Group Royal Engineers). While Ritchie's XII Corps flowed across and turned left to complete the siege and capture of Hamburg, Ridgway's XVIII Airborne Corps (US 7th Armored, 8th Infantry and 82nd Airborne Divisions), loaned to Second Army for the purpose, joined British 5th Infantry, 6th Airborne and 11th Armoured Divisions for their drive to the Baltic. Their collective mission was to advance with all haste to Wismar and Lübeck before the Soviets in order to prevent them from entering Denmark. The 5th Infantry and 11th Armoured dashed towards Lübeck later on 2 May, where they would eventually witness the sinking of the prison ships.

The 6th Airborne troops, with no transport of their own, riding in trucks or on the Shermans of the Royal Scots Greys (2nd Dragoons), set off for Wismar early on 2 May, with instructions to arrive that evening. In the vanguard was the Canadian Parachute Battalion, whom we last met jumping into Germany on 24 March, during *Varsity*. 'I never knew a Sherman tank could do sixty miles an hour,' observed one of the Canadians. Although its top speed was actually around thirty, this felt extremely fast to the Canuck paratroopers, thundering down good roads, past long columns of despondent German soldiers. All of the latter were fully armed, but few made any attempt to resist. The forty miles they covered amounted to the longest single day's advance of the Greys during the war, reaching the port after lunch.

At about 16:00 the Red Army arrived, none too impressed that they had been beaten to their objective, and insistent on following the coast further westwards to Lübeck. After fruitless negotiation, Major General Eric Bols, the 6th Airborne's commander, eventually turned to his interpreter and raged, 'Tell this bugger I have a complete airborne division and five regiments of guns. If he does not clear off, I will open fire.' The Soviets appreciated the strong retort, their General broke into a broad grin, and backed down. The BBC's Wynford Vaughan-Thomas was present and, without referring to the stand-off, broadcast on 3 May, 'Two great armies, British and Russian, have met. German prisoners were desperately trying to get across the barrier. A Russian guard gave me a wink and said "Siberia". And everybody I must say has no pity for them at all. It's the end, the dead end of Hitler's Reich.'[64]

It was on 3 May that Dönitz first sent peace emissaries to Second Army's headquarters in Lüneburg's Cavalry Barracks. They were redirected to Dempsey's quarters in the Villa Möllering in a southern suburb, Häcklingen. Warning his superior by radio that the Germans were on their way, Dempsey then sent them to Montgomery's TAC headquarters, five miles to the east. The latter's caravans had been set up two days earlier on the summit of Timeloberg hill on Lüneburg heath, south-east of the town. Shy and retiring by nature, the Second Army commander thereafter played no further part in the surrender proceedings, rightly judging this to be 'Montgomery's moment'.

On meeting the German delegation, Montgomery's Canadian liaison officer, Trumbull Warren, recollected that his field marshal was clad 'in a pair of corduroy trousers, washed so many times they were bleached white, and had no crease, and a grey turtle-neck sweater.' Bradley, who disapproved both of the man and his mode of dress, once called the Briton's appearance that of a 'Bohemian painter'. Above his office caravan, covered with camouflage netting, a Union Jack pulled restlessly in the spring breeze. 'Who are these men?' Montgomery demanded from his TAC intelligence officer, Colonel Joe Ewart, and interpreter, Captain Derek Knee. 'What do they want?' He knew full well but was determined to humiliate his foes. Their leader, Generaladmiral Hans-Georg von Friedeburg, Dönitz's former deputy and now in charge of the Kriegsmarine, introduced himself. Wearing the familiar double-badged beret, very sure of himself, hands behind his back, Montgomery glowered back. Then he spat out the words, 'Never heard of you.'[65]

With Friedeburg was Konteradmiral Gehard Wagner, Flag Officer; General Eberhard Kinzel, 'a magnificent looking officer about six-foot-five, complete with monocle; a real professional Prussian'; Dönitz's army advisor; and two staff officers, Oberst Fritz Poleck and Major Hans Jochen Friedel. They tried to negotiate, aware that each extra hour ensured more Germans could escape to the West. After giving them lunch, the Briton, who was wise to their game, took every opportunity to dress them down. He mentioned Coventry, whose city centre had been destroyed by the Luftwaffe on 14–15 November 1940, to widespread shock throughout Britain. Then he tongue-lashed them about Belsen.

With a threat to unleash 10,000 bombers on the remains of Germany if an unconditional surrender did not materialise within twenty-four hours, Montgomery sent them on their way. As they departed, a pre-arranged flight of Allied fighter-bombers zoomed fast and low over the area, to reinforce the point. Friedeburg returned the next day with his team and agreement to all Montgomery's demands. The field marshal was more soberly dressed on this occasion, with a special tent, and tables and chairs arranged for an alfresco ceremony. 'There was the sober air of a school prize-giving, or village fête where award-winning vegetables were being judged,' recorded Sergeant Major Ronald Playforth, of the TAC staff.[66]

Watched by war correspondents, at 18:30 (19:30 in British Double Summer Time) the deed was done in silence, interrupted only by the flapping of the Union Jack outside. 'German forces in Holland, in north-west Germany, including all islands, and in Denmark' agreed to unconditionally cease all hostilities on land, on sea and in the air by 08:00 on Saturday 5 May. It was Dunkirk in reverse: the Germans had snatched two days to evacuate tens of thousands more away from the Soviets. The Wehrmacht mostly complied, although the Kommandant of the Danish island of Bornholm and his garrison of 12,000 soldiers, who appear to have been overlooked, surrendered only on 9 May.

To reinforce the message of defeat, Major Sydney Radley-Walters of the Sherbrooke Fusiliers (2nd Canadian Armoured Brigade) was ordered to make a show of force through Emden. The officer, who had three tanks destroyed from under him and was twice wounded, recalled getting into his scout car, 'and we rolled through Emden with the swastika flag tied to the back and dragging in the mud, with the rest of the regiment's armour following'. Among the tanks was 'Bomb', the only survivor of all their Shermans to have landed in Normandy and make it to Germany, without being destroyed or knocked out.[67] Opposite, the perimeter of the Dutch port of Delfzijl, to where the defenders of Groningen had decamped, was protected by the guns of Emden, with the Germano-Dutch border running down the centre of the Ems estuary. After a ten-day siege, and acknowledging that the end of hostilities was around the corner, its garrison commander had surrendered on the evening of 2 May. More than 4,000 prisoners fell into the hands of the 5th Canadian Armoured Division, marking the end of its war.

Private Floyd McCulloch of the Cape Breton Highlanders recalled the last hours. 'Delfzijl was the toughest battle we were ever in. I sometimes think that I can still smell the burning buildings, but we took the place. After I got out of battle, I fell asleep in an old building. Sergeant MacGregor woke me up and said, "She's over, we won!" I told him I didn't think I could have gone into battle again.' Beginning with the crossing of the Rhine on 24 March and extending to the end of hostilities, Canadian Army casualties totalled 6,298, of whom 1,482 were killed. Their losses for the entire North West European campaign beginning on 6 June 1944 were 44,339, of whom 961 officers and 10,375 other ranks paid the ultimate price.[68]

Throughout the Netherlands, 5 May is known as *Bevrijdingsdag* (Liberation Day), and is celebrated with festivals in Amsterdam and the twelve Dutch provincial capitals. It was on this day that Charles Foulkes of I Canadian Corps summoned Generaloberst Johannes Blaskowitz to Hotel de Wereld in Wageningen, ten miles west of Arnhem, to sign a surrender document at 17:00. Attending as the Commander-in-Chief of his armed forces was Prince Bernhard of the Netherlands. His own complicated ancestry gave him greater insight than most into the Netherlands' struggle with her larger neighbour, for he was a German prince by birth. His brother was an officer in the German Army, but when Bernhard married Princess Juliana in 1937, he swore allegiance to the House of Orange, cutting off contact with his own family, who were Nazis. No paper soldier, Bernhard spent his war in England, flying combat missions as a Wing Commander in the RAF, while his wife Juliana and three daughters lived in Ottawa. Although the negotiations took place in the Hotel de Wereld, the actual signing took place in the nearby University auditorium.

On 7 May, as Amsterdammers gathered in the central Dam Square of their capital, a firefight broke out between German Marines and Dutch interior forces, disarming them. Thirty-two civilians, who had until that moment been celebrating the return of peace, were killed and 231 others wounded. Over the border, the port of Wilhelmshaven finally fell on 6 May to General Stanisław Maczek's Polish Armored Division, still part of the First Canadian Army. Colonel Antoni Grudzinski, second in command of the Polish 10th Armoured Brigade, recalled of the surrender negotiations, 'An officer on my staff translated every sentence into German. When the words "Polish Division" were uttered by him, the Germans blanched, and sheer terror flashed in their eyes. I enquired if they understood. "Jawohl," they replied. As they left, I thought, "This is for September 1939." '[69]

Apart from taking the surrender of ten infantry divisions, the Poles captured three cruisers – *Prinz Eugen*, *Nürnberg* and *Leipzig* – fifteen destroyers, eleven torpedo-boats, eighteen U-boats and 150 other Kriegsmarine vessels. Maczek's men had every reason to be proud of their achievements. Since landing in Normandy, they had covered more than 800 miles, captured 52,000 prisoners, destroyed 320 armored vehicles and 310 artillery pieces and downed thirteen aircraft. Their own losses were 5,000 men and 350 vehicles. They were joined in occupation by the 1st Polish Independent Parachute Brigade, who had earlier contested Arnhem. More widely, Poland had fielded over 250,000 soldiers, sailors and airmen in every theatre in Europe, Africa and the Middle East, making it the fourth largest Allied army, and the only one that fought from the first day of the war to the last.

Faced with piecemeal surrenders in Italy, southern Germany (to Devers), the north (to Montgomery), and numerous towns and cities, but no uniform capitulation, and none to the Soviets, SHAEF decided on the legal need for a general surrender document. Generaladmiral von Friedeburg was flown to SHAEF's headquarters in the Rheims Technical College, arriving at 17:00 on Saturday, with the surrender to Montgomery in force for twelve hours. He tried to insist that he had instructions to surrender only to the Western Allies but was overruled. Friedeburg was not empowered to sign a final surrender and had to request Dönitz to send someone who could. The following day Generaloberst Alfred

Jodl, deputy head of the High Command of the German Armed Forces, flew in, landing at 17:00 on Sunday 6 May. He dragged his feet until 02:00 on Monday 7 May.

CBS journalist Charles Collingwood described Eisenhower's map-lined war room as 'bathed in the hot glow from the blinding lights the photographers have set up. At one end is a long wooden table, the top side of which is painted black. Around this are fourteen chairs. Twelve of them are arranged around one side, and the other two, with their backs to us, occupy one whole side of the table. This is where General Jodl and Admiral Friedeburg had to sit. Major Wilhelm Oxenius, Jodl's aide, and Oberst Fritz Poleck, Friedeburg's assistant, stood behind their masters, the pair dressed in green, with a darker green collar, wide red stripes on flared breeches and black leather boots.'

Facing them were a range of senior SHAEF figures, presided over by General Bedell Smith, the chief of staff, with, in addition, the French Generals François Sevez and Alphonse Juin, and the Russian, Ivan Susloparov. The ink was soon dry. It was a little before three in the morning. After signing, Jodl asked for permission to speak. Collingwood recalled that 'he stood up stiffly, like a man holding himself in against some unbearable pain. In a strangled voice, like a sob, he said: "With this signature the German people and the German Armed Forces are, for better or worse, delivered into the victor's hands. In this hour, I can only express the hope that the victor will treat them with generosity."' Up to this moment, Eisenhower and his deputy, Air Chief Marshal Tedder, had absented themselves. Then Jodl and Friedeburg were taken to them. 'The Germans bowed and stood there. Through his interpreter, Eisenhower asked them curtly whether they had understood the terms of surrender and whether they agreed to carry them out. The pair said "Ja" and were taken away.'[70]

Eisenhower then addressed the media in his humble and generous way. 'The unconditional surrender has been achieved by teamwork; teamwork not only among all the Allies participating but almost all the services – land, sea, and air. To every subordinate that has been in this command of almost 5,000,000 allies, I owe a debt of gratitude that can never be repaid. The only repayment that can be made to them is the deep appreciation and lasting gratitude of all free citizens of all the

United Nations.'[71] Susan Hibbert, a British sergeant working in SHAEF, then signalled the War Office in London: 'The mission of this Allied Force was fulfilled at 02:41 local time, 7 May 1945.' To allow official messages to reach every headquarters of both sides, 8 May was designated VE-Day. The building, at 12 Rue Franklin Roosevelt, now houses a fine little museum detailing the event.

And yet. Susloparov had earlier sent the proposed text to Moscow for authorisation, which failed to arrive by the time of the Rheims ceremony. He signed with the caveat that another formality might be necessary for his own government. As he sent a report on his actions to Moscow, he saw a freshly arrived order *not* to sign the surrender document. True to form, Stalin had wanted his own observance and he insisted on it being held at the Soviet military HQ in Karlshorst, a former officers' mess of the Wehrmacht Pioneer School, six miles south-east of central Berlin. Chosen simply because it was one of the few buildings in the capital left with intact windows and a roof, the formalities were presided over by the captor of the city, Marshal Georgy Zhukov, and Stalin's French-speaking personal representative, Andrei Vyshinsky, who had flown in from Moscow for the occasion.

This time, it was Generalfeldmarschall Wilhelm Keitel, Jodl's superior, accompanied by the now-exhausted Friedeburg, who read over a near-identical document. As well as Tedder acting for SHAEF, Susloparov was again present, along with Carl Spaatz and de Lattre, whom de Gaulle had dispatched from southern Germany. Newsmen were unaware of the diplomatic spat that delayed proceedings over the fact that no French *tricolore* was in evidence among the standards and pennants decorating the surrender room. The first Soviet solution hilariously produced a Dutch flag. To pacify an even-more outraged de Lattre, a Red Army seamstress was summoned to run up the appropriate banner. More delays ensued while the Allies bickered over the order of signatures and witnesses. After the mollifying effects of vodka and some food, it was agreed that de Lattre and Spaatz would sign as witnesses, but on a line lower than that of Tedder and Zhukov. Finally, it was noticed, several sentences were missing from the Russian text; it took a further hour to translate, insert and reproduce the correct words to everyone's satisfaction, which is why the ceremony began shortly after midnight.

Cameras captured Keitel in full dress uniform, arriving in pompous mood. Flashlights caught the glint of his many medals, and the arrogant flourish of his marshal's baton, held with gloved hands. He gazed around the room, haughty contempt written across his face. The Generalfeldmarschall removed only his right glove, screwed his monocle into his left eye and applied a fountain pen to the two-page, typewritten document on behalf of the German Army. Generaladmiral Friedeburg did likewise for the navy and Generaloberst Hans-Jürgen Stümpff for the Luftwaffe. Clifford Webb of the London *Daily Herald* reported that 'the Soviet press surged forwards until they all but engulfed the top table, pushing and struggling amongst themselves, to thrust their cameras within inches of Keitel's furious face. Reporters stood on chairs until other reporters pushed them off.'[72]

It was 00:16 local time on Wednesday 9 May, which became Soviet Victory Day and remains so in Eastern Europe. Karlshorst, from where the Soviet sector of Berlin was administered, soon became known as the Little Kremlin, the name replacing Dachau as a place of fear and loathing for Germans. It, likewise, hosts a Russian-orientated museum, dedicated to the Great Patriotic War, and eventual German surrender. Later that day, Tedder and Spaatz departed on a motor tour of central Berlin, and newsreels captured their astonishment at the handiwork of their bomber fleets in reducing the German capital to blackened walls and smoking rubble.

Now the clock began ticking in the opposite direction, as various German groups resisted capitulation after VE-Day, or were overlooked. It took more than a week before all the German garrisons on the British Channel Islands finally yielded, after their five-year occupation. The 3,000 Axis troops on Alderney remained in control of the small island until 16 May, or V+8. Kapitänleutnant Johann-Heinrich Fehler with U-234 was in the mid-Atlantic, bound for Tokyo, when he learned of the surrender. He decided to press on with his cargo of a disassembled Messerschmitt-262 jet, two Japanese scientists, and the new chief of Luftwaffe liaison in Tokyo, General Ulrich Kessler. Significantly, U-234 was also carrying uranium oxide to aid a last-ditch Japanese atomic weapon. When apprehended by a fifteen-man boarding party from USS *Sutton* on 14 May, the Japanese committed suicide, while the uranium was diverted to the Manhattan Project.[73]

Another submariner, Oberleutnant zur See Heinz Schäffer, had put to sea with U-977 from Norway on 2 May with orders to sink warships off southern England, but he abandoned his mission and headed instead for Argentina, to request political asylum. After a spectacular voyage, sixty-six days of which were spent submerged, he arrived off the South American coast on 17 August, V+101. He had been preceded by another submarine, U-530, which had arrived in the same port, Mar del Plata, on 10 July. Both vessels and crews were immediately turned over to the US Navy. The arrival of these two boats fanned rumours then, which have continued unabated to this day, of senior Nazis, shipments of gold, or secret weapons aboard, none of which have been substantiated in any way.[74]

On V+12, Canadians from Simonds' II Corps arrived on the Dutch island of Texel to find a civil war in progress. Much earlier, on 5 April, in expectation of an Allied landing, its mostly-Georgian garrison had risen up against their Wehrmacht overlords and massacred around 400 German troops as they slept. Aided by the Dutch underground, they fought on when German reinforcements arrived to suppress the mutiny. The reaction was merciless, with more than 500 Georgians executed. Meanwhile, as the Germans on the mainland had surrendered to Montgomery, the retribution force was, in turn, stranded. Before further escalation, Canadian troops landed on 20 May to disarm both factions, by which time 1,500 Georgians and Germans had died, plus some Dutch civilians aiding the rebels. There are several monuments to this bizarre struggle, considered the final battle of the European war, across the fifteen-mile-long island.[75]

The final armed Germans to surrender were from a weather-reporting station on remote Svalbard (Spitzbergen). They had been overlooked in the events of early May, and when faced with no response to their reports, the eleven-man team started broadcasting on Allied distress channels. A Norwegian seal-hunting ship was sent to retrieve them. The crew and the meteorologists shared a meal together, after which Leutnant Wilhelm Dege handed his pistol to the Norwegian captain by way of official surrender. The date was 4 September 1945, V+119 – exactly four months after the ceremony with Montgomery on Lüneburg Heath.[76]

Who were the last soldiers to die in battle from the British and Canadian forces? As Montgomery was signing his surrender document on 4 May, to take effect on the 5th, the Protestant chaplain of the Canadian Grenadier Guards (4th Armoured Division), Padre Albert McCreery, set off, with Lieutenant Norman Goldie, to bring in some wounded Germans. Within hours, McCreery was discovered dead, and Goldie posted missing in circumstances which remain obscure. That evening, General Crerar received news of the German surrender at 20:35, first via the BBC, confirmed immediately afterwards by Twenty-First Army Group. However, south of Rastede, a small German town midway between Wilhelmshaven and Bremen, patrols from 'C' and 'D' Companies, the Algonquin Regiment, had already set out to round up German troops from nearby woods.

At about 20:00, 'C' Company ran into a party of aggressive opponents and in the ensuing firefight Private Arthur Donald was killed, several Germans died, and twelve surrendered. Meanwhile, at last light a two-man reconnaissance had also set out from the same regiment. At some stage, Private Charles 'Bones' Sheffield became separated from his colleague and was discovered dead the next day. It is probable that Sheffield was captured on patrol and killed before Donald died in the skirmish. These two, aged twenty-four and forty, respectively, were probably the last Canucks to die in combat.[77] Fighting under Canadian command, the last Pole killed in battle appears to have been Lance Corporal E. Strzelecki of the *Strzelców Podhalanskich* (Podhale Rifle) Battalion, killed on 27 April.

It is relatively simple to identify the last casualties of the First World War, but with a far more fluid situation in May 1945, it has proven unexpectedly challenging to pinpoint the last British soldier to die in combat, in North West Europe. The Commonwealth War Graves register lists one Royal Marine Commando and 228 army deaths between 1 and 8 May, buried in Germany alone.[78] Some will have been killed in action, others died of wounds, or from booby traps, more in accidents. In this category was eighteen-year-old Edward Hemmings of the 2nd Oxfordshire and Buckinghamshire Light Infantry (6th Airborne Division) who died on 1 May, rounding up prisoners of war from local farms and woods on the way to Lübeck. It was while examining captured weapons that

Hemmings accidentally shot himself with a Luger pistol, a week before peace. Near him in the same cemetery lies Reginald Cadd, aged seventeen, from the same regiment, who died three days before the end.[79] Some twenty-three soldiers died in Germany and eight in Holland on 7–8 May 1945; one of these will have been the last.

The V Corps historian, Master Sergeant Forrest C. Pogue, remembered the last day of the European War, D+336, in the Czech city of Pilsen. As he recorded in his diary: 'Heard the official announcement of VE Day. Was glad I heard it in Czechoslovakia; one of the first of Germany's victims. No blackouts: to many of the fellows, that was the best thing they had ever seen.'[80] Sergeant Henry Giles, whom we last met at Remagen, reported, 'Today is VE-Day. We heard Churchill's victory message on the radio. It made you blink back the tears. He reminded the British people that five years ago all he had to promise them was blood, sweat and tears. Now we have victory. I'm still afraid I'll wake up and find I've been dreaming.'[81]

In London, George Beardmore, a local government official living in the British capital, noted, 'the blackout curtains were left undrawn, and all the searchlights shone in the sky. I must be anti-social because I find that rejoicing with a hundred thousand others isn't my idea of fun. We are clouded by impending trouble with Russia over the future of Poland. We have come to the end of it all, but food is scarce.'[82] More sociable was the parliamentarian Harold Nicolson, whom we last met worrying about Hitler's Alpine Redoubt. He observed 'the glow above a floodlit Buckingham Palace under a cone of searchlights, which joined together like a Maypole above our heads. The statue of Nelson was picked out by a searchlight. The National Gallery was alive with every stone outlined in floodlighting, and there was Big Ben with a grin upon his illuminated face.'[83]

Across the divide, near Ulm, journalist Ursula von Kardorff confided to her diary on 8 May. 'It is midnight. Unconditional Surrender comes into effect from this moment. All over the world they are singing hymns of victory and the bells are ringing out. And what about us? We have lost the war. But if we had won it, everything would have been more horrible still.'[84]

Every major German city had been reduced to stinking ruins by aerial bombing and ground combat. Nuremberg was no exception. These two contrasting views of the ancient Hauptmarkt (market square) emphasise the destruction. Renamed the Adolf-Hitler-Platz on 25 March 1933, twelve years later, on 20 April 1945, victorious GIs of the 3rd 'Marne' Division rechristened it 'Iron Mike Place', after their commander, Major General John O'Daniel. The latter ordered it renamed 'Roosevelt Place', in honour of their recently deceased president, though in time it has reverted to being the Hauptmarkt.

20

Aftermath

Hitler had named Karl Dönitz as his successor. He was formerly *Befehl-shaber der Unterseeboote* (Chief of U-boats) and later of the entire German Navy. He spoke English due to the fact that, when serving in the Kaiser's submarine service in 1918, he had been captured off Malta with his U-boat and spent a period of imprisonment in a prison camp near Sheffield.[1] It was Dönitz who broadcast to the Reich the news of his predecessor's demise, and who set up a new German government in the Fatherland's most northern unoccupied city, Flensburg. Hitler's other likely successors – Göring, Himmler and Kesselring – had ruled themselves out by trying to negotiate peace settlements or surrenders without Hitler's knowledge. In the spring of 1945, for example, Himmler had met Folke Bernadotte, a Swedish nobleman and diplomat, and as the military situation turned sour, had attempted to negotiate behind Hitler's back, using his camp inmates as bargaining chips. Bernadotte rescued 15,000 of them, but Himmler's cynical and unrealistic talks went nowhere.

The Admiral was surprised to have been appointed. Reich Propaganda Minister Goebbels had originally been designated as Chancellor, with Dönitz as President and Commander of the Armed Forces. Bormann's signal to him on 1 May read, 'In place of former Reichsmarschall Göring, the Führer has appointed you, Herr Grossadmiral, as his successor. Written authorisation is on the way. You are to order all measures that are required by the present situation.' As Goebbels, trapped in the Berlin Führerbunker with his family, had committed suicide the day after Hitler, Dönitz became the senior Reich government minister.

He oversaw a mere sliver of territory, no more than a Nazi Theme-Park, centred on the Naval Officers' Academy at nearby Mürwik, where he spent most of his three-week tenure removing soldiers and civilians from Russian clutches. One useful thing Dönitz accomplished was to cancel the Werewolf programme. German radio, broadcasting from Flensburg early on 6 May, duly carried his appeal that German men and women 'abstain from any underground fighting in the Werewolf or any other organisations . . . that can only be to the detriment of our people.'[2]

With the arrest of the Admiral and his government on 23 May, a brief power vacuum ensued until the dissolution of the Third Reich on 5 June, when the United States, Russia, Great Britain and France assumed direct control of the administration of Germany, with absolute powers. As a result of the international conference held at Potsdam, over 17 July to 1 August 1945, Nazi organisations began to be terminated and their activities prohibited. On 30 August, the Allied Control Commission, then running Germany (sub-divided into its four occupation zones on 30 July), prohibited the wearing of German military uniform. The Nazi Party was formally disbanded on 10 October and on 12 November, the German Armed Forces.

Curiously, the only organisations permitted to keep their uniforms and sidearms were the Feldgendarmerie (Military Police) and Feldjägerkommando III, the latter being the outfit who had conducted many of the drumhead courts martial and executions during March–May 1945, in the West. The Feldjägerkorps was established in 1943; its members were identified by a crescent-shaped metal gorget worn around the neck and possessed the same level of authority as an Army commander. They were given legitimacy to punish any officer or enlisted soldier, from any branch of the military, Waffen-SS included. With their reputation of wielding such awesome power, the Feldjägers remained in being, at the disposal of the US Army, to maintain discipline amongst German prisoners of war until formal disbandment on 23 June 1946. The National Socialist-era eagles, another sign of the Reich, still adorning many civic buildings, had their swastikas erased, in accordance with an Allied Control Commission Directive of September 1946. Thus, it is perhaps difficult to state definitively the moment the Third Reich disappeared for good.[3]

The use of German units to police their own goes some way to challenging the contention that the Allies deliberately starved to death up to a million German prisoners after the war. Certainly, the presence of 3.5 million German troops in Western Allied POW camps by July 1945 stretched Eisenhower's logistics beyond breaking point. Around twenty mass *Rheinwiesenlagern* (Rhine meadow camps) were established along the banks of Germany's great waterway to house them, administered by British, French and American forces. Perhaps unwisely, SHAEF designated these prisoners as Disarmed Enemy Forces, which removed all rights to which they were entitled under the Geneva Convention. This was partly an administrative device, due to SHAEF shortages, to supply a lower daily calorific intake than Geneva recommended, but also a form of blackmail to deter German Werewolf activity in the post-war Fatherland.

Though the miserable Rhine camps, guarded by other Germans, and only ever a temporary expedient, were shut down in September 1945, prisoner abuse undoubtedly took place and up to 10,000 may have died from disease, malnutrition and neglect. The men were behind wire, in the open and without shelter. This was certainly not the US Army's finest hour (though the French were, in some respects, worse, for they required their hordes of disarmed Germans to perform hard labour), but the casualties were nothing like those claimed by some writers.[4] Thereafter, many Germans have since told me of their desperation to obtain their *Persilschein* (Persil ticket), a document certifying they had a clean political past and were not closet National Socialists. Essentially a 'whitewash' for minor Party functionaries and SS, and named after Germany's most popular pre-war soap powder (which washed 'whiter than white'), the certificate was the conclusion of an individual's denazification process, without which legal employment was impossible.

In 1945 there were 7 million more women than men left in Germany, so it was the *Trümmerfrauen* (rubble women) who had to clear up the ruins of the Third Reich. Newsreels captured long chains of them, piling up bricks for re-use, salvaging materials to repair their roofs and windows, and recovering timber for heating and cooking. There was little running water, and what there was came from street pumps. With around 3.5 million German soldiers killed, another 5 million detained as prisoners or missing, and the forced labourers set free, most agriculture ground to a halt.[5] There would be no harvest in 1945, and starvation threatened for the coming winter. Only Allied generosity – more forthcoming in the British zone than the American or French – would drag the Germans through their first post-war wintertide.[6]

None of the Allies had planned the occupation particularly well or foresaw they would remain in the Fatherland for decades. Initial policies were harsh, though the British, with most industrial capacity in their zone of 20 million people, realised the ban on fraternisation (which could include talking to Germans, as well as forming relationships with them) would have to be abandoned and replaced by friendly cooperation. Major Ivor Crosthwaite with the 4th Grenadiers (6th Guards Tank Brigade) recollected that 'Within fourteen days of Lüneburg, Monty came to inspect us. We gathered round his Jeep as he told us: "The War is over. No one's interested in it any more, except the historians. Every man-jack of you will have leave before 31 July. You'll be demobilised by age and length of service. What are we here for? To see the Germans get back into their homes, get the crops in and get the coal up before the winter, and to show them how to become good neighbours."'[7] Unspoken was that setting Germany back on her own feet in the British zone would also reduce the financial burden on a United Kingdom already bankrupted by the war.

Crippling Germany's future manufacturing and agricultural capabilities with a ruthless Carthaginian Peace, such as that imposed by Rome at the end of the Punic wars, would be to no one's benefit, although this was precisely the suggestion of Henry Morgenthau Jr, US Secretary of the Treasury, in 1944. The Western Allies soon feared such a vengeful policy would drive Germans eastwards into the hands of their Communist counterparts. Thus, Britain became the first Allied nation to change its policy from keeping Germany down, to setting that nation back on its feet again. For the most part, pursuing the perpetrators of many of the crimes against humanity we've explored, the process of *Vergangenheitsbewältigung* (coming to terms with the past) would have to be left to the Germans themselves.[8]

This process was not thorough, and although twenty-four top surviving Nazis, including Göring, Dönitz and Speer, were indicted by the

International War Crimes Tribunal at Nuremberg in 1945–6, and a further 183 soldiers, lawyers, doctors and industrialists were tried in the wake of the first trial, by 1958 as few as 6,093 former members of the NSDAP or its military offshoots had been convicted of committing a crime. This was complicated by a substantial number, as we have seen, committing suicide. Others had died in combat before the war's end; and more were detained within the Soviet Union or East Germany, both of whom resolutely refused to extradite their captives.

As the continued de-classification of government files demonstrates, not a few were recruited as military technicians, informers, and intelligence operatives in the Cold War fight against what came to be the Warsaw Pact nations. Shady deals were done in smoky coffee shops to exempt these former Nazis from post-war justice. The *Persilschein* process also came to be used as a more formal whitewash for junior members of the Party, SA, SS, Hitlerjugend, police, judiciary and others, to reintegrate them as servants of the new West German state, established on 23 May 1949. Within two years, a recorded 792,176 former NSDAP functionaries, out of 8.5 million Party members, had been legitimately readmitted to public life despite their past sinister behaviour.[9]

Across Germany, the immediate post-war imagery was staggeringly awful. Lieutenant Colonel Wilfred Byford-Jones, on Montgomery's staff, passing through railway stations, found 'men and women who had lost, together with their homes, families and property, all human dignity and had become animals, sleeping on the floor'. In refugee camps – former barracks, schools, quarantine stations, Red Cross centres – he 'saw such human degradation, depravity and tragedy that I was physically sick after a few hours of it'.[10]

Eisenhower and Montgomery became the military governors of their respective occupation zones, with the Foreign Office diplomat Sir William (later Lord) Strang advising the field marshal. At the time, Strang observed of Allied policy, 'The primary purpose of the occupation was to disarm and demilitarise Germany and to uproot the Nazi party, not to promote Anglo–German friendship or to bring about the economic revival of Germany, though these were laudable objectives which might well be consequently achieved.' In retrospect, Montgomery's governorship of May 1945 to October 1946 was strikingly successful yet remains one of the unsung achievements of his military career. It was he who in October 1945 first observed, with considerable foresight, that 'an Army of occupation would be required in Germany for at least ten, and possibly twenty years. The [British] field army should normally be kept and trained in Germany, where the cost would be borne by the Germans and where training facilities were magnificent.'[11]

Later Strang, Montgomery, and the chief of staff in Germany, General Sir Brian Robertson, realised that Anglo–German friendship and detente were preferable to West Germany falling under the Communist spell, and thus began the nation's astonishing, but unplanned, economic revival. Yet touring the British zone in 1945, Strang documented how the 'Villages and small towns off the main roads were intact; towns and villages at crossroads often smashed; larger centres like Münster and Osnabrück, half or three quarters demolished; industrial cities like Dortmund almost totally in ruins, except round the fringes.'[12]

George Clare, an Austrian Jew who had escaped in 1938, returned as a British officer after the war. He was more struck by the silence of German cities, which he reminisced, had been 'a medley of blaring car horns, squeaking brakes, snorting buses, clanging trams, shouting newspaper sellers'. Now he heard only 'the clip-clop of often wooden-soled footsteps, the rattle of a handcart or an occasional tram, the chugging of a wood-fuelled bus, the gear-clash of an Allied army lorry. This absence of the constant roar of city life was more unsettling than the sight of bombed and shelled buildings, of jagged outlines of broken masonry framing bits of blue sky. I had been prepared for that, but not for a city hushed to a whisper.'[13]

'My daily route through Hamburg was less by streets, than by a series of unpleasant meanders that zig-zagged between piles of debris,' Major John Maddock, a staff officer posted to north-west Germany in 1945–6, told me. 'Those damn road surfaces were so uneven. Shards of metal and glass slashed at our tyres, which we replaced weekly. Cobblestones and bricks had been blown to one side or other, and now awaited the rubble girls sorting them into neat piles. They were strong individuals. I mean mentally as well as physically. Hardly a day passed without them finding human remains from the raids. Mostly what had once been women and children. Wooden or metal stakes topped by rusty cans or rotted fabric acted as markers to indicate the presence of the unburied or the unexploded. I can still picture metal tubes sticking up from the wreckage, smoking chimneys, telling one of the troglodytes, mostly I think, DPs, for none spoke German, who subsisted in the cellars below.'

Maddock recalled that Hamburg was 'incredibly depressing, a city of sagging ruins, without straight lines. I remember all the lampposts were leaning at crazy angles. Signposts too. I don't recall seeing a single window left intact, just gaping holes. Facades were blackened by fire but spotted with marks from bombs which exposed the lighter stone beneath. Timber and trees had long gone for firewood. Telephone and power lines dangled down in every direction, reminding me of my mother's knitting. Only that first winter snow hid the apocalypse and softened the brutal lines of our sector. Everywhere was a ghastly smell of human waste and damp and concrete dust. Medieval. Rats scuttled everywhere. Occasionally I had to wrestle with the thought that our side had done this.'[14]

An outstanding account of what was left was penned by diplomat Ivone Kirkpatrick, British political advisor to Eisenhower at SHAEF, and later High Commissioner of the British Occupied Zone in Germany. In his autobiography he recollected, 'Germany was then an astonishing sight. Everything which modern man considers necessary to the maintenance of life in a civilised society had disappeared. There was no governmental authority, no police. No trains, trams, or cars; no factories working, no postal service, no telephones, no newspapers, no banks. No shop was open, and it would have been impossible to buy a loaf of bread, a glass of beer or an aspirin. Every bridge was blown, and the available rolling-stock could be seen marooned between the ruins. In the Rhine hundreds of sunken craft showed their upper works whilst the giant bridges lay collapsed in the riverbed. In the countryside the sudden departure of the foreign labourers had halted agricultural work.'[15]

Lieutenant Colonel Charles Carrington, a British veteran of 1914–18, recollected that the end of the Great War was unexpected until the last moment, 'like a sleeper suddenly awakening from a hideous nightmare.' In contrast, he and his colleagues could see the end of World War Two in Europe approaching from a long way off. Yet when it happened,

Carrington wrote of being gloomy and exhausted, as 'VE-Day meant no more than the war, which might go on for years, had shifted its ground from Europe to Asia.'[16]

On the minds of soldiers with long service was getting home, but the uncertainty of an even more ferocious opponent in Japan loomed large for most. Eisenhower particularly was under pressure from Marshall to announce Redeployment Day, when eligible GIs – calculated on points, determined by length of overseas service, married status, number of dependents, bravery awards and time in combat – could begin to return by sea and air to the United States. Eventually he agreed to an R-Day for Americans of 12 May 1945, with most over the next year being repatriated via staging camps at the ports of Marseilles, Antwerp and along the north French coast, named after cigarette brands. Hence the 'tent cities' of *Philip Morris*, *Old Gold*, *Lucky Strike* and *Pall Mall*. Though anxious to demobilise, most in the smaller British and Canadian armies expected to continue serving as an occupation force in the Fatherland or take part in Operation *Downfall*, the planned land invasion of Japan's home islands, scheduled to begin in November 1945. Before this, all would have been given home leave, as Montgomery had promised.

Meanwhile, the former servants of the Reich were considering their own futures. Many opted for a personal Wagnerian *Götterdämmerung*. Of the German capitulation signatories, Admiral von Friedeburg committed suicide on 23 May after his exhausting round of three surrender ceremonies; on the same day, General Kinzel shot himself with his mistress in their stationary car. Jodl and Keitel were tried at Nuremburg and hung on 16 October 1946. Hermann Göring, who surrendered on 9 May 1945 to Brigadier General Robert Stack, of the 36th Texas Division, a Seventh Army formation, died the day before his appointment with the hangman. He had likewise been found guilty at Nuremberg but cheated his executioner by taking poison smuggled to him the night before. Another suicide was Heinrich Himmler, head of the SS, police and Gestapo, who had been detained by the British on 21 May 1945. Admitting his identity two days later, he bit into a cyanide capsule on being searched. Johannes Blaskowitz, who surrendered Army Group 'H' to Crerar in the Netherlands, ended his life by throwing himself off a balcony in 1948, possibly fearing SS intimidation. Blaskowitz had been a particular opponent of the SS, first complaining to his army superiors about their murderous behaviour during the Polish campaign of 1939. Although the war was over, the enmity of the SS to him had not.

Of the other German commanders, Field Marshal Gerd von Rundstedt, already at retirement age when the war began, died of ill health in 1953. Günther Blumentritt, his chief of staff, who later succeeded Alfred Schlemm in leading the 1st Parachute Army for the last eight weeks of the war, penned an appreciation of his old boss, *Von Rundstedt: The Soldier and the Man*, in 1952. Rundstedt's successor as Commander-in-Chief West, Albert Kesselring, was captured at Saalfelden, near Salzburg, on 9 May, and came under the protection of Maxwell Taylor of the 101st, who allowed him to retain his pistol, medals and field marshal's baton. Tried for war crimes, Kesselring was found guilty in 1947 and condemned to death, but the sentence was commuted to life, and he was released for health reasons in 1952. The following year he published his autobiography, *A Soldier to the Last Day*, and died following a heart attack in 1960.

General Hermann Foertsch, who surrendered to Devers, was acquitted of war crimes and worked for the West German intelligence service before dying in 1961. Gustav-Adolf von Zangen, commanding the 15th Army opposite Simpson's *Grenade*, surrendered in the Ruhr pocket and died in 1964. Stümpff of the Luftwaffe was the only German signatory to live into old age, dying aged seventy-eight in 1968, after two years in British captivity. Generalmajor Franz Fehn, the defender of Augsburg, likewise had a light captivity, on account of his half-hearted resistance, and died in Bayreuth in 1972. So, too, for Alwin Wolz, Kampfkommandant of Hamburg, who followed him six years later. The much-reviled Ferdinand Schörner, the dedicated Nazi and ruthless hangman of his own troops, was convicted of war crimes by many nations. He eventually died in his bed in 1973 and was one of the reasons why the Bundeswehr abolished the rank of field marshal.

Grossadmiral Karl Dönitz was tried with Jodl, Keitel and Göring at Nuremberg and imprisoned for ten years in Spandau Prison in Berlin. He remained an unrepentant anti-Semite and Nazi, maintaining he had done nothing wrong. His memoirs came out in 1959, titled *Ten Years and Twenty Days*, the length of his prison sentence. After release, Dönitz retired to north-west Germany, where he died of a heart attack on Christmas Eve, 1980. He was followed the next year by his fellow Nuremberg defendant,

Albert Speer, who oversaw the mass use of slave labour. In 1969, he published *Inside the Third Reich*, a highly profitable memoir, though later found to be riddled with falsehoods. This last surviving Nazi minister died of a stroke on a visit to London in 1981. General of Paratroops Alfred Schlemm, who contested Operation *Veritable*, was later wounded in an air attack, but was one of the last Second World War generals to die, in 1986.

'I was very proud of being a Jew who arrested one of the most notorious gangsters in Nazi Germany,' said Sergeant Norman Turgel of 53rd Field Security Section, Intelligence Corps, of SS-Hauptsturmführer Josef Krämer, Kommandant of Belsen. In an unusually happy ending to a Holocaust saga, Turgel would soon marry Gina Goldfinger, one of his charges who had nursed the dying Anne Frank in Belsen and survived Auschwitz and Buchenwald. Their wedding took place in October 1945, officiated by Jewish padre Captain Leslie Hardman, who had helped liberate the camp. The bride's dress, now an exhibit at the Imperial War Museum, London, was sewn from British army parachute silk.[17] Krämer and chief female warden Irma Grese became the very personification of evil for a whole generation of Britons, in presiding over the largest 'horror camp' uncovered by Montgomery's forces. The pair, along with ten of the surviving staff, including two other women jailers, were tried by a British military court at Lüneburg, and on 13 December 1945, all were hanged at Hamelin prison, for their part in the atrocities.[18]

The shadow of World War Two dominated United States foreign policy for the next couple of decades after 1945, in Korea, Vietnam and via NATO in Europe. The man who made Eisenhower, George C. Marshall, went on to serve as Secretary of State in 1947–9, then Defence, in 1949–50. He spent the next ten years as chairman of the American Battlefields Monuments Commission (ABMC). In 1953, the year he also won the Nobel peace prize, Marshall led the American delegation to the coronation of Queen Elizabeth II. According to my grandfather who was present as a presiding bishop, when Marshall walked up the aisle of Westminster Abbey to take his seat, those present rose in respect. Humbly, Marshall looked behind to see who was following then realised the congregation had stood for him. Dying in 1959, the legacy of this great man includes the George C. Marshall Center for Security Studies, based in Germany, for whom I lecture occasionally.

Dwight Eisenhower became military governor of the US Occupation Zone, headquartered in the I.G. Farben building in Frankfurt after VE Day, before returning to Washington to follow Marshall as Army Chief of Staff. He became NATO's First Supreme Allied Commander Europe (SACEUR) in 1951–2 before entering politics as a popular and successful two-term president of the United States, practising what he had already become: a collaborative and diplomatic international leader. Succeeded by the youthful John F. Kennedy, Eisenhower retired to Gettysburg, a town and battlefield he had first visited when a student at West Point. He and his wife bought their 189-acre Gettysburg farm in 1950, which he used as a retreat from the presidency, before moving in full-time until his death in 1969, brought on by his life-long sixty-a-day smoking habit. 'Ham' Haislip, wartime commander of XV Corps, was one of the pall-bearers at his funeral.

Ike's close colleague and SHAEF Chief of Staff, Walter Bedell Smith, was appointed Director of the CIA, 1950–3, later becoming Under Secretary of State, 1953–4. He later narrated the voice-overs for Audie Murphy's movie *To Hell and Back* of 1955. After suffering a heart attack at home, he died in an ambulance on the way to hospital in 1961. Murphy, by then a movie star, whose film was based on his own bestselling 1949 memoir of the same name, had started to campaign vociferously for veterans' affairs. America would have heard more from him, were it not for his demise in an air crash in 1971, aged forty-six.

Eisenhower was followed as Army Chief of Staff by a succession of his former subordinates: Omar Bradley, J. Lawton Collins, Matthew Ridgway and Maxwell D. Taylor. Of these, Bradley ended his service in 1953, but lived out a very full retirement, lauded with honours, dying in 1981. Likewise, Collins, who was Army Chief of Staff through the Korean War. Ridgway, having taken command of the 82nd from Omar Bradley, succeeded one of Patton's corps commanders, Walton Walker, in running Eighth Army in Korea, then followed Eisenhower as SACEUR. He died in 1993.

Maxwell Taylor, who led the 101st Airborne until 1945, succeeded another wartime corps commander, James Van Fleet, at Eighth Army in Korea, and was then appointed by Kennedy as Chairman of the Joint Chiefs of Staff, 1962–4. Afterwards, he succeeded Henry Cabot Lodge

(Devers' former liaison officer to the French), as ambassador to South Vietnam, dying in 1987. Lodge, whose fascinating military career needs more examination, had re-entered the Senate in 1946 and is credited as the principal driver behind Eisenhower's decision to run for president in 1952. However, he worked so hard on the Eisenhower campaign that he neglected his own Massachusetts seat, narrowly losing it to John F. Kennedy. His consolation prize was the ambassadorship to the United Nations. He served in several ambassadorial roles until 1977, dying in 1985.

When the Sixth Army Group was disbanded in 1945, Jacob Devers soldiered on for four more years until his retirement, afterwards settling into the role of a West Virginian cattle rancher as well as consulting in industry, dying in 1979. Succeeding Marshall as chairman of the ABMC, Devers represented Eisenhower at the tenth anniversary ceremonies for Operation *Dragoon* in 1954, and for the dedication of three US military cemeteries, including that of Épinal, where Alexander Patch had buried his son in 1944.

'Sandy' Patch, who had suffered bouts of ill health since his service in the Pacific, relinquished Seventh Army when it joined Bradley's Twelfth Army Group on 16 May 1945, and immediately returned to Texas, where he died of a lung complaint in November the same year. Truth to tell, he still hadn't recovered from the death of his soldier son in October 1944. He was succeeded by the wartime XV Corps commander and Eisenhower's colleague, Wade Haislip. Hodges of the First, who was the same age as his exact contemporaries, Montgomery and Devers, but never possessed the same energy or presence, moved to the Pacific to prepare his army to invade Japan, but with the cessation of hostilities was invited to witness the official surrender in Tokyo Bay of 2 September 1945. He retired from service life four years later and died in 1966. After VE-Day, Bill Simpson of the Ninth undertook a mission to China in July 1945 before returning stateside to command the Second Army that October. Illness soon forced him into retirement, where he lived and worked on the boards of several local corporations in San Antonio, Texas. Far less well known than he deserves, 'Texan Bill' died in 1980.

George Patton, legendary commander of Third Army, became governor of Bavaria. He famously fell out with Eisenhower over his retention of National Socialist functionaries in his regional government, and more specifically because of his public anti-Soviet rhetoric. In September 1945 he lost his governorship, and Third Army the following month. He handed the latter over to Lucien Truscott, who had served under him in Sicily, when commanding the 3rd (Marne) Division, the 'Blue and White Devils', whom we first met in Utweiler.

On 9 December Patton was pheasant shooting with his chief of staff, Hobart 'Hap' Gay, when his car collided with a US military truck and the General hit his head on the glass partition in the back. Taken to a hospital in Heidelberg, Patton had received a broken neck rendering him paralysed from the neck down. The great warrior did not die as he had wished, clipped by a shell, standing on a tank in battle, but in his sleep of heart failure on 21 December 1945, aged sixty. It was an accident. There was no conspiracy to silence him as some have speculated. Patton was buried at the head of his troops in Luxembourg US military cemetery.

Throughout the war, with an eye to posterity, he had kept a daily journal. After his death it was edited by his wife Beatrice and published posthumously in 1947 as *War As I Knew It*. Self-centred and full of maxims and quotes about soldiering and leadership, the dedication from *Pilgrim's Progress* hints at how Patton saw himself. 'My sword I give to him that shall succeed me in my pilgrimage, and my skill and courage to him that can get it. My works and scars I carry with me, to a witness for me, that I have fought His battle who now will be my rewarder. So he passed over and all the trumpets sounded for him on the other side.' Patton's successor at Third Army, Lucien Truscott, enjoyed an exciting second career coordinating CIA activities in Europe during 1951–8 and died in 1965. John 'Iron Mike' O'Daniel, who took over the Marne Division from Truscott, rose to lead US forces in the Pacific. He retired as a Lieutenant General in 1955, commended by the then Army Chief of Staff, Maxwell Taylor. In 1945 it had been O'Daniel's destiny to beat Taylor to Berchtesgaden. The Marne's distinguished commander died in 1975.

In his last months, Patton had taken command of Fifteenth Army, originally led by Leonard 'Gee' Gerow, which had readied units for European combat. After the war, its role was to gather data for campaign histories of the European Theater of Operations, a semi-retirement role suited to Patton's love of history. On his death, Hobart Gay, Patton's chief of staff, inherited both Fifteenth Army and its mission. After service in the Korean War, on his death in 1983, Gay left an extensive account of Third Army's war under Patton, which I consulted in the US Army Military History Institute in Carlisle, Pennsylvania.

William Hoge, who did so well at Remagen, led IX Corps in Korea then took over Patch's old command, Seventh US Army, briefly in 1953, before handing it over to Anthony McAuliffe, wartime commander of 103rd Division. Hoge then went on to serve as Commanding General of US Army Europe, again succeeded by McAuliffe, before retiring in 1955. Hoge died in 1979, four years after McAuliffe. James Van Fleet, who replaced John Millikin at III Corps, Hoge and McAuliffe had all been colonels in 1943; within a decade all three had risen to full General. They are good examples of how the careers of already outstanding leaders can be boosted by stellar performance in war.

Of the Frenchmen under Eisenhower, Jean de Lattre stayed on to run his occupation zone, the result of his army's hard-fought campaign. After the humiliation of 1940, he made sure his fellow countrymen could enjoy the fruits of their victory with numerous parades, concerts and ceremonies at which he entertained visiting dignitaries. Yet de Gaulle sensed a rival in 'Le Roi Jean' and moved him back to Paris to undertake a series of administrative posts, which involved frequent rows with Montgomery. In 1950 de Lattre became commander in Indochina and was seemingly unbeatable against the Việt Minh. However, the death in action of his only son Bernard in May 1951 depressed him greatly. Prostate cancer forced his return to Paris, where he died in 1952.

Outside France, de Lattre's subordinate, Leclerc, remains better known than his chief, mainly on account of his liberation of the French capital in August 1944. Appointed inspector of land forces in North Africa after the war, his personal B-25 crashed in Algeria in November 1947, robbing France of one of her great generals. Leclerc's body was returned to France, where it was conveyed to Paris along the same route his division had taken in 1944. Like de Lattre, he was posthumously elevated to the rank of Marshal of France, an honour shared with only twelve others in the twentieth century.

In London, after his stint of governing Germany, Montgomery succeeded his mentor, Brooke, as Chief of the Imperial General Staff (CIGS) from 1946 to 1948. He later moved on to NATO positions, eventually becoming deputy SACEUR to Eisenhower from 1951. Like Patton, he was not a successful peacetime commander, though he did ensure the post-war British army was never again reduced to the pitiful state in which it had been in 1939. His elevation to the peerage as Viscount Montgomery of Alamein increased his sense of self-importance and led him to bicker with many friends and allies. With the British army thoroughly 'Montyfied', officers found their careers cut short if they took an opposing view to their field marshal. On retirement in 1958, his forthright *Memoirs* caused fresh howls of outrage, or – in Eisenhower's case – dignified silence. However, Montgomery brought to the army the highest standards of training and a sense of self-respect, both of which have lasted long after his death in 1976.

His principal subordinate, Miles Dempsey, is in danger of fading from the history books altogether. He remained completely unknown to the British public during the war and ensured he remained so after it. Montgomery wanted him to follow him as CIGS, but Dempsey preferred to retire, remained silent, pursued a successful career advising industries and developed his fine eye for racehorses. Committing his ire and frustrations to his diary, he ordered it be burned on his death in 1969, seven years before that of his chief.

Instead, it was the XXX Corps commander, Brian Horrocks, who became far better known during the war and afterwards. In 1949 he was appointed gentleman usher of the Black Rod, a ceremonial, but high profile, position within the House of Lords, which he held until 1963. At the same time, he wrote books and presented several documentaries, instantly at ease in front of the new medium of black and white television. As well-known as his friend and contemporary Dempsey was obscure, the jovial Horrocks died in 1985. Harry Crerar retired in 1946, accepting positions on the boards of several companies and undertaking diplomatic missions abroad for his country. Awkward and reserved, his reputation has not survived well since his death in 1965, assessed as more of a bureaucrat than a great battle captain, which as much reflected the state of the Canadian inter-war army as his personality.

The final map of the Victory Campaign, though holding with SHAEF's broad expectations, changed radically in the last hundred days, even if post-war narratives suggest otherwise. All had anticipated taking Berlin, though none, save de Gaulle, had suspected the French would carve for themselves a substantial occupation zone, won with greater martial élan than the Anglo-Americans had thought possible. Crossing the Rhine had proved easier and far less costly than expected, for the Reich had already expended its human and military capital in the Battle of the Bulge and defence of the western Rhineland. SHAEF's snail-like speed to take advantage of the Remagen bridgehead was disappointing. By contrast, the encirclement of Army Group 'B' in the Ruhr was a late stratagem, but a game-changer. The alternative was that Model's dispersed forces could have drawn out the struggle in the West for far longer. As it was, under Eisenhower's leadership, once the Rhine had been breached, the Third Reich had collapsed in just six weeks, though at huge human cost.

It seems odd that the wisdom of lingering to capture the workshop of Germany and its defenders in the Ruhr, rather than (to use Monty's phrase) cracking on to Berlin, continues to be questioned today. As some writers have pointed out, more than forty Allied divisions had crossed the Rhine by early April, but only eight were positioned north of the Harz mountains and on a direct road to Berlin. However, over thirty – including Patch's Seventh Army – were to the south or in the Ruhr. It was the three fronts of Zhukov, Rokossovsky, and Konev, with 150 divisions and sixty mechanised and armoured brigades, with 6,250 tanks, 7,500 aircraft, 41,600 artillery pieces and 3,255 truck-mounted Katyusha rocket launchers, totalling 2.5 million men (including 78,000 soldiers of the First Polish Army), that attacked Berlin. Of these, 1.1 million were later awarded the Soviet Victory Medal for the capture of the capital of the Reich.[19]

The city was never going to fall to the Western Allies ahead of the Soviets. Denying the city to the Western Allies was not an anti-British move, for it affected and dismayed American troops equally. Eisenhower was also wise, for Bradley's estimate of 100,000 casualties was far short of the mark. Post-war analysis suggests the Red Army suffered 300–400,000 killed and wounded in taking Berlin, albeit incurred in Soviet ruthless fashion.[20] History has come to regard those Allied commanders who turned their backs on the capital as discerning and insightful, big men who cared for the lives of those under them.

Even in early 1945, no senior commander would have predicted the possibilities of Werewolves, or a final German redoubt, even if both threats proved empty. The pointless final attacks, the German executions of their own and the wave of mass suicides took everyone, except the Russians, who operated with the same degree of ruthlessness, by surprise. The uncovering of the camps, the piles of corpses and the pitiful state of the survivors and slave labourers, was an evil beyond the wildest nightmares of Allied generals, even as they crossed the Rhine in March.[21] Many of their men never recovered from the trauma and no attempts were made to help them do so.

We can view the victory campaign in North West Europe as a durable and elaborate Roman arch, planned by the finest military architects, crafted by the most expert of martial stonemasons, and on which no expense had been spared. Its keystone was the person of Dwight David Eisenhower. He held the structure together, ensuring that military weight and responsibility was shared evenly among the Western Allies forming the sides. It was balanced and solid enough to absorb the earthquake of the Ardennes attack, and several disruptive personalities above, or under, his command. The arch was so reliable that it remains today, in the form of the North Atlantic Treaty Organization, founded less than four years after V E-Day, on 4 April 1949. Its military authority was based on the experience of SHAEF, which was restyled Supreme Headquarters Allied Powers Europe (SHAPE). It was appropriate that Eisenhower commanded both.

On 8 May 1945, Eisenhower's seven armies and three army groups delivered in full measure. Through Fire and Steel, they enabled the Victory in the West. It was the destiny of the Supreme Commander to keep the whole expedition on course, deaf even to the remonstrations of Churchill, Montgomery and de Gaulle. It was the Eisenhower arch, a collective effort, but governed by its keystone, that ensured the Third Reich ended 988 years short of its planned millennium, never to return.

Acknowledgements

It was shortly after completing the manuscript of this book that my attention was drawn to Sonderkommando Blaich. For those of you who cannot immediately call the story to mind, Theo Blaich was a professional adventurer and plantation owner (how I'd love that on my visiting card), a blend of the Hungarian cartographer Count László Almásy (of *English Patient* fame) and Indiana Jones. An amateur pre-war pilot who enjoyed nothing more than pottering over the Sahara in his Messerschmitt-108, the aforesaid Herr Blaich had, in 1941, worked out the importance of Fort Lamy, a war-time hub in French equatorial Africa. Its strategic position enabled the British to ferry supplies and aircraft from the west coast of the continent to their forces fighting Rommel. Allied pilots welcomed the pit stop at the airbase, where they poured fuel into their aircraft, croissants and café au lait into themselves, and followed the occasion with some professional snoozing.

Now, our enterprising friend had since become Hauptmann Blaich of the Luftwaffe. He thought it would be a jolly good wheeze to bomb the living daylights out of this remote Free French base in Chad, thus interdicting an important supply route for Montgomery. Rommel agreed with him and in January 1942, using a Heinkel-111 bomber, Blaich did just that, scattering sixteen bombs that interrupted the garrison's siesta, destroying 80,000 gallons of Allied fuel, important stocks of croissants and red wine, plus ten aircraft, and all before the somnolent defenders could find the keys to their lockers of anti-aircraft ammunition.

Naturally, I turned to social media and on the anniversary of his ingenious raid (21 January 1942), showered praise on his resourcefulness. And yet, and yet. I was immediately taken to task by the assembled online multitude. 'It wasn't just Blaich. What about the rest of the

Heinkel's crew?' some of you demanded. In fact, Blaich's team, which included an Italian, was accompanied by a second aircraft that ran out of fuel, and had to be rescued from the middle of nowhere by a third plane. The ensuing fury of Facebook, outrage on Instagram, ruffled feathers of LinkedIn and typhoon on Twitter was quite correct. I had overlooked that Hauptmann Theo's achievement was in fact one perpetrated by Messrs. Blaich & Company, a corporate team effort.

This is a particularly verbose way of saying that this volume is the result of many helpful suggestions, much invaluable advice and inspirational mentoring, without which I would still be pondering Chapter Five. Let's now forget about Herr Blaich and picture an aircraft carrier. Its sailors are responsible for every aspect of the onboard aircrew's life support and fighting capability. Thus, too, the lot of a writer. I am a humble scribe, honoured to be in the capable hands of a large assemblage of experts. Among the senior officers on board – let us name our carrier the *Intrepid* – is Lord High Admiral Trevor Dolby, who a decade ago commissioned my two 'monties' – *Monty and Rommel* and *Monte Cassino* – and then was visionary enough, with his fellow admiral and coalition partner, Tim Bent of Oxford University Press in New York, to give the green light to my World War Two trilogy, of which this volume is the last.

Trevor's place as ship's captain has now been taken by Admiral Nigel Wilcockson, whose expertise has been navigating the *Intrepid* through the rough waters of that global pandemic. He has also had to cope with his pilots flying with abnormally large bomb loads, as anyone who has attempted to lift *Sand and Steel*, my volume on D-Day, will acknowledge. The Bent-Wilcockson supreme command has helped keep this volume slim, to the relief of bookshops, delivery drivers and readers worldwide. Manning guns, radar screens and engine rooms, are Nigel's well-drilled team, including Hope Butler, Laura O'Donnell, Elena Roberts and Rose Waddilove; the officer in charge of maps and charts is Darren Bennett. My copy-editor, Katherine Fry, accomplished the Herculean task of battling with the gorgons of the author's prose and bashing it into the shape before you. Just as the real Admiral Horatio Nelson kept his own prize agent (Alistair Davison, responsible for determining the value of captured ships) close to him on his various men o' war, also near the helm of the *Intrepid* is my agent, Vice Admiral Patrick Walsh, who has now seen me through five meaty volumes. Without the magnificent help of this bridge of admirals (apparently their formal collective noun), your humble scribe would still be grounded.

The *Intrepid* is a weapon, designed and built to change perceptions and understanding of World War Two history. It would be inert without a slick and efficient flight deck. In charge of air operations, particularly in gathering intelligence, selecting targets and ensuring this pilot has the correct weapons load, is my wise old friend, Vice Admiral James Holland, who is often joined at the microphone by his salty seadog colleague, Vice Admiral Al Murray. In-mission communications, courtesy of Commander Tony Pastor, are frequently via their 'We Have Ways of Making You Talk' podcasts. You should listen in some time, for both entertainment and enlightenment. Mission control has been assisted by several staff officers of international repute, including professors (therefore rear admirals aboard the *Intrepid*) Alan Allport, Chris Bellamy, Jeremy Black, Philip W. Blood, Rob Citino, Saul David, John C. McManus (who kindly read some of the manuscript), Michael S. Neiberg, David O'Keefe, Alexandra Richie, Andrew Roberts, Gary Sheffield, Angeliki Vasilopoulou and Geoff Wawro.

They are friends all, whose counsel I have often sought, and which has been freely given. Professor John Buckley, who once had the privilege of attempting to teach me, has been ever ready to pull out of his head new angles on the 1939–45 period, with his razor sharp intellect and habit of posing searching questions. Two senior officers require special mention. Paul Beaver is a real senior officer, pilot, and authority on military aviation, who has served in all three services (we actually met when wearing army green) and has been a sage to me on anything to do with wings. Steve Prince is the real deal of being a senior nautical fellow, serving as the Royal Navy's chief historian, and right hand man of many a Sea Lord. A true friend, he has been my nautical advisor on anything that floats or lurks beneath the briny blue. However, as I see the *Intrepid* is already bulging at the seams with admirals, I will navigate this metaphor into a safe berth and continue with my thanks on dry land.

At this stage, I always like to pay tribute to my old boss, the late Brigadier and Professor Richard Holmes, who died far too young, in 2011, and whose loss I feel every day. The genesis of this book came from several staff rides I led for NATO forces and civilian groups. Amongst them, Colonel Peter Herrly of OSS gave me many opportunities to escort USAEUR (US Army Europe) groups to battlefields. I have always promoted the belief to my colleagues that walking the battle terrain is as much a primary source as an original document or personal account. Throughout the 1990s, in the aftermath of German reunification, with the generous help of the US Army and the British Army of the Rhine, I explored many of the central Fatherland's battlefields of fifty years before. In each case, by day I followed the nuances of combat, by night I discussed shot and shell over schnapps with a range of original eye-witnesses. Notably, in 1999, I accompanied the Royal Engineers of 1st (UK) Armoured Division to explore the Reichswald and Rhine crossing sites, accompanied by several British and German wartime participants.

Almost twenty years later, I visited more sites in Germany, guiding groups from the National World War II Museum, often with Professor Alexandra Richie of the Collegium Civitas, Warsaw, either following the famed Band of Brothers, from southern England all the way to Berchtesgaden, or exploring Berlin, Dresden and the meeting of East and West at Torgau. On other occasions, Aschaffenburg, Bremen, Colditz, Cologne, Hamburg, Heilbronn, Leipzig, Magdeburg, Stuttgart, Schweinfurt plus Würzburg and various concentration camps, were my destinations. Thus, I made it my business to explore every location described in the text.

It was good to roll up my sleeves and inhale the dust of various archives again. Alas, the global Plague ensured I undertook more online research and consulted more e-books than I would have liked. Books and documents have a tactile quality of their own, and there is always a squeak of excitement at handling papers personally read and signed by those who left big footprints – on this occasion, for example, Bradley, Churchill, Collins, Dempsey, Devers, Eisenhower, Kesselring, Model, Montgomery, Patch, Patton and Simonds. However, I fear a whole generation of younger scholars will fall into the trap of relying solely on what they can access in the virtual world.

For access to these documents and other materials, and visits to battlefields, I am most grateful to Clive Harris and Julian Whippy of Battle Honours Tours; David J. Bercuson, Centre for Military & Strategic

Studies, University of Calgary; Alice B in Berlin helped me better understand Marlene Dietrich's contribution to World War Two; the team at Schloss Colditz taught me of the castle's 1945 liberation; more wisdom came from the staff of the various concentration camp documentation centres at Belsen, Buchenwald, Dachau and Nordhausen (Germany), Mauthausen (Austria) and Vught (Holland); Major General Alastair Bruce of Crionaich; the Churchill Archives Centre at Churchill College, Cambridge; Andrew Whitmarsh and his motivated crew at the D-Day Story Museum, Portsmouth; the team at the Friedensmuseum bruecke von Remagen; Schloss Hartenfels in Torgau; and Dan Hill, a wonderfully motivated guide of combat terrain.

Major General Graham and Leslie Hollands kindly entertained me for weeks in Normandy; I owe many thanks to the Department of Documents, the Sound Archive and the Photographic Collection of the Imperial War Museum, London, and their outstation at Duxford; Mike Peters of the International Guild of Battlefield Guides; colleagues at the Joint Services Command and Staff College, Shrivenham, while Jean Jammes, one of the last fighters of the French Resistance (then aged 16), spent time explaining his generation's attitude to French military service, and the Germans. Important, also, have been the Liddell Hart Centre for Military History at King's College, London; Joël Stoppels and Liberation Route Europe; Professor Alexander Mikaberidze at Louisiana State University, Shreveport; Dr James Lacey at the US Marine Corps University, Quantico, Virginia; and Marshall University, Huntington, West Virginia, for access to Ken Hechler's papers.

In Caen, Normandy, I found archives that stretched far beyond 1944 at Le Mémorial Museum and Archive; helpful, too, were the Lee Miller Archives, East Sussex, and Professor Kathryn Barbier at Mississippi State University, Starkville. The late David Montgomery, Second Viscount and Monty's son, kindly spent time discussing his father with me, as, by coincidence, did Walther Model's son, Hans-Georg. In similar vein, I spent a memorable hour (or was it two?) with Manfred Rommel discussing the field marshal in his family. The UK National Archives, and their American and Canadian equivalents (the National Archives and Records Administration, and Libraries and Archives of Canada), were invaluable for access to war diaries, photographs and other materials.

So, too, were staff at the National Army Museum, Chelsea, London; also Professors Rob Citino and Nick Mueller, and Jeremy Collins, Nathan Huegen and Sarah Kirksey, all at the National World War II Museum in New Orleans, Louisiana. They have been kind enough to appoint me as a Presidential Counsellor to their august institution. Dorothea de la Houssaye and her team at the Normandy Institute, Château de Bernaville, Picauville, France, and the NS-Dokumentationszentrum der Stadt Köln, also enlightened me. Additional help with research and ideas came from Cristina de Santiago in Madrid; Dr Greg Pedlow of the SHAPE Historical Office, Mons, Belgium; historian extraordinaire and broadcaster Dan Snow; the US Army Heritage and Education Center at Carlisle, Pennsylvania; David Willey and his staff at the Tank Museum, Bovington, Dorset; and Paul Woodadge, friend and accomplished battlefield guide.

Of my fellow writers and historians, and others who have showered me with advice, I must especially doff my cap or throw up a spectacular salute to Nick Budd, Prit Buttar, Roger Cirillo, Dustin du Cane, and Eain Findlay, who is fighting to keep the story of the 6th Guards Tank Brigade alive. Brigadier Ben Kite, Laura in Princeton, Stewart McCartney, Toby McLeod; Andrew Rawson (who also read part of the manuscript), Sarah Rose, Guy Walters, Jonathan Ware, Major General Dave Zabecki and Steve Zaloga have been further advisors. Helen and Ed Haislmaier have kindly accommodated me in Washington DC; as did the honorary Brit, Chaz Mena, of New York City and Florida. My good friends, Richard & Gina Goldsbrough and Dr Harry Woodruff also very kindly entertained me in Hampshire.

The Great Plague was responsible for the positive side of finding fellow souls online, keen to share their knowledge, particularly amongst the Independent Company of enthusiasts ('the afflicted'). It was Covid that nudged me into understanding that the digital world has much to offer in terms of solid scholarship and inquisitive minds. The downside, of course, is that one gets so used to the ingenious virtual identities of that universe – Bagels over Berlin; the bard of Bognor; Blitzkrieg in Airfix; Clausewitz's Adjutant; Gary Antoinette; Lawrence of Bessarabia; Montgomery's Barman; Pretzels and Panzers; Rhine or Bust; SO3 Port & Stilton; the Stonehenge Ranger; Strangelove's Revenge; Tanks for the

Memory; the Texan Highlander, and all the rest – that one quite forgets their real names. To those in this category, if overlooked, please feel the field marshal's baton waved purposefully in your direction.

Finally, the good burghers, shopkeepers and restaurateurs of *grad* Poreč, Croatia, my top secret Istrian base, have been most tolerant, but in turn proud and puzzled by their mysterious *Englez*. My frequent comings and goings, dark glasses and snappy mode of dress make it obvious (at least to them) that I am no author, but an international *špijun* (spy) of some repute. I must also pay tribute to Boris, aka Mr. Bor, a young English Setter who has attached himself to my entourage, without whose infectious enthusiasm and energy for walks, games and swimming, this volume would have been finished in half the time.

Notes

Prologue

1. *US Army Pocket Guide to Germany, 1944* (reprint by Riva Verlag, 2015), pp. 22–3.
2. Martha Gellhorn, *The Face of War* (Hart Davis, 1959), p. 170.
3. And three would die in 1939–45. Details courtesy of http://www.denkmalprojekt. org/2018/utweiler_gde-gersheim_saarpfalz-kreis_wk1_wk2_saar.html
4. Stephen J. Ochs, *A Cause Greater Than Self* (Texas A&M University Press, 2012), p. 124.
5. In 1939, some 125 inhabitants were registered in Utweiler; its population is 65 today.
6. The US 12th Armored Division had seized Utweiler on 21 December 1944 but had relinquished their gains to stem the German assault further north in the Ardennes – the Battle of the Bulge.
7. 3rd Infantry Division Operations Order N.28, 15 March 1945, paragraph one.
8. Pournoy-la-Chétive, five miles south of Metz, was completely destroyed in serving as an American training site; its 500 inhabitants lived in barracks after the war until a new village was built and only the 1932 war memorial remains of the pre-World War Two site.
9. German reports (not always accurate) contradict this, and reference 'At midnight a barrage went off for several hours, including phosphorus shells. At the same time as the fire rolled, the Americans broke into our positions at the front of the grenadiers.'
10. Much of this account is courtesy of Earl A. Reitan's *Riflemen: On the Cutting Edge of World War II* (self-published, 2008), and his undated essay, 'Disaster at Utweiler'.
11. Local German armour comprised the 18–20 tracked assault guns (StuGs) of Sturmbannführer Karl Hohmann's 17th SS Panzer Battalion. Nathan W. White, *From Fedala to Berchtesgaden: A History of the Seventh United States Infantry in World War II* (self-published, 1947), pp. 235–239.
12. Kleiboeker Family archives at https://www.kleiboekercousins.org/hubie-and-wwii. html
13. Ted Tripp, 'Hero in Our Midst: Staff Sgt Eldon Berthiaume, Infantryman WWII' (*Valley Patriot*, North Andover, Massachusetts, August 2006).

14. Courtesy, Yankton (South Dakota) Veterans website @Yanktonarea WorldWar2Veterans.

15. Robert Cook, 'Uweiler [sic] 1945', The Watch on the Rhine (Newsletter of the Society of the Third Infantry Division March–April 2010), p. 26.

16. However, the Germans possessed no Tigers in the area at this time. For a fuller account, see John McManus, American Courage, American Carnage: The 7th Infantry Regiment's Combat Experience, 1812 through World War II, Vol. 2 (Forge Books, 2009).

17. German reports detail the capture of 262 GIs, but these would have included some of the US 15th Infantry Regiment, also attacking nearby.

18. Cited as 25,977 casualties, including 4,922 killed in action, 18,766 wounded and a further 636 who died of wounds (the remainder were posted as missing, captured, injured, suffering serious illness or battle fatigue), in North Africa, Sicily, Italy, France, Germany and Austria, during 531 consecutive days of combat; the division's GIs earned 36 Medals of Honor during the war (source: Army Battle Casualties & Nonbattle Deaths in World War II, Final Report, 1 December 1941 – 31 December 1946).

19. Earl E. Swanson is buried in Fort Snelling National Cemetery, Hennepin, Minnesota.

20. On 10 January 1945, Standartenführer Hans Lingner was captured when his car overturned on a slippery road; Oberst Gerhard Lindner, one of the army officers recently transferred to the division, took over until the arrival of Oberführer Fritz Klingenberg, who was in turn killed in action on 22 March.

21. Eastern Europe celebrates Victory in Europe Day on 9 May each year, due to a later surrender document signed in Berlin with the Russians.

Introduction

1. Martin Blumenson (ed.), The Patton Papers, Vol. II: 1940–1945 (Houghton Mifflin, 1974), p. 615.

2. Dwight D. Eisenhower, Crusade in Europe (Heinemann, 1948), p. 426.

3. Stephen Robinson, The Remarkable Lives of Bill Deedes (Little, Brown, 2008), Kindle locstat 2216.

4. Alan Moorehead's Eclipse of 1946 devoted 50 out of 300 pages to March–May 1945; Chester Wilmot's Struggle for Europe (1952) allowed only 20 pages out of 800 for the same period; while Milton Shulman in Defeat in the West (1947) covered those events in 40 pages out of 400.

5. The Rhine passes through or borders Switzerland, Liechtenstein, Austria, Germany, France and the Netherlands.

6. Originally published in 1927 as A Guide to the American Battle Fields in Europe, Major Eisenhower researched and contributed to the expanded 1938 edition, American Armies and Battlefields in Europe (American Battle Monuments Commission, Washington DC, 1938, republished 1992).

7. There is a fierce debate as to what constitutes the Holocaust between 1933 and 1945. Was it specifically Jewish and tied to concentration camps and the SS, or were its victims from other groups also, detained in a wider range of prisons and labour camps? In acknowledging the biblical term Shoah for the murder of the European Jews, I am employing the widest definition here, of those Jews and non-Jews who suffered abuse, torture or death while imprisoned by the servants of the Third Reich – for this is what their liberators encountered in 1945. This is on the basis that, *at the time*, Allied soldiers were frequently unable to determine which victims were Jewish and what site was a concentration camp. Most stockades of malnourished, non-military prisoners and slave labourers were regarded simply as 'death camps' and their occupants as survivors, equally in need of help. Similarly, the dead needed burial and remembrance, irrespective of nationality or religion. Understanding who they were and why they were imprisoned would come with post-war research.

8. Christian Gerlach, *The Extermination of the European Jews* (Cambridge University Press, 2016), p. 184.

9. William I. Hitchcock, *Liberation: The Bitter Road to Freedom, Europe 1944–1945* (Simon & Schuster, 2009), p. 250.

10. Conversation with Nikolaus Wachsmann, author of the definitive study on the subject, during a National WWII Museum conference in New Orleans in 2019. See his *KL: A History of the Nazi Concentration Camps* (Little, Brown, 2015), p. 17. The first camps were overseen by the SA, to whom the SS was initially subordinate. Initial prisoners were political opponents of the Nazis, Social Democrats and Communists; the Jews would come later. Meanwhile, the SS gained independence from the SA on 26 July 1934.

11. There were also around a thousand classic prisoner-of-war *lagers* from which doughty Allied detainees attempted occasional 'home runs'. Also part of this total were the pre-war prisons taken over by the Third Reich where criminals were detained; institutions and asylums used for euthanising the elderly, mentally handicapped and infirm; other buildings for 're-educating' miscreant youths or Germanising likely civilians into becoming *Volksdeutsche*; transit camps for transporting victims to killing centres, usually by rail; and the 500 brothels filled with sex slaves, designed for the gratification of German troops and even trusted prisoners.

12. Raymond Gantter, *Roll Me Over: An Infantryman's World War II* (Presidio, 1997), p. 376. Gattner served with the US 1st Division and his memoir was written in 1949 but published posthumously only in 1997.

1: From Normandy to the Reich

1. Forrest C. Pogue, *Pogue's War: Diaries of a WWII Combat Historian* (University Press of Kentucky, 2001), pp. 335–336. The Ardennes campaign is analysed fully in Peter Caddick-Adams, *Snow and Steel: The Battle of the Bulge 1944–45* (Preface, 2014).

2. Janice Holt Giles, *The GI Journal of Sergeant Giles* (Houghton Mifflin, 1965), p. 241.

3. Eisenhower enumerated his losses as 733 tanks and tank destroyers and 77,000 men, although the human casualties have since been revised upwards to 89,500, including 1,408 Britons. German losses are estimated at 554 tanks and armoured vehicles and 88–98,000 casualties; see Dwight D. Eisenhower, *Crusade in Europe* (Doubleday, 1948).

4. Omar Bradley, *A Soldier's Story* (Henry Holt, 1951), p. 492.

5. From West to East, XXX Corps (Horrocks), XII Corps (Ritchie), II Canadian Corps (Simonds), VIII Corps (O'Connor), I Corps (Crocker).

6. Landed in southern France in October 1944 were: 524,894 tons (total 1,309,184 tons in all French and Belgian ports), November: 547,602 tons (total 1,402,080), and December: 501,568 tons (total: 1,555,819); see Jeffrey Clarke and Robert Smith, *Riviera to the Rhine* (US Army Center of Military History, Washington DC, 1993), p. 576.

7. Toulon was opened for shipping on 5 September and Marseilles on the 15th. The Dragoon beaches were closed on 25 September, by which time 400,000 personnel, 68,480 vehicles and 360,000 tons of cargo had been landed. FM Sir Henry Maitland Wilson, *Report by Supreme Allied Commander Mediterranean to the CCS on Operations in Southern France, August 1944* (HMSO, 1946), pp. 43–5. Roland G. Ruppenthal, *Logistical Support of the Armies, Vol. II: September 1944 – May 1945* (Office of the Chief of Military History, Department of the Army, 1953), pp. 156–60.

8. Seventh Army finished the war with 14 divisions – 3rd, 36th, 42nd, 44th, 45th, 63rd, 86th, 100th, 103rd, 12th, 10th, and 20th Armored, French 2nd Armoured and 101st Airborne.

9. Patrick Delaforce, *The Black Bull: From Normandy to the Baltic with the 11th Armoured Division* (Alan Sutton, 1993), p. 127.

10. Eileen Younghusband interview courtesy of *WW2 The People's War*, BBC, at http://www.bbc.co.uk/history/ww2peopleswar/stories/16/a2093816.shtml

11. Bernard Montgomery, *The Memoirs of Field-Marshal the Viscount Montgomery of Alamein, KG* (Collins, 1958), p. 243.

12. Tony Foster, *Meeting of Generals* (Methuen, 1986), pp. 415–16, 533–4.

13. SHAEF Directive, 28 October 1944, SHAEF Files, Eisenhower Library; see also John A. Adams, *General Jacob Devers: World War II's Forgotten Four Star* (Indiana University Press, 2015), p. 276.

14. Ibid., pp. 299–301.

15. Led by a captain, each Quartermaster Corps Amphibian Truck Company included 7 officers, 180 enlisted men, 50 DUKWs, plus 4 other vehicles. Ordinary truck companies were similarly equipped with 6x6 vehicles.

16. H. H. Dunham, *US Army Transportation in the European Theater of Operations, 1942–1945* (Office of the Chief of Transportation, Army Service Forces, June 1946), p. 287.

17. Charles Whiting, *America's Forgotten Army: The Story of the US Seventh Army in WWII* (Sarpedon, 1999), p. 81.

18. Often incorrectly stated to be the Heritage Hotel, but there has never been a hotel of that name in Vittel. The manager of the art deco Hôtel de l'Hermitage (now part of Club Med) confirmed to the author that a very senior American general had stayed there in the winter of 1944–5. See also James Scott Wheeler, *Jacob L. Devers: A General's Life* (University Press of Kentucky, 2015).

19. Interviews with Devers by Forrest Pogue (12 August 1958) and Thomas Griess (29–30 December 1969, 17–20 August 1970), cited in Clarke and Smith, *Riviera to the Rhine*, p. 438.

20. Ibid.

21. Brigadier General Daniel Noce, chief G-3 (operations) at AFHQ (Algiers), who interviewed both Major General Walter Bedell Smith (Eisenhower's chief of staff) and Major General David G. Barr (Devers' chief of staff), Daniel Noce Papers (US Military Academy, West Point).

22. Headquarters 6th Army Group G-3 Section, *Final After Action Report* (Heidelberg, 1945), para 162.

23. Clarke and Smith, *Riviera to the Rhine*, p. 437.

24. David P. Colley, *Decision at Strasbourg: Ike's Strategic Mistake to Halt the Sixth Army Group at the Rhine in 1944* (Naval Institute Press, 2008).

25. Blumenson (ed.), *Patton Papers*, p. 583.

26. John Frayn Turner and Robert Jackson, *Destination Berchtesgaden: The Story of the US Seventh Army in World War II* (Ian Allen, 1975), p. 99.

27. US casualties in the Bulge are generally reckoned to be 80–90,000, similar to those of the Germans. See Garrison H. Davidson, *Grandpa Gar: The Saga of One Soldier as Told to His Grandchildren* (private publication, 1976), pp. 94–5.

28. Courtesy, René Chevrolet, Responsable documentation et recherches historiques, Centre européen du résistant déporté, Site de l'ancien camp de concentration de Natzweiler-Struthof, and Diana Mara Henry, author of https://www.frontseattowar.com

29. Milton Bracker, 'Alsace Nazi Prison Neat and Efficient', *New York Times*, 5 December 1944.

30. On 31 August, the SS had begun evacuating the inmates into Germany, tidying as they went. Plans had been made to destroy the camp, but the American advance had been too swift.

31. Nearby, run by the German Army, not the SS, was yet another kind of stockade – Vittel *Internierungslager* (internment camp), where British and American nationals and European Jews with foreign passports were detained for potential exchange with Germans held abroad. Several Vittel children remembered 'Kiki', the monkey glove puppet handmade by PFC Eldon G. Nicholas, an ambulance driver with the 36th Division, which brought smiles to the survivors of Vittel while they waited to start new lives after the Germans had left.

32. Explained fully in Terry Copp, *Cinderella Army: The Canadians in Northwest Europe, 1944–45* (University of Toronto Press, 2007).

33. Estimates of German casualties sustained during Operation *Bagration* and in France at that time vary from around 350,000 for each theatre to as high as 500,000.

34. Allied casualties were around 28 per cent of those of the USSR's; Carlo D'Este and Antony Beevor hover around 225,000 Allied losses, whereas Major Ellis in the UK official history and Michael Tamelander and Niklaus Zetterling suggest the slightly higher figure of 226,000.

35. Ian Kershaw, *Hitler, 1936–1945* (Allen Lane, 2000), p. 888.

36. Charles B. MacDonald, *US Army in World War II: ETO, The Last Offensive* (Office of the Chief of Military History, US Army, Washington DC, 1973), p. 478.

37. Maréchal Jean de Lattre de Tassigny, *History of the French First Army* (Allen and Unwin, 1952), p. 53.

38. The younger Patch graduated on 29 May 1942, when his class was addressed by George C. Marshall. See https://www.marshallfoundation. org/library/digital-archive/speech-to-the-graduating-class-united-states-military-academy/

39. General Patch to Julia Patch, 24 February 1945, courtesy Patch Papers, US Military Academy Special Collections & Archives.

2: Allied Leadership

1. George C. Marshall was clearly the front runner for the supreme command, but it became apparent that he was the key link in Washington DC and that Roosevelt had come to rely on him. Thus, Marshall nominated Eisenhower, his star pupil, who had already been Mediterranean supremo and had previously authored draft invasion plans for France.

2. Field Marshal Lord Alanbrooke (ed. Alex Danchev & Daniel Todman), *War Diaries 1939–45* (Orion, 1999), pp. 546–7.

3. Desmond Scott, *Typhoon Pilot* (Leo Cooper, 1982), p. 103.

4. Interviews, George Chambers and William Brown, 1988 (sound archive 10415, Imperial War Museum).

5. Letter, Montgomery to Brooke, 4 April 1943 (BLM 49/25, Imperial War Museum).

6. Norman Kirby, *1100 Miles with Monty: Security and Intelligence at Tac HQ* (Alan Sutton, 1989), p. 32.

7. Alistair Horne and David Montgomery, *Monty 1944–1945* (HarperCollins, 1994), p. 106; and conversations with David Montgomery, 2nd Viscount, 2010.

8. The portrait was painted in the spring of 1952, when Montgomery was deputy to Eisenhower at SHAPE. Letter to Major General 'Pug' Ismay, 14 January 1959, Eisenhower Diary, courtesy Dwight D. Eisenhower Presidential Library & Museum, Abilene, Kansas.

9. Rommel was killed in a traffic accident in Holland on 18 December 1944.

10. Forrest Pogue, *The Supreme Command* (US Army Center of Military History, 1954), pp. 276–7. The technical college in Reims which once housed the SHAEF war room

at 12 rue Franklin Roosevelt is now the Lycée Polyvalent Franklin Roosevelt. Today, it hosts the Musée de la Reddition, where the German surrender was signed by Jodl.

11. Throughout his life, Devers was an innovator and experimenter. Between the two world wars he was a staunch advocate of mechanisation at a time when the idea of losing their horses met antipathy from conservative gunners, as in Britain. During the war, he sponsored development of the DUKW, upgraded tank weaponry from 37mm to 75mm, and introduced first the M4 Sherman and later M26 Pershing tanks. Afterwards, in 1948, Devers would be responsible for purchasing 50 OH13s from the struggling and obscure Bell helicopter company. Known as the Sioux, the bubble-canopied aircraft was designed for artillery spotting, but equally associated with stretcher-bearing to MASH medical facilities in Korea.

12. Adams, *General Jacob Devers*, p. 303.

13. Allegedly rechristened *Dragoon* on 1 August 1944 at Churchill's behest, to acknowledge the British had been 'dragooned' into an operation they did not want, due to the drain of men and resources from Italy.

14. Jeffrey Clarke and Robert Smith, *US Army in WWII: ETO, Riviera to the Rhine* (US Army Center of Military History, Washington DC, 1976), p. 577.

15. General Jacob L. Devers, 'Operation Dragoon: The Invasion of Southern France', *Military Affairs* (Summer 1946), p. 31.

16. Clarke and Smith, *Riviera to the Rhine*, p. 229.

17. Maitland Wilson, *Report*, p. 45; De Lattre, *History*, p. 157; Major Rebecca E. Beard, Footnote in History: *Sixth Army Group Operations in the Second World War and Lessons for Contemporary Planners* (Monograph, School of Advanced Military Studies, US Army Command & General Staff College, Fort Leavenworth, Kansas, 2016), p. 11.

18. For example, see Russell Weigley, *Eisenhower's Lieutenants* (Indiana University Press, 1981), p. 580; Rick Atkinson, *The Guns at Last Light* (Henry Holt, 2014), p. 366.

19. Adams, *General Jacob Devers*, p. 451.

20. Lodge was the namesake and grandson of an earlier Republican senator from Massachusetts who opposed Woodrow Wilson's plans for the League of Nations after World War One.

21. Devers Papers, York County Heritage Trust, Pennsylvania.

22. Adams, *General Jacob Devers*, p. 210.

23. De Lattre, *History*, p. 53.

24. Ibid., p. 75.

25. Clarke and Smith, *Riviera to the Rhine*, p. 578.

26. Keith E. Bonn, 'Most Underrated General of World War II: Alexander Patch' (100th Infantry Division Association Newsletter, July 2003), courtesy Marshall Foundation Archives. Alas, Patch would not long survive the war, dying from one of his periodic bouts of pneumonia on 21 November 1945, and perhaps this as well as his natural

modesty are the reasons his name (and his Seventh Army) has not endured to the same extent as those of his contemporaries, Mark Clark, George Patton or Omar Bradley. He wrote no memoirs, though his letters to his wife reside in the archives at West Point. He was posthumously promoted to full general on 19 July 1954.

27. De Gaulle's call to arms is detailed in Chapter 1 of Peter Caddick-Adams, *Sand & Steel: A New History of D-Day* (Hutchinson, 2019). Maxime Weygand (1867–1965) was Pétain's first minister of defence until September 1940, when posted to French North Africa, where he practised only limited collaboration with the Germans; he was dismissed in November 1941 at Hitler's request, later arrested and imprisoned at Itter Castle in Austria until May 1945.

28. Anthony Clayton, *Three Marshals of France: Leadership After Trauma* (Brassey's, 1992), pp. 95–105.

29. For a full account, see: Peter Caddick-Adams, *Monte Cassino: Ten Armies in Hell* (Preface, 2011).

30. G-3 Section, *Headquarters, Twelfth Army Group, Report of Operations. (Final After Action Report), Part II* (Weisbaden Kurier, 1945), p. 36.

31. Omar N. Bradley, *A Soldier's Story of the Allied Campaigns from Tunis to the Elbe* (Eyre & Spottiswoode, 1951), p. 180.

32. Ibid., p. 226.

33. David W. Hogan Jr, *A Command Post at War: First Army Headquarters in Europe, 1943–1945* (US Army Center of Military History, 2000), p. 212.

34. Blumenson (ed.), *The Patton Papers*, p. 517.

35. Hogan, *A Command Post*, p. 122.

36. It is surprising that the extraordinarily able Henry L. Stimson (1867–1950) is not better known. He served both Republican and Democrat administrations as Secretary of War (1911–13) under President Taft, Secretary of State (1929–33) under Hoover, and Secretary of War (1940–45) under Roosevelt and Truman.

37. Ironically, in retirement, Bradley still underwrote Patton's reputation, to his own cost. In 1969–70 he agreed to be the historical advisor for the movie *Patton*, with its Oscar-winning performance by George C. Scott and screenplay by Francis Ford Coppola, based on Bradley's own memoirs. It revitalised the Patton brand, at the expense of wider public understanding of Bradley's role in winning World War Two.

38. The author can remember nursing his head after a 2nd Armored Division cocktail party and dinner in Germany, just prior to the Persian Gulf War in 1990.

39. George Forty, *Patton's Third Army at War* (Ian Allen, 1978), p. 46.

40. Steve Dietrich, 'The Professional Reading of General George S. Patton, Jr', *Journal of Military History*, October 1989.

41. Conversations with Helen Ayer Patton, the general's granddaughter, 2018–19.

42. Simpson's Ninth had originally been designated Eighth Army in America, but on arrival in the United Kingdom it was renumbered to avoid confusion with Montgomery's Desert Rats formation of the same number. This also reflected the fact

that US field armies in Europe were given odd numbers, while those in continental USA and the Pacific had even numbered designations.

43. Thomas R. Stone, 'General William Hood Simpson: Unsung Commander of US Ninth Army', *Parameters, Journal of the US Army War College*, Vol. XI/2 (1981).

44. The US Fifth Army was in Italy; Second and Fourth Armies remained in the USA preparing troops for combat, while the Sixth, Eighth and Tenth fought in the Pacific; Fourteenth Army was a non-existent 'Phantom' formation, supposedly deployed to England as part of the 'Fusag' and 'Quicksilver' deceptions associated with D-Day.

45. The Fifteenth went on to oversee the Occupation of Germany; Gerow remained in command until 21 October 1945 when replaced by Patton (who had been fired from Third Army). By then the Fifteenth's task was confined to denazification and historical analysis. After Patton's death on 21 December, command passed to his chief of staff, Hobart Gay.

46. Now preserved at the Imperial War Museum, Duxford (north London) site.

47. The British Army did not adopt the American (later NATO) system of numbered G[eneral Staff] branches until after the war.

48. Bradley, *A Soldier's Story*, p. 322.

49. Robert W. Love and John Major (eds), *The Year of D-Day: The 1944 Diary of Admiral Sir Bertram Ramsay* (University of Hull Press, 1994), p. 129; Alanbrooke, *War Diaries*, p. 586.

50. Correspondence, Field Marshal Lord Carver to author, 1999.

51. Peter Caddick-Adams, 'General Sir Miles Christopher Dempsey (1896–1969) – Not a Popular Leader', *RUSI Journal*, Vol. 150/5 (October 2005).

52. Brian Horrocks, Eversley Belfield and Hubert Essame, *Corps Commander* (Sidgwick & Jackson, 1977), pp. 182 –3.

53. Mark Zuehlke, *On To Victory: The Canadian Liberation of the Netherlands, 23 March–5 May 1945* (Douglas & McIntyre, 2010), p. 35.

3: The Colmar Pocket

1. Major General Sir Guy Salisbury-Jones, *So Full A Glory: a Biography of Marshal de Lattre de Tassigny* (Weidenfeld & Nicolson, 1954), p. 161.

2. For a full account, see: Peter Caddick-Adams, *Snow & Steel: The Battle of the Bulge, 1944–45* (Preface, 2014).

3. Donald Joseph Carner Papers, courtesy California State Military Museum Archives, Sacramento, CA, pp. 4–5.

4. Turner and Jackson, *Destination Berchtesgaden*, p. 106.

5. Frank Yarosh (1924–2008) was sent by cattle car to Limburg, then transferred to Stalag XI-B POW camp in Fallingbostel, where he was liberated by British 7th (Desert Rats) Armoured Division on 16 April 1945. He received a Bronze Star, and when I interviewed him had just written *World War II Is Not Over: A Combat*

Infantryman's Experiences in a German POW Camp (self-published, 1992), as an antidote to the PTSD he suffered from his war years.

6. Cited in Jonathan Trigg, *To VE-Day Through German Eyes* (Amberley, 2020), p. 182.

7. Martin Gilbert, *Winston Churchill: Road to Victory*, Vol. VII (Heinemann, 1986), pp. 1139–40.

8. Adams, *General Jacob Devers*, p. 354.

9. Bedell Smith's temper cited in Trigg, *To VE-Day*, p. 177.

10. Pogue, *The Supreme Command*, p. 398; Winston Churchill, *The Second World War*, Vol. 6 (Cassell, 1954), p. 245.

11. De Lattre, *History*, p. 413.

12. Army Group 'G' was originally commanded by Blaskowitz from its creation on 8 May 1944 until 21 September; then by Hermann Black until 24 December; he was succeeded by Blaskowitz again until 29 January, when replaced by Hausser.

13. Number of German divisions by front in World War Two. Based on Georg Tessin, *Verbände und Truppen der deutschen Wehrmacht und Waffen-SS 1939–1945* (19 volumes); courtesy Ron Klages and John Mulholland, *Axis History*, 19 April 2015.

14. The 100th and 103rd arrived in Marseilles in October 1944, the 42nd, 63rd and 70th in December 1944, and the 71st in January 1945.

15. De Lattre, *History*, p. 365.

16. Omar N. Bradley and Clay Blair, *A General's Life* (Simon & Schuster, 1983), pp. 335–7. In his earlier memoir, *A Soldier's Story*, Bradley was not nearly so forthright, barely mentioning the issue.

17. Adams, *General Jacob Devers*, p. 371.

18. Courtesy, US Army Heritage and Education Center (AHEC), Carlisle, November 2019.

19. De Lattre, *History*, p. 338.

20. Author's interview with Robert F. Lynch in 1984. See his *A Letter Marked Free* (Dog Ear Publishing, 2007), pp. 136–7; Lynch later retired to Florida, and died in 2016.

21. Audie Murphy, *To Hell and Back* (Henry Holt, 1949), pp. 242–4, 247; Murphy commanded Company 'B', First Battalion, 15th Infantry; Lynch served in Company 'K' of the regiment's 3rd Battalion.

22. Charles K. Blum, *Personal Experience, 3rd Platoon, Company 'E', 3rd Division, Colmar Pocket 22–23 January 1945* (Advanced Infantry Officers Course No. 1, Infantry School, Fort Benning, Georgia, 1947–8).

23. M. Bedford Davis, *Frozen Rainbows: The WWII Adventures of a Combat Medical Officer* (Meadowlark Publishing, 2003), p. 229, and author's correspondence with Dr Davis. A Georgian, Davis (1918–2015) served in the 28th Division 1943–5, in the Hürtgen Forest, Colmar Pocket and in Germany.

24. Davis, *Frozen Rainbows*, p. 232.

25. De Lattre, *History*, p. 356.

26. Ibid.

27. Blum, *Personal Experience*.

28. Ibid.

29. Murphy, *To Hell and Back*, p. 169.

30. Ibid., p. 266.

31. Victor Failmezger, *American Knights: The Men of the 601st Tank Destroyer Battalion* (Osprey, 2015), p. 247.

32. Lynch, *A Letter Marked Free*, p. 142.

33. Failmezger, *American Knights*, p. 252.

34. Known to Frenchmen as the 1re Division de Marche d'Infanterie (1re DMI).

35. Charles de Gaulle, *The Complete War Memoirs of Charles de Gaulle*, trans. Jonathan Griffin and Richard Howard (Carroll & Graf Publishers, 1998), pp. 699–703.

36. Marcel Vigneras, *United States Army in World War II Special Studies: Rearming the French* (US Army Center of Military History, 1956), p. 402.

37. De Lattre, *History*, p. 360.

38. The French casualties were lost between 26 and 28 January 1945.

39. The location is usually given as Rosencranz, the German word for rosary – which perfectly describes the road layout of the locale. It is marked by a memorial adjacent to the busy E25 autoroute that now bisects the area of Valdez's heroism.

40. Sergeant Elmer C. Brawley, *Complete Description of Service Rendered* (3-page typewritten and sworn affidavit, 1 March 1945, submitted to MOH Decorations Board for consideration, 18 April 1945), Records of the Army Staff, 1903–2004, *Personnel File, Audie Murphy* (RG-319, NARA).

41. Murphy, *To Hell and Back*, pp. 247–53; De Lattre, *History*, p. 361.

42. De Lattre, *History*, pp. 360–4.

43. James E. Hatcher, *Blood and Fire: With the 63rd Infantry Division in World War II* (63rd Infantry Division Association, Radcliff, Kentucky, 1986), p. 38.

44. Metal US Army dog tags generally contained five lines of text: 1. first name, middle initial, last name; 2. army serial no., tetanus dates, blood type; 3. next of kin; 4. street address for next of kin; 5. city and state, and religious preference – C (Catholic), P (Protestant), H (Hebrew), or left blank for no preference. Bill Gold, 'My Combat Experiences', *Blood and Fire* (Newsletter of the 63rd Division Association, Vol. 59/1, February 2007), p. 16.

45. Karl-Heinz Münch, *Combat History of the 654th Schwere-Panzerjäger-Abteilung* (J.J. Fedorowicz, 2001), p. 450.

46. De Lattre, *History*, pp. 360–4.

47. Courtesy, Stand Where They Fought website/Jebsheim.

48. Sergeant Robert Ross, *We Fought for Peace: World War II Memoirs* (US Army Heritage & Education Center, Carlisle, Pennsylvania), p. 37.

49. De Lattre, *History*, pp. 257, 269.

50. Lynch, *A Letter Marked Free*, pp. 146–7.

51. De Lattre, *History*, pp. 367–8.

52. Davis, *Frozen Rainbows*, p. 233.

53. Troy D. Cox, *An Infantryman's Memories of World War II* (Brown Line, 2003), pp. 156–7.

54. W. Bert Craft, *The Agony of Hell* (Turner Publishing Company, 1994), pp. 84, 92–3.

55. De Lattre, *History*, p. 395.

56. Edgar B. Mooney, *Seventh United States Infantry Regiment, 22 Jan–8 Feb 1945: The Colmar Pocket* (Seventh Army, 1945), pp. 57–8.

57. Luc Capdevila, 'The Mobilization of Women in Combatant France (1940–1945)', *Clio: Femmes, Genre, Histoire*, 2000.

58. See Chris Dickson, *Americans at War in Foreign Forces: A History, 1914–1945* (McFarland, 2014).

59. Interview, Thomas Moulton (son), September 2016; see also George Rock, *History of the American Field Service 1920–1955* (AFS/The Platen Press, 1956), Chapter One. The appeal read: 'Field Service Makes Appeal to Harvard For Volunteers. The American Field Service, the organization which sends men, and ambulances to save G.I., Tommy, and Free French lives on the Italian & Burma fronts, has appealed to Harvard for volunteer ambulance drivers. Volunteers must buy their own uniforms & pay their transportation to the point of embarkation. The AFS, which is under the British command, since it served in France before America entered the war, takes no responsibility for the health of its members. Training is done en route & at points overseas.' *The Harvard Crimson*, 17 March 1944 (AFS Records).

60. William M. Pena, *As Far as Schleiden* (self-published, 1992), pp. 162–3.

61. The French 5th Armoured (like American formations) was split into three combat commands during battle. Mayer was attached to Colonel Lecoq's CC4. Interview with Mayer's son, Thomas Moulton, 23 April 2017.

62. Richard Johnston, 'Colmar Residents Calm on Release', *New York Times*, 4 February 1945.

63. General der Infanterie Helmut Thumm, *LXIV Corps: 6 Dec 44–28 Jan 45* (Foreign Military Studies, 1946).

64. Davis, *Frozen Rainbows*, p. 238.

65. (No author), *Seventh United States Army in France & Germany, 1944–1945, Report of Operations* (Gräf, Heidelberg, 1946), p. 178.

66. De Lattre, *History*, p. 272; de Lattre fixed the Franco-American losses from the January–February fighting at 2,137 killed and 11,253 wounded, with the US 3rd Division suffering 317 out of the 542 American dead. With losses sustained in Colmar in late 1944, the Allied death toll was certainly higher.

4: Veritable Mud

1. TAC moved in on 12 November 1944. Zonhoven today has quadrupled in size from its small wartime population of 5,000. The house where Monty stayed is alternatively known as the 'Villa Mommen'. See: Horne and Montgomery, *The Lonely Leader*, p. 295.

2. Citation, *London Gazette*, 16 March 1945; Charles Whiting, *The Poor Bloody Infantry* (Hutchinson, 1987), pp. 236–8.

3. Pronounced Santen.

4. Philip Warner, *Horrocks: The General Who Led from the Front* (Hamish Hamilton, 1984), p. 72.

5. Philip Warner, quoted in obituary of Sir Brian Horrocks, *Los Angeles Times*, 10 January 1985.

6. Robert Boscawen, *Armoured Guardsmen: A War Diary, June 1944–April 1945* (Leo Cooper, 2001), p. 179.

7. Martin Lindsay, *So Few Got Through* (Collins, 1946), pp. 178–9.

8. Sergeant Trevor Greenwood, *D-Day to Victory*, ed. S.V. Partington (Simon & Schuster, 2012), pp. 326–9.

9. Sir Brian Horrocks with Eversley Belfield and Hubert Essame, *Corps Commander* (Sidgwick and Jackson, 1977), p. 184.

10. R.M. Wingfield, *The Only Way Out: An Infantryman's Autobiography of the North-West Europe Campaign August 1944–February 1945* (Hutchinson, 1955).

11. Brigadier George Taylor, *Infantry Colonel* (self-published, 1990), p. 164.

12. Obituary, Brigadier George Taylor, *The Times*, 20 July 1994.

13. Brian Horrocks, *British Army of the Rhine (BAOR) Operation Veritable, Battlefield Tour* (Students Edition) (BAOR, 1947), Introduction.

14. *21st Army Group Report on Operation Veritable*, March 1945 (WO205/93, UK National Archives).

15. Taylor, *Infantry Colonel*, p. 164.

16. The early commercial versions were known as Alligators; later armoured, military marks as Water Buffaloes. See Major Alfred D. Bailey, USMC, *Alligators, Buffaloes & Bushmasters: The History of the Development of the LVT Through WWII* (History & Museums Division, USMC, Washington DC, 1986).

17. Horrocks, *British Army of the Rhine*.

18. Ian C. Hammerton, *Achtung! Minen! The Making of a Flail Tank Troop Commander* (Book Guild, 1991), pp. 130–4.

19. Brian Horrocks, Eversley Bellfield and Hubert Essame, *Corps Commander* (Sidgwick & Jackson, 1977), pp. 186–7.

20. Taylor, *Infantry Colonel*, p. 165.

21. Lindsay, *So Few Got Through*, p. 187.

22. *History of the East Lancashire Regiment in the War of 1939–45* (privately printed, 1953), pp. 153–4.

23. Lindsay, *So Few Got Through*, p. 193.

24. Interview with Andreas Herdina (son), February 2021.

25. Hubert Essame, *The 43rd Wessex Division at War* (Clowes, 1952), p. 213.

26. G.J.B. Watkins, *War History of the 4th Battalion Dorset Regiment* (Rowe, 1956), p. 54. I am indebted to Professor John Buckley for drawing my attention to this reference.

27. John McGregor, *The Spirit of Angus: The War History of the County's Battalion of the Black Watch* (Phillimore Books, 1988), pp. 170–3.

28. Ibid.

29. Commanded by Lieutenant Colonel Ian Freeland (later GOC Northern Ireland in 1969–70), the 1/5th Queen's Royal Regiment (West Surrey) were a Territorial Infantry Regiment of 131st Brigade.

30. Wingfield, *The Only Way Out*, pp. 167–9.

31. Of these, 379 officers and 6,325 other ranks belonged to XXX Corps, though 111 officers and 1,683 other ranks were Canadians, a staggering loss rate neither could afford. See Terry Copp, 'Operation Blockbuster Begins', *Legion Magazine*, 1 January 2003.

32. G.N. Barclay, *History of the 53rd Welsh Division in the Second World War* (Clowes, 1955), pp. 178–9.

33. Copp, 'Operation Blockbuster Begins'.

34. XXX Corps, *Medical Dairy, March/April 1945* (WO 171/357, UK National Archives). I am indebted to Professor John Buckley for drawing my attention to this reference.

35. Obituary, Stan Perry, *Guardian*, 2 November 2021.

36. Wingfield, *The Only Way Out*, pp. 170–2.

37. Ibid., p. 187.

38. Extract from 30 Corps Operational Instruction No. 47, Appendix of 30 Corps Report On Operation *Veritable* 8 February (10 March 1945), cited in Horrocks, *British Army of the Rhine*.

39. *Blockbuster* involved the following divisions, from left (adjacent to the Rhine) to right (adjacent to the Maas): under II Canadian Corps: 43rd (Wessex), 2nd Canadian Infantry, 4th Canadian Armoured, 3rd Canadian Infantry, 11th (British) Armoured; under XXX Corps: 3rd (British) Infantry, Guards Armoured, 15th (Scottish), 53rd (Welsh), 51st (Highland), 52nd (Lowland).

40. Greenwood, *D-Day to Victory*, pp. 340–2.

41. Ibid.

42. Brigadier W.F.H. Kempster's 9th Brigade comprised: 2nd Lincolns, 2nd Royal Ulster Rifles, and 1st King's Own Scottish Borders.

43. 3rd (Tank) Battalion Scots Guards, *War Diary* (WO 171/5150, UK National Archives).

44. Ibid.

45. Tony Colvin in *The Noise of Battle: The British Army and the Last Breakthrough Battle West of the Rhine, February–March 1945* (Helion, 2016), pp. 357–83, argues that part of the citation for Runcie's MC referred to Sergeant Alldred's actions, but the 3rd Scots Guards CO blocked a further bravery award for the NCO.

46. Colonel C.P. Stacey, *Official History of the Canadian Army in the Second World War, Vol. III, The Victory Campaign, Operations in North-West Europe, 1944–1945* (Duhamel, Ottawa, 1966), Chapter XIX, 'The Battle of the Rhineland, Part II: Operation Blockbuster, 22 February–10 March 1945'.

47. Copp, 'Operation Blockbuster Begins'.

48. General der Fallschirmtruppen Alfred Schlemm, *First Parachute Army, 20 November 1944–21 March 1945* (Foreign Military Studies B-084); see also Major Milton Shulman, interview with General Schlemm, October 1945, cited in Shulman, *Defeat in the West* (Secker & Warburg, 1947), p. 333.

49. RG-24, Vol. 15001 (National Archives of Canada).

50. Shulman, *Defeat in the West*, p. 336.

5: The Road to Cologne

1. General der Infanterie Gustav von Zangen, *Defensive Battles on the Roer and Rhine, Fifteenth Army, 15 November 1944–28 February 1945* (Foreign Military Studies B-811 & B-812, 1947–8).

2. Viewed at https://archive.org/details/ADC-3791.

3. Nathan N. Prefer, *The Conquering Ninth: US Ninth Army in World War II* (Casemate, 2020), p. 157.

4. Montgomery claims he decided the date.

5. Headquarters US XIII Corps, *Artillery After Action Report*, 11 March 1945 (NARA), p. 3.

6. Cooper, *Death Traps*, p. 223.

7. Headquarters 84th Division, *After Action Report, February 1945* (15 March 1945, NARA), p. 19.

8. Lieutenant Colonel Charles R. Measey, 'Roer River Crossing at Linnich, Germany', *Armored Cavalry Journal*, Vol. VII/3 (May–June 1948), pp. 54–6.

9. Theodore Draper, *The 84th Infantry Division in the Battle for Germany* (Viking Press, 1946), pp. 143–8.

10. General der Infanterie Friedrich Köchling, *Defensive Combat of the LXXXI Armeekorps During the Period 25 January –13 April 1945* (Foreign Military Studies B-576), pp. 33–34.

11. See Brian Bond, *Liddell Hart: A Study of his Military Thought* (Cassell, 1977).

12. Zangen, *Defensive Battles on the Roer and Rhine*.

13. Lieutenant Colonel Donald E. Saurenman, Headquarters, 1115th Engineer Group, *Report on Roer River Crossing* (17 March 1945, NARA).

14. Ibid.

15. MacDonald, *US Army in World War II*, p. 172.

16. Harold E. MacGregor, *28th Infantry Regiment, 8th Infantry Division* (published by the Regiment, 1946), p. 41.

17. Not to be confused with Lev Allen, Bradley's army group chief of staff.

18. Gerald Astor, *Terrible Terry Allen: Combat General of World War II – The Life of an American Soldier* (Presidio, 2003), pp. 309–10.

19. Generalmajor Rudolf Langhaeuser, *12th Volksgrenadier Division, 23 February–March 1945* (Foreign Military Studies, B-080, 1946).

20. Astor, *Terrible Terry Allen*.

21. John H. Light, *An Infantryman Remembers World War II* (Beidel Printing House, 1997), p. 112.

22. Cooper, *Death Traps*, p. 226.

23. From the popular metal toy construction sets incorporating strips, plates, angle girders, wheels, axles and gears, which, using nuts and bolts, enabled the building of working models and machinery. It was known in the USA by the brand name, Erector.

24. James Graff, *Recollections of a Combat Infantryman* (Courtesy of the Museum of the Kansas National Guard).

25. Ibid.

26. Ibid.

27. Patrick Delaforce, *Red Crown and Dragon: 53rd Welsh Division in North-West Europe 1944–1945* (Tom Donovan, 1996), p. 160.

28. Every German commander in their post-battle analysis after the war felt this was a missed opportunity. See Foreign Military Studies B-084 (General Alfred Schlemm), B-147 (General Leo, Geyer von Schweppenburg), and A-965 (Generalmajor Karl Wagener).

29. Chester Wilmot, *The Struggle for Europe* (Collins, 1952), p. 755.

30. Henry T. Ford's investment in Cologne was a result of his rivals, General Motors, buying an 80 per cent controlling interest in Opel in the same year.

31. Cooper, *Death Traps*, pp. 237–8.

32. Ibid., p. 239.

33. Astor, *Terrible Terry Allen*, p. 298.

34. John T. Greenwood, *Normandy to Victory: The War Diary of General Courtney H. Hodges and the First US Army* (University Press of Kentucky, 2008), Chapter 6.

35. Ibid.

36. Ibid.

37. Frank Woolner, *Spearhead in the West: The 3rd Armored Division in WWII* (Nashville Battery Press, 1980), p. 122.

38. MacDonald, *US Army in World War II*, p. 169.

39. Andy Rooney, *My War* (Times Books, 1995), pp. 259–61.

40. MacDonald, *US Army in World War II*, p. 169.

41. Adam Makos, *Spearhead: An American Tank Gunner, His Enemy, and a Collision of Lives in World War II* (Ballantine Books, 2019), p. 137. One GI reacted tongue-in-cheek: 'I got it – the dog was disgusted – he hanged the family and then committed suicide!'

42. Greenwood, *Normandy to Victory*, Chapter 6.

43. Steve Novak, '74 years after his famous WWII tank battle, Allentown veteran gets his Bronze Star', www.lehighvalleylive.com, 19 September 2019.

44. Adam Makos built his book *Spearhead* around the story of Clarence Smoyer and the duel with the Panther in Cologne. Pleasingly, seventy-five years after it took

place, in September 2019, Makos lured Smoyer to the Pentagon for a book signing, but had actually arranged a surprise ceremony to award him and the rest of the crew, living and dead, a Bronze Star for their success that day.

45. Makos, *Spearhead*, p. 167.

46. Harald Jähner, *Aftermath: Life in the Fallout of the Third Reich, 1945–1955*, trans. Shaun Whiteside (W.H. Allen, 2021), p. 100.

47. Walter Isaacson, *Kissinger: A Biography* (Simon & Schuster, 1992), pp. 48–53. Private Kissinger was later promoted to sergeant and reassigned to the US Army Counter Intelligence Corps (CIC), to lead a team in Hanover tracking down Gestapo officials, for which he was awarded the Bronze Star. Later still, he was made Commandant of Bensheim, twenty miles north of Heidelberg.

48. NS-Dokumentationszentrum der Stadt Köln. The prison at Appellhofplatz 23–25 has been preserved as a memorial; Guy Walters, 'The wall of love and sorrow: What would you write to your loved ones if you only had hours to live? Read these haunting messages scratched in a Gestapo cell', *Daily Mail*, 23 December 2013.

6: The Saar and the Siegfried

1. Paul F. Jenkins (1916–2007), oral interview. OH-146, Wisconsin Veterans Museum Research Center, 2000.

2. Paul Roley (ed.), Bruce Egger and Lee M. Otts, *'G' Company's War: Two Personal Accounts of the Campaigns in Europe, 1944–45* (University of Alabama Press, 1992), Kindle locs 3320–61.

3. Ibid.

4. The widely used term for government-issued 'Victory' tobacco, V-cigarettes, was also applied to other commodities such as matches, soap and chewing gum, as well as V-mail. V-mail, written by GIs to loved ones, was photographed, reduced to thumbnail-size, sent home by air, where it was reproduced as an early form of photocopy.

5. Jähner, *Aftermath*, p. 190.

6. This has not changed. When peacekeeping in the Yugoslav Wars of the 1990s, the author discovered the preferred common currency on the streets of Sarajevo was a pack of Marlboro cigarettes, which could be bartered for anything.

7. *Newsweek*, 8 January 1945; *Life* magazine, 26 March 1945; *Yank* newspaper, 4 May 1945.

8. Amarilla Blondia, 'Cigarettes and Their Impact in World War II', *Perspectives*, Vol. 137; US issue tobacco was only discontinued in 1975.

9. See Charles Glass, *The Deserters: A Hidden History of World War II* (Penguin, 2013).

10. Roley (ed.), Egger and Otts, *'G' Company's War*, Kindle loc. 3362.

11. Leonard D. Heaton (Foreword), *Medical Department of the United States Army in World War II: Preventive Medicine, Volume V: Communicable Diseases Transmitted Through Contact* (Office of the Surgeon General, Department of the Army, Washington DC, 1958), Appendix 'D', Summary of Venereal Disease Statistics.

12. *Report to the President and Prime Minister of the Agreed Summary of Conclusions Reached by the Combined Chiefs of Staff at the Octagon Conference* (US Department of State Archives, Second Quebec Conference & Related Conversations at Hyde Park, Military Conclusions of the Conference, 16 September 1944), Document 287, Paragraph 9.

13. Lynch, *A Letter Marked Free*, p. 150.

14. Not to be confused with the 76mm Gun Motor Carriage M18 *Hellcat* tank destroyer.

15. PFC Harris Peel, *The Trail of the 254th: Through Blood and Fire* (254th Infantry Regiment, 1945), p. 5.

16. Sergeant Joseph D. Buckley, *A History of the 50th Armored Infantry Battalion* (*c*.1945, printed in Germany).

17. The unfortunate choice of a yellow swastika on a red background was made in 1924; it was replaced by the Thunderbird in 1939.

18. Notes to Ken Burns' *The War* PBS documentary TV series (2007). Recipient of a Bronze Star and Two Purple Hearts, Paul Fussell would become a professor, wide-ranging literary scholar, and prolific author. He is particularly remembered for his *The Great War and Modern Memory* (1975), a descriptor of World War One but penned drawing on his own World War Two experiences. Its counterpart, *Wartime: Understanding and Behavior in the Second World War* (Oxford University Press, 1989), was equally well received. Paul Fussell, *Doing Battle: The Making of a Skeptic* (Little Brown, 1996).

19. Though devastating to a single battalion, this action at Utweiler merits so little attention in official narratives and memoirs that it is frequently misspelled Uttweiller, Ottweiler or Uweiler.

20. Lynch, *A Letter Marked Free*, p. 151.

21. Kay Evans Little, courtesy of 25north21st, Instagram, 9 October 2017.

22. Antonio J. Munoz, *The Iron Fist Division: A Combat History of the 17 SS Panzer-Grenadier Division Goetz von Berlichingen, 1943–1945* (Europa Books, 1999).

23. Frank Garahan, *Easy Company Goes to War 1944–1945: The Story of Captain Thomas H. Garahan & the 100th Infantry Division Combat Tour of WWII. An Historical Account in His Own Words & a Retracement of His Journey by His Son* (courtesy, www.garahanhistory.com, 2017).

24. Captain Alejo Rivera-Morales, *Personal Experience: Operations of the 100th Division at Bitche, Alsace-Lorraine, 15–17 March 1945* (Advanced Infantry Officers Course, Infantry School, Fort Benning, Georgia, 1949–50).

25. Garahan, *Easy Company*.

26. Headquarters 781st Tank Battalion *After Action Report* (NARA). See also: Westin Ellis Robeson, *Buttoned Up: American Armor & the 781st Tank Battalion in World War II* (Texas A&M University Press, 2017); John T. Mitzel, *Duty Before Self: The Story of the 781st Tank Battalion in World War II* (Schiffer Publishing, 2014). By the end of the war, Lieutenant Colonel Zehner had earned two DSCs, a Silver Star, three Bronze Stars and two purple hearts.

27. This was the HVSS (horizontal volute spring system), a vast improvement on the previous VVSS (vertical volute spring system). About 12,000 Shermans were manufactured to this later specification.

28. Dean Joy, *Sixty Days in Combat: An Infantryman's Memoir of World War II in Europe* (Presidio, 2004), Kindle loc. 1589.

29. Captain John H. Atterbury, Jr, *Memoir* (Courtesy of *The Eagle* (newspaper), Bryan, Texas & worldwartwoveterans.org). Ulysses Lee, *US Army in World War II, Special Studies: The Employment of Negro Troops* (Center of Military History, Washington DC, 1966), pp. 672–4. US Army segregation ended with Executive Order No. 9981, signed by President Truman on 26 July 1948, prohibiting discrimination against military personnel on grounds of race, colour, religion or national origin.

30. Paul Fussell, 'My War', essay in *Harper's Magazine* (1982).

31. Jimmy Gentry interview, courtesy Veterans' Oral History Project, Center for the Study of War and Society, Department of History, University of Tennessee, 22 July 2000.

32. Sergeant Jay D. Baxter, *Siegfried Line March 1945*, courtesy Texas Military Forces Museum, 10 June 2007.

33. John D. Heyl, 'The Construction of the Westwall, 1938: An Exemplar for National Socialist Policymaking', *Central European History*, Vol. 14/1 (March 1981), pp. 63–78.

34. On 22 December 1945, US Army Directive No. 22 directed that all military buildings in the Reich be destroyed. This work started in the summer of 1946 and was carried out in the Rheinland-Pfalz region until the spring of 1950. Most *Westwall* buildings were destroyed, though a handful of bunkers have been preserved by local historical groups.

35. Failmezger, *American Knights*, p. 266.

36. Lynch, *A Letter Marked Free*, p. 151.

37. G. Hudson Wirth, *I was an Eighteen-Year-Old Infantry Replacement* (self-published, 1997); 'Hud' Wirth (1926–2012) also wrote another war memoir, *Five GIs in Battle – World War II*.

38. Ibid.

39. Charles B. MacDonald, *US Army in World War II: European Theater of Operations, The Last Offensive* (US Center of Military History, Washington DC, 1973), p. 261.

40. Joseph Driscoll, 'Mystery Division at Rhine: Patton's Forces Chasing Germans on Road Back', *New York Herald Tribune*, 22 March 1945.

41. Buckley, *A History of the 50th Armored Infantry Battalion*.

42. Joy, *Sixty Days in Combat*, Kindle loc. 1681.

43. Colonel Charles K. Graydon, *With the 101st Cavalry During World War 1940–45* (US Army Center for Military History/Marshall Foundation).

44. MacDonald, *The Last Offensive*, op. cit., p. 261.

45. Headquarters 157th Infantry Regiment, *After Action Report, March 1945* (NARA).

46. Lee, *Employment of Negro Troops*, op. cit., pp. 672–4.

47. See Caddick-Adams, *Snow & Steel*, pp. 220–1; David Edgerton's *The Shock of the Old: Technology and Global History* (Oxford University Press, 2006) deals more broadly with this point.

48. Murphy, *To Hell and Back*, pp. 197–8; Murphy is referring here to the destruction of a German horse-drawn column outside Montélimar the previous August.

49. Turner and Jackson, *Destination Berchtesgaden*, p. 148.

50. H.R. Trevor Roper (ed.), *Hitler's War Directives 1939–1945* (Sidgwick & Jackson, 1964), pp. 293–4.

51. Dietrich's US Army ID card stated she was a Non-Combatant Captain, Sieber being her legal, married surname.

52. Russell Weiskircher (then a lieutenant in the 157th Infantry Regiment, 45th Division), interview May 1984; Brigadier General Weiskircher died in 2015.

53. From my own experiences in Bosnia, Iraq and Afghanistan, I can personally attest that soldiering in a war far from home is a lonely business. Hence the lifeline provided by Dietrich, Lynn and their colleagues.

54. Weiskircher interview.

55. Author's interview (1984) with Colonel Frederick C. Clinton (1927–2020). Clinton entered the army aged 16 in 1943; he was later commissioned and fought in Korea and Vietnam, retiring in 1974.

56. Buckley, *A History of the 50th Armored Infantry Battalion*.

57. Oberst Gruppenführer Paul Hausser, *Central Europe: Fighting of Heeresgruppe 'G' from 22 March to 4 April 1945* (Foreign Military Studies B-026 & B-600, 6 May 1946); Colonel Horst Wilutzky (G-3 [Ia] of Army Group 'G'), *The Fighting of Army Group G in the West: The Final Battle in Central & Southern Germany until Capitulation 22 Mar–6 May 1945* (Foreign Military Studies B-703).

58. Eisenhower, *Crusade in Europe*, p. 421.

59. Lester M. Nichols, *Impact: The Battle Story of the Tenth Armored Division* (Bradbury, Sayles, O'Neil Co., 1967), p. 204.

60. De Lattre, *History*, p. 415.

61. Tristan Lecoq, 'Refaire l'Armée française (1943–1945): L'outil militaire, l'instrument politique, le contrôle opérationnel' (*Guerres mondiales et conflits contemporains* 2015/1), pp. 137–54.

62. De Lattre, *History*, p. 418.

63. Bradley, *A Soldier's Story*, p. 516. The Château de Namur is now a superb five-star hotel, and I must thank their management and staff for their excellent hospitality.

64. Roger Boas, *Battle Rattle: A Last Memoir of WWII* (Stinson Publishing, 2015), Kindle locs 2227, 2290.

65. Robert S. Allen (ed. John Nelson Rickard), *Forward With Patton: The WWII Diary of Col. Robert S. Allen* (University Press of Kentucky, 2017), pp. 182–6.

66. Major General William H. Morris (Introduction, *Terrify and Destroy: The Story of the 10th Armored Division* (Stars and Stripes, Paris, 1945).

67. Allen, *Forward With Patton*, p. 187.

68. Ibid., p. 190.

69. Hobart Winebrenner (ed. Michael McCoy), *Bootprints: An Infantryman's Walk Through World War II* (Camp Comamajo Press, 2005), pp. 199, 214–15.

70. Bradley, *A Soldier's Story*, p. 518.

71. Boas, *Battle Rattle*, Kindle loc. 2157.

72. Colonel Allen described the incident: 'Patton has relieved Brig Gen Charles Kilburn, twitchy little CG of 11th Armored Division, & it's about time. Patton has been raising hell with him from way back at Bastogne. Threatened to bounce him, & finally did. Sent him to 4th Armored to learn how to command Armor. What they should have done is bust him & send him home as a Lt Col. But he's a cavalryman & an old friend of Gay's & Patton's, so they are taking care of him.' (*Forward With Patton*, p. 185).

73. J. Ted Hartman, *Tank Driver: With the 11th Armored from the Battle of the Bulge to VE Day* (Indiana University Press, 2003), pp. 78–9, 84–5.

74. William S. Nance, *Patton's Iron Cavalry – The Impact of the Mechanized Cavalry on the US Third Army* (University of North Texas Denton, Texas, 2011), pp. 223–8.

75. Roley (ed.), Egger and Otts, *'G' Company's War*, Kindle locs 3941, 3971, 4187.

76. Morris, *Terrify and Destroy*.

77. Roley (ed.), Egger and Otts, *'G' Company's War*, Kindle loc. 4206.

78. *Time Magazine*, Vol. XLV, No. 13, 26 March 1945.

79. Buddy's War – Following Buddy Lehman, Company 'C', 80th Medical Battalion, Tenth Armored Division, courtesy of his son at https://www.buddyswar.com

80. Based on an average strength of 250–300 tanks per division, including a battalion of tracked tank destroyers.

81. Allen, *Forward With Patton*, p. 189.

82. Major E. Dave Wright, *Mechanized Cavalry Groups: Lessons for the Future of Reconnaissance and Surveillance* (School of Advanced Military Studies, United States Army Command and General Staff College, Fort Leavenworth, Kansas, 2013), pp. 28–33.

83. Nance, *Patton's Iron Cavalry*, p. 228.

84. Winebrenner, *Bootprints*, pp. 221–4.

85. Headquarters 80th Medical Battalion, attached 10th Armored Division, *After Action Report, 1 March–31 March 1945* (NARA). After a brief four-day respite before crossing the Rhine on 28 March, the 10th Armored Division were assigned to the Seventh Army and would spearhead its drive all the way to the Bavarian and Austrian Alps.

86. Bradley, *A Soldier's Story*, p. 519.

87. Roley (ed.), Egger and Otts, *'G' Company's War*, Kindle loc. 4206.

7: The Bridges at Remagen

1. Greenwood, *Normandy to Victory*, Chapter 6.

2. Prym was jailed after the war. Some of his collection of unique automobiles – superior loot – 'disappeared' during First Army's tenure, surfacing in the United States

in the 1970s. Sarah Dean, 'The long road home: Nazi-era industrialist's Mercedes that was stolen by Allied troops is seized and returned to his German family – who are now selling it for £6 million', *Daily Mail*, 3 August 2016. Part of the Prym business still operates today.

3. Ken Hechler, *The Bridge at Remagen: The Amazing Story of March 7, 1945 – The Day the Rhine River was Crossed* (Ballantine, 1957), p. 26.

4. For example: 39th Infantry Regiment: Nudge; 47th Infantry: Nostril; 60th Infantry: Nutmeg; 26th Field Artillery Bn: Nudist; 34th FAA Bn: Normal; 60th FA Bn: Nuptial; 84th FA Bn: Notary; 9th Medical Bn: Nostrum; 9th Division Signal Co: Nora; 9th QM Co: Nougat; 15th Engineer Bn: Noxema; 376th AAA Auto Weapons Bn (Mobile): Noble; 610th TD Bn (Towed): Nuisance; 709th Ordnance Co: Nutty; 607th TD Bn: Nylon. Within US regiments, each battalion was designated a colour, 1st Battalion = Red; 2nd = White; 3rd = Blue. US Companies followed the phonetic alphabet: 1st Battalion: A = Able; B = Baker; C = Charlie; D = Dog; 2nd Battalion: E = Easy; F = Fox; G = George; H = How; 3rd Battalion: I = Item; K = King; L = Love; M = Mike. Platoons were numbered. Thus, Nutmeg Red Able One was 1st Platoon of Company A, 1st Battalion, 60th Infantry Regiment.

5. Greenwood, *Normandy to Victory*, Chapter 6.

6. Eisenhower, *Crusade in Europe*, pp. 366–7. The destruction at Bari was magnified by the presence of 2,000 Allied mustard gas bombs which were ignited, killing 83 of 628 hospitalised military victims. The incident was covered up by the Allies for nearly forty years, until records were declassified, and payments made to veterans. I am grateful to Andrew Rawson for drawing my attention to SHAEF's concerns over the V-weapon blitz on Antwerp.

7. General Erich Ludendorff (1865–1937) rose to become the German Army's first quartermaster general under Paul von Hindenburg, its chief of general staff during 1914–18. Andrew Rawson, *Crossing the Rhine: Remagen Bridge: 9th Armoured Infantry Division* (Battleground Europe/Pen & Sword, 2004), p. 46.

8. General William M. Hoge, *Engineer Memoirs* (US Army Corps of Engineers, 1993), pp. 143–4.

9. Ibid.

10. Ibid.

11. Greenwood, *Normandy to Victory*, Chapter 7.

12. Rooney, *My War*, pp. 250–1.

13. Eisenhower, *Crusade in Europe*, p. 415.

14. Bradley, *A Soldier's Story*, pp. 510–12.

15. Ibid., p. 252.

16. Hogan, *A Command Post*, p. 253.

17. The Ju-87 was the infamous Stuka, hopelessly obsolete by 1944.

18. The jets came from II. /KG 51 (Me-262) and Oberstleutnant Robert Kowalewski's III. /KG 76 (Ar-234). Rawson, *Crossing the Rhine*, op. cit., p. 222.

19. '99th Infantry Division: Crossing the Rhine', courtesy of *Weapons and Warfare*, 15 October 2018.

20. Greenwood, *Normandy to Victory*, Chapter 7.

21. Simon Forty, *Across the Rhine, January–May 1945* (Casemate, 2020), p. 94.

22. Hartman, *Tank Driver*, pp. 80–1.

23. Rooney, *My War*, p. 252.

24. Alfred M. Beck, Abe Bortz, Charles W. Lynch, Lilia Mayo and Ralph F. Weld, *US Army in World War II, Corps of Engineers: The War Against Germany* (US Army Center of Military History, Washington DC, 1984), Chapter 22, pp. 505–6.

25. 'German Court Reviews Execution Over Failure To Blast Remagen Bridge', article in *Park City Daily News* (Bowling Green, Kentucky), 1 February 1967, p. 25.

26. See: Peter Caddick-Adams, *Sand & Steel: A New History of D-Day* (Hutchinson, 2019), Chapter 34.

27. Interview with Oberst Hans-Joachim Krug, October 2000.

28. Hoge, *Engineer Memoirs*, pp. 143–4. By the war's end, William M. Hoge (1894–1979) was commanding 4th Armored Division, followed by a meteoric military career.

29. Rundstedt (1875–1953) had served in three armies, that of the Kaiser, Weimar Republic and Third Reich. His ability to carry on serving Hitler, whom he loathed, is best understood by the fact that virtually all the Rundstedt males since the time of Frederick the Great had served in the Prussian Army, including his father, who had fought in the Franco–Prussian War. They regarded military service not as political, but part of the Rundstedt blood.

30. Greenwood, *Normandy to Victory*, Chapter 7.

31. Allen, *Forward With Patton*, p. 188.

32. Greenwood, *Normandy to Victory*, Chapter 7.

33. For the rest of the 16 March, they captured German trucks driving along the autobahn, unaware of the Lightning Division's presence.

34. Hogan, *A Command Post*, p. 254.

35. Robert H. Berlin, *US Army World War II Corps Commanders: A Composite Biography* (Combat Studies Institute, US Army Command and General Staff College, Fort Leavenworth, Kansas, 1989), pp. 17–20.

36. James Van Fleet (1892–1992) won three Distinguished Service Crosses and three Silver Stars, served with distinction in Korea, rose to four-star general commanding the US Second Army then the Eighth and died aged 100 in 1992.

37. Giles, *The GI Journal of Sergeant Giles* (Houghton Mifflin, 1965), pp. 309–10.

38. Beck et al., *US Army in World War II*, pp. 511–12.

39. Hechler, *The Bridge at Remagen*, pp. 146–7.

40. Major William S. Nance, *Forgotten Glory: US Corps Cavalry in the ETO* (PhD thesis, University of North Texas, 2014), p. 259.

41. Courtesy of http://www.holocaustresearchproject.org/euthan/hadamar.html; and see Doris L. Bergen, *War & Genocide: A Concise History of the Holocaust* (Rowman

& Littlefield, 2003); Henry Friedlander, *The Origins of Nazi Genocide: From Eutha-nasia to the Final Solution* (University of North Carolina Press, 1995); Eugen Kogon, Hermann Langbein and Adalbert Rückerl (eds), *Nazi Mass Murder* (Yale University Press, 1993); Robert Jay Lifton, *The Nazi Doctors: Medical Killing & the Psychology of Genocide* (Macmillan, 1990).

42. Leila Levinson, *Gated Grief: The Daughter of a GI Concentration Camp Liberator Discovers a Legacy of Trauma* (Cable Publishing, 2011), pp. 30–1. Levinson cites Marino (1919–2015) as 12th Armored, who were not in First Army or this area at the time. In photographs, Marino clearly wears the Indianhead badge of 2nd Infantry Division; see also Marino interview, courtesy University of Texas at Austin, Voces Oral History Project, 2001.

43. Jaeger interview courtesy of the US Association for Diplomatic Studies & Training (ADST), at https://adst.org/2014/11/a-soldier-uncovers-the-horrors-of-the-nazis-hadamar-camp/

44. Ibid.

8: Third Army

1. Five miles per hour.

2. Headquarters Third US Army, G-4, *After Action Report, Part V, March 1945* (US Army Heritage Center, Carlisle), p. 60.

3. Middleton's Mayor of Koblenz message was transmitted on 19 March. Allen, *Forward With Patton*, p. 190.

4. Bradley, *A Soldier's Story*, p. 519.

5. George S. Patton, *War As I Knew It* (Houghton Mifflin, 1947), p. 276.

6. Samuel Eliot Morison, *History of US Naval Operations in World War II, Vol. II: The Invasion of France and Germany* (Little, Brown, 1957), pp. 317–18; Beck et al., *US Army in World War II*, p. 506.

7. Allen, *Forward With Patton*, p. 192.

8. Ibid., p. 197.

9. Ibid., p. 195.

10. Ibid., p. 196.

11. Lieutenant Colonel Frank E. Stevenson, *Third Army's Planning for the Crossing of the Rhine River* (US Army Command and General Staff College, Fort Leavenworth, Kansas).

12. Major Robert J. Liddell (Staff Group leader) et al., *Rhine River Crossing: Offensive, Deliberate Assault, River Crossing conducted by the Third US Army & the 5th Infantry Division 22–24 March 1945* (Combat Studies Institute, Fort Leavenworth, Kansas, 1984), Chapters 3 and 4: Intelligence (G-2), Operations (G-3).

13. Roley (ed.), Egger and Otts, *'G' Company's War*, Kindle loc. 4206.

14. Headquarters Naval Task Unit [TU] 122.5.2, *After Action Report, 6 April 1945* (RG-38, NARA); *Recollections of Lieutenant Commander William Leide, Commanding*

Officer of US Naval Unit Two, attached to the US Third Army during the crossing of the Rhine River (US Naval History and Heritage Command, 2017).

15. Headquarters 5th Division, G-1 Section, *After Action Report, 3 April 1945* (NARA), pp. 1–3.

16. The 1135th Engineer Combat Group noted ruefully after the Rhine, 'The remainder of the war was anti-climactic. Six weeks of clearing fallen trees along the roadways and replacing an occasional destroyed bridge brought us to the Czechoslovak border.'

17. Valderrama memoir courtesy of the American Veterans Center, Arlington, VA, info@AmericanVeteransCenter.org

18. Brigadier General P.H. Timothy, *Twelfth Army Group Engineer Operations – The Rhine Crossing* (Wiesbaden, 1945), p. 37.

19. MacDonald, *US Army in World War II*, pp. 272–3.

20. Liddell et al., *Rhine River Crossing*, p. 44 *et seq.*

21. Patton, *War As I Knew It*, p. 283.

22. *New York Times*, 25 March 1945.

23. Bradley, *A Soldier's Story*, pp. 521–2.

24. Allen, *Forward With Patton*, p. 197.

25. Courtesy Jack Schweitzer (son), *From Bastogne to the Rhine*: http://www.kilroy-washere.org/009-Pages/Schweitzer/Schweitzer.html

26. Richard Manchester, *Personal Accounts, WWII Memoirs, Part 5: Crossing the Rhine* (courtesy 87th Division Association).

27. Phil Leveque, *General Patton's Dogface Soldier of WWII* (privately printed, 1960).

28. (No author), *Rolling Ahead! The Story of the 89th Infantry Division* (Stars and Stripes, Paris, 1945).

29. 'Oscar Friedensohn Recalls Leading an Assault Boat Across the Rhine River', *World War II* magazine, April 2005.

30. *Rolling Ahead!*

31. Her name, *Lorelei*, aptly translates as 'murmuring rocks'.

32. 'Oscar Friedensohn Recalls'.

33. Ed Quick, *Rhine Crossing* (89th Infantry Division Association Personal Stories, November 2001).

34. *Rolling Ahead!*

35. In 2008, it emerged that Barack Obama's great-uncle, PFC Charles T. Payne, had served with Company 'K' of the 355th Infantry Regiment, 89th Division, in the final months of the war.

36. Headquarters 80th Infantry Division, *G-3 After Action Report*, March 1945 (NARA).

37. Headquarters *Naval Task Unit [TU] 122.5.3*, *After Action Report, 6 April 1945* (RG-38, NARA).

38. Headquarters 80th Infantry Division, *G-3 After Action Report* (NARA).

39. A Medium Maintenance Company of 175 personnel included Administrative and Ordnance Supply Platoons, which looked after the unit, plus an Automotive

Platoon, overhauling vehicles, and an Armaments Platoon, repairing weapons. Within the latter was an Instrument Section which repaired equipment like watches and binoculars.

40. Roy Altenbach, 'Memoir: How Patton's Third Army Marched Across Europe to Beat the Nazis', *The National Interest* magazine (11 April 2020).

41. Martin Blumenson (ed.), *The Patton Papers, Vol. II, 1940–45* (Houghton Mifflin, 1974), p. 661; Patton, *War As I Knew It*, p. 284.

42. Altenbach, 'Memoir'.

43. Barry W. Fowle (ed.), *Builders and Fighters: US Army Engineers in World War II* (Office of History, US Army Corps of Engineers, 1992), pp. 463–76.

9: Montgomery

1. Bernd Horn, 'Hell in a Small Place: the Canadian Paratroopers of Operation Varsity', courtesy of *Warfare History Network*, accessed 29 August 2020; also: Tim Saunders, *Operation Varsity: Rhine Crossing, The British and Canadian Airborne Assault* (Pen & Sword, 2008); Terry Copp and Robert Vogel, *Maple Leaf Route: Victory* (Maple Leaf Route, 1988).

2. The strength of Twenty-First Army Group as of 5 May 1945 included 801,399 Britons, 184,664 Canadians and 34,518 'Others', which included Poles, Czechs, Dutch, Belgians and Luxembourgers, all of whom furnished divisions, brigades or battlegroups or varying sizes, commanded by their own national leaders, but subordinate to Montgomery.

3. RG.24/Vol. 18502/File 133.009/D-6 (Canadian National Archives), cited in George G. Blackburn, *The Guns of Victory* (McClelland & Stewart, 1996), p. 382.

4. The UK official history, Major L. F. Ellis with Lieutenant Colonel A. E. Warhurst, *Victory in the West, Vol. II: The Defeat of Germany*, HMSO, 1968, p. 378) states 4,000 tank transporters to move 662 tanks, but this seems excessive, and 400 more likely. I can find no evidence there were that number available. Some 6,500 American Diamond T and 500 British Scammel units were manufactured in total, and it seems unlikely that 57 per cent of the total Allied transporter fleet built was allocated to Twenty-First Army Group, with equal calls on Twelfth, Sixth and Fifteenth Army Groups at the same moment.

5. Peter White, *With the Jocks: A Soldier's Struggle for Europe 1944–45* (Sutton Publishing, 2001), p. 261.

6. Of the latter, Twenty-First Army Group later calculated that Simpson's GIs were supported by 624 guns of 25-pounder or larger size.

7. British 'land mattresses' were in imitation of the German *Nebelwerfer* and Soviet *Katyusha* rocket batteries, fired in salvoes of 16 or 30, and eventually mounted on some Sherman tanks before the war's end. The name implied the specific target area these could achieve.

8. Blackburn, *The Guns of Victory*, pp. 243, 402.

9. Ibid., p. 402.

10. Interview courtesy of Veterans' Affairs, Canada.

11. Patrick Delaforce, *Monty's Ironsides: From the Normandy Beaches to Bremen with the 3rd Division* (Alan Sutton, 1995), p. 172.

12. Delaforce, *The Black Bull*, p. 206.

13. White, *With the Jocks*, p. 263.

14. C.P. Stacey, *The Victory Campaign, Volume 3 of the Official History of the Canadian Army in the Second World War* (Government Printing Office, 1960).

15. BAOR Battlefield Guide, *Operations of XII British Corps crossing the River Rhine 23–25 March 1945 Operation PLUNDER* (Spectator Edition, HQ BAOR, 1947).

16. Alan Moorehead, *Eclipse* (Hamish Hamilton, 1945), pp. 203–4.

17. Peter Allen, *One More River: The Rhine Crossings of 1945* (J.M. Dent, 1980), p. 248.

18. White, *With the Jocks*, p. 262.

19. Moorehead, *Eclipse*, p. 204.

20. Allen, *One More River*, p. 241.

21. Ibid., p. 246.

22. Ibid., p. 247.

23. Robin Neillands, *The Raiders: The Army Commandos 1940–46* (Weidenfeld & Nicholson, 1989).

24. Allen, *One More River*, p. 253.

25. Ibid.

26. Allen, *One More River*, p. 250.

27. Ian Robertson, *From Normandy to the Baltic: The Story of 44th Lowland Infantry Brigade of the 15th Scottish Division from D-Day to the End of the War in Europe* (privately printed, 1945), p. 146. I am indebted to Professor John Buckley for this reference.

28. A very few unarmoured early models of LVT Alligators were used at both Omaha and Utah from 7 June onwards, but purely for conveying supplies from ship to shore, and not in an aggressive infantry-carrying assault role.

29. Moorehead, *Eclipse*, p. 205.

30. White, *With the Jocks*, p. 265.

31. Ibid., p. 263.

32. Horn, 'Hell in a Small Place'.

33. Moorehead, *Eclipse*, p. 206.

34. General der Infanterie Gustav von Zangen, *Fifteenth Army (15 Nov 1944–22 Feb 1945): Defense on the Roer and Rhine Rivers* (Foreign Military Studies B-811, 1947, NARA), and *Fifteenth Army (23–28 Feb 1945): In Holland and Northern Germany* (Foreign Military Studies B-812, 1948, NARA).

35. Generalmajor Heinz Fiebig, *84th Infantry Division (19 Jan–25 Mar 1945): West of the Lower Rhine from the Reichswald to Wesel* (Foreign Military Studies B-843, NARA).

36. However, 45 per cent of the vehicles, 29 per cent of the 75mm pack howitzers, 50 per cent of the 25-pounder artillery pieces and 56 per cent of the 17-pounder anti-tank guns delivered by gliders were damaged or destroyed.

37. These included Tedder, Ike's deputy, Kenneth Strong, J-2, Morgan, deputy chief of staff, and 'Jock' Whiteley, deputy J-3.

38. Field Marshal Montgomery, Personal Diary, 29 March 1945 (LMD 69/1, Imperial War Museum).

39. Churchill, *The Second World War*, Vol. 6, pp. 365 *et seq.*

40. Alanbrooke Papers 13/7 (King's College London Archives).

41. Moorehead, *Eclipse*, p. 206.

42. Taylor, *Infantry Colonel*, p. 192.

43. Copp, *Cinderella Army*, p. 261.

44. Major Edward P. Ludington, *Operations of the 313th Infantry (79th Infantry Division) in the Preparation and Crossing of the Rhine, 9–24 March 1945* (Advanced Infantry Officers Class No. 1, Fort Benning, Georgia, 1949–50), pp. 4–9; Major Richard P. Koch IV, *Combat Engineers of World War II: Lessons on Training & Mobilization* (MA thesis, US Army Command and General Staff College, Fort Leavenworth, Kansas, 2014), pp. 72–6.

45. Headquarters Ninth US Army, *Engineer Operations in the Rhine Crossing* (30 June 1945, NARA).

46. Lieutenant Colonel John C. Dalrymple, *The Operations of the 1117th Engineer Combat Group on the Rhine River Crossing* (student paper, School of Combined Arms Regular Course 1946–1947, Command and General Staff College, Fort Leavenworth, Kansas, 1947).

47. MacDonald, *US Army in World War II*, p. 304.

48. These were outfits trained in tactical deception activities and not to be confused with Special Forces-type units.

49. Headquarters Ninth Army, *G-2 After Action Report* (March 1945, NARA).

50. Eisenhower, *Crusade in Europe*, p. 425.

51. Assault boats, carrying seven men and a crew of two, were powered by 55hp motors; double assault boats (fourteen men and a crew of three) were driven by 22hp motors.

52. David Lippman, *Operation Plunder: Crossing the Rhine* (Warfare History Network, accessed 22 August 2020).

53. MacDonald, After Action Combat Interview with Lieutenant W.O. Refvem (1921–88) of Colorado (NARA).

54. Ludington, *Operations of the 313th Infantry*, p. 13.

55. Roy Morris Jr, 'The Race to the Rhine: How the US 79th Division Took Down the Nazis', MHQ, *Quarterly Journal of Military History*, Vol. 33/3, Spring 2021.

56. Ibid., p. 18.

57. Ibid.

58. Morris, 'The Race to the Rhine'.

59. Ludington, *Operations of the 313th Infantry*, p. 20.

60. Ibid., p. 21.

61. Graff, *Recollections of a Combat Infantryman*.

62. Dalrymple, *The Operations of the 1117th Engineer Combat Group.*

63. Despite its advantages, the C-46 had one drawback, the lack of self-sealing fuel tanks, which caused the majority of its losses in *Varsity.* Ridgway had them withdrawn from paratroop duties afterwards.

64. Headquarters 680th Glider Artillery Battalion, G-3, *After Action Report, Operation Varsity* (March 1945, NARA).

65. Eisenhower, *Crusade in Europe,* p. 426.

66. Bart Hagerman, 'Operation Varsity: Allied Airborne Assault Over the Rhine River' (*World War II* magazine, February 1998).

67. Matthew J. Seelinger, *Operation Varsity: The Last Airborne Deployment of World War II,* Army Historical Foundation, 2010.

68. Hagerman, 'Operation Varsity'.

69. Figures cited in MacDonald, *US Army in World War II,* p. 309; Eisenhower in *Crusade in Europe* (p. 426) gives slightly different figures.

70. Graff, *Recollections of a Combat Infantryman.*

71. Seelinger, *Operation Varsity.*

72. Graff, *Recollections of a Combat Infantryman.*

73. Field Marshal Bernard Montgomery, 'Order of the Day', issued to troops 23 March 1945: paper message in author's possession.

10: Sixth Army Group

1. *The Seventh United States Army in France and Germany, 1944–1945: Report of Operations* (Heidelberg, 1946), Part Two, p. 1013; De Lattre, *History,* p. 422.

2. Timothy, *Twelfth Army Group Report of Operations,* Introduction.

3. *Twelfth Army Group Report of Operations,* Vol. III (Wiesbaden, 1945), p. 747.

4. Klages and Mulholland, *Number of German divisions by front in World War II.*

5. On 30 January 1945 Hitler broadcast to his shrinking nation on the twelfth anniversary of his coming to power: 'I expect every German to do his duty to the last and that he be willing to take upon himself every sacrifice he will be asked to make; I expect every able-bodied German to fight with complete disregard for his personal safety; I expect the sick and the weak or those otherwise unavailable for military duty to work with their last strength; I expect city dwellers to forge the weapons for this struggle and I expect the farmer to supply the bread for the soldiers and workers of this struggle by imposing restrictions upon himself; I expect all women and girls to continue supporting this struggle with utmost fanaticism . . . However grave the crisis may be, it will, despite everything, finally be mastered by our unalterable will, by our readiness for sacrifice and by our abilities. We shall overcome this calamity, too, and this fight, too, will not be won by central Asia but by Europe; and at its head will be the nation that has represented Europe against the East for 1,500 years and shall represent it for all times: our Greater German Reich, the German nation.' In other words – victory or death.

6. Ursula von Kardorff, *Diary of a Nightmare: Berlin 1942–5* (Rupert Hart-Davis, 1965), p. 145.

7. Bernard L. Kahn, *Fight On: A GI's Odyssey Back to Nazi Germany* (Cable Publishing, 2013), Kindle loc. 3899.

8. Lynch, *A Letter Marked Free*, p. 158.

9. Captain Clayton H. Moore Jr, *Operations of Company 'F', 30th Infantry (3rd Infantry Division) in the crossing of the Rhine River near Worms, Germany, 26–27 March 1945* (Advanced Infantry Officers Course No. 1, Infantry School, Fort Benning, Georgia, 1948–9), pp. 10–15.

10. Alex Kershaw, *The Liberator* (Crown Publishers, 2012), p. 229.

11. Captured in huge quantities by US forces, panzerfäuste proved handy for attacking not only panzers, but houses concealing infantry.

12. On 15 August 1944, twelve DD tanks from three American tank battalions, the 191st, 753rd and 756th (total 36), were used in Operation *Dragoon*.

13. Moore, *Operations of Company 'F'*, pp. 37–9.

14. When promoted to brigadier general by Patton in 1943, Garrison 'Gar' H. Davidson (1904–92) was the youngest one-star commander in the US Army. He later commanded Seventh and First Armies before retirement in 1964.

15. Kershaw, *The Liberator*, p. 230.

16. Kevin M. Hymel, *A Sergeant in the 12th Armored Division*, courtesy Warfare History Network.

17. *Marvel B. Rowland's Story of WWII*, courtesy World War II Memorial Museum, Abilene, Texas, pp. 24–5.

18. Kevin M. Hymel, *Inside an M5 Stuart: A Tanker's WWII Tale in His Own Words*, courtesy Warfare History Network.

19. De Lattre, *History*, p. 421.

20. Joy, *Sixty Days in Combat*, Kindle loc. 2078.

21. De Lattre, *History*, p. 428.

22. Victor Hugo quote courtesy of James M. Markham, 'Watching the Rhine', *New York Times*, 24 August 1986.

23. Nos. 326–329, 340–347 Squadrons, RAF.

11: Tensions with the French

1. Stephen G. Fritz, *Endkampf: Soldiers, Civilians, and the Death of the Third Reich* (University Press of Kentucky, 2004), p. 307.

2. Klages and Mulholland, *Number of German divisions by front in World War II*.

3. Edward M. Bedessem, *Central Europe, 22 March–11 May 1945* (US Army Center for Military History, Washington DC, 1996), p. 3.

4. See Caddick-Adams, *Snow & Steel*, pp. 98–102.

5. *Daily Herald* (UK), 7 April 1945. Cited in Nathan Morley, *Radio Hitler: Nazi Airwaves During the Second World War* (Amberley, 2021), p. 236.

6. Louis Hagen, *Ein Volk, Ein Reich: Nine Lives Under the Nazis* (History Press, 2011), p. 212.

7. Perry Biddiscombe, *The Last Nazis: SS Werewolf Guerrilla Resistance in Europe 1944–1947* (History Press, 2004), p. 175.

8. *Seventh United States Army Report of Operations*, p. 1059.

9. Heinz Risel, *Concentration camp in Heilbronn: The SS Steinbock Labour Camp in Neckargartach* (self-published, Nordheim, 1987).

10. J. Glenn Gray, *The Warriors. Reflections on Men in Battle* (University of Nebraska Press, 1959), pp. 203–4.

11. Steven R. Welch, 'Harsh but Just? German Military Justice in the Second World War: A Comparative Study of the Court Martialling of German and US Deserters', *German History*, 173 (1999), pp. 369–99. Manfred Messerschmidt and Fritz Wüllner observe that by mid-1944 there had been some 440,000 military judgements, of which only 13,000–15,000 were cases of desertion or *Wehrkraftzersetzung*, with the remainder split equally between absence without leave, theft and fraud. These resulted in 11,664 documented executions, of which 9,372 had been for *Wehrkraftzersetzung*-related offences. By May 1945, they assess that the Third Reich military justice system issued about 30,000 death sentences for all offences, of which 23,000 were carried out; Messerschmidt and Wüllner, *Die Wehrmachtjustiz im Dienste des Nationalsozialismus: Zerstörung einer Legende* (Wehrmacht Justice in the Service of National Socialism: Destroying a Legend), (Nomos, 1987). However, Erich Schwinge cites more than 40,000 German soldiers sentenced to death (not all carried out), and over a million imprisoned, in 'A Human Life is for Nothing: Military Justice in the Third Reich', *Der Spiegel* (26 October 1987). Rüdiger Overmans calculates these 30,000–40,000 capital sentences equate to under 2 per cent of the minimum of 18 million who served in the Heer (13.6m), Luftwaffe (2.5m), Kriegsmarine (1.2m) and Waffen-SS (0.9m), besides uncounted Volkssturm, police, Hitler Youth, Labour Service and Organisation Todt personnel, during 1939–45. By contrast only 18 German soldiers were executed for desertion in 1914–18. Overmans, *Deutsche Militärische Verluste im Zweiten Weltkrieg* (German Military Losses in World War II), (Oldenbourg, 2004), p. 215.

12. The United States tried over 21,000 GIs for desertion during World War Two, issuing 49 death sentences, but Slovik's was the only one to be carried out. However, 102 executions did take place for rape or unprovoked murder of civilians.

13. Robert Tessmer, *Eric Levi Returns to Boyhood Home and Saves Village* (courtesy of Personal Memory Collection, Library & Archives, George C. Marshall Foundation, Lexington, Virginia), p. 1.

14. *Kreisleiter*, or District Leader, was the political rank below *Gauleiter*.

15. *Ortsgruppenleiter* (Local Group Leader) was the political rank beneath *Kreisleiter*.

16. As regional historians note, 'For his brutality, indiscriminate murder and responsibility in the final agony of their city, Drauz (1894–1946) remains a figure of

contempt in Heilbronn to this day.' Unrepentant when charged with a variety of war crimes, he was found guilty and hanged at Landsberg Prison on 4 December 1946.

17. Rufus Dalton, *Two Days of Hell at Heilbronn* (courtesy of Personal Memory Collection, Library & Archives, George C. Marshall Foundation), p. 3.

18. Ibid, p. 1.

19. In contrast to the M10 (75mm gun) and M36 (90mm) tank destroyers modelled on a Sherman chassis, the M18 Hellcat utilised a new suspension and hull, and was smaller, lighter, more comfortable and significantly faster than its forebears, but carried the same gun as the Sherman 76mm models.

20. Nichols, *Impact*, p. 231.

21. Morris, *Terrify and Destroy*.

22. A.I. Goldberg (1904–73), '10th Armored Sweats It Out' (Associated Press), *New York Times*, 9 April 1945.

23. Ibid.

24. Lee Reese, *The Last Battle, Maybe* (Personal Memory Collection, George C. Marshall Foundation), p. 2.

25. Typical of late-war battlegroups, *SS-Kampfgruppe Dirnagel* was formed on 25 March from the Munich SS Flak Training and Replacement Regiment and consisted of two battalions of anti-aircraft gunners fighting as infantry, plus a flak battalion, totalling 2,500 men, and led by *SS-Obersturmbannführer* Dirnagel.

26. Clifford H. Peek Jr (ed.), *Five Years, Five Countries, Five Campaigns with the 141st Infantry Regiment* (141st Infantry Regiment Association, Munich, 1945), Chapter XIV: 'The Last Ten Days of the War'.

27. Fritz, *Endkampf*, pp. 216–224. Also see: Oskar von Miller, *Incident at Brettheim, 1945* (Realschule, Rothenburg ob der Tauber and Goethe Institute, 1998). Bizarrely, Simon (1899–1961) was thrice tried for his role in the Brettheim affair and acquitted each time.

28. Graydon, *With the 101st Cavalry*.

29. Donald R. Jerge (1925–2007) interview, New York, 1984.

30. Nichols, *Impact*, p. 243.

31. Jerge interview.

32. Dalton, *Two Days of Hell*, p. 8.

33. Ibid., p. 4.

34. Ibid.

35. Ibid., p. 5.

36. Robert Bauer, *Heilbronner Tagebuchbätter* (Heilbronn Diaries), (self-published, Heilbronn, 1949), entry for 25 April 1945 (my translation).

37. For example, *Destination Berchtesgaden*, the Seventh Army's history by John Frayn Turner and Robert Jackson, appears to go out of its way in avoiding any mention of the French. Bradley's *A General's Life* is consistently anti-French.

38. De Lattre, *History*, p. 407.

39. Lieutenant General Reuben E. Jenkins Papers, *Battle of the National Redoubt* (US Army Military History Institute, Carlisle, PA).

40. Salisbury-Jones, *So Full A Glory*, pp. 194–5.

41. De Lattre, *History*, p. 485.

42. The two states merged in 1952 to become Baden-Württemberg.

43. De Lattre, *History*, p. 196.

44. Yaffa Eliach and Brana Gurewitsch, *The Liberators: Eyewitness Accounts of the Liberation of Concentration Camps* (Center for Holocaust Studies, Documentation and Research, 1981), pp. 8–10.

45. Later Général de Brigade Jacques de Parisot de Durand de la Boisse, Commandant at St Cyr, died 26 January 1999 aged 98, whom I interviewed in August 1975. De Lattre's recollection is from his *History of the French First Army*, p. 441.

46. See http://www.stolpersteine-gp.de/en/stolperschwelle-geislingen/

47. Including Russia, Hungary, Poland, Greece, France, Holland, Italy, Lithuania, Spain, Belgium and Germany.

48. Friederike Schröder, 'The Stuttgart US Army Airfield as a Place for Learning and Remembrance', PowerPoint presentation (Geschichtswerkstatt KZ-Außenlager Echterdingen-Bernhausen), at http://www.sfa-auvillar.com/JETE/2009_Tubingen/JETE_Tue09_schroeder_geschichtswerkstatt.pdf, accessed 7 July 2019.

49. De Lattre, *History*, pp. 196–7.

50. Devers' diary, 27 April 1945, *Devers papers* (Eisenhower Presidential Library, Abilene, Kansas). The final count of rapes was estimated at between 1,500 and 2,000, around 10 per cent of the 20,000 initially claimed in the Allied media.

51. 'Alsos' was a nod to the brigadier general, being Greek for 'grove'.

52. Contrary to rumours then and now, analysis indicates the German nuclear and biological weapons programmes were less threatening than had been feared. Compared to the Manhattan Project, they were woefully underfunded, disorganised and conducted on such a small scale (reflecting the Führer's disregard and ignorance of scientific research, and scepticism that weapons of mass destruction were even possible) that they lagged far behind the Anglo-American project.

53. Boris Pash, *The Alsos Mission* (Charter Books, 1969), pp. 201–17. Both Leslie Groves (*Now It Can Be Told: The Story of the Manhattan Project*, Harper & Row, 1962) and the chief Alsos scientist, Samuel A. Goudsmit (*Alsos*, Henry Schuman, 1947), also wrote accounts of their Alsos adventures.

54. Courtesy Bill McElvain, *In My Father's Words: Letters From a World War II Soldier* (Lulu, 2011), Chapter 12.

55. Author's interview, September 2002.

56. Robert C. McFarland (ed.), *History of the 15th Infantry Regiment in World War II* (Society of the Third Infantry Division, 1990), p. 289.

57. *Seventh Army, Report of Operations*, p. 1111.

58. Martin Gilbert, *Winston S. Churchill, Vol. VII: 1941–45, Road to Victory*, p. 1313.

59. Salisbury-Jones, *So Full A Glory*, p. 197.

60. Eisenhower, *The War Years: Volume 4, Part X: Victory; January 1945 to May 1945* (Johns Hopkins University Press, 1970) pp. 2657–8.

61. Devers' diary, 13 May 1945, *Devers papers*.

62. Charles E. Marshall, *Discovering the Rommel Murder* (Stackpole, 2002), pp. 182–201.

63. Intriguingly, Manfred's deposition sits in the Montgomery Papers in London's Imperial War Museum, at BLM/1/91. We now know that Desmond Young's biography, *Rommel: The Desert Fox* (Collins, 1950), tells only part of the true story, and scholars today have surmised there is no firm evidence for Rommel's involvement in the 20 July 1944 plot. It may be that it was a fabrication of the surviving plotters, led by Rommel's chief of staff Hans Speidel, who was connected with the coup attempt. Discussed more fully in Peter Caddick-Adams, *Monty and Rommel: Parallel Lives* (Preface/Arrow, 2011), pp. 476–9.

64. The trio were Generalmajor Richard Bazing (89th Division), Generalleutnant Karl Faulenbach (719th Division) and Generalmajor der Reserve Rudolf von Oppen (352nd Division), all part of SS-Obergruppenführer Georg Keppler's XVIII SS Corps.

65. Bielenberg was the niece of newspaper owners the Harmsworth brothers (later Lords Harmsworth, Northcliffe and Rothermere), meeting and marrying Peter Bielenberg in 1934. They initially lived in Berlin until Allied bombing forced her to the Black Forest in 1943. As they had moved in the circle of the Stauffenberg plotters, Peter was interned in a camp. She secured his release and engineered his disappearance until the end of the war. This is from her excellent memoir, *The Past is Myself* (Chatto & Windus, 1968), pp. 275–86.

66. Von Kardorff, *Diary*, pp. 183–8.

67. Eisenhower, *Crusade in Europe*, p. 452.

68. Salisbury-Jones, *So Full A Glory*, pp. 197–8.

69. Author's meeting with Dr Manfred Rommel, CBE, 23 October 2002, London.

12: Aschaffenburg, Würzburg and Schweinfurt

1. Alois Stadtmüller, *Aschaffenburg im Zweiten Weltkrieg* (Geschichts- und Kunstverein Aschaffenburg, 1971).

2. Contrary to several authors, Major Lamberth was never a 'von'. Formerly CO of *Pionier-Ersatz-und-Ausbildungsbatallion* 9 (9th Engineer Replacement and Training Battalion), Lamberth's garrison included four Hungarian companies, modestly equipped with 1,700 rifles, 32 machine-guns and a few mortars. Later, panzerfäuste, hand grenades, assault rifles & ammunition arrived.

3. There was never an accurate count of Lamberth's garrison; 5,000 may include neighbouring Volksgrenadier units which technically were not his. Some contemporary US G-2 military estimates assess his strength as 3,500.

4. Singular is *panzerfaust*, plural is *panzerfäuste*.

5. Author's interview with Herr Manfred Baunach, US Army Staff Ride to Aschaffenburg, November 1999; there were about 6,000 slave labourers working locally, who helped build the defences before being evacuated when the battle began. Major Quentin W. Schillare, *The Battle of Aschaffenburg: An example of Late World War II Urban Combat in Europe* (master's thesis, US Army Command and Staff College, Fort Leavenworth, Kansas, 1989), p. 73.

6. Some references suggest that Lamberth ordered the majority of the town's 30,000 residents to flee eastwards on 5 March, when promoted to fortress commander, but I can find no orders to this effect.

7. Kershaw, *The Liberator*, p. 231.

8. Translation of captured documents, *US Army, XII Corps, G-2 Periodic Reports, 1–31 March 45* (Combined Arms Research Library), p. 3.

9. Robert F. Lynch, interview and letter home, 29 March 1945, *A Letter Marked Free*, p. 155.

10. The boundary change was effective 00:01 hours on 27 March.

11. Mark J. Reardon, 'Aschaffenburg, 1945: Cassino on the River Main', Chapter 7, in John Antal and Bradley Gericke (eds), *City Fights: Selected Histories of Urban Combat from World War II to Vietnam* (Ballantine, 2003), p. 198.

12. Captain Harold B. Henderly, *Personal Experience of a Company Commander: The Operations of Company 'D', 191st Tank Battalion, at Aschaffenburg, Germany, 28 March–3 April 1945* (Advanced Infantry Officers Course No. 1, Infantry School, Fort Benning, Georgia, 1948–9), p. 9.

13. Napalm had been used sparingly in aerial bombs for raids and tactical attacks by the USAAF since its first use by strategic bombers on Berlin, 6 March 1944.

14. *The Story of Aschaffenburg* booklet (45th Infantry Division, May 1945).

15. Courtesy, http://45thinfantrydivision.com/index11.htm. The barracks later became the headquarters of US Army units stationed in the region.

16. For fuller accounts of the battle, see: Felix L. Sparks, 'The Aschaffenburg Battle', *157th Infantry Association Journal* (July 1982); Flint Whitlock, *The Rock of Anzio: From Sicily to Dachau, A History of the US 45th Infantry Division* (Westview Press, 1998); Emajean Jordan Buechner, *Sparks: The Combat Diary of a Battalion Commander (Rifle) WWII, 157th Infantry Regiment, 45th Division, 1941–1945* (Thunderbird Press, 1992); Kershaw, *The Liberator*, Chapter 22.

17. Rather unfairly, Lamberth survived and was tried for the executions after the war; he was found guilty and sentenced to four years in prison, although the sentence was later reduced because the defence succeeded in alleging Lamberth was pressurised by local SS officials.

18. Reardon, 'Aschaffenburg, 1945'.

19. Kershaw, *The Liberator*, p. 243.

20. Signed on 2 December 1944.

21. Stimpson Papers, George C. Marshall Foundation Library, Lexington, Virginia.

22. Pogue, *The Supreme Command*, p. 53.

23. This class included the Stauffenberg conspirators, who initially welcomed Hitler's accession to power, and even the humbling of the French in 1940. However, they decided earlier than the rest that their loyalty to their profession and Germany was being compromised and exploited by National Socialism.

24. Ian Kershaw, *The Führer Myth: Image and Reality in the Third Reich* (Oxford, 1987), pp. 206, 214.

25. Von Kardorff, *Diary*, p. 167.

26. Headquarters Sixth Army Group G-2, *Weekly Intelligence Summaries* (RG-332, NARA).

27. Headquarters 10th Armored Division, G-2, *Report, April 1945* (NARA), p. 1120.

28. Elisabeth von Berrinberg, *The City in Flames: Recollections of the Bombing of Würzburg* (Berrinberg/Smith House Press, 2013). Incendiary devices, often incorporating magnesium, are designed to burn at high temperature, destroying wooden roof joists and beams, whereas napalm is a petroleum jelly that sticks to what it burns and is impossible to extinguish with water.

29. Fritz, *Endkampf*, pp. 245–50.

30. Dr Otto Hellmuth, Gauleiter of Lower Franconia (*Gau Unterfranken*), lived in Würzburg on Ludendorffstraße, now Rotterdorfer Straße.

31. Gentry interview, University of Tennessee.

32. Rudolf Decker, 'The Battle for Würzburg', *Rainbow Reveille* (Rainbow Division's Veterans Association Journal, January 1993), courtesy of Archives & Special Collections, University of Nebraska–Lincoln.

33. Gentry interview, University of Tennessee.

34. Entry for Randolph Boling McDavid, class of 1943, Clemson University Corps Records, South Carolina.

35. Carner Papers, pp. 13–15.

36. Decker, 'The Battle for Würzburg'.

37. Carner Papers.

38. Hans-Peter Baum, *List of American soldiers killed in the Battle of Würzburg* (Mainfränkisches Jahrbuch für Geschichte und Kunst, 2019).

39. William George Hansult Jr, *The Final Battle: An Untold Story of WW II's Forty-Second Rainbow Division* (Mill City Press, 2018).

40. Gentry interview, University of Tennessee.

41. Martin Middlebrook, *The Schweinfurt-Regensburg Raid* (Allen Lane, 1983), Chapter 20.

42. Courtesy, Dr Victoria Taylor, 'Blitzmädels an die Front: A Lesser Known Female War Film', *Women's History Network* (December 2018) https://womenshistorynetwork.org/blitzmadels-an-die-front-a-lesser-known-female-war-film/

43. Karl Heinz Schlesier, *Flakhelfer to Grenadier: Memoir of a Boy Soldier 1943–5* (Helion, 2014), p. 126.

44. Lynch, *A Letter Marked Free*, p. 155.
45. Gentry interview, University of Tennessee.
46. Thomas Garahan, letter home, 13 April 1945, *Easy Company Goes to War*.
47. 'Secret Illnesses of the Presidents: Franklin D. Roosevelt – Disability and Deception', paper (University of Arizona, Health Sciences Library); see also Robert Ferrell, *Choosing Truman: The Democratic Convention of 1944* (University of Missouri Press, 1994), and *The Dying President: Franklin D. Roosevelt 1944–1945* (University of Missouri Press, 1998).

13: Patton's April

1. Set up as a German Army training camp in 1893, Hammelburg was technically two camps, divided into Oflag XIII-B (for 1,300 officers) and Stalag XIII-C (housing 5,000 enlisted men), though by 1945 all the Americans of whatever rank were in the Oflag, and the other nationalities in the Stalag.
2. *Camp Histories: Stalag XIII-C Hammelburg* (WO 208/3279, UK National Archives). The Americans were from the 14th Cavalry Group, and 28th, 99th and 106th Infantry Divisions, mostly the latter, captured in the Bulge. See Caddick-Adams, *Snow & Steel*.
3. Combat Command B, *After Action Report, March 1945* (24 April 1945, NARA).
4. Captain Abraham J. Baum, HQ 4th Armored Division, *Notes on Task Force Baum* (10 April 1945, NARA).
5. Lieutenant Colonel Frederick E. Oldinsky, 'Patton & the Hammelburg Mission', *Armor* magazine (July–August, 1976), pp. 13–18; Martin Blumenson, 'The Hammelburg Affair', *Army* magazine (October 1965), pp. 16–18, 20, 22–24, 26, 28, 30.
6. Richard Baron, Major Abe Baum and Richard Goldhurst, *Raid! The Untold Story of Patton's Secret Mission* (Putnam's, 1981), p. 196; Captain Sheldon L. Thompson, *Operations of Task Force Baum, 4th Armored Division, Between Aschaffenburg and Hammelburg, Germany, 27–28 March 1945* (Personal Experience of a PW at Oflag XIII-B, Advanced Infantry Officers Course, No. 2, Infantry School, Fort Benning, Georgia, 1948–9).
7. Patton's posthumous memoirs were first published in the *Saturday Evening Post*, in August 1948, Peter Domes and Martin Heinlein, *Alarm! Die Panzerspitze kommt!* (Hofmann-Buch, 2008).
8. Baum's route was dictated by the extant bridges over the River Main. Today's equivalent is via the 26 out of Aschaffenburg, crossing the Main at Lohr, joining the 27 at Karsbach and thence to Hammelburg; Michael K. Robel, 'Patton's Hammelburg Raid: Mission Assessment & Lessons Learned', *Command* magazine (November 2000), pp. 28–32; Herndon Inge, Jr, 'The Hammelburg Raid', *Military Magazine*, Vol. XVIII/10 (March 2002), pp. 5–8; Interview, Herndon Inge, Jr, 'Witnessing Patton's Failure: A Prisoner's View of the Task Force Baum Raid' (Warfare History Network, 28 December 2018).

9. Bradley, *A Soldier's Story*, p. 531.

10. These exchanges are in Eisenhower, *Crusade in Europe*, pp. 437–40.

11. Horne and Montgomery, *The Lonely Leader*, p. 320.

12. Ibid., p. 321.

13. Major Kenneth O. McCreedy, *Planning the Peace: Operation Eclipse and the Occupation of Germany* (School of Advanced Military Studies, US Army Command and General Staff College, Fort Leavenworth, Kansas, 1995); John McKenzie, *On Time, On Target: The World War II Memoir of a Paratrooper in the 82nd Airborne* (Presidio Press, 2000), p. 156; James Megellas, *All the Way to Berlin: A Paratrooper at War in Europe* (Presidio Press, 2003) writes in a similar vein.

14. Charles Whiting, *Battle of the Ruhr Pocket* (Pan Ballantine, 1971), pp. 158–9.

15. Stephen E. Ambrose, *Eisenhower and Berlin, 1945: The Decision to Halt at the Elbe* (W.W. Norton & Co., 1967); James M. Gavin, *On to Berlin* (Viking, 1978), p. 288; see also Forrest Pogue, *US Army in World War II: The Supreme Command* (Washington, 1954), chapters XXIII and XXIV.

16. Cable, Churchill to Eden (in USA), 19 April 1945, cited in *The Second World War*, Vol.VI *'Triumph and Tragedy'* (Cassell, 1953), pp. 515–16.

17. Allen, *Forward With Patton*, p. 207.

18. Ibid., p. 202; Hodges was not popular in Patton's headquarters, being rated privately by Allen 'as aggressive as a flabby hamburger, a soggy dishrag', p. 204.

19. Winebrenner, *Bootprints*, p. 229.

20. Allen, *Forward With Patton*, p. 207.

21. Mikael Levin, *War Story: Retracing my Father's Footsteps* (Kehayoff, Munich, 1997), pp. 119–23.

22. Joseph Borkin, *The Crime and Punishment of I.G. Farben* (Free Press/Macmillan, 1978); Peter Hayes, *Industry and Ideology: I.G. Farben in the Nazi Era* (Cambridge University Press, 2001); Diarmuid Jeffreys, *Hell's Cartel: I.G. Farben and the Making of Hitler's War Machine* (Henry Holt & Co., 2008).

23. Allen, *Forward With Patton*, pp. 209, 207.

24. The surname was changed to Windsor on 17 July 1917, due to public anti-German sentiment and specifically air raids on London of the previous month, carried out by German Gotha bombers.

25. Helga Raschke, *Josef Ritter von Gadolla and the Last Days of the War in Gotha* (Raschke Eigenverlag, 2007).

26. When Auschwitz was liberated on 26–27 January by the Soviet 322nd Rifle Division, they found 7,500 prisoners alive and over 600 corpses; among items found by the Soviet soldiers were 370,000 men's suits, 837,000 women's garments and 7.7 tons of human hair; at the time its liberation received little attention partly because of competing news from the Allied summit at Yalta and Stalin's purpose in minimising Jewish suffering and stressing that of the Soviet Union. Due to the vast extent of the camp area, at least four divisions took part in liberating Auschwitz: 100th Rifle, 322nd Rifle, 286th Rifle and 107th Motor Rifle Divisions.

27. David Cohen, 4th Armored Division, interview, *GIs Remember* (National Museum of American Jewish Military History, Washington DC, 1994).

28. Robert H. Abzug, *Inside the Vicious Heart: Americans and the Liberation of Nazi Concentration Camps* (Oxford University Press, 1985), p. 22.

29. Ibid., p. 21.

30. Sarah Boxer, 'Into the "Black Heart" of Evil: The Bodies, the Overgrowth, the Lies', Photography Review, *New York Times*, 7 March 1997.

31. Christopher Miskimon, 'Liberating the Camps: The U.S. Soldiers Who Liberated Nazi Concentration Camps Could Never Forget What They Saw', https://warfare-historynetwork.com/2019/01/12/liberating-the-camps/

32. Courtesy of *Gadsden Times* (Alabama), http://www.gadsdentimes.com/article/20090504/NEWS/905049993/1017/NEWS?Title=World-War-II-veteran-recalls-liberation-of-death-camp

33. Stewart's target on 25 February 1944, when leading the 445th Bomb Group, was Fürth in Bavaria, but it was over Gotha where he was hit. After a gruelling nine-hour flight home, when his shrapnel-perforated bomber landed, its fuselage buckled. As the crew climbed out and looked over their crippled aircraft, Stewart mused, 'Sergeant, somebody sure could get hurt in one of those damned things.'

34. Eddy was evacuated to the USA with extreme hypertension one week later, on 19 April, and was succeeded at XII Corps by Major General Stafford LeRoy Irwin, then commanding 5th Infantry Division.

35. Headquarters 358th Infantry Regiment: *After Action Report, Mar–May 45* (NARA); Colonel B. Bernstein to Brigadier General F. J. McSherry, *Report of developments in removal of Treasure from Kaiseroda at Merkers, Germany, Apr. 18, 1945*; Secretariat, G-5 Division, General Staff, Financial-Germany, *Discoveries of Gold & Other Valuables, Aug 43–Jul 45*, SHAEF/G-5/1/13; Information Branch, General Staff, *Special Report on Discovery & Disposition of German Gold*, File 105, Historical Section, G-5 Division, SHAEF (All NARA).

36. Winebrenner, *Bootprints*, p. 237.

37. Levinson, *Gated Grief*.

38. Patton, *War As I Knew It*, p. 293.

39. Charles R. Codman, *Drive* (Little, Brown, 1957), p. 283.

40. Eisenhower, *Crusade in Europe*, pp. 408–9.

41. Bradley, *A Soldier's Story*, p. 539.

42. Ohrdruf Nordlager (Ohrdruf North camp) passed to the Red Army in July 1945, when Thuringia became part of the Soviet occupation zone. Two memorials to the dead were erected at the time. Since 1993 it has been under Bundeswehr control.

43. Patton, *War As I Knew It*, p. 298.

44. Duff Hart-Davis (ed.), *King's Counsellor: Abdication and War, The Diaries of Sir Alan Lascelles* (Weidenfeld & Nicolson, 2006), p. 314; Ed Murrow, 'They Died 900 a Day in "the Best" Nazi Death Camp', CBS Sound Archives, 16 April 1945.

45. Levinson, *Gated Grief*, p. 151; aged 91, Nathan Futterman of New Rochelle, New York, died in 2017.

46. The Jewish Levin reported as Mike Levin, accompanied by a French Jewish photographer, Eric Schwab.

47. Levin, *War Story*, pp. 143–54.

48. Miskimon, 'Liberating the Camps'.

49. Winebrenner, *Bootprints*, p. 223.

50. *Atrocities and Other Conditions in Concentration Camps in Germany*, 79th Congress, 1st Session, Senate Document No. 47 (Washington DC, 1945), p. 1.

51. Gilbert, *Road to Victory*, p. 1306; Hart-Davis, *King's Counsellor*, p. 317. Their report is Command No. 6626, *Buchenwald Camp: The Report of a Parliamentary Delegation*.

52. Gilbert, *Road to Victory*, p. 1307.

53. Joseph Pulitzer, 'A Report to the American People' (*St Louis Post-Dispatch*, 1945), p. 94.

54. Hartman, *Tank Driver*, pp. 97–8.

55. Ibid., p. 98.

56. Winebrenner, *Bootprints*, p. 244.

57. Ben C. Ferencz and Ken Keyes Jr, *PlanetHood: The Key to Your Survival and Prosperity* (Vision Books, 1988). I am deeply indebted to Ben Ferencz's many inspiring works on contemporary security, international law and morality, including *Less Than Slaves: Jewish Forced Labor and the Quest for Compensation* (Indiana University Press, 2002).

58. John Colby, *War From the Ground Up: The 90th Division in WWII* (Nortex Press, Texas, 1991), pp. 463–4.

59. The former III Corps commander relieved by Hodges on 17 March. Millikin took over from Major General John B. Wogan, who was wounded on 17 April.

60. Hartman, *Tank Driver*, pp. 100–3.

61. Ibid., p. 103.

62. Cindy Goodman, Frank Murphy and Dave Kanzler, 'The Liberation of Moosburg', *Splasher 6 – Newsletter of the 100th Bomb Group (Heavy) Foundation*, Vol. 33/2, Summer 2002.

63. Willetts had been awarded a DSO in 1942 and was station commander at RAF Oakington when captured on a mission over Berlin on 24 August 1943; Goode was commanding the 175th Infantry Regiment (29th Division) when made a POW at Carentan on 13 June 1944.

64. Manuel Eser, 'World War II: Liberation of Moosburg Plunges City into Chaos and Violence' (1 May 2020, Merkur.de).

65. Flynn's experiences in the Battle of the Bulge were followed in Peter Caddick-Adams, *Snow & Steel*. See Alice M. Flynn, *Unforgettable: The Biography of Capt. Thomas J. Flynn* (Sky Blue Publishing, 2011).

66. Jim Lankford, 'The 14th Armored Division and the Liberation of Stalag VII-A', Army Historical Foundation.

67. Goodman, Murphy and Kanzler, 'The Liberation of Moosburg'. Old Glory was the prized possession of First Lieutenant Martin Allain, a 23-year-old bomber pilot who had sewn it between two German blankets for concealment. It was he who shimmied up the German flagpole, removed the swastika and replaced it with his flag.

68. Goodman, Murphy and Kanzler, 'The Liberation of Moosburg'.

14: First and Ninth Armies: From the Ruhr to the Elbe

1. John P. Irwin, *Another River, Another Town: A Teenage Tank Gunner Comes of Age in Combat, 1945* (Random House, 2002), Kindle locstat. 590.

2. Andrea Jacobs, 'Who was Maurice Rose?', *Intermountain Jewish News* (Colorado), 21 February 2013.

3. Daniel P. Bolger, *The Panzer Killers* (Caliber Random House, 2021), pp. 267–71.

4. General Rose's helmet was given to his family in Denver, Colorado, and subsequently donated to the Rose Memorial Hospital there, before being made over to the Patton Museum at Fort Knox.

5. I interviewed a former member of Schwere Panzer-Abteilung 507 on this subject in 2000, on condition of anonymity. After the war, he asserted, once it was known their column had killed Rose, the surviving panzermen discussed this at length among themselves. The tank commander who had fired the fatal shots survived the war and felt huge remorse. Even at the time he knew he had panicked and over-reacted. The rest of the Abteilung agreed to keep his identity a secret and thus it has remained.

6. Irwin, *Another River, Another Town*, locstat 712.

7. Mark Mazower, *Hitler's Empire: How the Nazis Ruled Europe* (Penguin, 2008), Chapter 10.

8. James Robert Parish, *It's Good to Be the King: The Seriously Funny Life of Mel Brooks* (Wiley, 2007); https://www.usace.army.mil/About/History/Historical-Vignettes/Sports-Entertainment/109-Mel-Brooks/

9. Greenwood, *Normandy to Victory*, p. 368.

10. The barracks was named after the German World War One fighter ace, Oswald Boelcke, and used for Mittelbau-Dora's sick and dying from early January 1945.

11. Courtesy of https://www.tracesofevil.com/Nordhausen

12. Hans Massaquoi, interview with Studs Terkel, *The Good War: An Oral History of World War Two* (Pantheon, 1984), p. 501.

13. Used as a tactical missile (their original role was envisaged as a less-accurate area weapon), V-2s were eventually aimed at targets on German soil, including the Ludendorff Bridge, Remagen, on 17 March 1945. The final V-2s aimed at Britain fell on Kynaston Road, Orpington in Kent, ten days later.

14. Courtesy of Geoff Walden, *The Third Reich in Ruins*, at http://www.thirdreichruins.com/mittelwerk.htm

15. David Malachowsky interview courtesy of Eliach and Gurewitsch, *The Liberators*, pp. 11–14.

16. Levinson, *Gated Grief*, p. 25.

17. Letter dated 3 April 1945 from 'Deep in Germany', ibid., pp. 247–8.

18. Jim Garamone, 'Remembering the Holocaust', American Forces Press Service, 26 April 2000.

19. Lou 'Louch' Baczewski interview courtesy of Steve Ossad, 'The Liberation of Nordhausen Concentration Camp', *Warfare History Network*, 31 December 2019.

20. Nico Wingert, 'How Laura Bush's Father Fought in Germany', *Stern*, 9 May 2008.

21. Al Newman, 'Nordhausen: A Hell Factory Worked by the Living Dead', *Newsweek*, 23 April 1945, p. 51.

22. 'I Was There: Moving Testimony of Providence College's Fr. Edward P. Doyle', *The Cowl*, 6 February 1997.

23. Ilan Ben Zion, 'When my Great-uncle Liberated a Nazi Concentration Camp', *Times of Israel*, 30 May 2016.

24. He is discussed at length in Robert Forczyk, *Walther Model* (Osprey/Bloomsbury, 2013).

25. Rob Citino, *Death in the West: The Battle of the Ruhr Pocket* (National World War II Museum, New Orleans), 16 April 2020.

26. Trial Papers of Judge H. C. Anderson, *Military Tribunal III in Nuremberg, August 1947– July 1948* (Jean and Alexander Heard Libraries, Nashville, TN).

27. Andrew Williams, *D-Day To Berlin* (Hodder, 2004), p. 314.

28. Ralf Blank, 'Die Nacht vom 16. auf den 17. Mai 1943 – Operation Züchtigung: Die Zerstörung der Möhne-Talsperre', *Landschaftsverband Westfalen-Lippe* (May 2006).

29. Rüdiger Hachtmann, 'Fordism and Unfree Labour: Aspects of the Work Deployment of Concentration Camp Prisoners in German Industry between 1941 and 1944', *International Review of Social History*, Vol. 55/3, December 2010, pp. 485–513.

30. See http://www.monoculartimes.co.uk/city-tours/research-dortmund/1945.shtml

31. In the lottery of post-war justice, Florian was detained, charged with the execution of the *Aktion Rheinland* plotters, fined and sentenced to six years' detention. He remained a convinced Nazi to the end and died in his bed in 1975.

32. Williams, *D-Day To Berlin*, p. 316.

33. Ibid., p. 317.

34. Pogue, *The Supreme Command*, p. 440.

35. Conversation with Brigadier General (retired) Hans-Georg Model (1927–2016), Bad Neuenahr, December 2000.

36. Citino, *Death in the West*.

37. Prefer, *The Conquering Ninth*, p. 273.

38. Robert Browning, *The Pied Piper of Hamelin* (1842), lines 3 and 4.

39. Levinson, *Gated Grief*, p. 170.

40. Ibid.

41. Ernst Jünger, *A German Officer in Occupied Paris: The War Journals, 1941–1945* (Columbia University Press, 2019), p. 404.

42. Kenneth Ayers interview, 12 October 2008, courtesy of Michael Hirsh, Concentration Camp Liberators Oral History Program, University of South Florida, Tampa Library, Ref C65-00006.

43. Headquarters 30th Division, 105th Medical Battalion, *Medical Detachment Diary & Log* (NARA).

44. Wayne Robinson, *Move Out, Verify: The Combat Story of the 743rd Tank Battalion* (Germany, no publisher, 1945), pp. 162–3.

45. Headquarters 743rd Tank Battalion, *After Action Report, April 1945* (NARA).

46. Klaus Neumann, *Shifting Memories: The Nazi Past in the New Germany* (University of Michigan Press, 2000), pp. 20–5; Richard Overy, *War and Economy in the Third Reich* (Oxford University Press, 1995), pp. 98–114 .

47. Allen H. Mick, *With the 102nd Infantry Division Through Germany* (Battery Press, 1982), p. 171; see also Staff Group B: Majors Trinidad, Buffington, Correa, Flora, Gustafson, Justice, Lovelady, Luckenbill, Morelock, Pingley, Ruth, Shelaren, Tetarenko and Williams, *The Last Pursuit: The 2nd Armored Division's Exploitation from the Rhine to the Elbe, 24 March–14 April 1945* (Combat Studies Institute CSI Battlebook 21-B, US Army Command & General Staff College, Fort Leavenworth, Kansas, 1984).

48. Levin, *War Story*, pp. 98, 212–13.

49. *17th Armored Engineer Battalion Unit History, July 1940–May 1945* (Office of History, US Army Corps of Engineers, Alexandria, Virginia).

50. 'Surgeon is Cited for Heroism', *Cincinnati Enquirer* (Hamilton, Ohio), 28 September 1945, and obituary, 4 August 1953.

51. Greenwood, *Normandy to Victory*, p. 271.

52. Colonel Edwin 'Buckshot' Crabill, *The Ragtag Circus from Omaha beach to the Elbe* (Vantage, 1969), p. 86.

53. Cornelius Ryan, *The Last Battle* (Simon & Schuster, 1966), pp. 331–2.

54. Helmut Menzel, 'The End of the War in Magdeburg in 1945', *Sachsen-Anhalt Journal*, Vol. 2/2020.

55. Headquarters 30th Division, *Capture of Magdeburg, After Action Report* (April 1945, NARA).

56. For an account of Major Werner Pluskat (1912–2002) on D-Day, see Caddick-Adams, *Sand and Steel: A New History of D-Day* (Hutchinson, 2019), pp. 633–4.

57. Holbrook Bradley, *War Correspondent From D-Day to the Elbe* (iUniverse, 2007), p. 157.

58. Prefer, *The Conquering Ninth*, p. 312.

59. Joseph C. Harsch, 'Why Eisenhower Halted at the Elbe', *Christian Science Monitor*, 10 April 1995.

15: April: Northern Flank

1. Deployed to wherever necessary, including with US forces, it was the three regiments of 31st Armoured Brigade that were equipped with Crocodile flame-throwing tanks: 1st Fife and Forfar Yeomanry; 141st Regiment Royal Armoured Corps (The Buffs, Royal East Kent Regiment) and 7th Royal Tank Regiment.

2. Headquarters 7th Canadian Infantry Brigade, *War Diary, March 1945* (Canadian National Archives).

3. Camp Erika was named for the surrounding heather, *Erica* being the shrub's Latin name.

4. Headquarters 1st Black Watch of Canada, *War Diary, April 1945* (Canadian National Archives).

5. Headquarters 8th Canadian Reconnaissance Regiment, *War Diary, April 1945* (Canadian National Archives), p. 5. My thanks to Joël Stoppels for interpreting the SAS role for me.

6. Reference courtesy of Joël Stoppels.

7. Headquarters 8th Canadian Infantry Brigade, *War Diary, Lessons Learned, March 1945* (Canadian National Archives).

8. Frank P. Holm, *A Backward Glance: The Personal Story of an Infantry Signaller with the Calgary Highlanders in World War II* (self-published, 1989).

9. Interview with Andreas Herdina (son), February 2021.

10. The Dutch Jews died in Auschwitz, Sobibor, Mauthausen, Bergen-Belsen and Theresienstadt between July 1942 and September 1944.

11. Kingsley Brown, *Semper Paratus: History of the Royal Hamilton Light Infantry* (RHLI Historical Association, 1977), pp. 332–3. However, Major Doering of 'D' Company also reported: 'These Jewish women had apparently been starved in more ways than one, and 'D' Coy personnel were heavily taxed in quenching their thirst, the results of five years of isolation. The 'D' Coy boys do not like the prospects of leaving the place.' The good major found 'some difficulty' in rounding up his men, a challenge only completed at 0300hrs. Headquarters Royal Hamilton Light Infantry, *War Diary, April 1945* (Canadian National Archives), pp. 16–17 and Mark Zuehlke, *On To Victory: The Canadian Liberation of the Netherlands* (Douglas & McIntyre, 2010), p. 251.

12. Brigadier W. Murphy's Canadian 1st Armoured Brigade comprised the 11th, 12th and 14th Armoured Regiments (Ontario, Three Rivers and Calgary Regiments); Kenneth J. West, *An' It's Called A Tam-o'-Shanter* (privately printed, 1985), p. 219.

13. Brigadier Erroll Prior Palmer's 8th Armoured Brigade comprised the 4th/7th Royal Dragoon Guards, 13th/18th Hussars, Sherwood Rangers Yeomanry, 12th Battalion (King's Royal Rifle Corps, mobile infantry battalion) and Essex Yeomanry (Royal Artillery, with Sexton self-propelled guns).

14. Delaforce, *Monty's Ironsides*, p. 185.

15. Greenwood, *D-Day to Victory*, p. 360.

16. White, *With the Jocks*, p. 267.

17. Noel Bell, *From the Beaches to the Baltic: The Story of 'G' Company, 8th Battalion, the Rifle Brigade, during the Campaign in North-West Europe* (Gale & Polden, 1947).

18. Headquarters 11th Armoured Division, *War Diary, March 1945* (UK National Archives).

19. Moorehead, *Eclipse*, p. 212.

20. Ibid., p. 213.

21. J. Glenn Gray, *The Warriors: Reflections on Men in Battle* (University of Nebraska Press, 1959), p. 203.

22. One of the SAS originals from 1941, Reg Seekings (1929–99) was awarded a DCM and MM during the war; Ben Macintyre, *SAS: Rogue Heroes: The Authorized Wartime History* (Viking, 2016), p. 303.

23. Warren Manger, 'I Found SAS Hero Who Saved Me in Belsen and Now We'll be Friends for Life', *Daily Mirror*, 10 April 2015; Alexander van Straubenzee, 'The Gate of Hell', *Daily Telegraph*, 10 April 2005.

24. Jack Bailey interview courtesy of *WW2 The People's War*, BBC, 2004.

25. Leslie Hardman, *The Survivors: The Story of the Belsen Remnant* (Vallentine, Mitchell, 1958); Isaac Levy, *Witness to Evil: Bergen-Belsen 1945* (Halban, 1995); David Cesarani, Tony Kushner, Jo Reilly amd Colin Richmond (eds), *Belsen in History and Memory* (Frank Cass, 1997).

26. Hardman, *The Survivors*; obituary, *Guardian*, 13 October 2008; 'Leslie Hardman was one of the first to enter Belsen concentration camp', obituary, Wales Online, 22 October 2008.

27. Doon Campbell, *Magic Mistress: A 30-Year Affair With Reuters* (Tagman Press, 2000), p. 100.

28. British Movietone, two reels with sound in AP Archives (30 April 1945); see also Rev. T.J. Stretch Papers, army chaplain with 10th Garrison Detachment (Mil. Govt), Imperial War Museum, Documents, 11561.

29. 'Irish priest remembers role in Bergen-Belsen concentration camp liberation: Fr Michael Morrison was with the British and Canadian troops who entered the camp on 15 April 1945', IrishCentral, 15 April 2017.

30. *Epsom College OE Magazine* (2007), pp. 32–4; interview courtesy of Wellcome Library, ref. RAMC 1218.

31. Joy Trindles (née Taverner) interview courtesy of *WW2 The People's War*, BBC, 2003.

32. Boscawen, *Armoured Guardsmen*, pp. 200–5.

33. *The War Diary of Julius Neave, A Personal Chronicle, Winter 1942–3 to May 1945* (privately printed by the regiment), p. 322, courtesy of the Regimental Museum of the Light Dragoons.

34. Stephen Robinson, *The Remarkable Lives of Bill Deedes* (Little, Brown, 2008), Kindle loc. 2216.

35. Ibid., locstats. 2118–2190.

36. Captain J.A. Brymer, *History of the 33rd Field Regiment, Royal Artillery* (privately printed, 1945).

37. Sydney Jary, *Eighteen Platoon* (self-published, 1994), p. 116.

38. Bell, *From the Beaches to the Baltic.*

39. Courtesy Sally B. McGlone.

40. Ian Hammerton interview, 2000.

41. Hammerton, *Achtung! Minen!*, pp. 144–6.

42. David H. Lippman, *Crossing the Rhine: How the Western Allies Crushed the Nazi Regime Once and For All* (courtesy, Warfare History Network, 21 December 2018).

43. Readers may be interested to meet King and his battalion in Caddick-Adams, *Sand & Steel*, pp. 811–12.

44. Norman Scarfe, *Assault Division: A History of the 3rd Division from the Invasion of Normandy to the Surrender of Germany* (Collins, 1947).

45. Part of Oberst Wolfgang Maucke's veteran 15th PanzerGrenadier Division.

46. Bill Ashley interview 4 July 2005, courtesy of *The People's War* (BBC).

47. 'Edward Charlton VC', *After the Battle* magazine, No.49 (1985); Lord Ashcroft, 'The Last Victoria Cross Hero Before VE Day Who Was So Brave Even the Enemy Marvelled' (*Daily Mail*, 2 May 2020). Von Bülow (1911–72), a pre-war lawyer, was a member of the Mecklenburg noble family.

48. Robin McNish and Charles Messenger, *Iron Division: History of 3rd Division 1809– 1989* (3rd Armoured Division, 1990), p. 132.

49. Whiting, *Bloody Bremen*, p. 195.

50. Gordon Blake, *Mountain and Flood: History of the 52nd Lowland Division* (Jackson, 1950), pp. 168, 203–5.

51. Letter of 4 May 1945, from P.B. Reynier, MC, courtesy of his son, Mark. See htttp:// ww2today.com/25-april-1945-the-royal-scots-fusiliers-enter-bremen, accessed 20 August 2020.

52. *War Diary of Julius Neave*, pp. 339–40, & 348.

53. Report by Dr H.O. Engel, 'Organisation for the Relief of Concentration Camps', *Journal of the Royal Army Medical Corps*, 2003/No. 149, pp. 340–3.

54. Bohdan Dembiński obituary, *Jeziorski* (newspaper),1 November 2019, courtesy of his son, Michael Dembiński.

55. What sets Sandbostel apart from nearly every other site is the preservation of 25 out of the original 150 camp barrack blocks. Elsewhere (Bergen-Belsen, for example), they were destroyed in 1945 and what you see are reconstructions, not originals.

56. Patrick Delaforce, *Churchill's Desert Rats: From Normandy to Berlin with 7th Armoured Division* (Alan Sutton, 1994), p. 161.

57. Richard Brett-Smith, *The 11th Hussars (Prince Albert's Own)* (Leo Cooper, 1969).

58. Delaforce, *Churchill's Desert Rats*, p. 161.

59. Lindsay, *So Few Got Through*, p. 264.

60. Mathilde Wolf-Mönckeberg, *On the Other Side: To My Children From Germany 1940–45* (Peter Owen, 1979), p. 128.

61. Anke Settekorn, 'April 1945: Young Soldiers Die in Vahrendorf in a Senseless Attack on the British Army', *Kreiszeitung-Wochenblatt*, 1 May 2020, courtesy of anke.settekorn@kreiszeitung.net; see also Wolfgang Buchwald, *Endkampf* (Buchwald, 1990), and Ulrich Saft, *The Fight for Northern Germany: The Bitter End between Weser and Elbe in 1945* (Beltheim-Schnellbach, 2011).

62. Noble Frankland and Charles Webster, *The Strategic Air Offensive Against Germany, 1939–1945, Volume II: Endeavour, Part 4* (HMSO, 1961), pp. 260–1.

63. Martin Middlebrook, *The Battle of Hamburg* (Allen Lane, 1980), p. 333.

64. Simon Gaskell, 'Berlin Burning Seen From 19,000 Feet was the Most Beautifully Horrible Sight I Have Ever Seen' (*Wales Online*, 14 September 2013).

65. Conversations with Frederick Taylor; see his *Dresden: Tuesday 13 February 1945* (Bloomsbury, 2005), p. 434.

66. Wolf-Mönckeberg, *On the Other Side*, p. 124.

67. Harry Leslie Smith, *Love Among the Ruins: A Memoir of Life and Love in Hamburg, 1945* (Icon Books, 2015).

68. Brigadier D. Mills-Roberts' 1st Commando Brigade comprised: No. 3 Commando, No. 4 Commando, No. 6 Commando, No. 45 (RM) Commando, and No. 10 (Inter-Allied) Commando. Brigadier W.D.C. Greenacre's 6th Guards Tank Brigade included: 4th Coldstream Guards, 4th Grenadier Guards, and 3rd Scots Guards.

69. Ray Griffiths, 'The Teutoburger Wald Story 9AD and 1945 Part 2', courtesy *WW2 The People's War*, BBC, interview, February 2002.

70. Delaforce, *The Black Bull*, pp. 214–15.

71. Ibid., p. 215.

72. Bill Close, *A View from the Turret: A History of the 3rd Royal Tank Regiment in the Second World War* (Dell & Bredon, 2002).

73. Delaforce, *The Black Bull*, p. 217.

74. Horne and Montgomery, *The Lonely Leader*, p. 330.

75. Patrick Forbes, *6th Guards Tank Brigade: The Story of Guardsmen in Churchill Tanks* (Sampson, Low & Marston, 1949); see also 'Night Fighting: Stadensen, April 1945', *Weapons & Warfare*, 16 December 2019.

76. Headquarters 4th Grenadier Guards, *War Diary, April 1945* (WO 171/5146, UK National Archives).

77. Edward Ardizzone, *Diary of a War Artist* (The Bodley Head, 1974), p. 197.

78. When captured, prisoners passed through a *Dulag* (*Durchgangslager*, transit camp) where they were interrogated and registered as a *Kriegsgefangener* (POW). Following this, they were sent to a *Stalag* (*Stammlager*, army POW camp), *Stalag Luft* (camp for air force personnel), *Marlag* (*Marinelager*, for naval servicemen) or *Oflag* (*Offizierslager*, camp for officers).

79. Courtesy of The Army Leader website, https://thearmyleader.co.uk/rsm-lord/, accessed 20 April 2019.

80. Richard Alford, *To Revel in God's Sunshine: The Story of RSM J.C. Lord* (self-published, 1981/2013).

81. Ardizzone, *Diary of a War Artist*.

82. Campbell, *Magic Mistress*, p. 99.

83. Eric Stephenson, 'Experiences of a Prisoner of a War: World War 2 in Germany', *Journal of Military and Veterans' Health*, Vol. 18/2.

84. John Nichol and Tony Rennell, *The Last Escape: The Untold Story of Allied Prisoners of War in Germany 1944–45* (Viking, 2002), pp. 268–76.

85. John L. Frisbee, 'Valor: Lest We Forget', [US] *Air Force Magazine* (September 1997), p. 130.

86. Yarosh interview; see also his *World War II Is Not Over*.

87. Courtesy of Kevin Greenhalgh, Fallingbostel Military Museum.

88. Kirby, *1100 Miles With Monty*, p. 112.

89. Horne and Montgomery, *The Lonely Leader*, p. 335.

16: First Army: To Leipzig and the Elbe

1. Michael N. Ingrisano Jr, *Valor Without Arms: A History of the 316th Troop Carrier Group 1942–1945* (Merriam Press, 2001), pp. 283–5.

2. Greenwood, *Normandy to Victory*, p. 370.

3. Ibid., p. 374.

4. Martin Wolfe, *Green Light! A Troop Carrier Squadron's War From Normandy to the Rhine* (Center for Air Force History, 1993), pp. 417–21; Hogan, *A Command Post*, pp. 262–4.

5. Greenwood, *Normandy to Victory*, p. 382.

6. Captain Felder L. Fair, *The Operations of Company 'B', 26th Infantry Regiment, in the Reduction of Enemy Positions in the Harz Mountains, 17–18 April 1945* (Personal Experience of a Company Commander, Advanced Infantry Officers Course, Fort Benning, Georgia, 1947–8), p. 8.

7. Headquarters 16th Infantry Regiment, *After Action Report, April 1945* (NARA).

8. Ibid., pp. 22–3.

9. Ibid., p. 26.

10. Ibid.

11. Headquarters 4th Mechanized Cavalry Group, G-3, *After Action Report* (April 1945, NARA).

12. Blum interview courtesy of *Unspoken, Now Told* (Soldier Stories, 4250 Veterans Memorial Hwy, Suite 420E, Holbrook, NY).

13. Interview with Walter Morison, DFC, April 1995; he was shot down flying with No. 103 Squadron on 6 June 1942; later the author of *Flak and Ferrets: One Way to Colditz* (Sentinel, 1995), Morison died in 2009.

14. As well as Shaughnessy's CCR, the 3rd Battalion/273rd Infantry Regiment (US 69th Infantry Division) also converged on Colditz, whose PFC Alan Murphey accepted the surrender of Hauptmann Eggers in the courtyard. The castle's keys were swiftly souvenired by Lieutenant Richard Morgan (Royal Ulster Rifles and No.

2 Commando), who later donated them to the Imperial War Museum in London; see Eric Narveson, 'Ordeal of Liberation at Colditz', *Fighting 69th Infantry Division Bulletin*, No.46/3, May–August 1993, pp. 30–6.

15. P.R. Reid, *The Latter Days at Colditz* (Hodder & Stoughton, 1952), pp. 226–7.

16. Nance, *Forgotten Glory*, p. 268.

17. Colonel Walter D. Buie, *History of the 272nd Infantry, The Battleaxe Regiment* (privately printed, June 1945).

18. Ibid.

19. Headquarters 272nd Infantry Regiment, *After Action Report, April 1945* (NARA).

20. Ibid.

21. Ibid.

22. A selection of Capa's images from Leipzig appeared in the Victory edition of *Life* magazine, 14 May 1945.

23. Charles B. MacDonald, *Company Commander* (Infantry Journal Press, 1947), pp. 348–57. Recipient of a Silver Star for his leadership in the Bulge, MacDonald (1922–90) was also the author of *US Army in World War II: The Last Offensive*, the official US Army account of this campaign, in which he downplayed his activities in Leipzig.

24. Headquarters 69th Division, G-3, *After Action Report, 30 April 1945* (NARA).

25. *War Report: A Record of Dispatches Broadcast by BBC War Correspondents 6 June 1944–5 May 1945* (Oxford University Press, 1946), pp. 381–2.

26. 69th Division, G-3, *After Action Report*.

27. https://www.frankfallaarchive.org/prisons/zoschen-forced-labour-camp/, accessed 6 August 2019.

28. W.F. Craven and J.L. Cate, *The Army Air Forces in World War II: Vol. III: Argument to VE-Day* (University of Chicago Press, 1951), Chapter 2, 'Big Week', pp. 30–40.

29. https://www.zwangsarbeit-in-leipzig.de/en/nazi-forced-labour-in-leipzig/abtnaundorf-memorial/long-text/, accessed 20 July 2019.

30. Margaret Bourke-White, *Dear Fatherland, Rest Quietly: A Report on the Collapse of Hitler's Thousand Years* (Simon & Schuster, 1946), p. 49.

31. https://legionmagazine.com/en/2020/03/the-evolution-of-war-photography/, accessed 10 March 2019.

32. Antony Penrose and Edward Scherman (eds), *Lee Miller's War: Photographer and Correspondent with the Allies in Europe 1944–45* (Bullfinch Press, 1992), pp. 161, 176.

33. Christian Goeschel, *Suicide in Nazi Germany* (Oxford University Press, 2009), p. 153.

34. Abzug, *Inside the Vicious Heart*, pp. 74–80.

35. Headquarters VII Corps, G-3, *War Diary, April 1945* (NARA).

36. Forrest Pogue, *Pogue's War*, pp. 371–3.

37. Greenwood, *Normandy to Victory*, p. 387.

38. I am grateful to the National World War II Museum of New Orleans, with whom I have travelled to Berlin, Dresden, Torgau and Berchtesgaden, for providing me

with many valuable insights contained in this and other chapters. Also relevant have been edition nos 16, 88 and 130 of *After the Battle* magazine, edited by Winston G. Ramsay. I owe him a huge debt of gratitude for helping me since 1975, when we first met, to study numerous World War Two campaigns.

17: Southern Flank: Nuremberg and Augsburg

1. Lynch, *A Letter Marked Free*, p. 161.
2. Courtesy of the US Army, I last enjoyed a visit to Bamberg (now a UNESCO World Heritage Site) in 1999.
3. Various articles in *Fürther Heimatblätter*: Gottlieb Wunschel, 'The Surrender of Fürth on 19 April 1945' (1965/1), pp. 7–16; Manfred Mümmler, '19 April 1945: The End of the Second World War in Fürth' (1985/1), pp. 1–12; Helmut Mahr, 'A Regime is Dissolving, or Whatever You Can do with People' (1985/1), pp. 13–34; Barbara Ohm, 'Fürth in 1945' (1995/2), pp. 29–63; Helmut Mahr, 'The Occupation of the District and City of Fürth by the US Army in April 1945' (1998/1), pp. 1–70.
4. Ethan Fowler, 'WWII Veteran Recalls Rough Memories', *Powder Springs (Cobb County, Georgia) Patch* (29 March 2011).
5. Master Sergeant Charles Senteney, *From Utah Beach to Salzburg, Austria: The ETO with HQ Battery, 144th Field Artillery Group* (typewritten memoir, California State Archives), p. 166.
6. *Seventh Army, Report of Operations*, p. 1076.
7. William Shirer, *Berlin Diary: The Journal of a Foreign Correspondent 1934–1941* (Alfred A. Knopf, 1941), entry for 4 September 1934.
8. See Martin Middlebrook, *The Nuremberg Raid* (Allen Lane, 1973).
9. Headquarters 45th Infantry Division, *After Action Report, April 1945* (RG-407, NARA).
10. Glenn L. Kappelman, *Through My Sights: A Gunner's View of WWII* (Sunflower Publishing, 2003).
11. Ochs, *Cause Greater Than Self*, p. 160.
12. Captain Paul L. Peterson, *Operations of Company 'E', 180th Infantry Regiment (45th Division) in the battle of Nuremberg, Germany, 17–20 April 1945* (Advanced Infantry Officers Course, Infantry School, Fort Benning, Georgia, 1948–9), pp. 7–9.
13. Ibid., pp. 14–18, 38–9.
14. Headquarters 645th Tank Destroyer Battalion, *After Action Report, April 1945* (NARA).
15. George Wilson, *If You Survive* (Presidio, 1987), p. 258.
16. Peterson, *Operations of Company 'E', 180th Infantry*, p. 25.
17. Ibid., pp. 162–4. It took Daly (1924–2007) a full year to recover, and he received his Medal of Honor personally from President Harry S. Truman in the East Room of the White House on 23 August 1946.

18. *Blue and White Devils: History of the 3rd Infantry Division* (Stars and Stripes, Paris, 1945).

19. The exchange is oft-quoted, but the decoration is never explained. It was the Deutsche Orden, the highest award of the party, bestowed only ten times, and worn on the left breast. Telegrams cited in *Seventh Army, Report of Operations*, p. 1081.

20. Peterson, *Operations of Company 'E', 180th Infantry*, p. 36.

21. See Sidney Kirkpatrick, *Hitler's Holy Relics: A True Story of Nazi Plunder and the Race to Recover the Crown Jewels of the Holy Roman Empire* (Simon & Schuster, 2010); after an extensive hunt and the interrogation of numerous SS and civic officials, the imperial treasures were found by the US Army in August 1945 and eventually returned to Vienna where they currently reside.

22. Headquarters 7th Infantry Regiment, *Narrative Account of Operations for Period 15 Mar 45 to 10 May 45* (27 May 1945, RG-735017, NARA), p. 15.

23. *Seventh Army, Report of Operations*, p. 1082.

24. So named because Count von Zeppelin demonstrated his first airship there in 1907.

25. *Narrative Account of 7th Infantry Operations*, p. 15.

26. Failmezger, *American Knights*, pp. 281–2.

27. Adams, *General Jacob Devers*, p. 412.

28. Readers can discover more about this campaign in Caddick-Adams, *Snow & Steel*.

29. Harold Nicolson, (ed. Nigel Nicolson), *Diaries & Letters 1939–45* (Collins, 1967), p. 445.

30. This was General Wenck's Twelfth Army, who never had a hope of forcing open a relief corridor. To my mind Hitler's fury is captured well by the famous scene in *Der Untergang/Downfall* (2004).

31. Seventh Army G-2 History for April–May 1945, cited in *Seventh Army, Report on Operations*, pp. 1102–3. There is extensive literature on Hitler's last days in Berlin. Easily the most scholarly (and recent) is Luke Daly-Groves' *Hitler's Death: The Case Against Conspiracy* (Osprey, 2019); see also his 'Seventy-four years on, Hitler's suicide is still shrouded in politics and propaganda', *New Statesman*, 30 April 2019; and 'The FBI, Hitler's Death and Rumours of Escape to Argentina', *The American*, 16 April 2019.

32. SHAEF G-2, *Weekly Intelligence Summary, 15 April 1945* (RG-332, NARA).

33. Captain R.S. Maddock interview, June 1994.

34. Headquarters 103rd Infantry Division, G-3, *Journal, 26 April 1945* (NARA).

35. Frank J. Waldeck, Company 'C', 411st Infantry, interview, Mississippi Oral History Program, World War II Veterans/National WWII Museum (University of Southern Mississippi, 2015), p. 6.

36. Author's interview with Richard H. McCullough (1918–2003), 1984.

37. Wendell H. Hall, *Reminiscences of World War II* (self-published, 2003), p. 20.

38. *Joint Intelligence Objectives Agency, German Underground Installations, Vol. 1, Unique Design & Construction Methods* (HMSO, 1945); E. Raim, *Die Dachauer KZ-Außenkomandos Kaufering & Mühldorf. Rüstungsbauten und Zwangsarbeit im letzten Kriegsjahr* (Neumeyer, 1992).

39. The three incomplete hangars were vast, code-named Weingut II, Diana II and Walnuss II, and planned to be 400 metres (1,300 feet) long, 28.4 metres (93 feet) high (more than 5 storeys), with a concrete roof 3 metres (9.8 feet) thick.

40. Levinson, *Gated Grief*, pp. 177–8; Bland died in 2018 but left numerous interviews of his wartime career, including one with the Library of Congress (American Folklore Center) Veterans' History Project.

41. Stephen E. Ambrose, *Band of Brothers* (Simon & Schuster, 1992), pp. 262–3. Although this was heralded as the best episode of the series, Ambrose devoted less than a page to the liberation of Kaufering IV. Of the 11 sites only Kaufering VII remains today, which I visited in 2019.

42. Charles Larson interview, Alex McRae and Megan Almon, *Benicia Times-Herald*, 2007.

43. Louis Vecchi interview, Rachel Raskin-Zrihen, *Benicia Times-Herald*, 25 September 2007.

44. Eugene Cook interview, Alex McRae and Megan Almon, *Benicia Times-Herald*, 24 December 2007.

45. Readers may have already met J. D. Salinger on 6 June 1944 at Utah beach in Caddick-Adams, *Sand & Steel*, pp. 541–2. Margaret A. Salinger, *Dream Catcher: A Memoir* (Washington Square Press, 2000), pp. 53–54; Eberhard Alsen, 'How Salinger's Nervous Breakdown Twisted His View of Nazis', *Daily Beast* (28 April 2018); Jonah Cohen, 'J.D. Salinger and the Nazis', *Times of Israel* (16 March 2020); Sarah Churchwell, 'Even in Death, the Writer's Battle with his Biographers Continues to Rage. But Revelations about the Man are No Substitute for an Understanding of his Work', review of *Salinger* by David Shields and Shane Salerno, *Financial Times*, 13 September 2013.

46. Rich Tenorio, 'These US soldiers liberated Dachau while their own families were locked up back home', *Times of Israel*, 29 May 2017.

47. Daniel Blatman, *The Death Marches: The Final Phase of Nazi Genocide* (Harvard University Press, 2013), p. 202; Norman Brody and John Malone interviews courtesy of the GIs Remember Project, NMAJMH.

48. Fritz, *Endkampf*, pp. 290–291.

49. *Beachhead News*, 22 April 1945.

50. Later a lieutenant colonel in Vietnam, Charles Ippolito (1920–2008) and William Riddell received Silver Stars for their actions at Dillingen; Hymel, *A Sergeant in the 12th*; *Hellcat News*, Vol. 3/2, 26 May 1945.

51. His vehicle was an M16 half-track armed with one 37mm cannon and twin 0.50-in machine-guns. Citation, US Seventh Army, General Order No.585/6 October 1945. A resident of Colorado County, Texas, the grave of Miculka (1916–45) resides in

Forest Park Cemetery, Houston. That Schoenke lies in the Lorraine American Cemetery, St Avold, France, and Miculka in Texas, reflects the wishes of their next of kin.

52. John Woodbridge and Maurice Possley, *Hitler in the Crosshairs: A GI's Story of Courage and Faith* (Zondervan, 2011), Chapter 11. See also Lieutenant Palm's *Operations of Company 'B', 179th Infantry Regiment (45th Division) in the Rhine River crossing north of Worms, Germany, 25–26 March 1945* (Advanced Infantry Officers Course No. 1, Infantry School, Fort Benning, Georgia, 1948–9).

53. British Army 15th Psyops Group presentation, Chicksands, 1998.

54. MacDonald, *US Army in World War II*, p. 436.

55. Melanie Förschner, *The US Garrison in Augsburg after the Second World War* (Gymnasium Königsbrunn Kollegstufenjahrgang, 2006).

56. Hermann Winter, *The War and Postwar Period in Augsburg 1939–45* (self-published, 2011), pp. 49–52.

18: 'The bloody dog is dead'

1. Lieutenant Hugh C. Daly, *42nd Rainbow Division Combat History of World War II* (Army & Navy Publishing, Baton Rouge, 1946), pp. 89–96.

2. Ibid. Dachau was still two days away, but the first, Ohrdruf, had been found on 4 April, and Buchenwald on the 11th.

3. 'Salute to Veterans: C Company at Dachau', *Daily Republic*, Solano County, California, 11 November 2017.

4. *Seventh Army, Report of Operations*, p. 1085.

5. *Narrative Account of 7th Infantry Operations*, p. 20.

6. Wheeled vehicles included 450 Jeeps, 460 2½-ton trucks and 54 M8 armoured cars.

7. Von Kardorff, *Diary*, pp. 189–90.

8. *Seventh Army, Report of Operations*, p. 1140.

9. Roland Eggleston, 'WWII: 60 Years After: Everyday Germans Recount Horrors of War's Last Days', Radio Free Europe/Radio Liberty, 10 May 2005.

10. Obersturmführer Josef Bachot, Unterscharführer Gaston Koeken and Unterscharführer Jean Moens were later tried in the 1960s for these murders.

11. Headquarters XV Corps, G-5, *Log, April 1945* (RG-4865, NARA).

12. These were at Erpting, Germering, Langerringen, Lauingen, Schrobenhausen, Schwabach, Schwabing and Türkheim.

13. Levinson, *Gated Grief*, pp. 87–8.

14. Ibid., p. 170; Barbara Helfgott Hyett, *In Evidence: Poems of the Liberation of Nazi Concentration Camps* (University of Pittsburgh Press, 1986).

15. The killing of the Dachau guard force has occupied many books and articles and was the subject of an investigation by the Seventh Army's assistant inspector general, Lieutenant Colonel Joseph Whitaker. His 120-page report of 8 June 1945 concluded that 'while there had probably been a violation of international law, in the

light of the conditions which greeted the eyes of the first combat troops, it is not believed that justice or equity demand that the difficult and perhaps impossible task of fixing individual responsibility now be undertaken'. See also Whitlock, *The Rock of Anzio*, Chapter 13.

16. Martha Gellhorn, 'Dachau', *Collier's Magazine*, 23 June 1945.
17. Rabbi Bohnen to his wife Eleanor, 1 May 1945, courtesy of GIs Remember Project, NMAJMH.
18. Eli Heimberg interview courtesy of GIs Remember Project, NMAJMH.
19. Morris Eisenstein interview courtesy of GIs Remember Project, NMAJMH.
20. Gellhorn, 'Dachau'.
21. *Narrative Account of 7th Infantry Operations*, p. 20.
22. *Seventh Army, Report of Operations*, p. 1141. After the war this became a DP camp for Ukrainians, then the US Army's Warner Barracks.
23. *Narrative Account of 7th Infantry Operations*, p. 21.
24. Fritz, *Endkampf*, p. 151. Chaplain Boice (1916–2003) was awarded a Silver Star and two Bronze Stars for his war service. He continued to serve as chaplain of the 22nd Infantry after the war, providing pastoral services and guidance to its veterans, their spouses and children of the regiment.
25. *Narrative Account of 7th Infantry Operations*, p. 21.
26. Fritz, *Endkampf*, p. 154.
27. The Volksbund Deutsche Kriegsgräberfürsorge (German War Graves Commission), founded in 1919; Jean-Loup Gassend, *Operation Dragoon: Autopsy of a Battle* (Schiffer, 2013), p. 307.
28. Robinow's citation for his Silver Star (dated 10 August 1945) is at https://valor.militarytimes.com/hero/115436
29. Charles Hawley, 'Remembering World War II: The US Soldier Who Liberated Munich Recalls Confronting the Nazi Enemy', *Der Spiegel*, 29 April 2005.
30. 'Salute to Veterans', *Daily Republic*.
31. 'Hitler's copy of *Mein Kampf* sells for $20,655', AFP newswire, 19 March 2016.
32. This is the apartment where Hitler's niece and probable mistress Geli Raubal (23) was found dead by gunshot wound on 19 September 1931. Murder or suicide was never ascertained. Ira Palm story: Woodbridge and Possley, *Hitler in the Crosshairs*, Chapter 15.
33. Ana Veciana Suarez, 'Jewish soldier's WWII letter, written on Adolf Hitler's stationery, sent to museum', *Sydney Morning Herald*, 22 January 2015.
34. Courtesy of https://www.leemiller.co.uk
35. BBC broadcast reported on page 3 of *New York Times*, 2 May 1945.

19: Eight Days of Agony and Ecstasy

1. 'Death of Hitler in the Berlin Chancellery', *Guardian*, 2 May 1945.
2. Requisition for Pacific Maps: Seventh Army G-3, *Journal, 29 April 1945* (NARA).

3. *Hellcat News*, Vol. 3/2, 26 May 1945.

4. David Kenyon Webster, quoted in Ambrose, *Band of Brothers*, p. 267.

5. Cited in John C. McManus, 'The Race to Seize Berchtesgaden', *World War II* magazine, May 2005; William Rosson (1918–2004) had won a DSC at Anzio, would later serve on Eisenhower's staff, and retired as a full general, commanding SOUTH-COM (1973–5). He had just taken a degree in International Relations at Oxford when I heard him lecture in Washington DC in 1984.

6. Ibid. Lieutenant General Heintges (1912–94) was born in Koblenz and emigrated to America in 1920, his infantry officer father having been killed at the front. He advised on the creation of the Bundeswehr, served in Korea and Vietnam, and became Deputy Commander-in-Chief United States Army Europe (USAREUR) in Heidelberg.

7. Lieutenant Colonel Sherman W. Pratt, *Autobahn to Berchtesgaden: A Combat Soldier's View of His Role in World War II as Seen from the Lower Ranks Looking Up* (Gateway Press, 1992).

8. Ibid.

9. Oscar White, *Conqueror's Road* (Cambridge University Press, 1996), pp. 61–2.

10. McManus, 'The Race to Seize Berchtesgaden'.

11. Author's visits to Lanson, 1975 and 1982, and Laurent-Perrier, 1975, 1980, 1986, 1990, 1997, 2010 and 2016; 'Champagne boss who blew open Hitler's cellar dies', Radio France International, 31 October 2010; Giles Fallowfield, 'Bernard de Nonancourt dies', *Decanter*, 2 November 2010; and see Don & Petie Kladstrup, *Wine & War: The French, the Nazis and France's Greatest Treasure* (Hodder & Stoughton, 2001), pp. 218–25.

12. I have to thank the National World War II Museum in New Orleans for the opportunity to guide one of their 'Easy Company: England to the Eagle's Nest Tours' in 2018, on which I have based my up-to-date observations of the area.

13. Interview with Mayer's son, Thomas Moulton, 23 April 2017.

14. Turner and Jackson, *Destination Berchtesgaden*, p. 186.

15. Filmed by Lieutenant Byars, Signal Corps.

16. Levin, *War Story*, p. 206. Levin later wrote a novel, *The Stronghold* (Simon & Schuster, 1956), on the drama. The full story is contained in Stephen Harding, *The Last Battle: When US and German Soldiers Joined Forces in the Waning Hours of World War II in Europe* (Da Capo Press, 2013).

17. Other prisoners included Austrians, Britons, Czechs, Danes, French, Germans, Greeks, Hungarians, Italians, Poles, Slovaks, Soviets, Yugoslavs and one each from Holland, Latvia, Norway and Sweden.

18. This drama is explained fully in Ian Sayer and Jeremy Dronfield, *Hitler's Last Plot: The 139 VIP hostages Selected for Death in the Final Days of World War II* (Da Capo Press, 2019).

19. Celia Sandys and Jonathan Littman, *We Shall Not Fail: The Inspiring Leadership of Winston Churchill* (Portfolio, 2003), p. 210.

20. Patton, *War as I Knew It,* p. 331. Ladislas Farago, *Patton: Ordeal and Triumph* (Arthur Barker, 1966), p. 528.

21. Charles R. Huebner, 'V Corps From Belgium to Czechoslovakia', *Army and Navy Journal,* No. 83, 4 December 1945.

22. Lieutenant Colonel Edgar Wilkerson et al., *V Corps Operations in the ETO 6 January 1942–9 May 1945* (668th Engineer Topographical Company, c.1946).

23. Farago, *Patton,* p. 528.

24. Ibid., p. 531.

25. Two books by Zdenek Roucka are most helpful on Third Army's liberation of Western Czechoslovakia: *Americans in West Bohemia 1945* (ZR and T, 2000) and *Plzen under the Swastika* (Bohemia Hobbies, 2001).

26. Holysov was administered by Flossenbürg. Recollections of Col. Antoni Skarbek (nom de guerre *Bohun*) to *The Jewish Voice* (New Jersey); and see Dr Marek Jan Chodakiewicz, *Narodowe Siły Zbrojne: "Ząb" przeciw dwu wrogom* (Fronda, 1999).

27. Raymond Gantter, *Roll Me Over: An Infantryman's World War II* (Presidio Press, 1997), pp. 360–368.

28. Ibid.

29. Ibid., p. 365.

30. Samuel Fuller appears in Caddick-Adams, *Sand & Steel*, pp. 350 and 646–7.

31. Marsha Orgeron, 'Liberating Images? Samuel Fuller's Film of Falkenau Concentration Camp', *Film Quarterly*, Vol. 60/2, pp. 38–47; Sam Fuller, *A Third Face: My Tale of Writing, Fighting, & Filmmaking* (Alfred A. Knopf, 2002), pp. 105, 114, 214, 217.

32. Schörner was arrested ten days later, charged with war crimes by the Soviets in 1952 and later by the West Germans. Released in 1960, he died in 1973.

33. 'Charles Havlat: The Last GI Killed in Action, a Czech-American, Died in Bohemia after the European Cease-fire', Radio Prague International, 9 May 2005; Kevin Knodell, 'PFC Charley Havlat: The Last American Combat Death of World War II', *Coffee or Die Magazine*, 8 May 2019.

34. *Brave Rifles: The 3rd Cavalry Reconnaissance Squadron (Mecz.) in World War II 9 August 1944 to 9 May 1945* (published in Germany 1945. Ref C 455, 877, courtesy of University of Michigan Library).

35. Abzug, *Inside the Vicious Heart*, p. 121.

36. 'Those who served: Veteran recalls World War II', *Oakland Press*, Michigan, 25 May 2009; Sam Klein died in Southfield, Michigan, in April 2020 as I was writing this chapter.

37. Kenneth Colvin interview courtesy of GIs Remember Project, NMAJMH; and see transcript of Colvin interview, International Liberators Conference (27 October 1981), courtesy of US Holocaust Memorial Museum.

38. *Brave Rifles.*

39. Sam Klein interview courtesy Holocaust Memorial Centre, Farmington Hills, Michigan, 14 February 2019.

40. Olivia B. Waxman, 'We Weren't Prepared for This – Inside the Accidental Liberation of a Concentration Camp', *Time Magazine*, 26 January 2018.

41. Eliach and Gurewitsch, *The Liberators*, pp. 48–9.

42. Concentration camps and DESt were totally interlinked. They exploited prison labour to produce building materials for the Reich. DESt operated with all the early camps. Sachsenhausen (1936), Buchenwald (1937), Flossenbürg (1938), Mauthausen (1938), Natzweiler-Struthof (1939), Gross Rosen (1940) and Neuengamme (1940) were all chosen for their proximity to brickworks or stone quarries.

43. Paul Mitchell, 'Concentration Camp Buildings as Artifacts: The Archaeology of Buildings in the Mauthausen-Gusen Complex', *International Journal of Historical Archaeology*, Vol. 22/3 (2017), pp. 553–73; Dan Stone, *The Liberation of the Camps: End of the Holocaust & its Aftermath* (Yale University Press, 2015).

44. Drago Arsenijevic, *Voluntary Hostages of the SS* (Ferni Publishing, Geneva, 1979), pp. 188–98.

45. Other sources suggest up to 40,000 died at Gusen.

46. Hal D. Steward, *Thunderbolt: History of the Eleventh Armored Division* (Washington DC, 1948), Chapter 4.

47. Albert J. Kosiek, 'The Liberation of Gusen and Mauthausen', *Thunderbolt: The 11th Armored Division Association*, Vol. 8/7, May–June 1955.

48. Levinson, *Gated Grief*, p. 141; Edelsack became a senior nuclear physicist at the US Office of Naval Research (ONR) and died in 2017 aged 92.

49. Kosiek, 'The Liberation of Gusen and Mauthausen'.

50. Interview with camp survivor Éva Pusztai-Fahidi in Budapest, 2019.

51. Tobias Buck, 'Inside the Trial of a Nazi Concentration Camp Guard', *Financial Times* magazine, 6 February 2020.

52. Chester Wilmot, *The Struggle for Europe* (Collins, 1952), p. 719.

53. Hartmann, *Tank Driver*, pp. 112–13.

54. Dale Olson interview courtesy of South Dakota WWII Veterans, Tales from the Midwest project.

55. Oliver Sander, 'Smuggled Letter Saved Hamburg', *Kreiszeitung-Wochenblatt*, 1 May 2020; Norddeutscher Rundfunk (NDR) Archive, 3 May 2020.

56. Hubert Essame, *The Battle for Germany* (Batsford, 1969), p. 211; Rommel's former flak chief in Africa, Wolz (1897–1978) was detained as a POW for two years, but in later years headed the *Volksbund Deutsche Kriegsgräberfürsorge*, the German War Graves Commission.

57. Wolf-Mönckeberg, *On the Other Side*, p. 134.

58. 'The Drive on Hamburg', courtesy of *Weapons & Warfare*, 23 October 2020.

59. It supplied the same SS-owned Deutsche Erd- und Steinwerke (German Earth and Stone Works company – DESt), as Flossenbürg and Mauthausen camps.

60. Literally 'Ascension Squads'; *Valentin* measured 1,400-foot-long, 300-wide and 100-foot-high.

61. Patrick Delaforce, *Monty's Ironsides* (Alan Sutton, 1991), p. 201.

62. Nicholas Rankin, *Ian Fleming's Commandos: The Story of 30 Assault Unit in WWII* (Faber & Faber, 2011), pp. 292–295.

63. Jackson testimony courtesy of *Division des Archives des Victimes des Conflits Contemporains* (Caen, ref. 26 P 1256).

64. Wynford Vaughan-Thomas, 3 May 1945, *BBC War Report* (Oxford University Press, 1945), pp. 421–2.

65. Lieutenant Colonel Trumbull Warren, *Report on the Surrender of the German Armed Forces* (Archives of the 48th Highlanders of Canada).

66. 'Uncovered: The World's Only Colour Pictures of Germans' World War Two Surrender . . . Taken by a Clerk Hiding Behind a Tree', *Daily Mail*, 16 September 2009.

67. Mark Zuehlke, 'Heroes and Villains: Radley-Walters and Wittmann', *Canadian Legion Magazine*, 8 August 2017.

68. Alex Morrison and Ted Slaney, *The Breed of Manly Men: The History of the Cape Breton Highlanders* (Canadian Institute of Strategic Studies / Cape Breton Highlanders Association, 1994). My thanks to Joël Stoppels for this reference.

69. Evan McGilvray, *A History of the First Polish Armoured Division 1938–47* (Pen & Sword), p. 300.

70. Also detailed by Eisenhower, *Crusade in Europe*, pp. 454–5.

71. Courtesy Bill Downs, CBS Archives.

72. *Daily Herald*, back page, Wednesday 9 May 1945.

73. *USS Sutton* (DE-771) had already captured another submarine, U-1228, on 10 May. It took the U-234 to Portsmouth, New Hampshire, arriving on 19 May.

74. Heinz Schäffer, *U-977: The U-Boat That Escaped to Argentina* (Cerberus, 2005); first published in German as *U-977: 66 Tage unter Wasser* (Limes-Verlag, Wiesbaden, 1974).

75. Eric Lee, *Night of the Bayonets: The Texel Uprising and Hitler's Revenge, April–May 1945* (Greenhill Books, 2020).

76. Wilhelm Dege, *War North Of 80: The Last German Arctic Weather Station Of World War II* (University Press of Colorado, 2004).

77. The assertion of the pair being the last Canadians to die in battle is my own; my thanks to David Patterson @stemvik and Charles Boudreault @Solsticenator on Twitter for their diligent research. Colonel C.P. Stacey's *Official History of the Canadian Army in the Second World War, Vol. III, The Victory Campaign: Operations in North-West Europe, 1944–1945* (Queen's Printer, Ottawa, 1960), p. 611, notes, 'The record shows sixty Canadian Army casualties on 4 May (of which 20 were fatal) and ten on 5 May, of which three were fatal.' Some of those reported as of the 5th May actually have taken place on the 4th.

78. 4 May – 24; 5 May – 14; 6 May – 15; 7 May – 14 (incl. Royal Marine); 8 May – 10.

79. Four members of 6th Airborne Division, who died on the Elbe on 4–5 May, are buried together in Berlin.

80. Pogue, *Pogue's War*, pp. 492–3.

81. Giles, *The GI Journal of Sergeant Giles*, p. 355.

82. George Beardmore, *Civilians at War: Journals 1938–1946* (Oxford University Press, 1986), pp. 194–5.

83. Nicolson, *Diaries & Letters*, op. cit., p. 463.

84. Von Kardorff, *Diary*, pp. 193–4.

20: Aftermath

1. Dönitz (1891–1945) can be heard speaking English in the *World at War* TV series (1973–4) on YouTube at https://www.youtube.com/watch?v=oj9s87Iobrc. He describes how he devised his World War Two wolf-pack tactics while pondering the German defeat in his Yorkshire POW camp, 1918–19.

2. Earl F. Ziemke, *The US Army in the Occupation of Germany, 1944–1946* (US Army Center of Military History, Washington DC, 1990), Chapters 15–21.

3. Two years after the establishment of the Bundeswehr (on 12 November 1955, the 200th anniversary of the birth of Gerhard von Scharnhorst), in 1957, nearly every German military decoration awarded during 1933–45 was denazified by the removal of the swastika, for reissue to the many Bundeswehr personnel who had served in the Wehrmacht.

4. The chief proponent of the 'million deaths' argument, now much discredited by historians, in academic circles, and at historical conferences, was James Bacque (1929–2019). His two works, now debunked, *Other Losses: An Investigation into the Mass Deaths of German Prisoners at the Hands of the French and Americans After World War II* (Stoddard, 1989) and *Crimes and Mercies: the Fate of German Civilians Under Allied Occupation, 1944–1950* (Little, Brown, 1997), are assessed as having 'misread, misinterpreted, or ignored the relevant documents'. However, their contents gained wide traction in far-right circles.

5. These are a consensus approximation from countless German, American, British and Russian sources.

6. The key text here is Earl F. Ziemke, *The US Army in the Occupation of Germany 1944–1946* (US Army Center of Military History, Washington DC, 1975).

7. Ivor Crosthwaite, *A Charmed Life: Grenadier Guards 1936–1946* (self-published, 1996), p. 99.

8. This German compound noun is post-World War Two and has the specific meaning of 'public debate within a country on a problematic period of its recent history'. It was originally coined to refer to the German debate about the Holocaust, but latterly includes East Germany. See: Mary Fulbrook, *Reckonings: Legacies of Nazi Persecution and the Quest for Justice* (Oxford University Press, 2018), pp. 231–65; Norbert Frei, *Adenauer's Germany & the Nazi Past: The Politics of Amnesty and Integration* (Columbia University Press, 2002), pp. 23–4.

9. Daniel Lee, *The S.S. Officer's Armchair: Uncovering the Hidden Life of a Nazi* (Hachette, 2020), pp. 50–51.

10. Wilfred Byford-Jones, *Berlin Twilight* (Hutchinson, 1947), Book 1: 'Meeting the People', pp. 51–2.

11. Field Marshal Bernard Montgomery, *Notes on the Occupation of Germany* (Discussion Documents, October 1945, BLM 85–8, Imperial War Museum).

12. Lord (William) Strang, *Home and Abroad* (Andre Deutsch, 1956). Robertson (1896–1974) was the son of Field Marshal Sir William Robertson, commander of the first British Army of the Rhine, 1919–20. See David Williamson, *A Most Diplomatic General: The Life of General Lord Robertson of Oakridge* (Brassey's, 1996).

13. George Clare, *Berlin Days* (Macmillan, 1989).

14. Author's conversations in 1994 with Major (retd.) John Maddock, former British staff officer, Hamburg.

15. Sir Ivone Kirkpatrick, *The Inner Circle: The Memoirs of Ivone Kirkpatrick* (Macmillan, 1959). The latest analysis of this era is by Christopher Knowles, via his *How it Really Was* blog, and whose *Winning the Peace: The British in Occupied Germany, 1945–1948* (Bloomsbury, 2018), and edited collection of essays with Camilo Erlichman, *Transforming Occupation in the Western Zones of Germany: Politics, Everyday Life and Social Interactions, 1945– 55* (Bloomsbury, 2020), provide valuable insights into this little-studied aspect of the surrender and aftermath in Germany.

16. Charles Carrington, *A Soldier at Bomber Command* (Leo Cooper 1987), p. 204.

17. Interview, Gena Turgel, June 1995.

18. Eighteen other SS wardens were imprisoned, and fourteen acquitted.

19. Steven J. Zaloga, *The Polish Army, 1939–45* (Osprey, 1982), p. 27; David M. Glantz, *When Titans Clashed: How the Red Army Stopped Hitler* (University Press of Kansas, 1998), p. 261; Earl F. Ziemke, *Battle for Berlin* (Pan/Ballantine, 1969), p. 71.

20. Colonel General Grigoriy Krivosheev, *Soviet Casualties and Combat Losses* (Greenhill, 1997), pp. 157–8.

21. The warning signs of the Holocaust were there and already known. In the House of Commons on 17 December 1942, Foreign Secretary Anthony Eden discussed the plight of European Jews who were being 'transported, in conditions of appalling horror and brutality to . . . Nazi slaughter houses in Poland. None of those taken away are ever heard of again. The able-bodied are slowly worked to death in labour camps. The infirm left to die of exposure and starvation or are deliberately massacred in mass executions. The number of victims of these bloody cruelties is reckoned in many hundreds of thousands of entirely innocent men, women and children.' (*Hansard*, 17 December 1942, Vol. 385, columns 2082–7.) The sheer scale was not appreciated, and it seems that SHAEF and their subordinate military formations, were completely unprepared to encounter the results of these German racial policies.

Bibliography

The canvas of this volume is incredibly broad, involving the experiences of over 4 million Allied personnel over 100 days. The literature before you thus covers campaign narratives and unit histories; personal memoirs of soldiers, civilians, journalists and others; documents relating to the Holocaust, its camps and survivors; as well as the aftermath in Germany. The unpublished archives and published sources cited below scratch the surface of material consulted by the author.

Primary Sources

Correspondence and interviews

Douglas Austin (46 REME Workshop, att. 3rd Scots Gds, 6th Guards Tank Brigade); Lt (later Brig.) David Baines MBE (25/26 Medium Battery, 7th Med. Regt RA, 5th AGRA); Manfred Baunach (Aschaffenburg Hitler Youth); Maj. Winrich Behr (Staff Officer, Army Group 'B'); John William Bray (Sherman driver, 'A' Sqn, Staffs. Yeomanry, 27th Armd Brigade); Capt. (later Col.) Arnold L. Brown (Co. 'G', 358th Infantry, 90th US Division); David (later Lord) Campbell of Croy, MC & bar, (320 Battery, 131st Field Regt RA, 15th Scottish Division); Hauptmann Otto Carius, Knights Cross with Oakleaves (Schwere Panzerjäger-Abteilung 512); FM Lord Michael Carver (CO, 4th Armoured Brigade); Col. Frederick C. Clinton (254th Infantry, 63rd 'Blood and Fire' US Division); Brig. T.F.J. Collins, CBE (Dir. of Movements for Continental Ops); SSgt James K. Cullen (1st Platoon, Co. 'E', 36th Armd. Infantry, 3rd US Armored Division); SSgt Bernard Dargols (Counter Intelligence Corps, 23rd Infantry, 2nd US Division); M. Bedford Davis (US combat surgeon, author of *Frozen Rainbows*); Michael Dembiński (son of Bohdan Dembiński, survivor of Sandbostel camp); Bernard de Nonancourt, head of Lanson Champagne (Division-Leclerc at Berchtesgaden); Général de Brigade Jacques de Parisot de Durand de la Boisse (CO, 3rd Régiment de Tirailleurs Algériens, liberator of Vaihingen Camp); Howell E. Dodd Jr (war correspondent & war artist, US Army); Dustin du Cane (grandson of Mirosław Łebkowski, survivor of Auschwitz, Buchenwald and V-2 rocket welder at Mittelbau-Dora); Lt Col. Norman J.L. Field, OBE (planning staff, Allied airborne ops); Sir John Archibald Ford MC (Royal

Artillery, awarded MC at Kervenheim, Reichswald, March 1945); Sgt Herbie Fussell (22nd Independent Pathfinder Company); Cpl Bob D. Gladson (Sherman gunner, 712th Tank Bn, 90th US Division); Ian C. Hammerton, Croix de Guerre (1st Flail Troop, 'B' Sqn, 22nd Dragoons, 79th British Armd Division); Cpl Pat Hennessey (Sherman crewman, 'A' Sqn, 13/18th Hussars); Andreas Herdina (son of Kurt Herdina, 6th Fallschirmjäger Division); James Hudson (3rd Platoon, 3683 QM Truck Co., US Army); Signaller Colin J. Hughes (7th R. Warwicks & No. 4 Commando, 1st Special Service Brigade); Robert J. Hutchings (stenographer, SHAEF); Sydney Jary MC (18 Platoon, 'D' Co., 4th Somerset LI, 129th Brigade, 43rd Wessex Division); Lt Frank A. Johnson (B-26 pilot, 454th Sqn, 323rd Bomb Gp, RAF Earls Colne, 9th US Air Force); Oberst (later Gen.) Johann Adolf, Graf von Kielmansegg (staff officer, OKW); TSgt Victor B. Kramer (P-47 armourer, 404th Sqn, 371st Fighter Gp, RAF Bisterne, 9th US Air Force); Oberst Hans-Joachim Krug (Wehrmacht & Bundeswehr, inhabitant of Linz); Sgt George Laws (5th Army Film & Photographic Unit, British Army); Major Hans von Luck, Knight's Cross (21st Panzer Division, Operation *Nordwind*); Robert F. Lynch (104th 'Timberwolf' US Division, author of *A Letter Marked Free*); Sqn Ldr (later Lord) George Mackie of Benshie, CBE, DSO, DFC (Stirling & Lancaster navigator, 149 & 115 Sqns, No. 3 Gp, RAFs Mildenhall & Witchford); Richard H. McCullough (409th Infantry, 103rd 'Cactus' US Division, liberator of Landsberg); SSgt Elmer 'Lucky' McGinty (B-17 waist gunner, 336th Sqn, 95th Bomb Gp, RAF Horham, 8th US Air Force); Maj. John Maddock (former British staff officer, Hamburg); SSgt Louis 'Lou' Masciangelo (B-24 crewman, 389th 'Sky Scorpions' Bomb Gp, RAF Hethel, 8th US Air Force); David Montgomery, 2nd Viscount (son of FM Bernard Montgomery); Thomas Moulton (son of Philip Moulton Mayer, American Field Service); Brig. Gen. (retired) Hans-Georg Model (son of FM Walter Model); Walter Morison, DFC (author of *Flak and Ferrets: One Way to Colditz*); Lt Melbourne Hugh Neily (Canloan offr, 3rd Platoon, 'A' Co., 2nd East Yorks, 8th Brigade, 3rd British Division); Lt Eugene (Gene) N. Noble (C-47 pilot, 95th Sqn, 440th Tp Carrier Gp, 9th US Air Force); John Painter (8th Rifle Brigade, 29th Armd Brigade, 11th Armd Division); PFC George Perrine (Co. 'B', 82nd Recon Bn, 2nd US Armored Division); Capt. Eugene (Gene) Polinsky (Navigator, 856 & 36th Sqns, 492nd (Special Ops) Bomb Gp, RAF Harrington, 8th US Air Force); Éva Pusztai-Fahidi (survivor of Auschwitz and Buchenwald); Sgt Edward L. Reisinger (4th Signal Co., 4th US Division); Ldg Aircraftswoman Myra Roberts, WAAF (Nurse on C-47, 233 Sqn/RAF Blakehill Farm); Dr Manfred Rommel, CBE (son of FM Erwin Rommel); Feldwebel Heinz Ronig (116th Recon Bn, 116th Pz Division); Richard, Freiherr von Rosen (3rd Co., 503rd Heavy Tank Bn); Josef Szygowski (Doctor, 1st Polish Armd Division); Ldg Aircraftsman Willie Taylor (Typhoon wireless mechanic, 175 Sqn, 121 Wing, No 83 Gp, 2nd Tactical Air Force); Sgt Troy Thomason (552nd Anti-Aircraft Artillery Auto Weapons Bn); Gina Turgel (née Goldfinger, Belsen survivor, wife of Sgt Norman Turgel of 53rd Field Security Section, Intelligence Corps); Frank W. Weaver (Driver, Co. 'C', 691st Tank Destroyer Bn); Sgt Wilmot Clive Weightman (Royal Signals despatch rider, HQ 21st Army Group); Gen. Russell Weiskircher (157th

Infantry Regiment, 45th 'Thunderbird' US Division); Dean M. White (44th US Infantry Division).

Museums and unpublished archives

2nd Armored Division 'Hell on Wheels' Association, Naugatuck, Connecticut: operational papers.

3rd Infantry Division Museum, Fort Stewart, Georgia: operational orders and reports.

42nd Rainbow Division Association: online access to military reports and returns.

45th Infantry 'Thunderbird' Division Association & Museum, Oklahoma City: operational orders and personal memories of 157th Infantry Regiment.

63rd 'Blood & Fire' Division Association: online access to reports and returns.

American Veterans Center, Glebe Rd, Arlington, Virginia: Edgar Valderrama (11th Infantry, 5th Division), memoir.

Association of 3rd Armored Division Veterans: online access to newsletters, reports and papers.

BBC WW2 People's War: interviews: Bill Ashley; Lieutenant F.W. Gordon; Joy Trindles (née Taverner); Eileen Younghusband.

British Library Newspaper Archive.

Buchenwald and Mittelbau-Dora Memorials Foundation (Gedenkstätte Buchenwald, 99427 Weimar / KZ-Gedenkstätte Mittelbau-Dora Kohnsteinweg 20, 99734 Nordhausen): details of forced labour and satellite camps.

Buddy's War – Following Buddy Lehman, Company 'C', 80th Medical Battalion, Tenth Armored Division, courtesy of his son at https://www.buddyswar.com

Bundeswehr Truppenübungsplatz-Hammelburg: access to camp facilities to study Task Force Baum.

California State Archives: Master Sergeant Charles Senteney, 144th Field Artillery Group, From Utah Beach to Salzburg, Austria (typewritten memoir).

California State Military Museum Archives, Sacramento: Donald Joseph Carner Papers.

Canadian Dept of Defence, Directorate of Heritage & History: Artillery Notes on Operation *Plunder*, ref: 142.4F14011(D1).

Clemson University Corps Records, South Carolina: Randolph Boling McDavid, class of 1943.

Eisenhower Presidential Library, Abilene, Kansas: Jacob L. Devers diary.

European Holocaust Memorial Foundation (Europäische Holocaustgedenkstätte): details of Kaufering VII Camp; the OT (Todt Organisation) Ringeltaube factory bunkers.

Fallingbostel Military Museum: Kevin Greenhalgh.

Friedensmuseum bruecke von Remagen: details of 7–17 March 1945.

Gedenkstätte Bergen-Belsen, Anne-Frank-Platz, 29303 Lohheide: details of liberation.

Holocaust Memorial Centre, Farmington Hills, Michigan: Sam Klein interview.

Imperial War Museum, London & Duxford: interviews, George Chambers and William Brown, 1988 (Sound. 10415); Dr Arnold R. Horwell Papers (Docs, 1164); Norman Kirby interview (Sound, 16084); Julius Neave Papers (Docs, LBY 94 / 2194); Rev. T. J. Stretch Papers (Docs. 11561); Maj. WR Williams Papers (Docs, 3120); access to Montgomery's headquarters caravans; Memory of the Camps (Film, A70 515); Montgomery, personal diary, 29 March 1945 (LMD 69/1); Montgomery Papers (BLM 49/25).

KZ-Gedenkstätte Dachau, Alte Römerstraße 75, 85221 Dachau: details of camp liberation.

KZ-Gedenkstätte Mauthausen, Erinnerungsstraße 1, 4310 Mauthausen: details of liberation.

Lee Miller Archives, Chiddingly, East Sussex, BN8 6HW: photographs.

Library and Archives, Canada, 395 Wellington St, Ottawa, K1A 0N4: Intelligence Summaries (all RG-24): 1 Canadian Corps, April–May 1945; 5th Armoured Division, April 1945; War Diaries (all RG-24): 1st Canadian Parachute Battalion, March 1945; 8th Canadian Infantry Brigade, March–May 1945; Algonquin Regiment, February–May 1945; Black Watch of Canada, April–May 1945; British Columbia Dragoons, April–May 1945; Hastings & Prince Edward Regiment, April–May 1945; Lincoln & Welland Regiment, March–May 1945; Princess Patricia's Canadian Light Infantry, April–May 1945.

George C. Marshall Foundation, Lexington, Virginia, Library & Archives, personal memory collection: Henry L. Stimpson Papers; Rufus Dalton, 'Two Days of Hell at Heilbronn'; Lee Reese, 'The Last Battle, Maybe'; Robert Tessmer, 'Eric Levi Returns to Boyhood Home and Saves Village'.

Marshall University, Huntington, West Virginia: Kenneth Hechler Papers, Bridge at Remagen notes.

Museum of the Kansas National Guard: James Graff, 'Recollections of a Combat Infantryman'.

Nationaal Monument Kamp Vught, Holland: archives of liberation.

National Museum of American Jewish Military History, Washington DC: David Cohen interview (4th Armored Division); transcript of Kenneth Colvin interview at the International Liberators Conference (27 October 1981); letter, Rabbi Bohnen to his wife Eleanor, 1 May 1945, Eli Heimberg interview; Morris Eisenstein interview; Norman Brody and John Malone interviews.

National World War II Museum of New Orleans, Louisiana: access to exhibits, papers and memoirs.

New York State Military Museum & Veterans Research Center, Saratoga Springs, NY 12866: books.

NS-Dokumentationszentrum der Stadt Köln: Gestapo prison graffiti details.

Ohio University Libraries, Athens, Cornelius Ryan Collection of World War II Papers, Mahn Center for Archives and Special Collections: materials relating to The Last Battle.

Providence College, Rhode Island: copy of The Cowl: Testimony of Fr. Edward P. Doyle.

Regimental Museum of the Light Dragoons: War Diary of Julius Neave, A Personal Chronicle, Winter 1942–3 to May 1945.

Mark Reynier, Letters home from P.B. Reynier, MC, Royal Scots Fusiliers.

Schloss Colditz, Schloßgasse 1, 04680 Colditz: memoirs of liberation.

Brigadier General John C. L. Scribner Texas Military Forces Museum, Austin, Tx 78763: operational orders and reports for 36th Texas Division.

Site de l'ancien camp de concentration de Natzweiler-Struthof: details of capture.

The Tank Museum, Bovington, Dorset, BH20 6JG: access to Sherman, Pershing, Panther, Churchill and Comet tanks, M10 and M36 tank destroyers.

UK National Archives, Kew: XXX Corps, Medical Diary, March/April 1945 (WO 171/357); 3rd (Tank) Battalion Scots Guards, War Diary (WO 171/5150); 4th Grenadier Guards, War Diary, April 1945 (WO 171/5146).

US Army Heritage and Education Center (AHEC), Carlisle, Pennsylvania: papers and memoirs: Colonel Charles K. Graydon, 'With the 101st Cavalry During World War 1940–45'; Gen Hobart Gay papers; Sergeant Robert Ross, 'We Fought for Peace: World War II Memoirs'; Jim Lankford, 'The 14th Armored Division and the Liberation of Stalag VII-A'.

US Holocaust Memorial Museum, Washington, DC 20024-2126: materials relating to Hadamar psychiatric clinic and T-4 centre.

US Military Academy Special Collections & Archives, West Point: Brig. Gen. Daniel Noce Papers; Gen. Alexander Patch Papers.

US National Archives & Records (NARA), Foreign Military Studies, all 1946–1948: Gen. Gunther Blumentritt, *Why did the German soldier fight to the bitter end?* (B-338); *Provisional Army Blumentritt, 10 April–1 June 1945* (B-361); *First Parachute Army, 28 March–9 April 1945* (B-354); *Twenty-Fifth Army, 3 February–28 March 1945* (B-365); Generalmajor Heinz Fiebig, *84th Infantry Division (19 Jan–25 Mar 1945): West of the Lower Rhine from the Reichswald to Wesel* (B-843); Generalleutnant Heinrich Greiner, *Wehrkreis VII, 12 April–10 May 1945: The Last Days of the War Along & South of the Danube* (B-375); Oberst Gruppenführer Paul Hausser, *Central Europe: Fighting of Heeresgruppe 'G' from 22 March to 4 April 1945* (B-026 & B-600); Gen. Rudolf Koch-Erpach, *German morale & fighting strength in the spring of 1945* (B-413); Gen. Friedrich Köchling, *Combat of LXXXI Armeekorps, 25 January–13 April 1945* (B-576); Generalmajor Rudolf Langhäuser, *12th Volksgrenadier Division, 23 February–March 1945* (B-080); *6th Parachute Division, 19 November 1944–10 May 1945* (B-368); Gen. Alfred Schlemm, *First Parachute Army, 20 November 1944–21 March 1945* (B-084); Gen. Helmut Thumm, *LXIV Corps: 6 Dec 44–28 Jan 45* (B-050); Oberst Ulrich Ulms, *XII SS Corps: Between the Roer & Rhine, 26 January–4 March 1945* (B-410); Generalleutnant Martin Unrein, *Panzer Division Clausewitz, 1–21 April 1945* (B-350); Gen. Gustav von Zangen, *Battles on the Roer & Rhine, Fifteenth Army, 15 November 1944–28 February 1945* (B-811 & B-812); Oberst

Horst Wilutzky, *The Fighting of Army Group 'G' in the West: The Final Battle in Central & Southern Germany until Capitulation 22 Mar– 6 May 1945* (B-703); Generalleutnant Otto Witek, *Army Group 'G': Supply, 26 October 1944–6 May 1945* (B-366).

University of Nebraska–Lincoln, Archives & Special Collections: copies of *Rainbow Reveille* (Rainbow Division's Veterans Association Journal).

University of South Florida, Tampa Library, Concentration Camp Liberators Oral History Program: Kenneth Ayers interview, Ref C65-00006.

University of Southern Mississippi, Oral History Program with the National WWII Museum: Frank J. Waldeck interview.

University of Tennessee Veterans' Oral History Project, Center for the Study of War and Society, Department of History: Jimmy Gentry interview.

Geoff Walden, The Third Reich in Ruins, at http://www. thirdreichruins.com/mittelwerk.htm

Wisconsin Veterans Museum Research Center: Paul F. Jenkins (1916–2007), oral interview, OH-146, 2000.

York County Heritage Trust, Pennsylvania: General Jacob L. Devers Papers.

Published US military memoirs, diaries and papers

GIs Remember (National Museum of American Jewish Military History, Washington DC, 1994)

Allen, Robert S. (ed. John Nelson Rickard), *Forward With Patton: The WWII Diary of Col. Robert S. Allen* (University Press of Kentucky, 2017)

Boas, Roger, *Battle Rattle: A Last Memoir of WWII* (Stinson Publishing, 2015)

Bradley, Omar N., *A Soldier's Story of the Allied Campaigns from Tunis to the Elbe* (Eyre & Spottiswoode, 1951); and Clay Blair, *A General's Life* (Simon & Schuster, 1983)

Buechner, Emajean Jordan, *Sparks: The Combat Diary of a Battalion Commander* (Thunderbird Press, 1992)

Cooper, Belton Y., *Death Traps: The Survival of an American Armored Division in World War II* (Presidio, 1998)

Cox, Troy D., *An Infantryman's Memories of World War II* (Brown Line, 2003)

Craft, W. Bert, *The Agony of Hell* (Turner Publishing Company, 1994)

Davis, M. Bedford, *Frozen Rainbows: The WWII Adventures of a Combat Medical Officer* (Meadowlark Publishing, 2003)

Eisenhower, Gen Dwight D., *Crusade in Europe* (Heinemann, 1948); *The War Years: Volume 4, Part X: Victory; January 1945 to May 1945* (Johns Hopkins University Press, 1970)

Fuller, Sam, *A Third Face: My Tale of Writing, Fighting, & Filmmaking* (Alfred A. Knopf, 2002)

Fussell, Paul, *Doing Battle: The Making of a Skeptic* (Little Brown, 1996)

Garahan, Frank, *Easy Company Goes to War 1944–1945: The Story of Captain Thomas H. Garahan & the 100th Infantry Division Combat Tour of WWII. An Historical*

Account in His Own Words & a Retracement of His Journey by His Son (www.gara-hanhistory.com, 2017)

Gantter, Raymond, *Roll Me Over: An Infantryman's World War II* (Presidio, 1997)

Garrison H., *Grandpa Gar: The Saga of One Soldier as Told to His Grandchildren* (private publication, 1976)

Gavin, James M., *On to Berlin* (Viking, 1978)

Giles, Janice Holt, *The GI Journal of Sergeant Giles* (Houghton Mifflin, 1965)

Graff, James, *Recollections of a Combat Infantryman* (Museum of the Kansas National Guard)

Gray, J. Glenn, *The Warriors. Reflections on Men in Battle* (University of Nebraska Press, 1959)

Greenwood, John T. (ed.), *Normandy to Victory: The War Diary of General Courtney H. Hodges & the First US Army* (University Press of Kentucky, 2008)

Hartman, J. Ted, *Tank Driver: With the 11th Armored from the Battle of the Bulge to VE Day* (Indiana University Press, 2003)

Hoge, Gen. William M., *Engineer Memoirs* (US Army Corps of Engineers, 1993)

Irwin, John P., *Another River, Another Town: A Teenage Tank Gunner Comes of Age in Combat* (Random House, 2002)

Joy, Dean, *Sixty Days in Combat: An Infantryman's Memoir of World War II* (Presidio, 2004)

Kahn, Bernard L., *Fight On: A GI's Odyssey Back to Nazi Germany* (Cable Publishing, 2013)

Kappelman, Glenn L., *Through My Sights: A Gunner's View of WWII* (Sunflower Publishing, 2003)

Leide, Lt Cdr William, *Recollections of the crossing of the Rhine River* (US Naval History and Heritage Command, 2017)

Leveque, Phil, *General Patton's Dogface Soldier of WWII From A Foxhole* (privately printed, 1960)

Light, John H., *An Infantryman Remembers World War II* (Beidel Printing House, 1997)

Lynch, Robert F., *A Letter Marked Free* (Dog Ear Publishing, 2007)

MacDonald, Charles B., *Company Commander* (Infantry Journal Press, 1947)

McElvain, Bill, *In My Father's Words: Letters From a World War II Soldier* (Lulu, 2011)

McKenzie, John, *On Time, On Target: The World War II Memoir of a Paratrooper in the 82nd Airborne* (Presidio Press, 2000)

Manchester, Richard, *Personal Accounts: Crossing the Rhine* (87th Division Association)

Megellas, James, *All the Way to Berlin: A Paratrooper at War in Europe* (Presidio Press, 2003)

Murphy, Audie, *To Hell and Back* (Henry Holt, 1949)

Patton, George S., *War as I Knew It* (Houghton Mifflin, 1947); Martin Blumenson (ed.), *The Patton Papers, Vol. II: 1940–1945* (Houghton Mifflin, 1974)

Pena, William M., *As Far as Schleiden* (self-published, 1992)

Pogue, Forrest C., *Pogue's War: Diaries of a WWII Combat Historian* (University Press of Kentucky, 2001)

Pratt, Lt Col Sherman W., *Autobahn to Berchtesgaden: A Combat Soldier's View of His Role in World War II* (Gateway Press, 1992)

Quick, Ed (ed.), *Rhine Crossing* (89th Infantry Division Association, November 2001)

Reitan, Earl A., *Riflemen: On the Cutting Edge of World War II* (self-published, 2008)

Roley, Paul (ed.), Bruce Egger and Lee M. Otts, '*G*' *Company's War: Two Personal Accounts of the Campaigns in Europe, 1944–45* (University of Alabama Press, 1992)

Sparks, Felix L., 'The Aschaffenburg Battle', *157th Infantry Association Journal* (July 1982)

Wilson, George, *If You Survive* (Presidio, 1987)

Winebrenner, Hobart (ed. Michael McCoy), *Bootprints: An Infantryman's Walk Through World War II* (Camp Comamajo Press, 2005)

Wirth, G. Hudson, *I was an Eighteen-Year-Old Infantry Replacement* (self-published, 1997)

Yarosh, Frank, *World War II Is Not Over: A Combat Infantryman's Experiences in a German POW Camp* (self-published, 1992)

Published British, Canadian & French military memoirs, diaries and papers

Alanbrooke, FM Lord (ed. Alex Danchev & Daniel Todman), *War Diaries 1939–45* (Orion, 1999)

Bell, Noel, *From the Beaches to the Baltic: The Story of 'G' Company, 8th Battalion, the Rifle Brigade in NW Europe* (Gale & Polden, 1947)

Blackburn, George G., *The Guns of Victory* (McClelland & Stewart, 1996)

Boscawen, Robert, *Armoured Guardsmen: A War Diary, June 1944–April 1945* (Leo Cooper, 2001)

Carrington, Charles, *A Soldier at Bomber Command* (Leo Cooper, 1987)

Close, Bill, *A View from the Turret: A History of the 3rd Royal Tank Regiment* (Dell & Bredon, 2002)

Crosthwaite, Ivor, *A Charmed Life: Grenadier Guards 1936–1946* (self-published, 1996)

de Gaulle, Charles, *Complete War Memoirs of Charles de Gaulle* (Carroll & Graf Publishers, 1998)

de Lattre de Tassigny, Maréchal Jean, *History of the French First Army* (Allen and Unwin, 1952)

Dyson, Stephen W., *Tank Twins: East End Brothers-In-Arms* (Leo Cooper, 1997)

Greenwood, Sgt Trevor, *D-Day to Victory*, ed. S.V. Partington (Simon & Schuster, 2012)

Hammerton, Ian C., *Achtung! Minen! A Flail Tank Troop Commander* (Book Guild, 1991)

Hardman, Leslie, *The Survivors: The Story of the Belsen Remnant* (Vallentine Mitchell, 1958)

Holm, Frank P., *A Backward Glance: The Personal Story of an Infantry Signaller with the Calgary Highlanders in World War II* (self-published, 1989)

Horrocks Brian, Eversley Belfield & Hubert Essame, *Corps Commander* (Sidgwick & Jackson, 1977)

Jary, Sydney, *Eighteen Platoon* (self-published, 1994)

Kirby, Norman, *1100 Miles with Monty: Security and Intelligence at Tac HQ* (Alan Sutton, 1989)

Levy, Isaac, *Witness to Evil: Bergen-Belsen 1945* (Halban, 1995)

Lindsay, Martin, *So Few Got Through* (Collins, 1946)

Montgomery, Bernard, *Memoirs of FM the Viscount Montgomery of Alamein* (Collins, 1958)

Morison, Walter, *Flak and Ferrets: One Way to Colditz* (Sentinel, 1995)

Neave, Julius, *War Diary of Julius 13th/18th Hussars: A Personal Chronicle* (privately printed, 1994)

Scott, Desmond, *Typhoon Pilot* (Leo Cooper, 1982)

Taylor, Brig George, *Infantry Colonel* (self-published, 1990)

West, Kenneth J., *An' It's Called a Tam-o'-shanter* (privately printed, 1985)

White, Peter, *With the Jocks: A Soldier's Struggle for Europe 1944–45* (Sutton Publishing, 2001)

Wingfield, R.M., *The Only Way Out: An Infantryman's Autobiography of the NW Europe Campaign* (Hutchinson, 1955)

Published memoirs, diaries and papers of Allied & German artists, civilians, diplomats, reporters

(No author), *War Report: A Record of Dispatches Broadcast by BBC War Correspondents 6 June 1944–5 May 1945* (Oxford University Press, 1946)

Ardizzone, Edward, *Diary of a War Artist* (The Bodley Head, 1974)

Bauer, Robert, *Heilbronner Tagebuchbätter* [Heilbronn Diaries], (self-published, Heilbronn, 1949)

Beardmore, George, *Civilians at War: Journals 1938–1946* (Oxford University Press, 1986)

Berrinberg, Elisabeth von, *The City in Flames: Recollections of the Bombing of Würzburg* (Berrinberg/Smith House Press, 2013)

Bielenberg, Christabel, *The Past is Myself* (Chatto & Windus, 1968)

Bourke-White, Margaret, *Dear Fatherland, Rest Quietly: A Report on the Collapse of Hitler's Thousand Years* (Simon & Schuster, 1946)

Bradley, Holbrook, *War Correspondent From D-Day to the Elbe* (iUniverse, 2007)

Byford-Jones, Wilfred, *Berlin Twilight* (Hutchinson, 1947)

Campbell, Doon, *Magic Mistress: A 30-Year Affair With Reuters* (Tagman Press, 2000)

Clare, George, *Berlin Days* (Macmillan, 1989)

Decker, Rudolf, 'The Battle for Würzburg', *Rainbow Reveille* (Rainbow Division's Veterans Association Journal, January 1993)

Dege, Wilhelm, *War North of 80: The Last German Arctic Weather Station of World War II* (University Press of Colorado, 2004)

Eliach, Yaffa and Brana Gurewitsch, *The Liberators: Eyewitness Accounts of the Liberation of Concentration Camps* (Center for Holocaust Studies, Documentation and Research, 1981)

Gellhorn, Martha, *The Face of War* (Hart Davis, 1959)

Guderian, Heinz Günther, *Normandy to the Ruhr: With 116th Panzer Division* (Aberjona Press, 2001)

Jünger, Ernst, *A German Officer in Occupied Paris: The War Journals, 1941–1945* (Columbia University Press, 2019)

Kardorff, Ursula von, *Diary of a Nightmare: Berlin 1942–5* (Rupert Hart Davis, 1965)

Kirkpatrick, Sir Ivone, *The Inner Circle: The Memoirs of Ivone Kirkpatrick* (Macmillan, 1959)

Levin, Mikael, *War Story: Retracing my Father's Footsteps* (Kehayoff, Munich, 1997)

Levinson, Leila, *Gated Grief: The Daughter of a GI Concentration Camp Liberator Discovers a Legacy of Trauma* (Cable Publishing, 2011)

Nicolson, Harold (ed. Nigel Nicolson), *Diaries & Letters 1939–45* (Collins, 1967)

Rooney, Andy, *My War* (Times Books, 1995)

Schlesier, Karl Heinz, *Flakhelfer to Grenadier: Memoir of a Boy Soldier 1943–5* (Helion, 2014)

Shirer, William, *Berlin Diary: Journal of a Foreign Correspondent 1934–41* (Alfred A. Knopf, 1941)

Strang, Lord William, *Home and Abroad* (Andre Deutsch, 1956)

White, Oscar, *Conqueror's Road* (Cambridge University Press, 1996)

Wolf-Mönckeberg, Mathilde, *On the Other Side: To My Children From Germany 1940–45* (Peter Owen, 1979)

Secondary Sources

Third Reich, Holocaust and Post-war Germany

(No author), *Joint Intelligence Objectives Agency, German Underground Installations, Vol. 1, Unique Design & Construction Methods* (HMSO, 1945)

Abzug, Robert H., *Inside the Vicious Heart: Americans and the Liberation of Nazi Concentration Camps* (Oxford University Press, 1985)

Arsenijevic, Drago, *Voluntary Hostages of the SS* (Ferni Publishing, Geneva, 1979)

Bacque, James, *Other Losses: An Investigation into the Mass Deaths of German Prisoners at the Hands of the French and Americans After World War II* (Stoddard, 1989); *Crimes and Mercies: the Fate of German Civilians Under Allied Occupation, 1944–1950* (Little, Brown, 1997)

Bergen, Doris L., *War & Genocide: Concise History of the Holocaust* (Rowman & Little-field, 2003)

Biddiscombe, Perry, *The Last Nazis: SS Werewolf Guerrilla Resistance in Europe 1944–1947* (History Press, 2004)

Blatman, Daniel, *Death Marches: Final Phase of Nazi Genocide* (Harvard University Press, 2013)

Borkin, Joseph, *The Crime and Punishment of I.G. Farben* (Free Press/Macmillan, 1978)

Buchwald, Wolfgang, *Endkampf: das Schicksal des A. und E. Bataillons (Brigade) der 12. SS-Panzer-Division Hitlerjugend, genannt: Kampfgruppe Panzerteufel* (Buchwald, 1990)

Cesarani, David, Tony Kushner, Jo Reilly & Colin Richmond (eds), *Belsen in History & Memory* (Frank Cass, 1997)

Daly-Groves, Luke, *Hitler's Death: The Case Against Conspiracy* (Osprey, 2019)

Domes, Peter and Martin Heinlein, *Alarm! Die Panzerspitze kommt!* (Hofmann-Buch, 2008)

Ferencz, Ben C., *Less Than Slaves: Jewish Forced Labor & the Quest for Compensation* (Indiana University Press, 2002)

Forczyk, Robert, *Walther Model* (Osprey/Bloomsbury, 2013)

Frei, Norbert, *Adenauer's Germany & the Nazi Past: The Politics of Amnesty and Integration* (Columbia University Press, 2002)

Friedlander, Henry, *The Origins of Nazi Genocide: From Euthanasia to the Final Solution* (University of North Carolina Press, 1995)

Fritz, Stephen G., *Endkampf: Soldiers, Civilians, and the Death of the Third Reich* (University Press of Kentucky, 2004)

Fulbrook, Mary, *Reckonings: Legacies of Nazi Persecution & the Quest for Justice* (Oxford University Press, 2018)

Gerlach, Christian, *The Extermination of the European Jews* (Cambridge University Press, 2016)

Goeschel, Christian, *Suicide in Nazi Germany* (Oxford University Press, 2009)

Hagen, Louis, *Ein Volk, Ein Reich: Nine Lives Under the Nazis* (History Press, 2011)

Hayes, Peter, *Industry and Ideology: I.G. Farben in the Nazi Era* (Cambridge University Press, 2001)

Huber, Florian, *Promise Me You'll Shoot Yourself: Downfall of Ordinary Germans* (Penguin, 2019)

Jähner, Harald, *Aftermath: Life in the Fallout of the Third Reich, 1945–1955* (WH Allen, 2021)

Jeffreys, Diarmuid, *Hell's Cartel: I.G. Farben & the Making of Hitler's War Machine* (H. Holt, 2008)

Kater, Michael H., *Hitler Youth* (Harvard University Press, 2004)

Kershaw, Ian, *The Führer Myth: Image and Reality in the Third Reich* (Oxford, 1987); *Hitler, 1936–1945* (Allen Lane, 2000)

Knowles, Christopher, *Winning the Peace: The British in Occupied Germany, 1945–1948* (Bloomsbury, 2018); with Camilo Erlichman, *Transforming Occupation in the Western Zones of Germany: Politics, Everyday Life and Social Interactions, 1945–55* (Bloomsbury, 2020)

Koch, H.W., *Hitler Youth. Origin & Development 1922–45* (Barnes & Noble, 1975)

Kogon, Eugen, Hermann Langbein & Adalbert Rückerl (eds), *Nazi Mass Murder* (Yale University Press, 1993)

Lee, Daniel, *The S.S. Officer's Armchair: Uncovering the Hidden Life of a Nazi* (Hachette, 2020)

Lifton, Robert Jay, *Nazi Doctors: Medical Killing & the Psychology of Genocide* (Macmillan, 1990)

Mazower, Mark, *Hitler's Empire: How the Nazis Ruled Europe* (Penguin, 2008)

Miller, Michael D., and Andreas Schulz, *Gauleiter: The Regional Leaders of the Nazi Party & Their Deputies, 1925–1945* (Bender Publishing, 2012)

Miller, Oskar von, *Incident at Brettheim, 1945* (Realschule, Rothenburg ob der Tauber and Goethe Institute, 1998)

Morley, Nathan, *Radio Hitler: Nazi Airwaves During the Second World War* (Amberley, 2021)

Münch, Karl-Heinz, *History of the 654th Schwere-PanzerjägerAbteilung* (J.J. Fedorowicz, 2001)

Munoz, Antonio J., *The Iron Fist Division: A Combat History of the 17 SS PanzerGrenadier Division Goetz von Berlichingen, 1943–1945* (Europa Books, 1999)

Neumann, Klaus, *Shifting Memories: Nazi Past in New Germany* (University of Michigan, 2000)

Overy, Richard, *War and Economy in the Third Reich* (Oxford University Press, 1995)

Pulitzer, Joseph A., *Report to the American People* (St Louis Post-Dispatch, 1945)

Raim, E., *Die Dachauer KZ-Außenkomandos Kaufering & Mühldorf. Rüstungsbauten und Zwangsarbeit im letzten Kriegsjahr* (Neumeyer, 1992)

Raschke, Helga, *Josef Ritter von Gadolla and the Last Days of the War in Gotha* (Raschke Eigenverlag, 2007)

Smith, Harry Leslie, *Love Among the Ruins: Life and Love in Hamburg, 1945* (Icon Books, 2015)

Stadtmüller, Alois, *Aschaffenburg im Zweiten Weltkrieg* (Geschichts-und Kunstverein Aschaffenburg, 1971)

Stargardt, Nicholas, *The German War: A Nation Under Arms 1939–45* (Bodley Head, 2015)

Stone, Dan, *The Liberation of the Camps: End of the Holocaust & its Aftermath* (Yale University Press, 2015)

Tooze, Adam, *Wages of Destruction: Making & breaking of the Nazi Economy* (Allen Lane, 2006)

Trevor Roper, H.R. (ed.), *Hitler's War Directives 1939–1945* (Sidgwick & Jackson, 1964)

Trigg, Jonathan, *To VE-Day Through German Eyes* (Amberley, 2020)

Ullrich, Volker, *Hitler. Vol. I: Ascent, 1889–1939; Vol. II: Downfall, 1939–1945)* (Vintage, 2017/2021); *Eight Days in May: How Germany's War Ended* (Penguin, 2021)

Wachsmann, Nikolaus, *KL: A History of the Nazi Concentration Camps* (Little, Brown, 2015)

Wieland, Karin, *Dietrich & Riefenstahl: Hollywood, Berlin: a Century in Two Lives* (Liveright, 2015)

Winter, Hermann, *The War and Post-war Period in Augsburg 1939–45* (self-published, 2011)

Young, Desmond, *Rommel: The Desert Fox* (Collins, 1950)

Allied Official histories

(No author), *Seventh United States Army in France & Germany, 1944–1945, Report of Operations* (Gräf, Heidelberg, 1946)

(No author), *HQ Sixth Army Group G-3 Section, Final After Action Report* (Heidelberg, 1945)

(No author), *HQ Twelfth Army Group, G-3 Section, Final After Action Report* (Wiesbaden, 1945)

(No author), *The Seventh United States Army, 1944–1945: Report of Operations* (Heidelberg, 1946)

(No author), *US Army Pocket Guide to Germany, 1944* (Riva Verlag, 2015)

(No author), *17th Armored Engineer Battalion Unit History, 1940–1945* (Office of History, US Army Corps of Engineers, Alexandria, Virginia)

Beck, Alfred M. et al., *US Army in World War II, Corps of Engineers: The War Against Germany* (Center of Military History, Washington DC, 1984)

Bedessem, Edward M., *Central Europe, 22 March–11 May 1945* (Center of Military History, Washington DC, 1996)

Clarke, Jeffrey and Robert Smith, *US Army in World War II: ETO, Riviera to the Rhine* (Center of Military History, Washington DC, 1993)

Dunham, H. H., *US Army Transportation in the European Theater of Operations, 1942–1945* (Office of the Chief of Transportation, Army Service Forces, June 1946)

Eisenhower, Major Dwight D., *American Armies and Battlefields in Europe* (American Battle Monuments Commission, Washington DC, 1938)

Ellis, Maj L. F. with Lieutenant Colonel A. E. Warhurst, *Victory in the West, Vol. II: The Defeat of Germany* (HMSO, 1968)

Fowle, Barry W. (ed.), *Builders and Fighters: US Army Engineers in World War II* (Office of History, US Army Corps of Engineers, 1992)

Heaton, Leonard D. (Foreword), *Medical Department of the United States Army in World War II: Preventive Medicine, Volume V: Communicable Diseases Transmitted Through Contact* (Office of the Surgeon General, Department of the Army, Washington DC, 1958)

Lee, Ulysses, *US Army in World War II, Special Studies: The Employment of Negro Troops* (Center of Military History, Washington DC, 1966)

MacDonald, Charles B., *US Army in World War II: ETO, The Last Offensive* (Center of Military History, Washington DC, 1973)

Morison, Samuel Eliot, *History of US Naval Operations in World War II, Vol. II: The Invasion of France and Germany* (Little, Brown, 1957)

Pogue, Forrest C., *The Supreme Command* (Center of Military History, Washington DC, 1954)

Rock, George, *History of the American Field Service 1920–1955* (AFS/The Platen Press, 1956)

Ruppenthal, Roland G., *Logistical Support of the Armies, Vol. II: September 1944–May 1945* (Center of Military History, Washington DC, 1953)

Stacey, C.P., *Official History of the Canadian Army in the Second World War, Vol. III, The Victory Campaign, Operations in North-West Europe, 1944–1945* (Government Printing Office, 1960)

Timothy, Brig Gen P.H., *12th Army Group Engineer Operations: Rhine Crossing* (Wiesbaden, 1945)

Vigneras, Marcel, *US Army in World War II Special Studies: Rearming the French* (Center of Military History, Washington DC, 1956)

Wilkerson, Lt Col Edgar et al., *V Corps Operations in the ETO 6 January 1942–9 May 1945* (668th Engineer Topographical Company, 1946)

Wilson, FM Sir Henry Maitland, *Report by Supreme Allied Commander Mediterranean to the CCS on Operations in Southern France, August 1944* (HMSO, 1946)

Ziemke, Earl F., *The US Army in the Occupation of Germany, 1944–1946* (Center of Military History, Washington DC, 1975)

Allied Unit histories

(No author), *Rolling Ahead! The Story of the 89th US Infantry Division* (Stars and Stripes, Paris, 1945)

(No author), *Blue and White Devils: The 3rd US Infantry Division* (Stars and Stripes, Paris, 1945)

(No author), *Terrify and Destroy: The 10th US Armored Division* (Stars and Stripes, Paris, 1945)

(No author), *Brave Rifles: The 3rd Cavalry Recon Squadron in World War II* (Germany, 1945)

Barclay, G. N., *History of the 53rd Welsh Division in the Second World War* (Clowes, 1955)

Blake, Gordon, *Mountain and Flood: History of the 52nd Lowland Division* (Jackson, 1950)

Brett-Smith, Richard, *The 11th Hussars (Prince Albert's Own)* (Leo Cooper, 1969)

Brown, Kingsley, *Semper Paratus: History of the Royal Hamilton Light Infantry* (RHLI Historical Association, 1977)

Brymer, Captain J. A., *History of the 33rd Field Regiment, Royal Artillery* (privately printed, 1945)

Buckley, Sgt Joseph D., *A History of the 50th Armored Infantry Battalion* (Germany, 1945)

Buie, Col. Walter D., *History of the 272nd Infantry, Battleaxe Regiment* (privately printed, 1945)

Colby, John, *War From the Ground Up: The 90th US Division in WWII* (Nortex Press, Texas, 1991)

Crabill, Col. Edwin 'Buckshot', *The Ragtag Circus from Omaha Beach to the Elbe* (Vantage, 1969)

Daly, Hugh C., *42nd Rainbow Division Combat History of World War II* (Army & Navy Publishing, Baton Rouge, 1946)

Delaforce, Patrick, *The Black Bull: 11th Armoured Division, Normandy to the Baltic* (Sutton, 1993); *Churchill's Desert Rats: From Normandy to Berlin with the 7th Armoured Division* (Sutton, 1994); *Monty's Ironsides: 3rd Division, From the Normandy Beaches to Bremen* (Sutton, 1995); *Red Crown and Dragon: 53rd Welsh Division in NW Europe 1944–45* (Tom Donovan, 1996)

Draper, Theodore, *The 84th US Infantry Division in the Battle for Germany* (Viking Press, 1946)

Essame, Hubert, *The 43rd Wessex Division at War* (Clowes, 1952)

Failmezger, Victor, *American Knights: Men of the 601st Tank Destroyer Battalion* (Osprey, 2015)

Forbes, Patrick, *6th Guards Tank Brigade: Guardsmen in Churchill Tanks* (Sampson, Low & Marston, 1949)

Forty, George, *Patton's Third Army at War* (Ian Allen, 1978)

Graydon, Col. Charles K., *With the 101st Cavalry During World War 1940–45* (Germany, 1945)

Hansult, William George, *The Final Battle: An Untold Story of WW II's Forty-Second Rainbow Division* (Mill City Press, 2018)

Hatcher, James E., *Blood and Fire: With the 63rd US Division in World War II* (63rd Division Association, Radcliff, Kentucky, 1986)

Hogan, David W., *A Command Post at War: First US Army Headquarters in Europe, 1943–1945* (US Army Center of Military History, 2000)

McFarland, Robert C. (ed.), *History of the 15th Infantry Regiment in World War II* (Society of the Third Infantry Division, 1990)

McGilvray, Evan, *A History of the First Polish Armoured Division 1938–47* (Pen & Sword)

MacGregor, Harold E., *28th Infantry Regiment, 8th US Division* (published by the Regiment, 1946)

McGregor, John, *The Spirit of Angus: The War History of the County's Battalion of the Black Watch* (Phillimore Books, 1988)

McManus, John, *American Courage, American Carnage: The 7th Infantry Regiment's Combat Experience, 1812 through World War II, Vol. 2* (Forge Books, 2009)

McNish, Robin & Charles Messenger, *Iron Division: History of 3rd British Division 1809–1989* (3rd Armoured Division, 1990)

Mick, Allen H., *With the 102nd Infantry Division Through Germany* (Battery Press, 1982)

Mitzel, John T., *Duty Before Self: The 781st Tank Battalion in World War II* (Schiffer, 2014)

Mooney, Edgar B., *Seventh US Infantry Regiment: The Colmar Pocket* (Seventh Army, 1945)

Morrison, Alex and Ted Slaney, *The Breed of Manly Men: The History of the Cape Breton Highlanders* (Cape Breton Highlanders Association, 1994)

Neillands, Robin, *The Raiders: The Army Commandos 1940–46* (Weidenfeld & Nicolson, 1989)

Nichols, Lester M., *Impact: The Battle Story of the Tenth US Armored Division* (Bradbury, Sayles, O'Neil Co., 1967)

Peek, Clifford H. (ed.), *Five Years, Five Countries, Five Campaigns with the 141st Infantry Regiment* (141st Infantry Regiment Association, Munich, 1945)

Peel, PFC Harris, *The Trail of the 254th: Through Blood and Fire* (254th Infantry, 1945)

Prefer, Nathan N., *The Conquering Ninth: US Ninth Army in World War II* (Casemate, 2020)

Rankin, Nicholas, *Ian Fleming's Commandos: 30 Assault Unit in WWII* (Faber & Faber, 2011)

Robertson, Ian, *Normandy to the Baltic: The 44th Lowland Infantry Brigade* (privately printed, 1945)

Robeson, Westin Ellis, *Buttoned Up: American Armor & the 781st Tank Battalion in World War II* (Texas A&M University Press, 2017)

Robinson, Wayne, *Move Out, Verify: The Combat Story of the 743rd Tank Battalion* (Germany, 1945)

Scarfe, Norman, *Assault Division: A History of the 3rd British Division* (Collins, 1947)

Steward, Hal D., *Thunderbolt: History of the Eleventh US Armored Division* (Washington DC, 1948)

Turner, John Frayn and Robert Jackson, *Destination Berchtesgaden: The Story of the US Seventh Army in World War II* (Ian Allen, 1975)

Watkins, G.J.B., *War History of the 4th Battalion Dorset Regiment* (Rowe, 1956)

White, Nathan W., *From Fedala to Berchtesgaden: A History of the Seventh United States Infantry* (self-published, 1947)

Whiting, Charles, *America's Forgotten Army: The US Seventh Army in WWII* (Sarpedon, 1999)

Whitlock, Flint, *The Rock of Anzio: From Sicily to Dachau, A History of the US 45th Infantry Division* (Westview Press, 1998)

Woolner, Frank, *Spearhead in the West: The 3rd US Armored Division in WWII* (Nashville Battery Press, 1980)

Zaloga, Steven J., *The Polish Army, 1939–45* (Osprey, 1982)

Allied campaign histories and battlefield guides

Allen, Peter, *One More River: The Rhine Crossings of 1945* (J.M. Dent, 1980)

Allport, Alan, *Browned Off and Bloody-Minded: The British Soldier Goes to War 1939–1945* (Yale University Press, 2015)

Ambrose, Stephen E., *Eisenhower and Berlin, 1945: The Decision to Halt at the Elbe* (Norton, 1967); *Band of Brothers* (Simon & Schuster, 1992)

Atkinson, Rick, *The Guns at Last Light* (Henry Holt, 2014)

BAOR Battlefield Guide, *Operations of XII British Corps crossing the River Rhine 23–25 March 1945 Operation PLUNDER* (Spectator Edition, HQ BAOR, 1947)

BAOR Battlefield Guide, *Operation Veritable, Battlefield Tour* (Students Edition, HQ BAOR, 1947)

Baron, Richard, *Major Abe Baum & Richard Goldhurst, Raid! The Untold Story of Patton's Secret Mission* (Putnam's, 1981)

Caddick-Adams, Peter, *Monte Cassino: Ten Armies in Hell* (Preface, 2011); *Snow & Steel: The Battle of the Bulge, 1944–45* (Preface, 2014); *Sand & Steel: A New History of D-Day* (Hutchinson, 2019)

Churchill, Winston, *The Second World War, Vol. VI 'Triumph and Tragedy'* (Cassell, 1954)

Colley, David P., *Decision at Strasbourg: Ike's Strategic Mistake to Halt the Sixth Army Group at the Rhine in 1944* (Naval Institute Press, 2008)

Colvin, Tony, *The Noise of Battle: The British Army and the Last Breakthrough Battle West of the Rhine, February–March 1945* (Helion, 2016)

Copp, Terry, *Cinderella Army: The Canadians in Northwest Europe, 1944–45* (University of Toronto Press, 2007); and Robert Vogel, *Maple Leaf Route: Victory* (Maple Leaf Route, 1988)

Doubler, Michael D., *Closing with the Enemy: How GIs Fought the War in Europe, 1944–45* (University Press of Kansas, 1994)

Essame, Hubert, *The Battle for Germany* (Batsford, 1969)

Fenelon, James M., *Four Hours of Fury: The Untold Story of World War II's Largest Airborne Invasion and the Final Push into Nazi Germany* (Scribner, 2019)

Foster, Tony, *Meeting of Generals* (Methuen, 1986)

Gassend, Jean-Loup, *Operation Dragoon: Autopsy of a Battle* (Schiffer, 2013)

Hechler, Ken, *The Bridge at Remagen: The Amazing Story of March 7, 1945* (Ballantine, 1957)

Hitchcock, William I., *The Bitter Road to Freedom, Europe 1944–1945* (Free Press, 2008)

Krivosheev, Col. Gen. Grigoriy, *Soviet Casualties and Combat Losses* (Greenhill, 1997)

Lee, Eric, *Night of the Bayonets: The Texel Uprising and Hitler's Revenge, April–May 1945* (Greenhill Books, 2020)

Moorehead, Alan, *Eclipse* (Hamish Hamilton, 1946)

Rawson, Andrew, *Crossing the Rhine: Remagen Bridge: 9th Armoured Infantry Division*

(Pen & Sword, 2004); *In Pursuit of Hitler: A Battlefield Guide to Bavaria* (Pen & Sword, 2008); *Eyes Only: The Top Secret Correspondence Between Eisenhower and Marshall* (History Press, 2012)

Reardon, Mark J., 'Aschaffenburg, 1945: Cassino on the River Main', Chapter 7, in John Antal & Bradley Gericke (eds), *City Fights: Selected Histories of Urban Combat from World War II to Vietnam* (Ballantine, 2003)

Russell, John, *Theirs the Strife: The Forgotten Battles of British Second Army and Armeegruppe Blumentritt, April 1945* (Helion, 2020)

Ryan, Cornelius, *The Last Battle* (Simon & Schuster, 1966)

Saft, Ulrich, *The Fight for Northern Germany: The Bitter End between Weser and Elbe in 1945* (Beltheim-Schnellbach, 2011)

Saunders, Tim, *Operation Varsity: British & Canadian Airborne Assault* (Pen & Sword, 2008)

Seelinger, Matthew J., *Operation Varsity: The Last Airborne Deployment of World War II* (US Army Historical Foundation, 2010)

Shulman, Milton, *Defeat in the West* (Secker & Warburg, 1947)

Terkel, Studs, *The Good War: An Oral History of World War Two* (Pantheon, 1984)

Whiting, Charles, *Battle of the Ruhr Pocket* (Pan Ballantine, 1971); *The Poor Bloody Infantry* (Hutchinson, 1987); *Bloody Bremen* (Pen & Sword, 1998)

Williams, Andrew, *D-Day To Berlin* (Hodder, 2004)

Williams, Jeffrey, *The Long Left Flank. The Hard Fought Way to the Reich* (Leo Cooper, 1988)

Wilmot, Chester, *The Struggle for Europe* (Collins, 1952)

Ziemke, Earl F., *Battle for Berlin* (Pan/Ballantine, 1969)

Zuehlke, Mark, *On To Victory: The Canadian Liberation of the Netherlands, 23 March–5 May 1945* (Douglas & McIntyre, 2010)

Allied air campaign and unit histories

Craven, W.F. and J.L. Cate, *The Army Air Forces in World War II: Vol. III: Argument to VE-Day* (University of Chicago Press, 1951)

Frankland, Noble, and Charles Webster, *The Strategic Air Offensive Against Germany, 1939–1945, Volume II: Endeavour, Part 4* (HMSO, 1961)

Ingrisano, Michael N., *Valor Without Arms: A History of the 316th Troop Carrier Group 1942–1945* (Merriam Press, 2001)

Middlebrook, Martin, *The Nuremberg Raid* (Allen Lane, 1973); *The Battle of Hamburg* (Allen Lane, 1980); *The Schweinfurt-Regensburg Raid* (Allen Lane, 1983)

Taylor, Frederick, *Dresden: Tuesday 13 February 1945* (Bloomsbury, 2005)

Wolfe, Martin, *Green Light! A Troop Carrier Squadron's War From Normandy to the Rhine* (Center for Air Force History, 1993)

Other biographies and histories

Adams, John A., *General Jacob Devers: World War II's Forgotten Four Star* (Indiana University Press, 2015)

Alford, Richard, *To Revel in God's Sunshine: The Story of RSM J.C. Lord* (self-published, 1981)

Astor, Gerald, *Terrible Terry Allen: Combat General of World War II – The Life of an American Soldier* (Presidio, 2003)

Bolger, Daniel P., *The Panzer Killers: The Untold Story of a Fighting General & His Spearhead Tank Division's Charge into the Third Reich* (Caliber, 2021)

Bond, Brian, *Liddell Hart: A Study of his Military Thought* (Cassell, 1977)

Bonn, Keith E., 'Most Underrated General of World War II: Alexander Patch' (*100th Infantry Division Association Newsletter*, July 2003)

Caddick-Adams, Peter, *Monty & Rommel: Parallel Lives* (Preface/Arrow, 2011)

Clayton, Anthony, *Three Marshals of France: Leadership After Trauma* (Brassey's, 1992)

Edgerton, David, *The Shock of the Old: Technology & Global History* (Oxford University Press, 2006)

Farago, Ladislas, *Patton: Ordeal and Triumph* (Arthur Barker, 1966)

Ferrell, Robert, *Choosing Truman: The Democratic Convention of 1944* (University Press of Missouri, 1994); *The Dying President: Franklin D. Roosevelt 1944–1945* (University Press of Missouri, 1998)

Flynn, Alice M., *Unforgettable: Biography of Capt. Thomas J. Flynn* (Sky Blue Publishing, 2011)

Fussell, Paul, *Wartime: Understanding & Behavior in the Second World War* (Oxford University Press, 1989)

Gilbert, Martin, *Winston Churchill: Road to Victory, Vol. VII* (Heinemann, 1986)

Glass, Charles, *The Deserters: A Hidden History of World War II* (Penguin, 2013)

Goudsmit, Samuel A., *Alsos* (Henry Schuman, 1947)

Groves, Leslie, *Now It Can Be Told: The Story of the Manhattan Project* (Harper & Row, 1962)

Harding, Stephen, *The Last Battle: When US and German Soldiers Joined Forces in the Waning Hours of World War II in Europe* (Da Capo Press, 2013)

Hart-Davis, Duff, (ed.), *King's Counsellor: Abdication & War, Diaries of Sir Alan Lascelles* (Weidenfeld & Nicolson, 2006)

Hodgson, Godfrey, *The Colonel: The Life and Wars of Henry Stimson, 1867–1950* (Knopf, 1990)

Horne, Alistair and David Montgomery, *The Lonely Leader: Monty 1944–1945* (HarperCollins, 1994)

Isaacson, Walter, *Kissinger: A Biography* (Simon & Schuster, 1992)

Kershaw, Alex, *The Liberator: One World War II Soldier's 500-Day Odyssey from the Beaches of Sicily to the Gates of Dachau* (Crown Publishers, 2012)

Kirkpatrick, Sidney, *Hitler's Holy Relics: A True Story of Nazi Plunder & the Race to Recover the Crown Jewels of the Holy Roman Empire* (Simon & Schuster, 2010)

Kladstrup, Don & Petie, *Wine & War: The French, the Nazis & France's Greatest Treasure* (Hodder & Stoughton, 2001)

Makos, Adam, *Spearhead: An American Tank Gunner, His Enemy, and a Collision of Lives in World War II* (Ballantine Books, 2019)

Marshall, Charles E., *Discovering the Rommel Murder* (Stackpole, 2002)

Michaels, David, *Schulz and Peanuts. A Biography* (Harper, 2007)

Nichol, John and Tony Rennell, *The Last Escape: The Untold Story of Allied Prisoners of War in Germany 1944–45* (Viking, 2002)

Ochs, Stephen J., *A Cause Greater Than Self: The Journey of Captain Michael J. Daly, World War II Medal of Honor Recipient* (Texas A&M University Press, 2012)

Parish, James Robert, *It's Good to Be the King: Seriously Funny Life of Mel Brooks* (Wiley, 2007)

Pash, Boris, *The Alsos Mission* (Charter Books, 1969)

Penrose, Antony & Edward Scherman (eds), *Lee Miller's War: Photographer and Correspondent with the Allies in Europe 1944–45* (Bullfinch Press, 1992)

Reid, P.R., *The Latter Days at Colditz* (Hodder & Stoughton, 1952)

Robinson, Stephen, *The Remarkable Lives of Bill Deedes* (Little, Brown, 2008)

Salinger, Margaret A., *Dream Catcher: A Memoir* (Washington Square Press, 2000)

Salisbury-Jones, Guy, *So Full A Glory: a Biography of Marshal de Lattre de Tassigny* (Weidenfeld & Nicolson, 1954)

Sayer, Ian, and Jeremy Dronfield, *Hitler's Last Plot: The 139 VIP hostages Selected for Death in the Final Days of World War II* (Da Capo Press, 2019)

Warner, Philip, *Horrocks: The General Who Led from the Front* (Hamish Hamilton, 1984)

Weigley, Russell, *Eisenhower's Lieutenants* (Indiana University Press, 1981)

Wheeler, Scott, *Jacob L. Devers: A General's Life* (University Press of Kentucky, 2015)

Williamson, David, *A Most Diplomatic General: Lord Robertson of Oakridge* (Brassey's, 1996)

Woodbridge, John and Maurice Possley, *Hitler in the Crosshairs: A GI's Story of Courage and Faith* (Zondervan, 2011)

Academic and military papers, dissertations and articles

Altenbach, Roy, 'Memoir: How Patton's Third Army Marched Across Europe to Beat the Nazis', *The National Interest* (11 April 2020)

Bailey, Maj Alfred D., *Alligators, Buffaloes & Bushmasters: The History of the Development of the LVT Through WWII* (History & Museums Division, USMC, Washington DC, 1986)

Beard, Maj Rebecca E., *Footnote in History: Sixth Army Group Operations in the Second World War and Lessons for Contemporary Planners* (US Army Command & General Staff College, Fort Leavenworth, 2016)

Berlin, Robert H., *US Army World War II Corps Commanders: A Composite Biography* (Fort Leavenworth, 1989)

Blum, Capt. Charles K., *Operations of Company 'E', 3rd Division, Colmar Pocket 22–23 January 1945* (Infantry School, Fort Benning, 1947–8)

Blumenson, Martin, 'The Hammelburg Affair', *Army* magazine (October 1965)

Bradsher, Greg, 'Nazi Gold: The Merkers Mine Treasure', *Prologue*, Vol. 31/1 (Spring 1999)

Caddick-Adams, Peter, 'General Sir Miles Christopher Dempsey (1896–1969) – Not a Popular Leader', *RUSI Journal*, Vol. 150/5 (October 2005)

Capdevila, Luc, 'The Mobilization of Women in Combatant France 1940–1945' (Clio: Femmes, Genre, Histoire, 2000)

Copp, Terry, 'Operation Blockbuster Begins', *Legion* magazine (January 2003)

Dalrymple, Lieutenant Colonel John C., *Operations of the 1117th Engineer Combat Group on the Rhine River Crossing* (Student paper, Fort Leavenworth, 1947)

Dietrich, Steve, 'The Professional Reading of General George S. Patton, Jr.', *Journal of Military History* (October 1989)

Fair, Capt. Felder L., *Operations of Company 'B', 26th Infantry, in the Harz Mountains, 17–18 April 1945* (Advanced Infantry Officers Course, Fort Benning, 1947–8)

Gold, Bill, 'My Combat Experiences', *Blood and Fire* (Newsletter of the 63rd Division Association, Vol. 59/1, February 2007)

Goodman, Cindy, Frank Murphy and Dave Kanzler, 'The Liberation of Moosburg', *Splasher 6*, Newsletter of the 100th Bomb Group (Heavy) Foundation, Vol. 33/2 (Summer 2002)

Hachtmann, Rüdiger, 'Fordism and Unfree Labour: Aspects of the Work Deployment of Concentration Camp Prisoners in German Industry between 1941 and 1944', *International Review of Social History*, Vol. 55/3 (December 2010)

Henderly, Capt. Harold B., *Operations of Company 'D', 191st Tank Battalion, at Aschaffenburg, Germany, 28 March–3 April 1945* (Infantry School, Fort Benning, 1948–9)

Heyl, John D., 'The Construction of the Westwall, 1938: An Exemplar for National Socialist Policymaking', *Central European History*, Vol. 14/1 (March 1981)

Huebner, Gen. Charles R., 'V Corps From Belgium to Czechoslovakia', *Army & Navy Journal*, No. 83 (December 1945)

Inge, Herndon, 'The Hammelburg Raid', *Military Magazine*, Vol. XVIII/10 (March 2002)

Koch, Maj. Richard P., *Combat Engineers of World War II: Lessons on Training & Mobilization* (MA thesis, Fort Leavenworth, 2014)

Lecoq, Tristan, 'Refaire l'Armée française 1943–1945: L'outil militaire, l'instrument politique, le contrôle opérationnel' (*Guerres mondiales et conflits contemporains* 2015/1)

Liddell, Maj. Robert J. et al., *Rhine River Crossing: River Crossing conducted by the Third US Army & the 5th Infantry Division 22–24 March 1945* (Combat Studies Institute, Fort Leavenworth, 1984)

Little, Wendell E., '6th Army Group Logistical Problems', *Military Review*, Vol. XXV/11 (1946)

Ludington, Maj. Edward P., *Operations of the 313th Infantry in the Preparation and Crossing of the Rhine, 9–24 March 1945* (Advanced Infantry Officers Class, Fort Benning, 1949–50)

McCreedy, Maj. Kenneth O., *Planning the Peace: Operation Eclipse & the Occupation of Germany* (Fort Leavenworth, Kansas, 1995)

Measey, Lt Col. Charles R., 'Roer River Crossing at Linnich, Germany', *Armored Cavalry Journal*, Vol. VII/3 (May–June 1948)

Menzel, Helmut, 'The End of the War in Magdeburg in 1945', *Sachsen-Anhalt Journal*, Vol. 2 (2020)

Mitchell, Paul, 'Concentration Camp Buildings as Artifacts: The Archaeology of Buildings at Mauthausen-Gusen', *International Journal of Historical Archaeology*, Vol. 22/3 (2017)

Moore, Capt. Clayton H., *Operations of Company 'F', 30th Infantry, in the crossing of the Rhine River near Worms, 26–27 March 1945* (Infantry School, Fort Benning, 1948–9)

Morris, Roy, 'The Race to the Rhine: How the US 79th Division Took Down the Nazis', *Quarterly Journal of Military History*, Vol. 33/3 (Spring 2021)

Nance, Maj. William S., *Patton's Iron Cavalry – The Impact of the Mechanized Cavalry on the US Third Army* (University of North Texas, Denton, Texas, 2011); *Forgotten Glory: US Corps Cavalry in the ETO* (PhD thesis, Univ. of North Texas, 2014)

Narveson, Eric, 'Ordeal of Liberation at Colditz', *Fighting 69th Infantry Division Bulletin*, No.46/3 (May–August 1993)

Oldinsky, Lt Col. Frederick E., 'Patton & the Hammelburg Mission', *Armor* magazine (Jul–Aug, 1976)

Orgeron, Marsha, 'Liberating Images? Samuel Fuller's Film of Falkenau Concentration Camp', *Film Quarterly*, Vol. 60/2

Peterson, Capt. Paul L., *Operations of Company 'E', 180th Infantry, in the Battle of Nuremberg, Germany, 17–20 April 1945* (Advanced Infantry Officers Course, Fort Benning, 1948–9)

Rivera-Morales, Capt. Alejo, *Operations of the 100th Division at Bitche, Alsace-Lorraine, 15–17 March 1945* (Infantry School, Fort Benning, 1949–50)

Robel, Michael K., 'Patton's Hammelburg Raid: Mission Assessment & Lessons Learned', *Command* magazine (November 2000)

Schillare, Maj. Quentin W., *The Battle of Aschaffenburg: An example of Late World War II Urban Combat in Europe* (Master's thesis, Fort Leavenworth, 1989)

Stevenson, Lt Col. Frank E., *Third Army's Planning for the Crossing of the Rhine River* (Fort Leavenworth)

Stone, Thomas R., 'General William Hood Simpson: Unsung Commander of US Ninth Army', *Parameters*, Vol. XI/2 (1981)

Taylor, Dr Victoria, 'Blitzmädels an die Front: A Lesser Known Female War Film', *Women's History Network* (December 2018)

Thompson, Capt. Sheldon L., *Operations of Task Force Baum, 4th Armored Division, Between Aschaffenburg and Hammelburg, Germany, 27–28 March 1945* (Infantry School, Fort Benning, 1948–9)

Trinidad, Major et al., *The Last Pursuit: The 2nd Armored Division's Exploitation from the Rhine to the Elbe, 24 March–14 April 1945* (Fort Leavenworth, 1984)

Welch, Steven R., 'Harsh but Just? German Military Justice in the Second World War: A Comparative Study of the Court Martialling of German and US Deserters', *German History*, 173 (1999)

Wright, Maj. E. Dave, *Mechanized Cavalry Groups: Lessons for the Future of Reconnaissance and Surveillance* (Fort Leavenworth, 2013)

Index

Miller, Lee, 414, 463–4

Millikin, John, 59, 123, 124, 177–9, 180, 193–5, 197, 332, 405, 526

Million Dollar Tank Test, 150–51

Mills-Roberts, Derek, 226, 227, 228, 392

Model, Walter, 343, 349, 350, 351, 354–6, 528

Monchengladbach, Germany, 115, 117

Monmouthshire Regiment, 390, 391

de Monsabert, Joseph, 69, 153, 253, 274–5

Monte Cassino, battle of (1944), xxviii, 40, 131, 145, 224, 316, 441

Montgomery, Bernard, 2, 3, 9, 15, 17, 18, 22, 25, 32–5, 42, 48–55, 109, 177, 483, 526–7
  Operation *Veritable*, 85–7, 103, 105; Operation *Grenade*, 110, 123; Operation *Undertone*, 171; Battle of Remagen, 187, 188, 190, 194; Operation *Plunder*, 123, 171, 173, 181, 187, 188, 190, 195, 202, 209, 219–34; Operation *Varsity*, 241, 245; switch away from Berlin, 232, 316–17; Netherlands and Elbe campaigns, 367, 371, 377, 380, 393, 396; German surrender, 481; Operation *Enterprise*, 499; German surrender, 501–2, 504, 508; occupation begins, 517–18

Moore, Bryant, 118, 131, 343

Moorehead, Alan, 2, 225, 227, 229, 231, 233, 372–3

Moosburg, Germany, 314, 333–5

Moroccan Division, 163, 254, 256, 276

Morocco, xxviii, 40, 68, 151

Morris, William, 165, 280, 481

Moselle River, 165, 168, 202, 204

Mosquito pathfinders, 131, 472

Mountain Division, German 2nd, 71, 75

Mountain Division, German 6th SS, 61, 402

Mozart, Wolfgang Amadeus, 444, 469

Mulde River, 316, 343, 344, 405, 412, 415, 417

Munich, Germany, 130, 331, 333, 343, 449–64
  Beer Hall putsch (1923), 408, 449–50
  Braunes Haus, 464
  Czechoslovakia agreement (1938), 450
  Hitler's apartment, 462–4
  Oktoberfest, 464
  Reinheitsgebot (1516), 464

Münster, Germany, 357, 396, 518

Murphy, Audie, xxxv, 74, 77, 474, 523

Murphy, Frank, 333–5

Mussolini, Benito, 435, 465

Nancy, France, 139, 205, 250

Napoleon I, Emperor of the French, xxviii, 3, 46, 144, 254, 257, 296, 298
  Battle of Donauwörth (1805), 451
  Battle of Leipzig (1813), 404, 411
  Elba exile (1814–15), 404
  Franconia abolition (1803), 298
  Hamelin siege (1806), 357
  Magdeburg siege (1806), 362
  Ulm campaign (1805), 280–81, 282

National Guard, US, 60, 111, 144, 145, 146, 172, 235, 399

National Redoubt, 316, 319, 433–7, 463, 510, 529

Natzweiler-Struthof camp, 24–5, 276–7

Nazi Germany; Nazism, 291, 449–50
  Arminius, appropriation of, 390
  Aryan superman ideology, 162, 263, 291, 342, 463
  Blutfahne, 450, 464
  Braunes Haus, 464
  dissolution (1945), 514
  Enigma machine, 51, 61
  euthanasia programme, 198
  Four-Year Plan (1936–40), 360
  Franconia and, 298

Image Credits

Second plate section

All images courtesy of the National Archives and Records Administration, except
p.1: author's collection.
p.2: (top) author's collection, (bottom) © Manchester Daily Express / SSPL via Getty Images.
p.3: (bottom) © Imperial War Museums via Getty Images.
p.4: (top) © Keystone / Hulton Archive via Getty Images, (bottom) © Keystone-France / Gamma-Keystone via Getty Images.
p.5: (top) © Imperial War Museums via Getty Images, (bottom) © Photo 12 / Universal Images Group via Getty Images.
p.6: (bottom) © Keystone-France / Gamma-Rapho via Getty Images.
p.7: (top) © ullstein bild via Getty Images, (bottom) © Bettmann via Getty Images.
p.8: (top) © Photo 12 / Universal Images Group via Getty Images, (bottom) © Keystone-France / Gamma-Keystone via Getty Images.

The author and publisher gratefully acknowledge the permission granted to reproduce the copyright material in this book. Every effort has been made to trace copyright holders and to obtain their permission. The publisher apologises for any errors or omissions and, if notified of any corrections, will make suitable acknowledgment in future reprints or editions of this book.